GEORGE S. HILLS, senior partner in the New York City law firm of Rogers Hoge & Hills, has written numerous articles on subjects dealing with corporate law and the law of accounting. His interest in the law of meetings was developed during more than forty years' experience in handling meetings of directors, committees, and shareholders, as chairman, corporate secretary, or parliamentarian.

MANAGING CORPORATE MEETINGS

A Legal and Procedural Guide

GEORGE S. HILLS

MEMBER OF THE NEW YORK BAR

THE RONALD PRESS COMPANY • NEW YORK

ISBN 0-8260-4121-3
Library of Congress Catalog Card Number: 75–35288
PRINTED IN THE UNITED STATES OF AMERICA

To
A. G. H.

Preface

The style and proceedings of corporate meetings have changed dramatically over the past half-century. Attendance and participation by individual stockholders and their spokesmen have grown from gatherings attended by a mere handful to meetings of thousands in cavernous microphone-equipped auditoriums. The widely publicized scene of a presiding chairman berating an inquisitive stockholder—the so-called corporate "gadfly"—is largely a memory. The chairman has learned from experience that a meeting's success will invariably depend upon his own tact and fairness in carrying out his basically ministerial duties.

To serve the needs of the chairman as well as the secretary, director, and corporate lawyer who are concerned with annual and special meetings of stockholders is a major purpose of this book. It should also be of practical value to other members of the corporate management team, and groups outside the corporate sphere who are active in meetings of a private, quasi-public, or public nature.

The volume covers the law and practice of meetings as recorded in the case law and parliamentary manuals. Emphasis is on the meetings of business and membership corporations, ranging from the basic state corporation laws to the precepts of regulatory commissions created by federal law.

Included are the basic legal requirements of meetings from call to their final adjournment. The application of common parliamentary law and the rights and duties of the presiding chairman are considered, in addition to standards of fairness, decorum and the preservation of order, the rights of the public, and constitutional aspects of freedom of speech. Extensive use of examples and precedents, and citations to the case law enhance the book's usefulness for all concerned with the subject.

Grateful acknowledgements are due to my secretary, Mrs. Barbara K. Pond, who started this venture more than ten years ago, and to her successor, Miss Louise Gehrig, who carried the project through the final manuscript and printer's proofs. Both kept the ever expanding mass of material under control with patient and diligent care.

GEORGE S. HILLS

New York, New York
September, 1976

Contents

MANAGING CORPORATE MEETINGS

1

Need for Meetings

§ 1.1 Collective Body Doctrine

It is a general principle of law that the members of a collective body can act only at a meeting duly called and held. They must act concurrently, not individually, and an act or decision of individual members while not duly assembled as a body is not a valid act of the body. Unanimous consent in writing may obviate the need for a meeting only if permitted by a governing statute.

The basic rule is founded on the common law.[1] It is well de-

---

[1] The members of a corporation aggregate cannot separately and individually give their consent in such a manner as to obligate themselves as a collective body. This is the doctrine of the common and the Roman civil law. Duke v. Markham, 105 N.C. 131, 10 S.E. 1017, 1018 (1890), *quoted in* Davenport v. Pitt County Drainage Dist., 220 N.C. 237, 17 S.E.2d 1, 3 (1941).

The "common-law doctrine requiring stockholders to act at a proper meeting of the corporation" is not abrogated or modified by the enactment of a statute on the same subject. Kappers v. Cast Stone Constr. Co., 184 Wis. 627, 632, 200 N.W. 376 (1924).

It is a general rule of common law that, where several persons are authorized to do an act of a public nature, they must all meet and deliberate, although a majority may decide. Norfolk & W. Ry. Co. v. Virginian Ry., 110 Va. 631, 66 S.E. 863 (1910).

3

veloped,[2] particularly as to meetings of municipal and local legislative bodies,[3] state and national legislatures,[4] boards of directors,[5] and stockholders,[6] and to committees generally.[7]

[2] "Although there is little federal authority, the state courts universally require that official action of state commissioners, town counsels, county boards, school boards, church trustees, and corporation boards of directors must be conducted in formal meetings attended by the necessary quorum." T.S.C. Motor Freight Lines, Inc. v. United States, 186 F. Supp. 777 (1960) (footnotes and citations omitted), *aff'd sub nom.* Herrin Transp. Co. v. United States, 366 U.S. 419 (1961) (*per curiam*).

[3] "It is axiomatic that municipal governing bodies may take official action only at public meetings." Brazer v. Borough of Mountainside, 102 N.J. Super. 497, 246 A.2d 170, 173 (1968).

See, e.g., Turk v. Richard, 47 So. 2d 543 (Fla. 1950) (city council); People *ex rel.* Reilly v. City of Kankakee, 288 Ill. App. 192, 6 N.E.2d 260 (1937) (fire and police commissioners); Terre Haute Gas Corp. v. Johnson, 221 Ind. 499, 45 N.E.2d 484, 489 (1942), *modified,* 221 Ind. 499, 48 N.E.2d 455 (1943) (public service commission); Paola & Fall River Ry. v. Commissioners, 16 Kan. 302 (1876) (county board); Moore v. Babb, 343 S.W.2d 373 (Ky. 1961) (board of education); Prezlak v. Padrone, 67 N.J. Super. 95, 169 A.2d 852 (1961) (city council); Amity Holding Corp. v. Eden, 238 App. Div. 623, 265 N.Y.S. 23 (1933) (water commissioners); Stanley v. Board of Appeals, 168 Misc. 797, 5 N.Y.S.2d 956 (Sup. Ct. 1938) (board of zoning appeals); Board of County Comm'rs v. Carey, Lombard, Young & Co., 178 Okla. 13, 61 P.2d 736 (1936) (county commissioners); Edsall v. Jersey Shore Borough, 220 Pa. 591, 70 A. 429, 431 (1908) (borough council); McAllister v. City of Frost, 131 S.W.2d 975 (Tex. Civ. App. 1939) (city council); City of Floydada v. Gilliam, 111 S.W.2d 761 (Tex. 1937) (town council); King v. Guerra, 1 S.W.2d 373 (Tex. 1927) (city commissioners); Edwards v. Hylbert, 146 W.Va. 1, 118 S.E.2d 347 (1961) (municipal council); State v. Union Light, Heat & Power Co., 47 N.D. 402, 182 N.W. 539 (1921) (railroad commissioners); Fleming v. Board of Trustees, 112 Cal. App. 225, 296 P. 925 (1931) (school board); Stirman v. City of Tyler, 443 S.W.2d 354 (Tex. Civ. App. 1969) (city commission).

[4] The Congress of the United States can take no legislative action while it is not in session. United States v. Taylor, 116 F. Supp. 439 (D. Minn. 1953), *appeal dismissed,* 214 F.2d 351 (8th Cir. 1954).

[5] "As a general rule the directors of a corporation may bind a corporation only when they act at a legal meeting of the board. . . . If they purport to act at a meeting which is not a legal meeting, their action is not that of the corporation, and the corporation, absent ratification or acquiescence, is not bound." Stone v. American Lacquer Solvents Co., 345 A.2d 174, 176–77 (Pa. 1975).

Schuckman v. Rubenstein, 164 F.2d 952 (6th Cir. 1947), *cert. denied,* 333 U.S. 875 (1948); United States v. Interstate R.R., 14 F.2d 328 (W.D. Va. 1926).

§ 1.2   Exceptions for Regulatory Bodies

There are exceptions to this rule applicable to federal regulatory boards and commissions, founded on statutory grants to such agencies of broad power to conduct their "proceedings" in such manner as will be conducive to the proper dispatch of business. The courts have held that the designated agency may proceed with its members acting separately, in their various offices, rather than jointly in a

---

"An individual director has no authority as such; he can only act as agent by appointment, like other agents are appointed. Moreover, directors must act together as a board; the separate assent of a majority is not binding on the corporation. Neither can they vote by proxy. These rules arise from the very nature of corporate business, which must be conducted by agents. And, as between themselves, the majority rule prevails." Haldeman v. Haldeman, 176 Ky. 635, 197 S.W. 376, 381 (1917).

"The stockholders of a corporation have a right to expect from their directors a conscientious consideration of every proposition which is presented which involves any interest of the company, in conformity to the oath which they have subscribed. They have a right to have the individual viewpoint of the several directors expressed at a conference, for the purpose of obtaining the exchange view of the several persons in arriving at conclusions after deliberate consideration of any issue. It is fundamental that officers of boards can only act as such constituted boards when assembled as such, and by deliberate and concerted action dispose of the issue under consideration, and that they cannot act in an individual capacity outside of a formal meeting, and a majority of the individual expressions be the action of the board. The law believes that the greatest wisdom results from conference and exchange of individual views, and it is for that reason that the law requires the united wisdom of a majority of the several members of the board in determining the business of a corporation, and will not permit the business and concerns of a corporation to be delegated to any officers or men, however capable, or however high their standard for integrity and honesty may be, and that fraud will be implied upon the delegation of such power and right, and the exercise thereof by men who may be the controlling stockholders, even though, in their own conscience, they may believe that everything has been done to the very best interests of the concern; . . . . It is the failure to give that consideration to the interests of the minority which the majority would have them give were the positions reversed. The law, therefore, wisely places control of corporations in a board of trustees, and requires its action as a board." Ames v. Goldfield Merger Mines Co., 227 F. 292, 301, 302 (W.D. Wash. 1915).

[6] See § 1.3 *infra*.

[7] "By general acceptation, even without a by-law or rule, a committee must act as a group and have a majority concur." Local 6068, UMW v. Bizzell, 257 S.W.2d 527, 528 (Ky. 1953).

meeting. Action is taken by a "notation voting procedure" whereby the views and votes of the members may be recorded separately rather than in joint session and circulated to the remaining members for their attention.[8] There is also a minority view that the members of an administrative body may act without the formality of a meeting. The court noted that "members of this court do not meet in formal sessions to approve proposed opinions. There is no apparent reason to impose upon the Commission a burden of acting in a more formal manner. It is sufficient if a majority of the Commission signs the findings."[9] This exception is not available to business corporations, where corporate action cannot lawfully be taken at a split meeting or at separate incomplete meetings. For example, when a minority of the board of directors meets and votes at one time and other directors, also constituting a minority, meet and vote at a different time, the board of directors has not complied with the rule that a majority must meet and take action at the same time.[10]

§ 1.3 Prevailing Rule—Stockholder Meetings

In the area of corporation law, it is generally held that the power of the members or shareholders of a corporation to control its actions, or to approve action taken by management, can be exercised only at a duly called meeting, and that the consent of a majority of the shareholders expressed elsewhere than at a meeting, even though signed by all, is not binding on the corporation. An early Supreme Court decision established this principle.[11]

[8] Braniff Airways, Inc. v. CAB, 379 F.2d 453, 460 (D.C. Cir. 1967) (Civil Aeronautics Board).

Notation voting is an approved method of conducting business by a federal regulatory commission. T.S.C. Motor Freight Lines, Inc. v. United States, 186 F. Supp. 777 (1960), aff'd sub nom. Herrin Transp. Co. v. United States, 366 U.S. 419 (1961) (per curiam) (Interstate Commerce Commission).

See Eastland Co. v. FCC, 92 F.2d 467 (D.C. Cir. 1937), cert. denied, 302 U.S. 735 (1937) (notation voting).

[9] Erkman v. Civil Service Comm'n, 198 P.2d 238 (Utah 1948).

[10] Schuckman v. Rubenstein, 164 F.2d 952 (6th Cir. 1947), cert. denied, 333 U.S. 875 (1948).

[11] A conveyance of all the assets of a corporation is not within the power of the stockholders, even though they may all sign it, without formal action at a meeting held for that purpose. De La Vergne Refrigerating Mach. Co. v. German Sav. Inst., 175 U.S. 40 (1899).

This rule, derived from the common law, is based on the concept that "[t]he private procurement of a written assent, signed by a majority of the members, will not supply the want of a meeting. Such an expedient deprives those interested of the benefit of mutual discussion, and subjects them to the hazard of fraudulent misrepresentation and undue influence." [12]

A recent case explains the law as it now stands. "A corporation has been defined as a body of individuals united as a single separate entity. When corporate powers are vested in the shareholders or members, they repose in them collectively as a body and not as indi-

---

"A corporation is bound by the acts of its stockholders and directors only when they act as a body in a regular session or under authority conferred at a duly constituted meeting." Tuttle v. Junior Bldg. Corp., 228 N.C. 507, 46 S.E.2d 313, 315 (1948).

A trial court excluded testimony as to the acts of individual members of a borough council, under the general rule that authority must be exercised by the council acting at a meeting duly called. Edsall v. Jersey Shore Borough, 220 Pa. 591, 70 A. 429 (1908).

It is a fundamental principle that all business requiring the assent of stockholders must be transacted at a duly convened meeting, and the only legal concurrence of stockholders is to be expressed at such meeting, after full opportunity for discussion and debate and full permission to the opposition to attempt by persuasion to reverse the prevailing sentiment. Reiff v. Western Union Tel. Co., 49 N.Y. Super. 441 (1883).

As a rule authorized meetings are prerequisite to corporate action based upon deliberate conference and intelligent discussion of proposed measures. O'Neal v. Wake County, 196 N.C. 184, 145 S.E. 28, 29 (1928).

"A corporation is bound by the acts of its stockholders and directors only when they act as a body in regular session or under authority conferred at a duly constituted meeting. 'As a rule authorized meetings are prerequisite to corporate action based upon deliberate conference and intelligent discussion of proposed measures.' [citations]." Park Terrace, Inc. v. Phoenix Indem. Co., 241 N.C. 473, 85 S.E.2d 677, 680 (1955); accord, Tuttle v. Junior Bldg. Corp., 228 N.C. 507, 46 S.E.2d 313 (1948).

[12] Commonwealth ex rel. Claghorn v. Cullen, 13 Pa. 133, 143–44 (1850); accord, Commonwealth ex rel. Maurer v. Burns, 365 Pa. 596, 76 A.2d 383 (1950).

The assent of every member given individually is not equivalent to a resolution passed at a general meeting. Re George Newman & Co., [1895] 1 Ch. 674.

Where the exercise of corporate acts is vested in a select body, an act done by the individuals comprising that body at an informal gathering of all the corporators, is not a valid corporate act. Landers v. Frank Street Methodist Episc. Church, 114 N.Y. 626, 21 N.E. 420 (1889).

viduals. That is, individuals have no power to act as or for the corporation except at a corporate meeting called and conducted in accordance with law." [13] The practical effect of this basic rule is shown by another case holding that a shareholders' meeting does not become "nugatory and dispensable" because one stockholder owns enough shares to carry any resolution and can be expected to vote in favor of his own resolutions. "The vote is not legally predetermined simply because it seems practically predictable." [14] On the other hand, a court will not order shareholders to convene a special meeting where it would be a "fruitless gesture" under adverse conditions.[15] A duly convened meeting has the merit of affording all shareholders a full opportunity for "discussion and debate, and full permission of those opposed to any measure favored by a majority, to attempt by persuasion to reverse the prevailing sentiment." [16]

§ 1.3.1   Exceptions

However, the adoption of a resolution at a duly convened meeting may not be the only way to take corporate action.[17] There are

[13] Studebaker Corp. v. Allied Prods. Corp., 256 F. Supp. 173, 189 (W.D. Mich. 1966).

[14] The court also held: "A majority stockholding cannot legitimate a meeting based on misleading information by reference to its possession of votes that would suffice to end debate." Laurenzano v. Einbender, 264 F. Supp. 356, 362 (E.D.N.Y. 1966).

[15] A special meeting to change the corporate name would be a fruitless gesture in view of continued opposition and the financial burden of preparing, printing, and making the necessary notice and proxy material. Ainsile v. Sandquist, 270 F. Supp. 382 (D. Mass. 1967).

[16] Reiff v. Western Union Tel. Co., 49 N.Y. Super. 441, 453 (1883).

"It is not an answer that the outcome would in all probability be the same. All members must have an opportunity to be present and take part in a decision of a board even though action by a majority is fully adequate." Reilly v. Board of Selectmen, 345 Mass. 363, 187 N.E.2d 838, 840 (1963).

See Bannigan v. Heffernan, 115 N.Y.S.2d 889, 896, modified, 280 App. Div. 891, 115 N.Y.S.2d 444 (2d Dep't), aff'd, 304 N.Y. 729, 108 N.E.2d 209 (1952) holding that candidates for election at a political convention should, under a proper and democratic process, be nominated as the result of the "deliberations of the elected representatives of the party" and not by "conflicting factions." The court quoted: "Nominations must be the act of the party, not of a clique."

[17] Stockholders may agree among themselves to distribute a dividend without the formality of corporate action. In re Norton's Will, 129 Misc. 875, 224 N.Y.S. 77, 87 (Sur. Ct. 1927).

exceptions to the general rule founded on unanimous consent or vote of all members,[18] on statutory non-unanimous consent,[19] and on common law.[20]

§ 1.4   Consent, Unanimous

The most recent statutory exception recognizes the fact that large shareholder meetings are often unnecessary and thus wasteful of time and energy, especially where the purpose of the meeting is to consider and act upon specific proposals which are fully explained in the proxy or consent solicitation material. Most state corporation laws have heretofore sanctioned action by written consent only if it is unanimous.[21]

§ 1.5   Consent, Quorum

The Delaware Corporation Law was recently amended to authorize non-unanimous written consent. It provides that any action

---

[18] Any action which may properly be taken at a meeting of a board of directors may be effected and is binding without a meeting, if a consent in writing setting forth the action so taken is signed by each and every member of the board and filed with the secretary of the corporation. Stone v. Am. Lacquer Solvents Co., 345 A.2d 174 (Pa. 1975).

See, e.g., Guaranty Loan Co. v. Fontanel, 183 Cal. 1, 190 P. 177, 180 (1920) (all shareholders present); Commonwealth *ex rel.* Claghorn v. Cullen, 13 Pa. 133, 143 (1850) (written consent of all shareholders); Columbia Stamping & Mfg. Co. v. Reich, 28 Wis. 2d 297, 137 N.W.2d 45 (1965) (informal board meeting with all present).

[19] Modern corporation laws permit the board of directors or any committee to take action without a meeting if all of the members of the board or committee consent in writing to the adoption of a resolution authorizing the action. The resolution and consent should be filed with the minutes of the board or committee. *See, e.g.*, N.Y. BUS. CORP. LAW § 708 (McKinney Supp. 1973); Lohman v. Edgewater Holding Co., 227 Minn. 40, 33 N.W.2d 842, 844 (1948) (state statute).

[20] Philadelphia Life Ins. Co. v. Crosland-Cullen Co., 234 F.2d 780 (4th Cir. 1956) (one-man dominated corporation); Elyea v. Lehigh Salt Mining Co., 169 N.Y. 29, 61 N.E. 992 (1901) (sale of corporate property in good faith without formal meeting); Commonwealth *ex rel.* Claghorn v. Cullen, 13 Pa. 133, 143–44 (1850); *see* Handley v. Stutz, 139 U.S. 417 (1891).

[21] A statute allowing corporate action by unanimous written consent of stockholders without the necessity of a formal meeting requires strict compliance with its provisions. *In re* Louisiana Inv. & Loan Corp., 224 F. Supp. 274 (E.D. La. 1963), *aff'd,* 342 F.2d 999 (5th Cir. 1965).

which may be taken at a meeting of shareholders, may be taken without a meeting, without prior notice, and without a vote, provided a consent in writing is signed by shareholders having not less than the minimum number of votes that would be necessary to take such action at a meeting at which all shares entitled to be voted were present and voted. The first New York Stock Exchange (NYSE) listed company to take advantage of this form of mail vote without a meeting sought approval of its shareholders to acquire another company.[22]

The NYSE requires that actively operating companies solicit proxies for all meetings of shareholders. The purpose and intent of this rule is to afford shareholders a convenient method of voting on matters which may be presented at shareholders' meetings with adequate disclosure.[23] The solicitation by management of "consents" under the Delaware law, if accompanied by a proxy statement meeting the SEC proxy rules, is considered to be in compliance with the proxy solicitation requirements of the NYSE.

The consent of shareholders to a corporate action must be given with the knowledge that they are acting as shareholders for a corporate purpose. For example, where there was a casual gathering of all the shareholders, without notice, in the waiting room of a local hospital and the conversation was general and no specific business was conducted, such gathering was not in fact a corporate meeting, nor did the shareholders thereby comply with the statute allowing corporate action by consent without a meeting. The court ruled that this informal gathering was not held for the purpose of conducting corporate business, and said that the alleged meeting appeared to be a "mere afterthought or hindsight." [24] On the other hand, any deliberative gathering or informal session may be a "meet-

---

[22] DELAWARE CORP. LAW § 228 (as amended 1969). Greyhound Corporation consent meeting to acquire Armour & Co., Wall St. Journal, Jan. 20, 1970.

[23] Sec. A–8, NYSE Company Manual, at A–134.

[24] "Even when a meeting is informally held it must be a meeting called for the purpose of conducting corporation business. . . . However, the conversation was general and no specific business was conducted . . . in behalf of the corporation." *In re* Louisiana Inv. & Loan Corp., 224 F. Supp. 274, 276 (E.D. La. 1963), *aff'd*, 342 F.2d 999 (5th Cir. 1965).

See Paola & Fall River Ry. v. Commissioners, 16 Kan. 302 (1876).

ing" within the meaning of a public meeting statute, sometimes known as a "sunshine law." [25]

§ 1.6   Meetings of Directors

Legal principles underlying the rule for shareholder meetings, and the exceptions to the general rule, apply generally to the meetings of a board of directors.[26] The corporation laws of the state of incorporation should always be examined for statutory exceptions to the general rule. Of particular interest are recent amendments of state corporation laws which permit members of the board or of a committee thereof to have a "conference" call meeting. The amendment makes fully effective a member's participation in a meeting by means of a "conference telephone or similar communications equipment" call allowing all persons participating in the meeting to hear each other at the same time. Thus, all who participate in a telephone conference are deemed to be present in person at the meeting.[27]

Although it is a general rule that a board of directors must act as a board, it may delegate some of its powers to committees and individuals, provided it does not abdicate its other functions. Individual members of the board do not, however, "become mere automatons, bereft of the power of speech and action, except when the

---

[25] See § 7.8 infra.

[26] "Directors of a corporation act as members of a board, not as individuals; it is their joint action that becomes the act of the corporation. This requires that the directors meet together at the same place and at the same time with the result that the action of the board is directed to facts and conditions existing and considered at that time." Schuckman v. Rubenstein, 164 F.2d 952, 957–58 (6th Cir. 1947), cert. denied, 333 U.S. 875 (1948).

Directors have no authority to act as a board except at a regularly constituted meeting, in the absence of a consent in writing. A director is not to be "trapped" with attendance at a meeting against his will. Zachary v. Milin, 294 Mich. 622, 293 N.W. 770, 771 (1940).

A corporation can act only through its board of directors at a regularly called meeting. Kelly v. Galloway, 156 Ore. 321, 68 P.2d 474 (1937).

[27] See DELAWARE CORP. LAW § 141 (as amended 1969); N. Y. BUS. CORP. LAW (as amended 1975).

See Acampora v. Birkland, 220 F. Supp. 527 (D. Colo. 1963) (absent director voted by letter under Maryland law).

mechanism of the board is set in motion." They have the power and duty as individual directors to take action in emergencies without prior board direction. "If a bank director should discover a fire in his banking house he would not wait for a formal meeting of the board of directors to authorize him to make an attempt to extinguish the fire or to call out the fire department." For "[o]nce let it be known that a bank director can be made liable for nothing that is not done by an organized board of directors, and confidence in banks will be put to a crucial test, and a dishonest director will never be at a loss for means of escape." [28]

To constitute a valid meeting, members of the body must meet knowingly. "To hold that certain directors could form a quorum by coming upon another in a room, or in the street, and, despite the protests of the other, could, by merely declaring the body of persons so gathered together to be a meeting actually give it that complexion, would be illegal. . . . A director of a corporation is not to be trapped into attendance at a meeting against his will." [29] However,

[28] Cassidy v. Uhlmann, 170 N.Y. 505, 516, 519, 526 (1902).

[29] Zachary v. Milin, 294 Mich. 622, 293 N.W. 770, 771 (1940).

A director cannot be tricked into attending a "fake" meeting. "Mr. Allen's testimony was to the effect that, when these two gentlemen came to his office, he did not understand that they came to hold a directors' meeting. They talked in a conversational way about the contract. Then one of them made a motion, and the other seconded it. Then Mr. Allen understood for the first time that they were trying to hold a meeting. He went to the telephone, and communicated with his attorney, and, after getting his advice, left the room. He denied that he said that he recognized that there was a quorum present, and would have put any motion they made. There is no legal process by which a director of a private business corporation can be forced to attend a meeting, and he cannot lawfully be compelled by physical force to attend, nor can he be trapped into attendance against his will. It happened to be the fact that Mr. Allen's office was the office of the company, and he was there for his daily work, not expecting a meeting of the board. These gentlemen knew that they would find him there, knew the other directors would not be there, and they planned to force a meeting at which they would constitute a majority. We hold that that was not a lawful meeting of the board of directors." Trendley v. Illinois Traction Co., 241 Mo. 73, 145 S.W. 1, 6, 7 (1912).

When two members of a three-member executive committee entered the office of the third member unannounced and tried to trap him into holding a meeting, and he refused to comply and left the room, the court held that it was a triable issue whether there was a valid meeting. American Center for Educ. v. Cavnar, 26 Cal. App. 3d 26, 102 Cal. Rptr. 575 (1972).

a recent case affirmed that the rule against obtaining a quorum through trickery does not apply where the director who has allegedly been tricked not only attends the meeting but also remains and participates in the meeting and in its proceedings.[30]

A court decision holds that the attendance of members of a zoning board at a dinner during which zoning problems were discussed was not a "meeting" within the purview of a statute requiring that certain meetings be open to the public,[31] and a meeting of a school board to consider appointment of a superintendent was a "sham" when it did not give the community an opportunity to participate in considering available candidates.[32]

Exceptions to the general rule requiring director action only at duly convened meetings may be found in the case of informal close corporations where the directors are in frequent communication with each other,[33] and where the directors and shareholders are the same persons.[34] "The exception is founded upon principles of equi-

---

See Gieselmann v. Stegeman, 443 S.W.2d 127 (Mo. 1969) (nocturnal meeting of board of directors without notice and without a quorum present was usurpation of corporate powers and intentionally performed in violation of a court order).

[30] Dillon v. Berg, 326 F. Supp. 1214 (D. Del.), aff'd, 453 F.2d 876 (3d Cir. 1971).

[31] Adler v. City Council, 184 Cal. App. 2d 763, 7 Cal. Rptr. 805 (1960).

A meeting of a church society, regularly called to fix the salary of the pastor, was held not a valid meeting. "No organization was effected, no motion made, no vote taken, no record of the meeting kept. It seems to have been a social rather than a business meeting, for refreshments were first served." Landers v. Frank Street Methodist Episc. Church, 114 N.Y. 626, 627, 21 N.E. 420 (1889).

An informal meeting of three members of a city council, called by a councilman and not by the mayor, was not an "official meeting" and action taken at such informal meeting was without force and effect. The mayor did not preside at the meeting and no vote was taken on the issue. Tanksley v. Foster, 227 Ga. 158, 179 S.E.2d 257, 259 (1971).

A gathering of members of a board of commissioners at the county seat to consider the filing of an answer in a pending lawsuit is not a "regular" meeting, a "special" meeting, or a "called" meeting. Rockingham County v. Luten Bridge Co., 35 F.2d 301 (4th Cir. 1929).

[32] Cullum v. Board of Educ., 15 N.J. 285, 104 A.2d 641 (1954).

[33] In re Stylemaster Dep't Store, 154 N.Y.S.2d 58 (Sup. Ct. 1956).

[34] Gerard v. Empire Square Realty Co., 195 App. Div. 244, 187 N.Y.S. 306

table estoppel and is limited to instances in which the custom or
usage of the directors is to act separately or informally and not as a
board." [35]

§ 1.7   Joint Meetings

There are circumstances under which meetings of different bodies
can be held together at the same time and place, with each being a
valid meeting for its own purposes. For example, where the shareholders (or principal shareholders) and the directors of a corporation are the same persons and meet together, the meeting may be
viewed as a "joint meeting" or as two separate meetings.[36] However,

---

(2d Dep't 1921) (all directors owning all the stock agreed separately on
contract).

When the directors and stockholders are the same persons, the irregularity
of not holding separate director and stockholder meetings will be overlooked.
Murray v. Smith, 166 App. Div. 528, 152 N.Y.S. 102 (2d Dep't 1915), *modified,* 224 N.Y. 40, 120 N.E. 60 (1918).

[35] Sharon Herald Co. v. Granger, 97 F. Supp. 295, 301 (W.D. Pa. 1951),
aff'd, 195 F.2d 890 (3d Cir. 1952); Forrest City Box Co. v. Barney, 14 F.2d
590 (8th Cir. 1926); Superior Portland Cement v. Pacific Coast Cement Co.,
33 Wash. 2d 169, 205 P.2d 597 (1949).

The directors "informally, but not collectively as a board," considered and
approved an advertising program without adopting a resolution at a formal
meeting. The court held that liability could not be imposed on the directors
because they failed to adopt a resolution at a board meeting. "The same
informal practice followed in this transaction had been the customary procedure of the directors in acting on corporate projects of equal and greater magnitude." The directors "with all their loose procedure, have done very well
for the corporation." Bayer v. Beran, 49 N.Y.S.2d 2, 8, 11 (Sup. Ct. 1944).

"Informal concurrence or assent to a decision by a majority of the board
of directors, in meeting assembled, constitutes corporate action as effectively
as a formal resolution." Bown v. Ramsdell, 139 Misc. 360, 249 N.Y.S. 387,
392 (Sup. Ct. 1931).

[36] In a "joint meeting" of directors and principal shareholders, a possible invalidity of the directors' meeting could be remedied by virtue of ratification by
the stockholders. *In re* Kartub's Petition, 7 Misc. 2d 72, 152 N.Y.S.2d 34 (Sup.
Ct. 1956), *aff'd,* 3 App. Div. 2d 896, 163 N.Y.S.2d 938 (1st Dep't 1957).

Where all shareholders are also directors and were present when action was
taken to increase officers' salaries, it is immaterial that the increase was recorded as authorized by a meeting of shareholders, while the by-laws committed
authority over salaries to the directors. Murray v. Smith, 166 App. Div. 528,
152 N.Y.S. 102 (2d Dep't 1915), *modified,* 224 N.Y. 40, 120 N.E. 60 (1918).

where two bodies meet together, each meeting must have independent validity and the meeting of one body cannot legally act upon matters pertaining to the other body.[37]

A "gathering" of city council members and members-elect (not yet sworn) has been held to be a "meeting" of members of a governing body within the ambit of the Florida "sunshine law." "An individual upon immediate election to public office loses his status as a private individual and acquires the position more akin to that of a public trustee." [38]

The term "joint session" implies that the two houses of the legislature, sitting as a unicameral body, have met together and commingle, thereby acting as one body.[39]

The legal significance of a resolution is not changed because it was adopted at a joint meeting of stockholders and directors. *See* Kilsby v. Aero-Test Equip. Co., 301 S.W.2d 703 (Tex. 1957).

[37] The court said that, by no "magic alchemy" can the meeting of one union be commuted into a meeting of another union even though the membership and general set-up and purpose of both were identical. Marvin v. Manash, 175 Ore. 311, 153 P.2d 251, 254 (1944), *citing* Robert's Rules of Order.

In a joint meeting of village commissioners and zoning commissioners, each body must act within its own authority. State *ex rel.* Synod of Ohio v. Joseph, 139 Ohio St. 229, 39 N.E.2d 515 (1942).

See Brechner v. Incorporated Village of Lake Success, 25 Misc. 2d 920, 208 N.Y.S.2d 365 (Sup. Ct. 1960), *aff'd*, 14 App. Div. 2d 567, 218 N.Y.S.2d 1017 (2d Dep't), *motion denied*, 11 N.Y.2d 875, 182 N.E.2d 403, 227 N.Y.S.2d 913 (2d Dep't), *appeal dismissed*, 11 N.Y.2d 929, 183 N.E.2d 81, 228 N.Y.S.2d 678 (1962) (joint meeting of village board of trustees and planning board).

[38] Hough v. Stembridge, 278 So. 2d 288, 289 (Fla. App. 1973).

"Judicial interpretation fails in its purpose when it becomes entangled in wishful or opinionated semantics of flaying opponents. The distinction between a meeting of the commission and a meeting of commissioners or the distinction between a meeting and a gathering serves no purpose." Dayton Newspapers, Inc. v. City of Dayton, 23 Ohio Misc. 49, 259 N.E.2d 522, 532–33 (1970).

[39] Anderson v. Krupsak, N.Y. Ct. App., N.Y.L.J., July 9, 1976.

2

Purpose of Shareholder Meetings

§ 2.1 Annual Meetings of Shareholders—General

It is the custom and practice of publicly owned companies to hold a general meeting of shareholders annually for the election of directors and for the transaction of such business as may properly come before the meeting.[1] Annual shareholder meetings are contemplated by State general corporate laws, and are often imposed by statute.[2] Generally, an annual meeting for the election of direc-

---

[1] The annual stockholders' meeting is an "important annual event." The statutory duty to hold an annual meeting is mandatory. Vanadium Corp. v. Susquehanna Corp., 203 F. Supp. 686, 699 (D. Del. 1962).

The holding of an annual meeting of corporations is an "important requirement" of business corporation statutes. Studebaker Corp. v. Allied Prods. Corp., 256 F. Supp. 173, 189 (W.D. Mich. 1966).

An election of directors is to be considered a meeting of the stockholders within the provisions of a corporation law that directors are to be chosen by the vote of stockholders voting at such election. In re Election of Directors of Rapid-Transit Ferry Co., 15 App. Div. 530, 44 N.Y.S. 539 (2d Dep't 1897).

[2] See, e.g., Studebaker Corp. v. Allied Prods. Corp., 256 F. Supp. 173 (W.D. Mich. 1966); In re Louisiana Inv. & Loan Corp., 224 F. Supp. 274

tors is required by the charter or by-laws of business and social organizations. Special shareholder meetings also may be held from time to time for the purpose of considering and voting upon particular matters which require or recommend shareholder approval. The difference between a regular meeting and a special meeting is well recognized by parliamentary law and by statute.[3]

Companies with shares listed on a national securities exchange are required to hold annual meetings and must issue proxy statements upon the solicitation of proxies by the management. Companies not subject to the proxy-soliciting rules of the SEC may con-

---

(E.D. La. 1963), *aff'd*, 342 F.2d 999 (5th Cir. 1965); Steinberg v. American Bantam Car Co., 76 F. Supp. 426, 436 (W.D. Pa. 1948), *appeal dismissed*, 173 F.2d 179 (3d Cir. 1949); Commonwealth *ex rel.* Sheip v. Vandegrift, 232 Pa. 53, 81 A. 153, 156 (1911).

Failure to hold an annual meeting of shareholders may justify a demand for inspection of the corporation's books and records. *See* Raynor v. Yardarm Club Hotel, Inc., 32 App. Div. 2d 788, 302 N.Y.S.2d 353 (2d Dep't 1969).

The Delaware Corporation Law requires that an annual meeting of stockholders must be held for the election of directors. There may be mitigating circumstances excusing a delay in holding the meeting. *See* Tweedy, Browne & Knapp v. Cambridge Fund, Inc., 318 A.2d 635 (Del. Ch. 1974).

Under Delaware law the court may summarily order a meeting of stockholders for the election of directors when a meeting has not been held for thirteen months. Prickett v. American Steel & Pump Corp., 251 A.2d 576 (Del. Ch. 1969).

[3] "When the statute says a regular meeting, it does not mean a special meeting. . . . A special meeting is a meeting called for a special purpose. . . . A regular meeting is a meeting convened at a stated time and place pursuant to a general order, statute or resolution." Barile v. City Comptroller, 56 Misc. 2d 190, 288 N.Y.S.2d 191, 196 (Sup. Ct. 1968).

A by-law providing that an annual meeting be held at a certain time is mandatory. When not so held, it is the duty of the directors within a reasonable time thereafter to call the annual meeting. Steinberg v. American Bantam Car Co., 76 F. Supp. 426, 436 (W.D. Pa. 1948), *appeal dismissed*, 173 F.2d 179 (3d Cir. 1949); *accord*, Stabler v. El Dora Oil Co., 27 Cal. App. 516, 150 P. 643 (1915).

Where a by-law requires annual meetings at a stated time, the company must adhere, but this does not prevent the directors, trustees, or members from holding special meetings whenever considered necessary or advisable. Noremac, Inc. v. Centre Hill Court, Inc., 164 Va. 151, 178 S.E. 877, 881 (1935).

See Annot., Remedies to restrain or compel holding of stockholders' meeting, 48 A.L.R.2d 615 (1956).

duct effective and lawful meetings, annual and special, without compliance with its rules.[4]

§ 2.2   Transaction of Business

Generally, shareholders may transact any ordinary business which properly comes before an annual or general meeting,[5] but may not transact extraordinary or unusual business unless due notice thereof has been given to the shareholders. It is the general rule that no business can be transacted at a special meeting except that specified in the notice.[6] The corporate and parliamentary rights of shareholders, including the right to make appropriate motions from the floor, apply to both special and regular meetings alike.

§ 2.3   Corporate Democracy

Shareholder meetings are a forum for the election of directors, the transaction of company business, and the discussion and resolution of corporate policy.[7] Such meetings enable shareholders—the "real

---

[4] "It would scarcely be contended, for example, that the elections of directors in the thousands of unlisted corporations in this country are invalid because formal proxy statements in the form required by the Securities and Exchange Commission were not used in connection with such elections." Bresnick v. Home Title Guar. Co., 175 F. Supp. 723, 724–25 (S.D.N.Y. 1959).

[5] A notice of an annual meeting of stockholders did not specify the subjects to be considered. "Every stockholder, therefore, takes notice of the fact that all business which may be transacted by the stockholders is open for consideration and action at such meeting; and their powers at such a meeting are as vast and complete as the competencies of the corporation." Chicago, R.I. & P. Ry. v. Union Pac. Ry., 47 F. 15, 20 (C.C.D. Neb. 1891), aff'd, 51 F. 309, appeal dismissed, 163 U.S. 564 (1896). However, where a notice of an annual meeting of shareholders limited the purposes to the election of named officers and to action properly coming before the meeting in respect of such election, other matters could not be acted upon. Bushway Ice Cream Co. v. Fred H. Bean Co., 284 Mass. 239, 187 N.E. 537 (1933).

See §3.4 infra.

[6] See FLETCHER, CYCLOPEDIA OF CORPORATIONS at § 2016.

[7] "It is a basic property right of stockholders to call stockholders' meetings and to select directors. . . . This is a matter of such moment that the shareholders themselves should be the ones to elect the directors and not their agents, to wit, the board of directors. The true corporate owners should not be deprived of the right to determine basic corporate policy." Shareholders are the

owners" of the corporate property[8]—to practice the concepts of "corporate democracy"[9] and to exercise their "corporate suffrage."[10]

"true corporate owners." Starr v. Tomlinson, 7 Misc. 2d 916, 166 N.Y.S.2d 629, 631–32 (Sup. Ct. 1957).

[8] Stockholders, by giving power to the directors to make by-laws, do not lose their own power to make them. "It would be preposterous to leave the real owners of the corporate property at the mercy of their agents, and the law has not done so." Rogers v. Hill, 289 U.S. 582, 589 (1932).

Accord, In re A. A. Griffin Iron Co., 63 N.J.L. 168, 41 A. 931, *aff'd,* 63 N.J.L. 357, 46 A. 1097 (1899); Auer v. Dressel, 306 N.Y. 427, 433, 118 N.E.2d 590 (1954).

[9] The term "corporate democracy" was coined and popularized by Lewis D. Gilbert in his presentations at corporate meetings and in his book DIVIDENDS AND DEMOCRACY (1956). The New York Stock Exchange has adopted the term in its publication THE CORPORATE DIRECTOR AND THE INVESTING PUBLIC (1965) in the following passages: "Stockholder approval obtained through the solicitation of proxies is the essence of corporate democracy." *Id.* at 6. "Legally, directors have authority to act on a great many matters without referring them to shareowners for approval. These days, however, many directors feel that solicitation of shareowner views via the proxy route is a desirable procedure where matters of unusual importance are involved. The Exchange believes that an extension of this philosophy would make a valuable contribution to the cause of true corporate democracy." *Id.*

See Locke Mfg. Cos. v. United States, 237 F. Supp. 80, 87 (D. Conn. 1964), describing proxy contests as "a part of the corporate way of life" and noting that Congress intended in enacting the Securities Exchange Act of 1934 to promote "corporate democracy and shareholder participation in the affairs of the corporation."

See reference to "democratic processes" concerning corporate elections in Standard Power & Light Corp. v. Investment Associates, Inc., 29 Del. Ch. 593, 51 A.2d 572, 576 (Sup. Ct. 1947).

"Normally, the majority rule prevails under our democratic processes." Stansberry v. McCarty, 149 N.E.2d 683, 686 (Ind. 1958).

For principles of union democracy, *see* Navarro v. Gannon, 385 F.2d 512, 518, 519 (2d Cir. 1967), *cert. denied,* 390 U.S. 989, *rehearing denied,* 390 U.S. 1046 (1968).

For definition of proxy "contest," *see* Dyer v. SEC, 266 F.2d 33, 39–40 (8th Cir.), *cert. denied,* 361 U.S. 835 (1959).

[10] The Securities Exchange Act § 14(a) stemmed from Congressional belief that fair corporate suffrage is an important right that should attach to every equity security bought on a public exchange. J. I. Case Co. v. Borak, 377 U.S. 426, 431 (1964).

The Securities Exchange Act contemplated "a fair opportunity for the operation of corporate suffrage, within the presumable intelligence of ordinary

These rights, although of recent emphasis, are of long standing. In an early Massachusetts case Chief Justice Holmes remarked that "[i]f stockholders want to make their power felt, they must unite. There is no reason why a majority should not agree to keep together." [11] This pronouncement has been restated: "If stockholders cannot act together, they cannot act effectively." [12] A recent case alleging violation of the SEC proxy rules stated the present posture of "this phase of corporate suffrage" in the following words: "Individual shareholders have a right to join together for their mutual protection and to advance their mutual interests. When they become dissatisfied with management they should be free to discuss their grievances and seek to influence the votes of other shareholders in any legal manner." [13]

It is the owners of the corporation, the stockholders, who should fashion the standards of corporate conduct. A recent decision has held that the intent of the SEC proxy regulations is to enable shareholders "to control the important decisions which affect them in their capacity as stockholders and owners of the corporation." [14] In

---

stockholders." Dyer v. SEC, 266 F.2d 33, 39 (8th Cir.), *cert. denied,* 361 U.S. 835 (1959).

See SEC v. Transamerica Corp., 163 F.2d 511, 518 (3d Cir. 1947), *cert. denied,* 332 U.S. 847 (1948); American Crystal Sugar Co. v. Cuban–American Sugar Co., 276 F. Supp. 45, 50 (S.D.N.Y. 1967).

In an early English case it was stated that a general meeting was a source from which the shareholders could, as far as possible, manage their own affairs without interference by the court. Harben v. Phillips, 23 Ch. D. 14 (C.A. 1882).

See Annot., Proxies—Securities Exchange Act, 12 L. Ed. 2d 1235 (1965).

"Only at the annual or specially called meeting of the shareholders can the individual shareholders exercise their right of suffrage. . . . Fair and full disclosure is of the essence of free suffrage." Studebaker Corp. v. Allied Prod. Corp., 256 F. Supp. 173, 189 (W.D. Mich. 1966).

[11] McQuade v. Stoneham, 263 N.Y. 323, 329, 189 N.E. 234, 238 (1934), *quoting* Brightman v. Bates, 175 Mass. 105, 111, 55 N.E. 809, 811 (1900).

[12] SEC v. Transamerica Corp., 163 F.2d 511, 518 (3rd Cir. 1947), *cert. denied,* 332 U.S. 847 (1948).

[13] Greater Iowa Corp. v. McLendon, 378 F.2d 783, 797 (8th Cir. 1967).

[14] Medical Comm. for Human Rights v. SEC, 432 F.2d 659, 680–81 (D.C. Cir. 1970), *cert. granted,* 401 U.S. 973 (1971), *vacated and remanded as moot,* SEC v. Medical Comm. for Human Rights, 404 U.S. 403 (1972).

Shareholders have the right to determine basic corporate policy. Starr v. Tomlinson, 7 Misc. 2d 916, 166 N.Y.S.2d 629 (Sup. Ct. 1957).

an action to recover monies paid by a corporation to defray expenses [15] of rival candidates for election as directors, the court commented that "[i]t is their corporation and an alert, articulate ownership is in a position to settle these matters far more effectively than can a judicial tribunal." [16]

Recent cases support the Congressional purpose behind the SEC proxy-soliciting rules. They indicate that Congress intended to give "true vitality to the concept of corporate democracy" [17] and to effectuate "free corporate suffrage." [18]

Corporate management is obligated to call an annual meeting of shareholders as provided in the by-laws even if the company is doing well. "Management of a corporation may be in skilled hands; its

---

In large corporations with stock widely distributed among many stockholders, a compact united ownership of a substantial block of stock, although less than a majority, could be ample to control the operations of the corporation. *See* Gottesman v. General Motors Corp., 171 F. Supp. 661, *appeal denied,* 268 F.2d 194 (2d Cir. 1959).

[15] *See* Eisenberg, *Access to the Corporate Proxy Machinery,* 83 HARV. L. REV. 1489 (1970).

[16] Rosenfeld v. Fairchild Engine & Airplane Corp., 284 App. Div. 201, 132 N.Y.S.2d 273, 282 (2d Dep't 1954), *aff'd,* 309 N.Y. 168, 128 N.E.2d 291 (1955).

This holding is consistent with English common law. "No one can doubt that the Court ought not to interfere in the conduct of the company's business further than is absolutely necessary. A meeting of shareholders is at once looked to as the source from which help can come. People ought to be allowed as far as possible to manage their own affairs without interference by a Court of law." Harben v. Phillips, 23 Ch.D. 14, 36–37 (C.A. 1882).

[17] The court also said that Congress desired to make proxy solicitations "a vehicle for *corporate* democracy rather than an all-purpose forum for malcontented shareholders to vent their spleen about irrelevant matters." Medical Comm. for Human Rights v. SEC, 432 F.2d 659, 676, 678 (D.C. Cir. 1970), *cert. granted,* 401 U.S. 973 (1971), *vacated and remanded as moot,* SEC v. Medical Comm. for Human Rights, 404 U.S. 403 (1972).

[18] The court also said: "Only at the annual or specially called meeting of the shareholders can the individual shareholders exercise their right of suffrage. An undue delay in holding the annual meeting of shareholders might dilute or defeat their right of free suffrage in this case." Studebaker Corp. v. Allied Prods. Corp., 256 F. Supp. 173, 189 (W.D. Mich. 1966).

Another court states that the SEC proxy rules are directed to requiring disclosures that will assure stockholders' meetings "informationally competent to deliberate on corporate matters and decide them by stockholder vote." Laurenzano v. Einbender, 264 F. Supp. 356, 362 (E.D.N.Y. 1966).

policies may be in the best interests of the corporation; there may be no waste or wrongdoing of any kind in so far as the corporate interests are involved; and yet the stockholders may attack the right of the directors to act as such." [19]

On the other hand, the court will enjoin the holding of a shareholders' meeting and election of directors until all shareholders can be informed of the facts relating to the financial condition of the corporation, particularly when a substantial loss had been sustained over a prolonged period. The court will intervene "when necessary to secure a free and full explanation, and an accurate record of the will of the shareholders on the subject in question. . . . The election of the directors should be orderly and with a full and complete opportunity for a participation of all the stockholders after being fully informed and advised as to the detailed facts and circumstances which exist as to the affairs of the company." [20] Shareholders are entitled to all pertinent information whenever called upon to exercise their "right of corporate suffrage" including the views of those who oppose as well as those who favor a proposed action, and shareholders, once informed of the facts, "have a right to make their own decisions in matters pertaining to their economic self-interest, where consonant with or contrary to the advice of others, whether such advice is tendered by management or outsiders or those motivated by self-interest." [21]

§ 2.4   Proper Subjects for Corporate Action

The purposes and subjects which properly may be brought before a general or special meeting of shareholders either by the manage-

[19] Lazar v. Knolls Cooperative, 205 Misc. 748, 130 N.Y.S.2d 407, 410 (Sup. Ct. 1954).

[20] Steinberg v. American Bantam Car Co., 76 F. Supp. 426, 436–37 (W.D. Pa. 1948), *appeal dismissed,* 173 F.2d 179 (3d Cir. 1949).

But, to drench the shareholders with a flood of information may defeat the very purpose of the proxy rules. Doyle v. Milton, 73 F. Supp. 281, 285 (S.D.N.Y. 1947).

[21] The court remarked that management "adopts a paternalistic attitude toward shareholders when it suggests that they may be unduly influenced by the arguments of the opposition." American Crystal Sugar Co. v. Cuban–American Sugar Co., 276 F. Supp. 45, 50 (S.D.N.Y. 1967).

ment or by the shareholders are far broader than the matters which meet the definition of a "proper subject" for action by security holders under the Rules of the SEC. The latter term has been the theme of considerable court action and interpretive comment since an early decision holding, in effect, that any subject is a "proper subject" where there is no logical basis for concluding that it is not a proper subject for action by the security holders.[22] It seems that the SEC has developed its own "common law" relating to proper subjects for shareholder action.[23]

It is the general rule that shareholders may be brought together to consider not only those corporate matters on which they can or must act but also those on which they cannot take effective action. In an interesting New York case the requisite number of shareholders requested the president to call a special meeting to consider certain proposals critical of management. The president refused to call the meeting on the ground that none of the stated purposes was a proper one for stockholders' action. The court acknowledged that the shareholders, by expressing their approval or disapproval, would not be able to take effective corporate action, but held the stated purposes to be proper subjects for shareholder action, saying:

[22] SEC v. Transamerica Corp., 163 F.2d 511 (3d Cir. 1947), *cert. denied,* 332 U.S. 847 (1948); *see* Medical Comm. for Human Rights v. SEC, 432 F.2d 659 (D.C. Cir. 1970), *cert. granted,* 401 U.S. 973 (1971), *vacated and remanded as moot,* SEC v. Medical Comm. for Human Rights, 404 U.S. 403 (1972); Dyer v. SEC, 266 F.2d 33 (8th Cir.), *cert. denied,* 361 U.S. 835 (1959).

See generally:

Allen, *The Proxy System and the Promotion of Social Goals,* 26 THE BUS. LAW. 481 (1970);

Blumberg, *Introduction of the Politicalization of the Corporation,* 26 RECORD OF N.Y.C.B.A. 369 (1971);

Schwartz, *The Public-Interest Proxy Contract: Reflections on Campaign G M,* 69 MICH. L. REV. 419 (1971);

Note, *The SEC and "No-Action" Decisions Under Proxy Rule 14a–8: The Case for Direct Judicial Review,* 84 HARV. L. REV. 835 (1971);

Note, *Proxy Rule 14a–8: Omission of Shareholder Proposals,* 84 HARV. L. REV. 700 (1971).

[23] Medical Comm. for Human Rights v. SEC, 432 F.2d 659, 677 (D.C. Cir. 1970), *cert. granted,* 401 U.S. 973 (1971), *vacated and remanded as moot,* SEC v. Medical Comm. for Human Rights, 404 U.S. 403 (1972).

"[t]here is nothing invalid in their so expressing themselves and thus putting on notice the directors who will stand for election at the annual meeting." As to constituting a shareholders' meeting as a tribunal to hear charges made by certain shareholders against the directors, and the "incongruity of letting the stockholders hear and pass on those charges by proxy," the court merely held that the charges were not frivolous or inconsequential and that "all that we are holding as to the charges is that a meeting may be held to deal with them." The dissenting opinion stressed the point that none of the matters to be considered at the meeting could be voted upon legally, and that the vote of shareholders would be merely an "idle gesture." The dissenting opinion also noted disapproval that the directors would be subjected to "trial by proxy" and that they could be "adjudged guilty of fraud or breach of faith in absentia by shareholders who have neither heard nor ever will hear the evidence against them or in their behalf." [24]

This case laid the foundation for the growing practice of shareholders to submit proposals for action at a forthcoming annual meeting requesting that management consider a recommended action which the stockholders themselves would not have authority to effect

[24] Auer v. Dressel, 306 N.Y. 427, 432–35, 438–39, 118 N.E.2d 590 (1954). The proposals were: (a) voting upon a resolution endorsing the administration of a former president who had been removed by the directors and demanding that he be reinstated; (b) voting upon a proposal to amend the charter and by-laws to provide for filling of vacancies on the board; (c) voting upon a proposal to have the stockholders hear certain charges preferred against four directors and to determine whether the conduct of such directors was inimical to the corporation and if so to vote upon their removal; and (d) voting upon a proposal amending the quorum provisions of the by-laws.

The holding in Auer v. Dressel, supra, would have been approved at common law. An early English case held that shareholders did not have the power to remove a director unless granted by the charter, but concluded that "no one can doubt that the wish of a corporation that certain persons should not be directors may effectually be expressed by any meeting of shareholders duly called for such purposes. . . ." Harben v. Phillips, 23 Ch. D. 14, 39 (C.A. 1882).

A shareholder proposal to censure all existing directors and declare them disqualified for re-election at a meeting at which they were candidates was a campaign effort against them and the SEC could authorize management to omit the proposal from the proxy material. Dyer v. SEC, 289 F.2d 242 (8th Cir. 1961).

in the absence of prior enabling corporate action which would require at least the cooperation of the board of directors.[25]

It must be observed that the criteria for judging the propriety of such resolutions and attendant questions from the floor is not necessarily the same as for proposals which do, in fact, meet the SEC qualifications for inclusion as a "proper subject" in a notice of meeting or in a proxy statement by shareholder demand. The rules of the SEC which permit the inclusion of shareholders' proposals in proxy-soliciting material issued on behalf of management create a privilege which does not otherwise ordinarily exist in favor of shareholders. This privilege is necessarily subject to the imposition by its creator of reasonable conditions and limitations on the scope and manner of its enjoyment, with the result that only certain proposals may be privileged and others may be denied the privilege and thereby excluded from the proxy statement. It is important to recognize that action of the SEC in ruling that a certain proposal is not privileged or not a proper subject for shareholder action at a particular meeting has no bearing on the shareholder's separate corporate or parliamentary right to advance the same proposal in any other manner or to make the same proposal from the floor of the meeting. Thus, privileges granted by rules of the SEC impinge on neither the common law of company meetings nor the rights of shareholders under charter or by-law provisions. In a leading decision relating to the exclusion by the SEC of certain shareholder proposals from the management proxy-soliciting material, the court observed that "the exclusion of petitioners' proposals from management's proxy material did not, of course, in any way affect petitioners' independent right to make a proxy solicitation of their own or to bring up the excluded proposals from the floor of the meeting in accordance with by-law provisions."[26] However, a court of equity has denied

[25] The SEC has considered the propriety of advisory proposals that the directors "consider the advisability of adopting a resolution setting forth" the proposed action. *See, e.g.,* Medical Comm. for Human Rights v. SEC, 432 F.2d 659, 663 (D.C. Cir. 1970), *cert. granted,* 401 U.S. 973 (1971), *vacated and remanded as moot,* SEC v. Medical Comm. for Human Rights, 404 U.S. 403 (1972).

[26] Dyer v. SEC, 266 F.2d 33, 41 (8th Cir. 1959) (state corporation law did not restrict proposals to purposes stated in notice of annual meeting).

The "proxy inclusion-and-expression privilege is an element of regulation

a motion of a stockholder to enjoin the holding of a scheduled annual meeting when an injunction would, in effect, "nullify an interpretation" by the SEC of its proxy-soliciting rules.[27]

§ 2.5 Matters Becoming Moot on Holding of Meeting

Questions relating to the solicitation of proxies for a shareholders' meeting [28] and to the action to be taken at the meeting [29] may become moot upon the holding of the meeting, under the general principle of law that a question becomes moot when it appears that the thing sought to be prevented has been done and cannot be undone by any order of the court. However, there may be questions of such character or consequence that they cannot properly be regarded as

---

and not of license in corporate democracy." Dyer v. SEC, 287 F.2d 773, 783 (8th Cir. 1961).

[27] Curtin v. AT&T, 124 F. Supp. 197 (S.D.N.Y.), aff'd per curiam (2d Cir. April 4, 1954) (unreported).

"Rules and regulations adopted by administrative agencies pursuant to congressional authorization are best interpreted, in the first instance, by the agency which has been entrusted with power and authority to write them." Peck v. Greyhound Corp., 97 F. Supp. 679, 681 (S.D.N.Y. 1951).

The court will accept the SEC's judgment as to orders made in relation to the facts of a particular proxy solicitation. See Brooks v. Standard Oil Co., 308 F. Supp. 810, 813 (S.D.N.Y. 1969).

The judgment of the SEC as to the necessity or appropriateness of material for use in proxy solicitation is not subject to judicial scrutiny unless it has no possible rational basis, or is arbitrary, capricious, or otherwise irresponsible. Dyer v. SEC, 287 F.2d 773, 779 (8th Cir. 1961).

[28] Richland v. Crandall, 353 F.2d 183 (2d Cir. 1965) (motion for temporary injunction to restrain holding of special meeting of stockholders); accord, Klastorin v. Roth, 353 F.2d 182 (2d Cir. 1965).

See generally Dyer v. SEC, 251 F.2d 512, 513 (8th Cir. 1958), vacated and remanded, 359 U.S. 449 (1959); SEC v. Topping, 85 F. Supp. 63 (S.D.N.Y. 1949); Doyle v. Milton, 73 F. Supp. 281 (S.D.N.Y. 1947).

[29] Action by a stockholder to prevent use at a stockholders' meeting of proxies claimed to be misleading was rendered moot by holding the meeting to approve a merger advocated by the proxy statement. Sawyer v. Pioneer Mill Co., 300 F.2d 200 (9th Cir.), cert. denied, 371 U.S. 814 (1962).

An appeal from a motion to enjoin a special meeting illegally called was dismissed as "academic" on a showing that the meeting had been held and that action authorized at the meeting had been substantially completed. Kursch v. Board of Education, 7 App. Div. 2d 922, 183 N.Y.S.2d 689 (2d Dep't 1959).

having become dissolved or rendered inoperative by the holding of the meeting.[30]

An issue is not mooted by the holding of the meeting where the "cessation of illegal conduct did not diminish the risk of future similar conduct." [31] However, where the "wrongful behavior" of a corporation in refusing to include a stockholder proposal in its proxy statement for the current annual meeting could not "reasonably be expected to recur" at a subsequent meeting, the court may dismiss enforcement proceedings against the corporation by the SEC on the ground that the issues have become moot. If the corporation "were likely to repeat its illegal conduct," the case would not be moot.[32]

The court may also consider the possibility that its judgment might become moot by future events. One court refused to accept an appeal from an interlocutory injunction against the issuance by inspectors of a final report on the results of a corporate election at the annual meeting, on the ground that the court's determination might well be shortly mooted by another election at the next annual meeting.[33]

A mandamus proceeding to compel the chairman and secretary of a stockholders' meeting to declare that plaintiff had been elected a corporate director and to have the corporate minutes corrected to truly reflect the results of the election did not become moot upon expiration of the term of office of elected directors while the court had the case under consideration because the demand for correction of the minutes still remained.[34]

[30] See Dyer v. SEC, 266 F.2d 33, 46 (8th Cir. 1959).

[31] Navarro v. Gannon, 385 F.2d 512, 521 (2d Cir. 1967), cert. denied, 390 U.S. 989, rehearing denied, 390 U.S. 1046 (1968) (injunctive relief against threatened interference with local union meeting).

Proceedings to set aside an unlawful union election and require a new election are not mooted by the "happenstance intervention" of a subsequent unsupervised election. Wirtz v. Local 153, GBBA, 389 U.S. 463, 474 (1968).

The adoption of procedures (mailing ballot asking for a vote upon recall) in search for alternative relief does not moot court proceedings to restrain a recalled union president from acting as such. Talton v. Behncke, 199 F.2d 471 (7th Cir. 1952).

[32] SEC v. Medical Comm. for Human Rights, 404 U.S. 403, 406 (1972).

[33] Ronson Corp. v. Liquifin Aktiengesellschaft, 508 F.2d 399 (2d Cir. 1974).

[34] State ex rel. Dunbar v. Hohmann, 248 S.W.2d 49 (Mo. 1952).

Expiration of the term of Congress at which a Senate investigation committee was appointed does not render moot a question as to the power of the

§ 2.6   Dissolution

The dissolution of a corporation or the forfeiture of its charter terminates its corporate existence and destroys its every operating facility, including the capacity to hold meetings of stockholders or of the board of directors for the purpose of conducting business.[35]

However, the directors, officers, and stockholders of a dissolved corporation may continue to function for the purpose of winding up the corporation's affairs and distributing its assets. General corporation statutes may provide in such case that dissolution does not change quorum or voting requirements for the board or shareholders in the conduct of meetings or change provisions regarding amendment or repeal of by-laws or the adoption of new by-laws.[36]

Senate to compel the attendance of witnesses. McGrain v. Daugherty, 273 U.S. 135 (1926), *citing* Jefferson's Manual, Hinds' Precedents.

See The Mootness Doctrine in the Supreme Court, 88 HARV. L. REV. 373 (Dec. 1974).

[35] The rescinding of a forfeiture of charter does not legalize meetings held during the forfeiture period. Gieselmann v. Stegeman, 443 S.W.2d 127 (Mo. 1969).

A dissolved corporation is a nonentity and its purported acts are without legal effect. New Hampshire Fire Ins. Co. v. Virgil & Frank's Locker Service, Inc., 302 F.2d 780 (8th Cir. 1962).

[36] *See* N.Y. BUS. CORP. LAW § 1006 (McKinney Supp. 1975); N.J. BUS. CORP. ACT, N.J.S.A. 14A:12 (1971).

A dissolved Delaware corporation, while it is still holding assets "naturally retains a board of directors, holds meetings, issues reports and invests its assets." Johnson v. Helicopter & Airplane Services Corp., 404 F. Supp. 726, 735 (D. Md. 1975).

3

Procedure for Calling Meetings

CALL OF MEETING

§ 3.1 Duty and Authority To Call

The calling of a meeting must be distinguished from giving notice of a meeting. A call of a meeting, in the legal sense of the term, has been described as "a summons to the parties entitled to meet, directing them to meet." [1]

The duty and authority to call a meeting is usually specified in the charter or by-laws of the organization. The board of directors or the holders of a certain percentage of voting shares usually have the power to call a meeting of shareholders. As a rule, the president of a corporation has no power to call a meeting of shareholders unless the charter, by-laws, or a resolution of the board of directors grants that authority to him. [2] It is important that a meeting be lawfully called, for any action taken at a meeting which was not called in accordance with a charter or by-law is a nullity. [3] An illegal call cannot be cured by subsequent ratification. [4]

[1] P. & F.R. Ry. Co. v. Commissioners, 16 Kan. 302 (1876). The court further describes a call in the following words: "It involves something more than a mere purpose in the mind of the caller, or an expression of that purpose unheard, unseen, and unknown. It implies a communication of that purpose to the parties to be affected by it. How it shall be communicated, is sometimes prescribed by statute, or by by-law. It is sometimes provided that it shall be by publication in the newspaper, sometimes by printed notice served personally or at the residence, and sometimes by mere oral personal notice. But in some way or other notice must be given. . . ." *Id.* at 307.

A meeting of a religious corporation was regularly called although it was not announced from the pulpit as was customary, where there was no requirement in the charter that notice be given in that manner, and when notice of the meeting was given by published and written notice which was more effective than an announcement from the pulpit would have been, and no one complained of failure to receive notice. State Bank v. Wilbur Mission Church, 44 Wash. 2d 80, 265 P.2d 821 (1954).

[2] As a general rule, the president of a corporation has no power to call a meeting of shareholders, unless the by-laws or a resolution of the board of directors make it his duty to do so. State Bank v. Wilbur Mission Church, 44 Wash. 2d 80, 265 P.2d 821 (1954).

[3] A call for an annual stockholders' meeting restricting its purpose to election of named officers is a valid call. A holder of a majority of stock had no power to change the call. A call for a special meeting not issued in accordance with by-laws or statutes is invalid. Bushway Ice Cream Co. v. Fred H. Bean Co., 187 N.E. 537 (Mass. 1933).

When a meeting has been duly called, notice of the meeting must be sent to all members entitled to vote by the clerk or the secretary of the organization, acting in an administrative capacity.[5]

The duty to call a meeting cannot be ignored. It has been held, for example, that the president of a corporation may not refuse to call a meeting of the board of directors for fear that the board would interfere with his control and management; nor may he refuse to call a meeting of shareholders because of fear that they might elect a board of directors unfavorable to him. "The management of the corporation's affairs belongs to the board of directors, and not to the president."[6]

If no one is specifically empowered to call meetings, it is generally competent for the chief executive officer or the board of directors[7] or the "managing agents"[8] to do so. A meeting called by de facto officers, and otherwise regularly held, is a valid meeting, especially where the dissident shareholders have notice of the meeting and are present and participate."[9]

---

[4] Where by-laws provided that a special meeting could be called by three directors or by 10 per cent of the shareholders, a call by a shareholder which was later ratified by more than 10 per cent of the shareholders was not a valid call. Smith v. Upshaw, 217 Ga. 703, 124 S.E.2d 751 (1962).

[5] Where the president lawfully called a special meeting and the clerk refused to send out a notice of the meeting, a notice mailed by the president constituted valid notice and the meeting was legally called. Whipple v. Christie, 122 Minn. 73, 141 N.W. 1107 (1913).

[6] State *ex rel.* Dendinger v. Kerr Gravel Co., 158 La. 324, 104 So. 60, 61 (1925).

[7] "Where the statute or by-laws are silent as to who shall call or give notice of a meeting of stockholders, the rule is that it must be called by the directors or the President or General Manager." Port Chilkoot Co. v. Heinmiller, 12 Alas. 200, 212 (D. Alas. 1948).

Where the by-laws provide that the board of directors shall call a special meeting when requested by not less than one-half of the outstanding shares, a majority of the board cannot ignore a request by more than one-half. Maurer v. J. A. Maurer, Inc., 76 N.Y.S.2d 150 (Sup. Ct. 1947); *see* Citizens' Mut. Fire Ins. Co. v. Sortwell, 90 Mass. (8 Allen) 217 (1864).

[8] Streuber v. St. Mary's Pipe Co., 33 Pa. County Ct. 46 (1906).

When no one is specifically empowered to call meetings, it is competent for the "general agent" to do so as he is the person who is entrusted with the management and control of the company's affairs. Stebbins v. Merritt, 64 Mass. (10 Cush.) 27, 33 (1852).

See Fisher v. Harrisburg Gas Co., 1 Pearson 118 (Pa. C.P. 1857).

§ 3.2   By-law and Charter Provisions

By-law provisions must be read carefully. Where the by-laws state that "[t]he board of directors shall have power to provide for the general and special meetings," the president does not have such power since it is reserved for the board.[10] On the other hand, where the by-laws provide that special meetings of the shareholders may be called by the president or the secretary at the request of a majority of the shareholders, the shareholders themselves do not have the right to call a meeting.[11] Where the by-laws provide alternative methods of calling a meeting, as by the board of directors or by the president, one or the other must do so.[12]

Where the by-laws of a corporation give the president power to call special meetings of shareholders for any purpose, but do not grant any power to cancel a call, the board of directors has been held unable directly to cancel the president's call for a special meeting. Nor could the board do so indirectly by removing the president and appointing a new president for the purpose of cancelling the meeting.[13]

By-laws authorizing the call of meetings and specifying the manner in which they may be called will be given full recognition by the courts. Where the by-laws of a corporation authorize the president to call a special meeting of shareholders "for any purpose or purposes, other than those regulated by statute" it will be presumed that the purposes for which a meeting may be called embrace only matters which are appropriate for stockholder action. Thus, such purposes need not be in furtherance of the routine business of the corporation and may in fact involve policies not defined by the board

---

[9] Simon Borg & Co. v. New Orleans City R., 244 F. 617 (E.D. La. 1917).

A notice signed by a de facto vice president when the president was absent and the secretary and another vice president refused to issue a call was held valid. Moon v. Moon Motor Car Co., 17 Del. Ch. 176, 151 A. 298 (1930).

[10] Knoll v. Levert, 136 La. 241, 66 So. 959 (1914); State *ex rel.* Guerrero v. Pettineli, 10 Nev. 141 (1875).

[11] Young v. Janas, 103 A.2d 299 (Del. Ch. 1954).

[12] Pennington v. George W. Pennington Sons, 170 Cal. 114, 148 P. 790 (1915).

[13] Republic Corp. v. Carter, 22 App. Div. 2d 29, 253 N.Y.S.2d 280 (1st Dep't), *aff'd*, 15 N.Y.2d 661, 204 N.E.2d 206, 255 N.Y.S.2d 875 (1964).

of directors.[14] Limitations on the purposes for which a meeting may be called are also lawful and binding.[15]

A proxyholder with the right merely to vote the shares of his principal does not have the power to call a meeting of shareholders. This power cannot be implied from the general authority given the proxy-holder to vote.[16]

Where the rules of a political county committee provide that a meeting shall be called on the written request of 10% of the membership, it would seem that "orderly procedure would leave the time and place to the Chairman in order to avoid any conflicts between competing interests." To give any group the right to choose the date of the meeting "would be a negation of orderly procedure." [17]

The chairman often has broad powers in handling the arrangements for a meeting, especially when the membership is alert to the fact that a meeting must be held and all have received notice in time to attend. In a case involving a political party judicial convention for the nomination of candidates, the chairman of the state committee designated the time and place of the meeting and then, before the meeting was called to order or had taken any action, cancelled and revoked his designation because the meeting room did not have sufficient seating capacity for the delegates and alternates entitled to attend. Those present were informed that the meeting would be held at a place to be determined, and a new call was issued by the chairman designating another and apparently adequate meeting

---

[14] The court held that the president had authority to call a special meeting of shareholders to fill director vacancies, to amend the by-laws to increase the number of directors, and to remove certain directors and fill such vacancies. The fact that the by-laws also authorized the shareholders on their initiative to call a meeting for the purpose of filling vacancies on the board does not mean that the president is deprived of his by-law authority to call a meeting for that purpose. Campbell v. Loew's Inc., 36 Del. Ch. 565, 134 A.2d 852 (1957).

[15] A call for an annual stockholders' meeting limiting the purpose of the meeting to the election of directors and officers and to other action properly coming before the meeting in respect of such election. Bushway Ice Cream Co. v. Fred H. Bean Co., 187 N.E. 537 (Mass. 1933).

[16] The relation between stockholders and the holders of their proxies is that of principal and agent. The power merely to vote the stock as proxy at an election does not purport to give proxyholders the power to act in calling a meeting. That power cannot be implied from the general authority given to vote. Josephson v. Cosmocolor Corp., 31 Del. Ch. 46, 64 A.2d 35 (1949).

[17] In re Davie, 13 Misc. 2d 1019, 178 N.Y.S.2d 740, 742, 743 (Sup. Ct. 1958), citing Robert's Rules of Order.

room. Notice of the meeting was given by telegrams transmitted to the delegates in the afternoon of the day before the new time for the meeting. The trial court held that the cancellation of the convention because of insufficient seating capacity was arbitrary and unjustifiable and that one day's notice of the later meeting was inadequate. On appeal the higher court found no evidence that any delegate or alternate failed to receive notice of the meeting in time to attend or was otherwise prejudiced by the shortness of the notice and held that the action of the chairman in revoking the first designation was not arbitrary or capricious. The court further held that the subsequent meeting had been legally convened in another room and thus its proceedings were lawful and valid.[18]

When the charter provides that the annual meeting of shareholders shall be held for the election of directors, the directors cannot by an amendment of the by-laws so change the time of holding the annual election as to have the effect of continuing themselves in office, against the will of the majority of the stockholders.[19]

NOTICE OF MEETING

§ 3.3   Requirement of Due Notice

It has long been a general and settled rule of common law that due and proper notice must be given to all members or stockholders entitled to vote at a meeting. A leading Supreme Court case held: "Even when there is no provision, in statute or by-laws, for notice, it has been held that common-law principles require corporate meetings to be called by reasonable notice to stockholders." [1] This is a duty of management.[2]

[18] The trial court was critical of the one-day notice, particularly when called for a Friday night during the Labor Day holiday and because there was no proof as to when the telegrams were actually delivered. Bannigan v. Heffernan, 280 App. Div. 891, 115 N.Y.S.2d 444 (2d Dep't), *modifying* 115 N.Y.S.2d 889 (Sup. Ct.), *aff'd*, 304 N.Y. 729, 108 N.E.2d 209 (1952).

[19] Walsh v. State *ex rel.* Cook, 199 Ala. 123, 74 So. 45, 47 (1917).

[1] Toombs v. Citizens Bank, 281 U.S. 643, 646–47 (1930); *accord,* Commonwealth *ex rel.* Claghorn v. Cullen, 13 Pa. 133, 139 (1850).

"It is not only a plain dictate of reason, but a general rule of law, that no power or function entrusted to a body consisting of a number of persons, can be legally exercised without notice to all the members composing such body." People *ex rel.* Loew v. Batchelor, 22 N.Y. 128, 134 (1860) (board of aldermen).

"A stockholder, although in the minority, at least has the right to statutory notice. . . ." Jones v. Pearl Min. Co., 20 Colo. 417, 38 P. 700, 702 (1894).

It is a general rule of law that notice must be given to every person entitled to be present at a corporate meeting. Knoll v. Levert, 136 La. 241, 66 So. 959 (1914) (no statutory requirement).

Resolutions authorizing directors to apply for amendments to a corporate charter as they might deem advisable are fundamental, and notice of such purpose should be given. When not given, stockholders not present are not bound. Johnson v. Tribune Herald Co., 155 Ga. 204, 116 S.E. 810 (1923).

Every member of a municipal council is entitled to reasonable notice of special meetings, and no important action may lawfully be taken unless such notice has been given or unless members not notified attend and participate in the business of the meeting. Crook v. Township of Clark, 74 N.J. Super. 148, 180 A.2d 715 (1962) (city council).

"It is axiomatic that no functions entrusted to a board consisting of a number of persons can be validly exercised without notice to all, ... The failure to give notice was a fatal procedural defect. . . ." Cirrincione v. Polizzi, 14 App. Div. 2d 281, 220 N.Y.S.2d 741, 742–43 (4th Dep't 1961).

Meetings of municipal legislatures and administrative bodies which are open to the public may often be held only on such notice and at such times as may be specified or permitted by ordinance. See Green v. Beste, 76 N.W.2d 165 (N.D. 1956).

The necessity for notice of meetings to stockholders is to give those entitled to vote a voice in the management of the corporation. In re J. A. Maurer, Inc., 77 N.Y.S.2d 159 (Sup. Ct. 1947).

To make a corporate act valid "it should be passed at a meeting duly convened, after notice to all the members." Commonwealth ex rel. Claghorn v. Cullen, 13 Pa. 133, 142 (1850).

Where the charter is silent on time and place, full notice must be given. Knoll v. Levert, 136 La. 241, 66 So. 959 (1914).

Notice of a shareholder meeting need be given only to holders of record, and not to beneficial holders. See, e.g., Goldfield Corp. v. General Host Corp., 29 N.Y.2d 264, 327 N.Y.S.2d 330, aff'g 39 App. Div. 2d 125, 318 N.Y.S.2d 378 (1st Dep't 1971).

Term "shareholder" means shareholder of record. Cross Properties, Inc., v. Brook Realty Co., 37 App. Div. 2d 193, 322 N.Y.S.2d 773 (2d Dep't 1971), aff'd, 340 N.Y.S.2d 928 (1972).

See, e.g., DELAWARE CORP. LAW § 222; N.Y. BUS. CORP. LAW § 603 (McKinney 1963).

[2] A by-law requiring ten days' written notice of an annual meeting of stockholders imposes a duty on management to give such notice for the benefit of all stockholders. Furthermore, where an attempt is made to hold a shareholders' meeting without notice as required by the by-laws, the corporation is under a duty to point out that the by-law provision adopted for the benefit of the stockholders was not carried out. Gries v. Eversharp, Inc., 30 Del. Ch. 129, 67 A.2d 69 (1949), rev'd on other grounds, 69 A.2d 922 (1949).

§ 3.4 Statement of Purposes of Meeting

§ 3.4.1 Purposes of Meeting—General

The notice of meeting should state such items of business to come before the meeting as may be required by statute, or by the charter or by-laws of the organization. In the absence of higher authority, the notice should also specify any business of an extraordinary nature or of great importance to be transacted at the meeting.

The purposes of the meeting must be reasonably identified in the notice.[3] To this end, the notice of meeting should fairly and adequately apprise the shareholders of the objects and purposes of

[3] The New York Stock Exchange Company Manual, Sec. A8, requires that listed corporations give prompt notice to the Exchange of the calling of any meeting of stockholders which shall "indicate the date of the meeting, the date of record . . . , and shall describe the matters to be voted upon at the meeting, unless accompanied by printed material being sent to stockholders which describes those matters." Definitive copies of the proxy material must also be filed with the Exchange.

Under Rule 14a–3 of the SEC, no solicitation of proxies subject to regulation may be made unless each person solicited is concurrently furnished or has previously been furnished with a written proxy statement containing the information required in Section 14A. Under Rule 14a–4 the form of proxy shall "identify clearly and impartially each matter or group of related matters intended to be acted upon, whether proposed by the management or by security holders."

The Supreme Court has confirmed that the Securities and Exchange Act was intended to promote the free exercise of voting rights of stockholders by ensuring that proxies would be solicited with explanation to the stockholders of the real nature of the questions for which authority to cast their votes is sought. The question of materiality is an objective one, involving the significance of an omitted or misrepresented fact to a reasonable investor. Thus some information is of such dubious significance that insistence on its disclosure in a proxy statement may accomplish more harm than good. The general standard of materiality is: "An omitted fact is material if there is a substantial likelihood that a reasonable shareholder would consider it important in deciding how to vote." It does not require proof of a substantial likelihood that disclosure of an omitted fact would have caused the reasonable investor to change his vote. The standard contemplates "a showing of a substantial likelihood that, under all the circumstances, the omitted fact would have assumed actual significance in the deliberations of the reasonable shareholder." TSC Industries, Inc. v. Northway, Inc. (No. 74–1471, 44 LW 4852, June 14, 1976), *quoting* Mills v. Electric Auto-Lite Co., 396 U.S. 375 (1970).

the meeting, such as the election of directors and the transaction of identified items of business.[4] However, "there generally is no duty

[4] A notice of meeting "for the purpose of electing directors" has been held to be adequate, and not "insufficient or misleading in any way." *In re* William Faehndrich, Inc., 2 N.Y.2d 468, 473, 141 N.E.2d 597, 161 N.Y.S.2d 99 (1957).

A notice of annual meeting "to elect directors" has been held to be sufficient to include an increase in the number of directors as it was within the general nature of the specified business. Choppington Collieries Ltd. v. Johnson, [1944] 1 All E.R. 762; *see* Betts & Co. v. Macnagten, [1910] 1 Ch. 430.

A notice of annual meeting "to determine the general policies" to be followed for the succeeding year was held insufficient to include a proposed merger. Stone v. Dean, 344 P.2d 649 (Okla. 1959).

A notice of meeting specifying several items of business to be transacted "and related matters" was not sufficient to cover separate unrelated matters. Parrish v. Moss, 200 Misc. 375, 106 N.Y.S.2d 577 (Sup. Ct.), *aff'd*, 279 App. Div. 608, 107 N.Y.S.2d 580 (2d Dep't 1951) (board of education). *See* Kingsbury v. Centre School Dist., 53 Mass. (12 Metc.) 99 (1846).

A notice of special meeting of stockholders specifying certain items with the usual addition of "such further and other business as may be properly brought before the meeting" is not sufficient to permit the consideration of other business so important as the ratification of a long-term management contract. *See, e.g.*, United Hotels Co. v. Mealey, 147 F.2d 816 (2d Cir. 1945).

A notice of special meeting to increase the number of directors and to elect such additional directors, and to transact "any and all other business that may properly come before the meeting or any adjournment or adjournments thereof, in connection with the foregoing matters," cannot fairly be construed as indicating that the meeting was to be adjourned for the purpose of electing additional directors after the amended charter increasing the number of directors had been filed. Fierman v. Rose, 175 Misc. 102, 22 N.Y.S.2d 215 (Sup. Ct. 1940).

In calling a meeting to remove a corporate officer, notice to the officer that he appear at the meeting without disclosing the purpose for which his appearance is sought is not equivalent to notice that charges for removal will be presented at the meeting. Goller v. Stubenhaus, 77 Misc. 29, 134 N.Y.S. 1043, 1051 (Sup. Ct. 1912).

Newspaper items covering a discussion of the use of a schoolhouse for the following year as a scheduled subject for a meeting of the school district were held not to constitute adequate notice of a meeting to decide whether the school should be discontinued. Botens v. Board of Educ., 26 Misc. 2d 158, 204 N.Y.S.2d 266 (Sup. Ct. 1960), *aff'd*, 14 App. Div. 2d 485, 217 N.Y.S.2d 670 (4th Dep't 1961).

Notice must also be given whenever action taken at a previous meeting is to be reconsidered. Anderson v. Judd, 158 Colo. 46, 404 P.2d 553 (1965).

to specify the course of conduct contemplated by the directors after their election, and no requirement to explain the consequences that will follow from the action they plan to take." [5]

On the other hand, voluntary or extraneous matter in a notice of meeting does not necessarily impair its validity or create any binding obligations on the body issuing the notice. Thus, a statement in a notice of meeting that the city council would hear complaints and allegations from the taxpayers does not, in the absence of a duty imposed by law, require the council to listen to the complaints of any or all dissatisfied taxpayers. [6]

The foregoing indicate that a principal reason for an informative notice of meeting is to bring interested members to the meeting and give all members an opportunity for investigation and consideration in preparation for the meeting. [7]

A notice of a union meeting for a "discussion and action upon a report by the Official Board regarding *current problems*" was held to be "inept" for the purpose of considering a disaffiliation of the union. The court reasoned that "[w]hile technical nicety is not necessary, the notice must state what is fairly intended in order to bring to the meeting the members who are interested in the proposed action, particularly when that action is of the extraordinary nature of disaffiliation." Harker v. McKissock, 10 N.J. Super. 26, 76 A.2d 89, 94–95 (1950), *aff'd*, 7 N.J. 323, 81 A.2d 480, *aff'd*, 8 N.J. 230, 84 A.2d 723 (1951).

[5] *In re* William Faehndrich, Inc., 2 N.Y.2d 468, 473, 141 N.E.2d 597, 161 N.Y.S.2d 99 (1957).

[6] The court noted that, if otherwise, "any organized group could disrupt the orderly proceedings of representative government by monopolizing them to the exclusion of the elected representatives of the people." People *ex rel.* Powott Corp. v. Woodworth, 172 Misc. 791, 15 N.Y.S.2d 985, 995 (Sup. Ct. 1939), *rev'd on other grounds*, 260 App. Div. 168, 21 N.Y.S.2d 785 (4th Dep't 1940).

See § 3.5 *infra*.

[7] Randolph v. Mt. Zion Baptist Church, 139 N.J. Eq. 605, 53 A.2d 206 (1947) (church meeting), *citing* Hiscox' Directory.

The rationale for the salutary rule that all directors receive notice of meetings is that each member of a corporate body has the right of consultation with the others, and has the right to be heard upon all questions considered, and it is presumed that if the absent members had been present they might have dissented, and their arguments might have convinced the majority of the unwisdom of their proposed action and thus have produced a different result. Stone v. American Lacquer Solvents Co., 345 A.2d 174 (Pa. 1975).

"The purpose of a parliamentary procedural rule requiring the reading of a resolution in full before it is voted on is to provide assurance that those whose

§ 3.4.2 Purpose of Meeting—Statutory Restriction

At common law, the notice of a general or stated meeting of stockholders, such as notice of an annual meeting, need not set forth the items of business to be considered and acted upon at the meeting, unless it is intended that any unusual or extraordinary business is to come before the meeting. Also at common law, and generally by statutory requirement, the notice of a special meeting of stockholders must state the purpose or purposes of the meeting. No business other than that stated in the notice may be transacted at a special meeting.

State corporation statutes regarding the need and content of the notice of stockholder meetings lack uniformity. Some states have elaborate provisions and some have no statutory regulations as to the manner of calling or conducting meetings. Generally, state corporation laws prescribe that notice of the time and place (but not the purposes) of the annual meeting shall be given to all stockholders and, in the case of a special meeting, that the notice shall also state the purpose or purposes for which the meeting is called. Thus, under most corporation laws there is a statutory void as to noticing the purposes of an annual meeting other than the usual election of directors.

This void is filled in some state statutes, notably Massachusetts and New Jersey, by a provision that the notice of "all meetings" or of "every meeting" of stockholders shall state the purpose or purposes of the meeting.[8]   Other state statutes take the opposite view and specifically broaden the rights of stockholders to conduct any proper business by introducing proposals from the floor at an annual meeting. The Delaware statute, for example, states flatly: "Any other proper business may be transacted at the annual meeting." Connecticut is more verbose: "Any matter relating to the affairs of the corporation may be brought up for action at an annual meeting of shareholders, whether or not stated in the notice of the meeting

---

duty is to vote thereon may have some knowledge of its scope and terms before they cast their votes." Pasadena v. Paine, 126 Cal. App. 2d 93, 271 P.2d 577, 579 (1954).

[8] Mass. G. L., 156 B. § 36.
N. J. Bus. Corp. Act, 14A:5–4.

. . . ," with certain exceptions.[9] Accordingly, the corporation law and case law of the state of incorporation must be examined to determine whether any subjects not noticed may be considered and voted upon at an annual meeting of stockholders, irrespective of whether such matters are introduced at the meeting by management from the chair or by shareholders from the floor.

In this posture, the statutory treatment of the purposes of an annual meeting of stockholders is significant in determining whether a particular shareholder proposal is, "under the laws of the issuer's domicile, not a proper subject for action by security holders" under the proxy soliciting rules of the SEC.[10] Thus, where the items of business of an annual meeting of shareholders is limited by the law of the corporate domicile to the items specified in the notice of meeting, it may be said that no other matters may be brought before the meeting for a vote by shareholders. A leading Massachusetts case decided in 1933 has so held.[11] The restricted items would include shareholder proposals which were omitted from the proxy statement pursuant to the rules of the SEC. A 1976 proxy statement of a New Jersey domiciled corporation has taken this position. It states under the heading "Other Matters" that "In accordance with New Jersey law, under which the Company is incorporated, matters not properly noticed to shareholders other than procedural matters may not be made the subject of a vote by shareholders at the meeting."[12]

Presumably, a charter or by-law provision of a corporation limit-

[9] DELAWARE GEN. CORP. LAW § 211.
CONN. S.C.A. § 46, Supp. § 33–327.
[10] See SEC Rule 14A–8(c)(1).
[11] Bushway Ice Cream Co. v. Fred H. Bean Co., 187 N.E. 537 (Mass. 1933). Bushway must be distinguished from Dyer v. SEC, 266 F.2d 33 (8th Cir. 1959), holding that the exclusion of a stockholder proposal from management's proxy soliciting material did not affect the stockholder's right to make a proxy solicitation on his own or to bring up the excluded proposal from the floor of the meeting. The question of purposes, as stated in the notice of meeting, was not at issue. See reference to Bushway in SEC v. Transamerica Corp., 67 F. Supp. 326 at 331 (D. Del. 1946), modified and aff'd, 163 F.2d 511 (3d Cir. 1947), cert. denied, 332 U.S. 847 (1948).
[12] Notice of 1976 Annual Meeting and Proxy Statement, Eastman Kodak Company.

ing the business of an annual meeting to items stated in the notice of meeting would be valid and enforceable as an agreement between the corporation and its stockholders and between the stockholders themselves, generally recognized as valid by state corporation case law.[13]

§ 3.5   Opportunity To Deliberate

It appears to be a fundamental rule of parliamentary practice governing assemblies that the opportunity to deliberate, and if possible, to convince their fellows, is the right of the minority, of which they cannot be deprived by the arbitrary will of the majority. An adequate notice of meeting may also assist a stockholder in attempting to convince others to follow his recommendations.[14]

§ 3.6   Failure of Substantial Compliance—Actions Invalid

Substantial compliance with established rules and procedures is generally sufficient.[15] Notice is sufficient if it gives members information upon which they may "exercise an intelligent judgment."[16]

---

[13] *See, e.g.,* Bushway Ice Cream Co. v. Fred H. Bean Co., 187 N.E. 537 (Mass. 1933) (state statute and corporation by-law required that notice of all meetings state the purpose or purposes).
See § 21 *infra.*
[14] *See* § 12.8 *infra.*
[15] Where rules of city council required publication of ʌ ʼtice of meeting one day in advance of the meeting date, and council me on the day when notice of meeting was published but adjourned until ʌhe next day, it was held that there was substantial compliance with the rule and that proceedings taken on the latter day were valid. Whalen v. Wagner, 2 Misc. 2d 89, 152 N.Y.S.2d 386, 391–92 (Sup. Ct. 1956), *aff'd,* 3 App. Div. 2d 936, 163 N.Y.S.2d 225 (2d Dep't 1957), *aff'd,* 4 N.Y.2d 575, 152 N.E.2d 54, 176 N.Y.S.2d 616 (1958).
Notice by telephone to the wrong municipal officials, although not in technical compliance, held to be defect in "unsubstantial detail." Brechner v. Incorporated Village of Lake Success, 25 Misc. 2d 920, 208 N.Y.S.2d 365 (Sup. Ct. 1960), *aff'd,* 14 App. Div. 2d 567, 218 N.Y.S.2d 1017 (1961), *motion denied,* 11 N.Y.2d 875, 182 N.E.2d 403, 227 N.Y.S.2d 913, *appeal dismissed,* 11 N.Y.2d 929, 183 N.E.2d 81, 228 N.Y.S.2d 678 (1962) (joint meeting of village trustees and planning board).
Notice is sufficient when it indicates with substantial certainty the nature

It need not specify with exactness the business to be conducted nor disclose the full effects of any business transaction by the board of directors pursuant to their corporate powers, but it must be sufficient to advise a reasonably alert stockholder of the nature of the business to be transacted.[17] However, unless the notice of meet-

---

of the business to be acted upon. Tuckerman v. Moynihan, 282 Mass. 562, 158 N.E. 2 (1933).

Notice need only be sufficiently explicit to call the attention of voters to subjects to be considered and acted upon. Capone v. Nunes, 85 R.I. 392, 132 A.2d 80, 82 (1957).

Personal notice by the mayor to every member of the city council that a special meeting would be held on a certain night and describing the nature of the business to be transacted was held to be in substantial compliance with a statutory provision for notice. State ex rel. Oil Operators' Trust v. Hellman, 36 S.W.2d 1002 (Tex. Comm. App. 1931).

The court added: "The failure to give the notice required by the by-laws is a substantial omission, which should not be disregarded unless upon clear waiver by the stockholder." In re Keller, 116 App. Div. 58, 101 N.Y.S. 133, 135 (3d Dep't 1906).

[16] Gruber v. Chesapeake & Ohio Ry., 158 F. Supp. 593, 611 (N.D. Ohio 1957).

[17] Blum v. Latter, 163 So. 2d 189, writ refused, 167 So. 2d 301 (La. 1964).

Statute providing that the warrant (notice) shall state the subject to be acted upon means that "the subjects to be acted upon must be sufficiently stated in the warrant to apprise voters of the nature of the matters with which the meeting is authorized to deal." Blomquist v. Arlington, 338 Mass. 594, 156 N.E.2d 416, 419 (1959), quoting Robert's Rules of Order on another issue and remarking that Robert's Rules are of "dubious application" to town meeting government.

Where by-laws provided for a board of 5 to 15 and notice of annual meeting called for election of directors, the stockholders could determine, as incidental to the election of directors, how many directors they wished to have for the ensuing year, notwithstanding notice of intention to change number of directors at annual meeting had not been given. In re Fleetwood Bank, 283 N.Y. 157, 27 N.E.2d 974 (1940).

Notice of meeting to consider appointment of a school superintendent is sufficient to authorize appointment after consideration. Cullum v. Board of Educ., 15 N.J. 285, 104 A.2d 641 (1954).

"The statute does not give the form of the call or notice, and it will be deemed sufficient if it merely designate in general terms the purpose of the meeting. Details are unnecessary; only a designation of the subject or sub-

ing shall "fairly apprise stockholders of the scope of the matter" to be presented at the meeting, such matter cannot be voted upon.[18]

§ 3.7 Stated Meetings

In the absence of some legal requirement, such as a statute requiring that the notice of meeting must state its purposes,[19] it is not necessary to give notice of the business to be transacted at a regular annual meeting.[20] However, it is the better rule that notice should be given of any unusual business to come before a regular annual meeting for consideration and action.[21] It may be assumed that

---

jects of legislation or business to be considered at the called meeting of the council, is required." Reuter v. Meacham Contracting Co., 143 Ky. 557, 560, 136 S.W. 1028 (1911).

[18] Rosenfeld v. Fairchild Engine & Airplane Corp., 284 App. Div. 201, 132 N.Y.S.2d 273, 281–82 (2d Dep't 1954), aff'd, 309 N.Y. 168, 128 N.E.2d 291, 51 A.L.R. 2d 860, reargument denied, 309 N.Y. 807, 130 N.E.2d 610 (1955) (reimbursement of expenses incurred in proxy fight).

[19] See § 3.4.2 supra (statutory requirement that notice of annual meeting state its purposes).

[20] "Notice of an annual meeting need not contain a specification of the details of the business to be considered. . . ." A "technical elaboration" of the information contained in the notice and accompanying letter was unnecessary. These communications read in the light of surrounding circumstances were sufficient. There was no concealment either in the notice of the meeting or at the stockholders' meeting. Koplar v. Warner Bros. Pictures, 19 F. Supp. 173, 186 (D. Del. 1937).

Where by-laws contain no provision requiring notice, and it has not been the custom to send notice of regular meetings other than the annual meeting, an annual meeting held at the regular time and place was not illegal because held without notice. New York Elec. Wkrs. Union v. Sullivan, 122 App. Div. 764, 107 N.Y.S. 886 (1st Dep't 1907).

"Where the meeting is stated and general, notice of the time and place of holding it, or of the business to be transacted, is, in the absence of provision or regulation to the contrary, in no case required. This is the general law of private corporations." State v. Bonnell, 35 Ohio St. 10, 15 (1878).

[21] "It is not usually necessary to give notice of the business to be transacted at a regular annual meeting of the stockholders of a corporation, but it seems to be the better rule where some unusual business is to be transacted, such as selling all the corporate property, that notice should be given." Des Moines Life & Annuity Co. v. Midland Ins. Co., 6 F.2d 228, 229 (D. Minn. 1925).

Notice of regular meeting of a labor union must state purpose of the meet-

proper items not stated in the notice are likely to arise in the usual course of the meeting.[22]

In the absence of statutory or by-law requirements, notice of the time and place of general or stated meetings of a corporate body, as distinguished from special meetings, need not be given, and every member is bound by whatever is done at any stated meeting within the range of the ordinary duties of the body. Members are "bound to know what is apt to come before a meeting in the regular course" [23]

---

ing if any business to be transacted is of an extraordinary nature. Estes v. Tompkins, 371 P.2d 86 (Okla. 1962).

Notice of an annual meeting of stockholders for the election of directors does not require special notice of any additional business unless it is of an unusual or extraordinary nature not usually brought up at a general meeting. Josephson v. First Nat'l Bank, 42 N.J. Super. 461, 127 A.2d 210 (1956).

[22] Notice of annual meeting of stockholders did not specify the subjects to be considered. "Every stockholder, therefore, takes notice of the fact that all business which may be transacted by the stockholders is open for consideration and action at such meeting; and their powers at such a meeting are as vast and complete as the competencies of the corporation." Chicago, R. I. & P. Ry. v. Union Pac. Ry., 47 F. 15, 20 (C.C.D. Neb. 1891), aff'd, 51 F. 309, appeal dismissed, 163 U.S. 564 (1896).

"The notice of meeting which went out to the stockholders made no mention of a proposal to be passed on at the meeting for a change in the by-laws. This was natural, because the management in control contemplated no such change. The meeting being the annual one, however, no advance notice of a proposed change in the by-laws was required. . . . A proposal to amend the by-laws in this particular, in view of the quoted by-law, must be regarded as likely to arise in the usual course." Gow v. Consolidated Coppermines Corp., 19 Del. Ch. 172, 165 A. 136, 142 (1933).

"The meeting was an annual meeting of the stockholders and it was not necessary that advance notice of the proposed resolutions be set forth." Gottlieb v. McKee, 34 Del. Ch. 537, 107 A.2d 240 (1954).

[23] Where the by-laws fix the time and place of holding meetings, "the rule is that the by-laws themselves are sufficient notice to all the stockholders, and no further notice is necessary." Morrill v. Little Falls Mfg. Co., 53 Minn. 371, 55 N.W. 547, 549 (1893).

The by-laws themselves are sufficient notice to all stockholders; no further notice is necessary. Green v. Felton, 42 Ind. App. 675, 84 N.E. 166 (1908).

Where the by-laws require annual meetings at stated times, the shareholders must adhere to such times, but they may hold special meetings whenever desirable. Noremac, Inc. v. Centre Hill Court, Inc., 164 Va. 151, 178 S.E. 877, 881 (1935).

Presumption of knowledge of the times for holding stated meetings does

and that any action authorized by the constitution and by-laws might be taken at the meeting without advance notice.[24]

However, the court will not approve an "opposition meeting" held without notice on the date fixed in the by-laws as the annual meeting date, when management has, in good faith, delayed the annual meeting and noticed it to be held a week later.[25]

§ 3.8   Special Meetings

The rule of notice applicable to special meetings differs from the rule regarding general or stated meetings.[26] With respect to special

---

not include a presumption that a member, although absent, intuitively knows all that is done at the meeting so that when something is done which contemplates future action not at a future stated meeting, he is charged with notice of the appointed time. People *ex rel.* Loew v. Batchelor, 22 N.Y. 128 (1860).

See Fisher v. Harrisburg Gas Co., 1 Pearson 118 (Pa. C.P. 1857).

"As to 'stated meetings' generally, notice is to be presumed." Anderson v. Krupsak, N.Y. Ct. App., N.Y.L.J., July 9, 1976.

A director receiving notice of a meeting was "bound to know" that the meeting might be adjourned and the business might be transacted at the adjourned meeting. Seal of Gold Mining Co. v. Slater, 161 Cal. 621, 120 P. 15, 18 (1911).

[24] A director "took his chances" as to what might be done when he failed to attend a meeting of an unincorporated labor association which had no governing law other than its constitution and by-laws. "Though he was bound to know that any action authorized by the Constitution and By-Laws might be taken by the Board, he did not attend. Obviously it does not lie within his right now to complain that he had no advance notice of the amendment. He was bound to know that it might be made." Talton v. Behncke, 199 F.2d 471, 473, 474 (7th Cir. 1952).

[25] Gries v. Eversharp Inc., 69 A.2d 922 (Del. Ch. 1949).

After a corporation has voluntarily abandoned its organization for 17 years, stockholders have no right, without notice, to meet on the day which would have been election day if the organization had not been abandoned, and proceed to reorganize the corporation. Morrill v. Little Falls Mfg. Co., 60 Minn. 405, 62 N.W. 548, 550 (1895).

[26] Sometimes there is a question whether a meeting is a general meeting or a special meeting.

Where the by-laws could not be changed except at a general meeting on notice to all shareholders, they could not be amended at a meeting called annually for the election of directors even when the unbroken custom or usage of the company for many years had been to regard the annual election of di-

meetings, notice of the time, place and purpose or purposes is required as a matter of common and statutory law. Notice may be waived but, in the absence of failure to give notice of a special meeting, renders actions taken at the meeting invalid.[27]

The general rule has been stated in a case holding that an executive committee had convened without proper notice because an absent member had not received notice of the meeting. "[S]ince each is entitled to take part in the exercise of the power, each is entitled to notice. Notice may be given by the adoption of rules fixing times for stated meetings; constructive notice will be sufficient if some rule, legally prescribed, declares it sufficient; but for special meetings, in the absence of a rule for constructive notice, actual notice must be given. In the absence of such notice, a special meeting will not be legally convened. These rules apply to the corporators of incorporated companies, the directors and any committee thereof." [28]

---

rectors as a meeting at which any of the company's business could be transacted. The court regarded the election of directors as a special meeting and not a general meeting. Mutual Fire Ins. Co. v. Farquhar, 86 Md. 668, 39 A. 527 (1898).

The fact that ordinary business was sometimes transacted at meetings specially designated by the charter to canvass votes after municipal elections, does not give such meetings the standing of regular meetings. Thorne v. Squier, 264 Mich. 98, 249 N.W. 497 (1933).

[27] A special meeting held without notice to some or any directors and in their absence is illegal. Stone v. American Lacquer Solvents Co., 345 A.2d 174 (Pa. 1975).

Where a directors' meeting was a special meeting, notice to the directors was required, and, although notice could be waived, failure to notify directors of a special meeting rendered actions taken at the meeting invalid. An unqualified allegation that one director did not receive notice of the mailing should be sufficient to put the adequacy of notice in issue. Rapoport v. Schneider, 29 N.Y.2d 396, 328 N.Y.S.2d 431 (1972).

Where a notice of special meeting of a city commission stated it was for the purpose of submitting a proposed ordinance to electors, the meeting did not have power to fill vacancies in the commission as that subject was not noticed. Burns v. Stenholm, 310 Mich. 639, 17 N.W.2d 781 (1945).

However, it has been held that a notice of a special meeting of a board of directors need not specify the purpose of the meeting when not required by the statute. Seal of Gold Mining Co. v. Slater, 161 Cal. 621, 120 P. 15 (1911).

[28] Metropolitan Tel. Co. v. Domestic Tel. Co., 44 N.J. Eq. 568, 573, 14 A. 907 (1888).

§ 3.9   Waiver of Notice—Participation

Notice of a meeting may be waived by an instrument in writing [29] or by participation in the meeting without protest. "It is settled beyond question that no matter where a stockholders' meeting is held or how defectively the members are notified, the proceedings will bind all who appear at the meeting and participate in it without dissent. . . . In other words, statutory and other requirements for

[29] A stockholder may expressly or by his acts waive his right to have a notice of a corporate meeting served upon him. *In re* Hammond, 139 F. 898, 900 (S.D.N.Y. 1905).

A stockholders' meeting held outside the state of incorporation is valid when all stockholders consented in writing and participated. Ellsworth v. National Home & Town Builders, 33 Cal. App. 1, 164 P. 14 (1917).

Where all directors attended a meeting and none objected to a lack of formal notice, the business transacted was not invalid. Osborne v. Locke Steel Chain Co., 153 Conn. 527, 218 A.2d 526, 532 (1966).

A resolution authorizing a mortgage was valid when all directors were present at a meeting, although not held pursuant to notice. Sorge v. Sierra Auto Supply Co., 47 Nev. 217, 218 P. 735 (1923), *rehearing denied*, 221 P. 521 (1924).

Waivers signed after the meeting may be effective. Prentice v. Knickerbocker Life Ins. Co., 77 N.Y. 483 (1879).

Waivers previously signed, with date of meeting left blank, may be effective. Johnson v. Busby, 278 F. Supp. 235 (N.D. Ga. 1967).

General corporation laws often provide that failure to give notice or defects in a notice of a meeting may be waived before or after the meeting. *See, e.g.,* Goldfield Corp. v. General Host Corp., 29 N.Y.2d 264, 327 N.Y.S.2d 330 (1971), *aff'g* 39 App. Div. 2d 125, 318 N.Y.S.2d 378 (1st Dep't 1971) (New York statute).

Subsequent waiver by absent directors of notice of a past meeting cannot validate action taken at that meeting. United States v. Interstate R.R., 14 F.2d 328 (W.D. Va. 1926).

Waiver subsequent to a meeting may be ineffective. Lippman v. Kehoe Stenograph Co., 11 Del. Ch. 80, 95 A. 895 (1915).

A proxy to "vote and act" for the undersigned stockholder at all meetings for five years has been held to be insufficient to constitute a waiver of the statutory notice requirement. Société Anonyme D'Innovations Chimiques v. American Alcolac Corp., 8 Misc. 2d 166, 171 N.Y.S.2d 149 (Sup. Ct. 1957).

Under Pennsylvania law notice of a directors' meeting may be waived in writing by a director either prior or subsequent to the meeting. Stone v. American Lacquer Solvents Co., 345 A.2d 174 (Pa. 1975).

notice of meetings of stockholders may be waived by their presence and participation in the meeting." [30]   Where all members are present

[30] Sherrard State Bank *ex rel.* Moberg v. Vernon, 243 Ill. App. 122, 126 (1926).

"Petitioner should either have disregarded the notice and not attended the meeting or, if he attended, should have left the meeting immediately after voicing his objection to the validity thereof without further participation. He could not object to the legality of the meeting insofar as it related to the election of new directors and at the same time participate therein to the extent that it involved consideration of the financial statement of the corporation submitted to the meeting." Frankel v. 447 Central Park W. Corp., 176 Misc. 701, 28 N.Y.S.2d 505, 506 (Sup. Ct. 1941), *aff'd mem.* 263 App. Div. 950, 34 N.Y.S.2d 136 (1st Dep't 1942).

Stockholders present and voting at a meeting cannot attack the validity of the action taken on the ground that the officers who called the meeting were not legally qualified. Simon Borg & Co. v. New Orleans City R., 244 F. 617 (E.D. La. 1917).

Where an unincorporated society has no governing law other than its constitution and by-laws, a member is "bound to know" that any action authorized by such articles might be taken by the board at a meeting which he does not attend. "Obviously it does not lie within his right now to complain that he had no advance notice of the amendment." Talton v. Behncke, 199 F.2d 471, 473 (7th Cir. 1952).

Notice of a meeting of directors was waived by those present, who constituted a majority of the board, because they took part in the business of the meeting without protest. Clark v. Mutual Loan & Inv. Co., 88 F.2d 202 (8th Cir. 1937) (limited to emergencies).

Attendance at and participation in a stockholder meeting by a holder of record amounted to a waiver of any defect in the notice, over the objection of plaintiff as beneficial owner of the shares. Andrews v. Precision Apparatus, Inc., 217 F. Supp. 679, 685 (S.D.N.Y. 1963).

"It is generally held attendance at and participation in a meeting without objection waives any defect in the notice." Weise v. Land O'Lakes Creameries, Inc., 191 N.W.2d 619 (Iowa 1971).

The notice of business to be transacted at special meetings of stockholders is a provision for the benefit of the stockholders and may be waived and is waived by attendance at and participation in the meeting without objection. Synnott v. Cumberland Bldg. Loan Ass'n, 117 F. 379, 385 (6th Cir. 1902).

When all stockholders are present at a meeting it is immaterial that notice of the meeting was not published in a newspaper as required by statute. *In re* P. B. Mathiason Mfg. Co., 122 Mo. App. 437, 99 S.W. 502 (1907).

A meeting held on a day other than that provided in by-laws is legal where all shareholders attended and participated without protest. Camp v. Shannon, 162 Tex. 515, 348 S.W.2d 517 (1961).

Where all shareholders assented to an out-of-state meeting, it constituted

and acting, no notice of a special meeting is required.[31] In applying
the principle that attendance at a special meeting cures any irreg-

---

an effective waiver of irregularity. American Clearing Co. v. Walkill Stock
Farms Co., 293 F. 58 (S.D. Fla. 1923); *accord*, State *ex rel.* Parker v. Smith,
22 Minn. 218, 222–23 (1875) (city charter did not prohibit meeting by agreement of all).

"Certainly a member who failed to object to the calling of a meeting outside the state, and failed to object to the validity of a by-law adopted at such
meeting, when the first election was held pursuant thereto, should be considered to have acquiesced in the procedure adopted . . . ." George v. Holstein–
Friesian Ass'n of America, 238 N.Y. 513, 526, 144 N.E. 776 (1924).

Notwithstanding a claim of no notice, the challenger attended the meeting,
nominated, and voted. "Such active participation must be deemed . . . a
waiver of any preceding irregularities." Shamel v. Lite Prods. Sales, Inc., 131
Cal. App. 2d 33, 279 P.2d 1020, 1022 (1955).

Calling of a meeting to order by the presiding officer constitutes a waiver
of an alleged irregularity in the notice of the meeting, in the absence of due
objection. *In re* Ajello's Petition, 26 Misc. 2d 1026, 212 N.Y.S.2d 970 (1961)
(county political committee).

Where directors received notice and actively participated in a special meeting of stockholders, they could not complain that a request for the meeting
was never legally referred to the board of directors at a formal meeting. Where
directors of a close corporation are in frequent contact with each other, it is
unnecessary to hold a formal meeting to make a decision. *In re* Stylemaster
Department Store, 154 N.Y.S.2d 58, 61 (Sup. Ct. 1956).

Where a petitioner was present and participated actively in nominations
and elections at a special meeting without objecting to the holding of the
meeting on short notice, he waived the right to object. *In re* Roosevelt
Leather Hand Bag Co., 68 N.Y.S.2d 735 (Sup. Ct. 1947).

Stockholders who attended a meeting in person or by proxy for the purpose
of ratifying a sale of corporate assets are not in a position to object to the form
of notice of the meeting. Beggs v. Myton Canal & Irrigation Co., 54 Utah 120,
179 P. 984 (1919).

It is immaterial whether action is taken at a regular or a special meeting
when all members are present and participate. City of Belton v. Brown-
Crummer, 17 F.2d 70 (5th Cir. 1927).

Notice of an adjourned meeting is not required where complainant was
present with his attorney. Moskowitz v. City of St. Paul, 16 N.W.2d 745
(Minn. 1944).

Where all members of a city council were present at a special meeting, failure to give written notice as required by charter does not invalidate action
taken. Giesel v. City of Broadview Heights, 14 Ohio Misc. 70, 236 N.E.2d
222 (1968) (city council).

[31] "It is laid down by the weight of authority, in fact there is but little dissent from it, that a special meeting of a municipal board—which means, of

ularity in the notice, one court has held notice unnecessary where it was impracticable due to the absence of a member who was vacationing in the western part of the country.[32]

Those who are present at a meeting called on insufficient notice are not in a position to complain, either on behalf of themselves or on behalf of others who were not present or represented by proxy.[33] However, presence at a meeting does not preclude a member from suing on other grounds to set aside action taken at the meeting.[34]

There must be a clear waiver on the part of the objectors; otherwise a defective notice cannot be disregarded. The fact that the objectors knew the purpose of the meeting and that the results of a new meeting would be the same does not cure the invalidity of the action taken.[35] Also, knowledge that a meeting has been called does

---

course, a meeting held at any time other than that fixed for regular meetings, or by reason of valid adjournments therefrom—is legal when all the members are present and acting although no notice of the meeting was issued or served. It is said that when all are present and acting, everything has been accomplished which a notice would have secured." City of Biloxi v. Cawley, 278 So. 2d 389, 393 (Miss. 1973).

[32] Crook v. Township of Clark, 74 N.J. Super. 148, 180 A.2d 715 (1962).

[33] "Assuming that the published notice was insufficient, the appellants, who were present at the meeting, are not in a position to complain, either on behalf of themselves or on behalf of other shareholders who were not present or represented by proxy." Beutelspacher v. Spokane Sav. Bank, 164 Wash. 227, 2 P.2d 729, 731 (1931).

A majority of directors held an informal meeting without notice to the other directors and directed that the corporation carry out certain contract terms. No director objected for nearly three years. The court held that the corporation acquiesced and ratified action as taken by the majority of directors. Gorrill v. Greenlees, 104 Kan. 693, 180 P. 798 (1919).

[34] Stone v. Dean, 344 P.2d 649 (Okla. 1959) (proposal to merge with another association).

[35] Officers of a corporate beneficial owner, not a stockholder of record but having actual notice of a meeting, attended the annual stockholders' meeting in their individual capacities after being refused admission as representatives of the beneficial owner, and stated the owner's position contrary to that of management. The court held that, although officers of the beneficial owner attended the meeting and presented the owner's views, such actions did not constitute a waiver of notice since the persons were not allowed to participate by voice or to vote as representatives of the owner. Goldfield Corp. v. General Host Corp., 29 N.Y.2d 264, 327 N.Y.S.2d 330 (1971), aff'g 39 App. Div. 2d 125, 318 N.Y.S.2d 378 (1st Dep't 1971).

not cure a failure to give legal notice to all shareholders.[36] Mere attendance at a meeting without participation except to demand that no business be transacted is not deemed to be a participation sufficient to constitute a waiver of statutory notice, even where the stockholders had held meetings for 20 years by "common consent" without notice.[37]

Where the county members of a political party committee did not receive a requisite written notice of a meeting, any action taken at the meeting was invalid notwithstanding that had the county members attended the meeting their combined vote might not have changed the final result. "Who is to say what course the vote might have taken had all members of the committee been present at the meeting." Jones v. Malone, 200 Misc. 88, 101 N.Y.S.2d 895, 899 (Sup. Ct. 1950).

The fact that a president, presiding at a meeting of directors at which the secretary was directed to send out notices of a special meeting of stockholders, did not object to the form of the notice prior to the meeting does not constitute waiver of notice. In re 74 & 76 West Tremont Ave. Corp., 10 Misc. 2d 662, 173 N.Y.S.2d 154 (Sup Ct. 1958).

A shareholder does not waive the requirement of due notice because some attorneys representing him at later court proceedings did appear at the meeting but took no part in the election of directors and did not vote or otherwise assume to represent the shareholder. In re Keller, 116 App. Div. 58, 101 N.Y.S. 133, 135 (3d Dep't 1906).

[36] "While she may have had knowledge of this meeting, the fact remains that the notice failed to comply with the statutory and corporate requirements. Such an omission is ground for disaffirmance unless there is a clear waiver on the part of the stockholders, not present in this case." In re Melloh's Petition, 17 Misc. 2d 902, 187 N.Y.S.2d 203 (Sup. Ct. 1959).

Non-compliance with notice requirements of a political committee renders any action taken by the committee invalid. The fact that members eventually received actual notice of the meeting in time to attend does not remedy a defective notice. Jones v. Malone, 200 Misc. 88, 101 N.Y.S.2d 895 (Sup. Ct. 1950).

The fact that a member, who did not receive notice and did not attend a meeting, had knowledge of the meeting and intended to attend does not constitute a waiver of defective notice. In re Election of Directors of FDR–Woodrow Wilson Democrats, Inc., 57 Misc. 2d 743, 293 N.Y.S.2d 463 (1968).

[37] The action of one stockholder in continuing to remonstrate after business had been taken up by the meeting was not a participation therein waiving the right to notice. The action of another stockholder in being present until after the assumption of business, but remaining mute and withdrawing upon the failure of the first stockholder remonstrance, was also not a participation waiving notice. People ex rel. Carus v. Matthiessen, 269 Ill. 499, 109 N.E. 1056, 1057 (1915).

§ 3.10   Statutory, Charter, and By-law Requirements

Notice of the meeting should be given in the manner provided in the applicable statute, charter, or by-laws,[38] and must meet the standards of sufficiency.[39] Where a by-law provision for calling a meeting is disregarded, the court may compel compliance in an appropriate proceeding.[40] The statute may prescribe a single method

---

[38] Where there is a conflict between the by-laws and the statute, the latter is controlling. Grant v. Elder, 64 Colo. 104, 170 P. 198, 203 (1917).

By-law provisions for calling stockholder meetings are valid. Purported annual meeting held without notice as required by by-laws was illegal. *In re* Mississippi Valley Utilities Co., 2 F. Supp. 995 (D. Del. 1933).

A charter and by-laws may provide for longer notice than a general corporation statute. Davison v. Parke, Austin & Lipscomb, 165 Misc. 32, 299 N.Y.S. 960 (Sup. Ct. 1937), modified, 12 N.Y.S.2d 358 (1st Dep't 1939).

Where the by-laws provide that meetings may be called by persons holding a certain proportion of the stock, a call by less than the required amount is invalid. Josephson v. Cosmocolor Corp., 31 Del. Ch. 46, 64 A.2d 35, 36 (1949).

Notice of a meeting of a federal savings and loan association is governed by federal regulations. Pearson v. First Fed. Sav. & Loan Ass'n, 149 So. 2d 891 (Fla. 1963).

Where a charter is silent, the general statute applies. Merrion v. Scorup–Somerville Cattle Co., 134 F.2d 473 (10th Cir.), *cert. denied*, 319 U.S. 760 (1943) (personal service).

On statutory requirement of publication in a newspaper of general circulation, *see, e.g.*, Beutelspacher v. Spokane Sav. Bank, 164 Wash. 227, 2 P.2d 729 (1931).

[39] Telegraphic notice sent to a wrong address is not valid. *In re* Melloh's Petition, 17 Misc. 2d 902, 187 N.Y.S.2d 203 (Sup. Ct. 1959).

Oral notice by telephone is sufficient where written notice is not legally specified. Brechner v. Incorporated Village of Lake Success, 25 Misc. 2d 920, 208 N.Y.S.2d 365 (Sup. Ct. 1960), *aff'd*, 14 App. Div. 2d 567, 218 N.Y.S.2d 1017 (1961), *motion denied*, 11 N.Y.2d 875, 182 N.E.2d 403, 227 N.Y.S.2d 913, *appeal dismissed*, 11 N.Y.2d 929, 183 N.E.2d 81, 228 N.Y.S.2d 678 (1962).

Where by-laws provided that the date for an annual meeting was to be set by a board of directors with seven days' written notice to all members and, due to unanticipated other business, election of directors was not reached at the annual meeting, the election of directors at a subsequent meeting called by the president and secretary on five days' notice, was void. *In re* Election of Directors of FDR–Woodrow Wilson Democrats, Inc., 57 Misc. 2d 743, 293 N.Y.S.2d 463 (1968).

[40] Where the by-laws of a corporation provide that the president shall call a

or may provide alternative methods of giving notice.[41] Also, the statute may provide only that "due notice" of the meeting be given, in which case any reasonably effective time for giving notice should be sufficient.[42] Where the statute provided, for example, that the notice of a special meeting of a religious congregation be given at two regular services or by posting at the entrance to the services, a postal card notice mailed to members was held inadequate and all actions taken at meetings so called were a nullity.[43] And when a

---

special meeting of stockholders whenever requested to do so by a majority of the stockholders entitled to vote, and written requests signed by a majority have been submitted to the president requesting a meeting, the court may summarily enter an order requiring the president to call the meeting. Auer v. Dressel, 306 N.Y. 427, 118 N.E.2d 590 (1954), 48 A.L.R.2d 604 (1956).

Where by-laws empower a president to call a special meeting of directors and require him to call a meeting when two directors make such a request, compliance by the president could be compelled in an "appropriate proceeding" if he ignores their request. Futility in making the request would not justify disregard of by-law requirements. In re Ann-Jen Holding Corp., 15 Misc. 2d 74, 179 N.Y.S.2d 494, 496 (Sup. Ct. 1958).

The court will restrain defendants from interfering with convening and holding a duly called special meeting of stockholders in a proper case, notwithstanding an objection that to do so would constitute interference with the internal affairs and management of a foreign corporation. Starr v. Tomlinson, 7 Misc. 2d 916, 166 N.Y.S.2d 629 (Sup. Ct. 1957).

The president of a corporation protested that one of the stockholders (his wife) had not been notified (by himself) of a stockholders' meeting and announced he would protest the legality of the meeting. The court concluded that the president feared the stockholders might elect a board of directors unfavorable to him and remarked: "Such a position is, of course, untenable. It is the plain ministerial duty of the president to call said meeting, whether requested to do so or not; and, if the stockholders do anything they have no right to do, it will then be his privilege to complain." State ex rel. Dendinger v. J. D. Kerr Gravel Co., 158 La. 324, 104 So. 60, 61 (1925).

[41] Where a statute provides that notice may be given by publication, by personal service, or by mail, notice given only by mail is sufficient. M & E Luncheonette, Inc. v. Freilich, 218 N.Y.S.2d 125 (1961).

[42] Only four days' notice of a public meeting of a town planning board was given. The court did not hold the notice insufficient: "What is the most effective time for giving notice of such a hearing may be open to question. It is possible to give notice too early as well as too late." Town of Burlington v. Dunn, 318 Mass. 216, 61 N.E.2d 243, 244, cert. denied, 326 U.S. 739 (1945).

[43] Kupperman v. Congregation Nusach Sfard, 39 Misc. 2d 107, 240 N.Y.S.2d 315, 320–21 (Sup. Ct. 1963).

notice is deficient because it fails to indicate with substantial certainty the business to be acted upon, it cannot be cured by informal advertisements in a local paper and by announcements from a sound truck.[44] Yet, in another case, two notices of meeting, one mailed by the secretary and the other a letter from the president asking all to attend, together constituted "fair notice" although either one standing alone may not have been sufficient.[45] Supplying stock brokers with copies of the notice of meeting has been labelled an inadequate means of notifying shareholders to whom notice was not given.[46]

A distinction must be made between a notice which fails to comply with statutory or charter requirements and a notice which meets such requirements but does not comply with rules of procedure adopted by the body for the conduct of its own affairs. When, for example, a statute allowed a zoning board to fix the dates of meetings so long as the interval between dates of notice and of hearing was at least three weeks, and the board fixed a date for hearing 30 days after notice, a meeting called with only 29 days elapsing between notice and hearing was valid because the rules of procedure adopted by the board were subject to change by the board at any time.[47]

§ 3.10.1   Putting Matter on Calendar

Putting a matter on the calendar of a municipal board for a hearing does not meet the requirements of the controlling ordinance that the board shall fix the time for the hearing.[48] However, putting

---

When articles provide for personal notice only, leaving a copy at a usual place of abode is not sufficient. Bank of Little Rock v. McCarthy, 55 Ark. 473, 18 S.W. 759 (1892).

[44] Fish v. Canton, 322 Mass. 219, 77 N.E.2d 231 (1948).

[45] In re Ajello's Petition, 26 Misc. 2d 1026, 212 N.Y.S.2d 970 (1961).

Notice of a general meeting stating that a purpose was to receive a directors' report, together with such report, constituted sufficient notice of the meeting. Boschoek Proprietary Co. v. Fuke, [1906] 1 Ch. 148.

[46] Bryan v. Western Pac. R.R., 28 Del. Ch. 13, 35 A.2d 909 (1944).

[47] Ellis v. Stokes, 207 Ga. 423, 61 S.E.2d 806, 810 (1950).

[48] See Blum v. Board of Zoning and Appeals, 1 Misc. 2d 668, 149 N.Y.S.2d 5 (Sup. Ct. 1956).

Administrative law recognizes that a regulatory body has control over its own calendar. City of San Antonio v. CAB, 374 F.2d 326 (D.C. Cir. 1967).

a matter on the calendar of a board of education at a regular meeting by unanimous consent of all members present may cure a defective notice of an earlier special meeting which failed to state the substance of the matter to be voted upon.[49]   Under the Florida "sunshine law," a public body may taken action on a matter which has not been placed on an agenda, but it is prohibited from holding "a public meeting" without reasonable notice to the public.[50]

§ 3.11   Custom and Practice

Custom and past practice will be followed in the absence of adverse controlling authority. A meeting of a voluntary association without controlling rules, which held each meeting pursuant to a schedule fixed at the adjournment of the previous meeting and published in the local newspapers, has been approved as a regularly called meeting.[51] Meetings may be valid when held on inadequate

[49] When a board of education by unanimous consent of all members present voted to add certain resolutions to the calendar for a regular meeting and then by a vote of seven to zero adopted such resolutions, the board cured any procedural defects that may have existed in such resolutions as adopted at a previous special meeting, such as failing to state the nature or substance of such resolutions in the notice of the earlier meeting. By-laws provided that an item not calendared for a regular meeting could be considered by the board by unanimous consent. Parrish v. Moss, 200 Misc. 375, 106 N.Y.S.2d 577 (Sup. Ct.), aff'd, 279 App. Div. 608, 107 N.Y.S.2d 580 (2d Dep't 1951).

[50] "The agenda plots the orderly conduct of business to be taken up at a noticed public meeting as provided for by city charter or ordinance. [Statute] does not embody this subject matter nor does it contemplate the necessity for each item to be placed on the agenda before it can be considered by a public noticed meeting of a governmental body. Although the drawing up of an agenda is a matter related to a noticed public meeting, it essentially is an integral part of the actual mechanics and procedures for conducting that meeting and, therefore, aptly relegated to local practice and procedure as prescribed by city charters and ordinances. Furthermore, the necessity of items to appear on an agenda before they could be heard at a meeting would foreclose easy access to such meeting to members of the general public who wish to bring specific issues before the governmental body." Hough v. Stembridge, 278 So. 2d 288, 290–91 (Fla. App. 1973).

[51] Ostrom v. Greene, 20 Misc. 177, 45 N.Y.S. 852, 857 (Sup. Ct. 1897), aff'd mem., 30 App. Div. 621, 52 N.Y.S. 1147 (3d Dep't 1898), aff'd, 161 N.Y. 353, 55 N.E. 919 (1900).

See Walker Memorial Baptist Church v. Saunders, 285 N.Y. 462, 35 N.E.2d 42 (1941) (religious corporation).

notice when there has developed a custom or practice of not strictly complying with by-law requirements of a written notice to all members.[52] Also, previous participation in similar meetings under similar circumstances may constitute an estoppel and prevent raising the question of irregularity due to lack of adequate written notice.[53]

Early court decisions suggested that, in the absence of controlling charter or by-laws, the mode of notifying members or shareholders might depend upon their material interest in the organization. For example, where members have a direct interest in the properties of a corporation, such as shareholders of a business corporation, the notice should be personal, while in the case of members of a religious organization without any individual pecuniary interest, such strictness need not be required.[54]

§ 3.12 Failure To Give Proper Notice—Substantial Omission

Failure to give proper notice of a meeting is a "substantial omission" which should not be disregarded unless clearly waived.[55] The firmness of this rule is illustrated by an early English case which held that an action for assault will lie in favor of a vestryman who had been thrashed and thrown out of a meeting of select vestrymen, since one of the vestrymen did not receive notice of the meeting and therefore the meeting was not a select vestry duly assembled.[56]

[52] See Forrest City Box Co. v. Barney, 14 F.2d 590 (8th Cir. 1926) (informal meeting of resident members); American Exch. Nat'l Bank v. First Nat'l Bank, 82 F. 961 (9th Cir. 1897) (custom to hold bank meetings when sufficient members present); Johnson v. Busby, 278 F. Supp. 235 (N.D. Ga. 1967) (previous participation in similar meeting).

[53] Johnson v. Busby, 278 F. Supp. 235 (N.D. Ga. 1967).

[54] Madison Ave. Baptist Church v. Baptist Church, 31 N.Y. Super. 109, 119 (1869), rev'd on other grounds, 46 N.Y. 131 (1871), aff'g 28 N.Y. Super. 649 (1867).

[55] In re Keller, 116 App. Div. 58, 101 N.Y.S. 133, 135 (3d Dep't 1906).

A notice which fails to state the purposes of a meeting is clearly defective. Bushers v. Graceland Cemetery Ass'n, 171 F. Supp. 205 (E.D. Ill. 1958).

Procedural defects in a notice of a meeting (failure to state substance of matters to be acted upon) may be cured by readoption at a subsequent meeting where proper procedures are followed. Parrish v. Moss, 200 Misc. 375, 106 N.Y.S.2d 577 (Sup. Ct.), aff'd, 279 App. Div. 608, 107 N.Y.S.2d 580 (2d Dep't 1951).

[56] Dobson v. Fussy, (1831) 7 Bing. 305; Curry (Crew) at 21.

Proceedings at a shareholders' meeting convened on improper notice [57] or called by an unauthorized person [58] are void and without

---

Suspension of a member from a membership corporation is not valid at a meeting not legally called. Stein v. Marks, 44 Misc. 140, 89 N.Y.S. 921 (Sup. Ct. 1904).

[57] "There was no notice given to the third member of the executive committee of the special meeting of that committee, nor was there notice of the special meeting to holders of stock approximating somewhat toward one-fourth of the voting stock. This lack of notice is fatal to the action of both the stockholders and of the executive committee." Close v. Brictson Mfg. Co., 43 F.2d 869 (D. Neb. 1930).

In the absence of notice of a meeting, or waiver of notice, action taken at the meeting is illegal and has no effect. Gentry-Futch Co. v. Gentry, 90 Fla. 595, 106 So. 473 (1925).

When insufficient notice of a corporate election is given, there is no election and justice requires no further showing. In re Election of Directors of FDR–Woodrow Wilson Democrats, Inc., 57 Misc. 2d 743, 293 N.Y.S.2d 463 (1968).

The legality of an election of directors is not a matter of the "balance of equities" or the court's "concept of fairness," but a matter of compliance with governing provisions of law. "The provision for notice has always been regarded as an essential requirement. Its absence can only be avoided by proof of waiver." In re Green Bus Lines, 166 Misc. 800, 2 N.Y.S.2d 556 (Sup. Ct. 1937).

Failure to give a legal notice to all stockholders is ground for disaffirmance of the election of directors at an annual meeting. In re Melloh's Petition, 17 Misc. 2d 902, 187 N.Y.S.2d 203 (Sup. Ct. 1959).

Notice of special meeting of stockholders failed to state the purpose of the meeting and did not comply with statutes, and by-laws of corporation, cannot be disregarded unless there is a clear waiver on the part of the objecting stockholders. In re 74 & 76 West Tremont Ave. Corp., 10 Misc. 2d 662, 173 N.Y.S.2d 154 (Sup. Ct. 1958).

Notice of a meeting was sent to only 140 members living in greater Cleveland out of some 450 members in good standing throughout Ohio. The meeting was illegally convened and the directors elected were "usurpers of the offices they pretend to hold." Ohio v. Brandt, 185 N.E.2d 790, 792 (Ohio 1962), appeal dismissed, 190 N.E.2d 689 (1963).

An opposition group of stockholders held an annual meeting on the date fixed in the by-laws, without sending a written notice of the meeting to stockholders as required by the by-laws. It was held to be an illegal meeting. Gries v. Eversharp Inc., 69 A.2d 922 (Del. Ch. 1949).

A special meeting of a board of directors consisting of three members is not competent to proceed with the transaction of business when one member neither attended nor had notice thereof. Knox v. Commissioner, 323 F.2d 84 (5th Cir. 1963).

effect, unless it can be established that the defect was waived or did not deprive the shareholders of sufficient notice of the time, place, and purposes of the meeting.[59] The court will not direct a

---

Generally, failure to give notice of a meeting as required by statute will render an election at the meeting void, and a new election would be required even without a showing that the results of the election would, or might be, different. Goldfield Corp. v. General Host Corp., 29 N.Y.2d 264, 327 N.Y.S.2d 330 (1971), aff'g 39 App. Div. 2d 125, 318 NY.S.2d 378 (1st Dep't 1971).

[58] Counsel for an applicant before a zoning board posted the required notices of a meeting at city hall and at the county courthouse. "We hold that this ministerial act could properly be performed by counsel and complied with the statutory requirements." Carter v. City of Nashua, 308 A.2d 847, 852 (N.H. 1973).

Where a president called a stockholders' meeting as authorized in the by-laws, and a statute required that a meeting be called by the directors or two stockholders, the meeting was void. Grant v. Elder, 64 Colo. 104, 170 P. 198 (1917).

Action taken at a stockholders' meeting called by a person not authorized to do so under the by-laws is illegal and void. Kersjes v. Metzger, 292 Mich. 83, 290 N.W. 336 (1940).

Where the by-laws expressly gave power to trustees to convene meetings of stockholders, it was held that the president could not call meetings except by mutual agreement of all stockholders. State ex rel. Guerrero v. Pettineli, 10 Nev. 141, 146 (1875).

Where, upon the death of the president, his duties to call a special meeting fell upon the first vice-president pursuant to general parliamentary rules and by "common custom and usage," the secretary did not have authority to issue a notice of special meeting to fill the vacancy. There being a defective notice of meeting, all business transacted at the meeting was void. In re Davie, 13 Misc. 2d 1019, 178 N.Y.S.2d 740, 742–43 (Sup. Ct. 1958), citing Robert's Rules of Order.

[59] Plaintiff claimed that a notice was defective because it was signed by someone purporting to be an assistant secretary who in fact was not such at the time. The court held that the notice of the meeting accomplished its purpose whether properly signed or not. Andrews v. Precision Apparatus, Inc., 217 F. Supp. 679 (1963).

The naming of four nominees in the notice of a meeting, where only two are to be elected directors, is not defective notice since 14 days' advance notice was requested and some nominees may die, resign, or refuse to run. Catesby v. Burnett, [1916] 2 Ch. 325, 330.

Notice of a meeting is valid whether the meeting is called an "adjourned" meeting or a "recessed" meeting or a "continued" meeting. In re Election of Directors of FDR–Woodrow Wilson Democrats, Inc., 57 Misc. 2d 743, 293 N.Y.S.2d 463 (1968).

See People ex rel. Smith v. Peck, 11 Wend. 604 (N.Y. Sup. Ct. 1834).

company to call a meeting where the notice improperly calls for the election of additional directors under conditional circumstances,[60] and will grant a preliminary injunction against holding a proposed special meeting which was called on defective notice where it can be shown that irreparable damage would be done if the meeting were held.[61] A defective notice of a stockholders' meeting gives no rights to the corporation; all rights, if any, are "in the ignored stock-stockholder." [62]

§ 3.12.1 Exceptions Rarely Made

On rare occasions the courts have overlooked the failure to give notice to all shareholders where no injury had been shown.[63] In one case, notice was not given to one member because, prior to the meeting, he had left on a cruise for reasons of health.[64] Another case held that the failure to give notice of a special meeting of a municipal council to an absent member did not invalidate the meeting when it was established that it would have been impossible to reach the member since he was on an extended vacation trip by automobile through several western states.[65]

[60] A notice called for a meeting to amend a charter, increasing the number of directors, and for electing additional directors. Such increase could be made only on amendment of the charter and approval of the increase by the superintendent of insurance. Fierman v. Rose, 175 Misc. 102, 22 N.Y.S.2d 215 (Sup. Ct. 1940).

[61] Where by-laws provided that the secretary would call a meeting at the request of 25 per cent of the stockholders, and only 10 per cent requested, an injunction against holding such meeting was granted on finding that irreparable damage would be done if the meeting were held. Callister v. Graham-Paige Corp., 146 F. Supp. 399 (D. Del. 1956).

[62] Blue River Co. v. Summit County Devel. Corp., 207 F. Supp. 283, 292 (D. Colo. 1962) (discussion of defective notice on executory and executed contracts, whether void or voidable).

[63] Through oversight one stockholder was not notified of a special meeting. Under the circumstances the court held the meeting valid because the stockholder did not complain and did not show injury. Port Chilkoot Co. v. Heinmiller, 12 Alas. 200 (1948).

[64] Avien, Inc. v. Weiss, 50 Misc. 2d 127, 269 N.Y.S.2d 836 (Sup. Ct. 1966).

[65] Crook v. Township of Clark, 74 N.J. Super. 148, 180 A.2d 715, 719 (1962).

Failure to give notice of a committee meeting to one member invalidated the proceedings even where the member had previously intimated to the chair-

There is a further exception that a local governing body, in complying with a state legislative mandate, may act without public notice or a hearing.[66]

Under English company law an "accidental omission" to give notice of a meeting does not invalidate the proceedings. It has been held that failure to give notice due to an inadvertent misplacing of addressograph plates for nine names of members was an accidental omission,[67] but that failure to give notice under the erroneous impression that some members had transferred their shares was an error of law and not an accidental omission.[68] Notice need not be given to a director who has absented himself from all meetings and has abandoned his membership.[69]

§ 3.12.2   Defects in Notice

In calculating the number of days of notice required to meet a statutory or by-law minimum, it is recommended that both the day of mailing and the day of the meeting be excluded.[70] If mailed on time, a notice is not defective because it is not dated.[71] Furthermore, the inaccurate printing of certain words [72] or a misdating of

---

man that she could not attend. Young v. Ladies' Imperial Club, Ltd., [1920] 2 K.B. 523.

A city ordinance was not invalid where one alderman did not receive notice of the meeting and no attempt was made to notify him because he was absent from the state on his job with a railroad about 300 miles away. The court noted that an exception to the general rule requiring notice "excuses notice when it is not practicable to give it." Knoxville v. Knoxville Water Co., 107 Tenn. 647, 64 S.W. 1075 (1901), aff'd, 189 U.S. 434 (1903).

[66] Dobrovolny v. Reinhardt, 173 N.W.2d 837 (Iowa 1970).

[67] In re West Canadian Collieries Ltd., [1962] Ch. 370.

[68] Musselwhite v. C. H. Musselwhite & Son Ltd., [1962] Ch. 964.

[69] Dodge v. Kenwood Ice Co., 204 F. 577 (8th Cir. 1913).

[70] "At least," when referring to the number of days of notice, has been interpreted to mean full days. MacCrone v. American Capital Corp., 51 F. Supp. 462 (D. Del. 1943).

"Days," when not qualified, means in ordinary and common usage calendar days. Okanogan Indians v. United States, 279 U.S. 672 (1928).

[71] Clark v. Wild, 85 Vt. 212, 81 A. 536 (1911).

[72] Martin v. Flynn, 19 App. Div. 2d 653, 241 N.Y.S.2d 883 (2d Dep't 1963) (proposed legislation by city council).

a contract described [73] in a notice of meeting will not invalidate the notice if the inaccuracy or misdescription is not misleading.

A notice of meeting may be valid through unsigned, when printed words apprise the members that a meeting has been called.[74]

§ 3.12.3 Short Notice

The giving of an untimely or "short notice" will invalidate any action taken at the meeting.[75]

§ 3.13 Presumption of Regularity

In the absence of evidence to the contrary, it will be presumed that proper notice of a meeting was given and that the meeting was regularly and fairly conducted in compliance with applicable statutes, charter, and by-laws.[76] This is an ancient rule which was ap-

---

[73] Trendley v. Illinois Traction Co., 241 Mo. 73, 145 S.W. 1 (1912).

[74] Jones v. Malone, 200 Misc. 88, 101 N.Y.S.2d 895 (Sup. Ct. 1950).

[75] Hayes v. Canada, Atl., & Plant S.S. Co., 181 F. 289 (1st Cir. 1910) (one day's notice to attend meeting 24 hours distant by rail); Bannigan v. Heffernan, 203 Misc. 126, 115 N.Y.S.2d 889 (Sup. Ct.), *modified,* 280 App. Div. 891, 115 N.Y.S.2d 444 (2d Dep't), *aff'd,* 304 N.Y. 729, 108 N.E.2d 209 (1952) (telegram filed afternoon before meeting on Friday before Labor Day holiday); Brown v. Republican Mt. Silver Mines, Ltd., 5 F. 7 (C.C.D. Colo. 1893) (English company gave short notice to American shareholders who could not travel to London in time for meeting); *In re* Election of Directors of FDR–Woodrow Wilson Democrats, Inc., 57 Misc. 2d 743, 293 N.Y.S.2d 463 (1968) (only five days' notice of adjourned meeting where seven days required for original meeting); *In re* M. & O. Realty Corp., 16 Misc. 2d 562, 182 N.Y.S.2d 186 (Sup. Ct. 1958) (notice not meeting statutory requirements); Janaug, Inc. v. Szlapka, 6 Misc. 2d 84, 162 N.Y.S.2d 668 (Sup. Ct. 1957) (six days' notice instead of ten); Davison v. Parke, Austin & Lipscomb, 165 Misc. 32, 299 N.Y.S. 960 (Sup. Ct. 1937) (12 days instead of 30 days), *modified,* 12 N.Y.S.2d 358 (1st Dep't 1939).

See § 3.12.1 *supra.*

[76] "In the absence of evidence to the contrary, it will be presumed that a stockholders' meeting was held in accordance with the statutes, charter, and by-laws, and the burden is upon one who claims that the meeting is invalid to show facts that render it so." Gentry-Futch Co. v. Gentry, 90 Fla. 595, 106 So. 473, 478 (1925).

There is a legal presumption "that the notice of meeting was legally sufficient, or that due and legal notice thereof was given to all the directors, unless

plied even when the court did not know how the meeting was called.[77]

Where the records of the clerk show that a meeting was called for the purpose of transacting the very business which was transacted, and that every member was present and participated, the presumption is that the meeting was duly and regularly called.[78] The words "duly assembled" infer that each member has received proper notice or that notice of the meeting has been waived.[79] Also, in the absence of evidence to the contrary, it may be assumed that a town meeting took action on matters set forth in the notice in the order listed.[80]

And, when notice has been given, and no objection has been

---

it affirmatively appears that such was not the case." Leavitt v. Oxford & Geneva Silver Min. Co., 3 Utah 265, 1 P. 356, 358 (1883).

In the absence of evidence to the contrary, it will always be presumed that a corporate meeting was regularly and fairly conducted. Noremac, Inc. v. Centre Hill Court, Inc., 164 Va. 151, 178 S.E. 877, 881–82 (1935).

The court observed that "it would be hazardous to decide that every vote, passed by an aggregate body, is void, if it do not appear by the record that all were notified. We believe it is not usual, in corporate records, to state how the members were notified. The presumption, 'omnia rite acta,' covers multitudes of defects in such cases, and throws the burden upon those, who would deny the regularity of a meeting, for want of due notice, to establish it by proof." Sargent v. Webster, 54 Mass. (13 Metc.) 497, 504 (1847).

In the absence of evidence to the contrary, it will be presumed that all members of a school board had due notice of meetings. Kavanaugh v. Wausau, 120 Wis. 611, 98 N.W. 550 (1904).

A meeting of a town board was to open at 9 A.M., but the record showed adjournment at that time. The court inferred that the meeting "was, at most, but a few minutes before that time." Besides, the board members were acting under the sanction of an oath, and "some presumptions may fairly be indulged in favor of the legality of their action." Wisconsin Cent. R.R. v. Ashland County, 84 Wis. 1, 50 N.W. 937, 940 (1891).

[77] People ex rel. Locke v. Common Council, 5 Lans. 11 (N.Y. Sup. Ct. 1871).

[78] City of Greeley v. Hamman, 17 Colo. 30, 28 P. 460 (1891), citing Cushing, Law & Pr. Leg. Assem. on another point.

[79] Cirrincione v. Polizzi, 14 App. Div. 2d 281, 220 N.Y.S.2d 741 (1961).

A statement in the record of an annual town meeting that it was "legally warned" is not sufficient proof that the particular item of business was specified in the warning (notice). Bloomfield v. Charter Oak Bank, 121 U.S. 121 (1886).

[80] See Berger v. Wellesley, 334 Mass. 193, 134 N.E.2d 436 (1956).

made to the regularity of the notice, all objections on that ground
are conclusively waived.[81]

§ 3.14   Emergency Meetings

There may be circumstances involving an emergency where a
short or incomplete notice of an immediate meeting may be justified.[82]

Whether the circumstances justify a failure to abide by generally
required legal formalities depends on the facts of each case.[83]   One
court has disregarded all the legalities in holding that "[t]he management of a corporation cannot be paralyzed by every absence of
a director from its place of business or from the state at a time when
a meeting of the board seems necessary." [84]

PLACE OF MEETING

§ 3.15   Statutory and Charter Provisions

Meetings must be held at the place or places designated or permitted by the organic law, the charter, or the by-laws.[1]   Many early
state corporation laws provided that all corporate activities of domes-

[81] The court was "inclined to the opinion that all the stockholders being notified and present at the meeting, and no objection having been then made to
the regularity of the notification, all objections on that ground have been conclusively waived." Stebbins v. Merritt, 64 Mass. (10 Cush.) 27, 34 (1852).

[82] See Hayes v. Canada, Atl. & Plant S.S. Co., 181 F. 289 (1st Cir. 1910)
(no emergency in this case).

[83] The fact that a bank's assets had been converted by the president who
absconded did not validate a special directors' meeting without full notice when
the bank was in the superintendent's hands and a regular meeting could have
been held without notice. Richman v. Bank of Perris, 102 Cal. App. 71, 282
P. 801 (1929).

See Paducah & Ill. Ferry Co. v. Robertson, 161 Ky. 485, 171 S.W. 171
(1914) (postponement of sale of corporate property by auctioneer to avoid
sacrifice); see also Gorrill v. Greenlees, 104 Kan. 693, 180 P. 798 (1919) (majority of directors at informal meeting, without notice to others, directed corporation to perform contract).

[84] Stafford Springs St. Ry. v. Middle River Mfg. Co., 80 Conn. 37, 66 A.
775, 777 (1907) (four of seven directors held meeting pursuant to telephonic
notice; others signed waiver after meeting).

[1] Generally, the charter or by-laws establish the place where meetings

tic corporations including meetings of shareholders had to be held within the state of incorporation. Today corporation laws generally permit the holding of shareholder meetings within or without the state, or at such places as may be stated in the by-laws or otherwise approved by the shareholders.[2] In the absence of statutory, charter, or by-law restrictions, corporate shareholder and director meetings may be held at any convenient place.

Meetings need not be held at the official headquarters of the organization, but may be noticed for any time and place suitable under the circumstances, such as the home of the president of the organization.[3] On the other hand, when the law requires that meetings of a public school board be "open to the public," a meeting held in a private office 20 miles from the school district's territorial boundaries may not be a lawful meeting.[4]

---

may be held. *See, e.g.,* Alfred Kohlberg Inc. v. American Council, 185 Misc. 633, 56 N.Y.S.2d 788 (Sup. Ct. 1945).

The failure of a notice or resolution to fix the place for a city council meeting will not invalidate the meeting if it is held at its usual and customary place within the corporate limits. State *ex rel.* Oil Operators' Trust v. Hellman, 36 S.W.2d 1002 (Tex. Comm. App. 1931).

See § 7.1 *infra.*

[2] *See, e.g.,* Bank of Augusta v. Earle, 38 U.S. (13 Pet.) 519, 10 L. Ed. 274 (1839); Port Chilkoot Co. v. Heinmiller, 12 Alas. 200, 211 (D. Alas. 1948); Alfred Kohlberg Inc. v. American Council, 185 Misc. 633, 56 N.Y.S.2d 788 (Sup. Ct. 1945).

By-laws providing for meetings outside the state form an integral and important part of the contract between the corporation and its members, and are intended to regulate the conduct of its business. George v. Holstein–Friesian Ass'n, 238 N.Y. 513, 144 N.E. 776 (1924).

As to corporations incorporated in more than one state, the court has stated: "That a meeting in one of several States of the stockholders of a corporation chartered by all those States is valid in respect to the property of the corporation in all of them, without the necessity of a repetition of the meeting in any other of those States, is, we think, a sound proposition." Graham v. Boston, H & E R.R., 118 U.S. 161, 168–69 (1886).

[3] *In re* Serenbetz, 46 N.Y.S.2d 475 (Sup. Ct. 1943), *aff'd,* 267 App. Div. 836, 46 N.Y.S.2d 127 (2d Dep't 1944).

[4] To meet the requirements of a public meeting, the meeting should be held in a public place located within the territorial confines of the school district. Quast v. Knutson, 150 N.W.2d 199, 200 (Minn. 1967). *See* Annot., 33 L.R.A. 85, 87.

See § 7.1 *infra.*

§ 3.16   Notice May Anticipate Change of Place

The notice of meeting may anticipate and provide for the moving of the place of meeting under certain conditions. An example would be a notice that a meeting of churchwardens would be held in the church, but if a poll should be demanded, the meeting would be removed to the town hall.[5]

§ 3.17   Move of Meeting to Different Place

Unexpected problems can usually be handled in a manner which is not prejudicial to the members. Where a notice stated that the meeting would be held in the evening of a certain day at a specified room in a named hotel at a stated address, and on that day a notice was posted at such room stating that the meeting was moved to a designated suite in the same hotel, a meeting held in such suite at the appointed time has been regarded as having been duly and regularly called.[6] However, when a town meeting was noticed for the school house, and it was adjourned to a store at a distance of a mile without posting any indication at the school that the meeting place had been changed so that only a few voters attended, the adjourned meeting was not binding.[7]

[5] On a demand for a poll the chairman, without asking for a vote whether the poll should be taken, adjourned the meeting to the town hall. The adjournment was a part of the original appointment and not an interruption of the business of the meeting. "Those who summon a meeting of this kind must necessarily lay down some order for the proceedings: and I think it is competent to them to say that the meeting shall be held in one place, and, in a certain event which may require it, shall be removed to another." Rex v. Archdeacon of Chester, 1 Adolph. & E. 342, 345 (K.B. 1834).

See Rex v. Churchwardens of St. Mary, 1 Adolph. & E. 346 (K.B. 1832) (on demand of a poll, the meeting moved from schoolhouse to church).

[6] It was not shown that any members were prejudiced or deprived of a vote by the change of location of the meeting room. In re Havender, 181 Misc. 989, 44 N.Y.S.2d 213, 215 (Sup. Ct. 1943), aff'd mem., 267 App. Div. 860, 47 N.Y.S.2d 114, motion for leave to appeal denied, 267 App. Div. 901, 48 N.Y.S.2d 325 (1st Dep't 1944), citing Robert's Rules of Order on question of quorum.

[7] Chamberlain v. Dover, 13 Me. 466 (1836).

§ 3.17.1   *Suitable Quarters and Facilities*

Meetings may be moved to larger quarters for the convenience of those present. Where a notice of meeting indicated that a hearing was to be held in city council chambers, and there were 250 persons in the hallways unable to gain entrance, it was not improper to adjourn the meeting to the public library auditorium two blocks away so all persons could participate, in the absence of any claim that any person was misled or thereby denied an opportunity to express his views.[8] And where a board of local improvement met at city council chambers pursuant to notice and then adjourned to an armory building for larger space, a distance of about 1,000 feet, where it reconvened about 20 minutes later, the court held that there had been substantial compliance with the notice of meeting.[9] And, when the directors attending a meeting at the principal place of business find the door locked, they may hold the meeting in the hall outside the door [10] or on the adjacent sidewalk.[11]

It is important to plan ahead and select a meeting place which has adequate facilities for the expected gathering. For example, an attempt to conduct a political meeting in a hall where the facilities are not conducive to orderly proceedings, resulting in confusion and the failure of speakers to get recognition from the chair and to use the microphones, may constitute a deprivation of substantial rights and be an "irregularity" under the state election law sufficient to warrant a court order nullifying the meeting and directing a reconvened meeting.[12]

---

[8] Mason City v. Aeling, 209 N.W.2d 8 (Iowa 1973).

[9] City of Carbondale v. Walker, 240 Ill. 18, 88 N.W. 296 (1909).

[10] Seal of Gold Mining Co., 161 Cal. 621, 120 P. 15 (1911).

[11] *See* Clark v. Oceano Beach Resort Co., 106 Cal. App. 579, 289 P. 946 (1930).

[12] "The facilities furnished were not adequate. There was a microphone on the platform and two microphones in the hall where the committeemen were seated, one on each side of the hall. With over 1,485 committeemen present out of the total of 1,846, it was rather hard to be heard unless you could as a speaker obtain access to one of the microphones which necessitated leaving the seat which the committeemen occupied and proceeding to a microphone and then getting recognition. It does not appear from the record that anyone got recognition except those who by prearrangement were listed on the agenda sheet used for the chairman, . . ." Although denied by the respondents' witnesses, several of the petitioners' backers proved by a preponderance

An appellate court has upheld the action of the state chairman of a political party in revoking his designation of the time and place of holding a party judicial convention, when it was asserted that the designated meeting room did not have sufficient seating capacity to accommodate all the delegates and alternates entitled to attend, and in designating a later date and another apparently adequate room for the meeting. The appellate court reversed the trial court's conclusion that the chairman was not justified in cancelling the meeting in the absence of proof regarding how many of the persons gathered in the room were delegates entitled to vote or alternates.[13]

In another case the appellate court set aside an injunction against holding a meeting of a county political committee where the injunction was issued on the ground that the place selected was not sufficiently large to accommodate the committee members who were to attend. The appellate court held that the evidence consisted largely of conjecture and surmise as to the number of persons who might attend, especially in the light of contrary proof of prior experience of attendance at meetings of this nature.[14]

When there is proof that many of the members who attended the meeting could not be accommodated, thus making a determination of the result of the balloting impossible, the court will issue an order that the meeting be reconvened.[15] In addition, the court will intervene when one faction attempts to monopolize the meeting

---

of the evidence that they could not get recognition or use the microphones. All of this deprived the petitioners of a substantial right and was an irregularity sufficient to require a voiding of all proceedings and a new meeting and election. *In re* Ryan v. Grimm, 43 Misc. 2d 836, 839, 252 N.Y.S.2d 521 (Sup. Ct.), *aff'd*, 22 App. Div. 2d 171, 254 N.Y.S.2d 462 (4th Dep't 1964), *aff'd*, 15 N.Y.2d 922, 258 N.Y.S.2d 843, 206 N.E.2d 867 (1965).

[13] There were 392 delegates and alternates entitled to attend. The fire laws prohibited occupancy of the room by more than 250 persons. Bannigan v. Heffernan, 280 App. Div. 891, 115 N.Y.S.2d 444 (2d Dep't), *modifying* 115 N.Y.S.2d 889 (Sup. Ct.), *aff'd*, 304 N.Y. 729, 108 N.E.2d 209 (1952).

[14] The reason assigned by the trial court for enjoining the meeting was that the place (Cooper Union) would accommodate 1,800 persons, whereas the county committee consisted of 11,985 members. Blaikie v. Knott, 277 App. Div. 461, 100 N.Y.S.2d 665 (1st Dep't 1950).

[15] The court ordered the county committee of a political party to reconvene its organization meeting on proof that many committeemen who attended the first meeting could not be accommodated. Crawford v. Cohen, 291 N.Y. 98, 51 N.E.2d 665 (1943).

room with its followers, to the disadvantage of the other shareholders. An early case held that the preoccupation of the meeting room, before the hour fixed for a corporate election, by a large number of "rough, low class of men" who had been imported from another city and furnished proxies, was a "gross perversion and abuse" of the right to vote by proxy and a clear infringement of the rights of bona fide shareholders.[16]

§ 3.17.2   Test of Adequacy

On the other hand, although the meeting room is overcrowded and some members remain in the hall outside, the premises may meet the test of adequacy for the size of the meeting when the members are able to go in and out of the meeting and any member seeking recognition is permitted to have access to the floor.[17]

In practice, large meetings can and have been conducted in relatively close quarters.[18]

TIME OF MEETING

§ 3.18   Notice Fixing Time of Meeting

It is a general rule that the notice of a meeting should state the exact time and place of the meeting. However, if the time of a

[16] People v. Albany & S.R.R., 1 Lans. 308, 341 (N.Y. 1869), *modified on other grounds,* 5 Lans. 25 (1871), aff'd, 57 N.Y. 161 (1874).

[17] Testimony was received from cameramen, radio newsmen, and newspaper reporters as to whether the nays or yeas predominated. McDonough v. Purcell, 44 Misc. 2d 23, 252 N.Y.S.2d 752 (Sup. Ct. 1964).

[18] A meeting was attended by more than 2,000 union members in an open-air ball park. Harker v. McKissock, 10 N.J. Super. 26, 76 A.2d 89 (1950), aff'd, 7 N.J. 323, 81 A.2d 480, aff'd, 8 N.J. 230, 84 A.2d 723 (1951).

A union having more than 11,000 members held a meeting in a hall having a capacity of 600, at a time when one-third of its members were at work and unable to attend. Mamula v. United Steelworkers of America, 304 F.2d 108, 109 (3d Cir.), *cert. denied,* 371 U.S. 823 (1962).

A meeting room was not large enough, so several rooms had to be used, with people coming in and out while the vote was being taken. Regina v. Vestrymen and Churchwardens of St. Pancras, [1839] 11 Adolph & Ellis' Reports 15.

meeting is specified in the by-laws, it is not necessary to again state the time in the notice.[1]

Generally a meeting should take place substantially at the time designated in the notice, or designated in the charter or by-laws where notice is not required, as in the case of some stated meetings.[2] A meeting should not be convened before the appointed hour; but, as a practical matter, a meeting need not be convened precisely on time. If convened within a reasonable time after the noticed hour, it will be a valid meeting.[3] One court has said: "It would be the adoption of too strict a rule to hold that a meeting of a city council is illegal if it does not start exactly at the minute specified." [4]

[1] Seal of Gold Mining Co. v. Slater, 161 Cal. 621, 120 P. 15 (1911).

Where the by-laws do not fix the time or method of calling a meeting of an association, it seems "just and fair" that the notice would "reasonably be calculated to impart notice" to those interested. State *ex rel*. Craig v. Offutt, 121 Neb. 76, 236 N.W. 174 (1931).

[2] Shareholders are presumed to have knowledge of the corporation's by-laws expressly placing in the board of directors the discretion for fixing the date of the annual meeting in each calendar year within certain limits. *In re* Unexcelled, Inc., 28 App. Div. 2d 44, 281 N.Y.S.2d 173, 177 (1st Dep't 1967).

For the effect of postponing the holding of a shareholders' meeting on the solicitation of proxies, *see* Rosen v. Allegheny Corp., 133 F. Supp. 858 (S.D.N.Y. 1955).

Under New York corporation law the record date and time of annual meeting of stockholders are not subject to shareholder control. Northwest Industries, Inc. v. B. F. Goodrich Co., 301 F. Supp. 706 (N.D. Ill. 1969).

[3] Where a portion of the shareholders met and organized before the hour named in the by-laws and in the notice of meeting (15 to 30 minutes), and afterward when the hour arrived they passed resolutions previously prepared and elected directors (with the same chairman presiding and the same secretary), the court set aside the election because the organization of the meeting prior to the noticed hour was a "surprise and fraud" upon many of the shareholders and thus the meeting was "irregular and void." The by-laws provided that the polls should stay open from noon until 1:00 P.M. Keeping them open from 12:15 P.M. to 1:30 P.M. was also held permissible. People v. Albany & S.R.R., 1 Lans. 308, 320, 325 (N.Y. 1869), *modified on other grounds*, 5 Lans. 25 (1871), *aff'd*, 57 N.Y. 161 (1874).

[4] Some members were late in arriving at the meeting place and it was customary to delay the meeting from 8 o'clock to 9 o'clock in order that all members might be present. It was not shown that there was any sinister motive in delaying the meeting or that any one was misled thereby. State *ex rel*. Oil Operators' Trust v. Hellman, 36 S.W.2d 1002, 1004 (Tex. Comm. App. 1931).

When the meeting has convened it is the duty of those present to organize and proceed with its business.[5]

§ 3.19   Which Clock To Use

The notice must fix the hour scheduled for calling the meeting to order. That is usually the hour according to local time, such as Standard Time or Daylight Time.[6] Occasionally, through inadvertence, the wrong hour is set in the notice and the question arises whether the meeting can proceed as scheduled. Generally, if the noticed hour is earlier than the equivalent local hour, the meeting can proceed with preliminary organizational matters but cannot take any official action until the hour stated in the notice arrives. Conversely, if the noticed hour is later than the equivalent local hour, the meeting can proceed when the noticed hour arrives. The meeting may, of course, proceed at any time if all members consent.[7] An agreement of those present to meet at a later hour is, in effect, an adjournment to that time.[8]

§ 3.20   Starting on Time

Usage and custom furnish, in most cases, a sufficiently accurate test of what is reasonable as to the time of proceeding with the business of the meeting. "It is not usual to commence business at the

[5] "A majority of all the stock issued being represented, it was clearly the duty of those present to organize the meeting and proceed with the election." Commonwealth ex rel. Sheip v. Vandegrift, 232 Pa. 53, 81 A. 153, 155 (1911).

[6] Where there was a dispute as to the time when a meeting commenced, the court, after hearing conflicting evidence, held that the time shown on the company office clock was to be considered the correct time. People v. Albany & S. R.R., 1 Lans. 308, 328 (N.Y. 1869), modified on other grounds, 5 Lans. 25 (1871), aff'd, 57 N.Y. 161 (1874).

[7] The fact that a shareholders' meeting was called according to "sun time" (18 minutes earlier than standard time), and it was agreed to postpone the meeting to the same hour according to standard time, did not affect the legality of the meeting. It was also agreed that a certain person would hold the floor until the standard time meeting. Proctor Coal Co. v. Finley, 98 Ky. 405, 33 S.W. 188, 189, 191 (1895).

[8] State ex rel. Blackwood v. Brast, 98 W. Va. 596, 602, 127 S.E. 507 (1925) (relator consented to change of hour from 11 A.M. to 4 P.M. and attended later meeting without objection).

exact hour appointed. Delays are constantly met and habitually borne with—less in some kinds of business than in others—but to some extent in all. . . ." In 1863, the court suggested that a delay of an hour may in ordinary cases be well regarded as a reasonable time for a city council meeting.[9] A later court held that waiting an hour after the designated time for members of a city council to arrive was substantial compliance with the time designated in the notice.[10]

§ 3.21 Holidays

In the absence of a permissive statute or charter, regular meetings falling on a holiday cannot be held on the following business day. Under a by-law requiring regular monthly meetings of directors to be held on certain days, a meeting held on a day following a holiday (the date of the regular meeting) may be invalid when there is no adjournment from the regular day and no notice of the new date to some directors. The court said: "It was a matter of their own voli-

[9] The court remarked that: "No more definite rule can be laid down than this, that where parties assemble in pursuance of a notice or appointment, and remain together for the purpose of attending to the business as soon as it is found convenient or practicable, the proceedings will be held regular, though the delay may seem unreasonable to impatient persons, or to those who have engagements elsewhere; and no one of the persons thus assembled would be heard to object to the regularity of the proceedings, if he should go away without having made a suitable effort to induce the proper officers or persons to proceed with the business; and no third person would be heard to object, unless he could show that his rights were affected by the delay." The court noted that, in former times, the proceedings of a town meeting had been set aside by the legislature "where a party have been in attendance precisely at the hour, and have at once commenced and dispatched the business of the meeting, and adjourned finally, or dissolved the meeting before the arrival of the members of another party, who relying upon the usual dilatory mode of commencing such had made no haste, and had not arrived." Kimball v. Marshall, 44 N.H. 465, 467 (1863), *citing* Jefferson's Manual and Cushing's Manual.

[10] The court commented: "Of course, if the meeting of the council had been held before the appointed hour or at such a length of time thereafter as to operate as a surprise to those interested therein, so as to prevent their attendance at the meeting, then a different question would be presented." State *ex rel.* Oil Operators' Trust v. Hellman, 36 S.W.2d 1002, 1004 (Tex. Comm. App. 1931).

tion whether the members of the board should meet or not on the date stated, although their duty was to do so." [11]   Under the laws of some states, meetings of official administrative bodies held on Sunday are not lawful.[12]

§ 3.22   Court Intervention When Time Factor Abused

The courts will approve meetings which have the appearance of regularity, and will condemn meetings which have been conducted unfairly, depending in each instance on the attending circumstances. For example, where the record showed that a meeting adjourned at about the same time it was scheduled to open, the court inferred that the meeting was held a few minutes before that time.[13]   And when two independent meetings for the election of directors were held in the same room, both proceeding at the same time, the court held irregular and void one of such meetings because it was organized before the hour set forth in the by-laws and notice of meeting.[14]   In another case, the court set aside an election of directors held at a meeting which was jammed through in ten minutes and not conducted in a proper, regular, and fair manner.[15]   A court has also set aside as premature an election of officers conducted by a board of directors which purported to meet during a recess of the stockholders' meeting at which they were elected.[16]

[11] Cheney v. Canfield, 158 Cal. 342, 111 P. 92, 94 (1910).

[12] Under Texas law a hearing held on Sunday and a later hearing held without notice to defendant were void. Texas State Bd. of Dental Examiners v. Fieldsmith, 242 S.W.2d 213 (Tex. 1951).

[13] The court reasoned: "Besides, the board was composed of officers acting under the sanction of an oath, and some presumptions may fairly be indulged in favor of the legality of their action." Wisconsin Cent. R.R. v. Ashland County, 81 Wis. 1, 50 N.W. 937, 940 (1891).

[14] People v. Albany & S.R.R., 1 Lans. 308, 321 (N.Y. 1869), *modified on other grounds*, 5 Lans. 25 (1871), *aff'd*, 57 N.Y. 161 (1874).

[15] *In re* Kirshner, 81 N.Y.S.2d 435 (Sup. Ct. 1948).

[16] Under a by-law providing that the board of directors shall hold its first annual meeting for the year immediately after the annual stockholders' meeting, or immediately after the election of directors at such meeting, a so-called meeting of a quorum of directors held during a recess prior to adjournment of the stockholders' meeting for the election of officers, was premature and of no effect and the pretended election of officers was in vain. The court noted that the spirit of the by-law was to the effect that the first meeting of directors

Sometimes a delay in opening a meeting is due to causes beyond the control of the actors. In a leading case, the president of the corporation arrived at the meeting room in Wilmington to attend the annual meeting of shareholders an hour late because his train from New York City had been delayed by a wreck on the railroad. A dissident shareholder attempted to organize and conduct the meeting. However, the president arrived and assumed the chair before the shareholder had effected a permanent organization of the meeting. The court held that the lawful chairman had arrived in time and that the directors elected after he had taken the chair were legally elected.[17]

§ 3.23　Time of Closing Measured by Polls

The notice of meeting sets forth the hour at which the meeting is scheduled to open, but does not state the hour at which it will close for that depends on the progress of the meeting in conducting the business for which it was called. Court decisions on the opening and closing of the polls and the announcement of the results of the voting are helpful in determining when a meeting has come to an end.[18] It is obvious that the polls cannot be closed before the statutory closing time, unless all the voters have cast their votes and do not have the right to change their votes as cast.[19]

An early case held that it was not lawful to open the polls before the hour set forth in the by-laws (noon) but that the polls could be kept open as long after the by-law closing time (one o'clock), within a reasonable discretion, as would be necessary to receive the votes of all shareholders present, ready, and offering to vote.[20] When

---

should not be held until the personnel of the board for the ensuing year should be finally determined. Gow v. Consolidated Coppermines Corp., 19 Del. Ch. 172, 165 A. 136 (1933).

[17] Cavender v. Curtiss-Wright Corp., 30 Del. Ch. 314, 60 A.2d 102 (1948).

[18] See § 17.40 infra.

[19] See Holland v. Davies, 36 Ark. 446 (1880) (polls closed before statutory time of sundown).

[20] People v. Albany & S.R.R., 1 Lans. 308 (N.Y. 1869), modified on other grounds, 5 Lans. 25 (1871), aff'd, 57 N.Y. 161 (1874), cited in Young v. Jebbett, 213 App. Div. 774, 211 N.Y.S. 61, 66 (4th Dep't 1925).

Where all the voters are members in good standing entitled to vote, keeping

there is no time specified by law within which the polls must be kept open, the poll may be adjourned from day to day at the discretion of the inspectors.[21]

At common law, it might be possible to properly adjourn a meeting during the process of balloting even though "such a course may not be in conformity with ordinary practice, or the most approved rules of parliamentary proceedings." [22] Yet, one court has upheld votes cast after adjournment of a shareholders' meeting and before any canvass of the votes had commenced, where there was no specified time when the polls would be deemed closed and no fraud or bad faith.[23]

Another case questioned whether the by-laws can limit the time during which the polls are to be open. After the one hour allotted had elapsed the inspectors continued to take votes despite an objection. "I much doubt whether the time could by virtue of a by-law be tied up to a certain hour of the day; but in this case it was not attempted. I have no doubt, that in case of actual necessity, the business might have been extended even to the next day. Every principle of construction is in favor of full time, otherwise business may be badly done by being hurried, or embarrassed and defeated by the raising of dilatory objections and protracted examination and discussion." [24]

In another case, the notice of meeting provided that the polls would remain open until 12 noon. The chairman ruled that a ballot delivered to the inspectors at 12:29 P.M. could not be counted. The court overruled, holding: "The fact that one of the ballots was cast

---

the polls open after the time prescribed by the constitution and by-laws will not vitiate the election. Rudolph v. Southern Beneficial League, 23 Abb. N.C. 199, 7 N.Y.S. 135, 139 (1889).

[21] *In re* Election of Dirs. Chenango County Mut. Ins. Co., 19 Wend. 635 (N.Y. 1839).

[22] Penobscot & Kennebec R.R. v. Dunn, 39 Me. 587 (1855).

[23] Washington State Labor Council v. Federated Am. Ins. Co., 474 P.2d 98 (Wash. 1970).

[24] *In re* Election of Dirs. Mohawk & H.R.R., 19 Wend. 135 (N.Y. 1838).

The articles may fix the time for which a poll is to continue; otherwise it must be kept open for a reasonable time, and the chairman should not close it so long as votes are being tendered. Regina v. St. Pancras Local Board, [1839] 11 Adolph. & E. 356. *See* SHAW AND SMITH, THE LAW OF MEETINGS at 157.

shortly after the time for closing the polls by a stockholder who had presented himself to vote before the closing time and who was in the process of voting does not invalidate the votes so cast." [25] In fact, where numerous stockholders desired to vote, no abuse of discretion on the part of the committee on elections was found where the polls were kept open for six hours after the closing time specified in the notice of meeting.[26]

However, the polls need not be kept open merely on the chance that a voter may appear to exercise his franchise. In an English case, on a finding that no one was in fact prevented from voting, the court held that "the chairman was not bound to wait many hours to see if any person would come." [27]

Although the voting and tally at a corporate meeting ordinarily are completed in one day, the voting may extend over a longer period and the tally may continue for several days or weeks until the count has been completed and announced. It is generally in order for one director to be elected at one meeting, and another director elected at an adjourned or later meeting.[28]

Also, where school trustees met on June 1, as required by statute, to elect a superintendent and continued in session, balloting until he was elected, the fact that the election was made after midnight did not render it invalid.[29]

Inspectors of election have been held to have a duty, on the day following an election, to accept and count proxies which had been inadvertently overlooked when the count was taken immediately after the election and where the final results of the voting had not yet been announced. The court said that the fundamental rule of fairness "permits the correction of a mere mistake, when it can be made without prejudice to the rights of others, and before the final

[25] State ex rel. Dunbar v. Hohmann, 248 S.W.2d 49, 51 (Mo. 1952).

[26] The court also held that the committee on elections need not take formal action where it received and counted the votes, and the secretary announced that the polls were kept open with the approval of the committee. Clopton v. Chandler, 27 Cal. App. 595, 150 P. 1012 (1915).

[27] Regina v. Rector, Churchwardens & Parishioners, 8 Adolph. & E. 356, 362 (Q.B. 1838).

[28] In re Excelsior Ins. Co., 38 Barb. 297 (N.Y. 1862).

[29] State ex rel. Walden v. Vanosdal, 131 Ind. 388, 31 N.E. 79, 15 L.R.A. 832 (1892).

vote is announced," and concluded that although the polls had closed, the meeting was still in existence, awaiting the report of the judges.[30]

Balloting is not closed until a "formal announcement" has been made of the results. Thus, a shareholder can reconsider his vote while other ballots are being collected and counted, and even after the tabulation has been made but before the official announcement.[31] After the votes have been counted, and the results announced, the polls cannot be reopened and additional votes received.[32]

Care must be taken that the person announcing the final results of the voting has authority to do so. If he lacks authority, his announcement is not official and does not constitute a closing of the polls or the meeting.[33]

§ 3.24 Stopping the Clock

The practice of stopping the clock prior to the constitutional expiration of a legislative session so that voting may continue has been both criticized and condoned by the courts. Generally the courts will not question legislative records which clearly and unambiguously show the time of adjournment, but upon a proper showing that a bill was in fact enacted after expiration of the session, the court may adjudge the legislation invalid. "The mere stopping of a clock does not stop the passage of time." [34]

[30] Young v. Jebbett, 213 App. Div. 774, 211 N.Y.S. 61, 66 (4th Dep't 1925).

[31] A stockholder changed his vote from ordinary voting to cumulative voting, thereby being assured of election to the board of directors. State ex rel. David v. Dailey, 23 Wash. 2d 25, 158 P.2d 330, 333 (1945).

See § 17.11 infra.

[32] Young v. Jebbett, 213 App. Div. 774, 211 N.Y.S. 61, 66 (4th Dep't 1925).

[33] One of three tellers remarked to a candidate for election as a director that he had lost. This was not an official or formal announcement of the results of the voting by the chairman or the secretary of the meeting. State ex rel. David v. Dailey, 23 Wash. 2d 25, 158 P.2d 330 (1945).

[34] State v. Thornburg, 70 S.E.2d 73, 80 (W. Va. 1952); accord, State ex rel. Heck's Discount Centers, Inc. v. Winters, 147 W. Va. 861, 132 S.E.2d 374 (1963); State v. Heston, 71 S.E.2d 481 (W. Va. 1952).

For definition and computation of "legislative days" see Knapp v. O'Brien, 179 N.W.2d 88 (Minn. 1970).

§ 3.25 Statutory Requirement of Meeting Date

Provisions in a statute or by-law requiring the election of directors to be held on a specified day are regarded as directory only, and the election if not held on the regular day, may be held on a later day.[35] And, of course, a meeting held on a day other than that provided in the by-laws is legal where all attended and participated without protest.[36]

§ 3.26 Meeting Date—Advance or Postpone

The date of the annual meeting fixed in the by-laws may be advanced by management, but only if done for a proper purpose. A recent decision held that management may not utilize the corporate machinery and the Delaware Corporation Law to advance the date of the annual meeting of stockholders for the purpose of perpetuating itself in office and "to that end, for the purpose of obstructing the legitimate efforts of dissident stockholders in the exercise of their rights to undertake a proxy contest against management." These were "inequitable purposes contrary to established principles of corporate democracy" and "inequitable action does not become permissible simply because it is legally possible." [37]

[35] Beardsley v. Johnson, 121 N.Y. 224, 228, 24 N.E. 380 (1890). "It is of no consequence that the [shareholders'] meeting was held in the month of May instead of April as no question is raised that there was a failure to notify all shareholders of the meeting." In re Dollinger Corp., 51 Misc. 2d 802, 274 N.Y.S.2d 285, 288 (Sup. Ct. 1966). See Wampler v. State, 148 Ind. 557, 47 N.E. 1068 (1897).

See In re Tonopah United Water Co., 16 Del. Ch. 26, 139 A. 762 (1927) (annual meeting erroneously called for two days before by-law specified date due to printer's error; management could call an annual meeting for another date as prescribed by the by-laws).

[36] When all shareholders attend a meeting and participate in the election of directors, the presiding officer is estopped from questioning the conduct of the meeting and of the election, and cannot enjoin new directors from removing him on ground that the meeting was held on the wrong day and without sufficient notice. Camp v. Shannon, 162 Tex. 515, 348 S.W.2d 517 (1961).

[37] The court continued: "When the by-laws of a corporation designate the date of the annual meeting of stockholders, it is to be expected that those who intend to contest the reelection of incumbent management will gear their cam-

By the same token, a delay in holding the annual meeting is permissible so long as it does not prejudice the rights of shareholders. "Only at the annual or specially called meeting of the shareholders can the individual shareholders exercise their rights of suffrage. An undue delay in holding the annual meeting of shareholders might dilute or defeat their right of free suffrage in this case. Fair and full disclosure is of the essence of free suffrage. Because the annual meeting of Studebaker has already been delayed, this court should not countenance any undue delay in the holding of elections, for the benefit of Studebaker stockholders." [38]

---

paign to the by-law date. It is not to be expected that management will attempt to advance that date in order to obtain an inequitable advantage in the contest." Schnell v. Chris-Craft Industries, Inc., 285 A.2d 437, 439 (Del. Ch. 1971).

Advancement of the record date and time of an annual meeting of stockholders is within the powers of a board of directors and is not subject to attack in a minority stockholder's suit to enjoin the corporation from purchasing the remaining interest in a joint venture. Northwest Indus., Inc. v. B. F. Goodrich Co., 301 F. Supp. 706 (N.D. Ill. 1969).

In a decision approving the advancement by a board of directors of the date for holding an annual stockholders' meeting, with the resultant shortening of the terms of the directors by three or four months, it was noted in a dissenting opinion that "[t]his stratagem of the Board, in precipitately advancing the meeting, had the clear purpose of fending off an anticipated proxy contest, or is open to such an inference. In any event, the petitioners assert this was the result; having received no intimation of the Board's intent to schedule the annual meeting four months prior to the expiration of one year from the last 'annual' meeting, they were caught completely off guard. . . . A collateral effect was to abridge the terms of the incumbent directors from twelve to eight months, and also to make it possible that the next 'annual' meeting could be held again in July of the next year, allowing for a prolongation of the terms of office of incumbent reelected directors for an additional sixteen months. The maneuver also made it possible for the incumbent management to keep their chosen directors in office for a period of two years as against the legislative mandate calling for the annual election of directors." The dissenting opinion continued: "In my view, the majority disposition condones a want of fundamental fair play and good faith as exacted by the statutes for the public interest and protection." In re Unexcelled, Inc., 28 App. Div. 2d 44, 281 N.Y.S.2d 173, 178, 179 (1st Dep't 1967).

[38] The court concluded: "That federal courts have power to postpone annual meetings is clear. . . . The setting of the date of an annual meeting is not a

Where the statute requires that an annual meeting of stockholders be held for the election of directors, the court may issue an order compelling the corporation to hold a meeting unless there be a valid excuse for delay. "Not all delays in holding an annual meeting are necessarily inexcusable, . . . and certainly if there are mitigating circumstances explaining the delay or failure to act, they can be considered in fixing the time of the meeting." However, failure to receive clearance from the SEC on filed proxy-soliciting material is not a valid defense where the corporation has not held a stockholders' meeting to elect directors for more than fifteen months.[39]

An annual meeting has been postponed by the court to give ample time for obtaining new valid proxies, where the shareholder had signed illegal proxies obtained as a result of solicitations containing false and misleading statements, and would in effect be disenfranchised if the meeting were held on the scheduled day.[40]

---

drastic departure from this power." Studebaker Corp. v. Allied Prods. Corp., 256 F. Supp. 173, 189, 192 (W.D. Mich. 1966).

"Under New York law, the courts have been given the power to set aside corporate elections in appropriate circumstances." Wolpert v. First Nat'l Bank, 381 F. Supp. 625, 632 (E.D.N.Y. 1974).

See Lincoln Am. Corp. v. Victory Life Ins. Co., 375 F. Supp. 112 (D. Kan. 1974) (question of postponement of annual meeting in a proxy fight to afford stockholders seeking control more time to solicit proxies).

See Keefe v. Geanakos, 418 F.2d 359 (1st Cir. 1969) (refusal to issue temporary injunction against school committee meeting to vote on teacher's discharge).

[39] Tweedy, Browne & Knapp v. Cambridge Fund, Inc., 318 A.2d 635, 637 (Del. Ch. 1974) (citation omitted).

[40] SEC v. O'Hara Re-election Comm., 28 F. Supp. 523 (D. Mass. 1939).

A corporation was required by the court to postpone its annual meeting to permit a proper resolicitation of proxies which had been solicited in violation of the proxy rules of the SEC. SEC v. May, 134 F. Supp. 247 (S.D.N.Y. 1955), aff'd, 229 F.2d 123 (2d Cir. 1956).

Holding of stockholders' meeting to vote on a merger was enjoined for a period not earlier than 60 days from the date of the order to permit solicitation of proxies for a new meeting in accordance with applicable regulations of the SEC. The court refused to allow the meeting to be held on schedule with the understanding that action taken at the meeting would be set aside if it favored a faction which had engaged in unlawful solicitation. Union Pac. R.R. v. Chicago & N.W. Ry., 226 F. Supp. 400 (N.D. Ill. 1964).

See Central Foundry Co. v. Gondelman, 166 F. Supp. 429 (S.D.N.Y. 1958)

The court may also postpone a stockholders' meeting in a proxy contest where management has resorted to dilatory tactics in opposing a demand for inspection of the stockholder list and corporate records.[41]

An adjourned annual meeting may be further adjourned when the interests of justice would be served by allowing time for a shareholder to communicate to his fellow shareholders certain facts and circumstances which if known might result in a majority vote for a change in the board of directors. The court noted that "[c]oncepts of corporate democracy and self-determination by the shareholders are at stake in this action," and expressed its belief that the plaintiffs should be granted a reasonable, limited opportunity to "go to the people" for the election of a different management.[42]

§ 3.27   Meeting and Session, Defined

There has been some confusion between the terms "meeting" and "session," since they are often used interchangeably. In common parliamentary law, the term meeting is limited to the assembly of members for any length of time during which they are not separated for longer than a few minutes or hours. In contrast, regular weekly, monthly, or annual assemblies, and all special meetings, are distinct sessions within parliamentary parlance.[43] This distinction is recog-

---

(postponement of annual meeting where proxies had been solicited by an insurgent proxy committee without full disclosure); Shvetz v. Industrial Rayon Corp., 212 F. Supp. 308 (S.D.N.Y. 1960) (temporary injunction against holding special meeting to consider merger, denied).

[41] Susquehanna Corp. v. General Refractories Co., 250 F. Supp. 797 (E.D. Pa.), *modified,* 356 F.2d 985 (3d Cir. 1966).

[42] The court also noted that eminent counsel had expressed written opinions in the case but that "[c]oncepts of corporate democracy do not make the conclusions of these experts binding on the shareholders." Cooke v. Teleprompter Corp., 334 F. Supp. 467, 470, 471, 473 (S.D.N.Y. 1971).

See Rosenblatt v. Northwest Airlines, Inc., 435 F.2d 1121 (2d Cir. 1970) (minority stockholder did not make application to stay meeting called to act upon proposed merger, but filed motion to enjoin any tally or certification of the vote; denied).

[43] See Robert's Rules of Order at 22, 23.

An "extra" session of Congress is a new session which is called by proclamation of the President. Ashley v. Keith Oil Corp., 7 F.R.D. 589 (D. Mass. 1947).

nized by the courts in holding that "an adjournment from day to day does not bring the session to a close. It may terminate the meeting, but not the session. Adjournments taken from day to day, or even to a day certain, do not interrupt the business of the session. It proceeds as of the same session." [44]

Each legislative session is separate and distinct from every other session and is generally composed of different members. At the expiration of a legislative session, unless extended, the legislature ceases to have legislative power and any bill voted upon thereafter cannot become law.[45]

A session is to be measured by its duration; each day of its duration is not a separate session. Therefore, members are not entitled to mileage for every day's attendance at sessions of the board. Wallace v. Jones, 122 App. Div. 497, 107 N.Y.S. 288 (2d Dep't 1907), aff'd, 195 N.Y. 511 (1909).

See Ashley v. Keith Oil Corp., 7 F.R.D. 589 (D. Mass. 1947) (adjournment of Congress, citing Parliamentarian of House of Representatives and Jefferson's Manual).

But see Atterbury v. Consolidated Coppermines Corp., 26 Del. Ch. 1, 20 A.2d 743, 749 (1941), holding that the presence of a quorum at the original "session" answered a contention that a quorum was not present at an adjourned session because "all sessions were but a part of the same meeting."

An extraordinary session of the legislature can be the "first session," as used in the Constitution. People ex rel. Carter v. Rice, 135 N.Y. 473, 31 N.E. 921. See In re Oran's Petition, 45 Misc. 2d 616, 257 N.Y.S.2d 839 (Sup. Ct. 1965).

The confusion between "session" and "meeting" is illustrated in the case of a city council which "convened in regular session" on a certain date and by appropriate recessing orders was "continued in regular session" on four succeeding dates until the "regular meeting" was finally adjourned. The statute required that the minutes of the meeting be signed "within ten (10) days of the meeting." The court held that the 10 days began to run on the date of adjournment, noting that "the statute deals with the minutes of meetings, not with days of meetings." City of Biloxi v. Cawley, 278 So. 2d 389 (Miss. 1973).

An annual school district meeting convened on March 31 and reconvened on April 6 and April 7 in the school gymnasium except for the balloting which took place in the school cafeteria. The votes taken on each of those days were "during the session" for purposes of reconsideration of a resolution previously adopted. Byron v. Timberlane Regional School Dist., 309 A.2d 218, 221 (N.H. 1973), quoting Mason's Manual and Robert's Rules of Order.

[44] Intermela v. Perkins, 205 F. 603, 611–12 (9th Cir. 1913), cert. denied, 231 U.S. 757 (1914), citing Robert's Rules of Order.

[45] See, e.g., Petition of Special Assembly Interim Comm., 90 P.2d 304 (Cal. 1939) (dissenting opinion quotes CUSHING, LAW AND PRACTICE OF LEGISLATIVE ASSEMBLIES).

§ 3.27.1 Continuing Bodies

Parliamentary law also recognizes "continuous" or "continuing" bodies. A typical example is the United States Senate which is "a continuing body whose members are elected for a term of six years and so divided into classes that the seats of one third only become vacant at the end of each Congress, two thirds always continuing into the next Congress, save as vacancies may occur through death or resignation." The rules of the Senate remain in force from Congress to Congress except as they are occasionally changed. In contrast, the House of Representatives is not a continuing body. Its members are elected for the period of a single Congress, and its rules are readopted at the outset of each new Congress.[46]

Although the device of staggered elections "guarantees continuity in a legislative body," [47] a body can be "continuous" even if the terms of all members expire at the same time.[48]

Generally, a city common council is considered to be a "continuous body" or an "uninterrupted organization." Thus, proceedings begun by the council may be completed at later sessions, although new members have been elected to the council in the meantime. Also, no measure before the body abates or is discontinued by reason of the expiration of the term of office or removal of any member.[49]

[46] McGrain v. Daugherty, 273 U.S. 135, 181 (1926), citing Jefferson's Manual, Hinds' Precedents; see Gojack v. United States, 384 U.S. 702 (1966).

Each House of Representatives is a "distinct legislative body rather than a continuation of its predecessor." Powell v. McCormack, 395 U.S. 486, 560 (1969).

Whether a state legislative body is in regular session or special session is a matter of state law. Groppi v. Leslie, 311 F. Supp. 772, 777 n.4 (W.D. Wis.), rev'd, 436 F.2d 326 (7th Cir. 1970), rev'd, 404 U.S. 496 (1972).

See Constitution of the United States, Jefferson's Manual and Rules of the House of Representatives, H. R. Doc. No. 416, §§ 58–61 (1975).

[47] Roche v. Lamb, 26 N.Y.2d 544, 311 N.Y.S.2d 903, 905 (1970) (city council).

[48] Van Cleve v. Wallace, 216 Minn. 500, 13 N.W.2d 467, 472 (1944), citing Robert's Rules of Order (municipal council).

[49] People ex rel. New York Cent. & H. R.R. v. Buffalo, 123 App. Div. 141, 108 N.Y.S. 331, 333 (4th Dep't 1908) (city common council).

A city council is a continuing body and no measure before it abates or is discontinued by reason of the expiration of the term of office or removal of any members. Halpern v. Dassler, 135 N.Y.S.2d 8 (Sup. Ct. 1954).

A new city council may proceed where a prior council left off and, as a continuing body, the council may act on proceedings until a final determination. Humphrey v. City of Youngstown, 143 N.E.2d 321 (Ohio 1955).

A new city council may complete the unfinished business of the preceding council, including the final reading and passage of an ordinance which had its first reading and passage in the previous council. The court remarked that, although a council generally finishes its business before it goes out of office, it often leaves much unfinished business. When the council has a rule that it must complete all business before going out, such rule is a "matter of parliamentary custom" and is not followed as a matter of law. The courts "are not required to recognize all parliamentary rules that may be adopted by a body of legislative functions." Reuter v. Meacham Contracting Co., 143 Ky. 557, 562, 136 S.W. 1028 (1911); *accord,* Tuell v. Meacham Contracting Co., 145 Ky. 181, 140 S.W. 159 (1911), *citing* Robert's Rules of Order.

See also C. B. Nash Co. v. Council Bluffs, 174 F. 182 (S.D. Iowa 1909), *appeal dismissed,* 184 F. 986 (8th Cir. 1911) (new member of city council at adjourned meeting, not present at time of adjournment).

4

Committees

§ 4.1 Inherent Power To Appoint Committees

It is a general principle of the common law that a legislative body has the power, without statutory authority, to delegate certain of its powers to one or more committees appointed for general or special purposes.[1] A recent case supported the principle that an adminis-

---

[1] *In re* Gordon, 141 Misc. 635, 252 N.Y.S. 858 (1931) (state legislature); *accord,* Adams v. Plunkett, 274 Mass. 453, 175 N.E. 60 (1931) (town council); *In re* Holman, 197 Mo. App. 70, 191 S.W. 1109, *aff'd,* 270 Mo. App. 696, 191 S.W. 711 (1917) (municipal corporation); McMahon v. Salem, 104 N.H. 219, 182 A.2d 463 (1962) (town).

The right of a state legislature to work through a committee exists "by force of implication and continued usage." Liveright v. Joint Comm., 279 F. Supp. 205, 214 (M.D. Tenn. 1968).

The power of a legislative body to enact rules governing its proceedings includes the right to require that proposals to amend the constitution be referred to a committee. Opinion of the Justices No. 185, 278 Ala. 525, 179 So. 2d 155 (1965).

"The theory of a committee inquiry is that the committee members are

trative board, when authorized by statute to establish "rules and regulations for the administration and transaction of its business" and for the "control" of its funds, has the authority to delegate the administration of its funds to a committee, whose decisions are final and binding on the entire board without need for approval or ratification.[2]

§ 4.1.1   *Ministerial Acts and Exercise of Judgment*

While a federal or state legislative body may make lawful delegation of its powers in certain respects to a body it creates or to inferior governmental bodies, it has been held that local legislative bodies are more limited in the exercise of such powers. Thus, it may be

---

serving as the representatives of the parent assembly in collecting information for a legislative purpose. Their function is to act as the eyes and ears of the Congress in obtaining facts upon which the full legislature can act. To carry out this mission, committees and subcommittees, sometimes one Congressman, are endowed with the full power of the Congress to compel testimony." Watkins v. United States, 354 U.S. 178, 200 (1957).

A county political committee may delegate to committees or to individuals the power to administer party affairs. Bauman v. Fusco, 45 Misc. 2d 326, 256 N.Y.S.2d 855 (Sup. Ct.), aff'd, 23 App. Div. 2d 404, 261 N.Y.S.2d 85 (1st Dep't), aff'd, 265 N.Y.S.2d 102 (1965).

It has been held that public meeting "sunshine laws" apply to the activities of an advisory citizens' planning committee appointed by the town council. "It is axiomatic that public officials cannot do indirectly what they are prevented from doing directly. . . . The adoption of a comprehensive zoning plan and ordinance which undoubtedly will dramatically mold the future development of a town is 'governmental action' of the highest magnitude. It would be ludicrous to invalidate the actions of a *public body* which are the result of secret meetings of *that* body or members thereof while at the same time giving approval to actions which result from the secret meetings of *committees designated by such public body.*" IDS Properties, Inc. v. Town of Palm Beach, 279 So. 2d 353, 356 (Fla. App. 1973).

A single branch of the legislature has the power to appoint a committee to gather information and report recommendations as to the enactment of laws. *See Ex parte* Wolters, 144 S.W. 531 (Tex. 1912).

See Barsky v. United States, 167 F.2d 241 (D.C. Cir. 1947), *cert. denied,* 334 U.S. 843 (1948), *rehearing denied,* 339 U.S. 971 (1950) (Congressional committee).

[2] Ostrove v. New York State Teachers Retirement Sys. Bd., 32 App. Div. 2d 163, 300 N.Y.S.2d 663 (3d Dep't 1969), aff'd, 27 N.Y.2d 623, 313 N.Y.S.2d 757 (1970).

said that those duties which are purely ministerial and executive may be delegated to a committee, while those involving the exercise of judgment and discretion may not.[3] Generally, a committee appointed "with power" has all requisite powers to carry out its instructions.[4]

A board of directors of a corporation has a similar inherent power to appoint one or more committees of their number to act for the corporation in particular matters.[5] Generally, modern corporation laws permit a corporate board of directors to delegate policy-making power to its committees.[6] The majority of a board may be justified in creating an executive committee from which the minority directors are excluded, where the conduct of the minority at board meetings has been so reprehensible and continuously harassing that no intelligent discussion of company business could be had.[7]

[3] Brown v. Ward, 216 N.Y.S. 402 (Sup. Ct. 1926).

A city council cannot confer upon a committee the power to perform acts which relate to the government of the city, but the council may delegate to a committee the power to perform merely business acts, such as making purchases and doing work. Kramrath v. Albany, 127 N.Y. 575, 28 N.E. 400 (1891).

[4] See Robert's Rules of Order at 218.

The "full powers" of an executive committee are limited to conducting the ordinary business operations and do not include the general powers of the board of directors to make fundamental changes. Hayes v. Canada, Atl. & Plant S.S. Co., 181 F. 289 (1st Cir. 1910).

[5] Union Pac. R.R. v. Chicago, R.I. & P.R.R., 163 U.S. 564 (1895); Ford v. Magee, 160 F.2d 457 (2d Cir.), cert. denied, 332 U.S. 759 (1947); Social Security Bd. v. Warren, 142 F.2d 974, 977 (8th Cir. 1944); Syracuse Television, Inc. v. Channel 9, 51 Misc. 2d 188, 273 N.Y.S.2d 16, 26, 27 (Sup. Ct. 1966); Fensterer v. Pressure Lighting Co., 85 Misc. 621, 149 N.Y.S. 49 (1914).

"In providing for an executive committee to manage the business and affairs of the corporation, the board of directors clearly acted within its powers." Haldeman v. Haldeman, 176 Ky. 635, 197 S.W. 376, 382 (1917).

[6] See, e.g., Ostrove v. New York State Teachers Retirement Sys. Bd., 32 App. Div. 2d 163, 300 N.Y.S.2d 663 (3d Dep't 1969), aff'd, 27 N.Y.2d 623, 313 N.Y.S.2d 757 (1970).

Trustees may not delegate the supervision of hospital investments even to a committee of fellow trustees. However, a corporate director may delegate his investment responsibility to fellow directors, corporate officers, or even outsiders, but he must continue to exercise general supervision over the activities of his delegates. Stern v. Lucy Webb Hayes Nat'l Training School, 381 F. Supp. 1003 (D.D.C. 1974).

[7] Selama-Dindings Plantations, Ltd. v. Durham, 216 F. Supp. 104 (S.D.

§ 4.2　Definition and Types of Committees

A committee [8] is generally defined as a "body of persons delegated
to consider, investigate, or take action upon and usually to report
concerning some matter of business." [9]　A committee must be created by appropriate enabling action, usually pursuant to a by-law,
or by a standing rule or resolution, and cannot be created by mere
inference.[10] Custom and usage are also appropriate. The creation of
a Senate subcommittee by appointment of the chairman of the full
committee has been approved by the court over a contention that it
should have been created by resolution of the full committee, because the appointment followed the "unvarying practice" of the
Senate.[11]

Generally, the committees of deliberative bodies consist of standing committees, which are normally established by the constitution

---

Ohio 1963), *aff'd sub nom.* Selama-Dindings Plantations, Ltd. v. Cincinnati
Union Stock Yard Co., 337 F.2d 949 (6th Cir. 1964).

[8] The word "committee" in its generic sense includes a subcommittee. Ba-
renblatt v. United States, 240 F.2d 875 (D.C. Cir.), *vacated and remanded on
other grounds,* 354 U.S. 930 (1957).

[9] Webster's Third New International Dictionary states: "A committee . . .
is only an agency of the legislative body creating it and its function is usually
to investigate and recommend. . . . Pursuant to well-established rules confirmed by custom and usage, reference of any proposal to a committee entails
not only vesting the committee with power to investigate and recommend but
also transferring physical custody of the writing embodying the proposal from
the chief clerical officer of the parent body to the chairman of the committee."
State *ex rel.* Todd v. Essling, 268 Minn. 169, 128 N.W.2d 307, 314 (1964).

See Robert's Rules of Order § 49 at 206; South Georgia Power Co. v. Baumann, 169 Ga. 649, 151 S.E. 513 (1929) (committee to prepare and report on
rules); Armitage v. Fisher, 74 Hun. 167, 26 N.Y.S. 364 (1893) (committee to
report rules).

[10] A provision that officers "shall attend executive meetings" does not suffice
to create an executive committee. Mayulianos v. North Babylon Regular Dem.
Club, 198 N.Y.S.2d 511 (Sup. Ct. 1960).

Where the by-laws refer to an executive committee of five members but the
annual report discloses that the entire board consisted of five persons and the
executive committee of three persons, the by-laws were not determinative. An
executive committee's authority to execute a proxy by a 2–0 vote has been upheld. Levin v. Metro-Goldwyn-Mayer, Inc., 221 A.2d 499 (Del. Ch. 1966).

[11] Meyers v. United States, 171 F.2d 800, 811 (D.C. Cir. 1948), *cert.
denied,* 336 U.S. 912 (1949).

or by-laws of the organization to perform recurring functions, and special or select committees, which are appointed for a limited or special purpose.[12] The Supreme Court has noted that "[i]nvestigations, whether by standing or special committees, are an established part of representative government." [13]

It is the "universal rule and custom" that standing committees as well as select committees of any deliberative or organized body are always composed of members of the body.[14] Members of standing committees are usually appointed for a definite period of time, while members of special or select committees are appointed only for the life of the committee, which disbands when its duties have been completed.

Of particular importance is the committee of the whole, which consists of the whole membership of the body sitting as a committee and operating with its own chairman under informal and flexible rules for the purpose of considering a particular measure or some special business; [15] and the executive committee, which consists of selected members of the governing board and generally has full power to act when the board is not in session.[16]

[12] Statute relating to a standing committee of the legislature does not apply to a special joint legislative committee. *In re* Gordon, 141 Misc. 635, 252 N.Y.S. 858 (Sup. Ct. 1931).

[13] Tenney v. Brandhove, 341 U.S. 367, 377 (1951).

[14] Theofel v. Butler, 134 Misc. 259, 236 N.Y.S. 81, 83 (Sup. Ct. 1929).

[15] A committee of the whole may be described under "parliamentary law" as follows: "The practice of conducting business through the committee of the whole has for many years prevailed in legislative and deliberative bodies. Such a committee is no more than the assembly or body itself transacting a part of its business through what is termed the committee of the whole. The committee, therefore, as its name implies, amounts to this: That the particular body or assembly is carrying on a part of its legislative or deliberative functions as a committee composed of all its members. The committee, as is well known, cannot be in session unless the legal or parliamentary body of which it is composed is in session. It cannot adjourn to meet at some other time or place. Whenever it rises, it must at once report its conclusions to the main body, and that body either rejects, approves, or modifies any matter reported to it." Acord v. Booth, 33 Utah 279, 93 P. 734, 735 (*citing* Cushing, Law & Pr. Leg. Assem., Robert's Rules of Order, and Waples' Handbook Parliament. Pr.).

[16] Corporation statutes generally contemplate that an executive committee shall be composed only of directors, and thus, a committee of non-members is invalidly constituted. Steigerwald v. A. M. Steigerwald Co., 9 Ill. App. 2d 31, 132 N.E.2d 373 (1955); *accord*, Canada, Atl. & Plant S.S. Co. v. Flanders, 145

§ 4.3   Number of Members

A deliberative or legislative body has the right, in exercising its powers, to devolve upon a committee of one [17] or more members the authority to investigate and report. And the body, if it so determines at any time after conferring authority upon its committee, for any reason satisfactory to it, may, in whole or in part, dispense with the services of the committee and resume the exercise of its powers to such extent as it may see fit.[18] The body may also increase the committee by adding to the number first chosen, or the body may entirely revoke the powers given to the committee.[19] The right to appoint a committee or subcommittee of a single member with authority to act includes the power to authorize each member of a com-

---

F. 875 (1906), *aff'd*, 165 F. 321 (1st Cir. 1908); Jackson v. Republic Mut. Fire Ins. Co., 27 P.2d 296 (Kan. 1933).

As to the "full powers" of an executive committee, see Hayes v. Canada, Atl. & Plant S.S. Co., 181 F. 289 (1st Cir. 1910).

The calling of a meeting of the board of directors suspends the authority of the executive committee to act in governmental matters. Commercial Wood & Cement Co. v. Northampton Portland Cement Co., 190 N.Y. 1, 82 N.E. 730 (1907).

See Thayer v. Ganter, 174 Misc. 394, 22 N.Y.S.2d 6 (Sup. Ct. 1940) (executive committee of county political committee).

[17] A committee of one is a person who has been delegated to perform the duties of a committee. *See In re* Smith, 175 Misc. 937, 26 N.Y.S.2d 560 (Sup. Ct. 1940), *aff'd*, 260 App. Div. 1003, 24 N.Y.S.2d 992, 285 N.Y. 632, 33 N.E.2d 556 (1941); *In re* Gordon, 141 Misc. 635, 252 N.Y.S. 858 (Sup. Ct. 1931).

Under the Companies Act (England 1908) "it is quite clear on the authorities that there may be a delegation to a committee of one." *In re* Fireproof Doors, Ltd., [1916] 2 Ch. 142.

See United States v. Reinecke, 524 F.2d 435 (C.A.D.C. 1975) (Senate Committee of one) *citing* Robert's Rules of Order Newly Revised (1970).

[18] Barry v. United States *ex rel.* Cunningham, 279 U.S. 597 (1928).

See Watkins v. United States, 354 U.S. 178, 200 (1957); Emspak v. United States, 203 F.2d 54 (App. D.C. 1952), *rev'd*, 349 U.S. 190 (1955); United States v. Moran, 194 F.2d 623 (2d Cir.), *cert. denied*, 343 U.S. 965 (1952).

[19] Damon v. Inhabitants of Granby, 19 Mass. (2 Pick.) 345, 354–55 (1824). A school district may appoint a committee member at a regular meeting and later at an adjourned meeting appoint two more members to serve on the committee. Kingsbury v. Centre School Dist., 53 Mass. (12 Metc.) 99 (1846).

mittee to act as a subcommittee of one.[20] There is some question whether a committee, in carrying out its authority, may delegate its powers to an individual member. Generally, a committee can act only as a body and therefore cannot delegate its powers to a single member.[21] However, it has been held that a political party committee may delegate its entire power to an executive committee, which in turn can delegate its power in whole or in part to the chairman thereof.[22]

A committee of a public corporation is a public agency and its meetings are included in the term "public proceedings." [23]

§ 4.4   Common Law and Parliamentary Rules

A committee of a deliberative body is itself a deliberative body.[24] Its business is conducted according to established procedures, but generally without the formality required of larger bodies. It has power solely within its discretion, unless otherwise directed by statute, to establish its own rules and it is not the function of the court to attempt to regulate such procedures.[25] In speaking of a political committee one court said: "In the absence of rules adopted by a political organization, such organization is governed by the common-law rules that the act of the majority represents the act of the Committee." [26] This is consistent with the statement of another court

[20] *In re* Smith, 175 Misc. 937, 26 N.Y.S.2d 560, *aff'd*, 260 App. Div. 1003, 24 N.Y.S.2d 992 (1st Dep't 1940), *aff'd*, Smith v. Kern, 285 N.Y. 632, 33 N.E.2d 556 (1941) (special committee of N.Y. City Council to investigate Civil Service Commission and report findings).

[21] Young v. United States Mortgage & Trust Co., 156 App. Div. 515, 141 N.Y.S. 364 (1st Dep't 1913), *modifying* 131 N.Y.S. 33 (1911) (executive committee fixing compensation of officer).

[22] State *ex rel.* Pfeifer v. Stoneking, 74 N.E.2d 759 (Ohio 1946) (delegation of power of central committee to an executive committee as authorized by statute is not against public policy).

[23] Selkowe v. Bean, 249 A.2d 35 (N.H. 1969).

[24] Robert's Rules of Order, § 52 at 213.
See Peurifoy v. Loyal, 154 S.C. 267, 151 S.E. 579 (1930) (committee of board can act only when quorum is present).

[25] *In re* Withrow, 176 Misc. 597, 28 N.Y.S.2d 223 (Sup. Ct. 1941) (joint legislative committee conducting investigation).

[26] De Camilla v. Connery, 43 Misc. 2d 395, 251 N.Y.S.2d 305, 309, *aff'd*, 23 App. Div. 2d 704, 256 N.Y.S.2d 986 (3d Dep't 1965) (rules and regula-

that "rules of parliamentary practice and procedure are not necessary to be followed in all cases by party committees." [27]

§ 4.5   Acting as a Body

A committee must act as a body,[28] unless it has statutory authority
to act otherwise.[29] If permitted by statute, a corporate board of
directors may designate alternate members of any committee who
may replace any absent or disqualified member at any meeting of
the committee.[30] Standards of notice [31] and of quorum,[32] includ-

---

tions governing procedure of town committee of political party should come
from county committee).

Generally speaking, a committee of a corporation is subject to the same
rules as the directors. McNeil v. Boston Chamber of Commerce, 154 Mass.
277, 28 N.E. 245, 13 L.R.A. 559 (1891) (quorum of executive committee).

Same rules that govern the board will prevail in the executive committee
unless the latter adopt different rules. Santee v. Amateur Athletic Union, 2
Misc. 2d 990, 153 N.Y.S.2d 465 (Sup. Ct. 1956).

Special meeting of executive committee held without due notice to one
member is not a valid meeting. Close v. Brictson Mfg. Co., 43 F.2d 869 (D.
Neb. 1930).

[27] State ex rel. Pfeifer v. Stoneking, 74 N.E.2d 759, 763 (Ohio 1946) (political party committee delegating power to executive committee).

It is implicit in an election law requiring all political committees to be
formed in the manner provided by the party rules, that such committees shall
also be conducted according to such rules. Jones v. Malone, 200 Misc. 88, 101
N.Y.S.2d 895 (Sup. Ct. 1950).

[28] "By general acceptation, even without a by-law or rule, a committee must
act as a group and have a majority concur." Local 6068, UMW v. Bizzell, 257
S.W.2d 527 (Ky. 1953). Young v. United States Mortgage & Trust Co., 156
App. Div. 515, 141 N.Y.S. 364 (1st Dep't 1913), modifying 131 N.Y.S. 33
(Sup. Ct. 1911), rev'd, 214 N.Y. 279 (1915). But see Superior Portland Ce-
ment v. Pacific Coast Cement Co., 33 Wash. 2d 169, 205 P.2d 597 (1949).

[29] DELAWARE CORP. LAW § 141 (as amended 1969) permits members of a
board or committee to conduct meetings by "conference telephone or similar
communication equipment" where all persons participating can hear each other.

[30] See DELAWARE CORP. LAW § 141(c) (as amended 1969).

[31] Requirements for notice applicable to board of directors also apply to
executive committee of board. In re Empire State Supreme Lodge, 103 N.Y.S.
465 (Sup. Ct.), aff'd, 103 N.Y.S. 1124 (4th Dep't 1907).

[32] "The same rule governs the meetings of the committee as governs the
board of directors." Peurifoy v. Loyal, 154 S.C. 267, 151 S.E. 579, 586 (1930).

In the absence of some special provision, it is the general rule that a majority

ing the disqualification of interested members,[33] are basically the same as those of larger deliberate assemblies.[34] A majority

---

of a committee may function. DeWoody v. Underwood, 66 Ohio App. 367 1940).

There can be no meeting of a Congressional committee unless a quorum is present. Fleischman v. United States, 174 F.2d 519 (App. D.C. 1949), rev'd, 339 U.S. 349, rehearing denied, 339 U.S. 991 (1950).

Under an appropriate Senate resolution, one member of a committee could constitute a quorum. United States v. Moran, 194 F.2d 623 (2d Cir.), cert. denied, 343 U.S. 965 (1952).

In the absence of proof as to the number of members of an executive committee necessary to constitute a quorum, a majority is deemed to be sufficient. Marshall v. Industrial Fed'n of America, 84 N.Y.S. 866 (Sup. Ct. 1903). See Levin v. Metro-Goldwyn-Mayer, Inc., 221 A.2d 499 (Del. Ch. 1966).

A quorum in the House of Representatives is presumed to continue unless a roll call or division indicates otherwise, but the presence of a quorum must be affirmatively shown before a committee is deemed to have legally met. The power to raise a point of no quorum appears to be limited to the members of the committee. Christoffel v. United States, 338 U.S. 84, 88 (1949). See United States v. Bryan, 339 U.S. 323 (1950); Damon v. Inhabitants of Granby, 19 Mass. (2 Pick.) 345 (1824). See also BURLESON, HISTORY OF THE UNITED STATES HOUSE OF REPRESENTATIVES 82 (1965).

The Standing Rules of the U. S. Senate provide that each committee is authorized to fix the number of members, not less than one-third of its entire membership, who shall constitute a quorum for the transaction of business, and to fix a lesser number than one-third who shall constitute a quorum for the purpose of taking sworn testimony. Rule XXV 5(a), (b), Senate Manual § 25.5 at 42 (1975).

In a committee of the whole the quorum is the same as in the assembly; in any other committee the majority is a quorum unless otherwise provided. See Robert's Rules of Order at 259.

A political party committee may establish a rule that less than a majority would constitute a quorum. State ex rel. Pfeifer v. Stoneking, 74 N.E.2d 759 (Ohio 1946).

[33] Metropolitan Tel. Co. v. Domestic Tel. Co., 44 N.J. Eq. 568, 573, 14 A. 907 (1888) (executive committee); Marshall v. Industrial Fed'n of America, 84 N.Y.S. 866 (Sup. Ct. 1903) (executive committee).

A Congressional committee member's motives alone will not vitiate an investigation instituted by a house of Congress if the assembly's legislative purpose is being served. Wilkinson v. United States, 365 U.S. 399, rehearing denied, 365 U.S. 890 (1961); Watkins v. United States, 354 U.S. 178 (1957); United States v. Kamin, 136 F. Supp. 791 (D. Mass. 1956).

See also § 17.45 infra.

[34] However, a committee does not have power to punish its members for

constitutes a quorum and a majority of the quorum may act.[35]

Members of the parent body generally have the right to appear at committee meetings and present their views. However, during the deliberations of the committee, no one has a right to be present except members of the committee.[36]

The courts will follow parliamentary law in considering the constituency, powers, and limitation of a committee of a deliberative body. In considering the activities of a standing committee of a county political committee, one court has stated: "As the executive committee is a standing committee of the county committee, it is necessary to note the usual and peculiar functions of such a committee. And for that purpose common parliamentary rules in use by all deliberative assemblies in this country must be considered. . . . In parliamentary law, a committee may be appointed for one special occasion or it may be appointed to deal with all matters which may be referred to it during the life of the deliberative body." In the latter case it is called a "standing committee." [37]

§ 4.6 Application of Rules of Parent

Unless otherwise prescribed, a committee is subject to the parliamentary rules and procedures of its parent assembly. The Supreme Court, in a case relating to the quorum of a Congressional committee, has said that "in the absence of any showing of a rule, practice or custom to the contrary, this Court has the duty to presume that the conduct of a Congressional Committee, in its usual course of business conforms to both the written and unwritten rules of the House which created it." [38] The rules of a Congressional

---

disorderly conduct; it is limited to reporting facts to the body. *See* Robert's Rules of Order at 218.

[35] Canada, Atl. & Plant S.S. Co. v. Flanders, 145 F. 875 (1906), *aff'd,* 165 F. 321 (1st Cir. 1908); McNeil v. Boston Chamber of Commerce, 154 Mass. 277, 28 N.E. 245 (1891); Kingsbury v. Centre School District, 53 Mass. (12 Metc.) 99 (1846); State v. Jersey City, 27 N.J.L. 493, 495 (1859). *See* Brown v. District of Columbia, 127 U.S. 579 (1888); Local 6068, UMW v. Bizzell, 257 S.W.2d 527 (Ky. 1953); Metropolitan Tel. Co. v. Domestic Tel. Co., 44 N.J. Eq. 568, 573, 14 A. 907 (1888).

[36] *See* Robert's Rules of Order at 212.

[37] Theofel v. Butler, 134 Misc. 259, 236 N.Y.S. 81, 83 (Sup. Ct. 1929).

[38] Christoffel v. United States, 338 U.S. 84 (1949). This case related to a

committee are judicially cognizable, and its practices should be given weight by the courts in construing its rules.[39]

§ 4.7   Time of Committee Meetings

Notice of stated meetings pursuant to established rules need not be given, but notice of all special meetings must be given to all committee members.[40]

---

committee investigation of the political affiliations of an individual, rather than to a hearing on proposed legislation. The court decided, in effect, that a quorum of the committee must be actually physically present when a perjurious offense is committed.

"The Rules of the House are the rules of its committees and subcommittees so far as applicable. . . . Each subcommittee of a committee is a part of that committee, and is subject to the authority and direction of that committee and to its rules so far as applicable." Constitution, Jefferson's Manual, and Rules of the House of Representatives, H.R. Doc. No. 416 at §703(a) (1975); *see id.* at § 340.

"The same rule governs the meetings of the committee as governs the board of directors." Peurifoy v. Loyal, 154 S.C. 267, 151 S.E. 579, 586 (1930) (presence of quorum).

"While we have found no cases with respect to executive committee meetings which started, as it were, out of the blue, such law as there is on the subject concerning directors' meetings is summarized in. . . ." American Center for Educ. v. Cavnar, 26 Cal. App. 3d 26, 102 Cal. Rptr. 575, 579 (1972) *quoting* Fletcher, Cyc. Law of Priv. Corp.

[39] Yellin v. United States, 374 U.S. 109, 114, 116–17 (1963); Wheeldin v. Wheeler, 373 U.S. 647 (1963); Christoffel v. United States, 388 U.S. 84 (1949).

The Rules of a Congressional committee "must be strictly observed" by the committee where they apply to matters of importance. Gojack v. United States, 384 U.S. 702, 708 (1966).

Rules adopted by a Congressional committee are admittedly valid and have the force of law. Randolph v. Willis, 220 F. Supp. 355, 358 (S.D. Cal. 1963).

Where the Standing Rules of the House did not cover the subject of televising subcommittee hearings, and the Speaker had not made any formal interpretations of the Rules on this subject during the Congress in session but had made rulings during the preceding and other prior Congresses, the court will not imply the existence of a Rule. *See* Hartman v. United States, 290 F.2d 460 (9th Cir. 1961), *rev'd on other grounds,* 370 U.S. 724 (1962).

[40] Close v. Brictson Mfg. Co., 43 F.2d 869 (D. Neb. 1930); Metropolitan Tel. Co. v. Domestic Tel. Co., 44 N.J. Eq. 568, 573, 14 A. 907 (1888).

A school district which instructed its committee to do a certain thing was

In the absence of instructions to the contrary, a committee may select its own time and place of meeting, but without a special directive or unanimous consent of the parent it may not meet while the body of which it is a committee is in session.[41] However, the body may go into a committee of the whole at any time since the committee constitutes the whole body.[42]

§ 4.8 Regularity of Appointment

An irregularity in the appointment of a committee may not prevent it from being a committee de facto with authority to act effectively.[43] And members of a committee of the board of directors are charged with knowledge they possess or might possess had they diligently pursued their duties, regardless of whether the committee is "de jure, de facto or a nullity." The argument that a committee was created without specific authority is irrelevant.[44]

§ 4.9 Powers of Committee

A committee is in many respects a miniature deliberative assembly. Its powers are limited to those clearly expressed or neces-

---

bound when the committee did as instructed although the vote of the district was pursuant to a notice that it would "transact such other business as may be legal and proper." Kingsbury v. Centre School Dist., 53 Mass. (12 Metc.) 99 (1846).

In the absence of a statute, by-law, or practice fixing the time or method of calling a meeting of the executive committee, a reasonable notice is necessary to the validity of the meeting. The action of two members of an executive committee in calling at the office of the third and stating that there would be a meeting of the committee, and calling one to order at once, does not constitute reasonable notice, unless there is some emergency which justifies such action. Hayes v. Canada, Atl. & Plant S.S. Co., 181 F. 289 (1st Cir. 1910).

[41] It was in order for a budget committee to hold its meeting during a recess of a school board hearing, which then reconvened. Byron v. Timberlane Regional School Dist., 309 A.2d 218 (N.H. 1973), citing Mason's Manual and Robert's Rules of Order on other points.

[42] A legislative body is "in session" when sitting as a committee of the whole. Acord v. Booth, 33 Utah 279, 93 P. 734 (1908).

[43] See Williams v. School District, 38 Mass. (21 Pick.) 75 (1838).

[44] Syracuse Television, Inc. v. Channel 9, 51 Misc. 2d 188, 273 N.Y.S.2d 16, 27 (Sup. Ct. 1966).

sarily implied in the words of the resolution or other authority creating or authorizing the creation of the committee.[45] For example, an executive committee may authorize and direct the payment of a dividend, and the board of directors may ratify such action, but the directors alone are responsible for the payment of the dividend even though the board may have delegated the power to their committee.[46]

Members of an executive committee assume additional powers and authority by reason of their appointment; their responsibility

[45] An executive committee "only has such power as the board of directors or the by-laws of the corporation provide." Jackson v. Republic Mut. Fire Ins. Co., 27 P.2d 296, 297 (Kan. 1933).

The authority of a committee is limited to the powers granted to it. Ryder v. Bushwick R.R. Co., 134 N.Y. 83, 31 N.E. 251 (1892).

A city council cannot confer legislative powers on a committee, but it may delegate power to the committee to perform routine business acts. Kramrath v. Albany, 127 N.Y. 575, 28 N.E. 400 (1891).

A committee may have power over subordinate committees, including the power to create or to abolish other committees. *See* O'Neil v. O'Connell, 300 Ky. 707, 189 S.W.2d 965 (1945).

The powers of a committee of a city council are limited to those such as are clearly comprehended or necessarily implied within the words of the resolution creating the committee. *In re* Cole, 16 Misc. 134, 38 N.Y.S. 955 (Oneida County Ct. 1896).

For cases concerning the powers of a Congressional committee, *see* Gojack v. United States, 384 U.S. 702 (1966); United States v. Tobin, 195 F. Supp. 588, *rev'd*, 306 F.2d 270 (D.C. Cir.), *cert. denied*, 371 U.S. 902 (1962); United States v. Shelton, 148 F. Supp. 926, *aff'd*, 280 F.2d 701 (D.C. Cir. 1960), *rev'd*, Russell v. United States, 369 U.S. 749 (1962); Davis v. United States, 269 F.2d 357 (6th Cir. 1959), *cert. denied*, 361 U.S. 919 (1959); United States v. Bryan, 72 F. Supp. 58, *aff'd*, Barsky v. United States, 167 F.2d 241 (D.C. Cir. 1948), *cert. denied*, 334 U.S. 843 (1948), *rehearing denied*, 339 U.S. 971 (1950); United States v. Lamont, 18 F.R.D. 27, *aff'd*, 236 F.2d 312 (2d Cir. 1956); United States v. Cross, 170 F. Supp. 303 (D.D.C. 1959); United States v. Icardi, 140 F. Supp. 383 (D.D.C. 1956).

A Congressional committee cannot confer on any of its subcommittees greater powers than the committee possesses. United States v. Lamont, 18 F.R.D. 27, *aff'd*, 236 F.2d 312 (2d Cir. 1956).

[46] Aiken v. Insull, 122 F.2d 746 (7th Cir. 1941), *cert. denied*, 315 U.S. 806, *rehearing denied*, 315 U.S. 829 (1942).

A corporation by its board of directors can ratify and render binding upon it the acts of its executive committee which the board of directors could in the first instance have authorized. Boyce v. Chemical Plastics, 175 F.2d 839 (8th Cir.), *cert. denied*, 338 U.S. 828 (1949).

encompasses matters passed upon by the committee, and thus the diligence required of them is greater and their liability stricter than that of the other directors.[47]

The court in a leading case involving directors' liability noted that certain directors were members of the executive committee and, by attending meetings and discussing company business, "must have known what was going on." [48]

§ 4.10   Acts and Reports

An act taken by a committee is not an act of the parent body, and, except as specially authorized, is in no way binding on the parent.[49] Also, the adoption of a committee report by the parent body is of no more effect than an acknowledgment of the receipt of the report from the committee and a divestiture by the parent of any further authority over the subject by the committee. "Even the most inexperienced legislator understands that a motion to adopt a committee report is relatively insignificant in effect since it is neither designed nor intended to reach the merits of a committee recommendation." [50]

§ 4.11   Vote of Committee Member as Member of Parent

The question often arises whether a member of a committee appointed to study and recommend action by the body may, as a

[47] Syracuse Television, Inc. v. Channel 9, 51 Misc. 2d 188, 273 N.Y.S.2d 16, 27 (1966); *accord,* Masonic Bldg. Corp. v. Carlsen, 128 Neb. 108, 258 N.W. 44 (1934); Kavanaugh v. Gould, 147 App. Div. 281, 131 N.Y.S. 1059 (3d Dep't 1911).

[48] Escott v. BarChris Constr. Corp., 283 F. Supp. 643, 684 (S.D.N.Y. 1968).

[49] United States v. Northern Pac. Ry., 41 F. Supp. 273, 283 (D. Wash. 1941) (Congressional committee).

"A legislative body cannot delegate its final power to a committee, and, except as especially authorized, the committee's acts have no force but remain subject to approval, modification, or rejection of the parent body." State *ex rel.* Todd v. Essling, 268 Minn. 169, 128 N.W.2d 307, 314 (1964), *citing* Jefferson's Manual and Mason's Manual.

A city council may reject the advice of a committee appointed to advise and assist the council. Anderson v. Thomas, 166 La. 512, 117 So. 573 (1928).

[50] State *ex rel.* Todd v. Essling, 268 Minn. 169, 128 N.W.2d 307, 314, 316 (1964), *citing* Mason's Manual.

member of the body, vote on a motion to approve or disapprove the report and recommendation of the committee. It was established at an early date that committee members had the right to vote as members on the acceptance or rejection of a report of their committee.[51] That rule is still in effect and is in conformity with Robert's Rules of Order which provides that when a member has been tried by a committee and the committee reports to the body the result of the trial with its recommendations regarding punishment, "[t]he members of the committee should vote upon the case the same as other members." The court also said of Robert's Rules that "resort to that manual for light on relevant parliamentary usages of a deliberative assembly is permissible." [52]

When a unanimous vote of a committee is required by statute, a unanimous vote of more than a legal quorum, although less than the full committee, meets the statutory requirement.[53]

§ 4.12   Duration of Committee

The term of existence of a committee depends on its purpose and origin, and the authority of its parent body.[54] As may be expected, litigation in this area relates primarily to the power of a legislative committee to act after adjournment of the parent legislature.

Common law recognizes that a legislative body with power to prepare and enact laws has the inherent and implied power to appoint a committee for the purpose of obtaining information concerning proposed legislation and reporting its findings to the appointing body.[55] If the appointing body is one house of a bi-cameral

---

[51] Damon v. Inhabitants of Granby, 19 Mass. (2 Pick.) 345 (1824).

[52] Posner v. Bronx County Med. Soc., 19 App. Div. 2d 89, 241 N.Y.S.2d 540, 544 (1st Dep't), aff'd, 13 N.Y.2d 1004, 195 N.E.2d 59, 245 N.Y.S.2d 393 (1963), quoting Robert's Rules of Order.

[53] Wasserman v. Board of Regents, 13 App. Div. 2d 591, 212 N.Y.S.2d 884, 885 (3d Dep't 1961), aff'd, 11 N.Y.2d 173, 182 N.E.2d 264, 227 N.Y.S.2d 649, 95 A.L.R. 2d 869, cert. denied, 371 U.S. 861 (1962) (proceeding to determine charges against professional man).

[54] See, generally, Annot., Formalities and requisites of the creation of legislative committees, 28 A.L.R. 1154 (1915).

[55] See, e.g., Petition of Special Assembly Interim Committee, 83 P.2d 932, 935 (Cal. 1938), aff'd on rehearing, 13 Cal.2d 497, 90 P.2d 304 (1939); Ex

legislature,[56] it may appoint a committee to obtain information and report back to the appointing house during the session or during a constitutional recess between sessions, but not after adjournment to a succeeding house.[57] This is based on the principle of common law that a committee cannot exist after its parent body adjourns. When the legislative power of the parent dies, so does the power of its committee to act.[58]

§ 4.13 Power To Sit After Adjournment of Parent

However, it is generally held that where the appointing body had constitutional or statutory authority, it has the power to appoint committees by explicit enactment with authority to sit after adjournment of the appointing body and even to report to a succeeding

---

parte McCarthy, 29 Cal. 395 (1866). *See also* People v. Sharp, 107 N.Y. 427, 14 N.E. 319 (1887); *In re* Parker, 74 S.C. 466, 55 S.E. 122 (1906).

[56] "A single house is not the legislature." Petition of Assembly Interim Committee *In re* Southard, 13 Cal.2d 497, 498, 90 P.2d 304, 305 (1939).

[57] "The legislative powers are vested in a senate and house of representatives and not in either separately; that is, the legislative power is vested in the legislature, which consists of a senate and a house of representatives. Neither the senate nor the house of representatives may, by independent act, create an investigating committee with power to sit after adjournment of the legislature." State *ex rel.* Robinson v. Fluent, 30 Wash. 2d 194, 191 P.2d 241, 252, *cert. denied*, 335 U.S. 844 (1948).

Petition of Special Assembly Interim Committee, 83 P.2d 932, 935–36 (Cal. 1938), *aff'd on rehearing*, 13 Cal.2d 497, 90 P.2d 304 (1939); *Ex parte* Caldwell, 61 W. Va. 49, 55 S.E. 910, 10 L.R.A. (NS) 172 (1906).

See Fergus v. Russel, 270 Ill. 304, 110 N.E. 130 (1915) (committee members reporting to succeeding body after adjournment were acting as individuals without authority).

[58] When the powers of one branch of the legislature are ended, the powers of the other branch and of its committees are also ended. "The limb cannot exist ·after the body has perished. . . . If the branch cannot act, how can a committee act deriving its life from the branch?" *Ex parte* Caldwell, 61 W.Va. 49, 55 S.E. 910, 911, 10 L.R.A. (NS) 172 (1906); *accord*, Petition of Special Assembly Interim Committee, 13 Cal.2d 497, 90 P.2d 304, 309 (1939), *aff'g* 83 P.2d 932 (Cal. 1938).

A subcommittee has no power to act after the term of office of its parent committee expires. McDonald v. Heffernan, 196 Misc. 465, 92 N.Y.S.2d 382 (Sup. Ct.), *aff'd*, 275 App. Div. 1054, 92 N.Y.S.2d 426 (2d Dep't), *aff'd*, 300 N.Y. 488, 88 N.E.2d 722 (1949).

body.[59] This is in conformity with parliamentary law.[60] Whether the adoption of joint or concurrent resolutions is equivalent to an enactment by both houses depends on the law of the applicable jurisdiction.[61]

The Supreme Court has held that the United States Senate, as distinguished from the House of Representatives, may continue its committees through the recess following the expiration of a

[59] *See, e.g.,* Petition of Special Assembly Interim Committee, 13 Cal.2d 497, 90 P.2d 304 (1939); Fergus v. Russel, 270 Ill. 304, 110 N.E. 130 (1915).

[60] "What the Legislature may say in a statute applicable to legislative committees generally, it may say with the same validity in defining the life and the functions of a particular committee. Far from departing thereby from the principles and precedents of parliamentary procedure, it is following the very method to which consecrating usage has affixed the stamp of regularity." People *ex rel.* Hastings v. Hofstadter, 258 N.Y. 425, 434, 180 N.E. 106 (1932), *citing* Jefferson's Manual, Hinds' Precedents.

[61] For a discussion of the differences among the form, purpose, and use of concurrent and joint resolutions in Congress, see Jefferson's Manual § 396, Constitution, Jefferson's Manual and Rules of the House of Representatives; Constitution of the United States of America, Art. I, Sec. 7, Bills and Resolutions, 1975.

Also, see full discussion of joint and separate resolutions in People *ex rel.* Hastings v. Hofstadter, 258 N.Y. 425, 180 N.E. 106 (1932).

A concurrent resolution of the two houses is not a statute, and is not effective to modify or repeal a statutory enactment. That can be done only by a legislative act of equal dignity and import. Moran v. LaGuardia, 270 N.Y. 450, 1 N.E.2d 961 (1936), *citing* Cushing; *accord,* Bohrer v. Toberman, 227 S.W.2d 719 (Mo. 1950), *citing* Cushing.

In jurisdictions where the constitution or statute law expressly recognizes concurrent or joint resolutions as equivalent to laws enacted by bill, such resolutions are given the force and effect of laws. Thus, there is no difference in principle between a committee created by legislative act and one created by joint or concurrent resolutions. *See* State *ex rel.* Robinson v. Fluent, 30 Wash. 2d 194, 191 P.2d 241, *cert. denied,* 335 U.S. 844 (1948).

The fact that the legislature has for many years created interim committees by single house or concurrent resolutions, and such usage has never been challenged, is beside the point. Usage and custom, no matter how long continued, cannot create a right in the legislature that otherwise it does not possess. Petition of Special Assembly Interim Committee, 13 Cal.2d 497, 508, 90 P.2d 304 (1939); *accord,* Fergus v. Russel, 270 Ill. 304, 110 N.E. 130 (1915).

The construction of a joint resolution of Congress is to be governed by the rules applicable to legislation generally. Ann Arbor R.R. v. United States, 281 U.S. 658 (1930).

Congress.[62] The Senate is considered a continuing body because its members are so divided into classes that the seats of only one third become vacant at the end of each Congress. Usually, a state legislature is not considered to be a continuing body.[63]

§ 4.14 Immunity of Members

Constitutional provisions respecting the privileges and immunity of members of a legislature apply to the assembly and any part thereof, such as a committee appointed by the assembly.[64]

[62] Gojack v. United States, 384 U.S. 702 (1966); McGrain v. Daugherty, 273 U.S. 135, 181 (1926) (recalcitrant witness before Senate select committee) *citing* Jefferson's Manual and Hinds' Precedents. *See* Petition of Special Assembly Interim Committee, 83 P.2d 932 (1938), *aff'd on rehearing*, 13 Cal.2d 497 (1939), 90 P.2d 304 (1939).

A select committee of the Congress is functus officio not later than the close of the session at which it was appointed, and hence no member of the old committee has any authority to bind a new committee that may be created by the incoming Congress. Riley v. United States, 121 F. Supp. 574 (Ct. Cl. 1954).

See § 5.27 *supra.*

[63] *See* Petition of Special Assembly Interim Committee *In re* Southard, 13 Cal.2d 487, 90 P.2d 304 (1939); People *ex rel.* Hastings v. Hofstadter, 258 N.Y. 425, 180 N.E. 106 (1932).

[64] *See* § 19.2 *infra.*

5

Attendance at Meetings

§ 5.1 Directors' Meetings

Attendance at meetings of the board of directors is one of the factors cited by the courts in determining whether a director has been negligent in permitting or failing to halt the mismanagement of corporate affairs.[1]

[1] Not every "director" is required to attend meetings. Neither a director emeritus nor an advisory director of a corporation is a director or officer in the true sense. He is designated by the board of directors and, unlike regular directors, he is not elected by the stockholders. Generally, an advisory director has the privilege of attending directors' meetings and participating in discussions and deliberations, but does not have the right to vote. A director emeritus may have the privileges of an advisory director or may have no privileges whatever, depending upon the practices of the company. If the advisory or honorary director has the right to attend meetings of the board he will be classified as an "insider" subject to the reporting requirements of Section 16(a) of the Securities Exchange Act of 1934. Fort Worth Nat'l Corp., 1971 CCH Dec. ¶ 78,309.

The legal distinction between an advisory or honorary director and a regular director has not been clearly defined, although an attempt has been made to distinguish between the duties of an "advisory director" and a "director occupied in the daily management" of corporate affairs. See Briggs v. Spaulding, 141 U.S. 132, 157 (1891).

Regular attendance at meetings with active participation in the deliberations may be helpful in establishing a record of diligence and attention to the affairs of the company. On the other hand, directors who persistently and willfully fail to attend meetings may have the burden of proving their diligence. Attendance at a meeting without actively participating in the discussion of all or any matters being considered does not necessarily mean that a director fails to be diligent. Attention and comprehension as well as active participation are signs of diligence, and support intelligent decision making.[2]

§ 5.2   Duty To Attend Meetings

It is generally understood that a corporate director need not give continuous attention to the business of the corporation, and that he does not have an absolute duty to attend all meetings of the board, even when he fails to have an acceptable excuse for being absent.[3]

[2] Acceptance of a directorship "in name only" does not immunize the director from liability arising from mismanagement of corporate affairs. However, a "lackadaisical attitude toward corporate responsibilities," in and of itself, does not automatically result in personal liability. "Liability necessarily depends upon the particular facts obtaining in each individual case and cannot be determined by mere rote application of general prnciples." Harman v. Willbern, 374 F. Supp. 1149, 1162 (D. Kan. 1974).

In finding that certain directors "were not as naive as they claim to be" the court noted that they were members of the executive committee and that, at meetings of the committee, company business was discussed at length. "They must have known what was going on." Escott v. BarChris Constr. Corp., 283 F. Supp. 643, 684 (S.D.N.Y. 1968).

[3] Bank directors are "not bound to give continuous attention to the business of the bank; they are bound only to be present, so far as rationally practicable, at stated meetings of the board and of its committees." Prudential Trust Co. v. McCarter (Brown), 271 Mass. 132, 171 N.E. 42, 44 (1930), 25 A.L.R.3d 960, 1002.

While directors need not attend every meeting, absence from one or two meetings does not necessarily constitute consent to action taken at such meetings. See Murphy v. Penniman, 105 Md. 452, 66 A. 282 (1907).

In denying motions to dismiss a complaint seeking to base liability under the common law against directors "who persistently failed to attend meetings," the court said that a willful and continued failure on the part of a director to attend meetings of the board is a violation of the duty which the common law imposes upon directors. "Of course, a director is not required to attend every meeting, and it may be that some of the losses which were the result of actions which were not violations of any statute, taken at meetings at which some of

While it has been said that a concerted plan to abstain from attending directors' meetings may be improper under some circumstances, the court will not issue a mandatory injunction to compel individual directors to attend directors' meetings in the absence of good cause shown.[4]   One court has stated: "There is no legal process by which a director of a private business corporation can be forced to attend a meeting, and he cannot lawfully be compelled by physical force to attend, nor can he be trapped into attendance against his will."[5]

§ 5.3   Attendance With Reasonable Regularity

Generally, it has been held that directors are required to attend meetings of the board and of committees "with reasonable regularity,"[6] or "so far as rationally practicable, at stated meetings of the board and of its committees."[7]   If the by-laws require monthly meetings, directors should make diligent effort to be present.[8]   Cer-

---

the directors, who were occasionally absent, were not present, and who did not thereafter approve, expressly or substantially, such actions of the board, cannot be held liable for those losses.   But quite a different situation is presented by a willful and continued failure, during the whole course of one's directorship, to attend meetings of the board and give to the board the benefit of his judgment and advice."   Williams v. Brady, 232 F. 740, 744 (D.N.J. 1916).

[4] In Campbell v. Loew's Inc., 36 Del. Ch. 565, 134 A.2d 852 (1957), a stockholder requested a mandatory injunction to compel individual directors to attend directors' meetings, on the ground that directors were acting unlawfully in attempting to cause the absence of a quorum at meetings for the purpose of preventing the board from exercising its power.   The court denied an injunction, holding that the directors' action was not such a breach of fiduciary duty as to require an injunction, particularly where a stockholders' action was in the offing to fill the board.   134 A.2d at 866–67.

However, when trustees fail to meet on the day fixed by law, they may meet on a subsequent day as reasonably near as possible to that fixed by statute.   A mandamus may be invoked to compel the trustees to meet and take required action.   See, e.g., Wampler v. State, 148 Ind. 557, 47 N.E. 1068 (1897), citing Robert's Rules of Order and Cushing's Manual on quorum.

[5] Trendley v. Illinois Traction Co., 241 Mo. 73, 145 S.W. 1, 6 (1912).

[6] Harris v. Cheetham, 180 N.Y.S. 106, 107 (Sup. Ct. 1919) (derivative action against directors of bank).

[7] Prudential Trust Co. v. McCarter (Brown), 271 Mass. 132, 171 N.E. 42, 44 (1930); accord, Medford Trust Co. v. McKnight, 292 Mass. 1, 197 N.E. 649, 655 (1935).

[8] The custom of banks in New York City to entrust to the executive committee the supervision of detail management generally does not relieve di-

tainly, participating in meetings of the board of directors better enables the directors to rely on the reports of officers and on corporate records.[9]

An English case held that a director cannot, by wilfully refusing to attend board meetings, prevent a quorum from being present to consider the transfer of company shares, thereby frustrating the right of a shareholder to register the transfer of his shares. The court directed the company to rectify the register by giving effect to the transfers.[10]

Corporate directors have a nondelegable duty to be present at directors' meetings, and lack of attendance will not excuse them for failure to exercise independent supervision and control of corporate affairs.[11] "Having accepted a position on the board, it was his duty

---

rectors of responsibility. "If the by-laws require monthly meetings, they must make diligent effort to be present thereat. . . . If at their meetings, or otherwise, information should come to them of irregularity in the proceedings of the bank, they are bound to take steps to correct those irregularities. The law has no place for dummy directors." Kavanaugh v. Gould, 147 App. Div. 281, 131 N.Y.S. 1059, 1064 (1911).

[9] Derivative action against directors for damages allegedly sustained by a corporation by reason of antitrust violations. The appellate court held that directors were not liable. "At the meetings of the Board in which all Directors participated, these questions were considered and decided on the basis of summaries, reports and corporate records. These they were entitled to rely on, not only, we think, under general principles of the common law, but by reason of [Delaware law] as well, which in terms fully protects a director who relies on such in the performance of his duties." Graham v. Allis-Chalmers Mfg. Co., 188 A.2d 125, 130 (Del. Ch. 1963).

[10] *In re* Copal Varnish Co., [1917] 2 Ch. 349.

[11] One defendant nonresident director never attended a board meeting and was never physically present in New York (situs of directors' meetings) for the purpose of transacting corporate business. See discussion of "omission" and "commission" and the conclusion that an attempt to distinguish between them is inconsistent with the duties and responsibilities of corporate directors. Platt Corp. v. Platt, 42 Misc. 2d 640, 249 N.Y.S.2d 1 (1964), *aff'd*, 258 N.Y.S.2d 629 (1st Dep't 1965), *rev'd*, 270 N.Y.S.2d 408 (1966).

No meetings were held by the board of directors of a bank except the annual meeting and meetings to declare dividends, or on some special occasion. Briggs v. Spaulding, 141 U.S. 132 (1891).

Directors' failure to attend to affairs of the bank, including abandonment of all their duties except the holding of semiannual meetings, constitutes gross inattention and negligence. Trustees Mut. Bldg. Fund & Dollar Sav. Bank v. Bosseiux, 3 F. 817 (E.D. Va. 1880).

to attend the meetings and assist his associates in supervising the business. He did not attend any of the meetings and was in all respects wholly inattentive to the affairs of the company. He should be held personally liable for any losses which are shown to have resulted from his inattention to the business." [12]

Circumstances may impose a greater responsibility on a director to attend meetings of the board. For example, a dominant stockholder who sold his controlling stock and agreed to remain on the board of directors in order to insure a smooth transition of management had "the duty to attend and take an active part in any and all board meetings." [13]

Consideration has been given to the question whether nonresident directors of a national bank have the same duty to attend directors' meetings as do resident directors. Specifically, one court has asked whether losses to the bank "were caused by the nonattendance of [director] at the directors' meetings or by the neglect of [director]." In this case, the court held that it would be "manifestly unjust" to hold a nonresident director to the same degree of attention as a resident director and that, although the nonresident

---

Bank directors were negligent for failing to hold or attend monthly meetings of the board, as prescribed by the by-laws. Only a quorum of the 9 qualified directors was present at 18 of the 25 meetings held. Gamble v. Brown, 29 F.2d 366 (4th Cir. 1928), cert. denied, 279 U.S. 839 (1929).

A suit against a director of a mining company for failure to exercise care and diligence and to attend meetings of the board. Horn Silver Min. Co. v. Ryan, 42 Minn. 196, 44 N.W. 56 (1889).

An action against a director for negligence and failure to hold and attend directors' meetings as required by by-laws. Only two meetings were held in two years before the company was declared insolvent. Besselieu v. Brown, 177 N.C. 65, 97 S.E. 743 (1919).

The failure of a bank director to attend even one of 17 meetings of the board of directors held while he was a director constituted violation of the common-law duty of a director to act with ordinary care and diligence. Crews v. Garber, 188 Okla. 570, 111 P.2d 1080 (1941).

Directors did not meet weekly as required by by-laws, and met in some years only once or twice. Marshall v. Farmers' & Mechanics' Sav. Bank, 85 Va. 676, 8 S.E. 586 (1889), overruled, 128 S.E. 624 (1925).

A director cannot be charged with neglect in attending directors' meetings where, during his incumbency, he was present at one and had an adequate excuse for his absence from the other. Barnes v. Andrews, 298 F. 614 (S.D.-N.Y. 1924).

[12] Martin v. Hardy, 251 Mich. 413, 232 N.W. 197, 198–99 (1930).
[13] Harman v. Willbern, 374 F. Supp. 1149, 1163 (D. Kan. 1974).

director was negligent in failing to attend meetings and prevent illegal loans, the stockholders could not recover therefor from him.[14]

§ 5.4　Dummy Directors

A "purely perfunctory" attendance at meetings is not sufficient; the director must pay attention and at least try to understand what is going on.[15] Although it is common practice at board meetings for the president to read reports to the members present, directors are still liable for negligence in failing to discover conditions disclosed in the reports but suppressed when read by the president.[16]

---

[14] Wallach v. Billings, 277 Ill. 218, 115 N.E. 382 (1917).

The court has also considered whether failure of a director to attend meetings makes him responsible for failures which may befall his bank. "It does not follow, because a director has failed to attend meetings, that he is legally or morally responsible for the disasters that may have befallen his bank. In the present case the board had provided for a reasonably vigilant supervision of the cashier. The cause of the losses was the neglect of those who had been appointed to keep watch of the discounts. Those directors who attended the meetings, and had no reason to suppose that the members of the discount and examining committees were neglecting their duties, are not responsible for the losses, which are solely attributable to such neglect. The directors who did not attend the meetings are in no worse category. What could they have done or prevented, exercising common diligence, if they had been present? A director who has failed to act is not liable for the thefts or shortcomings of the cashier, unless it appears, inferentially, at least, that his omission had some proximate relation to the losses." Warner v. Penoyer, 91 F. 587, 598 (2d Cir. 1898).

[15] "It will not do, therefore, for these gentlemen to say that they did not have time to attend the meetings of the board, or that they knew nothing about the business . . . when the evidence shows that some of them failed to discharge any duties as directors by staying away from the meetings of the board, and that those who did attend seemed to have deliberately closed their eyes" to what the management was doing. O'Connor v. First Nat'l Investors' Corp., 163 Va. 908, 177 S.E. 852, 858, 860 (1935).

"Gross non-attendance in a director may make him guilty of the breaches of trust committed by officers and other directors." Trustees Mut. Bldg. Fund & Dollar Sav. Bank v. Bosseiux, 3 F. 817, 838 (E.D. Va. 1880).

[16] A bank president, in reading reports to directors at their weekly meetings, stated that he was reading all the criticisms contained therein, although he read portions incorrectly and omitted material and important portions altogether. The court noted that "[a]ppellants say that it was common procedure at bank directors' meetings generally for the president to read the reports but this defense is not conclusive in character in a case where the custom is a dangerous one." Atherton v. Anderson, 99 F.2d 883, 890 (6th Cir. 1938).

Whether a director would have known about certain unlawful or improper acts if he had attended meetings of the board or had been reasonably attentive to his duties, presents a question of fact.[17]

No one is compelled to be a director, but once the office is assumed, it carries with it the burden of action and diligent service. Even an arrangement with a director at the time of his election that he will accept the office as an "accommodation," [18] or that he is not expected to attend meetings or take an active part in the affairs of the company, does not relieve him of his responsibility.[19] The fact that a director resides a great distance from the office does not excuse abdication of his common-law responsibilities such as attending meetings.[20] Unless a director is "in a mood to suffer the inconvenience of travel" he should not accept the position.[21]

All directorships are on an equal footing of active duty.[22] "A

[17] Kavanaugh v. Commonwealth Trust Co., 223 N.Y. 103, 113, 119 N.E. 237 (1918).

[18] Minton v. Cavaney, 15 Cal. Rptr. 641, 364 P.2d 473 (1961).

[19] A trust company director, by arrangement when he became a director, was not expected to attend meetings or to take any active part in the affairs of the company. He testified that he never went near the trust company, knew nothing of its affairs, gave no attention to its business, and took no action except to resign. Kavanaugh v. Commonwealth Trust Co., 223 N.Y. 103, 106, 119 N.E. 237, 238 (1918).

See Wallach v. Billings, 277 Ill. 218, 115 N.E. 382 (1917) (a nonresident director of a national bank entered into a secret agreement with the president that so long as he was a director, he should do nothing by way of administering its affairs; the director did not attend directors' meetings for 3½ years).

[20] A national bank director resided 200 miles from the bank and failed to attend a single directors' meeting during the entire 5½ years of the bank's existence. Bowerman v. Hamner, 250 U.S. 504 (1919).

[21] "When one becomes a director of a private corporation, he assumes certain duties, which he cannot excuse by showing that he lives a great distance from where the books are kept, or where the business is carried on." Dinsmore v. Jacobson, 242 Mich. 192, 218 N.W. 700, 701 (1928).

A director domiciled in Florida who willfully undertook to assume directorship in a Delaware corporation which he knew conducted its affairs and had all of its assets in New York, and who never attended a meeting of the board and was never physically present in New York on company business, was subject to suit in New York which was the situs of the tortious acts of failing to attend directors' meetings. Platt Corp. v. Platt, 42 Misc. 2d 640, 249 N.Y.S.2d 1 (1964), *aff'd*, 258 N.Y.S. 2d 629 (1965).

[22] However, since all directors are individuals, each with different talents and habits, it is manifest the law should recognize that the duties which attach to

director owes loyalty and allegiance to the corporation he under-takes to serve and his willful derelictions are not excusable because his numerous directorates make his duties conflicting. He cannot choose which he will serve, so long as he chooses to serve all. No one is compelled to be a director, but once the office is assumed, it carries with it the light burden of active, diligent, and single-eyed service." [23] To permit a defense of absence on other business affairs would be "putting a premium on the failure to attend board meet-ings and a penalty on those who attend regularly." [24]

It has been succinctly put: "The law has no place for dummy directors." [25] In a leading case, the chairman of the board of a national bank attended only three of 26 regular and special meetings over a period of two years, and at some meetings board action was vitiated by the presence of a number of the chairman's "disqualified dummies." [26] "No custom or practice can make a directorship a

each director may differ. "They cannot be the same under all circumstances; nor can they be imposed with unvarying exactness upon all directors alike." Cassidy v. Uhlmann, 170 N.Y. 505, 516, 63 N.E. 554 (1902), *quoted in* Brod-erick v. Horvatt, 148 Misc. 731, 266 N.Y.S. 341, 343–44 (Sup. Ct. 1933).

[23] People v. Marcus, 261 N.Y. 268, 277, 185 N.E. 97 (1933).

[24] Rankin v. Cooper, 149 F. 1010, 1016–17 (C.C.W.D. Ark. 1907).

[25] Kavanaugh v. Gould, 147 App. Div. 281, 289, 131 N.Y.S. 1059, 1064 (1911), *quoted in* Michelsen v. Penney, 41 F. Supp. 603, 610 (S.D.N.Y. 1941), *rev'd,* 135 F.2d 409 (2d Cir. 1943); Platt Corp. v. Platt, 42 Misc. 2d 640, 249 N.Y.S.2d 1, 11 (1964), *aff'd,* 258 N.Y.S.2d 629 (1st Dep't 1965), *rev'd,* 270 N.Y.S.2d 408 (1966); Walker v. Man, 142 Misc. 277, 253 N.Y.S. 458, 462 (Sup. Ct. 1931).

Bank directors are not "merely gilded ornaments of the institution to en-hance its attractiveness." Gibbons v. Anderson, 80 F. 345, 350 (C.C.W.D. Mich. 1897).

Directors who are "mere figureheads" on the board, subject to orders of some other director, are equally liable for their neglect. O'Connor v. First Nat'l Investors' Corp., 163 Va. 908, 177 S.E. 852 (1935).

"Unfortunately some directors appear to think that they have fully dis-charged their duties by acting as figureheads and dummies; but this is a mistake and a delusion from which some of them are now and then awakened by a judgment for damages arising from allowing the corporation to be looted while they sat negligently by and looked wise." McEwen v. Kelly, 140 Ga. 720, 79 S.E. 777, 779 (1913).

"The director may not act as a dummy or a figurehead." Bayer v. Beran, 49 N.Y.S.2d 2 (Sup. Ct. 1944).

[26] Michelsen v. Penney, 41 F. Supp. 603, 628 (S.D.N.Y. 1941), *rev'd,* 135 F.2d 409 (2d Cir. 1943).

mere position of honor void of responsibility, or cause a name to become a substitute for care and attention."[27] Directors cannot simply "shut their eyes to what is going on around them" and thereby avoid the consequences by their failure to act.[28] Directors must do more than officiate as "figureheads."[29]

§ 5.5 Excuses for Failure To Attend

There is considerable case law regarding the validity of excuses for failing to attend meetings of the board of directors. Illness and advanced age seem to be the principal reasons for granting an excuse; however, each case stands on its facts. An early decision noted that the courts are "under perplexing restraint lest they

[27] Kavanaugh v. Commonwealth Trust Co., 223 N.Y. 103, 106, 119 N.E. 237, 238 (1918); accord, Barr v. Wackman, 36 N.Y.2d 371, 368 N.Y.S.2d 497 (1975); People v. Marcus, 261 N.Y. 268, 277, 185 N.E. 97 (1933).

A directorship is not "merely honorary." Trustees Mut. Bldg. Fund & Dollar Sav. Bank v. Bosseiux, 3 F. 817, 838 (E.D. Va. 1880).

Barnes v. Eastern & W. Lumber Co., 205 Ore. 553, 287 P.2d 929, 938 (1955) (election to the board of directors not "merely the bestowal of an honor").

Directors of a bank cannot be classified as "active" or "nonactive." Chicago Title & Trust Co. v. Munday, 297 Ill. 555, 131 N.E. 103, 106 (1921).

[28] Briggs v. Spaulding, 141 U.S. 132, 168 (1891) (dissenting opinion); Martin v. Webb, 110 U.S. 7, 15 (1884); Atherton v. Anderson, 99 F.2d 883, 890 (6th Cir. 1938); Bank of Commerce v. Goolsby, 129 Ark. 416, 196 S.W. 803, 810 (1917); Platt Corp. v. Platt, 42 Misc. 2d 640, 249 N.Y.S.2d 1, 6 (1964), aff'd, 258 N.Y.S.2d 629 (1st Dept. 1965), rev'd, 270 N.Y.S.2d 408 (1966).

[29] Briggs v. Spaulding, 141 U.S. 132, 165 (1891), quoted in Besselieu v. Brown, 177 N.C. 65, 97 S.E. 743, 744 (1919); cf. Robinson v. Hall, 63 F. 222 (4th Cir. 1894) (see for criticism).

State banking laws impose on directors the positive duty of management and control. They should not sit as "mere figureheads or dummies upon whom no responsible duty should rest." Eubank v. Bryan County State Bank, 216 F. 833, 838 (8th Cir. 1914); accord, Crews v. Garber, 188 Okla. 570, 111 P.2d 1080, 1083 (1941).

The common law does not require a director "to adopt a system of espionage" in relation to the officers and agents of the company nor "to set a watch upon all their actions." Scott v. Depeyster, 1 Edw. Ch. 513, 541, quoted in Briggs v. Spaulding, 141 U.S. 132, 162 (1891); and Cassidy v. Uhlmann, 170 N.Y. 505, 528, 63 N.E. 554 (1902) (dissenting opinion); see Atherton v. Anderson, 99 F.2d 883, 888 (6th Cir. 1938).

should, by severity in their rulings, make directorships repulsive to the class of men whose services are most needed." [30]

One court has noted that it would be reasonable to excuse a director who has missed some meetings if he had been "faithful in attendance at other times." [31] Another court, noting that one director had not attended meetings of the board as often as some of the others, remarked that this fact, in the absence of some good cause shown, "would only tend to prove that he was even more remiss and negligent in the discharge of his duties in this particular than were the other members who did attend." [32]

A director may take a leave of absence on account of ill health and need not resign his directorship. [33] However, a permissive absence should be limited to a passing illness, temporary in character, and a confirmed invalid has no right to remain a director, yet decline his corresponding responsibilities. [34] It has been held, for example, that a bank director is not chargeable with negligence in staying away from board meetings between the time of his physical collapse to the time of his resignation about seven months later, or in failing to resign earlier. [35]

---

[30] "These officers receive no compensation. They are under no compulsion to give regular attendance to directors' meetings, and to their official duties. They are chosen for their exceptional character and standing in the community, and for their supposed knowledge of its business, and of the pecuniary responsibility of those who borrow from the bank. The most valuable directors are those who are indifferent to any advantage or prestige which the position may give them, and who serve the bank from motives which could not be compensated by money." Robinson v. Hall, 63 F. 222, 225 (4th Cir. 1894).

[31] See Michelsen v. Penney, 41 F. Supp. 603, 616 (S.D.N.Y. 1941), rev'd, 135 F.2d 409 (2d Cir. 1943) (rundown condition, sinus trouble, fainting spells, trips abroad, injury to wife, etc.).

[32] Bank of Commerce v. Goolsby, 129 Ark. 416, 196 S.W. 803, 812 (1917).

[33] President of bank is not negligent in acting upon a leave of absence granted to him for one year on account of ill health instead of resigning. Briggs v. Spaulding, 141 U.S. 132 (1891).

[34] Rankin v. Cooper, 149 F. 1010 (C.C.W.D. Ark. 1907).

[35] Atherton v. Anderson, 99 F.2d 883 (6th Cir. 1938).

However, the director was held liable with other directors for permitting a faulty system of administration to be maintained during his long and active service on the board. The court also considered the case of a director who missed three meetings of the board due to professional engagements, missed meetings during his vacation, and then resigned when he received unsatisfac-

In addition, failure to attend a duly called directors' meeting in the belief that a quorum would not be present, is not excusable. Thus, when one director told another director that he would not attend the next meeting but nevertheless attended and participated with the majority present, his actions did not constitute a fraud upon the corporation and the meeting was authorized to transact business.[36]

§ 5.6   Negligent Non-Attendance

Although the absence of a director from a particular meeting of directors may relieve him from personal liability for unlawful acts taken at that meeting,[37] it is a basic legal principle that absence

---

tory answers from the chairman to questions asked at board meetings. *Id.* at 891.

Where articles provided that the office of director would be vacated whenever a director absented himself from meetings for three months, it was held that a director who became seriously ill and unable to travel did not absent himself from meetings where his failure to attend was involuntary. *In re* London & N. Bank (Mack's Claim), [1900] W.N. 114.

[36]"The mere circumstance that one of them was told that another would not attend, and believed that a quorum would not be present, is not enough to make it a fraud for a majority of the board, including the director who had stated that he would be absent, to meet pursuant to proper call and notice." Seal of Gold Mining Co. v. Slater, 161 Cal. 621, 120 P. 15, 18 (1911).

[37] A director did not attend any meetings of the board during his six years as a member, except the one meeting at which an illegal dividend was declared out of capital. He was held liable for failure to inform himself as to the company's condition. Suit dismissed as against another director who was absent from the meeting when the dividend was declared. Fell v. Pitts, 263 Pa. 314, 106 A. 574 (1919).

Even though it did not affirmatively appear that defendant was present and voted at the meeting declaring the illegal dividend, or that he failed to have his dissent recorded, he was liable because he "approved, ratified, and acquiesced" in the declaration and failed to take steps to recover back the dividend paid. Walker v. Man, 142 Misc. 277, 253 N.Y.S. 458, 467 (Sup. Ct. 1931). *See* City Investing Co. v. Gerken, 121 Misc. 763, 202 N.Y.S. 41 (Sup. Ct. 1924).

A director not present when an unauthorized dividend is declared is not liable under the statute even though he was present at a subsequent meeting when the minutes of the former meeting were ratified. Hutchinson v. Curtiss, 45 Misc. 484, 92 N.Y.S. 70 (Sup. Ct. 1904).

A director newly elected at a board meeting which he did not attend has no

from meetings does not relieve a director from personal liability for negligence, misfeasance, or malfeasance.[38] Conversely, regular attendance at directors' meetings will not necessarily excuse a director from personal liability for negligence.[39]

Certainly, the fiduciary responsibilities of a director or other official holding a similar position are such that he should attend and participate in all regular and special meetings of the organizations he serves to the best of his ability and to the full availability of his time. A director can act only when physically present at a directors' meeting and cannot act through an agent or a proxy.[40]

---

responsibility for action taken at that meeting. See United Hotels Co. v. Mealey, 147 F.2d 816 (2d Cir. 1945).

Under the North Dakota statute, directors assume a liability akin to suretyship as to creditors for illegal dividends. The obligation is that of the directors, as distinguished from that of the corporation. Crane-Johnson Co. v. Commissioner, 105 F.2d 740 (8th Cir. 1939), aff'd, 311 U.S. 54 (1940).

The fact that the presiding officer at a directors' meeting did not vote for an unlawful dividend does not absolve him from liability. Union Discount Co. v. MacRobert, 134 Misc. 107, 234 N.Y.S. 529 (Sup. Ct. 1929).

[38] "Non-attendance at meetings does not relieve a director of liability." Bentz v. Vardaman Mfg. Co., 210 So. 2d 35, 40 (Miss. 1968).

A finding of negligence may not be predicated on inattention to matters which transpired at meetings held after a director tendered his resignation effective "at the pleasure of the Board," and before its acceptance. Van Schaick v. Aron, 170 Misc. 520, 10 N.Y.S.2d 550, 565–66 (Sup. Ct. 1938).

[39] Regular attendance of a director at monthly, quarterly, and annual meetings of the board does not excuse a director from liability for failure to have knowledge of the condition and business of the company which he might have had through the exercise of due diligence. Darling & Co. v. Petri, 138 Kan. 666, 27 P.2d 255 (1933).

The duty of a director is not discharged by his attendance at meetings to which he was summoned. "It is not so much a question of holding meetings, as of examination, searching" and diligent study. Briggs v. Spaulding, 141 U.S. 132, 160 (1891).

[40] Since a board of directors has the duty to exercise deliberative control over the corporate business, the physical presence of a director at a board meeting is necessary; he cannot vote by proxy. Greenberg v. Harrison, 143 Conn. 519, 124 A.2d 216 (1956). Accord, Dowdle v. Central Brick Co., 206 Ind. 242, 189 N.E. 145 (1934).

Directors of a corporation cannot vote by proxy at a directors' meeting or be present by proxy for purposes of a quorum. In re Acadia Dairies, 15 Del. Ch. 248, 135 A. 846 (1927); Craig Medicine Co. v. Merchants' Bank, 14 N.Y.S. 16 (Sup. Ct. 1891).

Only by attendance at meetings can a director listen to arguments by the other directors and exercise his own judgment.[41] Thus, without attending he may not be able to discharge his corporate responsibilities in good faith and with the degree of diligence, care, and skill which ordinary prudent men would exercise in similar positions in like circumstances.

A recent case of first impression brought into judicial focus the nature and scope of corporate trustee obligations in a nonprofit charitable institution. There, the individual trustees had not only failed to supervise the management of investment or even attend meetings of committees charged with such supervision, but also failed to object when no meetings of the supervisory committees were called for over ten years. The court noted that "the modern trend is to apply corporate rather than trust principles in determining the liability of the directors of charitable corporations" and held that: "A director who fails to acquire the information necessary to supervise investment policy or consistently fails even to attend the meetings at which such policies are considered has violated his fiduciary duty to the corporation." [42]

Members of an executive committee of a trade association cannot vote by proxy "in spite of the fact that the business of the committee had customarily been conducted in that manner." The court ruled that "having recourse to the analogy of a board of directors, such discretionary powers could not be lawfully delegated." *In re* Tidewater Coal Exchange, 274 F. 1011 (S.D.N.Y. 1921).

[41] In matters involving legislative discretion, directors can bind the corporation only when acting together as a board. Therefore, "directors cannot effectively act as directors, except at duly held board meetings." United States v. Interstate R.R., 14 F.2d 328, 329 (W.D. Va. 1926).

Directors owe a duty to stockholders to act according to their best judgment. Others may urge upon the board considerations in favor of or opposed to any proposed course of action. *See* Miller v. Vanderlip, 285 N.Y. 116, 33 N.E.2d 51 (1941).

[42] Stern v. Lucy Webb Hayes Nat'l Training School, 381 F. Supp. 1003, 1013–14 (D.D.C. 1974).

A newly elected director is not responsible for the negligence of his predecessors. "While a director is required to be reasonably informed about the status of the financial accounts, the law does not require him to unreasonably search through the books with a view of finding whether at some time in the past some previous director might have caused damage to the corporation through the negligent performance of his duties." Jensen v. Republic Steel Corp., 32 Ohio Abs. 29, 37 (1940) (parent corporation directors).

Directors, charged with negligent failure and neglect to hold and attend directors' meetings, may not escape liability by claiming that the stockholders should have held meetings to correct the causes of mismanagement. Courts have generally refused to take judicial notice of the fact that, in the long period of directors' default, the stockholders themselves have not held their regular meetings. Thus, stockholders will not be found "guilty of contributory negligence barring recovery."[43] Further, a dominant director cannot avoid personal liability and shift the responsibility for corporate action to his associates by refusing to attend meetings.[44]

§ 5.7 Non-Attendance, Tort Liability

Absence of a director from a meeting of the board at which a tortious act was approved by a vote of the board generally will relieve the absent director from liability for injury or prejudice resulting to third parties.[45] This is an exception to the general rule that a corporate director who votes for, directs, or otherwise actively participates in the commission of a tortious act is personally liable for injuries or prejudice to third parties proximately resulting therefrom, regardless of whether he acted on his own account or on behalf of the corporation and regardless of whether the corporation may also be liable.[46] However, a director is not personally liable for the torts of his corporation unless he has personally voted for or otherwise participated in the wrongful act. General corporation law does not subject an officer or director to a tort liability simply by virtue of his office.[47]

[43] Besselieu v. Brown, 177 N.C. 65, 97 S.E. 743, 745 (1919).

[44] See Globe Woolen Co. v. Utica Gas & Elec. Co., 224 N.Y. 483, 121 N.E. 378 (1918).

[45] See Chapter 19 infra.

[46] See, e.g., Lobato v. Pay Less Drug Stores, Inc., 261 F.2d 406 (10th Cir. 1958) (injuries from sale of defective bicycle); United States ex rel. Marcus v. Hess, 41 F. Supp. 197 (W.D. Pa. 1941) (general rule).

In a derivative action to recover losses sustained by a bank due to alleged misconduct of directors and officers, all directors who were present and voted at a meeting of the executive committee and at a meeting of the directors were liable. Litwin v. Allen, 25 N.Y.S.2d 667 (Sup. Ct. 1940).

[47] Tillman v. Wheaton-Haven Recreation Ass'n Inc., 517 F.2d 1141 (4th Cir. 1975) (tortious civil rights discrimination). See same case, 410 U.S. 431 (1973); 367 F. Supp. 860 (D. Md. 1973); 451 F.2d 1211 (4th Cir. 1971).

Thus, failure of a director to attend a meeting, or attendance at a meeting without voting for or otherwise approving the tortious act, are factors in determining whether the director incurs personal liability. This anomalous situation received judicial attention in a case involving a board meeting at which eight directors were present and voted in favor of the resolution approving the tortious act, while three directors were absent and not voting. One of the absent directors had participated in the act and was held liable. The court noted its "natural inclination" to treat all the directors alike and the inequity of holding that the remaining two absent directors were not personally liable "simply because they failed to appear at a directors' meeting." [48]

The tort liability of a participating director persists even if the director is ignorant of the full consequences of the applicable law and his ignorance has been generated by the advice of his lawyers and corroborated by the federal district court and by the federal appeals court, prior to a final adverse decision of the Supreme Court.[49]

The unlawful expulsion of a shareholder from a meeting duly called, or of a person rightfully attending a public or private meeting, is a tort for which the presiding officer and other participants may be personally liable in damages.[50]

Active participation, such as attendance at a meeting and the act of voting, seems to be requisite to liability. See Kline v. Coldwell, Banker & Co., 508 F.2d 226 (9th Cir. 1974) (mere parallelism, membership-ratification, or adherence is not sufficient to establish antitrust violation).

Phelps Dodge Refining Corp. v. FTC, 139 F.2d 393 (2d Cir. 1943) (director never attended meetings or knew about the illegal activity); Tedrow v. Deskin, 265 Md. 546, 290 A.2d 799 (1972) (automobile mileage charge).

A person who was late in arriving at a board meeting, and prior to his arrival the board had elected him a director and had adopted a resolution to purchase shares of the company stock without statutory authority, acquired the status of a director with respect to the resolution the same as if he had been present and voting throughout the meeting when he was informed of all that had been done, as shown by the minutes, and gave his approval. Uffelman v. Boillin, 19 Tenn. App. 1, 82 S.W.2d 545 (1935).

[48] Aeroglide Corp. v. Zeh, 301 F.2d 420, 423 (2d Cir. 1962).

[49] Tillman v. Wheaton-Haven Recreation Ass'n Inc., 517 F.2d 1141 (4th Cir. 1975).

See § 15.20 infra.

[50] See Chapter 14 infra.

§ 5.7.1   Situs of Tort

The negligent failure of nonresident directors to attend meetings of the board of directors at the New York home office and to exercise independent supervision and control of corporate affairs, resulting in injury to corporate property or waste of corporate assets, has been held to constitute tortious action. Since this neglect of duty can be committed only at the place where the duty is to be performed, for purposes of litigation the situs of required performance is New York, where the board holds its meetings. The court noted that one nonresident director had never attended a board meeting and that the other had attended several meetings in New York. Both were held amenable to the jurisdiction of the New York courts. It was noted that both directors knew or should have known of the potential consequences of their acts of omission because they had sufficient "minimal contacts" with New York.[51]

§ 5.8   Compelling Attendance at Stockholder Meetings

A court of equity may not by injunction compel a shareholder to attend shareholder meetings. The shareholder has no legal obligation to attend or to vote at such meetings even though his inaction may frustrate the conduct of corporate business.[52]

---

[51] Platt Corp. v. Platt, 42 Misc. 2d 640, 249 N.Y.S.2d 1, 10 (1964), aff'd, 258 N.Y.S.2d 629 (1st Dep't 1965), rev'd, 270 N.Y.S.2d 408 (1966).

[52] "The very nature of the corporate form is the creation by statute of an entity separate and apart from the individuals who own, manage and operate it. One who acquires corporate stock obtains an interest in the corporate assets after payment of corporate debts and a right to participate in management which he may or may not exercise. [Citation] The holder of shares is under no obligation whatever to the corporation other than to make full payment of the consideration for which the shares are issued. [Citation] As participation by a shareholder in management of corporate affairs is voluntary, it necessarily follows that no shareholder may be compelled to attend or participate in shareholders' meetings. Any different rule would contradict the distinction which separates the corporate existence from the identity of its shareholders and which vests management responsibilities in the directors."

"Conceding that the failure of respondent Harry Hall to attend stockholders' meetings has injured appellant in preventing her from participating in the management of the corporation, if respondent is under no legal duty to participate, how may a court of equity compel him by injunction to attend and

§ 5.8.1   Legislative Meetings

The common law implies a duty on the part of members of a
deliberative body elected or appointed to serve in a legislative or
administrative capacity, to attend meetings with reasonable regularity and to express their judgment on matters coming before
them for consideration and action. This duty to attend meetings
is correlated with the duty of members to vote. An assembled
body can act only by a vote of the members.[53] The duty to attend
and to act is a "burden of office" imposed by law upon each member
and "it is his duty, as stated in the oath required of him, faithfully
to discharge the duties of the office to the best of his ability."
However, unless authorized by constitution or statute creating the
body, a legislature assembly (city council) has neither an express
nor an implied power to impose a fine or other penalty on a
member for a mere failure to attend a meeting, since the imposition
of a penalty has no tendency to aid the minority in compelling the
attendance of absentees.[54]

Every legislative assembly, when duly constituted, has the power
to compel the attendance of its members. This power is "one of

---

vote at a stockholders' meeting? No maxim of equity may be invoked to
destroy an existing legal right nor may equity create a right at law which does
not exist. . . .

"No allegation was made by appellant of any contractual obligation on the
part of respondent Harry Hall to attend and participate in stockholders' meetings and none exists by statute or rule of law. It therefore follows of necessity that a court of equity may not by injunction compel that for which no
legal duty lies. The trial court was correct in refusing to grant the mandatory
injunction requested." Hall v. Hall, 506 S.W.2d 42, 45 (Mo. 1974).

In declaring invalid a voting trust agreement which was irrevocable for
ten years, the court said: "Stockholders cannot evade the duty imposed upon
them by law of using their power as stockholders for the welfare of the
corporation and the general interest of its stockholders. A stockholder may
refuse to exercise his right to vote and participate in stockholders' meetings,
but he cannot deprive himself of the power to do so." Luthy v. Ream, 270
Ill. 170, 110 N.E. 373, 375 (1915).

See § 17.28 infra.

[53] See § 5.1 supra.

[54] City of Earlville v. Radley, 237 Ill. 242, 86 N.E. 624, 625 (1908) (statute
provided that less than a quorum may adjourn and "compel the attendance of
absentees").

its most undoubted and important privileges" and is founded on the right of the members of a legislative assembly to have the presence and attendance of other members.[55]

Where a statute empowered a city council to compel the attendance of absent members at a duly called meeting, the council was permitted to provide by ordinance that the absent members be arrested and brought in by the council sergeant or his deputies. When enough members were convened willingly or under compulsion to constitute a quorum, the meeting proceeded with its business.[56]

---

[55] "Every legislative assembly, when duly constituted, has power to compel the attendance of its members; but, until so constituted, it has no such power, as it has itself no legal existence; and the right of the members who are present for the purpose of organization to compel the attendance of other members depends wholly, as has been seen, upon the constitution or law to which each assembly is subject. The right of a legislative assembly, after it is regularly constituted, to have the attendance of all its members except those who are absent on leave, or in the service of the assembly, and to enforce it, if necessary, is one of its most undoubted and important privileges." CUSHING, ELEMENTS OF THE LAW AND PRACTICE OF LEGISLATIVE ASSEMBLIES § 264 at 101.

The Constitution of the United States provides that a majority of each House shall constitute a quorum, but a smaller number may adjourn from day to day, "and may be authorized to compel the Attendance of absent Members, in such Manner, and under such Penalties as each House may provide." U.S. CONST. Art. I, § 5.

[56] "In construing this act the legislative purpose must be kept in view, and that is to prevent the loss or failure of the meeting. This power, vested in less than a majority of the members, must not be given a construction so technical as to impair its efficacy. Moreover, under the general parliamentary law every legislative assembly, when duly constituted, has the power to compel the attendance of its members. Until so constituted, it has no such power, for it has no legal existence. Members who are present merely for the purpose of organizing cannot compel the attendance of others, unless authorized by the law to which it is subject. This statute does not say, as does the constitution of the United States of the congress, a smaller number than a quorum 'may be authorized' to compel attendance, but that they may compel it. Cush. Law & Prac. Leg. Assem. § 264. The legislature left the mode of compulsion to the council, and that body determined that it should be by the arrest and detention of members, if necessary to the accomplishment of the purpose. In the determination of this question of authority to compel attendance it is of no consequence that in the execution of the order of arrest the officers entered places into which they had no right to go, or by means which they could not legally employ. Such irregularities cannot affect the validity of the exercise of

And when the city charter gave the aldermen present at a city council meeting at which there was no quorum the power to require the mayor to issue a warrant to arrest and bring in the absent members, a majority of those present were able to keep the meeting alive by remaining in the aldermanic chamber (nearly two days) while an effort was made to bring in enough members to constitute a quorum.[57]

§ 5.8.2 Regulatory Agencies

Exceptions to the general rule that members of a collective body must attend meetings in person and also vote in person are founded on the enabling legislation creating certain federal regulatory boards and commissions. In holding that the CAB could proceed with its members acting separately rather than jointly in a meeting, the court noted that an earlier decision had found no error when assistants to CAB members had participated in meetings in place of their superiors and even had cast votes on tentative awards.[58]

§ 5.9   Abandonment of Office

Public officers cannot escape their duties by refusing to meet and act as a body, or by resigning from office. The common law allows the courts to administer a form of compulsory service under

---

the power with which they were clothed, although they may have been such as made the officers liable to an action for damages or a criminal prosecution for trespassing." Schmulbach v. Speidel, 50 W. Va. 553, 40 S.E. 424, 427 (1901).

[57] The court noted that it was unnecessary for the members in attendance actually to remain in their seats during the hours or days which elapsed before the absentees returned. State *ex rel.* Rylands v. Pinkerman, 63 Conn. 176, 28 A. 110 (1893).

[58] Cf. Braniff Airways, Inc. v. CAB, 379 F.2d 453, 461 n. (D.C. Cir. 1967); Eastern Air Lines, Inc. v. CAB, 271 F.2d 752, 758 (2d Cir. 1959), *cert. denied sub nom.* Capital Airways, Inc. v. CAB, 362 U.S. 970 (1960); T.S.C. Motor Freight Lines, Inc. v. United States, 186 F. Supp. 777 (S.D. Texas 1960), *aff'd per curiam sub nom.* Herrin Transp. Co. v. United States, 366 U.S. 419 (1961).

A quorum of a state tax commission need not attend all sessions, when those conducting hearings were commissioners at the time the decision was rendered and presumably all members had the benefit of the hearer's observations and conclusions. Olsen Co. v. State Tax Commission, 109 Utah 563 (1946).

the basic doctrine of public necessity. "Indeed, the common law would compel the acceptance of an office, and a refusal to assume it was indictable as an offense." [59]

In a leading case, three newly elected members of a city council refused for ten months to meet with other elected members, to take the oath of office, and to attend regular meetings, leaving the council without a quorum to act. As a consequence, the machinery of the city government was brought to a standstill without power to start again, and the council was unable to perform its duties to the public. In an action by the mayor, the court declared the offices of the members forfeited and vacated by abandonment.[60] This principle of law has become well established, but it does not apply to temporary non-occupation.[61]

In a similar case, 21 of 26 justices of a county court, attempting to evade obedience to a writ of mandamus, tendered their resignations, which, when accepted, left the county government without a quorum. It was decided at common law that a public officer held his office until his successor was qualified and that he could not surrender it before the election of his successor without the consent of the crown or other appointing power. "The services of officers are necessary to organized society; and any hiatus or interregnum tends to disorganization. If one's property, services as a soldier, his very life, in fact, may be taken to preserve society, there is no reason why his personal services, in an official capacity, may not be demanded and insisted on by the state. Enforced jury service furnishes a conspicuous example of the principle, as well as compulsory attendance of witnesses, and there may be other." [62]

In another case it was held that a majority of members of a

[59] United States *ex rel.* Watts v. Justices of Lauderdale County, 10 F. 460, 464 (W.D. Tenn. 1882).

[60] City of Williamsburg v. Weesner, 164 Ky. 769, 176 S.W. 224 (1915).

[61] Under certain conditions a public office may become vacant by reason of the abandonment thereof on the part of the incumbent. In such cases, however, it is necessary to show that the incumbent has manifested a clear intention to abandon the office and its duties, although such intention may be inferred from conduct. . . . temporary absence is not ordinarily sufficient to constitute an abandonment of office." State v. Green, 206 Ark. 361, 175 S.W.2d 575, 577–78 (1943).

[62] United States *ex rel.* Watts v. Justices of Lauderdale County, 10 F. 460, 464 (W.D. Tenn. 1882).

common council cannot avoid their public duties by resigning from office collectively so as to prevent, for lack of a quorum, the selection and qualification of their successors. Penalties may be imposed on an official who refuses to serve after having been selected for an elective office, a principle well settled at common law. Thus, mandamus will lie to compel a member to perform his duties as a councilman until his successor has been elected and qualified.[63]

[63] State ex rel. Westfall v. Blair, 87 W. Va. 564, 105 S.E. 830 (1921).

A town officer who tenders his resignation does not cease to be such until his resignation has been accepted. Edwards v. United States, 103 U.S. 471 (1880); United States ex rel. Watts v. Justices of Lauderdale County, 10 F. 460 (W.D. Tenn. 1882); Haine v. Googe, 248 F. Supp. 349 (S.D.N.Y. 1965).

6

Quorum

§ 6.1 Need for Quorum Rule

A quorum is the minimum number of members of any body whose presence is requisite for the transaction of business.[1] Action taken without a quorum present is not valid.[2]

[1] The term "meeting" means the lawful assemblage of the number or proportion of shareholders necessary to make a quorum; therefore the terms "meeting" and "quorum" are in a sense synonymous terms. Myers v. Union League, 17 Pa. Dist. 301, 304 (C.P. 1908).

It is "well established that a quorum is the minimum number of members required to be present to transact business and that in organizations of fixed numbers, such as the Commission, the existence of a quorum is not determined by the votes cast, but by the presence of the members." *In re* Chronicle Broadcasting Co., 20 F.C.C. 903, 907 (1969).

"By dictionary definition and in common parlance a 'quorum' means such a number of members of any body as is, when duly assembled, legally competent to transact business. The word 'quorum' implies a meeting, and so the action must be group action, not merely action of a particular number of committeemen as individuals." *In re* McGovern, 291 N.Y. 104, 107, 51 N.E.2d

The purpose of having a quorum is to permit a stated proportion of the membership to transact the business of the body, recognizing the impracticability of securing the attendance of all the members at many of its meetings.[3] No general rule can be stated as to the number of persons necessary for a quorum. That is generally either a matter of organic law applicable to the body or a matter entirely within the discretion of a self-constituted body, in each case usually depending on the size of the body and on the interest in or urgency of attendance at its meetings.

The first question is whether the meeting is subject to a rule of quorum, or whether its purposes can be fulfilled without the presence of a quorum. A recent case involved a meeting of a county council under a charter defining a quorum for the "transaction of business." The meeting was called to fill vacancies on a suburban commission, and the chairman announced before the hearing began that no action would be taken on the nominees until a later meeting of the council. A quorum was not present at all times during this meeting. The question before the court was whether there was

---

666, 667 (1943); *accord,* Harroun v. Brush Elec. Light Co., 152 N.Y. 212 (1897).

"A quorum is, for all legal purposes, as much the body to which it appertains as if every member were present. . . ." *In re* Brearton, 44 Misc. 247, 257, 89 N.Y.S. 893, 899 (Sup. Ct. 1904).

[2] In the absence of a quorum there is a "defect of power" of a legislature to pass a bill. People v. Supervisors of Chenango, 8 N.Y. 317, 328 (1853).

A legislative act passed without a quorum is unconstitutional. Moore v. Langton, 167 A.2d 558 (R.I. 1961); *accord, In re* Shapiro, 392 F.2d 397 (3d Cir. 1968) (local draft board).

See, e.g., Christoffel v. United States, 338 U.S. 84 (1949); WIBC, Inc. v. FCC, 259 F.2d 941 (D.C. Cir.), *cert. denied,* 358 U.S. 920 (1958).

[3] "A judicial or legislative body having a quorum present proceeds ordinarily as if every member was sitting in his place, and exercises all the powers with which it is invested. Any other rule would greatly embarrass the transaction of business in case of illness, or voluntary or enforced absence among the members." Harroun v. Brush Elec. Light Co., 152 N.Y. 212, 213–14 (1897) (court).

"The provision that a majority of the members shall be required to transact business does not mean that such majority must vote in favor of each and every act or action, great or small. Such a construction would be unusual, inconvenient, and detrimental to public interest. It means only to require a majority for a quorum." McMillin v. Neely, 66 W. Va. 496, 497, 66 S.E. 635, 636 (1909).

"any need for a quorum" at this first meeting. The court perceived that the "real purpose" of the meeting was to "give the citizenry an uninhibited opportunity to voice their approval or to vent their umbrage" in respect to one or more nominees, and that this did not constitute the "transaction of business." The court also noted that the council had adopted Robert's Rules of Order in all matters not otherwise provided, and that according to Robert's debate on a pending question can continue after a quorum is no longer present and until a member raises the point. In holding that a quorum was not required, the court said that the hearing "at no time rose to the level of a debate" and that no member present had suggested the absence of a quorum.[4]

§ 6.2   Common-Law Quorum

Under old English common law two or more members actually present at a duly convened meeting were sufficient to constitute a quorum.[5]

---

[4] Gemeny v. Prince George's County, 264 Md. 85, 285 A.2d 602, 606 (1972), *citing* Robert's Rules of Order, Newly Revised, § 39, at 296–97 (1970).

[5] At common law the word "meeting" used in the ordinary sense means "a coming together of more than one person." "In this case, no doubt, a meeting was duly summoned, but only one shareholder attended. It is clear that, according to the ordinary use of the English language, a meeting could no more be constituted by one person than a meeting could have been constituted if no shareholder at all had attended. No business could be done at such a meeting. . . ." Sharp v. Dawes, 2 Q.B.D. 26, 29, 46 L.J.Q.B. 104 (Eng. 1876). A later (1908) English case construing the Companies Act stated: "Though it is true that one shareholder cannot constitute a meeting [citing Sharp v. Dawes] . . . it is not clear that one director cannot form a quorum of a board of two, and it is quite clear on the authorities that there may be a delegation to a committee of one. . . ." *In re* Fireproof Doors, Ltd., [1916] 2 Ch. 142, 150.

But see Morrill v. Little Falls Mfg. Co., 53 Minn. 371, 377, 55 N.W. 547, 549 (1893), where the court said that the two-stockholder theory advanced in Sharp v. Dawes was "based upon a narrow lexicographical definition of the word 'meeting,' as the coming together of two or more persons,—a reason that does not commend itself to our judgment."

"The acts of a corporation are those of the major part of the corporators, corporately assembled . . . and, omitting the words 'corporately assembled,' this is declared by 33 Hen. VIII, c. 27, to be the common law. This means that, in the absence of special custom, the major part must be present at the

Early American common law developed a distinction between assemblies consisting of a definite number of members or votes, as in the case of a city council, a board of directors, a committee, or a stock corporation; and assemblies indefinite [6] in number, such as a labor union, fraternal association, or membership corporation.

In the former definite number class, a majority of the members or shareholders is required for a quorum, and a majority of a quorum is sufficient to perform the function of the body and transact business.[7] A leading case states simply "the general rule applicable to

---

meeting, and that of that major part there must be a majority in favour of the act or resolution." Mayor, Constables & Co. of Merchants of the Staple of England v. Governor & Co. of the Bank of England, 21 Q.B.D. 160, 165 (1887).

"The term [quorum] arose from the Latin words which were used in the commission formerly issued to justices of the peace in England, by which commission it was directed that no business of certain kinds should be done without the presence of one or more of certain justices specially designated." Tobin v. Ramey, 206 F.2d 505, 507 (5th Cir. 1953). The terms "congregation" and "assembly" connote the presence of three or more persons acting in concert. Kinoy v. District of Columbia, 400 F.2d 761 (D.C. Cir. 1968).

[6] A majority of members is not necessary in organizations where the number of members is "indefinite and changing." Alliance Co-Op Ins. Co. v. Gasche, 93 Kan. 147, 148, 142 P. 882, 883 (1914).

[7] The law has been concisely stated in these words: "It is a fundamental rule of parliamentary procedure, applicable as well to municipal and electing boards, that a majority of the members of a body consisting of a definite number constitutes a quorum for the transaction of business . . . and it is equally well settled that a majority of the quorum has power to act. . . . This rule derives from the common law and is of universal application unless modified by statute or some controlling regulation or by-law in the particular instance." The court cited the U. S. Constitution and Jefferson's Manual. Hill v. Ponder, 221 N.C. 58, 62, 19 S.E.2d 5, 8 (1942).

The quorum of a joint session of the legislature sitting as a unicameral body is "simply a majority of the total membership of the unicameral body, without regard to whether those members come from the Senate or the Assembly." Anderson v. Krupsak, N.Y. Ct. App., N.Y.L.J., July 9, 1976.

It is the common-law rule that when a definite body exists, a majority of the entire membership constitutes a quorum, and a majority of the quorum can perform any act which the body is empowered to perform. Prezlak v. Padrone, 67 N.J. Super. 95, 169 A.2d 852, 856 (1961) (city council).

Where a statute provides that a majority shall constitute a quorum, the legislature intended that a majority thereof is sufficient to conduct business. Olsen Co. v. State Tax Comm'n, 109 Utah 563 (1946).

"Under the common-law rule a majority of a body constituted a quorum, and if there were a quorum a vote of a majority of those present was sufficient for valid action." Town of Smithtown v. Howell, 31 N.Y.2d 365, 292 N.E.2d 10, 339 N.Y.S.2d 949, 957 (1972).

While less than a majority of a zoning board voted to approve an application, its action was not invalid, where, with a quorum present, at least a majority of those voting approved the action. Shaughnessy v. Metropolitan Dade County, 238 So. 2d 266 (Fla. 1970), *citing* Robert's Rules of Order on another point.

See discussion of terms "quorum," "members present," "two-thirds of that House," "two-thirds of members present," and "majority" as related to power to reconsider a bill a second time after a veto. Kay Jewelry Co. v. Board of Registration in Optometry, 305 Mass. 581, 27 N.E.2d 1, 3–4 (1940).

A board of directors can act by a majority of a quorum present and voting irrespective of the number of other directors who may be present at the meeting. Crowley v. Commodity Exchange, 141 F.2d 182, 188–89 (2d Cir. 1944).

See United States v. Ballin, 144 U.S. 1 (1892); Missouri Pac. R.R. Co. v. Kansas, 248 U.S. 276, 285 (1919); Dillon v. Berg, 326 F. Supp. 1214 (D. Del.), *aff'd*, 453 F.2d 876 (3d Cir. 1971); Dillon v. Scotten, Dillon Co., 335 F. Supp. 566 (D. Del. 1971); Benintendi v. Kenton Hotel, 294 N.Y. 112, 60 N.E.2d 829 (1945) (corporate board of directors); *accord*, Wesley v. Board of Educ., 403 S.W.2d 28 (Ky. 1966); Merrill v. City of Lowell, 236 Mass. 436, 128 N.E. 862, 863 (1920); Ezell v. City of Pascagoula, 240 So. 2d 700 (Miss. 1970); State *ex rel.* Kiel v. Riechmann, 239 Mo. 81, 142 S.W. 304, 310 (1911); McCormick v. Board of Educ., 58 N.M. 648, 274 P.2d 299, 308 (1954), *citing* Robert's Rules of Order; Blaikie v. Knott, 277 App. Div. 461, 100 N.Y.S.2d 665, 668 (Sup. Ct. 1950); Bray v. Barry, 91 R.I. 34, 160 A.2d 577 (1960) (school committee); Bedford County Hosp. v. Bedford County, 304 S.W.2d 697 (Tenn. 1957) (hospital corporation).

See also Launtz v. People *ex rel.* Sullivan, 113 Ill. 137, 142 (1885); State *ex rel.* Laughlin v. Porter, 113 Ind. 79, 14 N.E. 883, 884 (1888) (county trustees), *citing* Cushing, Parl. Law; Murdoch v. Strange, 99 Md. 89, 57 A. 628, 630 (1904); Paola & Fall River Ry. v. Commissioners, 16 Kan. 302 (1876); Seiler v. O'Maley, 190 Ky. 190, 227 S.W. 141, 142 (1921); Zeiler v. Central Ry., 84 Md. 304, 35 A. 932 (1896); Sargent v. Webster, 54 Mass. (13 Metc.) 497 (1847); Haskell v. Read, 68 Neb. 115, 96 N.W. 1007, *denying rehearing in* 68 Neb. 107, 93 N.W. 997 (1903); *In re* State Treasurer's Settlement, 51 Neb. 116, 70 N.W. 532, 534 (1897); Hutchinson v. Mayor of Belmar, 61 N.J.L. 443, 39 A. 643, 645, *aff'd*, 62 N.J.L. 450, 45 A. 1092 (1898); Barnett v. Mayor of Paterson, 48 N.J.L. 395 (1886); Cadmus v. Farr, 47 N.J.L. 208, 216 (1885); Wells v. Rahway White Rubber Co., 19 N.J. Eq. 402 (Ch. 1869); *In re* McGovern, 291 N.Y. 104, 107, 51 N.E.2d 666 (1943); *In re* Brearton, 44 Misc. 247, 89 N.Y.S. 893 (1904); Coles v. Trustees of Village of Williamsburgh, 10 Wend. 659, 664 (N.Y. Sup. Ct. 1833) (village trustees); State *ex rel.* Stanford v. Ellington, 117 N.C. 158, 23 S.E. 250, 252 (1895) (*citing* Cushing, Elect.) (state legislature); Fisher

parliamentary bodies is that, when a quorum is present, the act of
the majority of the quorum is the act of the body, except so far as
the terms of the organic law under which the body is assembled
limit that rule." [8]

In the case of assemblies indefinite in number, a majority of the
members present at a legal meeting, no matter how small a proportion of the whole,[9] constitutes a quorum, and a majority of those
present may act.[10] The common-law rule will prevail in the absence
of legislative modification.[11]

---

v. Harrisburg Gas Co., 1 Pearson 118, 120 (Pa. C.P. 1857); Leavitt v. Oxford
& Geneva Silver Min. Co., 3 Utah 265, 1 P. 356, 358–59 (1883); *In re*
Walters, 270 Wis. 561, 72 N.W.2d 535, 539 (1955); Board of Supervisors v.
Hall, 47 Wis. 208, 2 N.W. 291 (1879); Booker v. Young, 53 Va. 593, 594
(12 Gratt. 303, 305) (1855); *In re* Chronicle Broadcasting Co., 20 F.C.C.
903 (1969); *In re* International Paper & Power Co., 2 S.E.C. 792 (1937).

[8] Morris v. Cashmore, 253 App. Div. 657, 3 N.Y.S.2d 624, 628, *aff'd*, 278
N.Y. 730, 17 N.E.2d 143 (1938) (*following* Reed's Rules).

[9] This distinction was also present in early English common law. "It is a
well established rule, that in order to constitute a good corporate assembly in
the case of a corporation consisting of a definite and indefinite body, there
must be present a majority of that number of which the definite body consists,
although it is not necessary that there should be a majority of the indefinite
body." Blacket v. Blizzard, 9 Barn. & Co., 851, 860 (K.B. 1829).

For an American statement of this distinction, *see* People *ex rel.* Remington
v. Rector, Church Wardens & Vestrymen of the Church of the Atonement, 48
Barb. 603, 606 (N.Y. Sup. Ct. 1866); New York Elec. Wkrs. Union v. Sullivan, 107 N.Y.S. 886 (App. Div. 1907); Craig v. First Presbyterian Church,
88 Pa. St. Rpts. 42, 47–48 (1878).

[10] "The rule of the common law is where a society or corporation are composed of an indefinite number of persons, a majority of those who appear at
a regular meeting of the same, constitute a body competent to transact business." Field v. Field, 9 Wend. 394, 403 (N.Y. Sup. Ct. 1832).

"The common law rule is that a quorum of any body of indefinite number
for purposes of elections and voting upon questions requiring the sanction of
the members consists of those who assemble at any meeting regularly called
and warned although they may be a minority of the whole number; and a
majority of those present may elect unless there be a statute to the contrary."
The court noted that Robert's Rules of Order provides that a quorum is a
majority of those who attend a meeting regularly called. *In re* Havender, 181
Misc. 989, 44 N.Y.S.2d 213, 215 (Sup. Ct.), *aff'd*, 267 App. Div. 860, 47
N.Y.S.2d 114 (1st Dep't 1943) (*citing* Robert's Rules), *appeal denied*, 267
App. Div. 901, 48 N.Y.S.2d 325 (1944) (membership corporation).

"Where the charter and by-laws of a corporation are silent on the subject,
the common-law rule is that such of the shareholders as actually assemble at

a properly convened meeting, although a minority of the whole number, and representing only a minority of the stock, constitute a quorum for the transaction of business, and may express the corporate will, and the body will be bound by their acts." Morrill v. Little Falls Mfg. Co., 53 Minn. 371, 377, 55 N.W. 547, 549 (1893).

"Every question must be decided, and every election determined by the majority; or in other words, by the major part numerically, of those who are personally present, and voting." Taylor v. Griswold, 14 N.J.L. 222, 227 (1834).

In a voluntary association without a constitution or by-laws and with an indefinite number of members, a quorum consists of the members who attend the meeting even if less than a majority. Ostrom v. Greene, 20 Misc. 177, 45 N.Y.S. 852, 857 (Sup. Ct. 1897), aff'd, 30 App. Div. 621, 52 N.Y.S. 1147 (3d Dep't 1898); aff'd, 161 N.Y. 353, 55 N.E. 919 (1900); accord, Francis v. Perry, 82 Misc. 271, 144 N.Y.S. 167, 168 (Oneida County Ct. 1913); Madison Ave. Baptist Church v. Baptist Church, 28 N.Y. Super. 649 (1867), aff'd, 31 N.Y. Super. 109 (1869), rev'd on other grounds, 46 N.Y. 131 (1871).

Any minority of shareholders present, however small, may constitute a quorum. In re Argus Printing Co., 1 N.D. 434, 48 N.W. 347, 351 (1891).

Where the law is silent, "the common law both in England and in this country is well settled that the *majority* of the members-elect shall constitute the legal body." A majority cannot fix a larger number as a quorum. "For the body itself to attempt to fix a greater number is for the body to attempt to change a rule of the common law. . . . But it is well established in this state that even a statute law (much less a rule of procedure) that seems to alter a principle of the common law must do so in plain and direct terms." Heiskell v. Baltimore, 65 Md. 125, 149–50, 4 A. 116, 119 (1886).

In the absence of any contrary rule "the common law principle is that the majority of a deliberative body constitutes a quorum, and there being a quorum, that a majority of those present can transact business." *In re* Doyle, 7 Pa. Dist. 635, 24 Pa. County Ct. 27, 30 (1898).

See Standard Power & Light Corp. v. Investment Associates, Inc., 29 Del. Ch. 593, 51 A.2d 572, 575 (1947); Walling v. Lansdon, 15 Idaho 282, 97 P. 396 (1908); Green v. Felton, 42 Ind. App. 675, 84 N.E. 166 (1908); Alliance Co-Op Ins. Co. v. Gasche, 93 Kan. 147, 142 P. 882, 883 (1914); Gilchrist v. Collopy, 119 Ky. 110, 82 S.W. 1018 (1904); Darrin v. Hoff, 99 Md. 491, 58 A. 196 (1904); *In re* Serenbetz, 46 N.Y.S.2d 475 (Sup. Ct. 1943), aff'd, 267 App. Div. 836, 46 N.Y.S.2d 127 (2d Dep't 1944); *In re* P. F. Keogh, Inc., 192 App. Div. 624, 183 N.Y.S. 408 (1st Dep't 1920); Field v. Field, 9 Wend. 394 (N.Y. Sup. Ct. 1832); *In re* Argus Printing Co., 1 N.D. 434, 48 N.W. 347 (1891); Lawrence v. Ingersoll, 88 Tenn. 52, 12 S.W. 422, 424 (1889).

However, a law requiring concurrence of a majority of all members elected to a city council for the passage of an ordinance is not contrary to public policy. McLean v. East St. Louis, 222 Ill. 510, 78 N.E. 815 (1906).

The fact that by-laws permit action on certain matters, such as adjournment by less than a quorum, does not imply that the full number of the

The Supreme Court has recently held: "The almost universally accepted common-law rule . . . [is that] in the absence of a contrary statutory provision, a majority of a quorum constituted of a simple majority of a collective body is empowered to act for the body" and, where the organic act creating the body is silent on the question, the body is justified in adhering to such common-law rule.[12] The earlier leading decision of the Supreme Court held that "the general rule of all parliamentary bodies is that, when a quorum is present, the act of a majority of the quorum is the act of the body. This had been the rule for all time, except so far as in any given case the terms of the organic act under which the body is assembled have prescribed specific limitations." [13]

---

quorum must vote on all matters requiring a quorum. Del Prete v. Board of Selectmen, 220 N.E.2d 912 (Mass. 1966), *citing* Robert's Rules of Order.

[11] Prezlak v. Padrone, 67 N.J. Super. 95, 169 A.2d 852 (1961); *see, e.g.,* Morris v. Cashmore, 253 App. Div. 657, 3 N.Y.S.2d 624 (1st Dep't), *aff'd,* 278 N.Y. 730, 17 N.E.2d 143 (1938) (statutory rule and common-law rule); People v. Supervisors of Chenango, 8 N.Y. 317 (1853) (three different quorum rules).

[12] The five-member Federal Trade Commission is empowered to act on the concurrence of two out of three participating members. FTC v. Flotill Prods., Inc., 389 U.S. 179 (1967). *See* Frischer & Co. v. Bakelite Corp., 39 F.2d 247 (C.C.P.A.), *cert. denied,* 282 U.S. 852 (1930) (U. S. Tariff Commission); Atlantic Ref. Co. v. FTC, 344 F.2d 599, 607 (6th Cir. 1965).

"In the absence of a valid rule establishing a different criterion, a quorum of a legislative body is a majority of the membership." United States v. Reinecke, 524 F.2d 435, 437 (D.C. Cir. 1975), *citing* Robert's Rules of Order Newly Revised (1970).

In the absence of a statute, constitution, or by-law, a simple majority constitutes a quorum. Gunnip v. Lautenklos, 33 Del. Ch. 415, 94 A.2d 712 (1953); Strong v. Garvey Memorial Liberty Hall, 380 Pa. 236, 110 A.2d 244 (1955).

See Reed v. National Order of Daughters of Isabella, 95 Misc. 695, 160 N.Y.S. 907 (Sup. Ct. 1916), *aff'd,* 177 App. Div. 949, 164 N.Y.S. 1110 (4th Dep't 1917).

[13] United States v. Ballin, 144 U.S. 1, 6 (1892); *accord,* Drath v. FTC, 239 F.2d 452 (D.C. Cir. 1956), *cert. denied,* 353 U.S. 917 (1957); Frischer & Co. v. Bakelite Corp., 39 F.2d 247 (C.C.P.A.), *cert. denied,* 282 U.S. 852 (1930); Ezell v. City of Pascagoula, 240 So. 2d 700 (Miss. 1970); *In re* Brearton, 44 Misc. 247, 89 N.Y.S. 893, 899 (Sup. Ct. 1904).

"In the absence of persuasive circumstances or a statutory directive to the contrary, it is a well-recognized principle that a majority constitutes a quorum, and if a quorum is present the legislative, judicial or administrative body has

Where the legislature confers powers upon a board without pre-scribing the number of members who must be in agreement to exercise the powers so conferred, then the common-law rule of quorum prevails.[14] But where the legislature provides that a major-ity of the members of a city political committee who are present and voting on all questions and elections constitutes a quorum, a majority of such quorum is sufficient to adopt a proposal duly sub-mitted.[15]

§ 6.3   Majority, Defined

There is a distinction in parliamentary law between a "majority" and a "majority vote." The word "majority" means more than half.

authority to act in those matters coming within its jurisdiction." Bray v. Barry, 91 R.I. 34, 41–42, 160 A.2d 577, 581 (1960).

"As a general rule applicable to parliamentary bodies, when a quorum is present, the act of the majority of the quorum is the act of the body." Steers Sand & Gravel Corp. v. Village Bd., 129 N.Y.S.2d 403, 405 (1954). *See* Shaughnessy v. Metropolitan Dade County, 238 So. 2d 466 (Fla. 1970); Smith v. City of Fort Dodge, 160 N.W.2d 492 (Iowa 1968).

The court will take judicial notice that the majority rule pervades the United States. O'Neil v. Tyler, 3 N.D. 47, 59, 53 N.W. 434, 438 (1892); *citing* Cushing, Law & Pr. Leg. Assem.

See Brown v. District of Columbia, 127 U.S. 579 (1888); St. Joseph Township v. Rogers, 83 U.S. (16 Wall.) 644 (1873).

[14] There seems to be no dispute that where a statutory requirement is ab-sent, the common-law rule prevails. Action may be taken by a majority of the members of the council present, provided that they are sufficient in num-ber to constitute a quorum of the body. Savatgy v. Kingston, 51 Misc. 2d 251, 273 N.Y.S.2d 1, 3 (Sup. Ct.), *aff'd*, 26 App. Div. 2d 978, 274 N.Y.S.2d 852 (3d Dep't 1966), *aff'd*, 20 N.Y.2d 258, 229 N.E.2d 203, 282 N.Y.S.2d 513 (1967).

"In the absence of anything specifically contrary, a majority of a quorum is sufficient to adopt a proposal duly submitted at a meeting." Lamb v. Cohen, 40 Misc. 2d 615, 618, 243 N.Y.S.2d 647, 651 (Sup. Ct. 1963), *citing* Robert's Rules of Order; *accord,* Bray v. Barry, 91 R.I. 34, 160 A.2d 577, 581 (1960).

"Ordinarily, a quorum means a majority of all entitled to vote." Bedford County Hosp. v. County of Bedford, 304 S.W.2d 697, 704 (Tenn. 1957) (hospital board of directors).

See Tabak v. Holmes, 174 N.Y.S.2d 857 (Sup. Ct. 1958); *In re* Lake Placid Co., 274 App. Div. 205, 81 N.Y.S.2d 36 (3d Dep't 1948).

[15] Lamb v. Cohen, 40 Misc. 2d 615, 243 N.Y.S.2d 647, 650 (Sup. Ct. 1963).

The term "majority vote," when used without qualification, means more than half of the votes cast by persons legally entitled to vote at a meeting duly called with a quorum present.[16] The Supreme Court has defined a house of Congress in the following terms: "What constitutes a house? A quorum of the membership, a majority, one half and one more." [17]

It is fundamental that a quorum of shareholders is a majority of all the shareholders and not just that portion of them which would constitute a majority. "A majority cannot separate itself from the minority, and be a quorum. All present are the quorum." [18] Accordingly, less than a quorum of a board of directors cannot elect another director to constitute a quorum.[19]

[16] See generally Robert's Rules of Order, Newly Revised at 3 and 339 (1970); Robert's Rules of Order, Revised at 23–24, 43, 191, 202 (1951); ROBERT, PARLIAMENTARY LAW at 571.

[17] Missouri Pac. R.R. Co. v. Kansas, 248 U.S. 276, 284 (1919).

A quorum means such a number of members as is, when duly assembled, legally competent to transact business. In re McGovern, 291 N.Y. 104, 107, 51 N.E.2d 666 (1943).

"The term 'majority' when referring to three named persons and applied to a course of action by 'a majority of such thereof as shall act' means, I think, such action by more than half of those entitled to act. The term 'majority' is the antonym of 'minority' and the counterpart of it. There is no more a 'majority' where only one is concerned than there is a 'minority' and the same person cannot be both." Callister v. Graham-Paige Corp., 146 F. Supp. 399, 403 (D. Del. 1956).

The term "majority" does not mean numerical majority of the entire board but means a majority of those present and voting. Payne v. Petrie, 419 S.W.2d 761, 763 (Ky. 1967).

An affirmative resolution which does not receive a majority vote, or such greater vote as may be required, will fail of passage. On the other hand, the concurrence of a majority is not required to defeat a motion and conclude a "final determination" of the question before the body. For example, when the village laws provided that the concurrence of a majority of the village trustees was necessary to exercise the powers conferred on them, the court held that: "Such a concurrence was not required to deny the petition. The vote of less than a majority of the authorized membership in favor of the petition, was sufficient to defeat it." Steers Sand & Gravel Corp. v. Village Board, 129 N.Y.S.2d 403, 405 (Sup. Ct. 1954); followed in Albini v. Board of Appeals, 41 Misc. 2d 783, 246 N.Y.S.2d 506, 508 (Sup. Ct. 1964).

For methods of determining the presence of a majority, see § 6.2 infra.

[18] Hill v. Town, 172 Mich. 508, 138 N.W. 334, 337 (1912), quoting In re Rapid Transit Ferry Co., 19 Misc. 409, 43 N.Y.S. 538 (Sup. Ct. 1897).

The majority rule has been described as a part of the democratic process. "Outstanding among the democratic processes concerning corporate elections is the general rule that a majority of the votes cast at a stockholders' meeting, provided a quorum is present, is sufficient to elect Directors." [20] Another opinion relating to a state council held: "The powers of the Council reside in the majority, and action taken by any duly convened meeting at which a quorum is present constitutes the action of the Council even though supported by less than a majority of the Council, or less than a majority of the Councilors present, provided a majority of the votes cast support the action." [21]

§ 6.4 Minimum Quorums

Often there is a minimum number fixed by statute, charter, or by-laws, to constitute a quorum.[22] There can even be a quorum of

---

"The conventional significance of a minimum number as a quorum disappears when more than that number are present and vote. Then the total number present and voting constitutes the quorum. Otherwise it could not be determined who represented a quorum, and of more importance a minority of those present and voting might control the meeting." *In re* Lake Placid Co., 274 App. Div. 205, 210, 81 N.Y.S.2d 36, 40 (3d Dep't 1948).

[19] "The fact that the six directors who were present elected a seventh to complete the quorum does not change the situation. If a valid meeting could be held by six directors, there is no reason why it could not be held by any other number less than a quorum. Such procedure, if given the sanction of the court, would render nugatory the provision of the by-laws with reference to a quorum." *In re* Fidelity Assur. Ass'n, 42 F. Supp. 973, 983 (S.D. W. Va. 1941), *rev'd on other grounds*, 129 F.2d 442 (4th Cir. 1942), *aff'd*, 318 U.S. 608 (1943).

[20] Standard Power & Light Corp. v. Investment Associates, Inc., 29 Del. Ch. 593, 51 A.2d 572, 576 (1947).

Ordinarily a bare majority of votes is sufficient to officially determine the action of a parliamentary body in a "democratic system." Wesley v. Board of Educ., 403 S.W.2d 28 (Ky. 1966). *See* Moore v. Langton, 167 A.2d 558 (R.I. 1961).

"While simple majority rule is a basic tenet in our system, history and practice demonstrate that the rule is not invariable." Adams v. Fort Madison Community School Dist., 182 N.W.2d 132 (Iowa 1970).

[21] Opinion of the Justices, 98 N.H. 530, 98 A.2d 635, 636 (1953). *See* Attorney General *ex rel.* Woodbury v. Bickford, 77 N.H. 433, 92 A. 835, 836 (1914).

[22] For example, the by-laws may fix the number which may constitute a

one,[23] or a quorum may consist of "those who answer the roll call." [24]

§ 6.5   Courts of Law

The number of judges required to constitute the quorum of a court or a division thereof is usually determined by constitutional or statutory provisions.[25] In the absence of such provision, the term

---

quorum within certain limits, namely, not less than one-third, but if that be nine or more, then not less than nine. If the legal minimum number is present, the meeting has a legal quorum even when the by-laws are defective in not specifying the minimum number. *See In re* Havender, 181 Misc. 989, 44 N.Y.S.2d 213, 215 (Sup. Ct.), *aff'd*, 267 App. Div. 860, 47 N.Y.S.2d 114 (1st Dep't 1943), *motion to appeal denied*, 267 App. Div. 901, 48 N.Y.S.2d 325 (1944), *citing* Robert's Rules of Order.

A resolution or by-law providing for a minimum quorum of three directors is not against public policy. Avien, Inc. v. Weiss, 50 Misc. 2d 127, 269 N.Y.S.2d 836 (Sup. Ct. 1966).

And when the statute provides that the charter or by-laws may fix the number not exceeding a majority, it is controlling over a general statute providing that the members attending shall constitute a quorum. M & E Luncheonette, Inc. v. Freilich, 218 N.Y.S.2d 125 (Sup. Ct. 1961).

The by-laws may specify various minimum requirements. New York Elec. Wkrs. Union v. Sullivan, 107 N.Y.S. 886 (1st Dep't 1907).

Some states have a "constitutional quorum," being "a number prescribed by our constitution that shall constitute a quorum." In the absence of a constitutional quorum, the general rule is that a quorum is a majority of all the members of the legislative body, and "a majority of this majority may legislate and do the work of the whole." State *ex rel.* Stanford v. Ellington, 117 N.C. 158, 23 S.E. 250, 251, 252 (1895), *citing* Cushing, Elect.

See N. Y. NOT-FOR-PROFIT CORP. LAW § 608 (McKinney 1970), providing that a charter or by-laws may provide for a quorum less than a majority but not less than the number of members entitled to cast 100 votes or one-tenth of the total number of votes entitled to be cast, whichever is lesser.

[23] United States v. Moran, 194 F.2d 623 (2d Cir.), *cert. denied*, 343 U.S. 965 (1952); *see* Watkins v. United States, 354 U.S. 178, 201 (1957).

[24] Santee v. Amateur Athletic Union, 2 Misc. 2d 990, 153 N.Y.S.2d 465 (Sup. Ct. 1956).

[25] "The Supreme Court of the United States shall consist of a Chief Justice of the United States and eight associated justices, any six of whom shall constitute a quorum." 28 U.S.C. § 1 (1970).

"What then is the meaning of Section 46(d) of Title 28 of the United States Code, which provides that a majority of the number of judges authorized to

"quorum" is generally used in its ordinary or common-law meaning of a majority of the whole body.[26]

---

constitute a division of the court, as provided in paragraph (c), shall constitute a quorum? The word *quorum* as therein used means such a number of the members of the court as may legally transact judicial business. The term arose from the Latin words which were used in the commission formerly issued to justices of the peace in England, by which commission it was directed that no business of certain kinds should be done without the presence of one or more of certain justices specially designated. Webster's International Dictionary." Tobin v. Ramey, 206 F.2d 505, 507 (5th Cir. 1953), *cert. denied,* Hughes Constr. Co. v. Secretary of Labor, 346 U.S. 925 (1954).

"Two judges of a three-judge circuit court of appeals . . . ordinarily constitute a statutory quorum for the hearing and determination of cases." Ayrshire Collieries Corp. v. United States, 331 U.S. 132 (1946).

The number of judges authorized under 28 U.S.C. § 46 to constitute a United States Court of Appeals in banc is seven; four or more of them are clearly a quorum. Alltmont v. United States, 177 F.2d 971, 973 (3d Cir. 1949).

"When the Constitution provides that four justices shall constitute a quorum, it is in effect conferring upon four the powers with which five were invested. A quorum is the number of the members of a body competent to transact business.

"A judicial or legislative body having a quorum present proceeds ordinarily as if every member was sitting in his place, and exercises all the powers with which it is invested. Any other rule would greatly enhance the transaction of business in case of illness, or voluntary or enforced absence among the members." Harroun v. Brush Elec. Light Co., 152 N.Y. 212, 213, 214, 46 N.E. 291 (1897).

Statute providing that a majority of "all the justices constituting the quarterly county court" was sufficient to elect officials is construed to mean a majority of existing justices excluding vacancies. A vote of five members out of an authorized ten with only nine in office due to the death of one, is sufficient. Beckler v. Tennessee, 198 Tenn. 372, 280 S.W.2d 913 (1941).

[26] "It is to be noted that a majority of the Judges of the Court, which would be three in the present instance, may constitute a quorum. A quorum is defined as the number of persons that are members of a body when assembled who are legally competent to transact the business of such a body. Normally, without the constitutional provision, a majority is considered a quorum at common law. The Constitution could have fixed a different number, but did not. Three members of this Court, under the Constitution as well as at common law, constitute a quorum to do business. This Court, when so constituted, may render a 2–1 decision." Davidson v. Indiana, 221 N.E.2d 814 (Ind. 1966).

"The statute does not define a quorum. The word, therefore, must be held to be used in its ordinary meaning, and that meaning is a majority of the

There is some uncertainty as to whether the court can act only by a majority of the whole number of judges, or whether the court may act under the common-law rule by a majority of a quorum. A leading case, often cited in support of the "majority of the whole" rule commented: "Where courts are concerned, it has been uniformly held, so far as we can ascertain, that a clear majority of all the legally constituted members thereof shall concur or no valid judgment may be entered except such as may follow no decision." [27] However the Supreme Court has said that this dictum rests on a "doubtful premise." [28]

The controversy is furthered by a Federal statute stating simply that any six Justices of the nine-man Supreme Court constitute a quorum, without defining the number of affirmative votes necessary for effective action.[29] Typical is a recent decision of the Arizona Supreme Court refusing to invalidate an Arizona statute on the basis of a four-to-three decision of the United States Supreme Court because it had been rendered by less than a majority of the full nine-member Court. This decision represents an implication that a common-law majority of a common-law quorum cannot act for the United States Supreme Court in constitution matters,[30] although it must be recognized that many decisions of the United States Supreme Court have been rendered on many issues by a four-member majority.

§ 6.6 Federal Administrative Agencies

The common-law rule has been applied to the decisions of Federal administrative agencies which have quasi-judicial functions.

---

entire body." Mountain States Tel. & Tel. Co. v. People *ex rel.* Wilson, 68 Colo. 487, 190 P. 513, 517 (1920).

A court consisted of 37 members, with 19 necessary for a quorum. The Chancellor held that 10, a majority of 19, could competently decide a case provided 19 members were present when the decision was made, and the vote of 10 would decide even though the other 9 did not vote. McFarland v. Crary, 6 Wend. 297 (N.Y. Ct. Correction Errors 1830).

[27] Frischer & Co. v. Bakelite Corp., 39 F.2d 247, 255 (C.C.P.A.), *cert. denied,* 282 U.S. 852 (1930); *quoted in* Roofing Wholesale Co. v. Palmer, 108 Ariz. 508, 502 P.2d 1327, 1330 (1972).

[28] FTC v. Flotill Prods., Inc., 389 U.S. 179, 184 (1967).

[29] 28 U.S.C. § 1 (1970).

[30] Roofing Wholesale Co. v. Palmer, 108 Ariz. 508, 502 P. 2d 1327 (1972); see 86 Harv. L. Rev. 1307 (1973).

In a leading case the five-member Federal Trade Commission (FTC), with only three Commissioners participating, issued a decision with only two Commissioners concurring as to one of the alleged violations. The Court of Appeals refused to enforce that part of the order which was concurred in by only two Commissioners, holding that, without statutory authority to the contrary, it was necessary that three members of the five-member Commission concur to enter a binding order. The Supreme Court reversed, unanimously holding that the FTC was not inhibited from following the common-law rule that a majority of a quorum consisting of a simple majority of a collective body was empowered to act for the Commission.[31]

§ 6.7　Disqualifications, Vacancies, Absences, Abstentions

In counting the number of members necessary to constitute a quorum of a deliberative body having a fixed number, the question arises as to how disqualifications, vacancies, and absences are to be treated. In considering these matters it is helpful to remember the long established rule that members present and not voting should be counted in determining whether a quorum is present.[32]

[31] *See* FTC v. Flotill Prods., Inc., 389 U.S. 179 (1967).

This issue was again raised in a recent decision cf the United States Supreme Court in which the dissenting opinion of two Justices stated in part: "*Fuentes,* a constitutional decision, obviously should not have been brought down and decided by a 4–3 vote when there were two vacancies on the Court at the time of argument. It particularly should not have been decided by a 4–3 vote when Justices filling the vacant seats had qualified and were on hand and available to participate on reargument. Announcing the constitutional decision, with a four-Justice majority of a seven-Justice shorthanded Court, did violence to Chief Justice Marshall's wise assurance, in *Briscoe v. Bank of Kentucky,* 33 U.S. (8 Pet.) 118, 122 (1834), that the practice of the Court 'except in cases of absolute necessity' is not to decide a constitutional question unless there is a majority 'of the whole court.'" North Georgia Finishing, Inc. v. Di-Chem, Inc., 42 L. Ed. 2d 751, 763 (1975).

[32] This principle was established in the House of Representatives in 1890 when Mr. Speaker Reed was faced with the question whether members present but refusing to vote could break a quorum and obstruct business. The Speaker directed the Clerk to enter on the Journal as part of the record of a yea-and-nay vote the names of members present but not voting, thereby establishing a quorum of record. This action was sustained by the Supreme Court in United States v. Ballin, 144 U.S. 1 (1892), and thereafter the point of order as to a quorum was required to be that no quorum was present and not that no

§ 6.7.1   Disqualifications

The authorities are divided with respect to disqualification.[33] The weight of authority, and the preferred rule, is that a quorum must consist of members who are capable of voting on the business before the body. Thus, members who are personally disqualified from voting due to an interest in the subject matter of a pending resolution cannot be counted in making a quorum, even though they do not vote.[34] The organic law [35] or the corporate charter

---

quorum had voted. U. S. Constitution, Jefferson's Manual, and Rules of the House of Representatives § 54 (1975 ed.).

[33] "Generally, whether a particular interest is sufficient to disqualify is factual, depending upon the circumstances of the particular case. . . . The question is always whether the circumstances could reasonably be interpreted to show that they had the likely capacity to tempt the official to depart from his sworn public duty." Township Comm. of Hazlet v. Morales, 119 N.J. Super. 29, 289 A.2d 563, 565 (1972).

Mere family relationship does not disqualify or relieve a corporate director from performing his duties. Rocket Mining Corp. v. Gill, 25 Utah 2d 434, 483 P.2d 897 (1971).

A trustee voting for himself is illegal as against public policy. Hornung v. State ex rel. Gamble, 116 Ind. 458, 19 N.E. 151 (1888).

[34] "All the directors constituting a quorum must be qualified to act. If one of the directors whose presence is necessary to constitute a quorum, or whose vote is necessary to constitute a majority of a quorum, is disqualified by reason of his personal interest, any act done by the body is invalid." In re Webster Loose Leaf Filing Co., 240 F. 779, 785 (D.N.J. 1916); see In re Shapiro, 392 F.2d 397 (3d Cir. 1968) (local draft board); United Hotels Co. of America v. Mealey, 147 F.2d 816 (2d Cir. 1945) (interlocking directors); Piccard v. Sperry Corp., 48 F. Supp. 465 (S.D.N.Y. 1943), aff'd, 152 F.2d 462 (2d Cir.), cert. denied, 328 U.S. 845 (1946); In re Fergus Falls Woolen Mills Co., 41 F. Supp. 355 (D. Minn. 1941), modified on other grounds, 127 F.2d 491 (8th Cir. 1942) (dominant director); Colorado Management Corp. v. American Founders Life Ins. Co., 145 Colo. 413, 359 P.2d 665 (1961) (common directors); Giuliano v. Entress, 158 N.Y.S.2d 961 (Sup. Ct. 1957) (zoning board of appeals); Rocket Mining Corp. v. Gill, 25 Utah 2d 434, 483 P.2d 897 (1971); Booker v. Young, 53 Va. 593 (12 Gratt. 303) (1855); In re Greymouth Point Elizabeth Ry. & Coal Co., [1904] 1 Ch. 32.

See Annot., 133 A.L.R. 1257 (1941).

When a member of a village board disqualifies himself and does not vote, but a quorum is present and votes, there is no need to consider his voting status. See Steers Sand & Gravel Corp. v. Village Board, 129 N.Y.S.2d 403, 404 (Sup. Ct. 1954).

may, of course, change the general rule of eligibility for quorum purposes.[36] The law has been well stated in a case concerning a board of directors of a definite number. "A director, whose interest in a matter disqualifies him from voting upon a resolution concerning it, cannot, according to the better opinion, be counted for the purpose of ascertaining whether a quorum is present when the vote is taken. A director so disqualified by personal interest loses, pro hac vice, his character as a director, and so cannot be counted."[37] This rule rests upon "the broad principle that it is the duty of each director in acting for the corporation to do so in the best interest of the corporation. His duty to the corporation is first. It is a duty he cannot perform if his own interest is adverse to that of the corporation." So strictly is this principle adhered to that no question is allowed as to the fairness or unfairness of the transaction.[38]

A transaction in which directors are jointly interested may not be split into two or more resolutions so as to qualify each interested director to vote in favor of the transaction for the benefit of other interested directors but not for himself. An English court has held that the vote of an interested director "in favour of a resolution to alter the quorum for such a purpose really comes to the same thing

---

[35] See DELAWARE CORP. LAW § 144 (1971) and N. Y. BUS. CORP. LAW § 713 (McKinney 1963), which provide that common or interested directors may be counted in determining the presence of a quorum at a meeting of the board or of a committee under certain standards of disclosure and fairness.

See Sterling v. Mayflower Hotel Corp., 33 Del. Ch. 293, 93 A.2d 107, 38 A.L.R.2d 425 (1952), also holding that a charter provision permitting interested directors to be included in counting a quorum is not against public policy.

[36] Piccard v. Sperry Corp., 48 F. Supp. 465, 469 (S.D.N.Y. 1943), *aff'd*, 152 F.2d 462 (2d Cir.), *cert. denied*, 328 U.S. 845 (1946).

[37] Enright v. Heckscher, 240 F. 863 (2d Cir. 1917); *accord*, Goldie v. Cox, 130 F.2d 695, 717 (8th Cir. 1942) (director); *In re* Lone Star Shipbuilding Co., 6 F.2d 192, 195 (2d Cir. 1925) (director); Gallaher v. Texagon Mills, Inc., 67 F. Supp. 845 (S.D.N.Y. 1946) (director); *In re* Fergus Falls Woolen Mills Co., 41 F. Supp. 355 (D. Minn. 1941), *modified on other grounds*, 127 F.2d 491 (8th Cir. 1942) (dominant director); Oceano Beach Resort Co. v. Clark, 289 P. 950 (Cal. 1930) (director); Marshall v. Industrial Fed'n, 84 N.Y.S. 866 (Sup. Ct. 1903) (executive committee); *see In re* Shapiro, 392 F.2d 397 (3d Cir. 1968) (member of draft board).

[38] *In re* Webster Loose Leaf Filing Co., 240 F. 779, 785 (D.N.J. 1916).

as a vote by him in favour of the resolution for conferring the interest on himself." [39]

There is an exception based on a "rule of necessity." When the body is the only entity capable to act in a matter, the fact that some members have a personal interest in the result of action taken does not disqualify them from performing their duty.[40]

The same rule applies to members who have limited voting rights not founded on self-interest. For example, where the mayor has no voting rights in the city council except to break a tie, he cannot be counted for quorum purposes.[41] But when an ex officio member of a body has all the authority of the other members, his presence can be counted in forming a quorum.[42] Furthermore, a person who has been enjoined from serving as a director of a corporation, but who nevertheless attends meetings of directors and participates in its business, is not necessarily disqualified for purposes of a quorum. "I am of opinion that the fact that certain of these directors may have violated the law in serving as such directors would not render their acts as directors invalid." [43]

§ 6.7.2 Vacancies

With respect to vacancies,[44] it has been established by a recent decision of the Supreme Court that the common-law rule of a quo-

[39] *In re* North Eastern Ins. Co. Ltd., [1919] 1 Ch. 198; *see* Greymouth Point Elizabeth Ry. & Coal Co., [1904] 1 Ch. 32.

[40] Gonsalves v. City of Dairy Valley, 71 Cal. Rptr. 255, 258 (1968).

[41] City of Somerset v. Smith, 105 Ky. 678, 49 S.W. 456 (1899).

A village mayor who is not a trustee cannot be counted in making a quorum of a board of trustees. People *ex rel.* O'Neill v. Hill, 260 App. Div. 111, 20 N.Y.S.2d 874 (2d Dep't), *aff'd*, 283 N.Y. 766, 28 N.E.2d 977 (1940).

[42] Seiler v. O'Maley, 190 Ky. 190, 227 S.W. 141, 143 (1921).

[43] *In re* Fidelity Assur. Ass'n, 42 F. Supp. 973, 983 (S.D. W. Va. 1941), *rev'd on other grounds*, 129 F.2d 442 (4th Cir. 1942), *aff'd*, 318 U.S. 608 (1943).

[44] Whether a vacancy actually exists is a question of law and fact. "In parliamentary law . . . an office is vacated by refusal of the elected member to accept it, communicated to the proper authorities; refusal to qualify; resignation and death. In all other instances, such as expulsion, adjudication of a controverted election, disqualification by act of the party, and acceptance of an incompatible office, ascertainment of the fact and declaration of the existence of the vacancy are necessary." State *ex rel.* Hatfield v. Farrar, 89 W. Va. 232, 109 S.E. 240, 241 (1921) (removal from city of member of city commission), *citing* Cushing, Law & Pr. Leg. Assem.

rum consisting of a simple majority of a collective body of a fixed number is not affected by vacancies or by self-disqualification of members so long as a quorum consisting of a majority of the whole body is present.[45] This common-law rule is not vitiated by a statute providing for the establishment of municipal boards and commissions consisting of not less than a fixed number of members. Such a statute does not mean that there must be at least that number

---

The term "vacancy" is often defined by statute to include events such as death, resignation, declination, disqualification, removal of residence outside the district, and removal from office. *See In re* Fleetwood Bank, 283 N.Y. 157, 27 N.E.2d 974 (1940).

A member of a political committee whose membership became vacant due to change of residence outside the district is not eligible to vote. Hart v. Sheridan, 168 Misc. 386, 5 N.Y.S.2d 820 (Sup. Ct. 1938).

Filling a vacancy in a city council is not a legislative act and may be done by a bare majority of a quorum consisting of the remaining members. Prezlak v. Padrone, 67 N.J. Super. 95, 169 A.2d 852 (1961).

If vacancies arise on a council, the remaining members constitute a quorum for the purpose of filling vacancies under a statute providing that the majority of the council should constitute a quorum. Nesbitt v. Bolz, 13 Cal. 2d 677, 91 P.2d 879 (1939).

A de facto member of a city council may vote on the passage of an ordinance. In an action to enforce a lien, the court stated: "It is a well recognized rule that the acts of a de facto officer will not, in a collateral proceeding, be deemed void." Reuter v. Meacham Contracting Co., 143 Ky. 557, 561, 136 S.W. 1028 (1911).

When a person by appointment to an office for a fixed term and until his successor has been "appointed and qualified" is serving after expiration of the fixed term, and the appointing power is not authorized to appoint his successor until three persons have been nominated, a vacancy does not exist until such nominations have been made. DeWoody v. Underwood, 66 Ohio App. 367, 368–69 (1940).

The term "vacancies" does not apply to newly created offices, as distinguished from existing offices which have become vacant. Moon v. Moon Motor Car Co., 17 Del. Ch. 176, 151 A. 298 (1930).

One court has suggested the possibility that "absentees are counted as if their silence reflects acquiescence and half-hearted approval of whatever is done by a majority of those voting at a meeting attended by a quorum." Carroll v. New York, N.H.&H. R.R., 141 F. Supp. 456, 458 (D. Mass. 1956).

[45] Arguments were heard by the full five-member Federal Trade Commission but two members retired before the decision, and a new member, appointed to fill one of the vacancies, declined to participate in the decision because he had not heard the arguments. The Supreme Court held that the Commission could act on two votes, being a majority of a common-law quorum of three members. FTC v. Flotill Prods. Inc., 389 U.S. 179 (1967).

of members of the body at all times. A court holding to that effect
"would unduly burden, restrict, and impair the action of a commission, board, or council, and could prove disastrous in situations
where immediate action is required." [46]

The common-law rule has often been changed by constitutional
and statutory provisions, so that a majority or fixed percentage of
"all of the members" or of the "whole membership" of the assembly
is required to constitute a quorum.[47] In such cases, the quorum is
not reduced by existing vacancies.[48]

§ 6.7.3 Whole Membership Concept

The leading case involved a resolution requiring a two-thirds
vote which was adopted by the vote of six members of a ten-member
Commission with two vacancies due to the death of two members
prior to the vote. The court upset the resolution, holding that the
requirement of a vote of "two-thirds of the Commissioners" meant
a vote of "two-thirds of the whole commission and not two-thirds of
the survivors." The court said, "According to the rules which govern corporate bodies, and deliberative or elective assemblies composed of a definite number of persons, a majority of the whole
number is necessary to constitute a legal meeting, and the number
necessary to constitute a quorum remains the same even though
there may be vacancies in the membership." [49] This rule has received statutory approval [50] and permits the body to exercise its

[46] Smith v. City of Fort Dodge, 160 N.W.2d 492, 496 (1968).

[47] Ezell v. City of Pascagoula, 240 So. 2d 700, 702 (1970).

[48] Where a statute requires the vote of three-fourths of the council it means
three-fourths of the whole number constituting the council and not three-
fourths of a quorum. Simmons v. Holm, 229 Ore. 373, 367 P.2d 368 (1961).

Statute required a majority of a fully constituted board for a quorum and
a majority vote of such a board to act. With a board of five members with
one vacancy, two members voted in favor, one voted against, and one abstained. The resolution was not adopted. Rockland Woods, Inc. v. Incorporated Village of Suffern, 40 App. Div. 2d 385, 340 N.Y.S.2d 513 (2d Dep't
1973).

[49] Erie R.R. v. City of Buffalo, 180 N.Y. 192, 197–98, 73 N.E. 26 (1904).

"The statutory language 'two-thirds vote of such commission,' different and
distinguishable from other formulations of the vote required to take action in
a deliberative body, has generally been interpreted to require favorable votes
of two thirds of the entire commission. . . . Thus, absence or abstention of a
commission member does not dispense with the requirement of a two-thirds
vote of the entire commission. . . . Nor does a vacancy on the commission

authority even when a vacancy exists, so long as the lawfully required proportion of the whole number exercises the power.[51] It is

---

reduce the number of votes required." Town of Smithtown v. Howell, 31
N.Y.2d 365, 339 N.Y.S.2d 949, 957–58, 292 N.E.2d 10 (1972) (county planning commission).

"Majority of members of the board" means a majority of all members. Thus
a vote of 3 to 2 of a six-member school board is not sufficient. Houser v.
School District, 189 Neb. 323, 202 N.W.2d 621 (1972).

"It is well established that a majority means a majority of the whole number of directors and a quorum remains the same even though there may be
vacancies." Cirrincione v. Polizzi, 14 App. Div. 2d 281, 220 N.Y.S.2d 741,
743 (4th Dep't 1961).

Vacancies from death, resignation, or failure to elect cannot be deducted
in ascertaining a quorum of a village council. Clark v. North Bay Village,
54 So. 2d 240 (Fla. 1951).

A statute providing that "a majority of the board" shall constitute a quorum
"clearly means a majority of the officers constituting the board, and not a re-
siduum resulting from vacancies, disqualifications or absences." *In re* Crosby,
178 Misc. 746, 36 N.Y.S.2d 301, 303 (Sup. Ct.), *aff'd,* 265 App. Div. 92, 37
N.Y.S.2d 745 (3d Dep't 1942); *accord,* Avien, Inc. v. Weiss, 50 Misc. 2d 127,
269 N.Y.S. 2d 836 (Sup. Ct. 1960) holding, also, that vacancies in the board
due to resignation can be filled by a majority of directors then in office, notwithstanding absence of a quorum.

The fact that there are vacancies in a board does not prevent the remaining
members, if they constitute a majority of the entire board as it would be
constituted if all vacancies were filled, from holding lawful meetings and
conducting business. Currie v. Matson, 33 F. Supp. 454 (W.D. La. 1940).

[50] *See* N. Y. GEN. CONSTR. LAW § 41. The purpose of this law was to
change the common-law rule that, when the power to act was conferred by
statute upon several persons, all were required to meet before the power
would be exercised. Morris v. Cashmore, 253 App. Div. 657, 3 N.Y.S.2d 624,
630 (1st Dep't), *aff'd,* 278 N.Y. 730, 17 N.E.2d 143 (1938).

Baker v. Jensen, 30 App. Div. 2d 969, 295 N.Y.S.2d 283 (2d Dep't 1968);
Incorporated Village of Farmingdale v. Inglis, 17 App. Div. 2d 655, 230
N.Y.S.2d 863 (2d Dep't 1962); Downing v. Gaynor, 47 Misc. 2d 535, 262
N.Y.S.2d 837 (Sup. Ct. 1965); Tabak v. Holmes, 11 Misc. 2d 848, 174
N.Y.S.2d 857 (Sup. Ct. 1958); Steers Sand & Gravel Corp. v. Village Bd.,
129 N.Y.S.2d 403 (Sup. Ct. 1954).

The Board of Higher Education of New York City is not subject to the
General Construction Law. McArdle v. Board of Higher Educ., 181 Misc. 766,
49 N.Y.S.2d 333 (Sup. Ct. 1943). *But see* Gray v. Maislen, 17 Misc. 2d 161,
130 N.Y.S.2d 466 (Sup. Ct. 1954).

[51] Incorporated Village of Farmingdale v. Inglis, 17 App. Div. 2d 655,
230 N.Y.S.2d 863, 865 (2d Dep't 1962).

But see Gray v. Maislen, 17 Misc. 2d 161, 130 N.Y.S.2d 466 (Sup. Ct.
1954).

also established that failures to vote, regardless of the fact that they emanate from those present or from vacancies, cannot change the results of voting if a quorum was present and a majority of that quorum adopted the motion.[52]

The courts have not been consistent in applying the "whole membership" concept. It has been held, for example, that the terms "majority of the whole number of members"[53] and "a majority of the directors"[54] mean a majority of the remaining members and not a majority of the total authorized number of members. This conforms to the general rule that vacancies occurring in a board of directors by reason of resignations may be filled by a majority of directors then in office, notwithstanding absence of a quorum.[55] The purpose of this rule "is to prevent vacancies in the board from paralyzing the corporation. The presence or absence of a quorum is immaterial so long as a majority of the remaining directors vote to fill the vacancies."[56]

---

[52] Lamb v. Cohen, 40 Misc. 2d 615, 243 N.Y.S.2d 647, 651 (Sup. Ct. 1963).

[53] City of Nevada v. Slemmons, 244 Iowa 1068, 59 N.W.2d 793, 795, 43 A.L.R.2d 693 (1953).

[54] The court noted that the language "A majority of the directors shall constitute a quorum" is in itself susceptible of either meaning. However, where the controlling charter or by-law fixes a number greater than a majority for certain purposes, such as a three-fourths vote, then the fraction is based on the authorized membership of the board. Gearing v. Kelly, 29 Misc. 2d 674, 215 N.Y.S.2d 609 (Sup. Ct.), rev'd, 15 App. Div. 2d 219, 222 N.Y.S.2d 474 (1st Dep't 1961), aff'd, 11 N.Y.2d 201, 182 N.E.2d 391, 227 N.Y.S.2d 897 (1962).

[55] Generally, corporation law provides that vacancies in a board of directors may be filled by a vote of a majority of the directors remaining in office, even though less than a quorum remains, unless the by-laws provide otherwise. In re Caplan's Petition, 20 App. Div. 2d 301, 246 N.Y.S.2d 913 (1st Dep't), aff'd, 14 N.Y.2d 679, 249 N.Y.S.2d 877 (1964) (N.Y. Bus. Corp. Law); accord, Gearing v. Kelly, 29 Misc. 2d 674, 215 N.Y.S.2d 609 (Sup. Ct.), rev'd, 15 App. Div. 2d 219, 222 N.Y.S.2d 474, 477 (1st Dep't 1961), aff'd, 11 N.Y.2d 201, 182 N.E.2d 391, 227 N.Y.S.2d 897 (1962).

Newly created but unfilled vacancies on a board of directors need not be counted in determining the number necessary to constitute a quorum or a majority of directors. Rocket Mining Corp. v. Gill, 25 Utah 2d 434, 483 P.2d 897 (1971).

[56] Avien, Inc. v. Weiss, 50 Misc. 2d 127, 269 N.Y.S.2d 836, 843 (Sup. Ct. 1966).

§ 6.7.4 Absence

A quorum must be present before a meeting can be called to order and commence business.[57] The absence of members of a fixed membership body from the meeting when it is scheduled to commence does not reduce the number of members legally required to constitute a quorum for the conduct of business. Whether a quorum must be present at all times throughout the meeting is another matter.[58]

§ 6.7.5 Abstention

It is a general rule of parliamentary law that members of a deliberative body who abstain from voting are counted for purposes of a quorum, although they may not necessarily be counted in determining whether a resolution has been accorded a sufficient vote to constitute action of the body.[59] One court has said: "The exercise of law-making power is not stopped by the mere silence and inaction of some . . . who are present. An arbitrary, technical, and exclusive method of ascertaining whether a quorum is present, operating to prevent the performance of official duty and obstruct the business of government, is no part of our common law. . . . [T]he requirement of a quorum at [the time of voting] was not intended to furnish a means of suspending the legislative power and duty of a quorum." [60]

§ 6.8 Statutes and By-Laws Controlling

The common law may, of course, be set aside or modified by statute, by appropriate charter provisions, or by the by-laws, fixing

[57] In general the chair is not to be taken until a quorum for business is present. Kimball v. Marshall, 44 N.H. 465 (1863), *citing* Jefferson's Manual and Cushing's Manual.

"Mere abstention from the meeting of a sufficient number will prevent its existence, except perhaps for adjournment purposes." Hexter v. Columbia Baking Co., 16 Del. Ch. 263, 267, 145 A. 115, 116 (1929).

[58] Constitutional requirement of "two-thirds vote" of members of each house means two-thirds of quorum present and voting, not two-thirds of elected members of each house nor two-thirds of members present as shown on the opening roll call. Branton v. Parker, 233 So. 2d 278 (La. 1970).

[59] Shaughnessy v. Metropolitan Dade County, 238 So.2d 466, 468 (Fla. 1970), *citing* Robert's Rules of Order.

[60] *In re* Opinion of the Justices, 98 N.H. 530, 98 A.2d 635, 636 (1953).

a different quorum requirement for all or any purposes.[61]   It is firmly established that a statute or other dominant authority in derogation of the common law of quorum must be strictly construed.[62]

At common law only a majority of directors was needed for a quorum and a majority of that quorum could transact business. State corporation statutes generally have modified that common-law rule by giving corporations the privilege of enacting a by-law fixing its own quorum requirement within certain limits. The New York law, for example, allows a quorum of any fraction not less than one-third, nor more than a majority, of its directors. The court has noted: "But the very idea of a 'quorum' is that, when that required number of persons goes into session as a body, the votes of a majority thereof are sufficient for binding action." Thus it has been held that a corporate by-law requiring the unanimous vote of all directors to take action,[63] or providing that no business should be transacted without their being 75 per cent of the stock represented at the meeting,[64] is invalid as inconsistent with the statute.

Statutory intrusion in the common law may result in a legislative body's having two or more quorum requirements, depending on the act or business then before the meeting. For example, it has been held that a city council must have a statutory quorum present to adopt a "local law or resolution" but that the statute does not prevent action by a common-law quorum in intracameral matters such as to elect a vice-chairman, to appoint committee members, and to adopt rules. The court confirmed that the adoption of rules was a procedural matter and that "general parliamentary law was clearly intended to prevail." [65]

---

[61] The constitution or a statute creating the body may prescribe the number necessary to constitute a quorum or may delegate to the body the authority to so prescribe. *See, e.g.,* Seiler v. O'Maley, 190 Ky. 190, 192, 227 S.W. 141, 142 (1921); *In re* Walter's Appeal, 270 Wis. 561, 570, 72 N.W.2d 535, 539 (1955).

The common law of quorum does not apply to a corporation having a by-law providing a different rule. New York Elec. Wkrs. Union v. Sullivan, 107 N.Y.S. 886 (App. Div. 1907).

[62] *See, e.g.,* Prezlak v. Padrone, 67 N.J. Super. 95, 169 A.2d 852 (1961).

[63] Benintendi v. Kenton Hotel, 294 N.Y. 112, 119, 60 N.E.2d 829 (1945).

[64] Gentry-Futch Co. v. Gentry, 90 Fla. 595, 106 So. 473 (1925).

[65] Morris v. Cashmore, 253 App. Div. 657, 3 N.Y.S.2d 624, 630, 632 (1st Dep't), *aff'd,* 278 N.Y. 730, 17 N.E.2d 143 (1938).

Most corporation laws provide that a quorum for a meeting of shareholders shall consist of the holders of a majority [66] of the outstanding shares entitled to vote represented at the meeting in person or by proxy.[67] Modern corporation laws also permit greater or lesser requirements as to quorum within specified limits.[68] It is basic that such express statutory provisions found in legislative acts, charters, and by-law provisions supersede the common law and are controlling.[69]

[66] The term "majority," used in defining a quorum, means more than one half. *See* distinction between majority and plurality, ROBERT, PARLIAMENTARY LAW at 571.

For history of word "majority" see Smith, *A Majority Vote, Toward Understanding our Balloting,* 10 PARL. J. 7 (1969).

[67] Franklin Trust Co. v. Rutherford Elec. Co., 57 N.J. Eq. 42, 41 A. 488 (1898).

See Gilchrist v. Collopy, 119 Ky. 110, 82 S.W. 1018 (1904), where the common-law rule of quorum was applied in the absence of any statute, charter, or by-law provision stating what proportion of the shares constituted a quorum.

A by-law requiring not less than a majority of stock "owned by individuals" to constitute a quorum violates a statute fixing a majority of outstanding stock as a quorum. Webb v. Morehead, 251 N.C. 394, 11 S.E.2d 586 (1959) (state owned large block of stock).

[68] *See, e.g.,* N.Y. BUS. CORP. LAW §§ 608 and 616.

A by-law requiring a larger vote will prevail. *In re* Laser Tech, Inc., 35 App. Div. 2d 994, 317 N.Y.S.2d 853 (2d Dep't 1970).

In the absence of a by-law, a majority of the directors constitutes a quorum. *In re* Webster Loose Leaf Filing Co., 240 F. 779 (D.N.J. 1916).

[69] See discussion of voting requirements of a city council. At common law, action may be taken by a majority of the members present, provided they constitute a quorum of the body. The question is whether the common-law rule prevails or whether it has been superseded by general or specific statutory action. Savatgy v. Kingston, 51 Misc. 2d 251, 273 N.Y.S.2d 1, 3 (Sup. Ct.), *aff'd,* 26 App. Div. 2d 978, 274 N.Y.S.2d 852 (3d Dep't 1966), *aff'd,* 20 N.Y.2d 258, 229 N.E.2d 203, 282 N.Y.S.2d 513 (1967). A by-law quorum is invalid if it conflicts with the statute or declared public policy. Webb v. Morehead, 251 N.C. 394, 11 S.E.2d 586 (1959).

Darrin v. Hoff, 99 Md. 491, 58 A. 196 (1904); M & E Luncheonette, Inc. v. Freilich, 30 Misc. 2d 637, 218 N.Y.S.2d 125 (1961). *In re* Argus Printing Co., 1 N.D. 434, 48 N.W. 347 (1891). As between the charter and by-laws, the charter controls. Christal v. Petry, 275 App. Div. 551 (1st Dep't), *aff'd,* 301 N.Y. 562, 93 N.E.2d 450 (1950).

When by-laws do not specify number of trustees constituting a quorum, the general corporation law of quorum will apply. *In re* Lake Placid Co., 274 App. Div. 205, 81 N.Y.S.2d 36 (3d Dep't 1948).

A public corporation organized by special statutory authority must abide by the rules of quorum established by law and does not have the freedom of a "parliamentary body," or of a corporation organized under general law, to regulate its own proceedings.[70] It has also been held, for example, that a by-law requiring a quorum of two-thirds of outstanding shares at a special meeting was invalid when it contravened a statutory designation of not more than a majority as being sufficient to constitute a quorum.[71] On the other hand it has been held that, where the by-laws provide that "the majority in number of stockholders shall constitute a quorum," the majority in number and not the holders of a majority of the stock must be present to constitute a quorum.[72]

§ 6.9 When Quorum Must Be Present

The exact time when a quorum must be present at the meeting may depend on the language of the applicable by-law or parliamentary rule. For example, if the by-law provides that a majority shall constitute a quorum "at all meetings," the quorum must be

[70] Talbot v. Board of Educ., 171 Misc. 974, 14 N.Y.S.2d 340, 344–45 (Sup. Ct. 1939). *See* McArdle v. Board of Higher Educ., 181 Misc. 766, 49 N.Y.S.2d 333 (Sup. Ct. 1943).

[71] *In re* Election of Directors of William Faehndrich Inc., 2 N.Y.2d 468, 473, 141 N.E.2d 597, 161 N.Y.S.2d 99, 103 (1957).

Resolutions adopted by shareholders requiring that directors be elected by not less than 76 per cent of capital stock were held violative of state law and thus against public policy because the applicable statute authorized the election of directors by a plurality of votes. Globe Slicing Mach. Co. v. Hasner, 223 F. Supp. 589 (S.D.N.Y. 1963), *aff'd,* 333 F.2d 413 (2d Cir.), *cert. denied,* 379 U.S. 969 (1964).

A by-law provision that vacancies on a board may be filled by the "directors in office" (two out of three) is controlling over a by-law provision that a quorum shall consist of 75 per cent of the directors and a vote of 75 per cent is necessary for "transaction of any business." Jacobson v. Moskowitz, 27 N.Y.2d 67, 313 N.Y.S.2d 684 (1970).

See also Gentry-Futch Co. v. Gentry, 90 Fla. 595, 106 So. 473 (1925); Benintendi v. Kenton Hotel, 294 N.Y. 112, 60 N.E.2d 829 (1945); Lutz v. Webster, 249 Pa. 226, 94 A. 834 (1915).

[72] Where five shareholders owning a majority of the stock were present, out of a total of 14, it was held not to be a quorum. This is a strict reading of an unusual by-law. Thisted v. Tower Management Corp., 147 Mont. 1, 409 P.2d 813 (1966).

present at the outset of each meeting. If it provides that a majority shall constitute a quorum "for the transaction of business," this may mean only that a quorum must be present at all times when business is transacted.[73] Certainly, a meeting is not "duly organized" and cannot legally transact business unless a quorum is present at the beginning.[74]

Although the presence of a quorum may be presumed under common parliamentary law unless it is questioned at the meeting or unless the record shows that a quorum in fact is not present,[75] it is always desirable to establish at the outset of a meeting whether the members present in person or by proxy constitute a quorum.[76]

[73] Hexter v. Columbia Baking Co., 16 Del. Ch. 263, 145 A. 115, 116–17 (1929).

A public hearing conducted by a county council to receive nominations and comments does not constitute transaction of business under a charter requiring a quorum for "transaction of business," and the fact that less than a quorum may have been present throughout the meeting did not invalidate subsequent action taken by the council. Gemeny v. Prince George's County, 264 Md. 85, 285 A.2d 602, 606 (1972), *quoting* Robert's Rules of Order, Newly Revised (1970).

[74] Davidson v. American Paper Mfg. Co., 188 La. 69, 175 So. 753 (1937).

The presence of a quorum must be affirmatively shown before the House or a committee of the House is deemed to be legally met. Christoffel v. United States, 338 U.S. 84, 88 (1949).

Where by-laws define a quorum, they refer to a quorum for the transaction of business. Beale v. Columbia Sec. Co., 256 Mass. 326, 152 N.E. 703 (1926). *See In re* Gulla, 13 Del. Ch. 23, 115 A. 317; 13 Del. Ch. 1, 114 A. 596 (1921).

Where a union constitution provided that a quorum shall be two-thirds of the members of the executive committee, the presence of seven out of eleven members did not constitute a quorum, and a vote to expel a member was invalid. Leonard v. M.I.T. Employees' Union, 225 F. Supp. 937, 940 (D.Mass. 1964).

[75] *See* Citizens' Mut. Fire Ins. Co. v. Sortwell, 90 Mass. (8 Allen) 217 (1864); Coombs v. Harford, 99 Me. 426, 59 A. 529 (1904) (fraternal lodge).

Outside persons are entitled to assume that a proper quorum was duly summoned and attended. County of Gloucester Bank v. Rudry Merthyr Steam & House Coal Colliery Co., [1895] 1 Ch. 629, 633.

A member having the floor cannot be interrupted while speaking to make a point of no quorum. The debate may continue until the point of no quorum is raised while no one is speaking. *See* Robert's Rules of Order at 260.

[76] *See In re* Gulla, 13 Del. Ch. 23, 115 A. 317, 319; 13 Del. Ch. 1, 114 A. 596 (1921), where no attempt was made to count shares present at the start of a meeting and the master decided to proceed with the voting and let the

Often in large meetings the secretary presents a preliminary count at the opening of the meeting to establish the existence of a legal quorum and later presents the final count after the inspectors of election or judges of the voting have completed their tally. Where the rules of order merely provide for a call of the roll without stating exactly how it should be done, the chairman may follow precedent and use the same method as had been used in the past. It has been held that this method of roll call did not conflict with the rules and therefore was not an "irregularity." [77]

However, the presence of a quorum cannot be assumed on the basis of a partial roll call. In one case, at a political judicial convention, a delegate attempted to organize the meeting after it had been cancelled by the chaiman, and started to call the roll. Before reaching a quorum a motion was made and carried that the balance of the roll call be dispensed with, predicated on the unfounded claim that a quorum was present. Without any further call of the roll the delegate was elected chairman of the convention and proceeded with the nominations. The court held that failure to complete calling the roll constituted such irregularity as to render impossible a determination as to whether the candidates were rightfully nominated.[78] Nor can a quorum be established by speculation, such as by assuming the number of shares held by members who have left the meeting room.[79]

---

vote decide if a quorum was present. The court held that a quorum cannot be established by speculation, and said: "Shares of stock, to be counted as present must be on hand either in person or by proxy. If present as proxies, they must be filed with the secretary of the meeting. That some one claimed on a day prior to the meeting that he would have certain proxies at the meeting, and that such person was bodily present at the meeting, but departed therefrom before the business for which he was there was attended to, without even depositing his proxies, makes too weak a presentation to permit of serious consideration as a justification for counting as present the shares he is supposed to have represented." *See also* Commonwealth v. Vandegrift, 232 Pa. St. 53, 81 A. 153 (1911).

[77] *In re* Ryan v. Grimm, 43 Misc. 2d 836, 838, 252 N.Y.S.2d 521 (Sup. Ct.) *aff'd*, 22 App. Div. 2d 171, 254 N.Y.S.2d 462 (4th Dep't 1964), *aff'd*, 15 N.Y.2d 922, 206 N.E.2d 867, 258 N.Y.S.2d 843 (1965).

[78] Bannigan v. Heffernan, 203 Misc. 126, 115 N.Y.S.2d 889, 893 (Sup. Ct.), *modified*, 280 App. Div. 891, 115 N.Y.S.2d 444 (2d Dep't), *aff'd*, 304 N.Y. 729, 108 N.E.2d 209 (1952).

[79] *In re* Gulla, 13 Del. Ch. 23, 115 A. 317, 319 (Ch. 1921).

§ 6.9.1   *Continuation of Established Quorum*

Having established the existence of a quorum, it may be presumed that a quorum will continue to be present until it shall appear that there is no quorum. Some corporation laws so provide.[80] Parol evidence cannot be received to show that a quorum was not present throughout the meeting where the record shows that a quorum was present at the start of the meeting.[81]

"All the parliamentary authorities, including those cited by the Court, agree that a quorum is required for action, other than adjournment, by any parliamentary body; and they agree that the customary law of such bodies is that, the presence of a quorum having been ascertained and recorded at the beginning of a session, that record stands unless and until the point of no quorum is raised. This is the universal practice. If it were otherwise, repeated useless roll calls would be necessary before every action."[82] However, this

---

[80] "It is admitted by plaintiff that there must be a quorum present to do business, or, in this case, to elect the plaintiff to the office he claims. But he claims that it appearing there was a quorum present that morning, and it not appearing there had been an adjournment since, it will be presumed that there continued to be a quorum present. We think this is undoubtedly true,—that the quorum will be presumed until it shall appear there is not one." State *ex rel.* Stanford v. Ellington, 117 N.C. 158, 23 S.E. 250, 251 (1895), *citing* Cushing, Elect. (2d ed.) at 369.

See, e.g., N.Y. Bus. Corp. Law § 608(c) (McKinney 1963) stating: "When a quorum is once present to organize a meeting, it is not broken by the subsequent withdrawal of any shareholders."

[81] Where the official count shows that more than a quorum of voters was present at the beginning of the meeting, but that less than a quorum actually voted, it will be presumed that a quorum was present throughout and parol evidence will not be received to contradict that record. Del Prete v. Board of Selectmen, 351 Mass. 345, 220 N.E.2d 912 (1966), *citing* Robert's Rules of Order.

[82] Christoffel v. United States, 338 U.S. 84, 92 (1949), Jackson, J., dissenting, *citing* Hinds' Precedents and Cannon's Precedents.

Summary statement on quorum rule of the U. S. Senate: "Until a point of no quorum has been raised, the Senate operates on the assumption that a quorum is present, and even if only a few Senators are present, a bill may be passed. Any Senator in attendance could have suggested the absence of a quorum, which would stay any action by the Senate until a quorum was ascertained. Voice votes may be taken on the passage of a bill and if no question of a quorum is raised, that action is final, even though a majority of

presumption can be rebutted. For example, when the roll call at
the opening of a session of a state legislature showed that a quorum
had assembled for the transaction of business, but a roll call on the
election of an officer disclosed that less than a quorum had voted,
it was not presumed that a quorum was present at the time of the
election.[83]

There is a difference between procedures as regards the presence
of a quorum in the full House of Representatives and its committees.
In the full House, a quorum having been established, business may
be transacted on the assumption that a quorum is present at all
times, unless a roll call or a division indicates the contrary. In committee meetings, however, the presence of a quorum must be affirmatively shown before the committee is competent to act, and the
point of no quorum need not be raised before the committee but
can be raised at a later trial. In a case relating to the testimony of a
witness before a Congressional committee, the Supreme Court held
that a quorum of a committee of the House must be physically
present when a perjurious offense is committed, and suggested that

---

the Senators did not participate; the Senate operates on the absolute assumption that a quorum is always present until a point of no quorum is made.

"Once a point of no quorum has been raised, and the absence of a quorum
established by the Chair announcing that a quorum is not present, the quorum
call may not be called off, not even by unanimous consent, and no business in
the meantime is in order, not even debate, until a quorum of the Senators has
responded to the call. The Senate may in the absence of a quorum recess (if
an order to that effect has been agreed to before the quorum call started),
adjourn, or adopt motions to request or compel the attendance of absent Senators; it may not, however, proceed to take any further legislative action until
a quorum is established." Senate Procedure, Precedents and Practices, Senate
Document No. 93–21, 93d Cong. at 630 (1974).

A recent decision holds that Robert's Rules "may well be dispositive" of a
case where there was a bare quorum at the beginning and at the end of a
meeting, but not throughout the meeting, and where no member suggested
the absence of a quorum. The court also questioned whether the events of
the meeting "rose to the level of a debate." Gemeny v. Prince George's
County, 264 Md. 85, 285 A.2d 602, 606 (1972), quoting Robert's Rules of
Order.

See Robert's Rules of Order Newly Revised, § 39 (1970).

[83] State ex rel. Stanford v. Ellington, 117 N.C. 158, 23 S.E. 250 (1895),
citing Cushing, Parl. Law; accord, Moore v. Langton, 167 A.2d 558, 561
(R.I. 1961).

the power to raise a point of no quorum is limited to a member of the committee.[84]

§6.9.2 Intentional Absence of Shareholder

The fact that a shareholder intentionally prevented the existence of a quorum at a previous meeting does not estop such shareholder from demanding that a subsequent annual meeting be called. "Generally speaking, the motive that the stockholder may have for not attending the meeting or voting his shares is irrelevant. Even if petitioner deliberately failed to attend because she did not want to create a quorum, her reason for abstaining, if relevant, is not of a character which should preclude the relief granted." [85] However, a

---

[84] The Supreme Court in a 5-to-4 decision upset a conviction of perjury of a witness who denied under oath before a House committee any affiliation with Communism. The reversal was based on the ground that inasmuch as a quorum of the committee, which was present at the outset, was not present at the time of the alleged perjury, testimony before it was not before a "competent tribunal" within the sense of the District of Columbia Code. The dissenters argued that under the rules and practices of the House, a quorum once established is presumed to continue unless or until a point of no quorum is raised. Christoffel v. United States, 338 U.S. 84 (1949).

To convict a Congressional committee witness of perjury the government must prove that he gave false testimony before a competent tribunal. For a legislative committee to be competent, a quorum sufficient to conduct business at hand must be present and the government must prove that the false statement was made to a quorum of that committee. Where a Senate committee rule that one Senator would constitute a quorum for taking of testimony was not published before the statutory deadline, the rule was not valid. Thus, where the prosecutor proved only that one Senator was present at the session when the testimony was given, there could be no conviction. United States v. Reinecke, 524 F.2d 435 (D.C. Cir. 1975), citing Robert's Rules of Order Newly Revised (1970).

It does not necessarily follow, however, that a standing committee of the Congress is not a competent tribunal unless a quorum of its members is present throughout a hearing held preparatory to reporting legislation as distinguished from a hearing held to investigate individual conduct. As to the Senate, it appears that committees do not require the presence of a quorum for the taking of testimony, and that they do not consider the holding of a hearing as the transaction of business. See BURLESON, HISTORY OF THE UNITED STATES HOUSE OF REPRESENTATIVES, 82 (1965).

[85] In re Pioneer Drilling Co., Inc., 36 Del. Ch. 386, 130 A.2d 559 (1957).

shareholder who deliberately refrains from attending a meeting may be estopped from objecting to the action taken.[86]

Shareholders are free to attend meetings or to stay away, as they individually may prefer, and while in attendance they can participate in the deliberations and vote, or they can remain silent and abstain from voting. Shareholders who go to a meeting may depart and return at will without affecting the power of the majority that remains and constitutes a quorum to do business, and without prejudice to the legality of any action taken.[87]

An intentional and deliberate absence of a director from a meeting of a board of directors for the purpose of preventing a quorum and paralyzing the board may bar the objector from equitable relief.[88] However, where a quorum of directors is in office, the majority thereof cannot be considered "outsiders" merely because they cannot procure the attendance of a quorum at a meeting.[89]

§ 6.9.3 Presence at a Meeting

Related questions arise as to whether the presence of a member in person or by proxy at the outset of a meeting constitutes his presence for purposes of a quorum, and whether his withdrawal from a meeting before or after it has been organized can have the effect of preventing or breaking a quorum and invalidating all further business except recess or adjournment.[90]

It is well established that when a member of a body having a definite number is present at the outset of a meeting, he should be

---

[86] Shareholder deliberately refrained from attending a meeting, giving as his reason, not his inability to vote certain shares, but his assumption that the election would result as usual. The court held that the shareholder "should not now be relieved from the consequences of his own deliberate act." *In re* P. F. Keogh, Inc., 192 App. Div. 624, 183 N.Y.S. 408, 413 (1st Dep't 1920), *quoting from In re* Pioneer Paper Co., 36 How. Pr. 105, 109 (N.Y. 1864).

[87] The fact that members left the meeting or remained in the room does not affect the power of a remaining majority to conduct business. American Aberdeen-Angus Breeders' Ass'n v. Fullerton, 325 Ill. 323, 156 N.E. 314, 317 (1927).

[88] Gearing v. Kelly, 11 N.Y.2d 201, 207, 182 N.E.2d 391, 227 N.Y.S.2d 897 (1962), *aff'g* 15 App. Div. 2d 219, 222 N.Y.S.2d 474 (1st Dep't 1961).

[89] Campbell v. Loew's, Inc., 36 Del. Ch. 565, 134 A.2d 852, 863 (1957).

[90] Generally, *see* Annot., 43 A.L.R.2d (1955).

counted in determining whether a quorum is then in attendance.[91]
This rule applies to both houses of the Congress.[92]   When a member

[91] The courts "as well as law writers and parliamentarians generally," have
adopted a rational rule that if a member of a legislative body such as a city
council, is present at a meeting and thus helps to make a quorum, he will be
counted as present whether or not he refuses to answer to the roll call.
Cromarty v. Leonard, 13 App. Div. 2d 274, 216 N.Y.S.2d 619, 623 (2d Dep't),
aff'd, 10 N.Y.2d 915, 223 N.Y.S.2d 870, 179 N.E.2d 710 (1961).
     After an election has been properly proposed, whoever has the majority
vote, assembly being sufficient, is elected although a majority of the entire
assembly abstains from voting, since their presence suffices to constitute an
elective body and their neglect to vote is considered an assent to determination
of a majority of those who do vote.   State *ex rel.* Roberts v. Gruber, 231 Ore.
494, 373 P.2d 657 (1962).
     Respondent contended that those present at a meeting of a city executive
committee who did not vote could not be legally counted to make a quorum.
The court cited United States v. Ballin, 144 U.S. 1 (1892), and then said:
"It thus appears that, in the absence of any contrary rule, the common law
principle is, that the majority of a deliberative body constitutes a quorum, and
there being a quorum, that a majority of those present can transact business."
In re Doyle, 7 Pa. Dist. 635, 637, 23 Pa. County Ct. 27 (1898).
     "I am further of opinion, that if a majority be present and qualified to vote
and do vote, the election may be made by a majority of the votes given, although they be not a majority of the whole board; and this although others of
the directors be present, but do not vote."   Booker v. Young, 53 Va. 593 (12
Gratt. 303, 305) (1855).
     Generally, mere presence at a meeting, and not active participation in its
affairs, is sufficient for purposes of a quorum.   *See* Atterbury v. Consolidated
Coppermines Corp., 26 Del. Ch. 1, 20 A.2d 743 (1941).
     Questions of quorum must be determined by "precedent and parliamentary
usage."   If a majority is present to do business, their presence is all that is
required in order to make a quorum.   "The idea that silence can be stronger
than a negative vote seems to have been unknown to our ancestors.   It seems
to be a modern parliamentary fiction which has never been able to stand the
examination of courts where business questions were involved."   The court
quoted from REED, PARLIAMENTARY RULES, as follows: "The quorum required
to constitute an assembly and render it competent to transact business is a
present quorum and not a *voting* quorum.   In all cases, if the number necessary to make a quorum is present, it makes no difference how many or how few
actually participate in the decision. *Those who sit silent are regarded as consenting to the result.*"   Myers v. Union League, 17 Pa. Dist. 301, 304–5 (C.P.
1908).
[92] For many years the quorum of the House of Representatives was determined only by noting the number of members voting, with the result that
members by refusing to vote could often prevent or break a quorum.   But in

is present and assists in the organization of a meeting, there can be no question as to his being present for purposes of a quorum.[93] The required number must be present at the same time, and not separately.[94] However, a member present at a meeting in person or by proxy before a quorum exists can leave without being counted toward a quorum then or later.[95] When the meeting is a part of a session and, therefore, already organized, mere attendance is sufficient for quorum purposes.[96] Members of the body must meet knowingly. They cannot be tricked into attendance for the purpose of obtaining a quorum.[97]

Shareholders in attendance at a meeting who hold proxies necessary and sufficient to make a quorum cannot invalidate an election

---

1890 Mr. Speaker Reed directed the Clerk to enter on the Journal the names of members present but not voting, thereby establishing a quorum of record. This rule established the principle that members present and not voting may be counted in determining whether a quorum is present. The Supreme Court sustained the rule. "The Constitution provides that 'a majority of each [house] shall constitute a quorum to do business.' In other words, when a majority are present the House is in a position to do business. Its capacity to transact business is then established, created by the mere presence of a majority, and does not depend upon the disposition or assent or action of any single member or fraction of the majority present. All that the Constitution requires is the presence of a majority, and when that majority are present the power of the House arises." United States v. Ballin, 144 U.S. 1, 5–6 (1892). See IV Hinds' Precedents § 2904.

[93] Where a by-law requires a certain member to be present to constitute a quorum, the meeting cannot proceed unless a quorum is present. "Mere abstention from the meeting of a sufficient number will prevent its existence, except perhaps for adjournment purposes. But when the number is present, and assists in the organization, the situation is an entirely different one." Hexter v. Columbia Baking Co., 16 Del. Ch. 263, 145 A. 115, 116 (1929).

[94] The purpose of the quorum requirement is that a certain minimum number of persons shall convene and consider. "It is not a meeting when less than that quantity convene on a number of separate days, on no one of which a quorum was present." Textron, Inc. v. American Woolen Co., 122 F. Supp. 305, 312 (D. Mass. 1954).

[95] A stockholder has no duty to attend a meeting in the first place, and no duty to remain. His original presence does not permit that his shares be counted for quorum purposes after he has left. Id. at 311–12.

[96] See United States v. Ballin, 144 U.S. 1 (1892).

[97] Trendley v. Illinois Traction Co., 241 Mo. 73, 145 S.W. 1 (1912). See § 1.6 supra.

by refusing to submit their proxies to the meeting.[98] Proxies in the possession of a proxyholder who is physically present at a meeting should be counted for purposes of a quorum even though the proxies are not turned in until later.[99] A shareholder who is present at an annual meeting for short periods in a capacity of attorney for others is present both as a shareholder and as a proxy, and the shares represented by him in both capacities should be counted toward a quorum. Shares owned by a partnership, when a member–shareholder is present at the meeting, also must be counted.[100] However, when a shareholder attends a meeting solely for the purpose of protesting its illegality and consistently makes his position known, his shares are not to be counted toward a quorum.[101] Inasmuch as a corporate director cannot vote by proxy at a meeting of the board of directors, he cannot be present by proxy for the purpose of counting a quorum.[102]

There has been some question as to whether a record shareholder

[98] "When it is clear that a majority of the stock of the corporation was present, either in person or by proxy, at a meeting of stockholders regularly called for the purpose of electing directors, and that an election was held, it should not be declared invalid because certain stockholders holding proxies for stock necessary to make a quorum, and in attendance at the meeting, declined to submit their proxies to the meeting." Duffy v. Loft, Inc., 17 Del. Ch. 140, 151 A. 223, 17 Del. Ch. 376, 152 A. 849, 852 (1930).

[99] The court suggested that, by the same token, a shareholder could have revocations of proxies physically present. Textron, Inc. v. American Woolen Co., 122 F. Supp. 305, 311 (D. Mass. 1954).

[100] Atterbury v. Consolidated Coppermines Corp., 26 Del. Ch. 1, 20 A.2d 743, 749–50 (1941), citing Duffy v. Loft, Inc., 17 Del. Ch. 140, 151 A. 223, aff'd, 17 Del. Ch. 376, 152 A. 849 (1930).

[101] The shareholder refused to produce his shares or proxies and was so persistent in protesting the legality of the meeting that he was ejected before any votes were received. Leamy v. Sinaloa Explor. & Dev. Co., 15 Del. Ch. 28, 130 A. 282 (1925).

A shareholder who participates in a meeting cannot claim it was not duly convened. "Petitioner should either have disregarded the notice and not attended the meeting, or if he attended, should have left the meeting immediately after voicing his objections to the validity thereof without further participation." Matter of Frankel v. 447 Central Park West Corp., 176 Misc. 701, 702, 28 N.Y.S.2d 505 (Sup. Ct.), aff'd, 263 App. Div. 950, 34 N.Y.S.2d 136 (1st Dep't 1941).

[102] See, e.g., Craig Medicine Co. v. Merchants' Bank, 59 Hun 561, 14 N.Y.S.16 (Sup. Ct. 1891).

is present at a meeting by proxy for purposes of counting a quorum
when his proxy limits the right of the named proxyholder to vote
on certain specified matters. This often occurs when shares held by
a member of a national securities exchange for a customer's account
are registered in a "street name," and the member organization has
not received instructions from the beneficial owner as to voting on
a certain matter. Generally, a member organization may not give
a proxy to vote without instructions from the beneficial owner when
the matter to be voted upon affects substantially the rights or privileges of the stock, such as a merger or consolidation, authorization
or increase of stock, or change of voting rights.[103] In practice, member organizations usually recognize limited proxies as valid for
quorum purposes and often sign and forward proxies on behalf of
their customers saying they are for "quorum purposes" with the
proxy cards marked to specify that they are not to be voted on the
restricted matters.

It is the preferred rule that restricted proxies are valid for purposes of counting a quorum.[104] So far as the corporation is concerned each shareholder of record at the record date has the right
to vote. Self-imposed restrictions between the beneficial owner and
the record holder should not limit or vitiate the right or duty of the
corporation to recognize the voting rights of the record holder.

A shareholder cannot be present at a meeting for some purposes
and absent for other purposes. Certainly, where the proxyholder
has been given the right to vote on some matters (such as the election of directors or the appointment of auditors), and has been
given the discretionary right to vote on such other matters as may
come before the meeting, then the shareholder is present by proxy
for quorum purposes even if he has not specifically authorized his
proxyholder to vote on certain other matters that may come before
the meeting. And even when the proxyholder has not been authorized to vote on any matters to come before the meeting, the mere
fact that he has been empowered by the shareholder to attend the
meeting as proxy constitutes presence of the shareholder for purpose
of a quorum.

[103] See New York Stock Exchange Proxy Rules, Rule A–143.

[104] But see ARANOW AND EINHORN, PROXY CONTESTS FOR CORPORATE CON-
TROL 315–16 (2d ed.), stating that shares which may not be voted by a broker
at his discretion should not be included in the quorum count.

§ 6.10   Treasury Shares

Shares held in the treasury may not be voted [105] and therefore cannot be included in computing a quorum.[106]

§ 6.11   Rights of Minority

Although there are well reasoned decisions to the contrary,[107] it is generally acknowledged that "under ordinary parliamentary law a

[105] *See, e.g.,* Goldfield Corp. v. General Host Corp., 29 N.Y.2d 264, 327 N.Y.S.2d 330 (1971).

[106] Atterbury v. Consolidated Coppermines Corp., 26 Del. Ch. 1, 20 A.2d 743, 747 (1941).

Stock which cannot be voted (owned by controlled subsidiary) cannot be counted for quorum purposes. Italo Petroleum Corp. v. Producers' Oil Corp., 20 Del. Ch. 283, 174 A. 276 (1934). *See* Walsh v. State *ex rel.* Cook, 199 Ala. 123, 74 So. 45 (1917); Lawrence v. I. N. Parlier Estate Co., 15 Cal.2d 220, 100 P.2d 765 (1940); Monsseaux v. Urquhart, 19 La. Ann. 482 (1867).

[107] *See, e.g.,* Duffy v. Loft, Inc., 17 Del. Ch. 376, 152 A. 849, 853 (1930).

"The rule enunciated in the Duffy case is that a quorum once present cannot be destroyed by subsequent withdrawals or revocations of proxies. This is founded upon the policy that reasonable rules should prevail in aid of the accomplishment of the statutory purpose that meetings be held for the election of directors at the time fixed in the by-laws." The court held that "a shareholder or proxy holder once having attended a meeting, should be deemed present for quorum purposes, in the absence of some unusual circumstances. . . ." Atterbury v. Consolidated Coppermines Corp., 26 Del. Ch. 1, 20 A.2d 743, 749–50 (1941).

A resolution reducing the company's capital was validly passed although a stockholder left the meeting after it was organized and before the vote, and there was a quorum at the time of vote. *In re* Hartley Baird Ltd., [1955] 1 Ch. 143 (1954).

"But when a quorum is once present, the meeting organized and transacting business however little, there must under the authorities be some justifiable reason for withdrawal by any one to break the quorum, before such withdrawal can be allowed the effect of destroying the meeting. It has in substance been held by courts and stated by textwriters, that if the withdrawing stockholders are animated by a purpose solely to destroy the meeting by breaking a quorum because of whim, caprice or chagrin, the law will consider their action as unavailing and will permit the meeting to proceed." Hexter v. Columbia Baking Co., 16 Del. Ch. 263, 145 A. 115, 117 (1929) (citations omitted).

Even assuming a company regulation making the majority of stockholders in number a quorum, once organized, a majority of stockholders cannot with-

quorum must remain present throughout." [108] This practice is founded on the concept of majority rule "and though convenience requires and usage has established the right of acting by majorities, neither will sanction the exercise of the power by minorities." [109] Other parliamentary factors are applicable in deciding whether the action taken is valid. In ruling on the validity of an order signed by two members of a board of three commissioners, the court said: "It appears to be a fundamental rule of parliamentary practice governing assemblies that the opportunity to deliberate, and if possible, to convince his fellows is the right of the minority, of which they can not be deprived by the arbitrary will of the majority. . . . As we view it, the matter of a quorum is one separate and apart from the principle that all the members of a deliberative body must have a fair opportunity to participate in its action. This does not mean that a single member may be absenting himself prevent action by a quorum." [110]

Thus, if the attendance at a meeting falls below a quorum due to the departure of shareholders and if the lack of a quorum is called to the attention of the chairman, the transaction of further business

---

draw from the meeting and prevent the owners of a majority of the stock from electing directors. State *ex rel.* Fritz v. Gray, 20 Ohio App. 26, 153 N.E. 187, 190 (1925).

[108] Textron, Inc. v. American Woolen Co., 122 F. Supp. 305, 311 (D. Mass. 1954).

Where a statute provides that a majority of all stock must be present at an election of directors, the breaking of a quorum, even by an illegal adjournment, prevents the minority from proceeding with the election. Bridgers v. Staton, 150 N.C. 216, 63 S.E. 892, 894 (1909).

Further, whether the vote of a majority of a quorum is necessary for approval "must be determined by precedent and parliamentary usage." Myers v. Union League, 17 Pa. Dist. 301, 304 (C.P. 1908) (*citing* Hinds' Precedents and Reed's Rules).

[109] Eight out of sixteen members of the committee withdrew. "The minority left, under these circumstances, had no power to act or decide. . . . But we cannot think that if a major part withdraw in the belief that they, or any of them, are to be prevented from acting, the minority can assume the powers of the whole body. A major part of the whole is necessary to constitute a quorum and a majority of such quorum may act." Damon v. Inhabitants of Granby, 19 Mass. 366, 376 (2 Pick. 345, 355) (1824).

[110] Terre Haute Gas Corp. v. Johnson, 221 Ind. 499, 45 N.E.2d 484, 490 (1942), *modified on other grounds*, 221 Ind. 499, 48 N.E.2d 455 (1943).

must be suspended.[111]   If the lack of a quorum persists, all business and discussion must come to an end, with adjournment the ultimate act.[112]

The withdrawal or departure of members from a meeting must be a physical move by them away from the meeting place. Retiring to the back of the meeting room into a crowd of bystanders, but without leaving the room, does not break the quorum.[113]

There is a minority view applicable to shareholder meetings, usually meetings for the election of directors, that a quorum once present at a shareholders' meeting will continue throughout the

---

[111] An early decision states: "In general the chair is not to be taken till a quorum for business is present; unless, after due waiting, such a quorum is despaired of, when the chair may be taken and the house adjourned. And whenever, during business, it is observed that a quorum is not present, any member may call for the house to be counted; and being found deficient, business is suspended." Kimball v. Marshall, 44 N.H. 465, 468 (1863), *citing* Jefferson and Cushing; *followed in* State *ex rel.* Shinnich v. Green, 37 Ohio St. 227, 235 (1881).

If the majority withdraws so as to leave no quorum, the power of the minority to act, is, in general, considered to cease. Brown v. District of Columbia, 127 U.S. 579, 586 (1888) (board of public works). *See* First Parish v. Stearns, 38 Mass. (21 Pick.) 148 (1838); Board of Supervisors v. Hall, 47 Wis. 208, 2 N.W. 291 (1879).

See In re Hartley Baird Ltd., [1955] 1 Ch. 143 (1954).

See also question of quorum at political meeting at 3 A.M. *In re* Ryan v. Grimm, 43 Misc. 2d 836, 842; 252 N.Y.S.2d 521 (Sup. Ct.), *aff'd*, 22 App. Div. 2d 171, 254 N.Y.S.2d 462 (4th Dep't 1964), *aff'd*, 15 N.Y.S.2d 922, 206 N.E.2d 867, 258 N.Y.S.2d 843 (1965).

See § 6.9.1 *supra*.

[112] When a quorum is not present at a meeting, "Its only possible legal action was to adjourn." Kauffman v. Meyberg, 59 Cal. App. 2d 730, 740, 140 P.2d 210, 216 (1943).

Under some circumstances, the body may fill vacancies in the absence of a quorum. *In re* Caplan's Petition, 20 App. Div. 2d 301, 246 N.Y.S.2d 913 (1st Dep't), *aff'd*, 14 N.Y.2d 679, 249 N.Y.S.2d 877 (1964) (board of directors).

[113] Action to contest a school election. Three out of six trustees, after being in session eleven hours to midnight and conducting 236 ballots, said they would participate no more and retired to the back of the room, whereupon the remaining three trustees elected the defendant by casting three votes on the 237th ballot. The election was held valid. Because the retiring trustees stayed in the room there still was a quorum in the meeting room and a majority of those voting could elect. State *ex rel.* Walden v. Vanosdal, 131 Ind. 388, 31 N.E. 79 (1892).

meeting, irrespective of the number of subsequent withdrawals. Cases favoring this view have been criticized. "They proceed on the basis that stockholders' meetings are required, and that accordingly more lenient principles should apply. This seems a questionable doctrine, and one difficult of delineation." [114]

The court has disapproved a contention that a quorum at a shareholders' meeting, once present, is always present for quorum purposes at subsequent adjourned meetings. It was suggested in argument that it was "capricious" for a shareholder, having been present at the meeting for purposes of a quorum and being capable of being present at an adjourned meeting, not to appear at the adjourned meeting. The court said: "This is a dangerous suggestion. Is the presence of a quorum to depend upon a determination of the reason for some shareholders' disappearance? And if disappearance, why not non-appearance? There being no duty on a shareholder to attend a meeting in the first place, there can be none on him to remain." [115]

The courts will not enforce parliamentary discipline which leads to unreasonable or unfair consequences. Thus, if a meeting has been properly organized in the first instance and all the parties have participated, no shareholder or faction may then, by withdrawing capriciously and without just cause for the purpose of breaking a quorum, render the subsequent proceedings invalid.[116]

[114] Textron, Inc. v. American Woolen Co., 122 F. Supp. 305, 311 (D. Mass. 1954).

See Davidson v. American Paper Mfg. Co., 188 La. 69, 175 So. 753 (1937) (statute provided that shareholders present at a duly organized meeting can continue to do business until adjournment even though a quorum is broken by the withdrawal of stockholders).

[115] The court continued: "It seems no more logical to find a quorum because some stockholder left for a 'capricious' reason than because he stayed away altogether for the same reason." Textron, Inc. v. American Woolen Co., 122 F. Supp. 305, 311–12 (D. Mass. 1954).

But see Atterbury v. Consolidated Coppermines Corp., 26 Del. Ch. 1, 20 A.2d 743, 749 (1941), holding that the presence of a quorum at the original session continued throughout an adjourned meeting for "all sessions were but a part of the same meeting" and there was no by-law requirement that a quorum remain continuously throughout the meeting.

[116] The court reasoned that "a majority of all the stock issued being represented, it was clearly the duty of those present to organize the meeting and proceed with the election." Commonwealth ex rel. Sheip v. Vandegrift, 232

An early decision held that a majority stockholder having acquiesced and participated in the organization of the meeting could not afterward withdraw and organize another meeting. The court said that it was the duty of the majority stockholder to remain in the meeting and added that a minority "must have the right to insist that, after a meeting is organized, the majority shall not withdraw from it and organize another meeting, at which the minority must appear or lose their rights. Once concede the right, and there is no limit to the number of wrecked meetings which may, at the caprice of a majority, precede the transaction of any business." [117] By the same reasoning, when a quorum is present and the minority withdraws because of dissatisfaction with the action taken by the majority, those remaining can proceed with the meeting.[118]

Where a minority of 11 walked out of a city council meeting for the purpose of breaking the quorum, and the remaining 15 members, knowing that they were without a quorum (a quorum was 16), nevertheless continued the meeting and recorded the absent members as voting in the affirmative on all questions, the court described their actions as an "inexcusable outrage" but let stand the acts of inspectors so appointed illegally due to the necessities of the situation, and ordered that a lawful meeting be held immediately to designate inspectors to replace those illegally appointed.[119]

Pa. St. 53, 60, 81 A. 153, 155–56 (1911); *accord,* Commonwealth *ex rel.* McCullough v. Exchange Operators, Inc., 11 Pa. Dist. & Co. 465 (1928) 32 Dauph. Co. 59 (1929).

Even assuming a company regulation is valid making the majority of shareholders in number a quorum, once organized, a majority of stockholders in number cannot withdraw from the meeting and prevent the owners of a majority of stock from electing directors. State *ex rel.* Fritz v. Gray, 20 Ohio App. 26, 153 N.E. 187, 190 (1925).

See Duffy v. Loft, Inc., 17 Del. Ch. 376, 152 A. 849, *aff'd,* 17 Del. Ch. 140, 151 A. 223 (1930); Darrin v. Hoff, 99 Md. 491, 58 A. 196 (1904).

[117] The court also said: "It is true that mere irregularities in conducting a meeting will not vitiate an election, but when a meeting is once organized it is not a mere irregularity to withdraw from it, and start a new one. . . ." *In re* Argus Printing Co.. 1 N.D. 434, 48 N.W. 347, 351 (1891).

[118] Ostrom v. Greene, 20 Misc. 177, 45 N.Y.S. 852 (Sup. Ct. 1897), *aff'd,* 30 App. Div. 621, 52 N.Y.S. 1147 (3d Dep't 1898), *aff'd,* 161 N.Y. 353, 55 N.E. 919 (1900).

[119] "The minority were not justified in leaving the council, and the action of President Griggs in declaring the council adjourned was an outrage and

The motive for withdrawing from a meeting may be important. It has been noted that the withdrawal of shareholders from a meeting for the purpose of preventing an election of directors would, if approved by the court, mean the holding-over of the old board of directors, which would be exactly what the withdrawing shareholders wanted to accomplish.[120]

If shareholders have withdrawn for the purpose of breaking a quorum because of whim, caprice, or chagrin, the law will consider the action as unavailing, and will permit the meeting to proceed.[121] The court has stated: "Stockholders who attend a meeting, and then without cause voluntarily withdraw, are in no better position than those who voluntarily absent themselves in the first instance."[122]

§ 6.12 Methods of Determining Quorum

In the absence of charter or by-law provisions, there is no prescribed method for determining whether a quorum is present. Any method which is reasonably certain to ascertain the fact may be employed and will be approved by the courts. The Supreme Court in considering the presence of a majority in the House of Representatives has said: "But how shall the presence of a majority be determined? The Constitution has prescribed no method of making this determination, and it is therefore within the competency of the House to prescribe any method which shall be reasonably certain

---

cannot be excused. No presiding officer can arbitrarily adjourn a meeting in defiance of the majority present." Dingwall v. Common Council, 82 Mich. 568, 46 N.W. 938, 939 (1890).

[120] Hexter v. Columbia Baking Co., 16 Del. Ch. 263, 145 A. 115, 116 (1929).

[121] *Id.* The same rule applies to a quorum of an adjourned meeting. Atterbury v. Consolidated Coppermines Co., 20 A.2d 743 (Del. Ch. 1941).

But motive is not necessarily relevant. In holding that less than a majority of county trustees could not elect a county superintendent, the court said: "The motives that may have induced the absence of five of the trustees from the adjourned meeting does not affect the question. . . . However reprehensible their conduct may have been in that respect, the absence of a quorum at the adjourned meeting rendered it impossible for the members present to make any valid appointment." State *ex rel.* Laughlin v. Porter, 113 Ind. 79, 82, 83, 14 N.E. 883, 884, 885 (1888), *citing* Cushing, Parl. Law.

[122] Commonwealth *ex rel.* Sheip v. Vandegrift, 232 Pa. St. 53, 81 A. 153, 155–56 (1911).

to ascertain the fact. It may prescribe answer to roll call as the only method of determination; or require the passage of members between tellers, and their count as the sole test; or the count of the Speaker or the clerk, and an announcement from the desk of the names of those who are present. Any one of these methods, it must be conceded, is reasonably certain of ascertaining the fact, and as there is no constitutional inhibition of any of those, and no violation of fundamental rights in any, it follows that the House may adopt either or all, or it may provide for a combination of any two of the methods. That was done by the rule in question; and all that that rule attempts to do is to prescribe a method for ascertaining the presence of a majority, and thus establishing the fact that the House is in a condition to transact business." [123]

In another decision relating to an election of directors to be conducted by a court-appointed master, the court upheld a decision of the master to proceed with the voting and to let the results of the vote disclose whether a quorum was present.[124]

Even where there are established procedures for determining whether a quorum is present, the court is often called upon to make a determination based on conflicting evidence. For example, in holding that a quorum of a political committee was present for an election of officers, the court held that it "must accept the facts with respect to membership or lack of membership at the meeting." [125] Obviously, an announcement by the secretary of the number of shares present at a shareholders' meeting which is based on a "speculative estimate" without a roll call or deposit of proxies is of no weight.[126]

---

[123] United States v. Ballin, 144 U.S. 1 (1892). *See* Annot., 94 L. Ed. 924 (1950).

"An arbitrary, technical and exclusive method of ascertaining whether a quorum is present, operating to prevent the performance of official duty and obstruct the business of government, is no part of our common law." *In re* Doyle, 7 Pa. Dist. 635, 637, 24 Pa. County Ct. 27, 30 (1898).

[124] *In re* Gulla, 13 Del. Ch. 23, 115 A. 317, 319 (1921).

[125] The court also said that: "Reason, commonsense and experience" teach that there is generally present at a political committee meeting many persons who are not members. *In re* Ajello's Petition, 26 Misc. 2d 1026, 212 N.Y.S.2d 970, 975 (1961).

[126] Leamy v. Sinaloa Explor. & Dev. Co., 15 Del. Ch. 28, 130 A. 282, 283 (1925).

In determining whether a quorum is present at a legislative or quasi-judicial hearing, it is sometimes necessary to consider the movements and activities of the individual members, within the scope of the statute or rule defining a quorum. In one case it was held that, where oral argument had been requested before a Federal commission and had not been clearly waived, a commissioner should not have voted without hearing oral argument, and, his vote having been decisive in effecting entry of orders, such orders would be vacated.[127] Yet in another case involving the Civil Aeronautics Board, when the statute required a quorum of three but also provided that the Board shall "hear or receive argument" on the request of either party, the presence of two members at the oral argument and a receiving of the arguments by another member met the statutory requirement. "If a quorum does not hear, the quorum requirement may still be met by having the requisite additional number receive. . . . A quorum either heard or received argument either by being physically present or by reading the record and transcript." [128]

The decision of an administrative body is not defective if it fails to show on its face that a quorum was present when it was made and that the requisite vote of those present concurred.[129]

[127] WIBC, Inc. v. FCC, 259 F.2d 941 (D.C. Cir.), *cert. denied,* 358 U.S. 920 (1958).

[128] Sisto v. CAB, 179 F.2d 47, 54 (D.C. Cir. 1949).

[129] Olsen Co. v. State Tax Comm'n, 109 Utah 563 (1946).

7

Rights of Public

RIGHT TO ATTEND

§ 7.1   No Common-Law Right To Attend

It has been held that "the public has no common-law right to attend meetings of governmental bodies" and, therefore, any right of the public to attend such meetings must arise by reason of some ordinance or statute.[1] Presumably, there is no legal right of the public to attend the meetings of private deliberative bodies or assemblies unless they are otherwise authorized to be present.[2] Common parliamentary law recognizes the right of an assembly to be secret in its proceedings and debates.[3] There is also an individual and collective inherent right of privacy which the press cannot invade.[4]

The Supreme Court has made it clear that it is impractical in a complex society to give all members of the public an opportunity to

---

[1] Beacon Journal Publ. Co. v. Akron, 3 Ohio St. 2d 191, 209 N.E. 2d 399, 404 (1965).

The right to attend meetings of government bodies did not exist at common law. *See* Miami Beach v. Berns, 245 So. 2d 38 (Fla. 1971).

Members of the public, or of the press, have no right to attend meetings of a borough council. Tenby Corp. v. Meson [1908] 1 Ch. 457, *cited in* Shaw and Smith at 38.

[2] In holding that a pastor had authority to invite strangers out of or into a congregation when assembled for worship, the court said: "We do not doubt that the sovereign authority of a particular congregation, whether board, wardens, bishop, presbytery, ruling elders, council, consistory or the congregation itself, extends to designating the manner in which nonmembers may be admitted into communing or into membership." On remand the court added: "We do not doubt that it would be, in effect, an act of establishing a religion if a given congregation were shorn of the choice to admit or exclude members or worshipers according to the duly expressed will of the group." Johnson v. State, 7 Div. 720, 173 So. 2d 817, 822, 824, *rev'd on other grounds,* 7 Div. 650, 173 So. 2d 824 (Ala. 1964).

The court has no jurisdiction under the Labor–Management Reporting and Disclosure Act (labor "Bill of Rights") over persons attending a union meeting who are not members of the union. Johnson v. Local Union 58, Elec. Wkrs., 181 F. Supp. 734 (E.D. Mich. 1960).

[3] "A legislative assembly has, therefore, all the powers and privileges which are necessary to enable it to exercise in all respects, in a free, intelligent and impartial manner, its appropriate functions. . . . What powers and privileges, therefore, a legislative assembly takes by force and effect of its creation, are to be ascertained by a reference to the common parliamentary law. Those powers and privileges are classified by Cushing (p. 246) as follows: . . .

3. To establish its own rules of proceeding.

4. To have the attendance and service of its own members.

5. To be secret in its proceedings and debates."

Ex parte D. O. McCarthy, 29 Cal. 395, 403–4 (1866).

[4] *See* § 7.14 *infra.*

participate in the deliberations and to be heard at legislative meetings when decisions affecting the public are made. Mr. Justice Holmes observed: "Where a rule of conduct applies to more than a few people, it is impracticable that everyone should have a direct voice in its adoption. The Constitution does not require all public acts to be done in town meeting or an assembly of the whole. General statutes within the state power are passed that affect the person or property of individuals, sometimes to the point of ruin, without giving them a chance to be heard. Their rights are protected in the only way that they can be in a complex society, by their power, immediate or remote, over those who make the rule." [5]

§ 7.2 News Reporters

In an early American case, a reporter was ejected from the floor of a meeting of a board of education when he entered in violation of a previous resolution of the board excluding him from the floor at future meetings by reason of his misconduct at an early meeting. The public gallery remained open to him. In an action for assault and battery brought by the reporter, it was held that his presence on the floor was a privilege, not a right, and that he could not raise parliamentary points of order in his defense. "That under the rules of the board, reporters were privileged to the floor of the chamber, did not take away the power of the board to revoke the rules." [6]

A news reporter has been ejected from a legislative committee room for refusing to leave on demand. The court held that a state legislature or legislative committee has the power to conduct its

[5] Bi-Metallic Inv. Co. v. State Bd. of Equalization, 239 U.S. 441, 445 (1915); *accord,* Aikens v. Abel, 373 F. Supp. 425 (W.D. Pa. 1974).

A presumption of validity attaches to public proceedings and the formal recitations of public officials. Willapoint Oysters v. Ewing, 174 F.2d 676 (9th Cir.), *cert. denied,* 338 U.S. 860 (1949).

[6] The court continued: "It is argued, that by the rules, the privilege could only be withdrawn by suspension of the rules, or by an amendment, that should have been laid over until the next meeting . . . assuming there were such rules, the objection is upon a point of order, which if not taken by a member of the board, could certainly be of no avail to any one else." Corre v. State, 8 Ohio Dec. Reprint 715, 716 (Dist. Ct. 1883).

proceedings according to orderly procedures free from interference by non-members, such as representatives of the press. As broad as freedom of speech and of the press have been developed in American legal and political history, this right and power of a state legislature to protect itself against contemptuous and disorderly conduct on the part of non-members cannot be disputed. While a newspaper has the right in its columns or its editorial pages, and in other appropriate ways, to speak out against legislative practices, a representative of the newspaper has no right to demonstrate the newspaper's opposition to the extent of refusing to leave a meeting room when requested by the chairman of a legislative committee which intends to go into executive session. However, where a state legislature attempts by resolution conditionally to banish all representatives of a named publisher from the legislative floor for the remainder of the session, it may run afoul of freedom of the press as guaranteed by the first amendment.[7] A leading case under the Ohio public meeting statute holds that the freedom of speech and of the press clause of the Constitution does not grant to the press a legal right of entry and access to executive, informal, or private meetings of city commissioners. The Constitution grants the press a freedom, shared by all, but no special or other right to insure its success. The court gave this homely advice: "The right and duty of citizens and of the press to know what they are talking about is controlled by ability, initiative and opportunity, enjoyed by all whether it be Peter Pan, the PTA or the press. Since the public is not permitted to attend executive meetings, the press also is denied that right.

---

[7] Kovach v. Maddox, 238 F. Supp. 835, 840–41 (M.D. Tenn. 1965).

Plaintiff newspaper reporter was excluded from a meeting of the finance committee of the city council and sought an injunction to require that future meetings of the committee be held open to the public. The court held that committee meetings are included in the statutory term "public meetings" but that the finance committee could exclude the press from its executive sessions where it did not take any final actions or make any recommendations. Selkowe v. Bean, 249 A.2d 35 (N.H. 1969).

See SEC v. Wall Street Transcript Corp., 422 F.2d 1371 (2d Cir.), cert. denied, 398 U.S. 958 (1970) (meaning of "press" and "bona fide newspapers)"; Consumers Union of U.S., Inc. v. Periodical Correspondents' Ass'n, 515 F.2d 1341 (D.C. Cir. 1975), cert. denied, 44 L.W. 3398 (Jan. 13, 1976) (bona fide reporters entitled to privilege of accreditation to Congressional galleries).

The constitution does not appoint the fourth estate the spokesmen of the people. The people speak through the elective process and through the individuals it elects to positions it created for that purpose. The press has no right that exceeds that of other citizens. Equal rights is not an idle word." [8]

The common law has been summarized as follows: "At public meetings members of the Press are entitled to be admitted to the same extent as any other member of the public. With regard to other meetings, Press representatives have in general no better right to be admitted than that enjoyed by the public at large. This will normally be a mere right to attend by the permission of those in authority over the meeting." [9] And, of course, there is a clear im-

---

[8] "In this case it is necessary to rely, not upon semantics, but the plain and ordinary meaning of grants to the press and to charter cities and to determine between the two fundamental issues of constitutional power, rights and duties. Does the right of citizens and of the press to freely speak and to freely publish mean more than the state and federal constitutions say? Does the constitutional grant of unlimited local power and the charter grant of unlimited rule making power mean anything less? It requires no mental gymnastics to see that these rights are not antagonistic. The right to freely publish includes no right to freely collect, no right to freely acquire and no right to appropriate information with or without compensation. It includes no right to represent anyone else and no duty of any kind. It does not include the right to enter uninvited onto property or into a gathering of persons. It is equally clear that public officials with sovereign rule making or administrative power may, if not otherwise restrained by law, determine the rules by which they conduct governmental affairs entrusted to them. It is unthinkable that any court could deny to officials the power granted by the people or award to a private citizen or to a private group a right of entry or acquisition not provided in the constitution." Dayton Newspapers, Inc. v. City of Dayton, 23 Ohio Misc. 49, 259 N.E.2d 522, 533 (1970).

[9] Tenby Corp. v. Meson, [1908] 1 Ch. 457 (later modified by statute), *cited in* Shaw and Smith at 38.

·An early decision cited these words: "Then it has been urged upon you that conductors of the public press are entitled to particular indulgence, and have special rights and privileges. The law recognizes no such peculiar rights, privileges, or claims to indulgence. They have no rights but such as are common to all. They have just the same rights that the rest of the community have, and no more. They have the right to publish the truth, but no right to publish falsehoods to the injury of others with impunity." Sheckell v. Jackson, 10 Cush. 25 (Mass. 1852), *quoting from* Bradley v. Heath, 12 Pick. 163 (Mass.).

plication that "a journalist *is* entitled to access to information available to the general public." [10]

The right of the public, including news reporters, to attend meetings of public bodies required by statute to be "open to the public" has been the subject of considerable litigation principally in the distinction between public meetings and executive sessions of public bodies. A California court has strictly construed the statute in holding that it was improper to exclude newspaper reporters from an Elks Club luncheon attended by five county supervisors, the county counsel, the director of welfare, and members of the central labor council to discuss the county's action with respect to a strike. The luncheon was held to be a "meeting" within the statute although the statute was "somewhat ambiguous as it encounters peripheral gatherings or conversations among board members where public business is a topic." [11]

§ 7.2.1   Constitutional Rights

A recent Supreme Court case states: "It has generally been held that the First Amendment does not guarantee the press a constitutional right of special access to information not available to the public generally. . . . Despite the fact that news gathering may be hampered, the press is regularly excluded from grand jury proceedings, our own [Supreme Court] conferences, the meetings of other official bodies gathered in executive session, and the meetings of private organizations." [12] On the other hand, members of the

[10] Lewis v. Baxley, 368 F. Supp. 768, 776 (M.D. Ala. 1973); *accord*, Watson v. Cronin, 384 F. Supp. 652 (D. Colo. 1974).

[11] Sacramento Newspaper Guild v. Sacramento County Bd. of Supervisors, 263 Cal. App. 2d 41, 47, 69 Cal. Rptr. 480 (1968).

[12] Branzburg v. Hayes, 408 U.S. 665, 684 (1972).

Regulations prohibiting interviews between newsmen and prison inmates do not abridge freedom of the press since the regulations do not deny the media access to sources of information available to members of the general public. Saxbe v. The Washington Post Co., 417 U.S. 843 (1974); Pell v. Procunier, 417 U.S. 817 (1974).

The right to speak and publish does not carry with it an unrestricted right to gather information. "For example, the prohibition of unauthorized entry into the White House diminishes the citizen's opportunities to gather informa-

press have a limited constitutional right of reasonable access, and that includes the right to go where the public generally may go. "That right extends also to access to places where other members of the press may go and congregate in the ordinary course of events. In other words, there is a limited First Amendment right of access to the public galleries, the press rooms, and the press conferences dealing with state government. The right is limited, however, to these circumstances." [13]

A public official need not answer questions put to him by the news media. However, news reporters have a limited right to reasonable access to general news conferences on government matters which are held by a public official in a public office. For example, the statements of a mayor concerning municipal operations are "embryonic executive directives" and thus are "public communications" which do not become private when the press meeting is held in the mayor's inner office. "If he chooses to hold a general news conference in his inner office, for that purpose and to that extent his inner office becomes a public gathering place." [14]

---

tion he might find relevant to his opinion of the way the country is being run, but that does not make entry into the White House a First Amendment right." Zemel v. Dean Rusk, 381 U.S. 1, 17 (1965); *accord*, Watson v. Cronin, 384 F. Supp. 652 (D. Colo. 1974); *see* Consumers Union of U. S., Inc. v. Periodical Correspondents' Ass'n, 515 F.2d 1341 (D.C. Cir. 1975), *cert. denied*, 44 L.W. 3398 (Jan. 13, 1976).

See The Rights of the Public and the Press to Gather Information, 87 HARV. L. REV. 1505 (1974); The Supreme Court and the right of free speech and press, 93 L. Ed. 1151, 2 L. Ed. 2d 1706, 11 L. Ed. 2d 1116, 16 L. Ed. 2d 1053, 21 L. Ed. 2d 976.

[13] Lewis v. Baxley, 368 F. Supp. 768, 777 (M.D. Ala. 1973); *accord*, Borreca v. Fasi, 369 F. Supp. 906 (D. Hawaii 1974).

The Constitution grants each House of Congress authority "to extend to those members of the press determined eligible, and otherwise to deny, admission to the floors and galleries of Congress." Thus, refusal of a duly constituted committee and sergeants-at-arms to accredit an applicant for membership to the periodical press galleries was held to be a "nonjusticiable political question" because it involved matters committed by the Constitution to the legislative branch. Consumers Union of U. S., Inc. v. Periodical Correspondents' Ass'n, 515 F.2d 1341, 1343, 1347 (D.C. Cir. 1975), *cert. denied*, 44 L.W. 3398 (Jan. 13, 1976).

[14] Borreca v. Fasi, 369 F. Supp. 906, 910 (D. Hawaii 1974).

§ 7.3   Corporate Meetings

The public does not have a common-law right to attend the meetings of a private corporation. Those who are not shareholders at the time of the meeting have no right to complain about procedural remedies, lack of notice, absence of a quorum, or any action taken by the shareholders not within the purview of the call.[15]

Whether a shareholder has the right to be accompanied at a corporate meeting by someone who is not a shareholder has not been clarified by legal decision. In an unreported case a minority shareholder gave proxies for one share each to his attorney and to a newspaper reporter for the annual meeting of shareholders. To an allegation that such acts were for the purpose of forcing the minority to sell its shares, and thus were in bad faith, the court merely said: "The annual meeting of stockholders is not a secret conclave and the publication of what transpired at such meeting does not constitute bad faith." [16]

It may be assumed that a shareholder would have the privilege by courtesy to bring a member of his family to a meeting of shareholders, especially if that practice had been established by custom or usage.

The presence of unauthorized persons at a corporate meeting will not vitiate the proceedings of the meeting unless it appears that such persons voted, and that their votes were necessary to carry the resolutions which were claimed to be passed.[17]

§ 7.4   Legislative Bodies

A legislative body had the right, in the absence of a controlling statute, to determine whether its proceedings shall be public or private and who shall be admitted to meetings or invited to attend.[18]

[15] Texlite, Inc. v. Wineburgh, 373 S.W.2d 325 (Tex. Civ. App. 1963).

[16] *In re* Scheeler v. Buffalo Wire Works Co., New York Sup. Ct., County of Erie, June 22, 1965.

[17] Madison Ave. Baptist Church v. Baptist Church, 28 N.Y. Super. 649, 650 (1867), *aff'd*, 31 N.Y. Super. 109 (1869), *rev'd on other grounds*, 46 N.Y. 131 (1871).

Strangers may or may not be bound by the by-laws, depending on the circumstances. Pfister v. Gerwig, 122 Ind. 567, 23 N.E. 1041 (1890).

[18] Whether a Congressional committee hearing shall be public or private,

In legislation and rule making, there is no constitutional right to a hearing.[19]

The fact that a meeting is open to the public does not necessarily mean that members of the public may participate in its deliberations or actions. Public meetings and hearings, whether executive, legislative, or judicial, are most often "public" as to physical presence only, but not as to participation.[20] The statutory requirement that a meeting shall be "open to the public" means only that the public may attend and observe the proceedings. It does not entitle any member of the public to participate in the meeting or to be heard unless the body sees fit to invite participation by the public or to conduct a public hearing.[21] A charter provision that the public shall not be excluded from city council meetings does not allow the public to participate in the proceedings except at the pleasure of the council. It follows that in the absence of a duty imposed by law to hear the complaints of all persons who appear, a legislative body in its discretion may refrain from hearing their complaints. That is the "established prerogative of legislative bodies." [22]

---

and who shall be admitted or invited are questions for Congress. United States v. Hintz, 193 F. Supp. 325 (N.D. Ill. 1961).

A Congressional committee has wide discretion in determining whether hearings should be held in public or in executive session. United States v. Grumman, 227 F. Supp. 227 (D.D.C. 1964).

See legislative history of secret sessions and admissions of the press in Consumers Union of U. S., Inc. v. Periodical Correspondents' Ass'n, 515 F.2d 1341 (D.C. Cir. 1975), cert. denied, 44 L.W. 3398 (Jan. 13, 1976).

[19] Superior Oil Co. v. FPC, 322 F.2d 601 (9th Cir. 1963), cert. denied, 377 U.S. 922 (1964).

[20] United States v. Woodard, 376 F.2d 136, 139–40 (7th Cir. 1967) (Congressional committee hearing).

[21] Barnes v. New Haven, 140 Conn. 8, 98 A.2d 523 (1953).

The purpose of public meeting laws is to prohibit secret or "star chamber" sessions of public bodies. Such laws do not require the public body to allow any individuals or group to be heard on the subject being considered. Dobrovolny v. Reinhardt, 173 N.W.2d 837 (Iowa 1970).

But see § 7.8 and § 7.10 infra.

[22] People ex rel. Powott Corp. v. Woodworth, 172 Misc. 791, 15 N.Y.S.2d 985, 995 (Sup. Ct. 1939).

There are exceptions to the general rule. One case has construed a statute permitting a legislative body to lease a municipally owned airport provided

The same rules of civility apply to public courtroom proceedings. "It is essential to the public trial that there be access to spectators, but any particular spectator is quite dispensable, as are all the spectators if disorderly." A court has ruled simply that spectators in a courtroom "are absolutely nonactors with the right only to use their eyes and ears." [23]

§ 7.4.1 Use of Recording Devices

The right of a deliberative body to regulate its own proceedings includes the right to regulate the use of its meeting facilities. "It is essential that a legislative body have the right to regulate its own halls in the same manner as a judge must control the conduct of his courtroom." In a proceeding brought by a member of the public to require a city council to permit the petitioner to make electronic recordings of its deliberations and proceedings, the court held: "The fact that legislative halls or courtrooms are open to the public does not give the public a vested right to televise, photograph or use recording devices. The reasons such places are open to the public is to prevent the possibility of star chamber proceedings. It is unquestioned that people should have the right to see the legislative process in action and there is no denial of that right involved in this proceeding. If in the judgment of the legislative body the recording distracts from the true deliberative process of the body it is within their power to forbid the use of mechanical recording devices." [24] The majority of a board of directors may adopt a by-law

---

the governing body "shall have held a public hearing" on published notice, to mean that "all interested parties attending the hearing be accorded an opportunity to be heard." This is a minority view. Lamb v. Town of East Hampton, 162 N.Y.S.2d 94, 96 (Sup. Ct. 1957).

Another case relating to the Florida sunshine law speaks of the "right of the public to be present and to be heard during all phases" of local legislation and remarks that local boards and commissions should not be allowed to "deprive the public of this inalienable right." Board of Public Instruction v. Doran, 224 So.2d 693, 699 (Fla. 1969).

[23] *In re* Katz v. Murtagh, 28 N.Y.2d 234, 240 (1971).

[24] The petitioner alleged: "It is my contention that, so long as a meeting is public, members of the public must be admitted to see, hear, memorize, take notes of, tape record, wire record or even photograph the proceedings had at such a meeting provided only that the behavior of the members of

prohibiting the recording of its proceedings by anyone other than management, whether by stenographer or mechanical device, when such action is in the best interest of the company, as in the case of minority directors who not only refuse to follow parliamentary procedure but continuously harass the majority and disrupt the chairman.[25]

On the other hand, it has been held that a newspaper reporter may use a portable tape recorder which operates without noise and does not interfere with the proceedings of a city council. The court noted that constitutional provisions protecting a free press and free speech were not involved and that the tape recorder was merely a better method of recording the acts of a public body than pencil and paper.[26]

Another decision held that a television news reporter and his secretary were authorized at any public court hearing where they

---

the public at the size, shape, sound, order, manner of operating or location of any recording equipment used shall not be such as to disturb or interfere with the proper, orderly and peaceful conduct of the business of the meeting." The petitioner also stated that "any attempt by the Common Council to regulate the character of a public meeting by banishing recording devices serves to destroy the public notice of the meeting." Davidson v. Common Council, 40 Misc. 2d 1053, 244 N.Y.S.2d 385, 387–88 (Sup. Ct. 1963); see 39 St. John's L. Rev. 55 (1964).

A state court rule forbidding the taking of photographs in a courtroom or the vicinity of a court does not interfere with the constitutional right of freedom of speech or the press. Tribune Review Publ. Co. v. Thomas, 254 F.2d 883 (3d Cir. 1958).

On televising House Subcommittee hearings, see Hartman v. United States, 290 F.2d 460, 466–67 (9th Cir. 1961), rev'd on other grounds, 370 U.S. 724 (1962).

[25] Selama-Dindings Plantations, Ltd. v. Durham, 216 F. Supp. 104 (S.D. Ohio 1963), aff'd sub nom. Selama-Dindings Plantations, Ltd. v. Cincinnati Union Stock Yard Co., 337 F.2d 949 (6th Cir. 1964).

See In re Election of Dirs. of Bushwick Sav. & Loan Ass'n, 189 Misc. 316, 70 N.Y.S.2d 478 (Sup. Ct. 1947) (secretary to shareholder was present taking minutes of turbulent meeting; police refused to eject secretary when chairman asked her to leave).

[26] The court further said that the council could properly prevent the use of municipal electricity in a recording machine operated by a reporter, and that a rule could be made that a reporter could not occupy any more space than any other citizen. Nevens v. City of Chino, 233 Cal. App. 2d 775, 44 Cal. Rptr. 50 (1965).

were rightfully in attendance to take such notes as they might wish concerning the proceedings in any form selected by them so long as they did not interfere with the orderly conduct of the proceedings.[27]

It has also been held that the presence of microphones, television cameras, and photographers at a Congressional committee hearing does not create such a lack of decorum as to make the committee an incompetent tribunal,[28] and does not infect the proceedings with impropriety.[29] The televising of committee hearings does not invalidate the proceedings or provide a defense for unlawfully refusing to answer questions pertinent to the matter being investigated.[30]

§ 7.5   Decorum

Whether public or private, the meeting should be conducted with decorum. "If each spectator were privileged to shout or even speak at will, pandemonium would likely result. When, as here, activity engaged in by a spectator prevents the orderly continuation of the hearing, it falls within the prohibition of the statute." [31]

It is a general principle that a public building or other assembly facility need not be made available for public gatherings, but if that is done, it must be done in a reasonable and non-discriminatory manner.[32]

§ 7.6   Police Officers

Under English law it is the duty of a public officer to prevent the holding of a meeting should it be reasonably apprehended that a

[27] Wrather-Alvarez Broadcasting Co. v. Hewicker, 147 Cal. App. 2d 509, 305 P.2d 236 (1957).

[28] United States v. Moran, 194 F.2d 623 (2d Cir.), cert. denied, 343 U.S. 965 (1952).

[29] United States v. Hintz, 193 F. Supp. 325 (N.D. Ill. 1961).

[30] Hartman v. United States, 290 F.2d 460 (9th Cir. 1961), rev'd on other grounds, 370 U.S. 724 (1962).

See United States v. Kamin, 136 F. Supp. 791 (D. Mass. 1956) (television coverage of Congressional committee hearing).

[31] United States v. Woodard, 376 F.2d 136, 139–40 (7th Cir. 1967) (Congressional committee hearing), quoted in State v. Moore, 101 N.J. Super. 419, 244 A.2d 522, 525 (1968).

[32] Madole v. Barnes, 20 N.Y.2d 169, 229 N.E.2d 20, 282 N.Y.S.2d 225 (1967).

breach of the peace would occur if the meeting were held.[33] In executing his duty, a police officer is entitled to enter a public meeting convened in a private hall and remain on the premises.[34]

PUBLIC MEETINGS

§ 7.7   Right To Know—Sunshine Laws

It is a general statutory rule that all meetings of local governing bodies (city councils, school boards, public authorities)[1] must be open to the public where any resolution, ordinance, regulation, or other formal action is to be adopted or voted upon.[2] Such requirement did not exist at common law.[3] There is sometimes a further provision that any meeting where action is taken which is required by law, rule, or regulation to be recorded in the minutes or other official journal, is a meeting which must be open to the public.[4] One court has stated flatly: "It is axiomatic that municipal governing bodies may take official action only at public meetings."[5] However, another court has held that the vote of a zoning board was not in-

---

[33] Duncan v. Jones, [1936] 1 K.B. 218.

[34] Thomas v. Sawkins, [1935] 2 K.B. 249.

[1] For the meaning of "governmental bodies" or "governmental boards," see Raton Pub. Serv. Co. v. Hobbes, 76 N.M. 535, 417 P.2d 32 (1966).

[2] Sometimes called the "sunshine law." See, e.g., Shaughnessy v. Metropolitan Dade County, 238 So. 2d 466, 468 (Fla. 1970), citing Robert's Rules of Order on another point.

See Open Meeting Statutes: The Press Fights for the "Right to Know," 75 HARV. L. REV. 1199 (1962); Annot., 38 A.L.R. 3d 1970 (1971).

[3] See § 7.1 supra.

[4] A reporter was denied entrance and attendance at an unscheduled conference among members of a city commission. Beacon Journal Publ. Co. v. Akron, 3 Ohio St. 2d 191, 209 N.E.2d 399 (1965).

[5] Decisions reached by municipal governing bodies at informal meetings are nothing more than gentlemen's agreements about how members will vote at a later public meeting. Brazer v. Borough of Mountainside, 102 N.J. Super. 497, 246 A.2d 170, 173 (1968).

A city housing authority is subject to a "right to know" statute. Bogert v. Allentown Housing Authority, 426 Pa. 151, 231 A.2d 147 (1967).

However, the controlling statute or charter should be examined to determine whether a particular meeting must qualify as a "public meeting." See Beacon Journal Publ. Co. v. Akron, 3 Ohio St. 2d 191, 209 N.E.2d 399 (1965) (consideration of six types of boards, commissions, and committees which serve the city of Akron).

valid because it was taken at a closed meeting which followed deliberations at other closed meetings of which no notice had been given in compliance with an "imprecise" public meeting statute.[6]

The subject of public meetings is enmeshed in definitions of "public meetings" and "all meetings" as used in the relevant statutes.[7] Also, the right of the public to participate in the deliberations of the meeting as well as to attend and listen; the right of members of the body also to meet in executive and secret session or to caucus in private; the right of the body to make decisions in private before voting in public—all are subjects of court decisions which take into consideration statutory interpretations, constitutional rights of freedom of speech and of the press, the constitutional issue of separation of powers, the express and implied common-law power of a legislative body to provide its own rules for the conduct of meet-

[6] The court commented: "It would be arbitrary to let the validity of a meeting, held without public notice and unattended by the public, depend upon whether the meeting was declared 'open.' " Elmer v. Board of Zoning Adjustments, 343 Mass. 24, 176 N.E.2d 16 (1961).

[7] "Interpretation or construction is confined to the plain and ordinary meaning of the language used and the expressed or implied purpose of the document. Neither should be distorted by fancy footwork or additions and subtractions from the intent expressed. Judicial interpretation fails in its purpose when it becomes entangled in wishful or opinionated semantics of flaying opponents. The distinction between a meeting of the commission and a meeting of commissioners or the distinction between a meeting and a gathering serves no purpose." Dayton Newspapers, Inc. v. City of Dayton, 23 Ohio Misc. 49, 259 N.E.2d 522, 532 (1970).

"Attempts to define 'meeting' by synonyms or by coupling it with modifying adjectives involve a degree of question-begging. . . . There is nothing in the Brown Act to demarcate a narrower application than the range of governmental functions performed by the agency. . . . To 'deliberate' is to examine, weigh and reflect upon the reasons for or against the choice." Thus, it is held that deliberative gatherings are "meetings." Sacramento Newspaper Guild v. Sacramento County Bd. of Supervisors, 263 Cal. App. 2d 41, 47, 69 Cal. Rptr. 480 (1968).

A gathering of members and members-elect of a city council may be a "meeting" under the sunshine law. A member-elect loses his status as a private individual and acquires a "position more akin to that of a public trustee." Hough v. Sternbridge, 278 So. 2d 288, 289 (Fla. App. 1973).

The intent of the sunshine law is to cover any "gathering of some of the members of a public board where those members discuss some matters on which foreseeable action will be taken by the board." Canney v. Board of Public Instruction, 278 So. 2d 260, 263 (Fla. 1973).

ings, the right to enter uninvited onto public or private property or into a gathering of persons, and other fundamental issues. The courts have also found it necessary to decide that the characterization of a decision-making process by a school board as "quasi-judicial" does not make the body into a judicial body or authorize the board to avoid the "sunshine law." [8]

Since the purpose of public meetings is to enable the public to attend and keep in touch with the proceedings, it is generally recognized that the public is entitled to have such meetings held at times specified by statute or local ordinance so as to prevent the body from doing business in secret meeting.[9] Statutory requirements that certain meetings be public have been held to be mandatory and not directory.[10]

§ 7.8 Meaning of "Public"

A requirement that proceedings shall be public means "public to the citizenry directly concerned" and without the necessity of their leaving the incorporated limits of the municipality to attend the meeting. Thus, a meeting of a city council held outside the limits of the city is not a "public" meeting, and all action taken at such meeting is void.[11] Whether a meeting held within the city limits, but outside the regular council chambers, qualifies as a public meeting is a question of fact depending on the circumstances in each case as determined by the trial court.[12] An interesting recent case has held that a general news conference conducted by a mayor in his

[8] Canney v. Board of Public Instruction, 278 So. 2d 260, 263 (Fla. 1973).
See Consumers Union of U.S., Inc. v. Periodical Correspondents' Ass'n, 515 F.2d 1341 (D.C. Cir. 1975), cert. denied, 44 L.W. 3398 (Jan. 13, 1976) (early custom of U. S. Senate to convene with closed doors and development of Congressional galleries for news media).

[9] Thus, a regular meeting cannot be adjourned without fixing a day certain for the resumption of business. Green v. Beste, 76 N.W.2d 165 (N.D. 1956).

[10] Town of Paradise Valley v. Acker, 100 Ariz. 62, 411 P.2d 168 (1966).

[11] Town of Paradise Valley v. Acker, 100 Ariz. 62, 411 P. 2d 168, 169 (1966); accord, Quast v. Knutson, 150 N.W.2d 199, 200 (Minn. 1967) (school board meeting held in private office 20 miles distant from school district territorial boundaries).

[12] Property Owners v. City of Anderson, 231 Ind. 78, 107 N.E.2d 3 (1952) (meeting adjourned from council chamber to mayor's office, held to be open to the public).

private inner office is a public and not a private meeting. If the mayor chooses to hold a general news conference in his inner office, for that purpose and to that extent his inner office becomes a "public gathering place." [13]

In deciding whether a meeting is open to the public, the court will consider the setting and the environment. Generally, a meeting open to the public means a meeting "in a public place where members of the public may attend and observe the action taken by those functioning as members of the authority." [14]

In a recent case, a committee of a Florida county commission took a fact-finding trip to Tennessee for the purpose of conducting interviews leading to the recommendation of a firm to reappraise taxable property. The committee selected a firm and then interviewed a representative of the chosen firm at a breakfast meeting in a public inn. While the breakfast meeting was not secret in the sense that it was behind closed doors, neither the press nor the public was apprised that the meeting would take place. The court noted that this meeting was no more public than the interview in Tennessee at which the committee made its selection. "The mere fact that the discussion took place in a public room cannot make it a public meeting for purposes of the Sunshine Law, because the advance notice and the reasonable opportunity to attend did not exist." [15]

On the other hand, another court held that a newspaper reporter could not be excluded from an Elks Club luncheon attended by five county supervisors, the county counsel, the director of welfare, and members of the central labor council because it was a meeting of the "legislative body" required under the statute to be "open and public." [16]

In holding that a meeting conducted in the second-floor bedroom of the home of a mayor (who was seriously ill) was not a public meeting, the court said that "a public meeting presupposes the right of the public freely to attend such meetings with the concurrent right freely to express any aproval or disapproval of any action or

[13] Borreca v. Fasi, 369 F. Supp. 906, 910 (D. Hawaii 1974).

[14] Barnes v. New Haven, 140 Conn. 8, 98 A.2d 523 (1953).

[15] Bigelow v. Howze, 291 So. 2d 645, 647–48 (Fla. App. 1974).

[16] Sacramento Newspaper Guild v. Sacramento County Bd. of Supervisors, 263 Cal. App. 2d 41, 69 Cal. Rptr. 480 (1968).

course about to be taken. Anything which tends to 'cabin, crib or confine' the public in this respect would be destructive" of the rights of the public.[17] On the other hand, a "public meeting" need not be held in a public place, and can be held in the living room of the residence of the chairman which had been designated by resolution of the board as its regular meeting place.[18] Also, in an emergency, the meeting of a town board need not be held at the Town House designated by resolution as the place for board meetings, but may be held at the home of the town supervisor who was incurably ill and could not leave his home.[19]

The distinction between a "public meeting" and a "private meeting" is significant in cases involving the disturbance of a public meeting or assemblage, or the use of a meeting or gathering to make an improper noise or diversion tending to a breach of the peace. Whether a gathering is a public meeting is a question of fact depending on the place and circumstances of each case. It is clear that a private meeting may be held in a public place and a public meeting in a private place; and that a meeting announced to be private may by circumstances become public. The circumstances generally relevant are those found in the notice of time and place, and in the qualifications of any of those who may be admitted.[20]

§ 7.9 Prevailing Rule

Under the prevailing rule, a statute requiring that "all meetings" of a city council "shall be held open to the public" means any "such

[17] Lexington v. Davis, 310 Ky. 751, 221 S.W.2d 659, 661 (1949), *quoted and followed in* Town of Paradise Valley v. Acker, 100 Ariz. 62, 411 P.2d 168, 170 (1966). The court in Lexington also quoted from Springfield v. People's Deposit Bank, 111 Ky. 105, 63 S.W. 271 (1901) (town council met in local saloon where women were prohibited from entering).

A resolution adopted at a meeting of county commissioners held in the chairman's home five miles from the county seat, due to the illness of the chairman, was not effective under a public meeting law providing that official meetings be publicly conducted at a known place in the county seat. Motes v. Putnam County, 143 Fla. 134, 196 So. 465 (1940).

[18] Smith v. Gilbertsville, 309 S.W.2d 162 (Ky. 1958).

[19] Roth v. Loomis, 54 Misc. 2d 39, 281 N.Y.S.2d 158 (Sup. Ct. 1967).

[20] Chicago v. Terminiello, 332 Ill. App. 17, 74 N.E.2d 45 (1947), *rev'd,* 337 U.S. 1 (1949) (meeting in rented private auditorium filled to capacity, with a mob demonstration outside auditorium).

formal assemblages of the council sitting as a joint deliberative body as were required or authorized by law to be held for the transaction of official municipal business." Thus, an executive session not open to the public is not a public meeting within the statute.[21]

Such statutes are said to be "primarily prophylactic" and not necessarily restricted to creation of a remedy for illegalities at particular public meetings from which the public is excluded.[22] They have been called "essential to the democratic process."[23] Public meeting statutes are generally interpreted to mean that the body can meet in executive session or in committee of the whole from which the public is excluded, to consider and discuss any matters, but that whenever effective action[24] is to be taken the meeting must

[21] The finance committee of a city council may properly meet in executive session for the purpose of reviewing the budget and receiving information relating to it, so long as no final action is taken and no recommendations to the city council are formulated or agreed upon. Selkowe v. Bean, 109 N.H. 247, 249 A.2d 35 (1969).

In the absence of evidence that a committee of the whole took any action concerning a proposed zoning ordinance, the enactment of such ordinance by the city council at a regular meeting was not invalid on the ground that the committee meeting was not public. Bigham v. City of Rock Island, 120 Ill. App. 2d 381, 256 N.E.2d 897 (1970).

"It is my view that under parliamentary procedure, all such matters affecting the public interest of the municipality should, by a special order of the city or town council or the board of aldermen, be referred to a special committee of the governing body. This committee could hold executive meetings not open to the public, whereby the interest of the municipality and of the people generally would be promoted." Turk v. Richard, 47 So. 2d 543, 544 (Fla. 1950).

See Adler v. City Council, 184 Cal. App. 2d 763, 7 Cal. Rptr. 805 (1960) (informal meeting of zoning commission to develop facts pertinent to zoning problems); Reilly v. Board of Selectmen, 345 Mass. 363, 187 N.E.2d 838 (1963) (hearings of board were in executive session while vote was taken at public meeting); Stoneman v. Tamworth School Dist., 320 A.2d 657 (N.H. 1974); State ex rel. Humphrey v. Adkins, 18 Ohio App. 2d 101, 247 N.E.2d 330 (1969) (Ohio code recognizes that executive sessions may be held but no action may be taken therein).

[22] Wolf v. Zoning Bd. of Adjustment of Park Ridge, 79 N.J. Super. 546, 553, 192 A.2d 305 (1963).

[23] Carter v. City of Nashua, 308 A.2d 847, 853 (N.H. 1973).

[24] "If they vote on the question, this is an 'act' which must be done publicly." State ex rel. Humphrey v. Adkins, 18 Ohio App. 2d 101, 247 N.E. 2d 330, 333 (1969).

be held in a public place on public notice where members of the public may attend and observe the action taken.[25]

A recent case stated simply: "A public meeting law requires that official business be conducted in public. Such a law is conditioned upon official conduct in the performance of an official act. If the conduct is not official or if no official act is performed, the law has no application."[26]

It is clearly established that any official action or vote taken at a closed meeting will be a nullity.[27] Hence, a perfunctory "rubber stamp" vote of approval at a subsequent public meeting on a verbatim resubmission of findings and conclusions does not operate to

[25] Only such business as involves no formal vote may be transacted at meetings from which the public is excluded. Barnes v. New Haven, 140 Conn. 8, 98 A.2d 523 (1953) (city parking authority).

Statute requiring that "[a]ll meetings of the legislative body of a local agency shall be open and public" was not directed to anything less than a "formal meeting of a city council or one of the city's subordinate agencies." Thus, the statute does not forbid members of a zoning commission from meeting informally to develop facts pertinent to zoning problems. Adler v. City Council, 184 Cal. App. 2d 763, 7 Cal. Rptr. 805, 807, 810 (1960).

Failure to give notice of meetings of a zoning board, "whether characterized as conferences, planning, review or work sessions," which were not decisive of legal issues and at which no final action was taken, did not affect the board's jurisdiction. Carter v. City of Nashua, 308 A.2d 847, 851 (N.H. 1973).

Members of a board of education may hold a closed conference where no official action is taken, and the fact that such conference was held does not render action taken at a subsequent public meeting invalid. Schults v. Board of Educ., 86 N.J. Super. 29, 205 A.2d 762 (1964), aff'd, 55 N.J. 2, 210 A.2d 762 (1965).

[26] Dayton Newspapers, Inc. v. City of Dayton, 23 Ohio Misc. 49, 259 N.E.2d 522, 530 (1970).

[27] All official action by a board of education must be taken at a public meeting, and not at a closed meeting at which only certain members of the public are permitted to attend. The court held irregular a special meeting to which only representative citizens were invited, at which it was unanimously agreed in closed session to call for a new vote on a previously rejected resolution. In re Flinn, 154 N.Y.S.2d 124 (Sup. Ct. 1956).

Fulton v. Board of Appeals, 152 N.Y.S.2d 974 (Sup. Ct. 1956) (official action taken at executive session); Wernert v. McHaffie, 158 N.Y.S.2d 438 (Sup. Ct. 1956) (village board action at closed session); Blum v. Board of Zoning & Appeals, 149 N.Y.S.2d 5 (1956) (vote taken at executive session).

"cure" the defective vote in the earlier executive session. A formal "re-run" does not constitute compliance with the statute.[28]

The unlawful exclusion of a non-member from an executive session or committee of the whole of a city council is actionable where a public meeting law provides that the city council "shall sit with open doors." In an early case, plaintiff was ordered to leave the council chamber, and failing to do so, the city marshal was ordered to eject him. To avoid forcible ejection plaintiff left the chamber and sued for suffering great humiliation, chagrin, and indignity. Judgment for the plaintiff was affirmed on appeal.[29]

Thus, it is generally recognized, in the absence of a statutory prohibition, that an administrative body may meet informally to develop facts pertinent to a problem which will be the subject of a public meeting.[30] After the public meeting has concluded, the body may meet in private to deliberate and reach a decision.[31]

[28] "If this court were to permit the actions of the board to stand, it would be tantamount to an express sanction to circumvent the requirements of [the statute]. Every commission, board and public authority would then be invited to vote in executive session and take the risk that the proceeding would go unchallenged. And if challenged on appeal, the administrative tribunal simply could meet the objection by hastily revoting at a public meeting. Clearly, such a procedure, even if taken in good faith, cannot be condoned." Kramer v. Board of Adjustment, 80 N.J. Super. 454, 194 A.2d 26, 31 (1963).

Where a town council held a public meeting but five councilmen then retired to a room closed to the public and the mayor and clerk did not join them, and thereafter one councilman came back to the council chambers and announced to the audience that the resolution had been tentatively approved, a formal passage of the resolution was merely a "perfunctory re-run" of the action taken by the five councilmen in closed session, and was a violation of the Right to Know Law requiring that the public shall be admitted to any meeting of a public body at which official action is taken. Scott v. Bloomfield, 94 N.J. Super. 592, 229 A.2d 667, 671, aff'd, 98 N.J. Super. 321, 237 A.2d 297 (1967), appeal dismissed, 52 N.J. 473, 246 A.2d 129 (1968).

[29] Acord v. Booth, 33 Utah 279, 93 P. 734, 735 (1908).

[30] Following is a description by one court of informal business: "The evidence is uncontradicted that the commissioners of the City of Dayton transact all official business at regular or specially called sessions as provided by the city charter and by [statute], if the latter is applicable to a charter city. In addition to the regular meetings the commissioners meet at other times to discuss among themselves—and with individuals directly interested—policy matters, agenda for regular meetings, personnel problems, employment of a new manager, prospects of federal assistance and other items which may arise at a regular meeting or are otherwise subject to their supervision and

§ 7.10 Strict Compliance Rule

On the other hand, there are public meeting statutes which have been construed to prohibit the transaction of any business or the conduct of any informal conference or caucus except openly and publicly. An interesting case demonstrating the legislative "muzzle" effect of "government in the sunshine" relates to the Florida law which provides that "all meetings" of a public body "at which official acts are to be taken are declared to be public meetings" and no "formal action shall be considered binding except as taken or made at such meeting." In a leading case, action was brought to enjoin the city, mayor, and city council from holding meetings other than in public and to restrain the city from prosecuting the petitioner for the offense of disorderly conduct for refusing to leave a closed or executive session of the council. The court held that the law did not permit any exceptions for "non-formal meetings" such as secret or executive sessions. On certiorari, the highest court held that when officials meet at a time and place to avoid being seen or heard by the public to transact or agree to transact public business at a future time in a certain manner, they violate the sunshine law regardless of whether the meeting is formal or informal. The court

---

control. Such additional gatherings of the commissioners at which no business is transacted are variously designated and differently conducted. Informal discussions and calendar sessions are open to the public and the press. In addition, discussions are held in private on policy, appointments, personnel, employment and other subjects at which either the commissioners or those with whom they are negotiating object to or do not desire public exposure at a preliminary stage of their conversations or investigations. The term executive meeting is not used. In a parliamentary sense this is precisely the character of the private sessions since both the public and the press are excluded. Similar private sessions are devoted to what may be described as doing their home work, gaining an understanding of problems, and preparing for the presentation and discussion of municipal business at public meetings." Dayton Newspapers, Inc. v. City of Dayton, 23 Ohio Misc. 49, 259 N.E.2d 522, 525 (1970).

[31] The court noted that for the past 14 years the board had "retired after the completion of the hearings, deliberated, reached a decision, recorded the decision and the vote of the members thereon (all of which then became a public record immediately available), and soon after notified the parties in interest by mail." Sullivan v. Northwest Garage & Storage Co., 223 Md. 544, 165 A.2d 881, 884 (1960) (zoning board of appeals).

then attempted to rationalize this legislative muzzle with a rule of reason and reference to the freedoms derived from "our American heritage." [32] Failure of a municipal or legislative body to comply with the open meeting law is not merely a "harmless error." [33] One court extended the public meeting statute to a meeting in closed session of members of a city council with the city attorney to discuss a legal proceeding to which the city was a party.[34] Yet another court modified an injunction to allow a board of supervisors to con-

[32] "The Legislature did not intend to muzzle lawmakers and administrative boards to an unreasonable degree. It would be contrary to reason and violate the right of free speech to construe the law to prohibit any discussion whatever by public officials between meetings. The practice of discussing politics and government is part of our American heritage enjoyed by public officials and private citizens. The evil of closed door operation of government without permitting public scrutiny and participation is what the law seeks to prohibit. If a public official is unable to know whether by any convening of two or more officials he is violating the law, he should leave the meeting forthwith. It is the law's intent that any meeting, relating to any matter on which foreseeable action will be taken, occur openly and publicly. In this area of regulating, the statute may push beyond debatable limits in order to block evasive techniques. An informal conference or caucus of any two or more members permits crystallization of secret decisions to a point just short of ceremonial acceptance." Miami Beach v. Berns, 245 So. 2d 38, 39–41 (Fla. 1971).

Another court concluded: "The members of a public body with rule making power may unveil their minds and expose their personalities if they choose, but they are not compelled to do so by open meeting laws except when they act officially on official business. The free and private exchange of ideas when the group is not formally gathered for the conduct of official business, cannot be controlled by outsiders. The mental gymnastics of each legislator operates in an unpredictable universe of its own, unfettered by law. Such mental operations are not confined to moments when all are assembled on the public stage. Any attempt to control them has no probability of success, constitutes an interference with the power of a separate branch of government and interferes with personal rights of privacy." Dayton Newspapers, Inc. v. City of Dayton, 23 Ohio Misc. 49, 259 N.E.2d 522, 530 (1970).

See Board of Public Instruction v. Doran, 224 So. 2d 693 (Fla. 1969).

[33] Stoneman v. Tamworth School Dist., 320 A.2d 657, 660 (N.H. 1974).

[34] Counsel for the city based his argument entirely on the attorney–client privilege. Laman v. McCord, 245 Ark. 401, 432 S.W.2d 753 (1968).

The effect of an open meeting statute is to waive the privilege of confidentiality existing in the attorney–client relationship on behalf of the board or commission governed by the statute. Times Publ. Co. v. Williams, 222 So. 2d 470 (Fla. 1969).

sult privately with their counsel and other attorneys representing the board, consistent with an evidence code assuring confidential lawyer–client conferences.[35]

The court has held, as would be expected, that a city council cannot escape its duties under a public meeting law by meeting as a committee of the whole, because under parliamentary law and practice a committee of the whole is a committee composed of all its own members.[36] The strict-construction courts have applied these strictures to the activities of a citizens' planning advisory committee, appointed by the town council, with no authority to do more than make recommendations. The court noted that the zoning ordinance recommended by the committee was not conceived at public meetings of the town council or the zoning commission but was the "product of the deliberations and actions" of the advisory committee "acting as the alter ego" of the town council.[37] A later case relating to a citizens' planning commission holds that the sunshine law should be construed so as to "frustrate all evasive devices." [38]

---

[35] Sacramento Newspaper Guild v. Sacramento County Bd. of Supervisors, 263 Cal. App. 2d 41, 69 Cal. Rptr. 480 (1968).

[36] Acord v. Booth, 33 Utah 279, 93 P. 734 (1908), *citing* Cushing, Law & Pr. Leg. Assem., Robert's Rules of Order, and Waples' Handbook Parl. Pr.

[37] "It is axiomatic that public officials cannot do indirectly what they are prevented from doing directly. Those to whom public officials delegate de facto authority to act on their behalf in the formulation, preparation and promulgation of plans *on which foreseeable action will be taken by such public officials* stand in the shoes of such public officials insofar as the application of the Government in the Sunshine Law is concerned. The adoption of a comprehensive zoning plan and ordinance which undoubtedly will dramatically mold the future development of a town is 'governmental action' of the highest magnitude. It would be ludicrous to invalidate the actions of a *public body* which are the result of secret meetings of *that* body or members thereof while at the same time giving approval to actions which result from the secret meetings of *committees designated by such public body*. To recognize this double standard is to defeat 'the right of the public to be present and to be heard during *all phases of enactments*. . . .' " IDS Properties, Inc. v. Town of Palm Beach, 279 So. 2d 353, 356 (Fla. App. 1973).

[38] "The Legislature would have no right to require meetings of civic organizations, unconnected with municipal government, to conform to the government in the sunshine law. However, a subordinate group or committee selected by the governmental authorities should not feel free to meet in

Whether the members of a legislative or administrative body which can take official action only at a meeting open to the public must vote openly, and not by secret ballot, is a question of statutory interpretation. One view is expressed in an opinion holding that the powers of a zoning board "must be exercised in a meeting open to the public at which each board member voting openly announces his vote at the time he gives it for recording by the clerk of the board." [39] Another view holds that a statute requiring meetings of a board of education to be open to the public does not preclude the board from reaching its decision by secret ballot.[40] And, when a statute directs the board to conduct hearings and decide the case within a reasonable time, it is clear that the decision of the board need not be made at the hearing. The court approved a decision after the hearing with a recording of the vote of the members and notification of the parties by mail, saying that it would be "unreasonable to require the calling of a new hearing or meeting . . . to announce a decision reached after private deliberations and irrational

---

private. The preponderant interest of allowing the public to participate in the conception of a proposed zoning ordinance is sufficient to justify the inclusion of this selected subordinate group, within the provisions of the government in the sunshine law. . . . One purpose of the government in the sunshine law was to prevent at nonpublic meetings the crystallization of secret decisions to a point just short of ceremonial acceptance. Rarely could there be any purpose to a nonpublic pre-meeting conference except to conduct some part of the decisional process behind closed doors. The statute should be construed so as to frustrate all evasive devices. This can be accomplished only by embracing the collective inquiry and discussion stages within the terms of the statute, as long as such inquiry and discussion is conducted by any committee or other authority appointed and established by a governmental agency, and relates to any matter on which foreseeable action will be taken. The principle to be followed is very simple: When in doubt, the members of any board, agency, authority or commission should follow the open-meeting policy of the State." Town of Palm Beach v. Gradison, 296 So. 2d 473, 476–77 (Fla. 1974).

[39] Blum v. Board of Zoning & Appeals, 149 N.Y.S.2d 5, 8 (Sup. Ct. 1956).

[40] The court noted that the statute did not prescribe the means by which the decision should be made, but suggested that if the board was required to keep minutes showing the vote of each member, then each member must openly announce his vote. Board of Educ. v. State Bd. of Educ., 79 N.M. 332, 443 P.2d 502 (1968).

to require the Board to convene to announce its decision to an empty room." [41]

In a recent case, students of a state law school brought suit against the dean and faculty seeking a judgment declaring that the Open Public Meetings Act was applicable to law faculty meetings. The court held that such Act applied to the law school faculty and required that students and the public in general be admitted to all official faculty meetings. The court noted that the faculty had been delegated extensive quasi-legislative authority by the university president, and was a "governing body" of a "public agency" as those phrases were used in the Act, despite the faculty's contention that its every act was subject to review by the university's president and board of regents. [42]

It has even been suggested that the public may have the right to participate in meetings required to be held open to the public. In a leading Florida case the court remarked: "The right of the public to be present and to be heard during all phases of enactments by boards and commissions is a source of strength in our country. During past years tendencies toward secrecy in public affairs have been the subject of extensive criticism. Terms such as managed news, secret meetings, closed records, executive sessions, and study sessions have become synonymous with 'hanky panky' in the minds of public-spirited citizens. One purpose of the Sunshine Law was to maintain the faith of the public in governmental agencies. Regardless of their good intentions, these specified boards and commissions, through devious ways, should not be allowed to deprive the public of this inalienable right to be present and to be heard at all deliberations wherein decisions affecting the public are being made." [43]

§ 7.11   "Sunburn"

However, even where the sunshine law is interpreted to require strict compliances, the court will find a way to permit secret sessions

[41] Sullivan v. Northwest Garage & Storage Co., 223 Md. 544, 165 A.2d 881, 883–84 (1960).

[42] Cathcart v. Andersen, 530 P.2d 313, 316 (Wash. 1975).

[43] Board of Public Instruction v. Doran, 224 So. 2d 693, 699 (Fla. 1969). The reference to a right of the public "to be heard" at a public meeting is contrary to prevailing law.

See § 7.8 *supra*.

when it is obvious that meaningful discussions would be impossible if the meeting was open to the public. For example, a school board may instruct and consult with its own labor negotiators in private session without being in violation of the sunshine law where the state constitution has guaranteed collective bargaining for employees. The court noted that such "intensity" of the "sunrays" under the sunshine law "could cause a damaging case of sunburn" to their employees and quite possibly would conflict with the "protective umbrella" of the constitutional guarantee. The court concluded that: "The 'sunshine' of the statute is still afforded in the debate and adoption of the ultimate employment contract at a public meeting but with the constitutional polaroid filter from the damaging 'ultra violet rays' of preliminary skirmishing." [44]

§ 7.12 Mass Meetings

A mass meeting is a public meeting called by the promoters or conveners of the meeting for some specific purpose. The call may specify the class of persons invited to attend, and admission may be denied to all others. If a vote is taken, all qualified persons attending may vote.

A mass meeting has no permanent organization, charter, or by-laws. Common parliamentary law applies to its rules of procedure, unless the promoters or the assembly adopt other rules of order in the call or at the opening of the meeting.[45]

A mass meeting is a form of public meeting. Its rights and procedures are founded on custom and practice, there being no codified law regarding such meetings.[46]

EXECUTIVE SESSIONS

§ 7.13 Definition

An assembly, or a committee of an assembly, may meet and act in executive or secret session. The expressions "executive session"

[44] Bassett v. Braddock, 262 So. 2d 425, 426 (Fla. 1972).

[45] ROBERT, PARLIAMENTARY LAW at 363, 571.

[46] *See* SHACKLETON, LAW AND PRACTICE OF MEETINGS at 1, 6, 10–11, 17–18, 75 (4th ed. 1958).

and "secret session," as applied to meetings of a body, are synonymous.[1] They have been adopted in parliamentary usage to signify
meetings from which the public has been excluded as distinguished
from meetings which are open to the public. "An executive session
is one from which the public is excluded and at which only such
selected persons as the board may invite are permitted to be present."[2] The test of an executive session is not whether all those
present are members or invited persons, but whether the meeting
was in fact open to the public. "If the meeting is open to the public
but no one chooses to attend it, except the members of the govern-

[1] The term "executive session" was derived from the custom of the United
States Senate to consider Presidential matters and executive business in secret
session.

The executive business of the Senate is handled separately from its legislative business, and the rules for the consideration of executive business are different and distinct from the rules for the consideration and disposition of legislative business. *See* Senate Procedure, Precedents and Practice, Executive
Business and Executive Sessions, Rule XXXVI at 475 (1974); Senate Manual
containing Standing Rules, Orders, Laws, and Resolutions Affecting the Business of the United States Senate, Rules XXXVI–XXXVIII, §§ 36–38, at 58–62
(Senate Doc. No. 94–1, 1975).

The Rules of the House of Representatives provide as follows: "Each meeting for the transaction of business, including the markup of legislation, of each
standing committee or subcommittee thereof shall be open to the public except
when the committee or subcommittee, in open session and with a quorum
present, determines by roll call vote that all or part of the remainder of the
meeting on that day shall be closed to the public. . . ." U. S. Constitution,
Jefferson's Manual, and Rules of the House of Representatives, Rule XI(g)(1),
§ 708 at 421 (H.R. Doc. No. 416, 1975).

The word "session" as used in "executive session" must not be confused with
the word "session" as distinguished from the word "meeting." *See* Toffolon v.
Zoning Bd. of Appeals, 236 A.2d 96, 99–100 (Conn. 1967).

In discussing the right of the press to attend executive sessions of city commissioners, a court said: "The term executive meeting is not used. In a parliamentary sense this is precisely the character of the private sessions since both
the public and the press are excluded." Dayton Newspapers, Inc. v. City of
Dayton, 23 Ohio Misc. 49, 259 N.E.2d 522, 525 (1970).

See § 7.7 *supra.*

[2] Blum v. Board of Zoning and Appeals, 1 Misc. 2d 668, 671, 149 N.Y.S.2d
5, 8 (Sup. Ct. 1956), *quoted in* Thomas v. Board of Trustees, 5 Ohio App. 2d
265, 215 N.E.2d 434, 436 (1966).

See, e.g., Selkowe v. Bean, 249 A.2d 35 (N.H. 1969); Beacon Journal Publ.
Co. v. Akron, 3 Ohio St. 2d 191, 209 N.E.2d 399 (1965).

mental body, the meeting is not legally an executive session of such body." [3]

§ 7.14 Inherent Rights

The power to hold executive or secret sessions is inherent in a legislative assembly and other deliberative bodies.[4] The Supreme Court recognizes that "the press is regularly excluded from . . . the meetings of other official bodies gathered in executive session, and the meetings of private organizations." [5] This doctrine is founded on common parliamentary law which recognizes the express and implied power and privilege of a legislative assembly to be secret in its proceedings and debates.[6] As one court indicated: "A governmental body that has complete rule making power has the inherent parliamentary or sovereign right to hold executive sessions. Nothing in the charter of the City of Dayton destroys that right." [7] There is also an individual and collective right of privacy which the press cannot invade. "Those who wish to consult or meet in private for

[3] Thomas v. Board of Trustees, 5 Ohio App. 2d 265, 215 N.E.2d 434, 436 (1966).

[4] A Congressional committee has wide discretion in determining whether hearings before a subcommittee should be held in public or in executive session. United States v. Grumman, 227 F. Supp. 227 (D.D.C. 1964); accord, United States v. Hintz, 193 F. Supp. 325 (D.C. Ill. 1961); see United States v. Kamin, 136 F. Supp. 791 (D.C. Mass. 1956).

For rights of a witness before a Congressional committee to request a hearing in executive session, under the rules of the committee, see Yellin v. United States, 374 U.S. 109 (1963).

[5] Branzburg v. Hayes, 408 U.S. 665, 684 (1972); accord, Lewis v. Baxley, 368 F. Supp. 768, 776 (M.D. Ala. 1973).

[6] Ex parte McCarthy, 29 Cal. Rep. 395, 403–4 (1866).

See Consumers Union of U. S., Inc. v. Periodical Correspondents' Ass'n, 515 F.2d 1341 (D.C. Cir. 1975), cert. denied, 44 L.W. 3398 (Jan. 13, 1976) (early custom of U. S. Senate to convene with closed doors and development of Congressional galleries for news media); Housh v. Peth, 165 Ohio St. 35, 133 N.E.2d 340 (1965) (history and meaning of "right of privacy" in the United States).

[7] Dayton Newspapers, Inc. v. City of Dayton, 23 Ohio Misc. 49, 259 N.E.2d 522, 529 (1970). The court added: "The right of privacy applies to individuals, corporations, associations, institutions and to public officials. The right responded slowly to modern developments but it is firmly established." Id. at 534.

the day-to-day conduct of public or business affairs may, in further-ance of their own common right to privacy, exclude the media." [8]

There was no common-law right of the public to attend meetings of governmental bodies.[9] The common law has been amended by public meeting laws, sometimes called "sunshine laws" or "right to know" statutes, which generally require that certain meetings of public bodies and other "public proceedings" be open to the public.[10]

§ 7.15   Appropriate Subjects for Private Discussion

Although executive sessions have been banned by the statutes of some states, the courts continue to recognize that there are certain matters which are commonly regarded as "appropriate subjects for consideration behind closed doors." [11] One court has noted that "the public interest, not only frequently but time and time again, is adversely affected by deliberations and discussions of governing municipal bodies open to the public. It is my view that under par-liamentary procedure, all such matters affecting the public interest of the municipality should . . . be referred to a special committee of the governing body. This Committee could hold executive meet-ings not open to the public, whereby the interest of the municipal-ity and of the people generally would be promoted." [12] A recent court decision explains the need for privacy and executive sessions: "A great portion of governmental operation cannot possibly be con-ducted in a public environment. The public interest in the opera-tion of government recognizes the policy of protecting public of-ficials, employees and even public buildings exclusively for the pur-pose of which they are dedicated." [13]

A state legislative committee has the power to hold secret or

---

[8] The court also noted: "An individual may refuse to be interviewed." Washington Post Co. v. Kleindienst, 357 F. Supp. 770, 772, aff'd after remand, 357 F. Supp. 779 (D.D.C. 1972), aff'd, 494 F.2d 994 (D.C. Cir.), rev'd and remanded, Saxbe v. Washington Post Co., 417 U.S. 843 (1974).

[9] See § 7.1 supra.

[10] See § 7.7 supra.

[11] Selkowe v. Bean, 249 A.2d 35, 36 (N.H. 1969).

[12] Turk v. Richard, 47 So. 2d 543, 544 (Fla. 1950) (Chapman, J., concur-ring).

[13] Dayton Newspapers, Inc. v. City of Dayton, 23 Ohio Misc. 49, 259 N.E.2d 522, 528 (1970).

executive sessions and, through its sergeant-at-arms, to exclude from the meeting room all non-members including all reporters and newspaper representatives. This has been held to be an acceptable and clearly valid method of enforcing the rules of the legislature adopted to secure orderly procedures free from the interference of strangers.[14] The court has described the "right to know" statutes and ordinances as a "rationalization developed by the fourth estate to gain rights not shared by others." [15] In fact, failure to exclude non-members from an executive session, other than attorneys for the board, may "exceed the scope of permissible deliberations at an executive session" and constitute improper conduct even if such action is not prohibited by statute.[16]

[14] Kovach v. Maddux, 238 F. Supp. 835 (M.D. Tenn. 1965).

See Selkowe v. Bean, 249 A.2d 35 (N.H. 1969); Beacon Journal Publ. Co. v. Akron, 3 Ohio St. 2d 191, 209 N.E.2d 399 (1965).

[15] "The constitution grants the press a freedom, shared by all, but no special or other right to insure its success. Every individual or group enjoys the same freedom through speech and print and through the press, radio or television. Assistance to the press could in certain circumstances be used as a practical way to infringe upon its freedom. The so-called 'right of the public to know' is a rationalization developed by the fourth estate to gain rights not shared by others and to usurp an ultra-legal and self appointed representative position on behalf of the people from which to assert incidents of sovereign power to improve its private ability to acquire information which is a raw asset of its business. The right and duty of citizens and of the press to know what they are talking about is controlled by ability, initiative and opportunity, enjoyed by all whether it be Peter Pan, the PTA or the press. Since the public is not permitted to attend executive meetings, the press also is denied that right. The constitution does not appoint the fourth estate the spokesmen of the people. The people speak through the elective process and through the individuals it elects to positions it created for that purpose. The press has no right that exceeds that of other citizens. Equal rights is not an idle word." Dayton Newspapers, Inc. v. City of Dayton, 23 Ohio Misc. 49, 259 N.E.2d 522, 533 (1970).

As to the rights of news reporters, the court added: "In the present situation, if one reporter has a legal right to enter and to join in executive, informal or private gatherings of officials or judges so have the members of all the media, others in publishing ventures and the public. The massive and sometimes dangerous congregation of competitive media with their heavy equipment and the boisterous crowds attracted to them could destroy or bring to a stop the governmental operation of the people and their chosen representatives." Id. at 537.

[16] State ex rel. Cities Service Oil Co. v. Board of Appeals, 21 Wis. 2d 516, 124 N.W.2d 809, 821 (1963).

§ 7.16 Prevailing Rule

Although the controlling statute may require that all meetings of a legislative or deliberative body, such as a municipal zoning board acting in a quasi-judicial capacity, must be open to the public, the weight of authority permits the board to go into closed executive session for the purpose of considering their decision,[17] There has been some question as to whether a board can vote in private, or whether it must schedule another public meeting for that purpose. There is authority allowing a vote in private. "It seems to us that voting is an integral part of deliberating and merely formalizes the result reached in the deliberating process."[18] Under a statute providing that all meetings of the body "must be open to the public," only action taken by the body when convened in a meeting open to the public attains the stature of an official determination. "Action taken by the Board while in executive session with the public excluded is illegal and void. To be effective, the powers of the [board] . . . must be exercised in a meeting open to the public at which each board member voting openly announces his vote at the time he gives it for recording by the clerk of the board."[19] Another decision holds that action taken by a municipal board in

[17] See § 7.9 supra.

[18] State ex rel. Cities Service Oil Co. v. Board of Appeals, 21 Wis. 2d 516, 124 N.W.2d 809, 821 (1963).

[19] Blum v. Board of Zoning and Appeals, 1 Misc. 2d 668, 671, 149 N.Y.S.2d, 5, 8 (Sup. Ct. 1956). The court referred to a decision of the Commissioner of Education that a board of education, although expressly authorized by statute to hold executive sessions, must take all action in a general session open to the public and that such action must be recorded in the minutes of the board. Matter of Kramer, 72 N.Y. St. Dept. Rep. 114; accord, In re Flinn, 154 N.Y. S.2d 124 (Sup. Ct. 1956); Fulton v. Board of Appeals, 152 N.Y.S.2d 974 (Sup. Ct. 1956).

It is contrary to statute for a board of education to adopt at a closed session a resolution to call a special meeting to vote on a school budget. However, the question was moot as the meeting had been held and the budget adopted. Kursch v. Board of Educ., 7 App. Div. 2d 922, 183 N.Y.S.2d 689 (2d Dep't 1959).

Under a "right to know" statute which authorized executive sessions of city council committees, if decisions made during such sessions are recorded and available for public inspection promptly, and if no official actions are finally approved, the council finance committee could meet in executive session so long as no final action was taken by the committee and no recommendation to

executive session was not invalid where the final vote was taken at a public meeting.[20]

§ 7.17 Caucus or Gathering

There is a difference between a formal meeting and a "caucus." The latter is described as an informal meeting to which the public is not admitted and of which no public record is made. Decisions reached at a caucus are held to be nothing more than "gentlemen's agreements" about how members will vote at a later public meeting.[21] Obviously, informal and unrecorded actions or expressions of views by members at a private meeting or an executive session have no legal effect,[22] and the fact that a matter was previously discussed at a private meeting does not invalidate subsequent actions taken at a public meeting.[23]

FREEDOM OF SPEECH AND ASSEMBLY, AND FREEDOM OF PRESS

§ 7.18 Freedom Presupposes Civility

Disturbance of a lawful meeting cannot be excused or justified on the grounds of free speech, free expression of religious, political, or social opinion, or the right of people peacefully to assemble.[1] Freedom presupposes civility and good behavior.

---

the city council was formulated or agreed upon. Selkowe v. Bean, 249 A.2d 35 (N.H. 1969). *See* Barnes v. New Haven, 140 Conn. 8, 98 A.2d 523 (1953).

[20] Reilly v. Board of Selectmen, 345 Mass. 363, 187 N.E.2d 838 (1963).

A vote taken at a closed executive session of a zoning board, which was immediately announced to members of the public who had gathered at city hall, was allowed to stand on a finding by the court that violation of the "right to know" law did not adversely affect the rights of the plaintiffs or of other citizens. Carter v. City of Nashua, 308 A.2d 847 (N.H. 1973).

[21] Brazer v. Borough of Mountainside, 102 N.J. Super. 497, 246 A.2d 170 (1968).

[22] 121–129 Broadway Realty, Inc. v. City of Schenectady, 23 App. Div. 2d 710, 257 N.Y.S.2d 226 (3d Dep't 1965).

[23] *In re* Housing Authority of Seattle, 62 Wash. 2d 492, 383 P.2d 295 (1963).

[1] "The principle of the freedom of press may be invoked by anyone in the country; it is not necessary that such person be an active newspaper reporter." Nevens v. City of Chino, 233 Cal. App. 2d 775, 777, 44 Cal. Rptr. 50 (1965).

Generally, *see* Annot., 93 L. Ed. 1151 (1950); 2 L. Ed. 2d 1706 (1958);

In considering the right of an assembly to regulate the conduct of business at its meetings to assure orderly procedures, and the concomitant right of the members to free speech and assembly, certain basic principles of orderly society clearly emerge. "The rights of free speech and assembly, while fundamental in our democratic society, still do not mean that everyone with opinions or beliefs to express may address a group at any public place and at any time. The constitutional guarantee of liberty implies the existence of an organized society maintaining public order without which liberty itself would be lost in the excesses of anarchy."[2] Thus spoke the Supreme Court in ruling on the right of certain individuals to assemble and speak at a public place in violation of local law.

§ 7.19　Freedom To Listen

A magistrate's court has expressed the concomitant view that those present at a lawful meeting have a right to listen. "The defendant had as absolute a right to listen to the speaker as had the speaker to speak, so long as he did not disturb the meeting or commit an act of disorderly conduct."[3]

A recent case involving the disturbance of a congregation which engaged in divine service expressed this basic principle in these words. "The constitutional right of *one* to freedom of speech is

---

11 L. Ed. 2d 1118 (1964); 16 L. Ed. 2d 1053 (1967). *See also* Note, *Regulation of Demonstrations*, 80 HARV. L. REV. 1773 (1967).

[2] Cox v. Louisiana, 379 U.S. 536, 554 (1965); *quoted* in United States v. Woodard, 376 F.2d 136, 142 (7th Cir. 1967); Zwicker v. Boll, 270 F. Supp. 131, 136 (W.D. Wis. 1967), *aff'd*, 391 U.S. 353 (1968) (*per curiam*).

The rights of freedom of speech and assembly are available to teachers and students within the schoolhouse as well as outside. Such freedoms do not end at the schoolhouse gate. A teacher's conduct resulted in a disturbance and interference with the quiet and good order of a school assembly, when he spoke several words and made a motioning gesture while walking to the rear and leaving an auditorium with several students following him out. State v. Besson, 110 N.J. Super. 528, 266 A.2d 175 (1970).

[3] People v. Rothenberg, 15 N.Y.S.2d 447, 448–49 (Magistrate's Ct. 1939).

Freedom of speech differs from freedom to remain silent; the latter is a freedom of privacy which is governed by different considerations. *See* Barsky v. United States, 167 F.2d 241, 249 (D.C. Cir. 1947), *cert. denied*, 334 U.S. 843 (1948).

counterbalanced by the right of the *many* to their constitutional freedom in the practice of their religion. Neither occupies a preferred position in the Constitution." [4]

The same doctrine applies to church services which are conducted in such a manner as to be a public nuisance. The abatement of such nuisance does not engender "prohibiting the free exercise of religious worship" in any constitutional sense.[5]

The Constitution affords some measure of protection to the free expression of all those present at a meeting—speakers, officials, and audience. "Nonetheless, the state retains a legitimate concern in ensuring that some individuals' unruly assertion of their rights of free expression does not imperil other citizens' rights of free association and discussion. . . . Freedom of everyone to talk at once can destroy the right of anyone effectively to talk at all. Free expression can expire as tragically in the tumult of license as in the silence of censorship." [6] The Supreme Court has stated flatly: "The hours and place of public discussion can be controlled." [7]

§ 7.20 Constitutional Rights Are Not Absolute

Thus, "Allowing the broadest scope to the language and purpose of the Fourteenth Amendment, it is well understood that the right

[4] Jones v. State, 219 Ga. 848, 136 S.E.2d 358, 363–64, *cert. denied,* 379 U.S. 935 (1964).

The defendants persisted in "applauding, yelling, standing on their seats, and making arm and finger gestures" in violation of the rights of other persons legally assembled. The court mused: "However extensive may be the right of a man, 'to step to the music which he hears.' . . . [t]here exists no co-extensive right to disturb, by beating his drum in his companions' ears." State v. Davis, 21 Ohio App. 2d 261, 257 N.E.2d 79, 86 (1969) (university commencement address in stadium).

[5] "It is not a question here of prohibiting the free exercise of religious worship in any constitutional sense. It is a question of peace and public order in a thickly populated community. The plaintiffs are entitled to maintain and practice any religious belief or religious principle, or teach any religious doctrine, which does not violate the laws of morality and property, and which does not infringe upon personal rights." Morison v. Rawlinson, 193 S.C. 25, 7 S.E.2d 635, 640 (1940).

[6] *In re* Kay, 83 Cal. Rptr. 686, 464 P.2d 142, 149 (1970) (public gathering).

[7] Saia v. New York, 334 U.S. 558, 562 (1948).

of free speech is not absolute at all times and under all circumstances." [8] Mr. Justice Holmes stated the basic principle in simple

[8] Chaplinsky v. New Hampshire, 315 U.S. 568, 571 (1942).

"No one would have the hardihood to suggest that the principle of freedom of speech sanctions incitement to riot. . . ." Cantwell v. Connecticut, 310 U.S. 296, 308 (1940).

First amendment rights are not absolute at all times and under all circumstances. "The first amendment does not guarantee the right of a spectator to shout during a legislative hearing or to disrupt the orderly processes of the proceeding. Also conceding that the defendant Woodard may have considered himself justified in attempting to regain admittance to the hearing room, it cannot be said that Woodard's action in resisting the lawful orders of the deputy marshals by falling on the floor so as to create a disturbance is entitled to the protection of the first amendment." United States v. Woodard, 376 F.2d 136, 142 (7th Cir. 1967).

Rights guaranteed by the first amendment are not absolute at all times and under all circumstances. Application for injunctive relief against deprivation of federal constitutional rights was denied to persons accused of disorderly conduct in disrupting interviews and classes in university buildings; Zwicker v. Boll, 270 F. Supp. 131, 136 (W.D. Wis. 1967), aff'd, 391 U.S. 353 (1968) (per curiam).

"A person's constitutional rights to freedom of speech and to freedom of assembly are qualified rights." United States v. Sroka, 307 F. Supp. 400, 402 (E.D. Wis. 1969).

First amendment freedoms must be gauged in the context in which they are asserted. They are not absolute and cannot be fully exercised at every place and at every occasion. The fact that a disturber disagrees with the particular activity then being conducted (government business) cannot serve to enlarge the rights he asserts. United States v. Akison, 290 F. Supp. 212 (D. Colo. 1968).

"It has always been recognized that there is no absolute right to exercise the First Amendment at any time and any place and that reasonable regulations, narrowly drawn, are necessary to permit the maintenance of order without which meaningful expression cannot flourish." Washington Activity Group v. White, 342 F. Supp. 847, 853 (D.D.C. 1971), aff'd, 479 F.2d 922 (D.C. Cir. 1973).

"Constitutionally protected rights, such as freedom of speech and peaceable assembly, are not the be all and end all. They are not an absolute touchstone. The United States Constitution is not unmindful of other equally important interests such as public order. To recognize the rights of freedom of speech and peaceable assembly as absolutes would be to recognize the rule of force; the rights of other individuals and of the public would vanish." State v. Zwicker, 41 Wis. 2d 497, 164 N.W.2d 512, 518 (1969).

"They do have a right to petition, but that right is not absolute. There is a

words: "The character of every act depends upon the circumstances in which it is done. . . . The most stringent protection of free speech would not protect a man in falsely shouting fire in a theatre, and causing a panic."[9] Lawlessness may not pass "in the garb of a constitutional guarantee"[10] and "obscenity is not protected by the First Amendment."[11]

The constitutional right to petition government and be heard is not absolute and is subject to reasonable regulation. Disturbance

---

time and place for everything." State v. McNair, 178 Neb. 763, 135 N.W.2d 463, 466 (1965).

Freedom of speech and protest is a fundamental right, but not an absolute freedom. A state may impose reasonable restraints of time and place upon the exercise of both speech and movement. State v. Wiggins, 272 N.C. 147, 158 S.E.2d 37 (1967), cert. denied, Wiggins v. North Carolina, 390 U.S. 1028 (1968).

There are places and times at which speeches and demonstrations may be prohibited. A legislative chamber is such a place and the duration of legislative proceedings is such a time. Groppi v. Froehlich, 311 F. Supp. 765, 770 (W.D. Wis. 1970).

"The right of peaceful protest does not mean that anyone wishing to express an opinion or belief may do so at *any* time or at *any* place." United States v. Cassiagnol, 420 F.2d 868, 875 (4th Cir.), cert. denied, 397 U.S. 1044 (1970).

A teacher made a speech at an orientation meeting by invitation of the district administration. She took occasion to speak against the school administration in general and against the superintendent of schools in particular. As a consequence she was dismissed. The dismissal was upheld. "Free speech and collective bargaining rights do not endow a teacher, as a school district employee, with a license to vilify superiors publicly. The employer–employee relationship restrains the right of the employee to the extent reasonably necessary to retain that harmony and loyalty which is necessary to the efficient and successful operation of the educational system. . . . An aggressive, contentious and, perhaps, controversial teacher working within the structure of a school district as a faculty member and/or as an education association representative may confidently look to the First Amendment as a protective shield for his or her activities; however, an intemperate, venomous employee, be he or she a teacher or otherwise, cannot claim constitutional protection when he or she attacks his or her superiors in public in brawling terms for no purpose discernible other than to satisfy some personal need." Pietrunti v. Board of Educ., 128 N.J. Super. 149, 319 A.2d 262, cert. denied, 42 L. Ed. 2d 654 (1974).

See Terminiello v. Chicago, 337 U.S. 1(1948), *rehearing denied*, 337 U.S. 934 (1949) (speech in full auditorium, stirring public anger).

[9] Schenck v. United States, 249 U.S. 47, 52 (1919).

[10] State v. Besson, 110 N.J. Super. 528, 266 A.2d 175 (1970).

[11] State v. Morgulis, 110 N.J. Super. 454, 266 A.2d 136, 140 (1970).

of a city council meeting by singing and marching to induce the council to favor a proposed ordinance is not "petitioning" within the First Amendment of the Constitution granting the right to petition the government for a redress of grievances.[12]

A demand to be heard on a day certain may be denied, although a demand to be heard at some convenient date may be the subject of mandamus. In an action by an individual petitioner seeking a court order to compel a city council to place his petition on its calendar for consideration and public hearing on a day certain, the petitioner contended that his "constitutional right to petition government has been abridged" by the refusal of the board to calendar and consider his petition. The court noted that petitioner had demanded a day certain and held that he had no constitutional or other right to compel the board to calendar and consider his petition and communication on the specific day he requested.[13] Fur-

---

[12] "Appellants' rights must be considered in conjunction with the rights of their neighbors. If we are to have a government of law and not of men, no one has a right to disrupt orderly proceedings because he cannot have his way. The laws apply to the appellants as well as to their neighbors. If their consciences and training in moral behavior do not make them realize the merits of their goal does not give them the right to take the law into their own hands, then they need retraining because their actions will in the long run imperil the very freedom they seek. If everyone who wanted to coerce the city council could disrupt the council proceedings whenever, to accomplish their purpose, they felt moved to do so, the business of the city would stagnate. The council would become a mere rubber stamp for the mob. Our constitutional safeguards are intended to protect against the very thing appellants attempt to do." State v. McNair, 176 Neb. 763, 135 N.W.2d 463, 466 (1965). "They cannot hide behind a patriotic song or a hymn, religious or otherwise, to take the law into their own hands to achieve their ultimate objective, regardless of the merits of that objective. If the law should wink at their conduct or hold that any right they might have must be preferred over the rights of their neighbors, we have no law. We have abdicated to the whim and caprice of the irresponsible enthusiasts. They virtually are elevated above the law. To do so is to take a step backward in the march of freedom, to return to anarchy or tyranny. This cannot be if we expect to preserve our individual freedoms. To depart from the rule of law is to return to the law of the jungle." Id. at 467.

[13] The court did not pass on the question whether a refusal to be heard on any date would be actionable, holding that in the absence of charter language making it mandatory to place petitions on the calendar at requested dates, it is discretionary with the board when to hear petitions and communications. Ungar v. Wagner, 20 Misc. 2d 403, 195 N.Y.S.2d 2, 4–5 (Sup. Ct. 1959).

thermore, a charter provision that the public shall not be excluded from council meetings does not allow the public to participate in the proceedings except at the pleasure of the council. "[O]therwise, any organized group could disrupt the orderly proceedings of representative government by monopolizing them to the exclusion of the elected representatives of the people." [14]

§ 7.21   Disturbance of Meetings

The courts have long held that the Bill of Rights cannot be relied upon to justify the disturbance of a meeting in violation of common-law or statutory prohibition. To a contention that the "constitutional rights" of a group of disturbers at a religious meeting had been violated because they were restrained at a meeting conducted in a publicly owned facility, the Court ruled: "The mere fact that they had a constitutional right to be present, if such be a fact, would not grant to them any immunity from the violation of a criminal statute." [15]

In upholding a verdict that defendant had disturbed a religious meeting, an early court decision held: "The guaranty of the Constitution of the United States of the free exercise of religious opinion, and the rights of the people peaceably to assemble and petition for a redress of grievances, would be but an idle mockery if meetings convened for such purposes can be invaded and disturbed with

[14] People ex rel. Powott Corp. v. Woodworth, 172 Misc. 791, 15 N.Y.S.2d 985, 995 (Sup. Ct. 1939), rev'd on other grounds, 260 App. Div. 168, 21 N.Y.S.2d 785 (4th Dep't 1940).

[15] Ford v. State, 210 Tenn. 114, 356 S.W.2d 726, 727, aff'g 210 Tenn. 105, 355 S.W.2d 102 (1962), cert. denied, Ford v. Tennessee, 377 U.S. 994, rehearing denied, 379 U.S. 870 (1964).

A disorderly conduct conviction does not violate the constitutional right of free speech. State v. Zwicker, 41 Wis. 2d 497, 164 N.W.2d 512 (1969).

The fourteenth amendment "does not imply that persons wishing to exercise the right to express their views may comport themselves in a manner which will constitute disorderly conduct as defined in penal statutes." People v. Martin, 43 Misc. 2d 355, 251 N.Y.S.2d 66, aff'd, 15 N.Y.2d 993, 259 N.Y.S.2d 152, cert. denied, 382 U.S. 828 (1965).

Constitutional immunity does not protect speech which incites an immediate breach of peace. People v. Knight, 35 Misc. 2d 216, 228 N.Y.S.2d 981 (Magistrate's Ct. 1962).

impunity." [16] And, in upholding the conviction of a suffragette for disturbing a political meeting, the court said: "There is no question of free speech or of oppression involved in this case, and it does not bulk large with incidental questions of liberty. There is but the simple question whether the defendant—a person—wilfully disturbed a meeting in violation of the statute." [17] Where a spectator at a Congressional committee hearing expressed his protest by jumping to his feet and shouting, and then claimed that his actions were protected by the First Amendment, the court replied that the defendant "had no constitutional right to voice his protest in the manner he adopted. The first amendment does not guarantee the right of a spectator to shout during a legislative hearing so as to disrupt the orderly processes of the proceeding." [18]

[16] Wall v. Lee, 34 N.Y. 141, 146 (1865).

Disruptive acts of demonstrators who entered a church deprived the church members of their rights of freedom of assembly, speech, and worship and of their right to use and enjoy their property. Gannon v. Action, 303 F. Supp. 1240 (E.D. Mo. 1969), modified, 450 F.2d 1227 (1971).

But see Gaddis v. State, 105 Neb. 303, 305, 180 N.W. 590 (1920), which held that, if permitted by precepts and usages, a member of a church congregation may interrupt a sermon to correct utterances by the minister which were at variance with established tenets or rites of the church. The court remarked: "Otherwise, freedom of worship and free speech might be impaired by bigotry and false doctrines." This case represents a minority view based on an alleged custom or practice. It has been cited in a court decision relating to a protest demonstration during a political speech at an Independence Day celebration in a public park. See In re Kay, 83 Cal. Rptr. 686, 464 P.2d 142, 148, n. 8, 150 (1970).

[17] People v. Malone, 156 App. Div. 10, 141 N.Y.S. 149, 153 (1913).

Standing in a public gathering in an orderly and peaceful fashion and holding an unoffensive sign, without interrupting the speaker or doing anything which would incite riot or cause disturbances, does not constitute disorderly conduct or disturbance of assembly. Pope v. State, 192 Misc. 587, 79 N.Y.S.2d 466, 471 (Sup. Ct.), aff'd, 277 App. Div. 1015, 99 N.Y.S.2d 1019 (4th Dep't 1950).

[18] United States v. Woodard, 376 F.2d 136, 142 (7th Cir. 1967).

In a prosecution for violation of a disorderly persons statute, defendant's resistance to efforts to remove him from a meeting chamber, with the noise necessarily generated by his removal, were held to have disturbed the quiet and good order of the chamber. The defendant resisted removal by locking arms with someone seated next to him and falling limp. The court said that his claim of "wholly passive" resistance "toys with words." State v. Smith, 46 N.J. 510, 218 A.2d 147, cert. denied, 385 U.S. 838 (1966).

The courts have also passed upon the right of a union member to freedom of expression under the labor "Bill of Rights." It has been held that the "outspoken remarks" of a union business agent at a union meeting are protected by the free speech provisions of the Act.[19] Such rights are individual rights subject to individual enforcement, and other union members have no standing "to complain to this court of an encroachment of the freedom of expression of a fellow union member." There is no basis for a class action, as no common right or common question of law or fact exists between the injured member and those seeking to champion his cause. "Sympathy with another's plight will not provide that interest." The court, in commenting on an alleged threat of a union president, while presiding at a union meeting, to tear up the objecting member's union book if he "had his way," wrote these words: "In determining whether [complainant's] freedom of expression was inhibited, this court must consider the setting in which the incident occurred, the statement made by the defendant [union president], and the effect upon the complainant. Not every ungentlemanly remark made by a local union's president to a member" is a denial of his statutory rights.[20] However, a public agitator who intention-

---

"Nor does a person carry with him into the United States Senate or House, or into the Supreme Court, or any other court, a complete constitutional right to go into those places contrary to their rules and speak his mind on any subject he pleases. It is a myth to say that any person has a constitutional right to say what he pleases, where he pleases, and when he pleases. Our Court has decided precisely the opposite." Tinker v. Des Moines Indep. Community School Dist., 393 U.S. 503, 522 (1969).

A defendant can lose his constitutional right to be present at his own criminal trial if, after he has been warned that he will be removed if he continues his disruptive behavior, he nevertheless insists on conducting himself in a manner so disorderly, disruptive, and disrespectful of the court that his trial cannot be carried on with him in the courtroom. Illinois v. Allen, 397 U.S. 337 (1970).

See Annot., 93 L. Ed. 1151 (1950), 2 L. Ed. 2d 1706 (1958), 11 L. Ed. 2d 1116 (1964), 16 L. Ed. 2d 1053 (1967), 21 L. Ed. 2d 976 (1969).

[19] The court also held that union officers and important union officials have "a greater obligation to speak up than do the ordinary members, because of the responsibility and prestige of their positions." DeCampli v. Greeley, 293 F. Supp. 746, 752 (D.N.J. 1968).

[20] Broomer v. Schultz, 239 F. Supp. 699, 702–3 (E.D. Pa. 1965), aff'd, 356 F.2d 984 (1966) (per curiam).

ally stirs up prejudice and hatred will not be permitted to use his constitutional privilege of freedom of speech as an instrument for abuse and incitement to violence.[21]

§ 7.22   Belief in Cause Not an Excuse

An unlawful disturbance cannot be excused because the conduct of the disturber was "in furtherance of a cause in which she believed." In upholding the misdemeanor conviction of a suffragette who was "dragged out" of a political meeting for persisting to interrogate the speaker and refusing to heed the orders of the chairman to resume her seat, the court noted that the principle of woman suffrage was supported by cogent arguments but remarked that "there is no argument in violations of law, and agitation in forms that fall foul of the penal law must be suppressed. If the courts overlook violations of such law for the sake of such propagandism of any cause as is in disobedience of such law, the courts fall into contempt and the lawless take heart. . . . If the law should blink at little things which are unlawful, irresponsible enthusiasts may be encouraged to commit grave offenses."[22] Nor is it a defense to a

---

A union president does not have the standing to sue to set aside an election on the ground that the constitution and by-laws did not prescribe procedures for selecting nominees, as he cannot enforce rights of other union members. Mamula v. United Steelworkers of America, 304 F.2d 108 (3d Cir.), *cert. denied,* 371 U.S. 823 (1962). *See* McGowan v. Maryland, 366 U.S. 420 (1961).

But see Schrank v. Brown, 192 Misc. 80, 80 N.Y.S.2d 452, 455 (Sup. Ct. 1948) which held: "Fair criticism is the right of members of a union, as it is the right of every citizen. A provision of a union constitution, which would suppress protests of members against actions of their officers which such members regard as improper or opposed to their best interests, would be illegal and unenforcible [sic]."

See also Schrank v. Brown, 194 Misc. 138, 86 N.Y.S.2d 209 (Sup. Ct. 1949).

[21] *See* Chicago v. Terminiello, 332 Ill. App. 17, 74 N.E.2d 45 (1947), *rev'd,* 337 U.S. 1 (1949).

[22] People v. Malone, 156 App. Div. 10, 141 N.Y.S. 149, 153 (2d Dep't 1913).

The fact that the disrupter disagreed with the particular activity then being conducted by the meeting (government business) cannot serve to enlarge the rights he asserts. United States v. Akison, 290 F. Supp. 212, 217 (D. Colo. 1968).

prosecution for disturbing a religious meeting that the disturber disagreed with the rules and practices of the church and tried to induce the church to change its rules by loud talking, shouting, and sitting on the floor.[23]

However, an orderly and peaceful display of a placard at a political meeting, not likely to incite a disruption of proceedings, does not constitute an unlawful disturbance. In one case the court held that the actor "was merely exercising his constitutional right of petition and freedom of speech in a somewhat unusual but perfectly lawful and orderly manner." [24] Also, it has been held that a speaker at an open meeting cannot expect an audience to remain passive while he asks provocative rhetorical questions, and that a listener who speaks out in answer has not committed an act of disorderly conduct.[25]

See Zwicker v. Boll, 270 F. Supp. 131, 135 (W.D. Wis. 1967), aff'd, 391 U.S. 353 (1968) (per curiam) where the court considered the first and fourteenth amendments and said that "conduct which is in fact disorderly is not insulated because it is perpetrated while engaged in a protest demonstration."

[23] Jones v. State, 219 Ga. 848, 136 S.E.2d 358, 364, cert. denied, 379 U.S. 935 (1964).

[24] Pope v. State, 192 Misc. 587, 79 N.Y.S.2d 466, 471 (Sup. Ct.), aff'd, 277 App. Div. 1015, 99 N.Y.S.2d 1019 (4th Dep't 1950).

[25] "The question before the court, if the defendant's version of the incident is believed, is whether a listener to a speaker at an open outdoor meeting, answering the question of a speaker, is committing an act of disorderly conduct. It is true that the speaker may have been making a rhetorical question and was not expecting an answer. At the same time, he takes just that chance. Ordinarily, the average person does not feel the urge to 'speak out in meeting' no matter what is said, but it can be well understood that the remarks of this speaker were so far from the truth, and in fact a direct insult to the race of the defendant, that it is reasonable to expect that he might give way to such an outburst when a direct question was asked, and the answer of the defendant can in no sense be considered disorderly conduct. It is true that a speaker has the right of free speech, and I would not limit that in the slightest degree, but a speaker at an open meeting cannot expect an audience to remain passive under such a provocation as in this case. The defendant testified that there had been a slight disturbance about fifteen minutes previously and at that time an officer had ordered him to move on and that he complied and moved to a different part of the audience. The defendant had as absolute a right to listen to the speaker as had the speaker to speak, so long as he did not disturb the meeting or commit an act of disorderly conduct." People v. Rothenberg, 15 N.Y.S.2d 447, 448–49 (Magistrate's Ct. 1939).

§ 7.23   Reasonable Parliamentary Rules

Reasonable rules of parliamentary law, properly applied by the chairman at a meeting, do not unlawfully interfere with a member's constitutional right of free speech.[26] However, the court will not even apply its own rules of practice where their application might have an inhibitory effect on freedom of speech.[27]

The rights of a free press, including the right of news reporters to attend meetings, are discussed elsewhere.[28]

ADVICE OF COUNSEL

§ 7.24   Liability for Negligence

Reliance on the advice of legal counsel may be asserted by a director or officer as a defense against personal liability for negligence and to show that he acted in good faith.[1] When a lawyer was present at a meeting for the purpose of advising the directors with respect to the legality of the proceedings, and dictated the minutes at the close of the meeting, evidence that the directors

---

[26] At a union meeting the chairman refused to put to vote for the third time a motion which had just been defeated for the second time only a month earlier. The court held: "The refusal to consider it again so shortly after the second defeat was not an interference with a member's right of free speech, but was a reasonable parliamentary rule." Broomer v. Schultz, 239 F. Supp. 699, 702 (E.D. Pa. 1965), aff'd, 356 F.2d 984 (1966) (per curiam).

[27] See United States v. Raines, 362 U.S. 17 (1960).

[28] See § 7.1 supra.

[1] "Counsel's opinion as to the law (even when erroneous) should, in our opinion, protect the officers acting in reliance upon it." Spirt v. Bechtel, 232 F.2d 241, 247 (2d Cir. 1956) (violation of fiduciary duty because of individual interest).

"Reliance upon the advice of counsel is a good defense. . . ." The appellate court remarked that the trial court had determined, in effect, that the directors "knew, or should have known, more Pennsylvania law than eminent Pennsylvania counsel." Gilbert v. Burnside, 13 App. Div. 2d 982, 216 N.Y.S.2d 430 (2d Dep't 1961), aff'd, 11 N.Y.2d 960, 229 N.Y.S.2d 10, 183 N.E.2d 325 (1962).

Directors, in approving a sale of corporate assets, "were entitled to reply [sic] on the advice of counsel, and in so doing were protected from charges of bad faith or negligence." Bown v. Ramsdell, 139 Misc. 360, 249 N.Y.S. 387, 394 (Sup. Ct. 1931).

acted on the advice of counsel was competent to show their good faith notwithstanding such defense was not pleaded.[2] In fact, it has been held that if a director feels any doubts as to the law, he may be charged with negligence if he fails to seek and be guided by competent legal advice.[3] One trial court has even suggested a breach in fiduciary duty of a director, who had relied on the advice of one lawyer, "in not procuring other additional legal advice." [4]

§ 7.25   Liability for Tort

On the other hand, reliance on the advice of counsel does not justify or constitute a defense against personal liability for committing an unlawful act.[5] Although the precaution in seeking the advice of legal counsel establishes the fact that directors acted with due care and hence could assert the defense of due diligence, it does not necessarily protect directors from personal liability who knowingly voted for or actively participated in an act held to be unlawful. "Their ignorance of the law, though engendered by

[2] See Uffelman v. Boillin, 19 Tenn. App. 1, 82 S.W.2d 545 (1935).

Where a director relies on the advice of counsel, and his counsel fails to perform his duty, the director is "bound by that failure." Escott v. BarChris Constr. Corp., 283 F. Supp. 643, 697 (S.D.N.Y. 1968).

In a stockholder's derivative action holding bank directors accountable for negligence in approving certain transactions, the court noted that the transactions were unusual and unique, "yet there was nothing in the record to indicate that the advice of counsel was sought." Litwin v. Allen, 25 N.Y.S.2d 667, 699 (Sup. Ct. 1940).

[3] Vance v. Phoenix Ins. Co., 4 Lea, 385 (Tenn. 1880), quoted in Uffelman v. Boillin, 19 Tenn. App. 1, 82 S.W.2d 545, 568 (1935).

[4] Blaustein v. Pan American Petroleum & Transport Co., 263 App. Div. 97, 31 N.Y.S.2d 934, 955 (1st Dep't 1941), modifying, 174 Misc. 601, 21 N.Y.S.2d 651 (Sup. Ct. 1940) (appellate court held that director had exercised his discretion honestly and in good faith).

See comments re disqualification of counsel giving advice, conflict of interest, legal advice permitting violation of fiduciary obligations, etc. Id. at 21 N.Y.S.2d 651, 729–31.

[5] "The fact that these defendants may have been advised by their attorney that this application of funds was legal, or the fact that no loss followed, would not constitute a defense or justify a violation" of the penal law. People v. Marcus, 261 N.Y. 268, 294, 185 N.E. 97 (1933) (misappropriation of safe deposit funds).

lawyers' advice and corroborated by lower federal courts, is no defense." [6]

§ 7.26   Presence of Counsel at Meetings

Whether a corporate director has the legal right, as an individual, to the presence and advice of his own counsel at meetings of the board, is not clearly established. One court has held that, as a general rule, an individual director has the right to have his counsel present in the meeting room when he deems it necessary, but that the majority may refuse to allow the minority directors to have their counsel present when the minority not only failed to follow parliamentary procedure but harassed the majority with abusive language in a reprehensible and inexcusable manner.[7] Another court has held that the board of directors, having the right to determine the manner of conducting directors' meetings, has the right as a board but not individually, to decide who might attend meetings other than the directors themselves; and has upheld the board in refusing to allow a director's personal attorney to be present at all meetings of the board.[8] A third approach has merit. It permits a director, in protecting the interests of the corporation and its shareholders, to every facility and assistance including the right to the advice and presence of counsel at meetings of the board and elsewhere.[9] This indicates a preferred rule that counsel may be present when it will facilitate or improve the deliberations of the board or any member, but not otherwise. There would be no legal right of an individual director to have his personal counsel present at any or all meetings unless there was reasonable justification for the need of his advice.

The New York law appears to follow the general principle that

[6] Tillman v. Wheaton-Haven Recreation Ass'n Inc., 517 F.2d 1141, 1146 (4th Cir. 1975) (tortious violation of civil rights).

See Chapter 5 *supra*.

[7] Selama-Dindings Plantations, Ltd. v. Durham, 216 F. Supp. 104 (S.D. Ohio 1963), *aff'd*, Selama-Dindings Plantations, Ltd. v. Cincinnati Union Stock Yard Co., 337 F.2d 949 (6th Cir. 1964).

[8] Burt v. Irvine Co., 224 Cal. App. 2d 50, 36 Cal. Rptr. 270 (1964).

[9] Posner v. Southern Exhaust & Blow Pipe Co., Ltd., 109 La. 658, 33 So. 641 (1902).

the courts will not interfere with the internal affairs of a corporation, in holding that the question of having counsel at a meeting of the board of directors is a matter of "internal corporate management" upon which the courts properly will decline to rule.[10]

Whether the presence on a board of directors of counsel for a litigant constitutes a conflict of interest and creates irreparable harm, is a question of law.[11]

Certainly there should be no objection to permitting a stockholder to bring his counsel to a stockholders' meeting of a publicly held corporation either as a proxy or individually as an attorney, provided that one or the other, but not both, may take the floor at the same meeting.

§ 7.27   Presence of Secretary

Whether a corporate director may have a stenographer at a board meeting is also still uncertain. If a stenographer accompanies counsel to a meeting, it may be presumed that the rule applicable to the presence of counsel will also apply to his stenographer. The courts will presumably approve the presence of a stenographer when counsel is authorized to be present,[12] and will refuse to allow the minority to record the proceedings of a directors' meeting, whether by stenographer or mechanical device, when minority counsel was not permitted to be present for good cause.[13]

Whether a shareholder may bring his secretary to a stockholders' meeting for the purpose of taking notes under circumstances which might contribute to the turbulence of the meeting, has been ques-

[10] Jacobson v. Moskowitz, 27 N.Y.2d 67, 261 N.E.2d 613, 313 N.Y.S.2d 684, 686 (1970).

[11] Ronson Corp. v. Liquifin Aktiengesellschaft, 508 F.2d 399 (2d Cir. 1974).

A stockholder is entitled to exercise his statutory right to inspect and to copy the stock ledger for the purpose of soliciting proxies for a forthcoming annual meeting even when he is an active member of an independent stockholders committee in which a fellow member was an attorney who had previously served as counsel to the corporation. Schnell v. Chris-Craft Industries Inc., 283 A.2d 852 (Del. Ch. 1971).

[12] See Jacobson v. Moskowitz, 27 N.Y.2d 67, 261 N.E.2d 613, 313 N.Y.S.2d 684 (1970).

[13] Selama-Dindings Plantations, Ltd. v. Durham, 216 F. Supp. 104 (S.D. Ohio 1963), aff'd, Selama-Dindings Plantations, Ltd. v. Cincinnati Union Stock Yard Co., 337 F.2d 949 (6th Cir. 1964).

tioned.[14] When the presence of a secretary or stenographer does not disturb or inconvenience the meeting there should be no objection to their presence for the purpose of observing or recording the proceedings on behalf of a stockholder or his attorney.

[14] *In re* Election of Directors of Bushwick Sav. & Loan Ass'n, 189 Misc. 316, 70 N.Y.S.2d 478 (Sup. Ct. 1947).

8

Adjournment

A meeting should be conducted in an orderly and expeditious manner, and its business concluded according to schedule without undue haste or unnecessary delay, if that is possible. An adjournment to a later hour or day should be avoided unless it was contemplated before the meeting started, or unless unexpected and uncontrollable events occur during the meeting which makes an adjourned meeting necessary.

§ 8.1   Definition

An adjournment is a termination of a physical sitting or session of an assembly or body. It is not a postponement nor a recess to a later time, unless so stated. When a meeting has in fact adjourned, having fulfilled its duties, it cannot reconvene and exercise further powers.[1]

[1] "When the [judicial] convention made their nominations and adjourned sine die [without any future date being designated] they became functus officio [having fulfilled their duties]. They could exercise no further power un-

An early English case describes the common law. "The sitting or meeting, as a whole, has a practical unity. It commences with the usual forms of opening, when the Speaker takes the chair, it is terminated by the adjournment of the House." The service of members at each sitting is continuous "and at each adjournment that service is interrupted, not to be renewed until after an interval of some hours, days, or weeks, or even months, as the case may be." [2]

A separation of the members for a time, with an intention of returning to the meeting, is in effect a recess as distinguished from an adjournment. Thus, when the members of a meeting become embroiled, abruptly disperse, and then return later in the afternoon, it is a recess, not an adjournment.[3] On the other hand, when all the members leave the meeting room and the floor of the building in which the meeting is held, the meeting is deemed to have been adjourned, even though the motion to adjourn was irregularly put to vote and was not lawfully adopted.[4]

When a meeting has been rightfully adjourned by the president in the presence of all the members, and no appeal has been taken from his ruling, an attempt by dissidents, after some time spent in consultation, to hold the meeting with less than a majority is for all substantial purposes a "new meeting."[5] A change of place

---

less ordered by the Court to reassemble. . . ." Aurelio v. Cohen, 44 N.Y.S.2d 145 (Sup. Ct.), aff'd, In re Aurelio, 266 App. Div. 603, 44 N.Y.S.2d 11 (1st Dep't), aff'd, 291 N.Y. 645, 51 N.E.2d 930 (1943).

However, a meeting may be adjourned during the process of balloting unless prohibited by law or corporate limitation. Penobscot & Kennebec R.R. v. Dunn, 39 Me. 587 (1855).

[2] Barton v. Taylor, 11 App. Cas. 197, 204 (P.C. 1886).

[3] State ex rel. Harnett v. Powell, 101 Iowa 382, 387 (1897).

A recess occurring during a session has no adverse effect upon the proceedings. See Mansfield v. O'Brien, 271 Mass. 515, 171 N.E. 487, 488 (1930).

[4] Western Cottage Piano & Organ Co. v. Burrows, 144 Ill. App. 350 (1908).

[5] It being impossible to hold an election because a few controlling shares were enjoined from voting, and all other shares were equally divided between the two sides, the presiding officer adjourned the meeting until the injunction proceedings could be determined. "We are inclined to think that this was within his powers as presiding officer, in view of the impossibility of doing any business at the meeting." Haskell v. Read, 68 Neb. 115, 96 N.W. 1007, denying rehearing of 68 Neb. 107, 93 N.W. 997 (1903), quoted and followed State ex rel. Industrial Fin., Ltd. v. Yanagawa, 484 P.2d 145 (Hawaii 1971).

for the convenience of taking a poll is not an adjournment.[6] Nor is an adjournment of a meeting the same as a dissolution[7] or a cancellation.[8]

A gathering of election officials to conduct a recount on a day after adjournment of a stockholders' meeting for the election of directors is not a meeting or an adjourned meeting at which directors are elected.[9]

The question sometimes arises as to whether an avowed "recess" is a final conclusion of the meeting or an adjournment to a specified time for a limited purpose. Care must be taken in deciding which posture is valid because a lawful adjournment terminates all unfinished business and incompleted proceedings.[10] A recess is not

[6] In an election of churchwardens, the notice provided that the meeting would be held in the church, but if a poll should be demanded the meeting would be adjourned to the town hall. The court remarked: "This is not properly an adjournment. May not the chairman appoint a convenient plan for taking the poll? . . . Those who summon a meeting of this kind must necessarily lay down some order for the proceedings: and I think it is competent in them to say that the meeting shall be held in one place, and, in a certain event which may require it, shall be removed to another." Rex v. Archdeacon, 1 Adolph. & E. 342, 344–45 [K.B. 1834].

In an election of churchwardens, a poll was demanded and the chairman moved the meeting from a schoolhouse to a church. It was held that this was not an adjournment but in reality the appointing of a place to take a poll. Rex v. Churchwardens, 1 Adolph. & E. 346 (K.B. 1832).

[7] There is no legal foundation for an argument that, if the moderator was not legally chosen, he could not put the question of adjournment; and that if a meeting was not sufficiently organized to elect officers it was not sufficiently organized to adjourn. See Attorney General v. Simonds, 111 Mass. 256 (1873).

[8] Revocation by state chairman of a designation of the time and place for a meeting of a judicial convention before it was called to order is in effect a cancellation of the meeting, and not an adjournment. It is suggested that a meeting cannot be cancelled after being called to order. Bannigan v. Heffernan, 115 N.Y.S.2d 889 (Sup. Ct.), modified, 280 App. Div. 891, 115 N.Y.S.2d 444 (2d Dep't 1952), aff'd, 304 N.Y. 729 (1952).

As to "cancellation" of a shareholders' meeting by management or by court order soon before it convened, see Union Pacific R.R. v. Chicago & N.W. Ry., 226 F. Supp. 400, 412–13 (N.D. Ill. 1964).

[9] Grip v. Buffelen Woodworking Co., 73 Wash. 2d 219, 437 P.2d 915 (1968).

[10] See City of Picayune v. Mississippi Power Co., 197 F.2d 444, 446 (5th Cir. 1952); In re Newcomb, 18 N.Y.S. 16 (Sup. Ct. 1891) (adjournment of meeting for election of directors before inspectors made final report).

an adjournment,[11] and to call a recess an adjournment or vice versa does not alter the fact.[12] However, a "postponed" meeting can be an "adjourned meeting." [13]

An adjournment of a meeting "without day" or "without day certain" has the effect of ending all unfinished business,[14] while an adjournment to a fixed day keeps the meeting alive for the transaction of business.[15] An adjournment "subject to call" without

[11] *See* Toffolon v. Zoning Board of Appeals, 236 A.2d 96, 100 (Conn. 1967).

When applied to a legislative body, "recess" means a temporary dismissal, and not an adjournment sine die. *See* Petition of Special Assembly Interim Committee, 90 P.2d 304 (Cal. 1939), *citing* Cooley.

[12] "Technically speaking, 'recess' probably applies to an intermission taken by a deliberative body from time to time during a day, and 'adjournment' when taken over a day, or to some definite time in the future, or without day." Intermela v. Perkins, 205 F. 603, 611–12 (9th Cir. 1913), *cert. denied*, 231 U.S. 757 (1914), *citing* Robert's Rules of Order.

A "recess" without setting a date for resumption of business amounts to an adjournment. Green v. Beste, 76 N.W.2d 165 (N.D. 1956).

An adjournment for the purpose of tabulating the ballots has been held to be "only a temporary recess." Salgo v. Matthews, 497 S.W.2d 620 (Tex. 1973).

Fact that adjourned meeting was described as a "session," instead of a "meeting," did not invalidate the meeting. Reference was made to another case in which an adjourned meeting was described by the clerk as a "recess." Stockton v. Powell, 10 So. 688, 698 (Fla. 1892).

[13] The minutes showed that a regular meeting of school trustees had been "postponed," there being no quorum present. The court said, "It is true the word 'postponed' is used instead of 'adjourned,' but, as used here, it cannot be seriously contended that it has a different meaning." People *ex rel.* Scott v. Nelson, 252 Ill. 514, 96 N.E. 1071, 1072 (1911).

[14] "Ordinarily, in the absence of any provision for stated meetings, an adjournment without day is notice to all concerned that matters which have been under consideration will not again be taken up unless initiated under the procedure established for new business. We are not disposed too rigorously to apply technical rules to the action of administrative boards and commissions, but a proper regard for established rules of procedure will cause little trouble and be likely at least to avoid such questions as have arisen in this case." Strain v. Mims, 123 Conn. 275, 193 A. 754, 758 (1937).

See Hill v. Goodwin, 56 N.H. 441, 446–47 (1876), *citing* Cushing's Manual, which provides at Rule 139: "An adjournment without day—that is, without any time being fixed for reassembling—would, in the case of any other than a legislative assembly, be equivalent to a dissolution."

[15] "There being no quorum present, according to parliamentary law the only business that could be transacted was to adjourn. If the adjournment had been

fixing a specific time or stating by call of whom, is not an adjournment to another time and the next meeting is not an "adjourned meeting."[16] Furthermore, an informal arrangement by a city council to postpone action on certain matters does not constitute an adjournment of such matters to the next regular meeting.[17] However, an "indefinite postponement" of a question is the equivalent of complete disapproval[18] and precludes further consideration of the subject during the entire session.[19]

Generally, legal distinctions are not critical where the results are fair. Where the majority stockholders were wrongfully excluded from a special meeting lawfully called at the company's office for the purpose of changing the management, their subsequent action in moving the meeting to a dwelling and electing new directors was lawful whether the moved meeting was regarded as a continuance or an adjournment of the meeting begun at the office.[20]

The adjournment of an invalid meeting held without due notice, and the giving of notice of the adjourned date sufficiently in advance to comply with any time requirements of original notice

---

without day, it might have ended the power of the board to act upon the petition upon its own initiative, but by adjourning to a day fixed one week later the regular meeting was kept alive for the purpose of transacting the business, including action upon the petition." People *ex rel.* Scott v. Nelson, 252 Ill. 514, 96 N.E. 1071, 1073 (1911).

[16] Village of Coon Valley v. Spellum, 190 Wis. 140, 208 N.W. 916 (1926).

[17] Smith v. City of Phillips, 174 Wis. 54, 182 N.W. 338 (1921).

A vote taken at a regular meeting to hold the next meeting on a certain date has been interpreted to be a vote to adjourn to such date. *See* Lafleur v. City of Chicopee, 352 Mass. 746, 227 N.E.2d 702 (1967).

[18] "Indefinite postponement by a body having only definite present existence is the equivalent of complete disapproval. This conclusion is confirmed by technical meaning, which the phrase has acquired in parliamentary usage. There is a consensus of opinion among writers on this subject that it means suppression of the question, and is equivalent to a negative vote." Wood v. Town of Milton, 197 Mass. 531, 84 N.E. 332, 333 (1908), *citing* Cushing, Law & Pr. Leg. Assem.; Crocker, Parl. Proc.; Jefferson's Manual; Reed's Rules.

[19] Under the rules of a city council, indefinite postponement of a question precludes further consideration of the subject to which the question must be referred during the entire session. Zeiler v. Central Ry., 84 Md. 304, 35 A. 932, 933 (1896).

[20] Byrne v. Morley, 78 Idaho 172, 299 P.2d 758 (1956).

of a meeting, did not cure the defect of want of notice in the first instance. The attempted adjourned meeting is not the equivalent of an original meeting.[21]

§ 8.2 Adjournment by Assembly

It was well established at English common law that the right to adjourn a meeting is in the assembly, and is not in the unlimited province of the chairman. Therefore the chairman cannot end a lawfully convened meeting without good cause; he must carry on and fulfill the obligations of his position, which are to "preserve order, and to take care that the proceedings are conducted in a proper manner, and that the sense of the meeting is properly ascertained with regard to any question which is properly before the meeting." If the chairman declares the meeting dissolved and leaves the chair at his own will, the meeting by itself can resolve to proceed and to appoint a new chairman to conduct the business of the meeting.[22]

§ 8.2.1 Common Law

American common law is in accord.[23] "At a meeting duly constituted and organized, a majority of the voters present, in the

[21]Gries v. Eversharp, Inc., 69 A.2d 922 (Del. Ch. 1949).

[22] National Dwellings Soc'y v. Sykes, [1894] 3 Ch. 159, 161–62. The court quoted from BURNS' JUSTICE OF THE PEACE, 29th Ed., Vol. VI, p. 336. "The right of adjourning the meeting is not in the minister or any other person as chairman . . . but in the whole assembly, where all are upon an equal footing."

An earlier case held that the vicar presiding at an election of churchwardens did not have power to declare the meeting adjourned over the opposition of the electors. "The power must arise from the custom, or common law. Here is no custom found, and I know of no book that shews how it stands at common law. . . . We must therefore resort to the common right, which is in the whole assembly, where all are upon an equal foot. And though there may be a difficulty in polling for an adjournment, yet as there is no other way, that must be taken." Stoughton v. Reynolds, 2 Strange 1045 [K.B. 1736].

The court, in discussing the right at common law to a poll, commented: "Cannot a meeting be adjourned at common law?" Regina v. Wimbleton Local Bd., 8 Q.B.D. 459, 463 (1882).

[23] A town meeting, or a meeting of any other assembly or body, may be adjourned from one hour to another, and to a different place, in the same day.

absence of any statute or other restraining authority to the contrary, have an implied right to adjourn the meeting to another time and place. But even this, we apprehend, must be fairly done, and for no improper purposes." [24]

"At a lawful meeting of the corporators, irrespective of any statutory grant or denial of power, a majority of those present would at common law, have the right as a power incident to all corporations, to adjourn the meeting to another time, either in the same or a future day, and to another place." People *ex rel.* Simonson v. Martin, 5 N.Y. 22, 27 (1851).

"Common parliamentary rules, in use by all deliberative assemblies in this country, may also be resorted to, in the absence of any made by the association itself, in considering the regularity of its proceedings. . . . The association, in the absence of rules, can adjourn its meetings from time to time according to the usual methods of parliamentary bodies, and transact business at any adjourned meeting without notice to the absentees." Ostrom v. Greene, 161 N.Y. 353, 362, 55 N.E. 919 (1900).

[24] Stone v. Small, 54 Vt. 498 (1882).

"It is inconceivable that a shareholders' meeting cannot be adjourned if it become [sic] necessary or advisable." *In re* Weinstein, 203 Misc. 975, 978, 119 N.Y.S.2d 457, 459 (Sup. Ct. 1953), *quoting In re* Election of Dirs. of Bushwick Sav. & Loan Ass'n, 189 Misc. 316, 318, 70 N.Y.S.2d 478 (Sup. Ct. 1947).

"We hold that the acts of the president in adjourning or attempting to adjourn said meetings were illegal; that, when he refused to preside further at said meetings, the stockholders had the right to proceed with the business of the meeting without him. . . ." State *ex rel.* Ryan v. Cronan, 23 Nev. 437, 49 P. 41, 45 (1897).

The right of adjournment rests primarily with the members and not with the presiding officer. In an election of corporate directors by cumulative voting, the chairman adjourned the meeting when the shareholders failed to elect a quorum of directors on the first ballot due to a tie vote. The adjournment was held to be arbitrary and illegal. State *ex rel.* Price v. DuBrul, 100 Ohio St. 272, 126 N.E. 87, 90 (1919).

A shareholders' meeting regularly convened "could not have been legally adjourned except by the act of the meeting itself." Chicago Macaroni Mfg. Co. v. Boggiano, 202 Ill. 312, 67 N.E. 17, 18 (1903).

A meeting has the power to adjourn to another day. Alliance Co-op Ins. Co. v. Gasche, 93 Kan. 147, 142 P. 882, 883 (1914).

"The rule, as we understand, applicable to all deliberative bodies, is that any number have power to adjourn, though they may not be a quorum for the transaction of business." Kimball v. Marshall, 44 N.H. 465, 467–68 (1863).

The same principle applies to a county political committee. "Such is the recognized rule as to corporation meetings and we see no reason why it should

The right of a body to adjourn the meeting must be duly exercised. An annual meeting which had been regularly convened was not legally adjourned where the motion to adjourn was defeated by holders of a majority of the stock represented at the meeting, even though a majority of the owners of stock voted in favor of adjournment and the chairman declared the meeting to be adjourned.[25] Where a motion to adjourn a meeting of corporate directors was apparently defeated, but was actually approved by a majority of the legally elected directors who were entitled to vote, the meeting was legally adjourned and subsequent action removing officers was ineffective.[26] Furthermore, the motion to adjourn must be made by a qualified member of the organization. Otherwise, the meeting is not legally adjourned.[27]

§ 8.2.2   Inherent Right To Adjourn

The right of an assembly to adjourn is inherent in its constitution.[28] "The association, in the absence of rules, can adjourn

---

not be equally applicable to a political meeting." Egan v. Kelly, 14 N.J. Super. 103, 81 A.2d 413, 414–15 (1951).

When a meeting is once fairly organized at the time and place appointed in the notice (warrant), it possesses the incidental power of adjourning to a future time. *See* Chamberlain v. Dover, 13 Me. 466 (1836).

[25] State *ex rel.* Fritz v. Gray, 20 Ohio App. 26, 153 N.E. 187, 190 (1925).

Where seven shareholders owning 1,724 shares voted to adjourn and left the meeting, and the remaining five shareholders owning 4,275 shares remained and elected directors, the election was held valid because the motion to adjourn was regulated by a statute giving each shareholder one vote per share owned. *In re* Alleged Election of Dirs. & Officers of Rochester Dist. Tel. Co., 40 Hun. 172, 174 (N.Y. 1886).

[26] Young v. Janas, 103 A.2d 299 (Del. Ch. 1954).

[27] Where a non-member moved to adjourn and the motion was seconded and declared by the chairman on voice vote, the meeting was held not legally adjourned as the moving party was not qualified. *In re* Ajello's Petition, 26 Misc. 2d 1026, 212 N.Y.S.2d 970 (Sup. Ct. 1961) (county political committee).

[28] "Once a stockholders' meeting is properly convened it may be adjourned from time to time without further notice to stockholders." *In re* Siebenmann, 32 Misc. 2d 92, 93, 222 N.Y.S.2d 707 (Sup. Ct. 1961).

It must be conceded that "the power to adjourn resides in the stockholders

its meetings from time to time according to the usual methed of
parliamentary bodies, and transact business at an adjourned meeting
without notice to the absentees. . . . It can elect a president at
each meeting, and in so doing would, by implication, remove the
preceding president." [29]

The adjournment of a meeting for the election of directors rests
primarily with the stockholders, and "should be for a reasonable
time, having this purpose in view, and should not be sine die
adjournment exercised by the chairman and forestalling such purpose." [30] This is consistent with the general principle that the
owners of the company have the right to decide on questions of
adjournment, while the presiding officer has only the right and
duty of presiding.[31]

Although it is generally conceded that the power to adjourn
inheres in the meetings of a deliberative assembly and may be
exercised by the body itself for all proper purposes,[32] such power

---

assembled at the meeting. This power was exercised, and a valid adjournment
resulted by the stockholders' action to another date, and the second meeting
was a continuation of the annual meeting, and the acts and proceedings which
could take place on the first day could also take place with like force on the
second day of the meeting, to which an adjournment had been taken by the
stockholders." Sagness v. Farmers Co-Op. Creamery Co., 67 S.D. 379, 293
N.W. 365, 368 (1940).

[29] Ostrom v. Greene, 161 N.Y. 353, 55 N.E. 919, 922 (1900).

[30] State ex rel. Price v. DuBrul, 100 Ohio St. 272, 126 N.E. 87, 90 (1919).

[31] "It would seem that if the right of adjournment at an annual meeting is
given to the shareholders in the absence of a quorum, it is idle to urge that
they are without this prerogative when they assemble as a duly constituted
body for effective action. It is the shareholders' meeting, the owners of the
company, who have the right to make a decision on a question of adjournment,
and not of the president who has only the duty of presiding." In re Dollinger
Corp., 51 Misc. 2d 802, 274 N.Y.S.2d 285, 287 (Sup. Ct. 1966), quoting
Robert's Rules of Order.

[32] A city council has inherent power, in the absence of provision to the contrary, to adjourn a regular meeting to a date certain without notice to absent
members of the time to which the meeting has been adjourned, and a meeting
so adjourned is but a continuation of the same meeting and in the absence of
some positive restriction the adjourned meeting may consider and act on any
matter which it could properly have considered during the course of the regular meeting. Del Greco v. Mayor, 294 N.E.2d 594 (Mass. 1973).

"Like all other similar bodies, the board of trustees had power to adjourn a
regular meeting when not restricted by statute and, unless such adjournment is

cannot be abused.[33] It has been held, for example, that a share-holders' meeting may not be adjourned "over the protest of the minority stockholders or any of them" for the purpose of preventing the minority stockholders from exercising their legal right to elect other directors, thereby permitting the old board of directors to remain in office.[34] Similarly, although a town meeting has the im-

---

an abuse of the power, it is not the subject of review." People *ex rel.* Scott v. Nelson, 252 Ill. 514, 96 N.E. 1071, 1072 (1911).

Adjournment is a regulatory proceeding within the common parliamentary rules which are available to all deliberative assemblies and parliamentary bodies. Ostrom v. Greene, 161 N.Y. 353, 55 N.E. 919, 922 (1900).

The right of adjournment of a stockholders' meeting rests primarily with the stockholders. State *ex rel.* Price v. DuBrul, 100 Ohio St. 272, 126 N.E. 87 (1919).

Village trustees have the implied right at common law to adjourn their meeting to another time or place. Stone v. Small, 54 Vt. 498, 502 (1882).

[33] "At a meeting duly constituted and organized, a majority of the voters present, in the absence of any statute or other restraining authority to the contrary, have an implied right to adjourn the meeting to another time and place. But even this, we apprehend, must be fairly done, and for no improper purpose." Stone v. Small, 54 Vt. 498, 502 (1882).

[34] The court concluded: "The minority stockholders of a corporation have property rights in the corporation and its assets and management, which the directors, their trustees, may not ignore and set aside. Nor can the majority of the stockholders, broad as their powers are, override the organic law of the corporation for the illegal purpose of preventing the minority from securing the representation in the directory which the shares of stock owned by them enable them to elect." West Side Hosp. v. Steele, 124 Ill. App. 534, 540, 542 (1906).

See discussion in Chapman v. Barton, 345 Ill. App. 110, 102 N.E.2d 565, 567 (1951), concluding that "[t]he illegality arose because the adjournment was for the deliberate purpose of depriving the minority of its rights."

One stockholder faction, having failed to organize the annual meeting, moved to adjourn to another building, and there proceeded with an election of directors. It was held that quo warranto was the proper remedy to adjudicate the right to corporate office, and the equitable action for an injunction should be dismissed. Grant v. Elder, 64 Colo. 104, 170 P. 198 (1917).

Where the majority stockholders of a banking corporation were wrongfully excluded from a special meeting lawfully called at the bank (for purposes of changing the management), their subsequent action in moving the meeting to a dwelling and voting out of office the directors who had excluded them from the meeting and electing a new board was lawful, whether the meeting was regarded as a continuance of the meeting opened at the bank or an adjournment thereof. Byrne v. Morley, 78 Idaho 172, 299 P.2d 758 (1956).

Stockholders were notified that the annual meeting for the election of di-

plied right to adjourn, this power cannot be "oppressively exercised, and lead to the defeat of the public will." [35]

§ 8.2.3 Right Cannot Be Abused

Where the by-laws specify when an adjourned meeting may be reconvened, and what is proper notice, such requirements must be observed.[36]

The courts will resist and undo illegal acts arbitrarily taken whether caused by the majority, by the minority, or by the chairman. In an interesting case involving the election of inspectors by a common council, the court found, in sequence, that the minority had no right to walk out of the meeting, that the action of the president in declaring the council adjourned was an "outrage" which could not be excused, and that the action of those remaining in "the counting of absent members, and recording them as voting in the affirmative" was also "an inexcusable outrage." [37] In another case it was held that a meeting, being illegally adjourned by the president, could properly be continued under a successor chairman, and that an ensuing election of officers was valid.[38] Courts have

---

rectors would be held at a certain hour of the day fixed by the charter. The corporation was restrained from holding an election on that day, in consequence of which no meeting was held until several hours after the time fixed in the notice. A small number of stockholders, without the knowledge of the others, met, organized, and adjourned until the next day, at which time an election was held by a majority of the stockholders without notice to others who were in the vicinity for the purposes of the meeting and might have been readily notified. It was held that the election was unfair and invalid whether the restraining order did or did not bind the stockholders. The court remarked: "To sustain an election held under such circumstances would, indeed, be a most dangerous precedent. The liberal rule which is extended to elections fairly but irregularly held, has no just application to this case." State v. Bonnell, 35 Ohio St. 10 (1878).

[35] People ex rel. Simonson v. Martin, 5 N.Y. 22, 27 (1851).

[36] A by-law providing that adjournment can be taken to a future date not less than 10 days hence, and notice of adjourned meeting must be given, is a valid by-law and must be observed. Commonwealth ex rel. McCullough v. Exchange Operators, Inc., 11 Pa. Dist. & Co. 465 (1928), 32 Dauph. Co. 59 (1929).

[37] Dingwall v. Common Council, 82 Mich. 568, 46 N.W. 938, 939 (1890).

[38] In re Ajello's Petition, 26 Misc. 2d 1026, 212 N.Y.S.2d 970 (Sup. Ct. 1961) (county political committee).

further held that an adjourned annual meeting of shareholders subject to call under the statute cannot be thwarted by calling another meeting in the interim between the annual meeting and the adjourned meeting.[39]

§ 8.3　Adjournment by Chairman

Although the power to adjourn is primarily vested in the assembly itself, the chairman has an inherent right to adjourn a meeting over which he presides when by so doing he can facilitate the business of the meeting.[40] Thus, where it has been the custom in prior years to conduct the annual company meeting in an informal manner and to select or retain directors by voice vote or agreement, the chairman was upheld by the court in adjourning the meeting until a lawyer could be consulted when a minority stockholder demanded a poll and began distributing ballots. The minority stockholder then proceeded with an election of directors by ballot. The court set aside the election, saying: "There is no legal basis whereby a fraction of a meeting may ignore the duly elected chairman and the rest of those in attendance, conduct some private manoeuvers of their own, and then assert that their actions consti-

[39] The court also said: "If during the pendency of the annual meeting the minority conceived that their rights were not being respected, and if the minority believed that no adjourned meeting would be held, they had the right to demand that the annual meeting be reconvened and, upon such demand being refused by the secretary, mandatory injunction would lie to compel giving the notice of such meeting." State *ex rel.* Webber v. Shaw, 103 Ohio 660, 134 N.E. 643, 645 (1921).

[40] In an early English case the rector adjourned a meeting of parishioners to take a poll on the election of churchwardens. His authority to adjourn for this purpose being questioned, the court affirmed, holding that the rector had power to adjourn the meeting, though against the wish of the majority present. "It is on him that it devolves [power to adjourn], both to preserve order in the meeting, and to regulate the proceedings so as to give all persons entitled a reasonable opportunity of voting. He is to do the acts necessary for these purposes on his own responsibility, and subject to the being called upon to answer for his conduct if he has done anything improperly." Regina v. D'Oyly, 12 Adolph. & E. 139, 159 [Q. B. 1840].

Where the articles provide that the chairman may adjourn the meeting with the consent of the members present, he is not bound to do so even though a majority of those present so desire. Salisbury Gold Mining Co. Ltd. v. Hathorn, [1897] A.C. 268.

tute the official acts of the meeting." [41] An adjournment of a parishioners' meeting from a church to the town hall to take a poll by show of hands was also held valid, if not as an adjournment, as a reasonable action of the chairman in appointing a convenient plan for taking the poll.[42] The chairman may also adjourn a meeting on his own responsibility without a vote of the members to conduct a poll where the constituency entitled to vote at the poll is so large as to be cumbersome.[43]

§ 8.3.1   Motion To Adjourn

The right of the chairman to entertain a motion to adjourn and put it to vote at any time during the proceedings has been approved

[41] Chapman v. Barton, 345 Ill. App. 110, 102 N.E.2d 565, 567 (1951).

Meeting was adjourned by unanimous vote to enable the president to take legal advice as to whether the chairman should be elected by voice vote or by a share vote. At the adjourned meeting another squabble occurred and the meeting was again adjourned by a voice vote put by the chairman. Western Cottage Piano & Organ Co. v. Burrows, 144 Ill. App. 350 (1908).

See Henderson v. Bank of Australasia, 45 Ch. D. 330, 346, 62 L.T.R. (n.s.) 869 (1890) (adjournment to take legal advice).

[42] Notice provided that a meeting would be held in the church but if a poll were demanded it would be adjourned to the town hall. Adjournment was held a part of the original appointment and not an interruption of business. To the argument that the right of adjournment was in the assembly at large and not in the chairman, the court replied: "This is not properly an adjournment. May not the chairman appoint a convenient place for taking the poll?" Rex v. Archdeacon, 1 Adolph. & E. 342, 344 (K.B. 1834). See Regina v. D'Oyly, 12 Adolph. & E. 139 [Q.B. 1840].

Meeting adjourned from schoolhouse to church by chairman on demand for a poll. Discussion of adjournment from room to room. See Rex v. Churchwardens, 1 Adolph. & E. 346 [K.B. 1832].

[43] Meeting of vestry for the purpose of electing new churchwardens, with about 1,500 rate payers present at the meeting. A poll being demanded, the presiding rector adjourned the meeting and directed the taking of a poll. The court said: "Then, who is to direct the adjournment? It is suggested that a majority of the voters should do so. But how is the majority to be ascertained in so large a constituency? And what is the situation of parties if the majority present decide against adjournment so as to leave no time for a considerable part of the rate payers to vote? Setting aside the inconvenience that might arise if a majority of the parishioners could determine the point of adjournment, we think that the person who presides at the meeting is the proper individual to decide this." Regina v. D'Oyly, 12 Adolph. & E. 139, 159 [Q.B. 1840].

by the court. During a union meeting, a member presented a motion to have her rights of arbitration reinstated. While she had the floor the chairman allowed her to be interrupted and then entertained a motion to adjourn, which was carried. The court approved, holding that the member had failed to allege that the motion to reconsider "was in order and proper for consideration at that time." [44]

On the other hand, the chairman need not put to vote a motion which in his opinion will serve no useful purpose. In a case on this point the court characterized the motion to adjourn as "obviously a stalling tactic," and held that "[i]t might have been more consonant with parliamentary law to have put the motion to adjourn to a vote; failure to do so, however, was not of such serious import as to deprive the dissenting stockholders of any substantial rights." [45]

§ 8.3.2 Adjournment for Valid Reason

Where the presiding officer does adjourn a meeting he must do so for some valid reason. "No presiding officer can arbitrarily adjourn a meeting in defiance of the majority present." [46]

In a case involving a stockholder election, the president, having concluded that an election of directors would be impossible because

[44] The majority opinion held: "Although freedom of speech is a union member's right that is protected by [statute], the exercise of the right at union meetings must accommodate itself to the union's correlative right to conduct its meetings in an orderly fashion and in accordance with its previously established rules. The statute itself places these conditions upon the rights of a member." Scovile v. Watson, 338 F.2d 678, 680–82 (7th Cir. 1964), *cert. denied*, 380 U.S. 963 (1965). *See* dissenting opinion holding that adjournment was contrary to the by-laws and in violation of federal statute.

[45] Bresnick v. Home Title Guar. Co., 175 F. Supp. 723, 726 (S.D.N.Y. 1959).

[46] A minority of city aldermen left the meeting to break the quorum and prevent further business. Adjournment by the presiding officer was called an "outrage." Dingwall v. Common Council, 82 Mich. 568, 46 N.W. 938, 939 (1890).

An unofficial meeting of those remaining after the chairman arbitrarily declared an adjournment against the vote of the majority cannot grant rights to directors already elected at the regular meeting. State *ex rel.* Reed v. Smith, 14 P. 814, 15 P. 386 (Ore. 1887).

two shares were enjoined from being voted and the other shares were evenly divided, adjourned the meeting until the injunction proceedings could be determined. The court sustained the president's ruling: "We are inclined to think that this was within his powers as presiding officer, in view of the impossibility of doing any business at the meeting." [47] In another case the chairman, having concluded that an election would not be possible because of opposing factions, declared the meeting dissolved and was upheld by the court.[48]

§ 8.3.3 Arbitrary Adjournment

The chairman should not adjourn a meeting arbitrarily. When in an election of directors there is a tie vote on the first ballot, either faction may insist that the voting proceed until it is demonstrated that further balloting would be futile, and an abrupt adjournment by the chairman is not warranted.[49] Where the chairman without justification and perhaps fearful of the trend of the meeting, pe-

[47] The court added: "However this may be, the only proper course for those who objected was to appeal from the ruling and put the matter to a vote." Haskell v. Read, 68 Neb. 115, 96 N.W. 1007, *denying rehearing of* 68 Neb. 107, 93 N.W. 997 (1903).

A majority of stockholders of a bank, having been excluded from a special meeting, met at the locked front door of the bank and moved, seconded, and carried a motion to "recess" to a dwelling and there elected new directors. Their action was held valid. Byrne v. Morley, 78 Idaho 172, 175, 299 P.2d 758 (1956).

[48] "The division of the meeting, brought about in part by differences of opinion, prevented the ascertaining and carrying out of the will of those entitled to participate in the election of directors." The court held that the meeting was dissolved without effective action. Alliance Co-Op Ins. Co. v. Gasche, 93 Kan. 147, 142 P. 882, 883 (1914).

[49] When a quorum of directors was not elected by cumulative voting on the first ballot due to a tie vote, an adjournment by the chairman was arbitrary and illegal. "Had this election proceeded by ballot for such a length of time as to demonstrate to the shareholders and their chairman that a board of directors could not be elected, in such an event either a postponement or adjournment of the meeting would be upheld. However, that situation did not develop in this case, as no opportunity was given by the chairman for compromise and adjournment, but the whole proceeding was declared at an end for the reason already stated." State *ex rel.* Price v. DuBrul, 100 Ohio St. 272, 126 N.E. 87, 90 (1919).

remptorily declared the meeting at an end and left the room, it was competent for the meeting to go on with the business for which it had convened and to appoint another chairman. "The meeting by itself . . . can resolve to go on with the business for which it has been convened, and appoint a chairman to conduct the business which the other chairman, forgetful of his duty or violating his duty, has tried to stop because the proceedings have taken a turn which he himself does not like." [50] And where the president arbitrarily declared an adjournment of a shareholders' meeting for four weeks against the wishes of a quorum present, to prevent the election of directors and the termination of his office, and then absented himself from the meeting, he "abdicated the Chair which automatically by such action became vacant." Another chairman was lawfully elected and the meeting proceeded to elect directors. "A quorum was present and if the wishes of the shareholders could be thwarted by the conduct of a single person it would violate all rules of fair play. Furthermore, if the president could adjourn the meeting for four weeks, the query presents itself as to how long the frustration of the shareholders could continue." [51]

In an interesting case the chairman of a political convention cancelled the convention before it was called to order or had taken any

[50] National Dwellings Society v. Sykes, [1894] 3 Ch. 159, 162, *quoted in* Arcus v. Castle, [1954] N.Z.L.R. 122, 130 (1953).

Where the chairman peremptorily declared a meeting at an end and left the room without justification, it was competent for the meeting to go on with the business for which it was convened and to appoint another chairman for this purpose. Arcus v. Castle, [1954] N.Z.L.R. 122 (1953).

When the president illegally attempted to adjourn a meeting, the shareholders had a right to adjourn the meeting to another place and to proceed with its business. State *ex rel.* Ryan v. Cronan, 23 Nev. 437, 49 P. 41 (1897).

[51] *In re* Dollinger Corp., 51 Misc. 2d 802, 274 N.Y.S.2d 285, 288 (Sup. Ct. 1966), *quoting In re* Ajello's Petition, 26 Misc. 2d 1026, 1034, 212 N.Y.S.2d 970, 978 (Sup. Ct. 1961).

French v. Roosevelt, 18 Misc. 307, 41 N.Y.S. 1080 (Sup. Ct. 1896) (temporary chairman refused to call certified roll of delegates at a political convention and left the room, whereupon majority present elected a chairman and continued business of the meeting).

The speaker of a city House of Delegates put a motion to adjourn to a viva voce vote and declared it carried. He and others then left the meeting, preventing an appeal. The remaining members, constituting a quorum, then removed the speaker and elected a new speaker in his place. The action was held valid. State *ex rel.* Fox v. Alt, 26 Mo. App. 673 (1887).

action because the meeting room did not have ample seating capacity for all delegates and alternates entitled to attend. After the meeting was cancelled a delegate mounted the platform and called for a continuance of the meeting and for the nomination of candidates. The trial court held that the action of the chairman in cancelling the meeting was arbitrary and unjustifiable and that the delegate was within his rights in attempting to organize the meeting and continue with its business, but that the continuance was irregular because a partial roll call taken by the delegate indicated that less than a quorum was present. The appellate court reversed, holding that the cancellation of the convention by the chairman was not arbitrary or capricious and that a later meeting called by the chairman at another room was a valid meeting.[52] In another case conflicting evidence with respect to an adjournment and subsequent election clearly indicated such irregularities that it was impossible to determine who was rightfully elected. The court ordered a new election.[53]

§ 8.3.4   Adjournment for Persistent Disorder

The authorities agree that the chairman has implicit power to adjourn a meeting without a motion being made and submitted to the body whenever persistent disorder or a serious emergency renders further orderly business impossible.[54] Generally the disorder must be so great that the assembly has ceased to be a deliberative body.[55] Adjournment may be for such period as is reasonably

[52] Bannigan v. Heffernan, 115 N.Y.S.2d 889 (Sup. Ct.), *modified,* 280 App. Div. 891, 115 N.Y.S.2d 444 (2d Dep't 1952), *aff'd,* 304 N.Y. 729 (1952).

[53] Connolly v. Cohen, 173 Misc. 288, 17 N.Y.S.2d 891 (Sup. Ct. 1939), *aff'd,* 17 N.Y.S.2d 621 (1st Dep't 1940).

[54] The chairman of a union meeting had power to recess a meeting which opened with "shouts, protests, confusion and general disorder." Ash v. Holdeman, 13 Misc. 2d 528, 175 N.Y.S.2d 135 (Sup. Ct. 1958), *modified,* 5 App. Div. 2d 1017, 174 N.Y.S.2d 215 (2d Dep't 1958), *citing* Robert's Rules of Order.

See Robert's Rules of Order at 237, 358.

[55] "That a presiding officer, who is merely the agency through which the assembly declares its will, does not ordinarily have the power of arbitrarily adjourning the meeting of his own motion, is a proposition which demands little, if any, discussion. While there is no statutory provision defining his duties in this respect, common parliamentary custom or law necessarily forbids such action on the part of a presiding officer of a legislative assembly. To

necessary to restore a sufficiently tranquil atmosphere for the proceedings to continue.[56] A meeting may be adjourned whenever necessary or advisable. "Certainly, if the meeting becomes so turbulent that it cannot be conducted peacefully and without the aid of police officers, an adjournment would seem to be in order."[57] In case of less violence, such as a common "squabble," the chairman properly can adjourn the meeting with the concurrence of a voice vote of the members present.[58]

In a recent case the court nullified a county political meeting due to irregularities and disorder, holding that it was the duty of the chairman to quiet the disorder or to adjourn the proceedings until a proper atmosphere had been restored. "If there was disorder it was incumbent upon the chairman to quiet the disorder or cease doing business until there was the proper atmosphere for the proper conduct of the meeting. Failure to do this was a grave irregular-

---

uphold such procedure would be to sanction his usurpation of the undoubted rights and privileges of the assembly. Unless the assembly acquiesces in an arbitrary announcement of an adjournment by the chairman, it would seem to be difficult to sustain such action, except upon the ground that the attending circumstances were of a very extraordinary character. If it appeared that there was great turmoil and disorder, and that the members or a substantial part of them refused to respond to the efforts of the chairman to preserve order, an adjournment might result as a necessary consequence of the situation; and the announcement of the chairman that the meeting was adjourned, without a motion being made for that purpose, might be deemed a valid exercise of his implied power. The occasion might be so urgent as to make such action necessary. Indeed, it has been said by a writer on parliamentary procedure: 'Should the disorder become so great that business cannot be transacted, and the chairman cannot enforce order, as a last resort he can declare the assembly adjourned.' Rob. Rules Ord. § 40, note. An urgent necessity arising from the attendant circumstances would seem to be the only justification for such action, in the absence of statutory authority or special rules of procedure. Whether the disorder is so great that the assembly ceases to be a deliberative body and is unable to perform its legislative functions, and whether the chairman is unable to preserve such a degree of order as is necessary for the transaction of legislative business, are principally questions of fact." Attorney General v. Remick, 73 N.H. 25, 58 A. 871, 873 (1904).

[56] SHAW AND SMITH, THE LAW OF MEETINGS at 73.

[57] *In re* Election of Dirs. of Bushwick Sav. & Loan Ass'n, 189 Misc. 316, 70 N.Y.S.2d 478, 481 (Sup. Ct. 1947).

[58] Western Cottage Piano & Organ Co. v. Burrows, 144 Ill. App. 350 (1908).

ity." [59] In another case involving a disorderly political meeting the
court affirmed the general rule applicable to both corporate and
political meetings, that the power to adjourn is vested only in the
meeting itself, but noted an exception to the rule: "[W]here there
is a dire threat of physical harm, riot or the like, the chairman may
adjourn the meeting to a place where it may be continued without
the threat of physical harm." [60]

The offending members or shareholders who cause the disorder
resulting in an adjournment of a meeting may not take advantage
of the disturbance to reorganize the meeting and attempt to gain
their objective. An interesting case involves the president of a corporation who, while serving as an inspector of election, was violently
interfered with in the discharge of his duties, and who might reasonably have expected further violence if he had attempted to continue. Under these circumstances, the court held that he was
justified in refusing to preside further or remain in attendance,
stating that "we cannot hold that those, whose violent acts caused
him to vacate his office as inspector, could take advantage of their
own lawless conduct to reorganize the meeting and recount the
votes." [61] However, if the chairman declares the meeting adjourned
because of disorder of a member and then withdraws without first
exhausting all his legitimate powers for preserving order before
declaring the meeting adjourned no matter how "reprehensible and
unparliamentary" the member's conduct may have been, it has been
held that the meeting was not legally adjourned. "Under such circumstances it was competent for the remaining members, who
constituted a quorum, to elect a chairman and a temporary clerk
for that meeting, and to proceed with the transaction of such business as it was competent for the council to transact." [62]

The court will look to common parliamentary law for guidance
in determining whether the chairman may act without concurrence
of the assembly. At a disorderly meeting of an unincorporated

[59] *In re* Ryan v. Grimm, 43 Misc. 2d 836, 840, 252 N.Y.S.2d 521 (Sup. Ct.
1964), *aff'd,* 22 App. Div. 2d 171, 254 N.Y.S.2d 462 (4th Dep't 1964), *aff'd,*
15 N.Y.2d 922, 206 N.E.2d 867, 258 N.Y.S.2d 843 (1965).

[60] Egan v. Kelly, 14 N.J. Super. 103, 81 A.2d 413, 415 (1951).

[61] Umatilla Water Users' Ass'n v. Irvin, 56 Ore. 414, 108 P. 1016, 1021
(1910).

[62] Attorney General v. Remick, 73 N.H. 25, 58 A. 871, 873, 874 (1904),
citing Robert's Rules of Order.

trade union, the presiding officer adjourned the meeting in view of
the disorderly arguments and fisticuffs. Despite adjournment the
dissidents continued the meeting. The Constitution of the union
provided that: "The meetings of this Union shall be governed by
the Robert's Rules of Order unless otherwise specified by this Constitution and By-laws." The court held that the meeting was validly
adjourned, citing Robert's Rules. "The trial judge also recognized
the rule that in the absence of any provision in the laws of an
association prescribing the manner in which its meetings may be
conducted, common parliamentary principles in use by all deliberative assemblies may be resorted to in considering the regularity of
the proceedings." The court quoted Robert's at § 58 and concluded
that the trial judge was fully warranted in holding, as applied to
this case, that "Robert's Rules of Order could be deemed to state
common parliamentary principles in general usage without any
other affirmative showing to that effect." [63]

It has been suggested that the chairman take caution in adjourning a meeting for disorder and that adjournment be taken only
when the exigent circumstances leave no room for the suggestion
that he was actuated by some arbitrary motive or bias. Clearly
the chairman has the power to declare a bona fide adjournment
during the course of a meeting "if circumstances of violent interruption make it unsafe or seriously difficult for the voters to tender
their shares. . . . In most of such cases, the question will turn
upon the intention and effect of the adjournment; if the intention
and the effect were to interrupt and procrastinate the business, such
adjournment would be illegal; if, on the contrary, the intention and
effect were to forward and facilitate it, and no injurious effects were
produced, such adjournment would, it is conceived, be supported." [64]

§ 8.4 Managerial Discretion

Although an adjournment differs from a cancellation, it has also
been suggested that a shareholders' meeting, called and soon to

[63] Marvin v. Manash, 175 Ore. 311, 153 P.2d 251, 253–54 (1944).

[64] SHAW AND SMITH, THE LAW OF MEETINGS at 73, *quoting* from Rogers,
Eccl. Law.

See Wall v. London & No. Assets Corp., [1898] 2 Ch. 469 (shareholders
voted in favor of terminating discussion and against adjournment of meeting,
whereupon chairman put the motion for which meeting was called).

convene, cannot be cancelled by management simply because the proxies received indicate an unfavorable result. However, cancellation may be justified as a reasonable exercise of managerial discretion if misleading information has been circulated among the shareholders preventing an intelligent and untainted decision.[65]

§ 8.5   Adjournment—Less Than Quorum

It is a generally accepted rule of parliamentary law applicable to all deliberative assemblies that a meeting may be adjourned by the chairman or by action of less than a quorum if a quorum is not present.[66] A board of aldermen adjourned several times for lack of

[65] "It does not follow, however, that management, having power to call a stockholders' meeting, may cancel it simply because the proxies returned indicate an unfavorable vote. Substantial expenditures in the proxy solicitation may raise an estoppel in the absence of good cause. If, however, misleading information has been circulated among the stockholders, preventing an intelligent and untainted decision, cancellation may be justified as a reasonable exercise of managerial discretion without regard to whether the circulation was made by the opponent in the proxy contest or by some unrelated third person. Neither the corporate interest nor the public interest is satisfied by the votes of misled stockholders simply because the misinformation was not distributed by either party." Union Pacific R.R. v. Chicago & N.W. Ry., 226 F. Supp. 400, 412–13 (N.D. Ill. 1964).

[66] The chairman of an annual meeting, ascertaining a lack of quorum, announced that he would adjourn the meeting if there were no objections. The meeting was adjourned and no motion was made to appeal the chair's ruling. After the adjournment a group of stockholders constituting less than a quorum voted to adjourn to a day certain. Such action was a nullity. "The adjournment declared by [the chairman] was sine die. In the absence of appeal, it became final and there was no meeting which could be adjourned to a certain date by a minority of the stockholders." State ex rel. Industrial Fin., Ltd. v. Yanagawa, 484 P.2d 145, 147 (Hawaii 1971).

The rule, as we understand, applicable to all deliberative bodies, is that any number have power to adjourn, though they may not be a quorum for the transaction of business." Kimball v. Marshall, 44 N.H. 465, 467–68 (1863), citing Jefferson's Manual (1813), and quoting Cushing's Manual (1856) as follows: "If at any time in the course of the proceedings notice is taken that a quorum is not present, and such appears to be the fact, the assembly must be immediately adjourned."

"It is elementary that any member of a board or deliberative body, in the absence of a quorum to transact business, may adjourn the meeting to a

quorum and, when a quorum was present, approved the assessment roll. The court, in approving the assessment, noted that "the approval here was valid for the reason that, while less than a quorum of a deliberative assembly is without power to transact business, less than a quorum thereof may adjourn, or take a recess, to a later time. It is true that no statute here so provides, but such is the general parliamentary rule." [67]

It has been argued that a meeting which has not been sufficiently organized for the choice of officers, and thus is without a presiding officer who could put the question of adjournment and declare the meeting adjourned, would not be sufficiently organized for the purpose of adjournment. In answer, the court has said: "But we do not consider this argument as having any legal foundation. It is not at all unusual, and never has been supposed to be unlawful,

---

day certain." Notice of the adjourned meeting was properly given to the absent commissioners. Therefore all business properly coming before the meeting was regularly transacted. Choate v. North Fork Highway Dist., 39 Idaho 483, 228 P. 885, 886 (1924).

Where a quorum was not present at a regular meeting "its only possible legal action was to adjourn." Kauffman v. Meyberg, 59 Cal. App. 2d 730, 140 P.2d 210, 216 (1943).

"Relators, being less than a quorum, could do nothing more than adjourn, as they did." Wampler v. State, 148 Ind. 557, 47 N.E. 1068, 1072 (1897), *citing* Robert's Rules of Order and Cushing's Manual.

"All the parliamentary authorities . . . agree that a quorum is required for action, other than adjournment, by any parliamentary body. . . ." Christoffel v. United States, 338 U.S. 84, 92 (1949) (Jackson, J., dissenting).

[67] It is the general parliamentary rule that the only business which can be transacted in the absence of a quorum is to take measures to obtain a quorum, to fix an adjournment date, to adjourn, or take a recess to a later time. Shelby v. Burns, 153 Miss. 392, 121 So. 113 (1929) (board of aldermen), *citing* Robert's Rules of Order.

Accord, Kauffman v. Meyberg, 59 Cal. App. 2d 730, 140 P.2d 210, 216 (1943) (family corporation); Hexter v. Columbia Baking Co., 16 Del. Ch. 263, 145 A. 115 (1929) (stockholders' meeting); Davidson v. American Paper Mfg. Co., 188 La. 69, 175 So. 753, 757 (1937) (stockholders' meeting); City of Rolla v. Schuman, 189 Mo. App. 252, 175 S.W. 241, 243 (1915) (board of aldermen); Kimball v. Marshall, 44 N.H. 465 (1863) (election of city clerk), *citing* Jefferson's Manual and Cushing's Manual; O'Neil v. Tyler, 3 N.D. 47, 53 N.W. 434, 438 (1892) (city council), *citing* Cushing, Law & Pr. Leg. Assem.

for meetings of corporations to be adjourned for want of a quorum, without transacting any other business." [68]

There is a conflict of authority on this point.[69] The minority view is that a number of members less than a quorum cannot legally adjourn a meeting unless there be statutory, by-law, or regulatory authority therefor.[70]

[68] Attorney General v. Simonds, 111 Mass. 256, 259–60 (1873).

See Davidson v. American Paper Mfg. Co., 188 La. 69, 175 So. 753, 757 (1937) (statute provided that "if a meeting cannot be organized because a quorum has not attended, those present may adjourn the meeting").

[69] "As to the right of less than a quorum of a body to adjourn to a certain time, in the absence of a constitutional or statutory provision allowing it, the authorities are in conflict." However, the legality of an adjournment of a meeting by less than a quorum to a certain time cannot be questioned by the courts, where at the adjourned meeting all members were present and participated in the transaction of business. C. B. Nash Co. v. Council Bluffs, 174 F. 182, 184 (C.C.S.D. Iowa 1909) (citing cases).

[70] "The by-laws of the corporation provided that a quorum should consist of five members, while in fact there were but two members of the board present when the adjournment was attempted to be made, and they alone assumed to order it. There can be no question but that less than a quorum of a board of directors have no authority to adjourn a meeting to any date whatever." Cheney v. Canfield, 158 Cal. 342, 111 P. 92, 94 (1910).

An annual meeting cannot adjourn unless a quorum is present, to any date whatever, unless the by-laws otherwise provide. Noremac, Inc. v. Centre Hill Court, Inc., 164 Va. 151, 178 S.E. 877, 882 (1935).

"It is usual, in the by-laws of private corporations . . . to provide that less than a quorum may adjourn from time to time until a quorum shall be present. That power for less than a quorum to act by way of adjournment is not found in the statute or in any by-law produced. An adjournment is not the act of individuals, but of the body itself, and, if the council is not present by a quorum, it cannot by way of adjournment act in the matter of stating a time in the future to reconvene." Pennsylvania Co. v. Cole, 132 F. 668, 678 (C.C.D. Ind. 1904) (city council).

Where a regulation of a fraternal order makes no "mention of adjournment, or power to adjourn, when no quorum was present at the first meeting," the regulation will be construed as requiring a further or second call on notice. DiSilvestro v. Sons of Italy Grand Lodge, 130 Misc. 494, 223 N.Y.S. 791 (Sup. Ct. 1927), aff'd, 225 App. Div. 844, 232 N.Y.S. 732 (4th Dep't 1929), modified, 228 App. Div. 14, 238 N.Y.S. 477 (4th Dep't 1930).

Assuming that an adjournment of a city council was irregular for want of a quorum, attendance at the adjourned meeting by all the members and participation in its proceedings create an assumption that all members acquiesced in the illegal adjournment. State ex rel. Parker v. Smith, 22 Minn. 218 (1875).

§ 8.6   Business at Adjourned Meeting

An adjourned meeting of either a regular or special meeting is but a continuation of the meeting of which it is an adjournment.[71] It is generally accepted that any business which could have been considered and acted upon at a regular meeting duly convened of a deliberative body may legally be considered and determined at an adjourned meeting.[72] However, no business can be transacted at an

[71] "An adjourned meeting of either a regular or special meeting is but a continuation of the meeting·of which it is an adjournment, and any business which could have been transacted at the original meeting may be transacted at the adjourned meeting. Thus meetings of the council or board on a day other than the stated one for regular meetings, assembled pursuant to adjournment of the regular meetings, are not special meetings, or a distinct class of meetings, but are regular meetings with all the power and authority for municipal affairs possessed on the stated day for assembling, and all municipal action taken at such meeting is as valid as if taken on the first day of the session." City of Biloxi v. Cawley, 278 So. 2d 389, 391 (Miss. 1973).

An adjourned meeting is but a continuation of the same meeting, and may consider and act upon any matter which it could properly have considered during the course of the regular meeting. Del Greco v. Mayor, 294 N.E.2d 594, 597 (Mass. 1973).

"The general rule is that a city council may adjourn and that its adjourned meeting is a continuation of the original meeting." Mason City v. Aeling, 209 N.W.2d 8, 11 (Iowa 1973).

"An adjourned meeting is legally the continuation of the meeting of which it is an adjournment." Strain v. Mims, 123 Conn. 275, 193 A. 754, 758 (1937), *quoting* TROW, THE PARLIAMENTARIAN at 76.

See, e.g., In re Hammond, 139 F. 898, 900 (S.D.N.Y. 1905); Attorney General v. Simonds, 111 Mass. 256, 259 (1873); Vogel v. Parker, 118 N.J.L. 521, 193 A. 817, 818 (1937); *In re* Weinstein, 203 Misc. 975, 119 N.Y.S.2d 457 (Sup. Ct. 1953); *In re* Election of Dirs. of Bushwick Sav. & Loan Ass'n, 189 Misc. 316, 70 N.Y.S.2d 478 (Sup. Ct. 1947); State *ex rel.* Balsinger v. Town of Madisonville, 435 S.W.2d 803 (Tenn. 1968).

[72] An adjourned meeting is simply "a session of the regular meeting" and it can do any business which could have been done at the original meeting. *In re* Hammond, 139 F. 898, 901 (S.D.N.Y. 1905).

A meeting can transact on the adjourned date any and all of the business that could have been transacted on the original date. *In re* Weinstein, 203 Misc. 975, 119 N.Y.S.2d 457, 459 (Sup. Ct. 1953) (election of directors at annual meeting).

"The notice given respecting the original meeting extends to all adjourned meetings and corporations may transact any business at an adjourned meeting which they could have done at the original meeting, it being but a continua-

adjourned meeting unless it could have been transacted at the original meeting,[73] and all "limitations imposed upon the governing body as regards action at the original meeting obtain at the adjourned meeting." [74]   Thus, if a special meeting is adjourned, nothing can be considered at such adjourned meeting unless it could have been considered and acted upon at the special meeting.[75]

---

tion of that meeting."   *In re* Election of Dirs. of Bushwick Sav. & Loan Ass'n, 189 Misc. 316, 70 N.Y.S.2d 478, 481 (Sup. Ct. 1947).

A duly adjourned meeting can do any business that could legally be done at the regular meeting.   People *ex rel.* Locke v. Common Council, 5 Lans. 11 (N.Y. Sup. Ct. 1871).

Stockholders may transact at an adjourned meeting any business which might have been transacted at the original meeting.   State *ex rel.* Ryan v. Cronan, 23 Nev. 437, 49 P. 41 (1897).

In a zoning board dispute it was held that "[w]hen a meeting is adjourned before the business is finished, and that meeting closes the session, the unfinished business may be introduced at the next session as new business on the same footing as if it had never been before the assembly."   Strain v. Mims, 123 Conn. 275, 193 A. 754 (1937), *quoting* TROW, THE PARLIAMENTARIAN at 76.

"It has been held that any business which may be properly transacted at a regular meeting may, if commenced but not completed at the regular meeting, be done at an adjourned meeting, which is simply a continuation of the regular meeting, and that no notice to the stockholders of the holding of such adjourned meeting is necessary."   State v. Bonnell, 35 Ohio St. 10, 16 (1878).

An adjourned meeting has power to transact any business which might have been transacted at the original meeting.   Seal of Gold Mining Co. v. Slater, 161 Cal. 621, 120 P. 15 (1911).

[73] Adjourned meetings are but continuations of the same meeting without any loss or accumulation of powers.   "Nothing could be transacted at any of the adjourned meetings, unless it could have been transacted at the called meeting."   Neill v. Ward, 103 Vt. 117, 153 A. 219, 224 (1930).

[74] An adjourned meeting is a continuation of the same meeting, and "the limitations imposed upon the governing body as regards action at the original meeting obtain at the adjourned meeting."   Vogel v. Parker, 118 N.J.L. 521, 193 A. 817, 818 (Sup. Ct. 1937).

[75] "That is, if a regular meeting is adjourned, any business which could have been proper for the council to consider at that meeting may be considered and acted upon at the adjourned meeting; but if it is a special or called meeting which is adjourned, nothing can be considered at such adjourned meeting unless it could have been considered and acted upon at the special meeting."   *Ex parte* Wolf, 14 Neb. 24, 14 N.W. 660, 663 (1883).

§ 8.6.1   Reconsideration at Adjourned Meeting

A meeting in adjournment may reconsider any action taken at the regular meeting,[76] except a valid election by ballot duly declared and entered of record.[77]

[76] "All deliberative or legislative bodies, during their session, have the power to do and undo, consider and reconsider, as often as they think proper, and it is the final result only which is to be regarded as the thing done." Neill v. Ward, 103 Vt. 117, 153 A. 219, 224 (1930).

It is within the power of a political convention before it finally adjourns to revoke a nomination previously made and to substitute another nominee at the same or at an adjourned meeting. *In re* Nash, 36 Misc. 113, 72 N.Y.S. 1057 (Sup. Ct. 1901).

A resolution of a city common council vetoed by the mayor may be passed over the veto at a later council in which several new members are sitting. "If the body is a continuous one when a proceeding is taken up in any of its phases, that is a reconsideration for it is the board of aldermen or board of councilmen as an entirety which reconsiders, and not its constituent members." People *ex rel.* New York Central & H. R.R. v. Buffalo, 123 App. Div. 141, 108 N.Y.S. 331 (1908).

"The power is inherent in every deliberative body to amend a resolution previously adopted by it. . . . By reasonable implication an amendment to a resolution may be also amended at a meeting subsequent to that when the resolution was passed." Simpson v. Berkowitz, 59 Misc. 160, 110 N.Y.S. 485, 487 (Sup. Ct. 1908).

A school committee elected a superintendent on the first ballot, then reconsidered its vote at the same meeting, and elected another person at an adjourned meeting. The members of a deliberative body may reconsider their vote and change it at an adjourned meeting. Wood v. Cutter, 138 Mass. 149 (1884).

A resolution of a common council to construct a sewer properly was reconsidered at an adjourned meeting. People *ex rel.* Locke v. Common Council, 5 Lans. 11 (N.Y. Sup. Ct. 1871).

"[U]nless some right of a third person intervenes, all deliberative bodies have a right to reconsider their proceedings during a session as often as they think proper, when not otherwise provided by law, and it is the final result only which is to be regarded as the thing done." Toffolon v. Zoning Bd. of Appeals, 236 A.2d 96, 99–100 (Conn. 1967).

[77] While a municipal body may set aside an election for irregularity or illegality before the election is declared, the court stated: "We are aware of no authority which holds that, when the election by ballot is declared and entered of record, it may be reconsidered at an adjourned meeting on a subsequent day, and a new election had." State v. Philips, 79 Me. 506, 11 A. 274, 275 (1887).

When it appeared that the stockholders of a cooperative association had adopted a resolution to amend the charter at the noticed meeting but the president was in doubt as to the exact number of outstanding common shares and thus was not able to state the vote and make a ruling on the results, a motion to adjourn to another day was properly adopted. At the adjourned meeting, a motion that all previous action "be rescinded and held for naught" was made and carried. Thereupon a motion was carried approving the amendment, and the president declared the resolution adopted. The court held that the shareholders had a right to adjourn, that the adjournment was made in good faith, that the adjourned meeting was a continuation of the first meeting, and that the proceedings which could take place at the first meeting could also take place with like force and effect at the second meeting.[78]

Where an election was duly held by a joint meeting of school committees and the chairman refused to declare that the respondent was elected, but on the contrary declared that there was no election and adjourned the meeting, it was held that the adjourned meeting had power to rescind the vote taken at the regular meeting and to conduct a new election.[79]

Reconsideration at an adjourned meeting cannot prejudice the rights of other parties which have intervened.[80] Also, where the purpose of the adjourned meeting is "expressly restricted to methods and means to effectuate that plan previously adopted, not to reconsider or undo the same," the adjourned meeting may not reconsider or undo the adopted plan.[81]

[78] Sagness v. Farmers Co-Op. Creamery Co., 67 S.D. 379, 293 N.W. 365, 366 (1940).

[79] Reed v. Barton, 176 Mass. 473, 57 N.E. 961 (1900). See opinion by Holmes, C. J.

[80] "Under the decisions here quoted and the general rules relating to powers of deliberative bodies of the character of city councils, we are of the opinion that, where such a body has finally voted upon a proposition and no motion for reconsideration or other motion is pending thereon, the city council, upon adjournment of its meeting, has no power to reconsider its action where the rights of other persons have intervened." City of Kankakee v. Small, 317 Ill. 55, 147 N.E. 404, 408 (1925).

See Terry v. Eagle Lock Co., 47 Conn. 141 (1879) (rescission of vote to increase capital stock).

[81] Naftalin v. La Salle Holding Co., 153 Minn. 482, 190 N.W. 887, 889 (1922) (increase of capital stock).

§ 8.6.2　Meeting Unlawfully Adjourned

All action taken at a meeting not lawfully called or organized is unauthorized and illegal, and by the same token, no legal action can be taken at an adjourned unlawful meeting or at a meeting unlawfully adjourned.[82] For example, an invalid hearing (for lack of quorum) cannot be validated by a subsequent vote at which a quorum is present. Where a zoning board proceeded with a hearing on an application for a variance with less than a quorum of disinterested members present, on the understanding that the hearing would be adjourned for a later decision by a lawful quorum, approval of the variance at the adjourned meeting did not validate the earlier hearing and therefore was a nullity.[83] There has been an exception to this rule applicable to deliberative bodies having a fixed or determinable number of members, such as a city council, where there is a full attendance and participation by the members at an adjourned meeting.[84]

[82] An adjourned meeting without a quorum cannot act. "The motives that may have induced the absence of five of the trustees from the adjourned meeting does not affect the question. . . . However reprehensible their conduct may have been in that respect, the absence of a quorum at the adjourned meeting rendered it impossible for the members present to make any valid appointment." State ex rel. Laughlin v. Porter, 113 Ind. 79, 14 N.E. 883, 884–85 (1888), citing Cushing, Parl. Law.

Where a quorum was not present at a reconvened meeting at which officers and directors of a corporation were elected, a preliminary injunction against continuation of the adjourned meeting was granted, thereby precluding announcement of the results of the vote. Textron, Inc. v. American Woolen Co., 122 F. Supp. 305 (D. Mass. 1954).

Statute required majority of stock to be present at all elections of directors. Thus, after the breaking of a quorum, the minority could not elect directors, although the adjournment which broke the quorum was illegally voted. Bridgers v. Staton, 150 N.C. 216, 63 S.E. 892 (1909).

Election of officers at an adjourned meeting held without a legal quorum present will be set aside. See DiSilvestro v. Sons of Italy Grand Lodge, 130 Misc. 494, 223 N.Y.S. 791 (Sup. Ct. 1927), aff'd, 225 App. Div. 844, 232 N.Y.S. 732 (4th Dep't 1929), modified, 228 App. Div. 14, 238 N.Y.S. 477 (4th Dep't 1930).

[83] Giuliano v. Entress, 158 N.Y.S.2d 961 (Sup. Ct. 1957).

[84] In the absence of proof that the adjourned meeting was not fully attended by all the members, it will be presumed that they did so attend and acquiesce in the irregular adjournment. "Illegality will not be presumed, but the contrary." State ex rel. Parker v. Smith, 22 Minn. 218, 223 (1875).

§ 8.7   Voting at Adjourned Meeting

The concept that an adjourned meeting of stockholders is a continuation of the regularly called meeting does not limit the right of attendance at the adjourned meeting to those stockholders who were present in person or by proxy at the called meeting. New stockholders of record and stockholders who were not present or represented at the regular meeting are entitled to attend the adjourned meeting and to vote their shares.[85] This meets the general principle that the right of a person to vote at an adjourned meeting is to be determined by his status as a stockholder at the time when such meeting is held.[86]

However, when an annual shareholders' meeting has been declared illegal and the court has ordered that a special meeting be held, the order may contain detailed provisions that shareholders qualified to vote would be, as nearly as practicable, those who were eligible to participate in the voided meeting.[87]

§ 8.8   Notice of Adjourned Meeting

A due notice of meeting extends to all adjournments of the meeting, and further notice of an adjourned meeting is not necessary unless the controlling law or by-laws so provide.[88] "Once a stock-

---

[85] The court commented: "The fact that more votes were cast at the adjourned meeting because of new votes obtained since the regular meeting does not seem to alter the situation." Sagness v. Farmers Co-Op. Creamery Co., 67 S.D. 379, 293 N.W. 365 (1940).

[86] The board of directors may change the record date for determining shareholders entitled to vote after adjournment of the original meeting. McDonough v. Foundation Co., 7 Misc. 2d 571, 155 N.Y.S.2d 67 (Sup. Ct. 1956).

"But even in an adjourned meeting stockholders not represented at the first meeting are entitled to vote. . . ." Bridgers v. Staton, 150 N.C. 216, 63 S.E. 892 (1909).

Where the voting power has shifted from the common stock to the preferred stock between the convening of the annual meeting and an adjourned session, the common stock may no longer be voted. Vogtman v. Merchants' Mortgage & Credit Co., 20 Del. Ch. 364, 178 A. 99 (1935).

[87] See Dillon v. Berg, 453 F.2d 876 (3d Cir. 1971).

[88] "The law holds the members of deliberative bodies, parties attending courts of justice and public meetings, bound to take notice of the time of ad-

journments, and to be present at the time and place of adjournment without special notice." Kimball v. Marshall, 44 N.H. 465, 468 (1836).

"The association, in the absence of rules, can adjourn its meetings from time to time according to the usual method of parliamentary bodies, and transact business at an adjourned meeting without notice to the absentees." Ostrom v. Greene, 161 N.Y. 353, 55 N.E. 919, 922 (1900).

The transaction of business at an adjourned meeting without further notice thereof is valid; and directors may be elected at an adjourned annual meeting. *In re* Hammond, 139 F. 898 (S.D.N.Y. 1905).

A zoning board of appeals is entitled to continue its public hearings at a later date without further notice. "This is in accordance with the general authorities." Shaughnessy v. Metropolitan Dade County, 238 So. 2d 466, 468 (Fla. 1970), *citing* Robert's Rules of Order on another point.

No notice of an adjourned meeting was required where complainant was present at the adjourned meeting with his attorney. Moskowitz v. City of St. Paul, 16 N.W.2d 745 (Minn. 1944).

Under a by-law authorizing a quorum to adjourn a meeting of directors from time to time, not exceeding a period beyond the next regular meeting, notice of the adjournment need not be given. "A director receiving notice of a meeting was bound to know that a quorum might adjourn, and that business might be transacted at the adjourned meeting. And this is in accordance with the general rule, which is that no notice of adjournment of a meeting regularly called need be given." Seal of Gold Mining Co. v. Slater, 161 Cal. 621, 120 P. 15, 18 (1911).

"It is generally known that at a school district meeting, or other similar meetings, the action is not concluded nor the final results known until final adjournment takes place. We hold that the warning and posting which was duly made for the annual meeting of March 31 effectively gave notice to the voters of any business to be transacted in the recessed or adjourned annual meeting until its final adjournment." Byron v. Timberlane Regional School Dist., 309 A.2d 218, 222 (N.H. 1973), *citing* Mason's Manual, Robert's Rules of Order.

A city council has inherent power to adjourn a regular meeting to a date certain without notice to absent members of the time and place to which the meeting has been adjourned. Del Greco v. Mayor, 294 N.E.2d 594 (Mass. 1973).

After a meeting has been convened by proper notice or waiver, and organized, it can adjourn from time to time without further notice or waiver. *In re* Election of Dirs. of Bushwick Sav. & Loan Ass'n, 189 Misc. 316, 70 N.Y.S.2d 478 (Sup. Ct. 1947).

Unless required by by-laws or statute, notice of an adjourned meeting is not necessary. Clark v. Wild, 85 Vt. 212, 81 A. 536, 539 (1911).

Where the regulations of a fraternal order make no mention of adjournment, or power to adjourn, when no quorum was present at the first meeting, a further or second call or notice is necessary. DiSilvestro v. Sons of Italy Grand Lodge, 130 Misc. 494, 223 N.Y.S. 791, 794 (Sup. Ct. 1927), *aff'd mem.*, 225

holder's meeting is properly convened it may be adjourned from time to time without further notice to stockholders." [89] The same rule generally applies when a duly noticed meeting is adjourned without fixing a date for a subsequent meeting.[90] However, a notice of meeting will not necessarily extend to an adjourned meeting unless the latter is held for the same purposes and be virtually a continuation of the original meeting.[91]

A reason for not requiring service of a notice of the date of an adjourned meeting is founded on the general parliamentary practice of announcing to the membership at large attending the original meeting that it has been adjourned to a specified time and place. One court observed: "Obviously, as all members are bound by proceedings at a duly called meeting, there is no need for further notice." Also, as a practical matter, the service of notice in person or by mail or publication on each member might unduly delay the holding of an adjourned meeting. If it is necessary to give notice of an adjourned meeting, such notice should meet all legal requirements of the notice required to be given of the original meeting. Thus, where the resolution of adjournment does not specify the time, but empowers an officer or a committee to set the time, the membership is entitled to receive full notice and need

---

App. Div. 844, 232 N.Y.S. 732 (4th Dep't 1929), *modified*, 228 App. Div. 14, 238 N.Y.S. 477 (4th Dep't 1930).

Majority of board had authority to adjourn the meeting to a subsequent day. Each member present had notice of the adjournment, and those not present at the adjourned meeting were charged in law with notice thereof. Stockton v. Powell, 10 So. 688 (Fla. 1892).

[89] *In re* Siebenmann, 32 Misc. 2d 92, 93, 222 N.Y.S.2d 707 (Sup. Ct. 1961).

[90] *See* Lander v. Mercantile Nat'l Bank, 186 U.S. 458 (1902).

[91] Notice is not required of an adjourned meeting, held in continuation of a prior one and for the purpose of completing its unfinished business. People *ex rel.* Loew v. Batchelor, 22 N.Y. 128 (1860).

An adjourned meeting is but a continuation of the meeting which has been adjourned. Shareholders may at the adjourned meeting consider and determine any corporate business that may lawfully have been transacted at the original meeting. However, when a notice of an adjourned meeting is given to transact some but not all of the items of business named in the notice of the original meeting, a proxy given to attend this adjourned meeting is limited to conducting the items of business thus noticed. Synnott v. Cumberland Bldg. Loan Ass'n, 117 F. 379, 385 (6th Cir. 1902).

not make inquiry of the management as to the adjournment date.[92]

It is good parliamentary practice to refer in the notice of meeting to "any adjournment or adjournments thereof" to be certain that the notice of meeting extends to all adjourned meetings.[93]

Reference in the notice of meeting to any other business which may properly come before the meeting or any adjournment thereof does not intimate that the meeting would be adjourned for the purpose of conducting any other business.[94]

Where a corporation has but one office, which is also its principal place of business, it is not necessary in taking an adjournment to designate the place at which the adjourned meeting would be held.[95]

---

[92] *In re* Election of Dirs. of FDR–Woodrow Wilson Democrats, Inc., 57 Misc. 2d 743, 293 N.Y.S.2d 463, 466 (Sup. Ct. 1968).

[93] It makes no difference whether a notice of "Annual Membership Meeting" is called an "adjourned" annual meeting or a "recessed" annual meeting or a "continued" annual meeting. It was an "annual meeting." *In re* Election of Dirs. of FDR–Woodrow Wilson Democrats, Inc., 57 Misc. 2d 743, 293 N.Y.S.2d 463, 466 (Sup. Ct. 1968).

[94] Notice of meeting referring to "any and all other business that may properly come before the meeting or any adjournment or adjournments thereof, in connection with the foregoing matters" does not intimate that the meeting would be adjourned for the purpose of electing additional directors if the certificate of amendment submitted to shareholders increasing the number of directors should be approved at the meeting and then approved by the superintendent of insurance. Fierman v. Rose, 175 Misc. 102, 22 N.Y.S.2d 215, 218–19 (Sup. Ct. 1940).

[95] Clark v. Oceano Beach Resort Co., 106 Cal. App. 579, 289 P. 946 (1930).

9

Rules of Order

POWER TO ADOPT RULES

§ 9.1   Inherent Power of Deliberative Assembly To Adopt

A deliberative assembly [1] possesses the ultimate authority peacefully to convene and act, and to conduct its affairs in an orderly fashion according to established rules.[2] Common parliamentary law

---

[1] The terms "legislative" and "deliberative" as used in case law generally apply to bodies or units which meet at scheduled intervals or upon call more frequently than once annually, and whose business is generally not transacted at a single session. A town meeting is "theoretically and nominally such, however it may be in fact. . . ." Hill v. Goodwin, 56 N.H. 441, 453 (1876).

A city council is a "deliberative body with prerogatives limited only by positive laws. As such, it had full power to make reasonable rules governing the election." State *ex rel.* Reed v. De Maioribus, 131 Ohio St. 201, 2 N.E.2d 506, 509 (1936); *accord*, City of Kankakee v. Small, 317 Ill. 55, 147 N.E. 404, 408 (1925).

A constitutional convention is a deliberative body. Wells v. Bain, 75 Pa. 39 (1874).

The First Baptist Church, in meeting assembled, is a "deliberative body." Gipson v. Morris, 31 Tex. Civ. App. 645, 73 S.W. 85, 87 (1903).

A board of supervisors is a corporate body with duties of such a nature as to make it a "deliberative assembly." Neal v. County of Franklin, 43 Ill. App. 267, 269 (1892).

[2] "The power is inherent and inseparably attached to the right of the body to convene and act. It is exercisable, when not restrained by some extrinsic law, at the will of the body." Hicks v. Long Branch Comm'n, 69 N.J.L. 300, 55 A. 250, 251 (1903).

"Deliberative assemblies, in order that the will of a majority of [their] members may be ascertained and registered in an orderly way, must, ex necessitate rei, be governed by rules of procedure to which each member thereof must conform." Witherspoon v. State *ex rel.* West, 138 Miss. 310, 103 So. 134, 137 (1925), *quoting* Robert's Rules of Order (State Senate).

Rules of procedure adopted by a legislative body are "intended for the orderly and proper disposition of the matters before it." Heiskell v. Baltimore, 65 Md. 125, 4 A. 116, 118 (1886).

Parliamentary rules are "intended as principles of conduct for the government of the members, and by which the speaker or presiding officer is to regulate their conduct." Coffin v. Coffin, 4 Mass. 1, 22 (1808), *citing* Jefferson's Manual.

The adoption of rules for the conduct of business is a step in the organization of a deliberative body and is within the power of a majority of a quorum. Morris v. Cashmore, 253 App. Div. 657, 659, 3 N.Y.S.2d 624, 633 (1st Dep't), *aff'd*, 278 N.Y. 730, 17 N.E.2d 143 (1938) (city council).

implies a right of self-protection necessary for the purpose of maintaining order and facilitating the conduct of business.[3] Without

---

A state statute may preserve to a town the right to establish procedure for
a particular meeting at which a vote is taken, including the right to compel a
vote by ballot at the meeting. Town of Exeter v. Kenick, 104 N.H. 168, 181
A.2d 638 (1962).

The common law implies that nonlegislative assemblies have incidental
powers of self-protection, although of inferior importance and dignity to bodies
constituted for purposes of public legislation. Barton v. Taylor, 11 App. Cas.
197, 203 (P.C. 1886).

[3] "A legislative assembly, when established, becomes vested with all the powers and privileges which are necessary and incidental to a free and unobstructed
exercise of its appropriate functions. These powers and privileges are derived
not from the Constitution; on the contrary, they arise from the very creation of
a legislative body, and are founded upon the principle of self preservation. . . .
A legislative assembly has, therefore, all the powers and privileges which are
necessary to enable it to exercise in all respects, in a free, intelligent and impartial manner, its appropriate functions.

"What powers and privileges, therefore, a legislative assembly takes by force
and effect of its creation, are to be ascertained by a reference to the common
parliamentary law." *Ex parte* McCarthy, 29 Cal. Rptr. 395, 403 (1866). The
court quotes CUSHING, LAW AND PRACTICE OF LEGISLATIVE ASSEMBLIES. The
text from which the court quoted is as follows (Chapter Third, §§ 610–11 at
246):

> 610. The rights and immunities, incident to or conferred upon a legis-
> lative assembly, considered as an aggregate body, are founded in the
> same general reason, upon which those of the individual members rest,
> namely, to enable the assembly to perform the functions with which it is
> invested, in a free, intelligent, and impartial manner.
>
> 611. The privileges of this kind, which belong to each branch of a
> legislative assembly, may be classified and arranged under the following
> heads, namely:—
>
> 1. To judge of the returns, elections, and qualifications of its mem-
>   bers:
> 2. To choose its own officers and remove them at pleasure:
> 3. To establish its own rules of proceeding:
> 4. To have the attendance and service of its members:
> 5. To be secret in its proceedings and debates:
> 6. To preserve its own honor, dignity, purity, and efficiency, by the
>   expulsion of an unworthy, or the discharge of an incompetent,
>   member:
> 7. To protect itself and its members from personal violence:

8. To protect itself and its members from libellous and slanderous attacks:
9. To protect itself and its members from corruption:
10. To require information touching public affairs, from the public officers:
11. To require the opinion of the judges and other law-officers, on important occasions:
12. To investigate, by the testimony of witnesses or otherwise, any subject or matter, in reference to which it has power to act; and consequently, to protect parties, witnesses, and counsel, in their attendance, when summoned, or having occasion to attend for that purpose:
13. To be free from all interference of the other coordinate branch, and of the executive and judiciary departments, in its proceedings on any matter depending before it.

Followed: Bohrer v. Toberman, 227 S.W.2d 719 (Mo. 1950); State *ex rel.* Robinson v. Fluent, 30 Wash. 2d 194, 191 P.2d 240, 246, *cert. denied,* 335 U.S. 844 (1948); *see* Moran v. LaGuardia, 270 N.Y. 450, 1 N.E.2d 961 (1936).

The adoption of parliamentary rules often depends on the type and purposes of the organization which they are to serve. One court has explained: "We believe much of the confusion in the trial and decision of this proceeding and in the presentation of the appeal has been caused by the failure of the parties to recognize certain fundamental principles of parliamentary law here applicable. Broadly speaking, an assembly of persons may be classified as (1) a permanent society; (2) an occasional or mass meeting; and (3) a convention. Again in broad terms a meeting of newly elected county committeemen partakes of the nature of a convention which initially is unorganized and is simply a mass meeting in that when called to order it has no constitution, by-laws, or officers. It must rely for guidance upon the rules adopted by a predecessor committee. It is for this reason that such a mass meeting must follow with precision the procedural steps outlined in the rules for an organization meeting and particularly the order of business. Once an unorganized convention has adopted rules, decided who is entitled to vote (frequently accomplished by a committee on credentials), and elected officers it becomes an organized convention with members, officers and rules and is ready to transact business as a deliberative assembly." *In re* Ryan v. Grimm, 43 Misc. 2d 836, 252 N.Y.S.2d 521 (Sup. Ct.), *aff'd,* 22 App. Div. 2d 171, 173, 174, 254 N.Y.S.2d 462 (4th Dep't 1964), *aff'd,* 15 N.Y.2d 922, 206 N.E.2d 867, 258 N.Y.S.2d 843 (1965), *citing* Robert's Rules of Order at 275–98.

A board of supervisors is a corporate body of such a character as to make it a "deliberative assembly." "It has, therefore, those rights which inhere in any such body, of which any one dealing with it must take notice." Neal v. County of Franklin, 43 Ill. App. 267, 269 (1892) (right to reconsider and annul action previously taken).

such authority, a deliberative assembly would be powerless to accomplish the purposes of its constitution.[4]

Common parliamentary law also recognizes the right of an assembly to establish its own rules of proceeding and judge the qualifications of its own members.[5] This principle has been confirmed in a recent case involving selection of the delegates to a national political convention. The Supreme Court held that the convention itself served a pervasive national interest and was the proper forum for determining intra-party disputes as to which delegates should be seated in accordance with party standards.[6]

This right to control their own procedures is "the established prerogative of legislative bodies,"[7] but the fact that these procedures are not in accordance with rules of parliamentary law is not fatal to any action taken.[8]

When a state constitution provides that the legislature "shall

---

[4] "[T]he power to commit and to expel its members was not given [explicitly] to the house and senate, respectively, because it was regarded as inherent, incidental and necessary, and must exist in every aggregate and deliberative body, in order to the exercise of its functions, and because without it such body would be powerless to accomplish the purposes of its constitution." Hiss v. Bartlett, 69 Mass. (3 Gray) 468, 475 (1855).

In a recent case the court upheld a charge to the jury that "a church has the right to establish its own practice and rules for the admission and seating of persons and if one refused to comply with the rules the church authorities had the right to use reasonable force to evict him." Defendant went to the church "for the purpose of getting the church authorities to change its rules and practices as to seating persons." Jones v. State, 219 Ga. 848, 136 S.E.2d 358, 364 (1964), cert. denied, 379 U.S. 935 (1964).

[5] Ex parte McCarthy, 29 Cal. Rptr. 395 (1866), citing Cushing.

[6] Cousins v. Wigoda, 419 U.S. 477 (1975).

[7] A city council, having authority under its charter to control its own procedures, is not required to hear complaints of every dissatisfied taxpayer even though the notice of meeting states that it would hear complaints. People ex rel. Powott Corp. v. Woodworth, 172 Misc. 791, 15 N.Y.S.2d 985, 995 (Sup. Ct. 1939), rev'd on statutory grounds, 260 App. Div. 168, 21 N.Y.S.2d 785 (4th Dep't 1940).

[8] Regarding the question of the discretion a city council has in adhering to and changing its own rules, the court quoted Ohio Jurisprudence as follows: "The fact that procedure is not in all respects in accordance with the rules of parliamentary law is not fatal to the action of the body, if the procedure was all that the statute requires, especially in the case of proceedings of a village council." Humphrey v. Youngstown, 143 N.E.2d 321, 323 (Ohio 1955).

determine the rules of its procedure," this authority is not limited to any particular power but is broad and unlimited in its scope.[9] These words have been held to be "about as broad and compre-

[9] The power to determine rules of procedure "does not restrict the power given to the mere formulation of standing rules, or to the proceedings of the body in ordinary legislative matters; but in the absence of constitutional restraints, and when exercised by a majority of a constitutional quorum, such authority extends to the determination of the propriety and effect of any action as it is taken by the body as it proceeds in the exercise of any power, in the transaction of any business, or in the performance of any duty conferred upon it by the Constitution." Crawford v. Gilchrist, 64 Fla. 41, 59 So. 963, 968 (1912).

The power of the state Senate to enact rules governing its proceedings is unlimited except as controlled by other provisions of the Constitution. And unless controlled by other constitutional provisions "the courts cannot look to the wisdom or folly, the advantages or disadvantages of the rules which a legislative body adopts to govern its own proceedings." This power "is not restricted to proceedings of the body in ordinary legislative matters; but such authority extends to the determination of the propriety and effect of any action taken by the body as it proceeds in the exercise of any power, in the transaction of any business, or in the performance of any duty conferred upon it by the Constitution." Opinion of the Justices No. 185, 278 Ala. 525, 179 So. 2d 155, 158 (1965), *citing* Jefferson's Manual.

The constitutional authority of the legislature to determine the rules of its proceedings "does not limit itself to any particular power which the Legislature has or is given but is broad and unlimited in its scope." State *ex rel.* Johnson v. Hagemeister, 161 Neb. 475, 73 N.W.2d 625, 628, 629 (1955), *citing* Gregg's Handbook Parl. Law.

It has been suggested that, when a meeting is organized or sponsored by some state or local government agency, the government may not establish meeting rules inconsistent with the guarantees of the First Amendment. *In re* Kay, 83 Cal. Rptr. 686, 464 P.2d 142, 150 (1970).

A statute empowering the FCC to "conduct its proceedings in such manner as will best conduce to the proper dispatch of business and to the ends of justice" explicitly and by implication delegates the power to resolve subordinate questions of procedure. FCC v. Schreiber, 381 U.S. 279 (1965).

Congress intends that the CAB be "free to work out application procedures reasonably adapted to fair and orderly administration of its complex responsibilities." No principle of administrative law is more firmly established than that of agency control of its own calendar. City of San Antonio v. CAB, 374 F.2d 326, 329 (D.C. Cir. 1967).

Constitutional power in each house of the legislature to determine its rules confers authority on either house to adopt the same rules as the other, and to make joint rules not inconsistent with the Constitution. Tayloe v. Davis, 212 Ala. 282, 102 So. 433 (1924).

hensive as the English language contains," and the court held it did not have the right to ingraft any limitation thereon.[10] Thus, proceedings in conformity with legislative rules are valid where not in conflict with the Constitution.

Often rules of procedure are mandated by a higher authority. In the absence of rules of procedure so established, deliberative bodies and other assemblies have an inherent and continuous power to adopt their own governing rules of procedure,[11] both standing

[10] Witherspoon v. State *ex rel*. West, 138 Miss. 310, 103 So. 134, 138 (1925), *citing* Robert's Rules of Order, *quoted and followed in* State *ex rel*. Johnson v. Hagemeister, 161 Neb. 475, 73 N.W.2d 625, 629 (1955), *citing* Gregg's Handbook Parl. Law.

[11] The power of a deliberative body (school board) to adopt and amend rules of order is well established. "The board had the right to adopt such parliamentary rules for the convenient dispatch of its business as it might deem proper. This is a power that is inherent in every public and private body, and mere parliamentary rules are, of course, not designed to be and are not binding upon any person or persons except the members of the body that adopts them; and they may be amended, suspended, or repealed at the pleasure of the body, or in any manner that it has prescribed for this purpose." Montenegro-Riehm Music Co. v. Board of Educ., 147 Ky. 720, 145 S.W. 740, 743 (1912).

"Each legislative body, when it meets, and unless restrained by the authority which created it, is without rules of procedure, and has inherent power to make its own rules without reference to the action of preceding bodies." South Georgia Power Co. v. Baumann, 169 Ga. 649, 151 S.E. 513, 515 (1929).

"The city council has a right to prescribe by ordinance, rules of procedure in the exercise of its powers." City of Carbondale v. Wade, 106 Ill. App. 654, 662 (1903).

"It stands to reason that the city council, a legislative body has the inherent power, by ordinance, to provide for and establish rules for its own procedure, and the rules thus adopted will not be interfered with or set aside by the courts, unless they are directly, or by necessary implication, in conflict with some provision of the statute." State *ex rel*. Bishop v. Dunn, 76 Neb. 155, 107 N.W. 236, 238 (1906).

An assembly has the right to exercise its parliamentary powers in an orderly way. "The power is inherent and inseparately attached to the right of the body to convene and act. It is exercisable, when not restrained by some extrinsic law, at the will of the body." Hicks v. Long Branch Comm'n, 69 N.J.L. 300, 55 A. 250, 251 (Ct. Err. & App. 1903).

"The council is a deliberative body with prerogatives limited only by positive law. As such it had full power to make reasonable rules governing the election." State *ex rel*. Reed v. DeMaioribus, 131 Ohio St. 201, 2 N.E.2d 506, 509 (1936).

A constitutional convention is a deliberative body, having all the necessary

rules [12] and those which affect the rights of others.[13] The assembly itself, by its very existence, is fully competent to decide the manner in which it shall conduct its business.[14] This decision may be made by the assembly or by its chairman at the opening of the meeting.[15]

---

authority to make rules for its own procedure, and to decide upon all questions falling within the scope of its authority. Wells v. Bain, 75 Pa. 39 (1874).

In the absence of requirement in a borough code, statute, or rule of law, a borough council has the "legal right to adopt its own rules of procedure or parliamentary usage." Commonwealth *ex rel.* Fox v. Chace, 403 Pa. 117, 168 A.2d 569, 571 (1961).

In the absence of statutory restraint, a city council may prescribe its own rules. County Court v. City of Grafton, 77 W. Va. 84, 86 S.E. 924, 925 (1915).

The courts recognize the right and necessity of administrative agencies to fashion their own procedural rules. Flotill Prods., Inc. v. FTC, 358 F.2d 224, 229–30 (9th Cir. 1966), *rev'd*, 389 U.S. 179 (1967).

Political parties are generally self-governing and can make their own rules. "As creations of free men, political parties are privileged to make their own rules and regulations and to establish machinery for making their organizations effective. They have plenary powers as to their government and other affairs in the absence of restrictive statutes, and the courts have no power in the absence of statute conferring jurisdiction to interfere with those operations, unless a legal right has been conferred by previous party action. . . . Party differences, like family or church disputes, should be settled within the organization or by its dominating authority." O'Neil v. O'Connell, 300 Ky. 707, 189 S.W.2d 965, 967 (1945).

A city planning board can adopt rules and procedures for its hearings. State v. Moore, 101 N.J. Super. 419, 244 A.2d 522 (1968).

Ordinarily the election of officers is regulated by charter or by-laws; if none exists, then by usage and the resolutions adopted from time to time. In the absence of these, resort may be had to the rules of parliamentary law in common use in deliberative assemblies. Oestereich v. Schneider, 187 S.W.2d 756 (Mo. 1945).

[12] Generally, standing rules are minor rules setting forth operating procedures such as the starting and closing time of meetings, appointment of inspectors, reading of minutes, and the like.

[13] The provision in the state constitution that each House "shall determine the rules of its proceedings" does not restrict the power given to the "mere formulation of standing rules, or to the proceedings of the body in ordinary legislative matters" but extends to the determination of the propriety and effect of any action in the exercise of any power conferred upon it by the constitution. Crawford v. Gilchrist, 64 Fla. 41, 59 So. 963, 968 (1912).

[14] The full measure of a meeting's powers is described by Lord Russell in the following words: "There are many matters relating to the conduct of a meeting which lie entirely in the hands of those persons who are present and constitute

§ 9.2   Statutory Right of Corporations

The constitutional authority of a corporation to adopt rules and regulations for the conduct of meetings of shareholders may be found in the corporation statutes of its state of incorporation, in its charter, or in its by-laws.[16] The typical statute authorizes corporations to adopt, amend, or repeal rules, not inconsistent with law, relating to the business of the corporation, the conduct of its affairs, the rights and powers of the corporation and of its shareholders, directors, and officers.[17] At common law, the ultimate corporate

---

the meeting. Thus it rests with the meeting to decide whether notices, resolutions, minutes, accounts, and such like shall be read to the meeting or be taken as read; whether representatives of the Press, or any other persons not qualified to be summoned to the meeting, shall be permitted to be present, or if present shall be permitted to remain; whether and when discussion shall be terminated and a vote taken; whether the meeting shall be adjourned. In all these matters, and they are only instances, the meeting decides, and if necessary a vote must be taken to ascertain the wishes of the majority. If no objection is taken by any constituent of the meeting, the meeting must be taken to be assenting to the course adopted. It is not a case, as was suggested in argument, of those present at a meeting waiving rights of those who have elected not to attend; it is a case of those who have elected to attend regulating the conduct of the meeting, a question in which those who have chosen to stay away have no voice." Carruth v. Imperial Chem. Indus., Ltd., [1937] A.C. 707 at 761.

[15] The chairman of a municipal planning board, at a public meeting in the city council chamber, outlined the procedure that would govern the hearing. Defendant demanded that the proceedings be governed by Robert's Rules of Order, and the chairman ruled him out of order several times, finally resulting in his removal from the hearing room. See State v. Moore, 101 N.J. Super. 419, 244 A.2d 522 (1968).

[16] Corporations have the common-law power "without any express words or authority" to adopt by-laws. Bank of the United States v. Dandridge, 25 U.S. (12 Wheat.) 64 (1827).

A voluntary association may "adopt a constitution, by-laws, rules and regulations which will control as to all questions of discipline, or internal policy and management, and its right to interpret and administer the same is as sacred as the right to make them." State ex rel. Givens v. Superior Court, 233 Ind. 235, 117 N.E.2d 553, 555 (1954).

See, e.g., United States v. Ballin, 144 U.S. 1 (1892); Richardson v. Union Congregational Soc'y, 58 N.H. 187 (1877).

[17] "It is a general rule that a corporation may enact any bylaw for its internal management so long as such bylaws are not contrary to its charter, a controlling statute, its articles of incorporation, or violative of any general law

regulatory power rests in the stockholders. When the procedures prescribed by the charter or by-laws fail to accomplish the purposes contemplated by them, so that necessary corporate action is frustrated, it is competent for the stockholders themselves to exercise the requisite regulatory powers.[18]

§ 9.2.1   Charter and By-Laws

Charter and by-law provisions relating to meeting procedures, standing alone without further rules, are mandatory and are strictly construed.[19] They may not be supplemented by common law or by

---

or public policy. Subject to the above qualifications, a corporation may adopt bylaws regulating the calling and conduct of corporate meetings and elections of its officers." Booker v. First Fed. Sav. & Loan Ass'n, 215 Ga. 277, 110 S.E.2d 360, 362 (1959), *cert. denied,* 361 U.S. 916 (1959).

A corporation may adopt any reasonable by-laws for the purpose of enabling it to carry out the purposes and objects of its organization, within the limitations that they shall not be in conflict with law. Gottlieb v. Economy Stores, Inc., 199 Va. 848, 102 S.E.2d 345, 352 (1958).

"The power of making rules and regulations, is necessarily incident to a corporation; and it is generally inserted in the act of incorporation, to define its nature and limit its extent." Mechanics' & Farmers' Bank v. Smith, 19 Johns. R. 115, 124 (N.Y. 1821).

[18] The established election procedures having failed, and such an "emergency and contingency" having arisen that the "ordinary forms of procedure prescribed and contemplated by the charter and laws regulating these elections had suddenly failed to accomplish the purposes contemplated by so much that under the circumstances the corporators themselves had the right to exercise the power themselves, and provide for the appointment of inspectors of election, and proceed in the manner they did. . . . I have abstained from considering the question whether those provisions of the law, giving directions as to the manner of holding these elections, and which were not observed in this case, are to be considered under ordinary circumstances directory, but prefer to place the case upon the ground that where those regulations, which were intended merely to preserve and regulate the rights of the stockholders tend, in their strict observance, to the destruction of those corporate rights, instead of their preservation, a departure from them by the corporators should be sustained in law." *In re* Wheeler, 2 Abb. Pr. N.S. 361, 364, 365 (N.Y. 1866).

[19] By-laws provided that Robert's Rules of Order should govern at all corporate meetings where not in conflict with by-laws. There being a conflict as to voting requirements, the by-laws prevailed. *In re* Koch (Koch v. Wadsworth), 257 N.Y. 318, 178 N.E. 545 (1931) (religious corporation).

In the absence of rules or regulations, by-law provisions are controlling. Eisenberg v. Fauer, 25 Misc. 2d 98, 200 N.Y.S.2d 749 (Sup. Ct. 1960).

parliamentary postulates. For example, common-law rules of procedure and parliamentary practice relating to corporate meetings do not apply to an unincorporated society which has no governing law except its constitution and by-laws. Such a decision may rest on the basic principle that the constitution and by-laws of an organization constitute a binding contract between the members and the society and its officers. "By this compact, plaintiffs, defendant and all other members were bound." Thus, if the constitution and by-laws so permit, meetings of the board may be held and action taken without advance notice.[20]

§ 9.3   Power To Adopt Not Exercised

The power to establish rules need not be exercised. A deliberative body having the right to adopt rules of procedure "is not bound to establish general rules of procedure, and the failure to make such general rules does not invalidate its action if otherwise legal." [21]

§ 9.4   Preferred Rule—Common Parliamentary Law

In the case of a deliberative body which has not adopted special rules of procedure and is not bound by rules imposed by a higher authority, it is the preferred rule that meeting procedures will be governed by "common-law rules" [22] or by generally accepted parlia-

---

[20] Talton v. Behncke, 199 F.2d 471 (7th Cir. 1952) (ousting of official at meeting held without full notice).

When the law is silent as to the mode of procedure, no particular formality need be adopted. It is only necessary that the meeting proceed according to the "will of the governing body." State ex rel. Balsinger v. Town of Madisonville, 435 S.W.2d 803, 805 (Tenn. 1968) (reading of ordinances).

[21] Armitage v. Fisher, 74 Hun. 167, 26 N.Y.S. 364, 367–68 (1893), rev'g 4 Misc. 315, 24 N.Y.S. 650.

[22] "In the absence of rules adopted by a political organization, such organization is governed by the common-law rules that the act of the majority represents the act of the Committee." DeCamilla v. Connery, 43 Misc. 2d 395, 251 N.Y.S.2d 305, 309 (Sup. Ct.), aff'd, 23 App. Div. 2d 704, 256 N.Y.S.2d 986 (3d Dep't 1965).

mentary law [23] which fits the attending circumstances.[24] In describing the authority of the presiding officer, an early decision

---

A legislative joint session sitting as a unicameral body without parliamentary rules "is governed by the generally accepted rules of parliamentary procedure which flow from general principles of common law." Anderson v. Krupsak, N.Y. Ct. App., N.Y.L.J., July 9, 1976.

[23] The By-laws of The Association of the Bar of the City of New York at II 3 provide simply: "The usual parliamentary rules of order shall govern all meetings of the Association, except in cases otherwise provided for by the Constitution or by-laws."

A city council adopted a regulation that "the general rules of parliamentary law," so far as applicable, were to be considered rules of the council. The court defined "parliamentary law" by quoting from Webster's International Dictionary and Bouvier's Law Dictionary as follows: "the rules and usages of Parliament, or of deliberative bodies" and "the recognized usages of Parliament and legislative assemblies, by which their procedure is regulated" respectively. Landes v. State ex rel. Matson, 160 Ind. 479, 67 N.E. 189, 193 (1903).

Jefferson's Manual is "entitled to great weight because since 1837 it has been, by virtue of a still effective rule of the House of Representatives, governing authority in that House in all cases where there is no conflict with the standing rules and orders of the House." Ashley v. Keith Oil Corp., 7 F.R.D. 589, 592 (D.C. Mass. 1947).

[24] "Deliberative assemblies . . . must be governed by rules of procedure to which each member thereof must conform. In the absence of special rules of procedure adopted by such an assembly, or for it by an outside power having the right so to do, its procedure is governed by the general parliamentary law." Witherspoon v. State ex rel. West, 138 Miss. 310, 103 So. 134, 137 (1925), citing Robert's Rules of Order.

"In the absence of a specific regulation to the contrary, the ordinary rules of parliamentary law should be observed in the conduct of meetings." Randolph v. Mt. Zion Baptist Church, 139 N.J. Eq. 605, 53 A.2d 206, 208 (1947).

"In the absence of the adoption of rules of procedure and in the absence of statutory regulation, the generally accepted rules of parliamentary procedure would control." McCormick v. Board of Educ., 58 N.M. 648, 274 P.2d 299 (1954).

"Common parliamentary rules, in use by all deliberative assemblies in this country, may also be resorted to, in the absence of any made by the association itself, in considering the regularity of its proceedings." Also, where there are no rules, a usage or custom cannot be ignored. Ostrom v. Greene, 161 N.Y. 353, 362, 55 N.E. 919, 922 (1900).

"In the absence of any guide from statute, constitution or by-laws, the commonly recognized rules of parliamentary procedure govern." Egan v. Kelly, 14 N.J. Super. 103, 81 A.2d 413, 414 (1951).

"In the absence of rules adopted by a political organization, such organiza-

stated: "The nature and extent of his authority as the presiding officer of the council, in the absence of rules of procedure adopted by the council and of statutory provisions upon the subject, can only be determined by such principles of parliamentary usage as have been generally adopted or observed in deliberative assemblies, and which are reasonably essential to the due execution of the legitimate business of the council." [25]

In speaking of a shareholders' meeting, one court stated flatly: "The ordinary parliamentary usages apply to meetings of this character." [26]   Another court said: "The trial judge also recognized the rule that in the absence of any provision in the laws of an association prescribing the manner in which its meetings shall be conducted, common parliamentary principles in use by all deliberative assemblies may be resorted to in considering the regularity of the proceedings." [27]   In fact, the rules applicable at any one time may consist of several levels of authority then in force.   It has been held, for example, that the mode of procedure to be used in ascertaining the "associative will" of a voluntary association regarding a given matter may be "regulated by the constitution and by-laws and any

---

tion is governed by the common-law rules that the act of the majority represents the act of the Committee." DeCamilla v. Connery, 43 Misc. 2d 395, 251 N.Y.S.2d 305, 309 (Sup. Ct.), aff'd, 23 App. Div. 2d 704, 256 N.Y.S.2d 986 (3d Dep't 1965) (political meeting).

"Each legislative body, when it meets, and unless restrained by the authority which created it, is without rules of procedure, and has inherent power to make its own rules without reference to the action of preceding bodies." South Georgia Power Co. v. Baumann, 169 Ga. 649, 151 S.E. 513, 515 (1930) (city council).

[25] Attorney General v. Remick, 73 N.H. 25, 58 A. 871, 872 (1904), citing Cushing, Law & Pr. Leg. Assem., Reed's Rules, and, on another point, Robert's Rules of Order.

[26] Commonwealth ex rel. Sheip v. Vandegrift, 232 Pa. 53, 81 A. 153, 156 (1911).

An association is governed by parliamentary law. Johnson v. South Bend Hill Cemetery Ass'n, 221 A.2d 280 (Me. 1966).

[27] Marvin v. Manash, 175 Ore. 311, 153 P.2d 251, 254 (1944). The court further held that the trial judge was fully warranted in holding that Robert's Rules of Order "could be deemed to state common parliamentary principles in general usage without any other affirmative showing to that effect."

motion or resolution duly adopted thereunder in accordance with the usual tenets of parliamentary law." [28]

§ 9.5   Minority Rule

A minority rule holds that an organization which has not adopted any procedures will not be presumed as a matter of law to be governed in its deliberations by commonly accepted parliamentary rules. In the leading case no rules had been adopted and there was no evidence as to what are "commonly understood or commonly accepted parliamentary rules governing deliberative societies." The court said that "it cannot be held as a matter of law that a voluntary association of persons, when assembled as a deliberative body, are bound by rules which they are not shown to have adopted and of which they may be entirely ignorant." [29]

The assembled members themselves may "determine what parliamentary rule is applicable to the business before them." [30] They may fashion rules to meet their own manner of conducting business, preferably in conformity with common law.[31] When rules have been adopted, enforcement must be by the assembly itself, and not

[28] United States Steel Corp. v. Wood, 40 Ala. App. 431, 114 So. 2d 533, 543 (1958), *rev'd on other grounds*, 269 Ala. 5, 114 So. 2d 551 (1959).

[29] Gipson v. Morris, 31 Tex. Civ. App. 645, 73 S.W. 85, 87, 88 (1903) (viva voce vote is conclusive unless poll is demanded).

[30] Rule of common council provided that general rules of parliamentary law would apply. "Who but the Council themselves are to determine what rules are general rules, within the meaning of their rule 29? And who but they are to determine what parliamentary rule is applicable to the business before them?" Landes v. State *ex rel.* Matson, 160 Ind. 479, 67 N.E. 189, 193 (1903).

[31] " 'Rules of Procedure' are rules made by any legislative body as to the *mode* and *manner* of conducting the business of the body. They are intended for the orderly and proper disposition of the matters before it. Thus, what committees, and upon what subjects they shall be appointed; what shall be the daily *order* in which the business shall be taken up; in *what order* certain motions shall be received and acted upon; and many other kindred matters,—are proper subjects of the rules of procedure. These rules operate nowhere except in the legislative hall that adopts them; and in this country . . . expire at the end of the session. But these rules of procedure never contravene the statute or common law of the land." Heiskell v. Baltimore, 65 Md. 125, 4 A. 116, 118 (1886) (city council).

by the court.[32] The right to adopt rules of procedure does not, of course, include the power to change any existing statute or the common law.[33] Any conflict between parliamentary rules and the constitution of the body must necessarily be resolved in favor of the latter.[34]

§ 9.6   Courts Will Not Question Compliance With Rules

Rules of procedure adopted for or by any assembly which effectively enable the chairman to conduct a meeting in an orderly fashion and to ascertain the sense of the meeting upon any resolution properly coming before it, are not subject to question by the courts.[35] It is well settled that, in considering the validity of a

[32] "In that connection the plaintiffs argue that the ordinance has been held in council committee for more than sixty days prior to the passage of the initiated ordinance. It is this court's feeling that the rules of council are something which must be enforced by council itself, and this court cannot enforce the rules of council. That legislative body will have to take its own steps within its own rules to bring the legislation out on to the council floor." Mihocka v. Ziegler, 28 Ohio Misc. 105, 274 N.E.2d 583, 586 (1971).

[33] In an early case it was held that rules of procedure adopted by a city council "which attempt to change the common law" are void. Such "rules of procedure never contravene the statute or common law of the land." It was held that the common law of quorum could not be modified even to the extent of increasing the number of members necessary for a quorum. Heiskell v. Baltimore, 65 Md. 125, 4 A. 116, 118, 119 (1886).

[34] Where a parent union's constitution made Robert's Rules of Order the parliamentary law of both parent and local unions, except in cases otherwise provided for, if there were any conflict between Robert's Rules and provisions of either constitution, such constitutional provisions would necessarily prevail. Gonzales v. International Ass'n of Machinists, 142 Cal. App. 2d 207, 298 P.2d 92, aff'd, 356 U.S. 617 (1958).

"The power to make rules cannot overturn those rules [statutes] relating to the course of pending legislation embedded in the Constitution." Tayloe v. Davis, 212 Ala. 282, 102 So. 433, 40 A.L.R. 1052, 1055 (1924).

[35] "The power to make rules is not one which once exercised is exhausted. It is a continuous power, always subject to be exercised by the House, and within the limitations suggested, absolute and beyond the challenge of any other body or tribunal." United States v. Ballin, 144 U.S. 1, 5 (1892), quoted in Humphrey v. City of Youngstown, 143 N.E.2d 321 (Ohio 1955).

"These rules have not, in any proper sense, the force of a public law. They are merely in the nature of by-laws, prescribed for a deliberative body for the orderly and convenient conduct of its own proceedings. The power that made them can unmake them, or disregard them. The rules of public deliberative bodies, whether codified in the form of a 'manual,' and formally adopted by the body, or whether consisting of a body of unwritten customs or usages, preserved in memory and by tradition, are matters of which the judicial courts, as a general rule, take no cognizance. It is a principle of the common law of England that the judicial courts have no conusance of what is termed the *lex et consuetudo parliamenti.* . . . And, although this doctrine is not acceded to, in this country, to the extent to which it has gone in England . . . we do not believe that respectable judicial authority exists, for the proposition that the judicial courts have power to compel legislative, or *quasi*-legislative, bodies to proceed in the conduct of their deliberations, or in the exercise of their powers, in accordance with their own rules." State *ex rel.* Fox v. Alt, 26 Mo. App. 673, 676–77 (1887) (rules of city House of Delegates).

Action to enforce the holding of a union election of officers. "A voluntary association may, without direction or interference by the courts, for its government, adopt a constitution, by-laws, rules and regulations which will control as to all questions of discipline, or internal policy and management, and its right to "interpret and administer the same is as sacred as the right to make them."

"As a general rule courts will not interfere to control the administration of the constitution and by-laws of such association, or to enforce rights springing therefrom." State *ex rel.* Givens v. Superior Court, 233 Ind. 235, 117 N.E.2d 553, 555 (1954).

A constitutional convention is a deliberative body having all necessary authority to make rules for its own procedure, and to decide upon all questions falling within the scope of its authority. If the convention decides to submit an amendment to the people, it must act in accordance with its own rules of procedure. But if the convention acts wrongly, no appeal lies to the courts. The people can accept or reject. "Mere errors of procedure will then be of no avail. The convention having in this matter acted within the scope of its undoubted power, we must take its decisions as final, and leave correction to the power to which it belongs." Wells v. Bain, 75 Pa. 39 (1874).

Disregard by a city council of its own rules of council proceedings is not a subject matter of judicial inquiry. Humphrey v. City of Youngstown, 143 N.E.2d 321, 327 (Ohio Ct. App. 1955).

The courts will not enjoin a state senate in submitting an amendment to the Constitution on a reconsidered vote, where its action was in compliance with its own rules (Jefferson's Manual), and there was no constitutional provision to the contrary. Crawford v. Gilchrist, 64 Fla. 41, 59 So. 963 (1912).

Rules of the House of Representatives which require the approval of the Speaker need not be followed where the Speaker has neither given or denied his approval after timely requests have been made to him. The court noted that it was unaware of any principles of law which require compliance with a regulation of the House which has been made impossible of performance by the person charged with administering it. Washington Activity Group v. White, 342 F. Supp. 847, 852 (D.D.C. 1971), *aff'd*, 479 F.2d 922 (D.C. Cir. 1973).

statute, the courts will not permit any inquiry to ascertain whether the legislature complied strictly with its own rules of procedure, and there is no constitutional provision to the contrary.[36]

§ 9.7   Rule of Reasonable Relation

The Supreme Court, in construing the constitutional authority of Congress to establish its own rules of procedure, has held that any method of proceeding which has a "reasonable relation" to the orderly results sought to be attained is beyond the challenge of any other body or tribunal even if "some other way would be better, more accurate, or even more just."[37] Consistent with this prin-

---

[36] The fact that a rule of the legislature "may have been overlooked or violated in the passage of the act did not impair its validity" where such rule was not required by the Constitution but was adopted for its own convenience. Goodwin v. State Bd. of Admin., 210 Ala. 453, 102 So. 718, 719 (1925).

[37] United States v. Ballin, 144 U.S. 1, 5 (1892). The court said: "Neither do the advantages or disadvantages, the wisdom or folly, of such a rule present any matters for judicial consideration. With the courts, the question is only one of power. The Constitution empowers each house to determine its rules of proceedings. It may not by its rules ignore constitutional restraints or violate fundamental rights, and there should be a reasonable relation between the mode or method of proceeding established by the rule and the result which is sought to be attained. But within these limitations all matters of method are open to the determination of the house and it is no impeachment of the rule to say that some other way would be better, more accurate or even more just. It is no objection to the validity of a rule that a different one has been prescribed and in force for a length of time. The power to make rules is not one which once exercised is exhausted. It is a continuous power, always subject to be exercised by the house, and within the limitations suggested, absolute and beyond the challenge of any other body or tribunal."

The manner in which a house or committee of Congress chooses to run its business ordinarily raises no "justiciable controversy." Yellin v. United States, 374 U.S. 109, 146, 147 (1963). *Followed,* Randolph v. Willis, 220 F. Supp. 355, 358 (S.D. Cal. 1963).

See discussion of "political question doctrine" and "internal administrative dispute" within the legislature. Anderson v. Krupsak, N.Y. Ct. App., N.Y.L.J., July 9, 1976.

"The Constitution commits to the Senate the power to make its own rules; and it is not the function of the Court to say that another rule would be better." United States v. Smith, 286 U.S. 6, 48 (1932).

The Senate of Alabama has the right and power to enact rules governing its proceedings and, unless controlled by other provisions of the constitution, the courts cannot look to the wisdom or folly, the advantages or disadvantages of

ciple of law is the concept that the court will approve "any method understood by the assembly which arrives at substantial results." [38] Another realistic approach has been described in these words: "Still, it is necessary that the council should proceed along some fixed, reasonable, and recognized rule, and, if their action comes within this requirement, it must be upheld." [39]

§ 9.8   Rules Are Judicially Cognizable

The Supreme Court has also held that rules adopted by Congress and by its committees are judicially cognizable,[40] and that they are admittedly valid and have the force of law.[41] Rules must be "strictly observed" when they apply to matters of importance, such as a rule that a major committee inquiry must be initiated by a vote of a majority of the committee. "When a committee rule relates to a matter of such importance, it must be strictly observed." [42] The

---

the rules which a legislative body adopts to govern its own proceedings. Opinion of the Justices No. 185, 278 Ala. 525, 179 So. 2d 155, 158 (1965).

Even trial procedures involving the death penalty need not be "the best of all worlds" nor conform to the preference of the court. Trials need only be "fairly conducted." McGautha v. California, 402 U.S. 183, 221 (1971).

[38] "Counsel . . . insists that strict parliamentary rules should not be applied to these municipal bodies exercising legislative functions; that if they adopt or pursue a method of proceeding understood by themselves, which arrives at substantial results, their action should not be overthrown upon any technical rules or strict construction of parliamentary law. We are of the same opinion." Whitney v. Common Council, 69 Mich. 189, 37 N.W. 184, 189 (1888).

[39] Tuell v. Meacham Contracting Co., 145 Ky. 181, 140 S.W. 159, 160 (1911) (challenge of city council ordinance).

[40] Christoffel v. United States, 338 U.S. 84 (1949).

"It has long been held that the rules of Congress and its committees are judicially cognizable." Wheeldin v. Wheeler, 373 U.S. 647, 663 (1963) (dissenting opinion).

The court may inquire into the language and application of rules of the House of Representatives when constitutional rights are affected. Washington Activity Group v. White, 342 F. Supp. 847, 852 n.14 (D.D.C. 1971), aff'd, 479 F.2d 922 (D.C. Cir. 1973).

[41] Rules of the House of Representatives "have the same force of law, and are equally binding upon the Committee members, the Committee staff, and witnesses as well." Randolph v. Willis, 220 F. Supp. 355, 358 (S.D. Cal. 1963); see Yellin v. United States, 374 U.S. 109 (1963).

[42] Gojack v. United States, 384 U.S. 702, 708 (1966).

presumption in favor of regularity of all official conduct requires that
it be assumed that a Congressional committee will not disregard its
own rules of the House.[43]

The Supreme Court has also decided that the courts "must give
great weight" to the Senate's construction of its own rules, although
a construction arrived at subsequent to the event in controversy
need not be conclusive.[44] A formal interpretation of the Standing
Rules of the House made by the Speaker during a term of Congress
may be effective during that Congress, but is not necessarily binding
on a succeeding Congress.[45]

The power of Congress to make rules is "absolute and beyond
the challenge of any other body or tribunal" if such rules do not
ignore constitutional restraints or violate fundamental rights,[46] and
if they do not affect persons other than members of Congress.[47]

[43] *See, e.g.,* Randolph v. Willis, 220 F. Supp. 355, 360 (S.D. Cal. 1963).

[44] United States v. Smith, 286 U.S. 6, 33 (1932).

[45] *See* Hartman v. United States, 290 F.2d 460, 466–67 (9th Cir. 1961),
rev'd on other grounds, 370 U.S. 724 (1962) (televising of subcommittee hearings).

[46] United States v. Ballin, 144 U.S. 1, 5, 6 (1892).

The House of Representatives may not by its rules "ignore constitutional
restraints or violate fundamental rights. . . ." Washington Activity Group v.
White, 342 F. Supp. 847, 852 n.14 (D.D.C. 1971), *aff'd,* 479 F.2d 922 (D.C.
Cir. 1973).

[47] In speaking of the United States Constitution, the Supreme Court said:
"The role that the courts play in adjudicating questions involving the rules of
either house must of necessity be a limited one, for the manner in which a
house or committee of Congress chooses to run its business ordinarily raises no
justiciable controversy. . . . However, when the application or construction of
a rule directly affects persons other than members of the house, 'the question
presented is of necessity a judicial one.'" Yellin v. United States, 374 U.S. 109,
143, 146–47 (1963).

The construction of a rule of the Senate presents a judicial question where
it affects persons other than members of the Senate. United States v. Smith,
286 U.S. 6 (1932) (executive employee).

The refusal of a Congressional committee to accredit an applicant publisher
and its representative to the periodical press galleries of Congress is immune
from judicial inquiry under the speech and debate clause and is a nonjusticiable
political question involving matters committed by the Constitution to the
legislative branch. Consumers Union of U.S., Inc. v. Periodical Correspondents' Ass'n, 515 F.2d 1341 (D.C. Cir. 1975), *cert. denied,* 44 L.W. 3398
(Jan. 13, 1976).

See Annots., Contempt of Congress or congressional committee, 97 L. Ed.

Authority to adopt rules to govern the proceedings of a municipal
body is often provided by statute, in which case it has been said
that the rules adopted by it are as binding upon it as the statute.[48]
But if the statute prescribes the rules of procedure which are to be
used, the body must abide by the rules so prescribed, and does not
have the freedom of a "parliamentary body" to regulate its own proceedings.[49] "Rules adopted pursuant to express authority granted
by statute are effective unless such rules run counter to some express provision of the organic law."[50]

§ 9.9   Political Parties

In the absence of statute, political parties generally are governed
by their own usages and establish their own rules of procedure.
They enjoy a "constitutionally protected right of political association."[51] They have been "a law unto themselves," and need not
follow common-law rules of "parliamentary practice and procedure."[52] And where the state legislature has manifested an in-

---

782 (1953), 99 L. Ed. 985 (1955), 3 L. Ed. 2d 1647 (1959), 10 L. Ed. 2d
1329 (1964); Power of court to pass upon rules of legislative body, 76 L. Ed.
967 (1932).

[48] Where a state statute empowers the city council to make and adopt rules
to govern its proceedings "it is doubtless true that rules adopted by it are as
binding upon it as the statute. . . . The rule would be otherwise if adopted
from the inherent authority of the council." Baker v. Combs, 194 Ky. 260, 239
S.W. 56, 59 (1922).

[49] A Board of Education organized by special statutory authority must abide
by rules of quorum established by law, and does not have the power of a corporation organized under general corporate law to regulate its own proceedings.
Talbot v. Board of Educ., 171 Misc. 974, 14 N.Y.S.2d 340, 344–45 (Sup. Ct.
1939).

Also, when a board or a commission is created by ordinance of a city council, the council has power to control its rules of procedure with regard to meetings. Beacon Journal Publ. Co. v. Akron, 3 Ohio St. 2d 191, 209 N.E.2d 399
(1965).

[50] Blaikie v. Knott, 277 App. Div. 461, 100 N.Y.S.2d 665, 668 (1st Dep't
1950).

[51] Cousins v. Wigoda, 419 U.S. 477 (1975).

[52] "It is established by the great weight of authority that political parties are
voluntary organizations and in the absence of legislative enactment they are
governed by their own usages and establish their own rules." To arguments
that in the absence of legislative enactment the common rule of quorum pre-

tention of non-interference with political party government by allowing parties to formulate their own rules, the court is not concerned with the motives in adopting rules but only with the legality of their adoption.[53]

However, the authority of a city political committee to adopt rules for its conduct and its functioning may be subject to and dependent upon rules and regulations laid down by the appropriate county political committee. When so adopted they are "the law" of the city committee and must be obeyed and enforced by the court.[54]

Such rules need not precisely follow recognized parliamentary law. "While municipal governing bodies usually adopt or recognize parliamentary law as their rules of order and proceedings, courts ordinarily will not annul or invalidate an ordinance enacted in dis-

---

vails, the court noted that voluntary associations often fixed the quorum at less than a majority and frequently delegated all powers to the central committee. The court concluded: "It has always been determined that rules of parliamentary practice and procedure are not necessary to follow in all cases by party committees." State *ex rel.* Pfeifer v. Stoneking, 74 N.E.2d 759, 762, 763 (Ohio 1946).

The court will not "invade the political arena." Franklin Nat. Bank v. Clark, 26 Misc. 2d 724, 212 N.Y.S.2d 942, 947 (Sup. Ct. 1961).

[53] Bauman v. Fusco, 45 Misc. 2d 326, 256 N.Y.S.2d 855 (Sup. Ct.), *aff'd*, 23 App. Div. 2d 402, 261 N.Y.S.2d 85 (1st Dep't 1965); Schleimer v. Knott, 181 Misc. 421, 46 N.Y.S.2d 302, 303 (Sup. Ct. 1944).

[54] Under the rules and regulations of the city committee, no requirement of cause or reason is necessary for the removal of a chairman who absents himself from three regular consecutive meetings. "This Court cannot say that this Rule, validly enacted and authorized by the County Committee Rules is unreasonable or in violation of any of the provisions of the Election Law under which the ultimate authority for their validity rests." Kiernan v. Mirante, 53 Misc. 2d 173, 278 N.Y.S.2d 278, 282 (Sup. Ct. 1967).

"Valid rules of a committee will be enforced by the Court." Lamb v. Cohen, 40 Misc. 2d 615, 243 N.Y.S.2d 647, 650 (Sup. Ct. 1963).

"As creations of free men, political parties are privileged to make their own rules and regulations and to establish machinery for making their organizations effective. They have plenary powers as to their government and other affairs in the absence of restrictive statutes, and the courts have no power in the absence of statute conferring jurisdiction to interfere with those operations, unless a legal right has been conferred by previous party action." O'Neil v. O'Connell, 300 Ky. 707, 189 S.W.2d 965, 967 (1945).

regard of parliamentary rule, provided the enactment is made in the manner provided by statute. The rules of parliamentary procedure are merely procedural, and not substantive." [55]

§ 9.10 Newly Organized Assemblies

When a newly elected assembly meets for organization, it may adopt any rules it desires to govern its future action, provided such rules do not contravene any statutory provision. A statute has been upheld by the court which provides that, until new rules are adopted, procedures should be governed by the rules of the outgoing assembly, and, in the event that new rules are not adopted at the organization meeting, the rules of the previous assembly would continue in effect.[56]

It should be noted that a parliamentary rule is not the same as an ordinance. The rules adopted by a legislative or municipal body cannot be deemed "ordinances," [57] and adoption of parliamentary rules is not the enactment of a "local law" or the passage of a "resolution." [58]

---

[55] City of Pasadena v. Paine, 126 Cal. App. 2d 93, 271 P.2d 577, 579 (1954).

[56] Schleimer v. Knott, 181 Misc. 421, 46 N.Y.S.2d 302, 304 (Sup. Ct. 1944).

Unless authorized by statute, "a deliberative body such as a town meeting cannot pass procedural rules which will bind similar bodies at subsequent meetings, since rules of procedure expire at the adjournment of the body adopting them unless readopted in the future." Town of Exeter v. Kenick, 104 N.H. 168, 181 A.2d 638, 641 (1962).

[57] "Such bodies adopt rules for their guidance in making ordinances or laws. A rule is defined to be 'the regulation adopted by a deliberative body for the conduct of its proceedings.' The word 'ordinance,' as applicable to the action of a municipal corporation, should be deemed to mean the local laws passed by the governing body." Armitage v. Fisher, 74 Hun 167, 26 N.Y.S. 364, 367 (1893), rev'd, 4 Misc. 315, 24 N.Y.S. 650 (1893).

[58] A statutory quorum was required to pass a local law or resolution. This did not prevent council from adopting intracameral matters such as parliamentary rules with a common-law quorum. Morris v. Cashmore, 253 App. Div. 657, 659, 3 N.Y.S.2d 624, 628, 633 (1st Dep't), aff'd, 278 N.Y. 730, 17 N.E.2d 143 (1938) (following Reed's Rules).

Adoption of rules by a legislative body need not be by resolution. Maickel v. Lundy, 155 N.Y.S.2d 581 (Sup. Ct. 1953).

§ 9.11　Failure To Adopt Rules in Compliance With Law

Failure of a deliberative assembly to adopt rules as required by law and to follow the rules so adopted may nullify a meeting. Where, for example, an election law provided that the organizational meeting of a county political committee should first call the roll and then adopt rules for the conduct of the meeting, the court nullified the meeting and held that failure to so adopt rules resulted in a meeting not "legally organized." In that case, the failure of the meeting to adopt and enforce rules of conduct resulted in such disorder that the court noted: "A reading of the transcript of what transpired at the meeting discloses that no rules having been adopted the proceedings not unexpectedly resembled in no way those of a deliberative assembly, but rather an unorganized, disorderly mass meeting." [59] Similarly, where by-laws setting forth rules of procedure were totally ignored and as a result there was "no organization or regularity in the proceedings," no action taken by those present was valid since no legal meeting was held.[60]

POWER TO AMEND RULES

§ 9.12　Power To Amend or Waive Rules

The power of a deliberative or legislative body, and of any lawful assembly, to adopt governing rules of order for the orderly

[59] The court suggested a simple, although perhaps inadequate, way to comply with the statutory requirement that rules of order be adopted by the organizational meeting. "Inasmuch as there must be a new meeting we point out that one recognized way to comply with this requirement is to adopt a resolution that 'The rules contained in [specifying the work of parliamentary practice] shall govern this meeting in all cases to which they are applicable, and in which they are not inconsistent with statute or the rules of this committee.'", citing Robert's Rules of Order at 268.

The court also expressed its belief that the parties to the litigation had failed to recognize "certain fundamental principles of parliamentary law," here applicable. See note 3 *supra*, page 248.

[60] Provision in the by-laws that the president shall preside at all meetings, and in his absence a president pro tempore shall be chosen, was totally ignored. "The president, although present, did not preside at the election, nor was there a president pro tempore chosen in his stead; and no person who participated in the proceedings was authorized to receive the ballots, or to declare the result;

conduct of its affairs is a continuous power which can be exercised at any time. "The power to make rules is not one which once exercised is exhausted. It is a continuous power, always subject to be exercised by the House, and within the limitations suggested, absolute and beyond the challenge of any other body or tribunal." [1] This principle expresses the inherent powers of an organization, such as a corporation, and its members or shareholders, to adopt from time to time such general or special rules of order as may be designed to enable the orderly and convenient conduct of business.

It is also a well accepted principle of law that legislative bodies and other deliberative assemblies are not bound by their own rules of procedure. Such rules are created by the body "to insure the orderly conduct of business and the same body which makes them can also waive or simply disregard them at pleasure." [2] The power

---

hence, it follows that there was no legal election. . . ." State *ex rel.* Guerrero v. Pettineli, 10 Nev. 141, 146 (1875).

[1] United States v. Ballin, 144 U.S. 1, 5 (1892) (Congress), *quoted,* Humphrey v. Youngstown, 143 N.E.2d 321, 324 (Ohio 1955) (city council).

This principle is equally applicable to a duly constituted legislative committee, which is itself a deliberative body. Yellin v. United States, 374 U.S. 109 (1963).

"The power of the society, derived from the charter and the laws under which it was organized, to enact by-laws, is continuous, residing in all regular meetings of the society so long as it exists. Any meeting could, by a majority vote, modify or repeal the law of a previous meeting, and no meeting could bind a subsequent one by irrepealable acts or rules of procedure. The power to enact is the power to repeal; and a by-law, requiring a two-thirds vote of members present to alter or amend the laws of the society, may itself be altered, amended, or repealed by the same power which enacted it." Richardson v. Union Congregational Soc'y, 58 N.H. 187, 189 (1877).

Each house of Congress may amend its rules without consulting the other. Amendment of rules of a house of Congress is not an "Act of Congress." Krebs v. Ashbrook, 275 F. Supp. 111 (D.D.C. 1967), *cert. denied,* 393 U.S. 1026 (1969).

[2] State *ex rel.* Todd v. Essling, 268 Minn. 169, 128 N.W.2d 307, 318 (1964), *citing* Robert's Rules of Order, Jefferson's Manual, and Mason's Manual.

"The rule here invoked is one of parliamentary procedure, and it is uniformly held that it is within the power of all deliberative bodies to abolish, modify, or waive their own rules of procedure, adopted for the orderly conduct of business, and as security against hasty action." Rutherford v. City of Nashville, 168 Tenn. 499, 79 S.W.2d 581, 584 (1935) (city council), *quoted in*

State *ex rel.* Balsinger v. Town of Madisonville, 435 S.W.2d 803, 805 (Tenn. 1968) (town board).

Rules of procedure passed by one legislative body are not binding upon a subsequent legislative body. "Courts ordinarily will not invalidate an ordinance enacted in disregard of parliamentary usage, provided the enactment is made in the manner provided by statute . . . 'Rules of parliamentary procedure are merely procedural, and not substantive.'" Ellis v. Stokes, 207 Ga. 423, 61 S.E.2d 806, 810 (1950).

"The only province of the courts is to inquire whether charter provisions have been followed. Charter provisions are structural, and the courts have a right to inquire whether they have been complied with. Parliamentary rules are merely procedural, and with their observance the courts have no concern. They may be waived or disregarded by the legislative body." South Georgia Power Co. v. Baumann, 169 Ga. 649, 151 S.E. 513, 515 (1929).

A village board can lawfully adopt an ordinance while its proceedings were "informal in the matter of parliamentary procedure." People *ex rel.* Gregory v. Strohm, 283 Ill. 580, 121 N.E. 223, 225 (1918).

"The board had the right to adopt such parliamentary rules for the convenient dispatch of its business as it might deem proper. This is a power that is inherent in every public and private body, and mere parliamentary rules are, of course, not designed to be and are not binding upon any person or persons except the members of the body that adopts them; and they may be amended, suspended, or repealed at the pleasure of the body, or in any manner that it has prescribed for this purpose." Montenegro-Riehm Music Co. v. Board of Educ., 147 Ky. 720, 145 S.W. 740, 743 (1912).

Where a city council failed to comply with one of its rules concerning unfinished business, the most that could be said was that the council "violated one of its own parliamentary rules." The court added: "The courts are not required to recognize all parliamentary rules that may be adopted by a body of legislative functions." Tuell v. Meacham Contracting Co., 145 Ky. 181, 140 S.W. 159, 161 (1911); *see* Reuter v. Meacham Contracting Co., 143 Ky. 557, 136 S.W. 1028 (1911).

"It is no objection to the validity of the assessment that the order did not receive, in either branch of the city council, two several readings before its passage, as required by the rules of the city council. It is within the power of all deliberative bodies to abolish, modify or waive their own rules, intended as security against hasty or inconsiderate action." Holt v. City Council, 127 Mass. 408, 411 (1879).

An order was passed in violation of the rules and orders of the common council. "But the answer to this is that the rules referred to are rules governing the order and routine of business, intended as securities against hasty and inconsiderate action, which, in every deliberative body, acting within the powers conferred, may be abolished, modified or waived at will." Bennett v. New Bedford, 110 Mass. 433, 437, 438 (1872).

Rules of parliamentary procedure may be disregarded by a city assembly. "Those rules have not, in any proper sense, the force of a public law. They are merely in the nature of by-laws, prescribed for a deliberative body for the orderly and convenient conduct of its own proceedings. The power that made them can unmake them, or disregard them." State *ex rel.* Fox v. Alt, 26 Mo. App. 673, 677 (1887).

"The adoption of rules is left entirely to the determination of the council. Here again, the matter is procedural, and the general parliamentary law was clearly intended to prevail. Rules, however, are always within the control of the majority, and may be changed at any time by a majority vote." Morris v. Cashmore, 253 App. Div. 657, 3 N.Y.S.2d 624, 632, 633, *aff'd*, 278 N.Y. 730 (1938) (N.Y. City Council).

Whether a parliamentary rule shall be insisted on or dispensed with rests exclusively in the discretion of the body. "A majority could dispense with the rule requiring the reconsideration to be moved by one who voted with the majority, and if the majority treat the motion as regularly made, it is to be considered as a tacit suspension of the rule. The members alone have the right to object to the violation of the parliamentary rule." People *ex rel.* Locke v. Common Council, 5 Lans. 11, 14, 15 (N.Y. Sup. Ct. 1871).

City commission adopted ordinance without complying with its parliamentary rules. "It has been decided by the courts of last resort of many states, and also by the United States Supreme Court, that a legislative act will not be declared invalid for noncompliance with rules." Dayton v. Woodgeard, 110 Ohio App. 326, 187 N.E.2d 921, 925 (1962).

A borough council has the legal right to adopt its own rules of procedure or parliamentary usage. "Further, rules of procedure are always within the control of the majority and may be changed at any time by a majority vote. . . . When such power exists, the rules under which it will proceed may be changed, suspended or waived at its pleasure. . . . The mere failure to conform to some defined parliamentary usage will not invalidate the action when the requisite number of members have agreed on the particular measure." Commonwealth *ex rel.* Fox v. Chace, 403 Pa. 117, 168 A.2d 569, 571 (1961).

Parliamentary rules are "mere rules of procedure." "Being rules of procedure adopted by the council for its own convenience and government in the enactment of ordinances, it is competent for the council to waive them, and certainly this is so with the consent of all the council present . . . such consent, in our opinion, may be implied." Bradford v. City of Jellico, 1 Tenn. Ch. App. R. 700, 719 (1901).

A legislative body may waive, modify, or disregard its own rules. However, statutory procedures under which the body must proceed cannot be ignored by the body. Anderson v. Grossenbacher, 381 S.W.2d 72 (Tex. 1964) (county commissioners).

A city council may prescribe its own rules for passing ordinances. "What rules of procedure the council has adopted are not disclosed by the record. Whatever they are, they may provide for suspension." County Court v. City of Grafton, 77 W. Va. 84, 86 S.E. 924, 925 (1915).

However, if the construction of the rules affects persons other than members of the body, the question presented is necessarily a judicial one. United

to waive includes the power to suspend.[3]   A leading case condensed
the law in these words: "The adoption of rules . . . is left entirely

States v. Smith, 286 U.S. 6 (1932) (appointment to office of regulatory agency).

Rules required publication of notice of meeting of council one day in advance of meeting date.   Where city council by more than two-thirds voted to
consider a certain matter, it in effect overruled any objections that it had violated the terms of its own rules. Whalen v. Wagner, 2 Misc. 2d 89, 152
N.Y.S.2d 386 (Sup. Ct. 1956), aff'd, 3 App. Div. 2d 936, 163 N.Y.S.2d 225
(2d Dep't 1957), aff'd, 4 N.Y.2d 575, 152 N.E.2d 54, 176 N.Y.S.2d 616
(1958).

Where a congressional committee rule confers upon a witness the right to
be heard in executive session, the witness should be permitted judicial review
of his defense based on a violation of such rule by the committee. Yellin v.
United States, 347 U.S. 109 (1963); see Gojack v. United States, 384 U.S. 702
(1966).

A federal regulatory commission may violate its own rules relating to hearings as they are "procedural" only. Pacific & S. Co. v. FCC, 405 F.2d 1371
(D.C. Cir. 1968).

Where an administrative agency has laid down its own procedures and regulations, they cannot be ignored by the agency itself, even where discretionary
decisions are involved. Smith v. Resor, 406 F.2d 141, 145–46 (2d Cir. 1969).

"First, it appears from the evidence that oral reading of proposed ordinances
has not been practiced in Anchorage for a number of years, it being considered
a useless formality. Because [statute] prescribes merely a rule of parliamentary
procedure, the council could, by its customary practice, waive the requirement
of oral reading." Jefferson v. City of Anchorage, 513 P.2d 1099, 1101 (Alas.
1973).

See Annot., Power of court to pass upon rules of legislative body, 76 L. Ed.
967 (1932).

[3] Rules of a city council were suspended by unanimous vote. "So far as appears, the rules so suspended were not rules prescribed by any superior authority, as by the constitution or laws of the state, but such rules as the council
itself had adopted, and which it was authorized to adopt to govern its own
proceedings. . . . Such rules might properly be thus suspended by unanimous
consent." City of Greeley v. Hamman, 17 Colo. 30, 28 P. 460, 461 (1891),
citing Cushing, Law & Pr. Leg. Assem.

Rules of procedure of a city council are directory and can be suspended by
the council acting as a legislative body for reasons deemed sufficient. Schoen-
feld v. City of Seattle, 265 F. 726 (W.D. Wash. 1920).

Statutory right of city council to suspend rule that ordinances should be fully
read on three different days. Vaughan v. City of Searcy, 199 Ark. 585, 135
S.W.2d 319 (1940).

The validity of a proposed local law adopted by a common council could
not be successfully attacked on the ground that it was never referred to a special
committee of the council as required by the rules of that body, because the

to the determination of the council. Here again the matter is procedural, and the general parliamentary law was clearly intended to prevail. Rules, however, are always within the control of the majority, and may be changed at any time by a majority vote." [4] The failure of a city council to comply with its own rules "would be an irregularity, not a jurisdictional defect." [5] In one case, the court merely commented: "But, if we should concede that the rule in question became applicable, the most that could be said is the council violated one of its own parliamentary rules." [6]

According to parliamentary law, where the body has made no

---

council which adopted the rule had power to suspend it. Commission of Pub. Charities v. Wortman, 255 App. Div. 241, 7 N.Y.S.2d 631 (3d Dep't), *aff'd*, 279 N.Y. 711, 18 N.E.2d 325 (1938).

"The statute specifically provides that the requirement of a reading at two separate meetings may be suspended by a vote of two-thirds of the members of the board. As shown, the requirement was suspended by a vote of all members of the board. Appellant contends that the Bowling Green council had never adopted any rules and, therefore, could not vote to suspend non-existing rules. We are unable to accept that argument and consider that the statutory suspension was appropriately adopted, and the ordinance was effectively enacted insofar as the reading at two separate meetings is concerned." Payne v. Petrie, 419 S.W.2d 761, 763 (Ky. 1967).

Presumably, a city council has authority to suspend its own rules. Meredith v. Connally, 38 App. Div. 2d 385, 330 N.Y.S.2d 188 (3d Dep't 1972).

"If a procedural restriction (such as an agenda requirement) is found in one of the rules of order of such a body and a second rule provides for the suspension of the operation of the first rule, the first rule may be dispensed with upon compliance with the requirements of the second rule." Del Greco v. Mayor, 294 N.E.2d 594, 597 (Mass. 1973).

"The board had power to suspend or disregard its rules of order by a vote of the majority; and to vote on the consideration of the nomination, in effect, suspend all rules inconsistent with such a vote." State *ex rel.* Rylands v. Pinkerman, 63 Conn. 176, 28 A. 110, 115–16 (1893) *citing* Cushing, Parl. Law.

[4] Morris v. Cashmore, 253 App. Div. 657, 3 N.Y.S.2d 624, 632 (1st Dep't), *aff'd*, 278 N.Y. 730, 17 N.E.2d 143 (1938) (*following* Reed's Rules).

[5] Meredith v. Connally, 38 App. Div. 2d 385, 330 N.Y.S.2d 188, 190 (3d Dep't 1972).

[6] The court noted that a rule may be adopted "as a matter of parliamentary custom" and need not be followed as a matter of law, and said that "the courts are not required to recognize all parliamentary rules that may be adopted by a body of legislative functions." Reuter v. Meacham Contracting Co., 143 Ky. 557, 562, 136 S.W. 1028 (1911) (Robert's Rules of Order had been adopted by the city council).

specific provision for suspending the rules, there seems to be no
other mode of suspending or dispensing with a rule than by general
consent; and where the body has adopted a particular parliamentary
manual which so provides, a rule can be suspended by unanimous
opinion of the body expressed informally, and not by means of
a vote.[7]

§ 9.13 Parliamentary Rules Are Procedural Only

Courts are prone to look upon the regulatory provisions of parliamentary rules and corporate by-laws as being procedural only,
and not substantive, with the result that the deliberative body may
alter them at will. It has been summarily stated by the court that
"[i]t is the uniform rule that parliamentary rules . . . are merely
procedural and not substantive. They may be waived or disregarded by the legislative body, and courts have no concern over
their observance. . . . Neither will the courts invalidate an ordinance enacted in disregard of parliamentary usage if complying
with statute."[8] When the rules of a state Senate permit amend-

---

[7] The board of education had adopted a rule providing that "the ordinary
parliamentary rules should be observed, and in case any disputed question arose,
Cushing's Manual should be taken as authority." Cushing provided that a rule
could be dispensed with or suspended by general consent, or if proposed informally, without objection. It was held that the rule could be suspended only
by unanimous consent, and not by a two-thirds vote. State *ex rel.* Krejsa v.
Board of Educ., 2 Ohio C.C.R. 510, 515–16 (Cir. Ct. 1887).

[8] State *ex rel.* Todd v. Essling, 268 Minn. 169, 128 N.W.2d 307, 319 (1964),
citing Robert's Rules of Order, Jefferson's Manual, and Mason's Manual.

The courts will determine only whether the legislature complied with the
Constitution. "Matters of parliamentary law and the failure of the legislature
to observe its rules of procedure, insofar as they are not required by the Constitution, must not be considered." Carlton v. Grimes, 237 Iowa 912, 923, 928,
23 N.W.2d 883 (1946).

"Provisions in corporate by-laws may, generally speaking, be divided into
two classes (a) those that are mere regulations governing the conduct of the internal affairs of the corporation. These may be repealed, altered and amended
at the will of the majority unless a greater vote is required by the by-laws
themselves or by statute; (b) provisions in the nature of a contract which are
evidently designed to vest property rights *inter se* among all stockholders.
These cannot be repealed or changed without the consent of the other parties
whose rights are affected." Bechtold v. Coleman Realty Co., 367 Pa. 208, 79

ment of its rules after one day's notice by a majority vote, and there is no constitutional prohibition against such action by a legislative body, the court would feel it "impertinent and lawfully unwarranted" to attempt to inject itself as a rule-making body for the Senate.[9]

§ 9.14   Waiver of Procedures Imposed by Parliamentary Manuals

The same right of waiver [10] applies to procedures imposed by a parliamentary manual which has been adopted by an assembly for the guidance of its deliberations and the conduct of its meetings. Case law establishes that parliamentary rules in standard published manuals [11] and in other specialized codes are procedural only [12] and

---

A.2d 661, 663 (1951); *accord,* Metzger v. George Washington Memorial Park, Inc., 380 Pa. 350, 110 A.2d 425 (1955).

[9] Opinion of the Justices No. 185, 278 Ala. 525, 179 So. 2d 155, 158 (1965).

[10] See § 9.13 *supra.*

[11] "This parliamentary guide [Robert's Rules of Order] is adopted by legislative bodies to expedite the transaction of their affairs in an orderly fashion. Such rules are therefore procedural and their strict observance is not mandatory. Consequently, a failure to observe one of them is not jurisdictional and does not invalidate action which is otherwise in conformity with charter requirements." Pasadena v. Paine, 126 Cal. App. 2d 93, 271 P.2d 577, 579 (1954) (city board).

"It is shown that the city council of Clinton adopted for its parliamentary governance Robert's Rules of Order. It is contended that, according to one of the rules, all unfinished business fell to the ground when the term of service of the outgoing aldermen expired. But if we should concede that the rule in question became applicable, the most that could be said is that the council violated one of its own parliamentary rules." McGraw v. Whitson, 69 Iowa 348, 28 N.W. 632, 633 (1886) (city council).

"It has been held repeatedly by the courts of this country that the mere failure to conform to some defined parliamentary usage will not invalidate the action when the requisite number of members have agreed on the particular measure." State *ex rel.* Todd v. Essling, 268 Minn. 169, 128 N.W.2d 307, 318 (1964) (state Senate), *citing* Robert's Rules of Order, Jefferson's Manual, and Mason's Manual.

"It is said also that the appropriation was made in violation of parliamentary law as expounded in Cushing's Manual and his Law and Practice of Legislative Assemblies. If it be assumed that these had been adopted as the rules of the city council, it is enough to say, without passing upon the question whether they were violated, that it is within the 'power of all deliberative bodies to

their strict observance may be disregarded. And, of course, a body without rules can change its practices from meeting to meeting.[13]

§ 9.15 Vote Required To Change or Waive

It has been held that where a body adopts rules for its own conduct by a majority vote and then provides that such rules shall not be changed except upon a three-fourths vote, a majority has the right to waive or change the rule. "To my mind it is clear that the power to make carries with it the right and power to unmake.

---

abolish, modify, or waive their own rules intended as security against hasty action'. . . ." Wheelock v. City of Lowell, 196 Mass. 220, 81 N.E. 977, 980 (1907) (city council).

City council had adopted Cushing's Manual to govern its parliamentary action. "But even if the council had acted out of harmony or in contradiction of the rules of the manual, it did no more than it legally might do, since such body is not bound to act in accordance with its rules or by-laws. Such bodies may, and perhaps do, oftener than otherwise, waive them." City of Sedalia v. Scott, 104 Mo. App. 595, 78 S.W. 276, 280 (1904) (city council); *accord,* City of Sedalia *ex rel.* Gilsonite Constr. Co. v. Montgomery, 109 Mo. App. 197, 88 S.W. 1014, 1017 (1904), *aff'd,* 127 S.W. 50 (1910) (city council).

Membership corporation adopted by-law providing: "The rule in Cushing's Manual shall govern all debates, except in cases herein specially provided for." The court held that procedure provided in Cushing should apply when action is taken against a member for disorderly words. Cushing was not followed and expulsion of the member was improper. People *ex rel.* Godwin v. American Inst., 44 How. Pr. 468, 471 (N.Y. Sup. Ct. 1873).

[12] "Those rules have not, in any proper sense, the force of a public law. They are merely in the nature of by-laws, prescribed for a deliberative body for the orderly and convenient conduct of its own proceedings. The power that made them can unmake them, or disregard them." State *ex rel.* Fox v. Alt, 26 Mo. App. 673, 677 (1887) (rules of city House of Delegates).

[13] "Common parliamentary rules, as used by all deliberative assemblies in this county, may also be resorted to, in the absence of any made by the association itself, in considering the regularity of its proceedings. . . . An association, however, without articles, constitution or rules, can make changes at will at any meeting duly held, except that it cannot expel a member without notice. . . . The association, in the absence of rules, can adjourn its meetings from time to time according to the usual method of parliamentary bodies, and transact business at an adjourned meeting without notice to the absentees. . . . It can elect a president at each meeting, and in so doing would, by implication, remove the preceding president." Ostrom v. Greene, 161 N.Y. 353, 55 N.E. 919, 922 (1900).

The same power which can make rules in the first instance can directly attack and unmake or repeal such rules. . . . Rules are made solely for the government of the body." The court continued: "The further proposition that a bare majority can repeal a rule which it has adopted, and by which there has been imposed limitations on the power of a bare majority is equally well settled by the sound case law of the land."[14] It has been ruled that a simple majority of the United States Senate has the power to amend Senate Rule 22 which requires a two-thirds vote to cut off debate.[15]

§ 9.16   Failure To Conform to Parliamentary Usage

Since parliamentary rules are merely procedural and not substantive, the failure to adhere thereto will not invalidate action taken when approved by the requisite number of members.[16]   How-

[14] State *ex rel.* Kiel v. Riechmann, 239 Mo. 81, 142 S.W. 304, 309 (1911).

[15] Ruling of Vice President Humphrey as President of the Senate, January 1967.

[16] "The important inquiry is whether the number required by law have agreed to the particular measure. If this be so, and it is expressed in a way not inconsistent with the statutory provisions, the fact that the niceties of every parliamentary rule have not been followed does not render the act illegal." State *ex rel.* Todd v. Essling, 268 Minn. 169, 128 N.W.2d 307, 318 (1964).

Rules of order are procedural and their strict observance is not mandatory. "Consequently, a failure to observe one of them is not jurisdictional and does not invalidate action which is otherwise in conformity with charter requirements." Pasadena v. Paine, 126 Cal. App. 2d 93, 271 P.2d 577, 579 (1954) (Robert's Rules of Order adopted).

City council had adopted Robert's Rules of Order for its parliamentary governance. It was contended that one of the rules was not followed in the passage of an ordinance. "But if we should concede that the rule in question became applicable, the most that could be said is that the council violated one of its own parliamentary rules. But if the statute was complied with, as we hold it was, in the passage of the ordinance, we think it was valid." McGraw v. Whitson, 69 Iowa 348, 28 N.W. 632, 633 (1886).

A mere failure of a city council to conform to parliamentary usage will not invalidate the action taken when the requisite number of members agree to a particular measure. City of Corinth v. Sharp, 107 Miss. 696, 65 So. 888 (1914).

The fact that the procedure followed by a city council is not in all respects in accordance with the rules of parliamentary law is not fatal to the action of the body, if the procedure was all that the statute requires." Humphrey v. City of Youngstown, 143 N.E.2d 321 (Ohio Ct. App. 1955) (city council).

ever, statutory and charter requirements defining the procedure necessary to suspend the rules or prescribing methods to be pursued, as distinguished from parliamentary rules, are mandatory.[17] Statutory procedures under which a legislative body must proceed cannot be ignored by that body.[18] Where the statute provides that amended rules may be adopted by a majority vote, attempted adoption by less than a majority is invalid.[19]

Violation of House rules, which are not required by the Constitution, but are adopted for convenience, does not impair the validity of a law. Goodwin v. State Bd. of Admin., 210 Ala. 453, 102 So. 718 (1925).

[17] "The rule here invoked is one of parliamentary procedure, and it is uniformly held that it is within the power of all deliberative bodies to abolish, modify, or waive their own rules of procedure, adopted for the orderly conduct of business, and as security against hasty action. . . . It is settled that charter requirements, prescribing the method to be pursued by a municipal body, are mandatory, and unless complied with, any attempted exercise of power is void." Rutherford v. City of Nashville, 168 Tenn. 499, 79 S.W.2d 581, 584 (1935).

"The only province of the courts is to inquire whether charter provisions have been followed. Charter provisions are structural, and the courts have the right to inquire whether they have been complied with. Parliamentary rules are merely procedural, and with their observance the courts have no concern. They may be waived or disregarded by the legislative body." South Georgia Power Co. v. Baumann, 169 Ga. 649, 151 S.E. 513, 515 (1929) (city council).

The court will take judicial notice of the provisions of a legislative charter under which a city is operating. "The authorities support the proposition that the requirements of the charter, properly construed, defining the procedure necessary to suspend the rules, are mandatory." Simmons v. Holm, 229 Ore. 373, 367 P.2d 368, 372 (1961).

"But a more solid and substantial legal answer . . . is that these rules of order for the government of the city council are mere rules of procedure adopted by itself for its guidance and convenience. They are no part of its legislative or legal charter, and rest upon no positive prescription of the statutes of the state." Bradford v. City of Jellico, 1 Tenn. Ch. App. 700, 719–20 (1901).

[18] Anderson v. Grossenbacher, 381 S.W.2d 72 (Tex. 1964).

Rules cannot be suspended unless a controlling statute or code so allows. City council action in adopting an ordinance within three days after filing, when the code required a five-day waiting period, was held invalid. Hukle v. City of Huntington, 134 W. Va. 249, 58 S.E.2d 780 (1950).

[19] Amended rules of a county political committee were not adopted by a majority vote of the county committee as required by election law, and therefore were invalid and their enforcement was enjoined. Theofel v. Butler, 134 Misc. 259, 236 N.Y.S. 81, 82 (Sup. Ct. 1929).

It is a general principle that any action taken by a deliberative body is subject to the implied condition that it is subject to further "ordinary parliamentary practice."[20] Thus, a deliberative assembly may, within defined limitations, reconsider or rescind a vote on action previously taken.[21] In deciding the "question of what discretion the council has in adhering to and changing its own rules," one court held that a city council may change its own rules by procedures not in accordance with the rules of parliamentary law if the procedures were all that the law required.[22]

§ 9.17　Rules To Be Observed Until Changed or Waived

Where rules have been adopted by the body, they must be observed until they have been regularly changed or waived. The adoption of new rules abrogates the old rules, and such new rules continue in force until they are amended or further new rules adopted.[23] An amendment of the rules takes effect only as of the

[20] Wood v. Cutter, 138 Mass. 149, 150 (1884) (reconsideration).

[21] See §§ 9.19 to 9.27 infra.

[22] Humphrey v. City of Youngstown, 143 N.E.2d 321, 323 (Ohio 1955).

[23] "There is a marked difference between a voluntary association with rules and one without. If lawful rules are made for the government of the members they must be conformed to until they are regularly changed. So long as they are in force they are the law of the association and must be obeyed." Ostrom v. Greene, 161 N.Y. 353, 362, 55 N.E. 919 (1900).

Where a political party committee, which had not held its initial organizing meeting, neither adopted new rules nor amended its predecessor's rules, those rules continued in effect pursuant to the election law. Baker v. Jensen, 30 App. Div. 2d 969, 295 N.Y.S.2d 283 (2d Dep't 1968), aff'd, 295 N.Y.S.2d 331 (1968).

Where the constitution of an unincorporated labor union provided that its meetings shall be governed by Robert's Rules of Order unless otherwise provided in the constitution and by-laws, the constitutional provisions governing its liquidation are controlling on the members until amended or repealed by approved procedure. Marvin v. Manash, 175 Ore. 311, 153 P.2d 251 (1944).

"Rules having been adopted by the Republican County Committee of New York County they must be conformed to until they are regularly changed. So long as they are in force they are the law of the Committee and must be obeyed. These Rules are not contrary or repugnant to any provisions of the Election Law and consequently must be enforced by this court." In re Davie, 13 Misc. 2d 1019, 178 N.Y.S.2d 740, 743 (Sup. Ct. 1958), citing Robert's

effective date of the amendment, and cannot be applied retroactively to make valid an election by members who were not permitted to vote under rules in effect at the time of election.[24]

§ 9.18   Rules Not Binding Except on Members

Rules of order adopted by an assembly are not binding upon any person except the members of the body which adopts them.[25] And, of course, neither the rules of procedure adopted by one deliberative body,[26] nor the custom or practice of a previous body,[27]

Rules of Order on another point; *accord,* Battipaglia v. Executive Comm., 20 Misc. 2d 226, 191 N.Y.S.2d 288 (Sup. Ct. 1959).

Extension of the life of a legislative committee, without limiting procedures already adopted by it, constitutes approval of such procedures. *In re* Withrow, 176 Misc. 597, 28 N.Y.S.2d 223 (Sup. Ct. 1941).

[24] Where the county committee of a political party elected members of the executive committee contrary to the rules then in effect, the elections were a nullity, and could not be validated by a subsequent amendment of the rules. A new election having been ordered by the court, it must be held in accordance with the amended rules then in effect. Broderick v. Knott, 94 N.Y.S.2d 43 (Sup. Ct. 1949), *aff'd,* 276 App. Div. 960, 95 N.Y.S.2d 346 (Peck, C. J., dissenting, holding that old rules should apply to new election), *aff'd,* 301 N.Y. 723, 95 N.E.2d 405 (1950).

See Morris v. Cashmore, 253 App. Div. 657, 3 N.Y.S.2d 624 (Sup. Ct.), *aff'd,* 278 N.Y. 730, 17 N.E.2d 143 (1938) (Reed's Rules); Bauman v. Fusco, 45 Misc. 2d 326, 256 N.Y.S.2d 855 (Sup. Ct.), *aff'd,* 23 App. Div. 2d 404, 261 N.Y.S.2d 85 (1st Dep't), *aff'd,* 16 N.Y.2d 952, 265 N.Y.S.2d 102 (1965) (legislative intention that political parties be allowed to formulate their own rules).

See also Walker Memorial Baptist Church v. Saunders, 285 N.Y. 462, 35 N.E.2d 42 (1941) (religious corporation—Hiscox' Directory).

[25] It was held that the board had "the right to adopt such parliamentary rules for the convenient dispatch of its business as it might deem proper. This is a power that is inherent in every public and private body, and mere parliamentary rules are, of course, not designed to be and are not binding upon any person or persons except the members of the body that adopts them; and they may be amended, suspended, or repealed at the pleasure of the body, or in any manner that it has prescribed for this purpose." Montenegro-Riehm Music Co. v. Board of Educ., 147 Ky. 720, 145 S.W. 740, 743 (1912).

[26] "Rules of procedure passed by one legislative body are not binding upon subsequent legislative bodies operating within the same jurisdiction. No legislative body can divest its successor of its legislative powers by passing ordinances or resolutions which deprive their successor of the power to exercise

is binding on a subsequent body operating within the same jurisdiction. Rules of procedure expire at the adjournment of the body
adopting them; they may of course, be readopted by a subsequent
body.[28] The new rules may differ materially from the prior rules
in any respect, including the vote required to adopt the new rules.[29]
While this is generally true, it is also acknowledged that "[a]n
unbroken legislative practice upon a question partaking so much

---

fully their legislative discretion. Each legislative body, when it meets, and
unless restrained by the authority which created it, is without rules of procedure, and has inherent power to make its own rules without reference to the
action of preceding bodies." South Georgia Power Co. v. Baumann, 169 Ga.
649, 151 S.E.2d, 513, 515 (1929), *quoted in* Ellis v. Stokes, 207 Ga. 423, 61
S.E.2d 806, 810 (1950) (county commissioners).

"The power of the society derived from its charter and the laws under which
it was organized, to enact by-laws, is continuous, residing in all regular meetings of the society so long as it exists. Any meeting could, by a majority vote,
modify or repeal the law of a previous meeting, and no meeting could bind a
subsequent one by irrepealable acts or rules of procedure. The power to enact
is the power to repeal; and a by-law, requiring a two-thirds vote of members
present to alter or amend the laws of the society, may itself be altered,
amended, or repealed by the same power which enacted it." Richardson v.
Union Congregational Soc'y, 58 N.H. 187, 189 (1877), *quoted in* Hornady v.
Goodman, 167 Ga. 555, 146 S.E. 173, 182 (1928).

It is well established that in legislative matters a town council cannot bind
its successors. Hanna v. Rathje, 171 N.W.2d 876 (Iowa 1969).

[27] "The council is a deliberative body with prerogatives limited only by
positive law. As such it had full power to make reasonable rules governing the
election. . . . Neither custom nor practice of previous councils is of determinative value." State *ex rel.* Smith v. Nazor, 135 Ohio St. 364, 21 N.E.2d 124,
126 (1939), *quoting* State *ex rel.* Reed v. DeMaioribus, 131 Ohio St. 201, 2
N.E.2d 506, 509 (1936).

[28] "It is also established that unless authorized by statute a legislative body
such as a town meeting cannot pass procedural rules which will bind similar
bodies at subsequent meetings, since rules of procedure expire at the adjournment of the body adopting them unless readopted in the future." Town of
Exeter v. Kenick, 104 N.H. 168, 181 A.2d 638, 641 (1962).

[29] "Where a city council resolves that the rules of the prior council be
adopted until a committee reports rules, the prior rules cease to be in force on
the report of the committee. . . . Although the rules of a prior council, temporarily adopted until new rules can be reported by a committee, provide that
they cannot be amended except by a two-thirds vote, the new rules, when reported, can be adopted by a majority vote." South Georgia Power Co. v.
Baumann, 169 Ga. 649, 151 S.E.2d 513, 515 (1929), *citing* Armitage v. Fisher,
74 Hun 167, 26 N.Y.S. 364 (1893).

of the nature of pure parliamentary law would be entitled to weight." [30]

However, if the failure to observe an established procedure is more than a technicality and results in an impairment of the fundamental rights of a member, the court is likely to uphold strict compliance with the procedural requirements.[31]

RECONSIDERATION AND RESCISSION

§ 9.19   Inherent Right of Assembly To Reconsider

Every deliberative assembly has the right, within certain stated limitations,[1] to reconsider or rescind action previously taken. An

[30] Nevins v. City Council, 227 Mass. 538, 116 N.E. 881, 885 (1917) (reconsideration of vote), *citing* Cushing, Law & Pr. Leg. Assem., Barclay's Digest, Fish's Manual, Spofford's Practical Manual, Wilson's Digest Parl. Law.

"The technical rules of a legislative body, formed for its own convenient action and government, are not of binding force on towns, unless such rules have been so acted upon and enforced by the town in their regular meetings, as to create a law for themselves and binding on the inhabitants." Hunneman v. Inhabitants of Grafton, 10 Met. 454, 457 (Mass. 1845).

[31] People *ex rel.* Godwin v. The American Inst., 44 How. Pr. 468 (N.Y. 1873). A member of the Institute was expelled for accusing other members of voting with self-interest. His conduct occurred at a meeting prior to the one which resulted in his expulsion. The by-laws had adopted Cushing's Manual, which forbade members at a subsequent meeting from punishing members for conduct occurring at a prior meeting. Because Cushing was not meticulously followed, the court awarded reinstatement of the expelled member.

"While the power to expel a member is primarily in the whole body of members constituting or representing the corporation, the better view is that such power may be exercised by a duly adopted by-law or resolution not contrary to its charter or the law." It is sufficient if the procedure adopted for expulsion of a member "is fair and reasonable, and made for justice rather than form." Gottlieb v. Economy Stores, 199 Va. 848, 102 S.E.2d 345, 351, 353 (1958).

[1] Generally, the right of a legislative body to reconsider a bill which has passed continues so long as the bill remains in the custody or under the control of the body, unless a special rule restrains the body.

See Annot., At what stage does a statute or ordinance pass beyond the power of legislative body to reconsider or recall?, 96 A.L.R. 1309 (1935).

Where a motion has been adopted or has failed of passage, and afterward a member who voted with the prevailing side feels that the action taken was not wise and wishes to have the question considered again in the hope of reversing or modifying the decision, such member may move to reconsider.

early case stated simply: "All deliberative assemblies, during their session, have a right to do and undo, consider and reconsider, as often as they think proper, and it is the result only which is done. . . . In this case, so long as the joint-meeting was in session, they had a right to reconsider any question which had been before them, or any vote which they had made." [2] A later court decision

---

Such motion may be seconded by any member. Although it is often difficult to determine how the member voted when the vote was taken by voice, by show of hands, or by secret ballot, the chairman generally will not challenge the words of one who claims he voted with the prevailing side. Generally, *see* DEMETER'S MANUAL OF PARLIAMENTARY LAW AND PROCEDURE at 152, 153; Robert's Rules of Order at 49, 156.

A state legislature had the right to recall from the Governor and reconsider a bill after it had been passed and signed by the Speaker of the House and the President of the Senate but before it was deposited with the Secretary of State as custodian. "As a deliberative body the Legislature had the right of reconsideration of the bill before it reached its final custodian, and while in continuous session." Doody v. State *ex rel.* Mobile County, 233 Ala. 287, 171 So. 504, 506 (1936).

See also Annot., Reconsideration of appointment, or confirmation of appointment to office, 89 A.L.R. 132 (1934).

[2] State v. Foster, 7 N.J.L. 101, 107, 108 (1823) (general assembly); *quoted in* Witherspoon v. State *ex rel.* West, 138 Miss. 310, 103 So. 134, 137, 138 (1925) *quoting* Robert's Rules of Order. *Also quoted in* Neill v. Ward, 103 Vt. 117, 153 A. 219, 224 (1930).

"However, it is well established that unless otherwise provided by law, 'all public bodies have a right during the session to reconsider action taken by them as they think proper and it is the final result only that is to be regarded as the thing done.' Mason, Manual of Legislative Procedure § 450 (1970)." Byron v. Timberlane Regional School Dist., 309 A.2d 218, 221 (N.H. 1973), *also quoting* Robert's Rules of Order.

The right to reconsider action is an attribute of all deliberative bodies. "All deliberative bodies, during their session, have a right to reconsider their proceedings as they deem proper, when not otherwise provided by law, and it is the final result only which is to be regarded as the thing done." Crawford v. Gilchrist, 64 Fla. 41, 59 So. 963, 969 (1912), *citing* Jefferson's Manual.

Generally, "unless some right of a third person intervenes, all deliberative bodies have a right to reconsider their proceedings during a session as often as they think proper, when not otherwise provided by law, and it is the final result only which is to be regarded as the thing done." Toffolon v. Zoning Bd. of Appeals, 236 A.2d 96, 99–100 (Conn. 1967).

"It should not be impossible to remedy hasty and ill advised action by those who took that action, but later discovered their mistake. It is elementary that any legislative body may reconsider and amend a proposition once adopted if no person or any vested interest is affected thereby . . . ; and where the legis-

lative power resides in the body of the voters, they may take such action. . . .
A common council may reconsider its action. . . . So may trustees of a village." *In re* Eiss (Eiss v. Summers), 205 App. Div. 691, 199 N.Y.S. 544, 548
(1st Dep't 1923), *appeal dismissed,* 236 N.Y. 638 (1923) (*see* citations *re*
town meetings and village trustees).

"It was objected that the ordinance was at the first meeting lost, and the
vote reconsidered, and laid upon the table, and passed at the next meeting.
The right of reconsidering lost measures inheres in every body possessing legislative powers." Mayor of Jersey City v. State, 30 N.J.L. 521, 529 (1863).

A board of directors adopted resolutions setting up procedures for bids to
lease a canal and later rejected the bids and accepted a lease made on the spot.
"The adoption and observance of one mode, did not preclude them from afterwards pursuing another, which in their judgment is equally or more advantageous. The first resolutions did not perpetually bind them to follow the formalities therein prescribed." Ricau v. Baquie, 20 La. Ann. 67 (1868).

"A municipal council, like other legislative bodies, has a right to reconsider,
under parliamentary rules, its votes and action upon questions rightfully pending before it, and rescind its previous action." People *ex rel.* MacMahon v.
Davis, 284 Ill. 439, 120 N.E. 326 (1918), *citing* Robert's Rules of Order.

"The power is inherent in every deliberative body to amend a resolution
previously adopted by it. . . . By reasonable implication an amendment to a
resolution may be also amended at a meeting subsequent to that when the resolution was passed." Simpson v. Berkowitz, 59 Misc. 160, 110 N.Y.S. 485, 487
(Sup. Ct. 1908).

A school board elected a superintendent on the first ballot and then reconsidered this vote and elected a different person at an adjourned meeting. "It
begs the question to say that the board had once definitely voted in pursuance
of the instructions of the town meeting, and therefore, was *functus officio,* and
could not reconsider its vote. The vote was not definitive if it contained the
usual implied condition, that it was not reconsidered in accordance with ordinary parliamentary practice, and it must be taken to have been passed subject
to the usual incidence of votes, unless some ground is shown for treating it as
an exception to common rules." Wood v. Cutter, 138 Mass. 149 (1884).

A school district voted at an annual meeting to raise money, then voted to
reconsider at a special meeting, and finally rescinded the vote at a second
special meeting. At neither of these special meetings did the ballots equal
one-half the number of voters in the district. It was held that one-half of the
votes were not necessary since rescinding was not an action to raise monies
under the statute. "Ordinarily, where no rights of third parties have attached,
as is the case here, a municipal corporation has the power to reconsider or
rescind any action previously taken. . . . And, in the absence of express regulation, 'a proposition is carried in a town-meeting, or other legislative assembly,
by a majority of the votes cast.' " Frost v. Hoar, 85 N.H. 442, 160 A. 51, 52
(1932).

Standing orders provided that any resolution may be revoked or altered by
a unanimous vote at the same meeting or by a majority vote at a subsequent

used these words: "It is a general principle that a parliamentary or deliberative body may during the same sitting treat proceedings already had as irregular and invalid, or may, unless some right of a third party may have intervened, reconsider action already taken and then take new and different action. This principle has been applied to elections as well as to measures of a more strictly legislative character." [3]

---

meeting. It was held not improper for the board to consider rescission a third time after two tie votes, each of which was broken by the casting vote of the Chairman. Arcus v. Castle, [1954] N.Z.L.R. 122, 128, 129 (1953).

Refusal of the chair to declare the results of an election allows reconsideration at an adjourned meeting. An adjourned meeting may rescind a former vote and vote anew on the subject. "It follows that the respondent Barton was elected at the first meeting, and should have been declared elected by the chair. The chairman, however, declared that there was no election and the meeting adjourned. At the adjourned meeting—which was a continuation of the same meeting . . . —it was voted 'to rescind the vote at the previous meeting whereby the convention voted to elect a superintendent of schools,' and this vote is treated by both sides as a rescission of the election, if that was within the power of the meeting. We are of opinion that it was within the power of the meeting to rescind its vote." Reed v. Barton, 176 Mass. 473, 57 N.E. 961, 962 (1900).

A county board of supervisors is a "deliberative assembly" and has the rights inherent in any such body. "If for want of due deliberation, ill advised action is taken, the interests of the public require that it should be permitted, at least at the same meeting, to reconsider and annul such action. It would be intolerable that such a public corporation should be restricted from so doing. . . . The inherent right of the board to rescind, may fairly rest on the theory that its deliberations as to any measure acted upon or under consideration extends over the whole period of such meeting." Neal v. County of Franklin, 43 Ill. App. 267, 269 (1892).

[3] The court made this comment: "Whatever may be said as to the apparent vacillation of members of the council who change their votes under conditions similar to those here disclosed, we think it must be held to be within the power of such a deliberative body as the joint convention here in question to change its mind, and of course this can be brought about only by a change of mind on the part of individual members." Mansfield v. O'Brien, 271 Mass. 515, 171 N.E. 487, 489 (1930).

"It will not be contended that had the town fixed upon a site for the meetinghouse by vote of the inhabitants at a regular meeting, they would not have had the right at another regular meeting to have rescinded the vote and to have designated another site. Surely then, they were not bound by the opinion of those whom they had appointed to select a spot for them." Damon v. Inhabitants of Granby, 19 Mass. (2 Pick.) 345, 354 (1824).

The inherent right of a legislative body to reconsider its actions, and adopt, if need be, the opposite course in all cases where no vested rights of others have intervened, is a continuing right up to the time when by conclusive vote, accepted as such by itself, a final determination has been reached.[4] A motion to reconsider has a "high priority in parliamentary procedure" and may properly be made at any time before final adjournment of the meeting or reconvened meeting.[5]

Generally, no question of "technical parliamentary procedure" is presented in considering the right of a parliamentary body to reconsider action taken by it.[6] It has been suggested, however, that technical rules of parliamentary law, although generally not binding on the assembled body [town meeting], may become binding where "such rules have been so acted upon and enforced by the town at their regular meetings, as to create a law for themselves."[7]

§ 9.20 Purpose of Reconsideration

The purpose of a motion to reconsider is to prevent hasty decisions previously adopted by the assembly, whether affirmative or negative, from being carried out until they can be reviewed and reconsidered.[8] Thus, this right to reconsider cannot be initiated

---

A municipal legislative body may reconsider and rescind its actions at any time before the rights of third parties have vested. Anderson v. Judd, 158 Colo. 46, 404 P.2d 553 (1965).

[4] The court quoted from Ohio Jurisprudence: "It is said to be a well-established rule that the action of municipal bodies respecting legislative or administrative matters is not always conclusive and beyond recall, but that they are possessed of inherent power to reconsider their action in matters of that nature, and adopt, if need be, the opposite course in all cases where no vested rights of others have intervened, the power thus to act being a continuing power." Humphrey v. City of Youngstown, 143 N.E.2d 321 (Ohio 1955).

[5] Byron v. Timberlane Regional School Dist., 309 A.2d 218, 222 (N.H. 1973), *citing* Robert's Rules of Order; Mason's Manual.

[6] *See* Mansfield v. O'Brien, 271 Mass. 515, 171 N.E. 487, 490 (1930).

[7] Hunneman v. Inhabitants of Grafton, 10 Met. 454 (Mass. 1845). *Cited in* Bullard v. Allen, 124 Me. 251, 127 A. 722, 727 (1925), holding it to be a "universal rule" that a town is free to act as it pleases within its legal scope. "It may impair intervening rights."

[8] "The purpose of reconsidering a vote is to permit correction of hasty, ill-

by a further resolution declaring that the action taken would not be reconsidered at an adjourned meeting.[9]

In parliamentary practice, if a motion to reconsider prevails, the reconsidered question is again brought before the body in the precise position it had reached when first decided, and the same questions are put in relating to it as if the vote to be reconsidered had never been passed. The adoption of a motion to reconsider has the effect of returning a resolution "to the stage in which it was before the final vote by which it was originally passed."[10] "A

---

advised, or erroneous action, or to take into account added information or a changed situation that has developed since the taking of the vote." Robert's Rules of Order, Newly Revised, § 36, at 265 (1970), *quoted in* Byron v. Timberlane Regional School Dist., 309 A.2d 218, 221 (N.H. 1973), *also citing* Mason's Manual.

In an early case the court remarked that "the general purpose of parliamentary rules is to restrain the hasty action of a bare majority." State *ex rel.* Krejsa v. Board of Educ., 2 Ohio C.C.R. 510, 517 (Cir. Ct. 1887), *citing* Cushing's Manual.

Parliamentary rules are intended as security against "hasty and inconsiderate action." Bennett v. New Bedford, 110 Mass. 433, 437, 438 (1872).

"It is within the power of all deliberative bodies to abolish, modify or waive their own rules, intended as security against hasty and inconsiderate action." Holt v. City Council, 127 Mass. 408, 411 (1879).

[9] A town meeting, immediately after voting to purchase engines, voted that they would not reconsider. It was held that the town meeting could not bind the town so as to prevent a future action on the resolution. "The technical rules of a legislative body, framed for its own convenient action and government, are not of binding force on towns, unless such rules have been so acted upon and enforced by the town in their regular meetings, as to create a law for themselves and binding on the inhabitants." Hunneman v. Inhabitants of Grafton, 10 Met. 454, 457 (Mass. 1845).

[10] "The plaintiff's claim for relief is based upon the fact that the common council reconsidered and subsequently postponed indefinitely the resolution authorizing the improvement, and that, consequently, all subsequent proceedings were invalid. If the question as to the legal effect of the action of the common council in resolving to reconsider its former action was still open to the plaintiffs, we would be inclined to hold that the resolution was, by the adoption of the motion to reconsider, brought back to the stage in which it was before the final vote by which it was originally passed. The vote on the resolution was reconsidered, and consequently the effect which it would otherwise have was lost." Ashton v. Rochester, 133 N.Y. 187, 192, 30 N.E. 965, 967 (1892), *citing* Jefferson's Manual, Robert's Rules of Order.

Adoption of a motion to reconsider immediately places the resolution before

vote adopting a resolution and a vote duly taken to reconsider the vote of adoption, 'like positive and negative quantities in equation, destroy one another and are as if they were expunged from the journals.' " [11]

Whether a motion to override a veto, having failed of passage, may then be reconsidered, is uncertain in the absence of parliamentary precedent or decisive legislative practice.[12] One court has held that, under parliamentary rules, the proper move is to reconsider the vote by which the motion was adopted.[13]

In a case deciding whether a state legislature had the power to "reconsider" a second time the question of passing a bill over a governor's veto, the court held: "[I]n our opinion the word 're-consideration' in the Constitution does not contain any implication that the reconsideration required is to result in a single vote which exhausts the power of the legislative body. It signifies rather that the bill is to be again before the legislative body for further consideration." [14] Hence, a common council may reconsider and enact at a later meeting a new resolution identical in language and intent with a resolution vetoed by the presiding mayor at a previous

---

the meeting "in the exact position it occupied the moment before it was voted on originally." Byron v. Timberlane Regional School Dist., 309 A.2d 218, 220 (N. H. 1973), *quoting* Robert's Rules of Order, § 36.

[11] Crawford v. Gilchrist, 64 Fla. 41, 59 So. 963, 969 (1912), *citing* Jefferson's Manual.

[12] Parliamentary writers seem to accept the precedent of the House of Representatives, holding that the vote cannot be reconsidered. But there is no harmony among legislative bodies, and this court favored granting the reconsideration. Nevins v. City Council, 227 Mass. 538, 546, 116 N.E. 881 (1917) (city council), *citing* Cushing's Law & Pr. Leg. Assem., Barclay's Digest, Fish's Manual, Spofford's Practical Manual, Wilson's Digest Parl. Law, none of which contained any discussion of the subject.

[13] "By parliamentary rules the proper action to be taken by a legislative body when a measure adopted by it has been returned to it with a veto by the proper authority, is to move to reconsider the vote by which the measure was originally adopted. If a majority of the legislative body adopt the motion to reconsider, it is then proper to move that the measure be adopted notwithstanding the veto, or that it be passed over the veto. If the required majority adopt that motion, the measure is adopted; if not, the veto stands." Rogers v. City of Mendota, 200 Ill. App. 254, 256 (1916).

[14] Kay Jewelry Co. v. Board of Registration, 305 Mass. 581, 27 N.E.2d 1, 3 (1940).

meeting.[15] Further, a resolution of a city council which was vetoed by the mayor may be passed over his veto by the required vote of a later council in which several new members were sitting.[16]

§ 9.21　Meaning of Reconsideration

A motion to reconsider differs from a motion to rescind. The latter is intended to cancel, void, or repeal a resolution previously adopted to the extent that it has not been carried out or otherwise executed in the meantime. Only affirmative action can be rescinded, not negative action.

A reconsideration is not a mere change in the voting; it is a separate and distinct parliamentary action. Where a five-member board voted on a resolution, two members for, one member against, and two members abstaining, it was held that the resolution failed for lack of a majority vote as required by statute. At a later meeting of the four remaining members (one having resigned) a new vote was taken and the resolution was adopted by unanimous affirmative vote. The court properly held that the resolution had not been reconsidered; that it could not be approved at a later meeting because of a mere change of the negative vote of one member and the voting of another member who had previously abstained; and that the resolution could only be approved "upon formal proceedings expressly taken by the body as a whole for a reconsideration of the matter." [17] Due notice must be given if the

[15] "It is claimed that a legislative body cannot adopt a new resolution, identical in language and intent with a resolution previously vetoed. [The city charter] provides for the procedure to be followed by the Council. There is nothing in the charter which prohibits the tabling of a vetoed resolution and the adoption of a new one. The only thing for the executive to do is to approve or disapprove the new resolution." Mott v. Gould, 122 N.Y.S.2d 89, 91–92 (Sup. Ct.), aff'd, 281 App. Div. 1072, 122 N.Y.S.2d 418 (4th Dep't 1953).

[16] "If the body is a continuous one when a proceeding is taken up in any of its phases, that is a reconsideration, for it is the board of aldermen or board of councilmen as an entity which reconsiders, and not its constituent members." People ex rel. New York Central & H.R.R. v. Buffalo, 123 App. Div. 141, 108 N.Y.S. 331, 334 (4th Dep't 1908). See Gollob v. Bevans, 5 Misc. 2d 958, 161 N.Y.S.2d 225 (Sup. Ct. 1957).

[17] Gollob v. Bevans, 5 Misc. 2d 958, 161 N.Y.S.2d 225, 228 (Sup. Ct. 1957). Reconsideration is not considered judicial in its nature but is executive, administrative or ministerial. Actions of a board of regents in reconsidering

action to be reconsidered or rescinded was taken at a previous meeting; a municipal legislative body lacks authority to reconsider and rescind action approved at a previous meeting unless taken at a meeting duly adjourned or at a subsequent meeting after due notice.[18]

A mere change of views before they have been promulgated is not a reconsideration by the body.[19] Where no definitive action has been taken, there is nothing which may be reconsidered.[20] And, of course, a resolution cannot be reconsidered or rescinded at a later meeting which is unlawful for lack of sufficient members present to make a quorum.[21]

A reconsideration cannot be effected by a subsequent declaration that a previous legal act was illegal. For example, where an election of directors has been legally held, resolutions adopted at a subsequent meeting undertaking to create vacancies by declaring that the previous election was illegal do not constitute a reconsideration of the vote previously taken.[22] Nor can a lawful election of

---

an application for a license after the board had previously granted the license is not reviewable until it has become final. Siegel v. Mangan, 258 App. Div. 448, 16 N.Y.S.2d 1000 (3d Dep't 1940).

The removal of a clerk by a local board through a resolution passed by the board was held to be an independent resolution and not a rescission of a former resolution appointing the clerk which would have required one month's notice. *Ex parte* Richards, [1873] L.R. 3 Q.B. Div. 368.

[18] Anderson v. Judd, 158 Colo. 46, 404 P.2d 553 (1965) (reconsider); Village of Coon Valley v. Spellum, 190 Wis. 140, 208 N.W. 416 (1926) (rescind).

[19] The members of a tax assessment commission changed their minds on the afternoon of the same day, before announcement of their decision. The court held: "All bodies, possessing a judicial capacity, have the competency to consult, resolve and reconsider, and they are not bound by their conclusions until such conclusions have been promulged [sic] by their authority. In the present instance there was nothing to prevent the further action of the board but an unannounced opinion, formed while in private consultation. . . . Under the circumstances, I see nothing wrong or illegal in the act of the commissioners in changing their views before such views had been officially announced or made known by them." State v. Crosley, 36 N.J.L. 425, 428 (Ct. Err. & App. 1872).

[20] Plantz v. Board of Supervisors, 122 Misc. 576, 204 N.Y.S. 27 (Sup. Ct. 1924) (an invalid election cannot be reconsidered).

[21] *In re* Acadia Dairies, 15 Del. Ch. 248, 135 A. 846 (1927).

[22] Clark v. Wild, 85 Vt. 212, 81 A. 536 (1911).

a city attorney by a city council be invalidated on a motion to reconsider or a motion to defer action.[23]

On the other hand, a second vote may have the legal effect of a reconsideration although it was not so intended. This occurred when a city council by viva voce vote elected a city assessor and the presiding officer declared the plaintiff elected, and then, in confusion but without criticism of the vote or the declaration, took a recess. After the recess a doubter moved, and it was voted to take a new roll call, which was ordered by the president. Two votes switched and the defendant was elected. The court held that the second vote was not a verification of the first vote, but a reconsideration.[24]

§ 9.22   Reconsideration at a Future Date

A motion entered in the minutes to reconsider at a future date differs from a simple motion to reconsider. It does not have the effect of a motion to reconsider and cannot be put to a vote on the same day it was made.[25]

[23] "Nor did the other proceedings of the council respecting deferring action and voting to reconsider the election invalidate the election, if relator was elected by the first formal ballot. The proceeding to reconsider was not regular even if the council had power to reconsider. The motion deferring action did not disturb the vote taken or change the choice of the three aldermen who voted for the relator, and the motion to reconsider was not passed upon until after the relator had filed his oath of office." State ex rel. Burdick v. Tyrell, 158 Wis. 425, 149 N.W. 280, 283 (1914). See People ex rel. Simpson v. Board of Police Comm'rs, 10 Misc. 98, 100, 31 N.Y.S. 112, 114 (Sup. Ct. 1894) (attempt to reconsider valid nomination).

[24] Mansfield v. O'Brien, 271 Mass. 515, 171 N.E. 487, 488 (1930).

[25] The purpose of a motion to reconsider at a future date is to prevent a temporary majority from taking action opposed to the true majority, and is often used in large societies having frequent meetings and small quorum requirements. "According to Robert's Rules of Order, Revised, pages 165–168, the motion of January 10th was a motion entered on the minutes to be considered at a future date. In discussing the difference between this type of motion and a simple motion to reconsider, Mr. Robert says that the former motion cannot be voted upon on the same day on which it is made, but must be taken up and voted on the day in the future fixed by the motion itself, where the regular business sessions of the assembly are as often as quarterly." First Buckingham

The right of a legislative body to reconsider a vote previously taken is not a matter for judicial consideration. "That is merely a matter of parliamentary procedure which each body, by special rule, may, and usually does, regulate for itself." [26] And, being a matter of parliamentary law or procedure, the inherent right of an assembly to amend or waive its rules or to change its procedures is applicable.[27]

An assembly may reconsider a resolution at any later time deemed to be reasonable under the circumstances.[28] Hence, where the clerk of a city council is required to lay a resolution before the body at a certain meeting and the council is required to proceed to consider or reconsider the motion, the body is expected to act with reasonable dispatch, but it is not essential that the action of the body "be ingrafted into a resolution at once," since new members not entirely familiar with the situation may need time for study and discussion.[29] But where the court has intervened and adjudged

---

Community, Inc. v. Malcolm, 177 Va. 710, 15 S.E.2d 54, 55 (1941), *quoting* Robert's Rules of Order.

See Rutherford v. Nashville, 168 Tenn. 499, 79 S.W.2d 581 (1935).

[26] Smith v. Jennings, 67 S.C. 324, 45 S.E. 821, 822–23 (1903), *cert. denied*, 206 U.S. 276 (1907); *see* Nevins v. City Council, 227 Mass. 538, 116 N.E. 881 (1917), *citing* Cushing's Law & Pr. Leg. Assem., Barclay's Digest, Fish's Manual, Spofford's Practical Manual, Wilson's Digest Parl. Law.

It is unquestionably competent for a common council to reconsider the vote by which an ordinance was lost. People *ex rel.* Locke v. Common Council, 5 Lans. 11 (N.Y. Sup. Ct. 1871).

[27] Standing order of city council allowed a motion to reconsider at the next regular meeting. "The rule here invoked is one of parliamentary procedure, and it is uniformly held that it is within the power of all deliberative bodies to abolish, modify, or waive their own rules of procedure, adopted for the orderly conduct of business, and as security against hasty action." Rutherford v. Nashville, 168 Tenn. 499, 79 S.W.2d 581, 584 (1935).

[28] Ordinance failed on first vote and was reconsidered and passed two months later. "Council unquestionably has a right to reconsider its action at any time, provided the motion is made within a reasonable time." This was a reasonable time based on facts and circumstances of the case. Tuell v. Meacham Contracting Co., 145 Ky. 181, 140 S.W. 159, 161 (1911), *citing* Robert's Rules of Order.

[29] The court also said: "If the body is a continuous one when a proceeding is taken up in any of its phases, that is a reconsideration, for it is the board of aldermen or board of councilmen as an entirety which reconsiders, and not its

that a resolution is in full force notwithstanding the adoption of a motion to reconsider and a further motion of indefinite postponement (more than a month after passage of the resolution), the action directed by the resolution must proceed.[30]

§ 9.23 Rights of Third Parties

There are, of course, circumstances under which a resolution cannot be reconsidered and where the right to reconsider presents a judicial question. Ordinarily, where no rights of third parties have attached, a deliberative assembly has the power to reconsider or rescind any action previously taken. Under such circumstances reconsideration and rescission of previous votes and orders may be effected at any time before the rights of third parties have vested.[31] However, it is well settled that reconsideration and rescission cannot adversely affect the rights of others. An early court decision said: "And though matters acted upon where no step has been taken in which the rights of others are affected, may be reconsidered and rescinded; yet when the subject of the votes has been so far carried into effect that rights and duties have grown out of such action, the town cannot, at an adjournment of the same meeting, by a mere reconsideration of their previous act, destroy or affect any right thus vested." [32] This is one of the "general rules relating to powers of deliberative bodies." [33]

---

constituent members." People *ex rel.* New York Central & H.R.R. v. Buffalo, 123 App. Div. 141, 108 N.Y.S. 331, 334, 335 (4th Dep't 1908) (action taken in 15 days).

[30] Ashton v. Rochester, 133 N.Y. 187, 191, 193, 30 N.E. 965 (1892), *citing* Jefferson's Manual, Robert's Rules of Order.

[31] People *ex rel.* New York, W. & B. Ry. v. Waldorf, 168 App. Div. 473, 153 N.Y.S. 1072 (2d Dep't 1915), *quoting* Dillon on Municipal Corporations.

[32] Hunneman v. Inhabitants of Grafton, 10 Met. 454, 456–57 (Mass. 1845).

[33] "Under the decisions here quoted and the general rules relating to powers of deliberative bodies of the character of city councils, we are of the opinion that, where such a body has finally voted upon a proposition and no motion for reconsideration or other motion is pending thereon, the city council, upon adjournment of its meeting, has no power to reconsider its action where the rights of other persons have intervened." The court concluded that "[w]hile a city council is given by statute the power to make its own rules of procedure, they may not be invoked to defeat the rights which have intervened by reason of a

Whether third parties have gained rights depends upon the circumstances of each case.[34] A leading precedent is a Supreme Court decision holding that the construction of a rule of the United States Senate (relating to reconsideration of action taken) presents a judicial question where it affects persons other than members of the Senate, in that case an executive appointment to a regulatory agency. The Senate could not reconsider its action after the President had acted upon notification from the Senate by issuing a commission, although the commission was issued within the period during which Senate Rules permitted reconsideration of its action.[35]

§ 9.24 Reconsideration More Than Once

Where standing orders provided that any resolution might be revoked or altered by unanimous vote at the same meeting at which it was passed or by a majority vote at a subsequent meeting, it was held that it was not improper for an assembly to reconsider rescission a third time after two tie votes, each of which was broken by the casting vote of the chairman.[36]

---

legal action of that body." Kankakee v. Small, 317 Ill. 55, 147 N.E. 404, 406, 408 (1925).

"When the city council has formally voted upon a proposition and there is no motion for reconsideration, it may not reconsider its action where the rights of other persons intervene." Getz v. City of Harvey, 118 F.2d 817, 824 (7th Cir.), *cert. denied,* 314 U.S. 628 (1941).

[34] *See* Harrison v. Village of New Brighton, 110 App. Div. 267, 97 N.Y.S. 246 (1st Dep't 1905) (rescission of resolution granting contract before any work was done).

[35] The question at issue was whether under the Senate's rules an order of notification empowers the President to make a final and indefeasible appointment if he acts before notice of reconsideration; or whether, despite the notification, he is powerless to complete the appointment until two days of executive session shall have passed without the entry of a motion to reconsider, as permitted by the rules. United States v. Smith, 286 U.S. 6 (1932). *Accord,* DeWoody v. Underwood, 66 Ohio App. 367, 34 N.E.2d 263 (1940) (appointment of civil service commission with consent of legislative body, appointee qualified, took oath and discharged duties). *Case distinguished,* State *ex rel.* Johnson v. Hagemeister, 161 Neb. 475, 73 N.W.2d 625, 631 (1955), *citing* Gregg's Handbook Parl. Law.

But see Thorne v. Squier, 264 Mich. 98, 249 N.W. 497 (1933).

[36] Arcus v. Castle, [1954] N.Z.L.R. 122, 128–29 (1953).

At common parliamentary law a resolution cannot be twice reconsidered

§ 9.25   Reconsideration of Election Results

An election may be set aside, and a new election had, if it is undertaken before the results of the first election are declared.[37] However, an election to office cannot be reconsidered after the results of the election have been declared and recorded.[38] Nor can proceedings for rescission or reconsideration of an election be effective when the election was in fact and law a valid election. That the electors made a mistake in computing the number of votes required to elect does not disturb the vote as taken or the choice

---

unless it was materially amended after its first reconsideration. *See* Robert's Rules of Order at 158.

[37] Where a corporate election of directors has been taken, but the election has not been declared, the majority may, before adjournment, reconsider the vote and have a new election although the minority faction has withdrawn from the meeting and thereby been deprived of its cumulative voting advantage. South Carolina *ex rel.* LeRoy Springs v. Ellison, 106 S.C. 139, 90 S.E. 699 (1910). *Accord,* Baker v. Cushman, 127 Mass. 195 (1879) (power of common council, before result of an election had been declared, to treat the proceedings already had as irregular and invalid, and to vote anew); *In re* Newcomb, 42 N.Y. St. R. 442, 18 N.Y.S. 16 (1891) (adjournment of stockholders' meeting before inspectors made final report on election of directors).

It is within the power of an adjourned meeting to rescind an election held at the previous meeting. Reed v. Barton, 176 Mass. 473, 57 N.E. 961 (1900) (school committee meeting for election of superintendent).

See Casler v. Tanzer, 134 Misc. 48, 234 N.Y.S. 571 (1929) (finality of election to office by common council) *citing* Cushing's Manual.

[38] "While a municipal body having the power of election may set aside a ballot by which it appears that an election is made, for some irregularity or illegality before the election is declared . . . we are aware of no authority which holds that, when the election by ballot is declared and entered of record, it may be reconsidered at an adjourned meeting on a subsequent day, and a new election had." State v. Philips, 79 Me. 506, 11 A. 274, 275 (1887) (board of aldermen).

Appointment by a city council is complete when a roll call is made and the result recorded, and the appointment was not subject to change thereafter by motion for reconsideration. Appointment of officers is executive in nature and cannot be affected by the requirement of subsequent clerical action or by subsequent parliamentary procedure. *See* discussion of Robert's Rules of Order, "concurred in by every accepted parliamentary procedure unless specifically excepted," which provides that motion to reconsider "must be made . . . by a member who voted with the prevailing side," which was not a fact in this case. MacAlister v. Baker, 139 Cal. App. 183, 33 P.2d 469, 471, 472 (1934).

made. Moreover, acceptance of and qualification for the office to which elected deprives the electors of power to reconsider the election and elect another.[39]

§ 9.26   Vote Required To Reconsider

It is a general parliamentary rule that a reconsideration requires only a majority vote, regardless of the vote necessary to adopt the motion being reconsidered.[40] Under this rule, a majority of a quorum can reconsider or rescind a resolution which had been adopted by a requisite larger vote.[41] However, the case law is not harmonious on this point. It has been held, for example, that a resolution requiring a two-thirds vote could not be rescinded by a mere majority,[42] and that a resolution requiring a majority vote for passage could not be rescinded except by a like vote.[43]

[39] However, if there were in fact mistake or fraud in the taking of a ballot (as distinguished from a mistake in computing the vote), another ballot may be taken and the irregular or fraudulent one rejected. State ex rel. Burdick v. Tyrrell, 158 Wis. 425, 149 N.W. 280, 283 (1914).

[40] Robert's Rules of Order at 158.

[41] A statute required approval of one-half of the voters in a school district to pass a resolution raising money for school purposes. It was held that a vote of less than one-half of the voters can rescind the resolution previously adopted by one-half, since a majority has the power to act, and a rescission is not an action to raise money. Frost v. Hoar, 85 N.H. 442, 160 A. 51, 52 (1932).

See Terry v. Eagle Lock Co., 47 Conn. 141 (1879) (rescission of vote to increase capital stock).

[42] "We think the moderator was correct in holding that a mere majority could not rescind the vote which had been required to be taken by a two-thirds vote, and had been so taken." Stockdale v. School Dist., 47 Mich. 226, 10 N.W. 349, 350 (1881) (school district meeting).

The court has reasoned that where the body has not adopted a rule regulating motions for reconsideration, the same vote should be required. "Two-thirds are satisfied with it as it then reads, and no reason exists why a majority less than two-thirds can bring the resolution again before the body for the purpose of changing its features or postponing action. There should be some stability in legislative action which is passed under the requirements of a law calling for a vote of two-thirds of its members, and it should remain as the two-thirds have passed it unless the same number desire a further consideration of the measure." Whitney v. Common Council, 69 Mich. 189, 37 N.W. 184, 190 (1888).

[43] A city charter required a majority vote of all members to adopt resolutions. "A corporate act, which can only be taken by a majority vote of all the

The voting requirements on a motion to rescind differ from those on a motion to reconsider. Under parliamentary law, the vote of two-thirds of those voting is required to rescind a resolution or order previously adopted, but if previous notice of intent to rescind is given, rescission may be effected by a majority vote. The purpose of this distinction is to permit a quick rescission by a vote larger than is required for a rescission after proper notice.[44]

§ 9.27   Motion by One Voting on Prevailing Side

Parliamentary law requires that the motion to reconsider be made by one who voted with the prevailing side on the motion proposed to be reconsidered.[45] But, under general principles of parliamentary law, this rule rests exclusively with the body and may be waived. A motion regularly made to reconsider will be treated as a tacit suspension of the rule and the members alone have a right to object to this violation of parliamentary law.[46]

---

aldermen elect, could not be rescinded except by a like vote." Naegely v. City of Saginaw, 101 Mich. 532, 60 N.W. 46, 48 (1894).

[44] See Robert's Rules of Order at 54.

Where there is a specific provision in the rules for a reconsideration or rescission of a resolution, the prescribed procedure must be stringently observed or the proposed action will be ineffective. See SHAW AND SMITH, THE LAW OF MEETINGS at 78, citing Rex v. Tralee Urban Dist. Council, [1913] Ir. K.B. 59.

[45] See Robert's Rules of Order at 156.

A member of a city council who failed to vote for an appointee on a roll call is not a member who voted on the "prevailing side." MacAlister v. Baker, 139 Cal. App. 183, 33 P.2d 469 (1934), quoting Robert's Rules of Order.

[46] "It was unquestionably competent for the board to reconsider the vote by which the ordinance was lost. Parliamentary law requires that the motion to reconsider be made by one who voted with the majority on the motion proposed to be reconsidered. But whether this shall be insisted on or dispensed with, and the motion made by one voting with the majority, rests exclusively in the discretion of the body whose action it is proposed to reconsider, and no other tribunal has a right to treat a reconsideration thus moved for as void. A majority could dispense with the rule requiring the reconsideration to be moved by one who voted with the majority, and if the majority treat the motion as regularly made, it is to be considered as a tacit suspension of the rule. The members of the body alone have the right to object to the violation of the parliamentary rule." People ex rel. Locke v. Common Council, 5 Lans. 11, 14–15 (N.Y. Sup. Ct. 1871), followed in Tuell v. Meacham Contracting Co., 145 Ky.

RATIFICATION

§ 9.28   Purpose

A motion to ratify is often made to confirm or to legalize action previously taken by an official or a committee, or action taken by an insufficient number of members of the main body. For example, when a quorum is not present to act upon business of an urgent nature, the members present sometimes proceed on the assumption that the body will ratify their action at the next meeting, a quorum then being present. Also, when there is some doubt as to whether action taken by an official was within his authority, a motion to ratify may be made to legalize his act.[1]

181, 140 S.W. 159, 160 (1911); Commonwealth *ex rel.* Fox v. Chace, 403 Pa. 117, 168 A.2d 569 (1961). MacAlister v. Baker, 139 Cal. App. 183, 33 P.2d 469 (1934).

See Sullivan v. Board of Education, 264 App. Div. 207, 34 N.Y.S.2d 900 (2d Dep't 1942) (by-law permitting a reconsideration of a vote cast at a prior meeting on the next succeeding meeting on motion of any member who voted with the majority, held not inconsistent with the education law).

[1] Proposed amendment of rules of city political party committee was not void as being contrary to county committee rules when the latter were subsequently so amended. "The position of the Committee is exactly the same as that of a corporation that is engaged in a transaction which, although beyond its powers in the first instance, can be validated by subsequent legislation if the transaction could have been authorized in the first instance." Lamb v. Cohen, 40 Misc. 2d 615, 243 N.Y.S.2d 647, 651 (Sup. Ct. 1963), *citing* Robert's Rules of Order on point of quorum.

The act of county commissioners in approving payment of cost of building a bridge, made in writing but not in meeting duly convened, can be ratified at a proper subsequent meeting by a quorum vote. Cleveland Cotton-Mills v. Cleveland County, 108 N.C. 678, 13 S.E. 271 (1891).

"Ratification is a conclusion of fact and not a conclusion of law." Pollitz v. Wabash R.R., 207 N.Y. 113, 131, 100 N.E. 721, 726 (1917).

Ratification by directors of transaction approved by executive committee, having knowledge of the transaction, makes directors liable. Ratification is "equivalent to prior acquiescence." Litwin v. Allen, 25 N.Y.S.2d 667 (Sup. Ct. 1940).

A corporation may ratify the unauthorized acts of its officers and directors by a vote of stockholders if such acts were within the corporation's powers. Bates Street Shirt Co. v. Waite, 130 Me. 352, 156 A. 293 (1931).

An assembly cannot ratify an action which it could not have legally taken in the first instance. But, almost any irregularity in a proceeding which would otherwise have been lawful may be cured by subsequent ratification by the body. "An assembly may ratify any action which it has the power to authorize in advance, in which case the ratification relates back to the date of the action ratified." [2] This rule applies to meetings of the board of directors, where it has been held that "meetings irregularly convened or conducted may be cured by acquiescence or subsequent ratification." [3]

[2] Harker v. McKissock, 10 N.J. Super. 26, 76 A.2d 89, 95, aff'd, 7 N.J. 323, 81 A.2d 480 (1950), aff'd, 8 N.J. 230, 84 A.2d 723 (1951) (ratification of disaffiliation of local union from national labor union).

The doctrine of ratification had its origin in the law of agency. A corporation may ratify and thereby render binding upon itself the originally unauthorized acts of its officers and agents. Ratification is equivalent to a prior authority and relates back and supplies the needed authority. "The test of the effectiveness of the ratification of an unauthorized act of an officer or officers of a corporation is whether the corporation or its board of directors making the ratification could in the first instance have authorized such an act. For example, if there is no power to make a contract there can be no authority to ratify it." Boyce v. Chemical Plastics, 175 F.2d 839, 842 (8th Cir.), cert. denied, 338 U.S. 828 (1949).

"We recognize the principle that a governing body may effectively ratify what it could theretofore lawfully authorize, and ratification after the act is as potent as authority before the act." Stirman v. City of Tyler, 443 S.W.2d 354, 359 (Tex. Civ. App. 1969).

[3] Redstone v. Redstone Lumber & Supply Co., 101 Fla. 226, 133 So. 882, 883 (1931).

"An act done at an illegal board meeting may be ratified and given a retroactive validity at a subsequent legally held board meeting." United States v. Interstate R.R., 14 F.2d 328, 329 (W.D. Va. 1926).

Directors can ratify at a legal meeting acts authorized by them, or some of them, at an illegal meeting or under circumstances which would render the original authorization invalid. Wright v. McLaury, 81 F.2d 96 (7th Cir. 1936).

Although stockholders can ratify action undoing an amendment which was approved at a previous meeting, to be effective, such ratification must not result in action substantially prejudicial to the rights of objecting or minority stockholders. Naftalin v. LaSalle Holding Co., 153 Minn. 482, 190 N.W. 887, 889 (1922).

Acts of directors at a meeting which was illegal because of want of proper notice may be ratified either expressly by the action of the directors at a subsequent legal meeting or impliedly by the corporation's subsequent course of conduct. Johnson v. Community Dev. Corp., 222 N.W.2d 847 (N.D. 1974).

§ 9.29   Cannot Ratify Action Initially Void

However, any action which was initially void cannot be retroactively cured. Where, for example, a union increased dues and
imposed an assessment on all members but failed to comply with
the voting standards of the so-called labor "Bill of Rights," such
irregularities could not be cured retroactively at a subsequent meeting.[4]

An attempted ratification must conform to all legal requirements.
Thus, an illegal action taken at an executive session of a zoning
board cannot be cured by an attempted ratification of its action
by the board at a subsequent executive session which does not
meet all statutory requirements.[5]   Furthermore, "ratification relates
back and is equivalent to some prior authority, and, when the
adoption of some form of procedure is necessary to confer the

---

[4] Peck v. Associated Food Distrib., 237 F. Supp. 113, 114 (D. Mass. 1965)
(labor union).

Action taken at a prior illegal and irregular stockholders' meeting cannot be
retroactively ratified at a subsequent legal regular meeting. Gentry-Futch Co.
v. Gentry, 90 Fla. 595, 106 So. 473 (1925).

A stockholders' meeting cannot cure by ratification an incompetent act of a
prior meeting of stockholders. Hotaling v. Hotaling, 193 Cal. 368, 224 P. 455
(1924).

An illegal call of a special meeting of shareholders cannot be cured by subsequent ratification. Smith v. Upshaw, 217 Ga. 703, 124 S.E.2d 751 (1962).

Ratification by board of supervisors of act of its committee is unavailing,
unless this board itself was authorized to do the things performed by the committee. Brown v. Ward, 246 N.Y. 400, 159 N.E. 184 (1927) (grant of unlawful construction contract).

However, when permitted by statute, a "confirmatory meeting" may be
held by a school district for the purpose of confirming and ratifying prior
illegal action taken by it at an unlawful meeting. Brochu v. Brown, 128 Vt.
549, 268 A.2d 745 (1970).

Action taken at a meeting not legally called cannot be validated by ratification at a subsequent meeting. American Center for Educ. v. Cavnar, 26 Cal.
App. 3d 26, 102 Cal. Rptr. 575 (1972).

[5] Blum v. Board of Zoning and Appeals, 1 Misc. 2d 668, 671, 149 N.Y.S.2d
5 (1956).

Where directors of a corporation were guilty of self-dealing, and used proxies
representing three-fourths of the stock which were given to them to "ratify"
their own acts, without giving notice that the transaction would be voted on
at the meeting, the corporation was not bound by the vote. Cumberland Coal
& Iron Co. v. Sherman, 20 Md. 117 (1863).

authority in the first instance, there can be no ratification except in the same manner." [6]

Ratification constitutes an assent or consent.[7] For example, directors alone are responsible for the payment by a corporation of illegal dividends, even though they may have delegated that power to a committee of their own and have ratified its action in declaring the dividend.[8]

"The general rule is well established that shareholders can ratify any action of the Board of Directors which they themselves could have lawfully authorized," [9] including action in which the directors have a disclosed self-interest and vote their own stock in their own behalf.[10] However, shareholders cannot validate illegal acts of directors and officers by ratification of such acts,[11] nor can ratification by shareholders render fair what is unfair.[12]

[6] Knapp v. Rochester Dog Protective Ass'n, 235 App. Div. 436, 257 N.Y.S. 356, 361 (4th Dep't 1932).

[7] The majority of directors at an informal meeting without due notice directed that the corporation carry out contract terms. There being no objection for nearly three years, it was held that the corporation acquiesced and ratified action taken by a majority of directors. Gorrill v. Greenlees, 104 Kan. 693, 180 P. 798 (1919).

[8] See Aiken v. Insull, 122 F.2d 746 (7th Cir. 1941), cert. denied, 315 U.S. 806, rehearing denied, 315 U.S. 829 (1942).

[9] Chambers v. Beaver-Advance Corp., 392 Pa. 481, 140 A.2d 808, 811 (1958).

Action by an interested director is not void, but voidable. "Such acts, which may be ultra vires, but not fraudulent, and which are voidable only, may be ratified by the majority of the stockholders." In re Franklin Brewing Co., 263 F. 512, 515 (2d Cir. 1920).

[10] A stockholder contended in a derivative action that stockholders could not ratify an action of directors in compromising accounts receivable, particularly after commencement of suit and when the directors had voted their own stock and proxies in their own interest. The court held that directors acting as stockholders are entitled to vote their own stock in their own self-interest so long as there is no fraud, overreaching, or attempt to intentionally dissipate the corporation's assets. Smith v. Brown-Borhek Co., 414 Pa. 325, 200 A.2d 398, 400 (1964).

[11] A fraudulent transaction cannot be ratified by a mere majority of shareholders. A transaction which is not fraudulent although irregular and unlawful is voidable, not void, and subject to repudiation or ratification by a duly had vote of a majority of shareholders. Pollitz v. Wabash R.R., 207 N.Y. 113, 100 N.E. 721 (1917).

Issuances of stock to directors and their breach of fiduciary obligation cannot by ratified by anything less than unanimous vote of stockholders after a full

§ 9.30   Ratification Implies Knowledge

Shareholder resolutions approving all acts of officers and directors do not absolve them from liability for unlawful acts, particularly in the absence of evidence that the shareholders as a body had notice of what had been done. Ratification "implies knowledge" on the part of the persons ratifying,[13] and "can never exist unless it is clearly shown that the party charged with ratification has full knowledge of all material facts."[14]

---

disclosure. Robbins v. Banner Indus., Inc., 285 F. Supp. 578 (S.D.N.Y. 1966).

Illegal acts of directors and officers cannot be validated by ratification of a majority of the stockholders. Legal acts of directors, when ratified by a majority of stockholders, cannot be disturbed by a minority of stockholders in the absence of fraud. Lewis v. Matthews, 161 App. Div. 107, 146 N.Y.S. 424 (1st Dep't 1914).

A director who approved, ratified, and acquiesced in the declaration of an illegal dividend and failed to take any steps to recover the dividend paid, is liable as if he had been present and voted in favor of the dividend. Walker v. Man, 142 Misc. 277, 253 N.Y.S. 458 (Sup. Ct. 1931).

[12] Ratification by stockholders of a long-term management contract at a special meeting called without sufficient notice of this item. "The resolution of ratification, therefore, is not binding on these stockholders. Moreover, ratification by stockholders cannot render fair what is unfair to general creditors, for they, too, constitute a part of that community of interest in the corporation which the law seeks to protect." United Hotels Co. of America v. Mealey, 147 F.2d 816, 819 (2d Cir. 1945).

[13] A shareholder resolution approving all acts of directors and officers does not absolve them of liability for fraudulent transfers and declaration of illegal dividends. Union Discount Co. v. MacRobert, 134 Misc. 107, 234 N.Y.S. 529, 534 (Sup. Ct. 1929); accord, Bowers v. Male, 111 App. Div. 209, 97 N.Y.S. 722 (1st Dep't), aff'd, 186 N.Y. 28, 78 N.E. 577 (1906) (cannot ratify unknown and hidden items).

One cannot ratify an action unless he was aware of the action sought to be ratified. Stone v. American Lacquer Solvents Co., 345 A.2d 174 (Pa. 1975).

[14] Colorado Management Corp. v. American Founders Life Ins. Co., 145 Colo. 413, 359 P.2d 665, 669 (1961) (approval by stockholders of all lawful acts of directors for the preceding year).

See Johnson v. Busby, 278 F. Supp. 235 (N.D. Ga. 1967) (ratification of all acts of board of directors by stockholders, including some who were directors absent from board meeting).

10

Standard of Fairness

FAIRNESS AND GOOD FAITH

§ 10.1   Standard of Fairness and Good Faith

Mr. Justice Holmes's reminder that "the machinery of government would not work if it were not allowed a little play in its joints" has particular applicability to parliamentary law.[1]

Where there are no established rules or procedures, reasonableness and fairness are the standards by which courts will judge the conduct of the proceedings. "In the absence of express regulations by statute or by-law, the conduct of meetings, including the election of directors, is controlled largely by accepted usage and common

---

[1] Bain Peanut Co. v. Pinson, 282 U.S. 499, 501 (1930), *quoted in* Lamb v. Danville School Bd., 162 A.2d 614, 616 (N.H. 1960).

practice. The fundamental rule is that all who are entitled to take part shall be treated with fairness and good faith." [2] This is a

---

[2] *In re* Young v. Jebbett, 213 App. Div. 774, 779, 211 N.Y.S. 61, 65 (1925) (contested election of officers based on incidents relating to voting). The court added: "In such proceedings courts are interested in the merits, rather than in the technique. Provided, always, that there is no surprise, and no unfair advantage taken, and there is no substantial prejudice sustained, and that all parties have had a fair opportunity to be heard, the niceties of procedural law may to a certain extent be disregarded, when the circumstances of the case demand it." *Id.* at 778. *Quoted in In re* Election of Dirs. of Bushwick Sav. & Loan Ass'n, 189 Misc. 316, 70 N.Y.S.2d 478, 481 (Sup. Ct. 1947). *See* discussion of this case in Burke v. Wiswall, 193 Misc. 14, 85 N.Y.S.2d 187 (1948). *See also In re* Kaminsky, 251 App. Div. 132, 295 N.Y.S. 989 (4th Dep't 1937), *aff'd*, 277 N.Y. 524, 13 N.E.2d 456, 2 N.Y.S.2d 336 (1938) (civil election in religious organization).

The principle that shareholders and officials at a general meeting must in all matters act "honestly and fairly" is founded on English common law. Wandsworth & Putney Gas-Light & Coke Co. v. Wright, 22 L.T. 404, 405 (1870).

In an early New York decision it was held, as to an election of corporate officers, that where "no particular mode of proceeding is prescribed by law, if the wishes of the corporators have been fairly expressed, and the election was conducted in good faith, it will not be set aside on account of any informality in the manner of conducting the same." Philips v. Wickham, 1 Paige (N.Y.) 590, 600 (1829).

An early Iowa case held that the method of voting by a city council was largely within the discretion of the majority, "the wholesome restriction always being that of a reasonable guaranty for fairly taking the sense of the entire body . . . a strict observance of parliamentary usage, especially adapted for larger bodies, is not essential. The important inquiry always is whether the number required by law have agreed to the particular measure. If this has been done in a way not inconsistent with statutory provisions, it is quite immaterial whether or not parliamentary procedure has been followed." Mann v. City of LeMars, 109 Iowa 251, 80 N.W. 327, 328 (1899).

Questions of "right, justice and fair play" are to be judged in the light of the attending circumstances. For example, at a meeting of a political club it is not "unfair" in law for one group to legally outmaneuver the others in the election of their candidates. *See In re* Serenbetz, 46 N.Y.S.2d 475, 481 (Sup. Ct.), *aff'd*, 46 N.Y.S.2d 127 (1943).

In a judicial review of corporate elections, the court is not confined to strict legal considerations but has broad equitable powers which should be exercised whenever an election is so clouded with doubt or tainted with questionable circumstances that standards of fair dealing require the court to order a new expression of the voters' will. Wyatt v. Armstrong, 186 Misc. 216, 59 N.Y.S.2d 502 (Sup. Ct. 1945); *accord, In re* Garrett, 132 N.Y.S.2d 373 (Sup. Ct. 1954).

general judicial policy which is equally applicable to the more severe penalty of expulsion of a member from a non-profit corporation. "It is sufficient if the procedure adopted and followed is fair and reasonable, and made for justice rather than form." [3] The concept of fairness applies with equal force to all concerned.[4] Rules of procedure should never be used "to defeat or even modify justice." [5]

The court will not interfere with a fair election (unincorporated association) even though many technical requirements of the constitution and by-laws were ignored, where the meeting was fairly conducted and there was no showing of a fraudulent attempt by the minority to "capture" the association by trickery or fraud. Zryd v. Chapman, 97 Cal. App. 2d 357, 217 P.2d 679 (1950).

"Moreover, to permit the technical rules as commonly applied to corporations in the case of close family corporation of two shareholders of equal ownership would serve to defeat such equality of ownership, impede justice and perpetuate fraud." Kauffman v. Meyberg, 59 Cal. App. 2d 730, 140 P.2d 210, 215 (1943).

Under New York law, the courts have been given the power to set aside corporate elections in appropriate circumstances. "In essence, the question is whether or not the election 'was conducted legally, fairly and in good faith.' Under this standard elections have been set aside for numerous reasons." Wolpert v. First Nat'l Bank, 381 F. Supp. 625, 632 (E.D.N.Y. 1974).

See People v. Albany & S.R.R., 1 Lans. 308 (N.Y. 1869), *modified on other grounds,* 5 Lans. 25 (1871), *aff'd,* 57 N.Y. 161 (1874); *In re* Election of Mohawk and Hudson R.R., 19 Wend. 135 (N.Y. 1838).

[3] Gottlieb v. Economy Stores, Inc., 199 Va. 848, 102 S.E.2d 345, 353 (1958).

[4] In a case considering the sufficiency of the notice of a county political committee meeting, the court said: "The petitioners' papers refer to the use of fair treatment. It strikes me upon consideration of all the matters herein that the question of fairness as to notice and procedure applies with equal force to both sides of this controversy. As an aside, the matter seems to be not so much fair treatment or fairness but whose fairness should prevail. With respect to fairness, what one side considers fair is not to be the yardstick but fairness in the overall should control." *In re* Ajello's Petition, 26 Misc. 2d 1026, 212 N.Y.S.2d 970, 974 (Sup. Ct. 1961).

[5] United-Buckingham Freight Lines v. United States, 288 F. Supp. 883 (D. Neb. 1968).

"Administrative procedures need not conform to the procedural niceties that surround the judicial process." United States v. Rasmussen, 222 F. Supp. 430 (D. Mont. 1963).

An administrative agency (ICC) is not bound by technical common-law principles of evidence or procedure. Fried v. United States, 212 F. Supp. 886 (S.D.N.Y. 1963).

§ 10.2   Adherence to Judicial Precedents Not Necessary

Formality and strict adherence to judicial precedents are not essential. In the case of corporate meetings "[m]atters for stockholder consideration need not be conducted with the same formality as judicial proceedings."[6] Hearings before a village board of trustees are not "circumscribed by the evidentiary rules against hearsay," and testimony may be admitted which would have been excluded in a court trial.[7] The hearings by a Congressional committee need not be conducted with the conventional and traditional formalities of a trial in a court of law, and rules of evidence applicable to a jury trial need not be followed.[8] Union officials on a trial board are not judges.[9] And, of course, witnesses in committee hearings "cannot be required to be familiar with the complications of parliamentary practice."[10]

§ 10.3   Manual of Rules of Order Not Applicable Unless Adopted

The assumption that any recognized parliamentary manual is applicable in all respects to company meetings, in the absence of any established rules of procedure, is wholly unfounded. "The plaintiff cites Robert's Rules of Order . . . as the binding proce-

[6] Campbell v. Loew's Inc., 36 Del. Ch. 565, 134 A.2d 852, 860 (1957).

In an action to remove directors, the court held that corporate bodies are not bound to act "with strict regularity which obtains in judicial proceedings." The court will limit its inquiry as to whether they acted within their powers, and whether they "exercised their powers fairly and in good faith." State ex rel. Blackwood v. Brast, 98 W. Va. 596 (1925).

[7] Dubato v. Board of Trustees, 8 Misc. 2d 346, 166 N.Y.S.2d 971 (1957).

[8] United States v. Deutch, 147 F. Supp. 89, aff'd, 280 F.2d 691 (App. D.C. 1960), rev'd, 367 U.S. 456 (1961); United States v. Kamin, 136 F. Supp. 791 (D.C. Mass. 1956); United States v. Fitzpatrick, 96 F. Supp. 491 (D.D.C. 1951).

[9] Union officials are not familiar with the delicate problems of truth or falsehood, privilege and "fair comment." Salzhandler v. Caputo, 316 F.2d 445 (2d Cir.), cert. denied, 375 U.S. 946 (1963).

Administrative bodies are not bound by the rigid exclusionary common-law rules of evidence. Smith v. General Truck Drivers, 181 F. Supp. 14 (S.D. Cal. 1960) (action under Labor–Management Reporting and Disclosure Act).

[10] Christoffel v. United States, 338 U.S. 84, 88 (1949).

dure to be followed by any and all corporations while conducting a stockholders' meeting. This contention cannot be sustained. Unless otherwise provided by its certificate of incorporation or by law, every corporation has the power to adopt, change, amend and repeal by-laws relating to the regulation of business and to the conduct of the affairs of the corporation." [11]

Furthermore, a particular parliamentary manual need not be considered or followed by a deliberative assembly which has adopted its own procedures for the conduct of public hearings. In a recent case the defendant tried to impose an authoritative parliamentary manual on a city planning board. He was arrested and convicted as a disorderly person for refusing to relinquish the floor microphone and for persisting in his efforts to quote and explain the manual, when the board had already adopted, and the chair had outlined, its own rules of procedure.[12] And, a school board, unless under

[11] Abbey Properties Co. v. Presidential Ins. Co., 119 So. 2d 74, 77 (Fla. Dist. Ct. App. 1960). The court added: "In addition to this liberal power to amend regulations relating to procedure to be followed at stockholders' meetings, it has been held that in the absence of evidence to the contrary, it will be presumed that the meeting was held in accordance with the statutes, charters, and by-laws."

Where there is no statutory provision requiring a school board to decide school matters by a vote of aye or nay, the members may take binding action at a full meeting after formal discussion and by finally declaring themselves, which is just as conclusive as though they had formally voted. The court commented that "[T]his formal action, however, has never been held to require strict adherence to the technical procedure approved by 'Robert's Rules of Order.'" Fleming v. Board of Trustees, 112 Cal. App. 225, 296 P. 925, 926 (1931).

But see MacAlister v. Baker, 139 Cal. App. 183, 33 P.2d 469, 472 (1934) in which the court quoted Robert's Rules "concurred in by every accepted parliamentary procedure unless specifically excepted." In this case Robert's Rules had been adopted by a city council. Since there was uncertainty as to which edition was adopted, the court held that the edition located in the local county law library had been adopted.

By-laws of a religious corporation provided that Robert's Rules were to govern at all corporate meetings when not in conflict with the by-laws. Conflict existed as to voting requirements, so the by-law provision applied. *In re* Koch (Koch v. Wadsworth), 257 N.Y. 318, 178 N.E. 545 (1931).

[12] The court noted that the defendant went to the microphone to quote Robert's Rules of Order as supporting a request from the floor by another speaker on a point of information. The chairman ruled the defendant out of order but he "persisted in his efforts to explain what *Robert's* held, so that the

some statutory restraint, can act without "strict adherence to the technical procedure approved by 'Robert's Rules of Order.'"[13] Thus, the fact that the "niceties of every parliamentary rule" have not been followed, and that there has been a failure to follow some defined parliamentary usage, does not render the proceedings illegal.[14]

Where a city council adopts Robert's Rules to govern its parliamentary procedure and also adopts its own ordinances covering the duties of the mayor and the council in procedural matters, both the mayor and the council are bound by such rules of procedure. "Neither the mayor nor city council is supreme. Each has its rights and duties prescribed by statute; each has its limitations." Thus the mayor as presiding officer of the city council does not have power to refuse to recognize a motion for the adoption of an ordinance, claiming that he has sole power to determine whether or not the ordinance or motion is valid. "Even if the mayor does not believe that a particular motion or ordinance is valid, it can still be considered by the city council. His remedy is not to refuse the right to consider but, rather, to veto the ordinance. . . . Though it may subsequently be proven in court to be invalid, the remedy is in the court house and not in the mayor's office."[15]

§ 10.4   Where Manual Has Been Adopted

Even where a particular parliamentary manual has been adopted by the assembly, it is not mandatory that the rules of the manual

---

chairman had to rule him out of order three more times." State v. Moore, 101 N.J. Super. 419, 244 A.2d 522, 523 (1968).

Where standing rules of a city council provided that Robert's Rules were to apply when not inconsistent with council rules, Robert's was not applied to the election of the president when the city charter provided a method. Van Cleve v. Wallace, 216 Minn. 500, 13 N.W.2d 467 (1944).

When by-laws provide for a majority vote, that is sufficient, and the requirement, under Robert's Rules, of a majority of the entire membership is not applicable as it exceeds anything conferred by the by-laws. Robert's Rules have "dubious application to town meeting government." Blomquist v. Arlington, 338 Mass. 594, 156 N.E.2d 416, 419 (1959).

[13] Fleming v. Board of Trustees, 112 Cal. App. 225, 296 P. 925, 926 (1931).

[14] Commonwealth ex rel. Fox v. Chace, 403 Pa. 117, 168 A.2d 569 (1961).

[15] Rudd v. Sarallo, 111 Ill. App. 2d 153, 249 N.E.2d 323, 325 (1969).

be followed at all times. For example, where a city ordinance adopted Robert's Rules of Order and a resolution was not read fully as provided by Robert's, the court upheld the resolution as validly adopted although the Rules had not been followed. "This parliamentary guide is adopted by legislative bodies to expedite the transaction of their affairs in an orderly fashion. Such rules are therefore procedural and their strict observance is not mandatory. Consequently, a failure to observe one of them is not jurisdictional and does not invalidate action which is otherwise in conformity with charter requirements." [16] A leading case involving a Massachusetts town meeting distinguishes between substantive law and procedural matters in deciding whether the provisions of an adopted parliamentary manual should be followed. The by-laws provided that "the duties of the moderator, and the government of the town meeting, not specially provided for by law, or by the foregoing rules, shall be determined by the rules of practice contained in Robert's Rules of Order [edition] so far as they are adopted to the condition and the power of the town." The moderator ruled that a motion to amend salary classifications was lost because it lacked a majority vote of the entire membership which he ruled was necessary under Robert's Rules. The trial court approved. The appellate court reversed, holding that "the imposition of a requirement of a vote of a majority of the entire membership is one of substance and not of practice," while Robert's Rules applied only to "procedural matters." [17]

On the other hand, where a particular parliamentary manual has been adopted, the courts often hold that the meeting procedures prescribed by that manual, if not in conflict with higher authority, should be followed especially where the results are fair and reasonable.[18] This conforms with a general principle of the common law

[16] City of Pasadena v. Paine, 126 Cal. App. 2d 93, 271 P.2d 577, 579 (1954).

[17] Blomquist v. Town of Arlington, 338 Mass. 594, 156 N.E.2d 416, 418, 419 (1959).

[18] Expulsion of a life member for using abusive language at a prior meeting was set aside by the court. The organization had adopted Cushing's Manual, which provided for prompt notice of offensive words and concurrent action calling the member to order, but did not authorize disciplinary action against a member at a subsequent meeting. People *ex rel.* Godwin v. American Inst., 44 How. Pr. 468, 471 (N.Y. Sup. Ct. 1873).

See MacAlister v. Baker, 139 Cal. App. 183, 33 P.2d 469 (1934) (recon-

that the intricate niceties of parliamentary procedure prescribed in
a specific manual, although adopted for or by the body and therefore generally applicable, must stand the test of "natural justice" and
"fair play." [19] Where such procedures are inappropriate, unreasonable, intricate or beyond the realm of common sense under the circumstances they may be waived or ignored by the assembly.[20]

---

sideration of an election vote), *citing* Robert's Rules of Order; Randolph v. Mt.
Zion Baptist Church, 139 N.J. Eq. 605, 53 A.2d 206 (Ch. 1947) (sale of
church property), *citing* Hiscox' Directory for Baptist Churches; Walker Memorial Baptist Church v. Saunders, 285 N.Y. 462, 35 N.E.2d 42 (1941), *citing*
Hiscox' Directory; Morris v. Cashmore, 253 App. Div. 657, 3 N.Y.S.2d 624 (1st
Dep't), *aff'd*, 278 N.Y. 730, 17 N.E.2d 143 (1938) (city council—following
Reed's Rules); *In re* Havender, 181 Misc. 989, 44 N.Y.S.2d 213 (Sup. Ct.
1943), *aff'd*, 267 App. Div. 860, 47 N.Y.S.2d 114 (1st Dep't), *motion appeal
denied*, 267 App. Div. 901, 48 N.Y.S.2d 325 (1944) (election of officers),
citing Robert's Rules of Order; First Buckingham Community, Inc. v. Malcolm, 177 Va. 710, 15 S.E.2d 54 (1941) (motion to reconsider), *citing* Robert's
Rules of Order.

A rule requiring that a resolution (purchase of new school books) should be
referred to a committee and should not be acted upon within four weeks from
its introduction is reasonable and binding. Krejsa v. Board of Educ., 2 Ohio
C.C. 510 (1887), *citing* Cushing's Manual.

[19] It was not contrary to "natural justice" or inconsistent with "fair play" for
members of a committee which had recommended a penalty to vote at a special
meeting of a medical society which considered a suspended member's appeal
from action of the committee; and such suffrage at the special meeting was
authorized by by-law providing that deliberations of the society should be
governed by parliamentary usage as contained in Robert's Rules of Order.
Posner v. Bronx County Med. Soc'y, 19 App. Div. 2d 89, 241 N.Y.S.2d 540
(1st Dep't), *aff'd*, 13 N.Y.2d 1004, 195 N.E.2d 59, 245 N.Y.S.2d 393 (1963).

[20] *See* § 9.12 *supra*.

Where the constitution of a labor union provided that members could be
expelled only by vote of a supreme quorum after such action was recommended
by a trial committee and the majority report of such committee did not recommend expulsion, their expulsion by the supreme quorum after adoption of the
minority report will not be sustained, notwithstanding the fact that Robert's
Rules of Order had been adopted under the by-laws as the standard of procedure and those rules permit the adoption of a minority report. "The union
voted to substitute the minority report for the majority report and to concur
therein. That this was a violation of the rule making the recommendation of a
Trial Committee a condition precedent to expulsion is so clear that further
comment is unnecessary. The fact that under the by-laws Robert's Rules of
Order were adopted as the standard of procedure and that those rules provide
for the adoption of a minority report cannot change the plain requirement of

Taking into account the many court decisions which adjudicate whether the rules of order promulgated by a particular authoritative parliamentary manual are binding on a private body or on a local public assembly which has adopted such rules for its own proceedings, it is evident that the courts will tend to uphold and require compliance with such rules if their employment leads to a fair and reasonable result, but will be inclined to set them aside as mere internal regulations adopted solely for the convenience of the body if their enforcement would lead to unfair or unreasonable consequences.

§ 10.5   Complexities of Parliamentary Law Ill-Suited for All Meetings

Practically speaking, the nice distinctions and complexities of parliamentary law are ill-suited for all meetings. One need not search far for the reasons why they are not suited to corporate meetings. Early English common law stated the basic concept simply. "Now I come to what is the critical question in this action. It appears to me that meetings of this kind are not bound to model all their proceedings strictly on the rules of the House of Commons. Those rules are very useful. . . . But they are too complex for the appreciation of the ordinary shareholders." [21]

§ 10.6   Town Meetings and Small Gatherings

Early American case law recognized that the intricate formalities of parliamentary law were not suitable for town meetings and vil-

---

the constitution nor convert by procedural sleight of hand the minority report into the recommendation of the committee which the constitution requires." Harris v. National Union of Marine Cooks & Stewards, 98 Cal. App. 2d 733, 221 P.2d 136, 138 (1950).

[21] Henderson v. Bank of Australasia, 45 Ch. D. 330, 333 [62 L.T.N.S. 869] (C.A. 1890). Chairman of shareholders' meeting refused to put to vote a motion to alter a proposed amendment. The moving shareholder did not appeal the ruling to the assembly. Chitty, J., whose words are cited in the text, felt this forbade the shareholder from challenging the result by suit. On appeal, the judges felt differently, holding that the chairman's refusal to entertain the shareholder's proposal prevented a material question from coming before the assembly.

lage councils.[22] "No doubt the ordinary rules of parliamentary law, as laid down in the manuals and rules of authority, are a very convenient aid to the orderly transaction of business; but its rules are in many matters complicated, and the distinctions subtle and nice;— and when the various champions of discussion engage in a game of parliamentary tactics, a town-meeting would very soon find itself entangled in the complicated meshes of parliamentary rules which would effectively stop all proceedings and bar all legitimate action, if they were of any binding force."[23]   It has also been held that de-

---

[22] For a statement of the essential and distinguishing characteristic of the town meeting form of government, *see In re* Opinion of the Justices, 229 Mass. 601, 119 N.E. 778 (1918). In brief, all qualified inhabitants meet, deliberate, act, and vote in their natural and personal capacities in the exercise of their corporate powers; each qualified inhabitant of the town has an undisputed right to vote upon every question presented, as well as to discuss it.

A town meeting is not a representative body but a "pure democracy" where the citizens, as to matters within their jurisdiction, administer the affairs of the town in person. A town is free to take action in one direction today and in another tomorrow. Technical rules of parliamentary law are ill adapted to a town meeting and hence they are not governed by the strict rules of legislative practice. Bullard v. Allen, 124 Me. 251, 127 A. 722, 727 (1925).

"The electors qualified to vote in a financial town meeting do not constitute the town. The inhabitants constitute the town as a body corporate. And the other qualified electors thereof have as great voting power as the taxpaying voters in the election of officers and the appointment of such agents." Capone v. Nunes, 85 R.I. 392, 132 A.2d 80, 83 (1957).

In Massachusetts the appropriate town body to adopt, repeal, or modify by-laws is the town meeting. These functions are legislative in character and historically are appropriately those of the town meeting. Russell v. Zoning Bd. of Appeals, 209 N.E.2d 337 (Mass. 1965).

The electors of a town at a town meeting represent the corporate authorities and have power to take all necessary measures and give directions for the exercise of the town's corporate powers. Anders v. Town of Danville, 45 Ill. App. 2d 104, 195 N.E.2d 412 (1964).

"It has long been recognized that town meetings do not consistently express their purposes with legal precision and nicety . . . and that votes adopted by such meetings will be liberally construed to give 'a legal effect to language inartificially employed to express the corporate purpose.' " McMahon v. Town of Salem, 104 N.H. 219, 182 A.2d 463, 464 (1962).

For a history of the town meeting *see* JOHNSON, TRUSTMAN, AND WADS-WORTH, TOWN MEETING TIME, A HANDBOOK OF PARLIAMENTARY LAW (1962).

[23] The court cited and discussed Cushing's Manual in holding that town meetings "are not suffered to be, nor are they in part governed by the strict rules of deliberative, legislative assemblies." Such meetings are run by the

moderator. It is not wise to compel the running of town meetings by strict rules, since men who run the meetings may be intelligent but without experience in the intricacies of parliamentary rules. Hill v. Goodwin, 56 N.H. 441, 453–56 (1876).

"Counsel for defendants insist that strict parliamentary rules should not be applied to these municipal bodies exercising legislative functions; that if they adopt or pursue a method of proceeding understood by themselves, which arrives at substantial results, their action should not be overthrown upon any technical rules or strict construction of parliamentary law. We are of the same opinion." Whitney v. Common Council, 69 Mich. 189, 201, 37 N.W. 184, 190 (1888), *quoted with approval*, Casler v. Tanzer, 134 Misc. 48, 234 N.Y.S. 571, 576 (Sup. Ct. 1929) (common council), Thorne v. Squier, 264 Mich. 98, 249 N.W. 497 (1933) (city commission).

A resolution of a county board need not be in "the language which one experienced in parliamentary proceedings would use in a resolution," and "it will not do to apply to the orders and resolutions of such bodies nice verbal criticism and strict parliamentary distinctions, because the business is transacted generally by plain men, not familiar with parliamentary law. Therefore, their proceedings must be liberally construed in order to get the real intent and meaning of the body." Hark v. Gladwell, 49 Wis. 172, 5 N.W. 323, 328–29 (1880), *quoted in* Wisconsin Cent. R.R. v. Ashland County, 81 Wis. 1, 50 N.W. 937 (1891).

In a leading case involving a town meeting where Robert's Rules of Order had been adopted as the rules of practice for the duties of the moderator and the government of the town meeting, the court remarked that "we are at once struck by its dubious application to town meeting government." Blomquist v. Arlington, 338 Mass. 594, 156 N.E.2d 416, 419 (1959).

"The technical rules of parliamentary law, designed for the regulation of deliberative assemblies, are in some respects ill adapted for the transaction of the affairs of a town meeting. Hence, although in general the action of town meetings conforms to parliamentary procedure, it never has been held that they are governed by the strict rules of legislative practice." Wood v. Town of Milton, 197 Mass. 531, 84 N.E. 332, 333 (1908), *citing* Cushing, Crocker, Jefferson, and Reed.

"It is not to be expected that the technical rules of parliamentary law, which are enforced for the convenience in governing and controlling legislative bodies, should be vigorously applied to the proceedings of a village council." Thus, the fact that the procedures followed were not fully in accordance with parliamentary law is not fatal to the action of the body if the procedures were all that the statute required. Madden v. Smeltz, 2 Ohio C.C. 168, 174, 1 Ohio C.D. 424 (Cir. Ct. 1887), *quoted in* Humphrey v. City of Youngstown, 143 N.E.2d 321, 324 (Ohio 1955).

"The technical rules of a legislative body, framed for its own convenient action and government, are not of binding force on towns, unless such rules have been so acted upon and enforced by the town in their regular meetings, as to create a law for themselves and binding on the inhabitants." Hunneman v. Inhabitants of Grafton, 10 Met. 454, 457 (Mass. 1854).

parture by the city council from the formal procedures prescribed for the passage of an ordinance will not affect the validity of such action unless the governing law makes such formality vital. The courts generally regard non-compliance with merely formal requirements in the manner of enacting an ordinance no ground for declaring it void. One court explained: "It is not to be expected that aldermen will be experts in parliamentary law. The objection is purely technical." [24]

Since town meetings do not consistently express their purposes with "legal precision and nicety," votes adopted by such meetings will be liberally construed to give a legal effect to language "inartificially employed to express the corporate purpose." [25]

Certainly, as to small gatherings, including the typical school board meeting,[26] and close family corporation,[27] the formalities of parliamentary procedure are not suitable.[28]

---

[24] "Here, neither the statute nor the ordinance on that subject declare the ordinance void unless a formal vote to reconsider be first adopted. The proper motion was made. The vote by which the ordinance was passed over the veto shows that the motion to reconsider would have been adopted if it had been put. It is not to be expected that aldermen will be experts in parliamentary law. The objection is purely technical. Six of the seven aldermen desired and intended to reconsider the vote and pass the ordinance. To reconsider does not necessarily require a formal vote." Rogers v. City of Mendota, 200 Ill. App. 254, 257 (1916).

[25] McMahon v. Salem, 182 A.2d 463, 464 (N.H. 1962).

[26] Votes at town and school meetings will be construed liberally "without regard to technicalities or the strict rules of parliamentary procedure." Irregularities of the moderator not violative of statute do not constitute valid objection to result. The court quoted Mr. Justice Holmes's reminder that "the machinery of government would not work if it were not allowed a little play in its joints," as having particular application to town and school meetings. Lamb v. Danville School Bd., 162 A.2d 614, 616 (N.H. 1960).

"If all of the members of a school board are present, or have knowledge of the meeting and have an opportunity to attend, and a majority of the members of the board, after a formal discussion . . . finally declare themselves as opposed to the election or discharge of the particular teacher under discussion . . . their decision will amount to a valid binding determination of the board just as conclusively as though they had formally voted by means of the ordinary signs of aye and nay. The results are just as definite and certain." Fleming v. Board of Trustees, 112 Cal. App. 225, 296 P. 925, 926 (1931).

[27] Mere irregularities in the transactions of a family corporation do not affect their validity. "Moreover, to permit the technical rules as commonly applied

The typical New England town moderator has full statutory powers exceeding those of a parliamentary chairman or presiding officer. One court held that "the ample powers possessed by moderators, recognized from earlier times and growing out of the imperative needs of the office, are inconsistent with many incidents of ordinary parliamentary law."[29] A moderator has "wide discretion in prescribing rules for the government of his meeting." In a school district case where the moderator did not conduct the meeting according to "the strict rules of parliamentary procedure" the court refused to interfere. The court observed that the allegations of irregularity were "instances where the moderator failed to observe the niceties of parliamentary procedure involving no violation of

---

to corporations in the case of a close family corporation of two shareholders of equal ownership would serve to defeat such equality of ownership, impede justice and perpetuate fraud." Kauffman v. Meyberg, 59 Cal. App. 2d 730, 140 P.2d 210, 215, 216 (1943).

[28] "In large bodies slight deviations from established practice might be fatal, because, in such bodies, the confusion consequent on departure from settled modes of transacting business may seriously impair or utterly destroy the rights of the minority to be heard in argument, to the end that they may convert an adverse majority into a minority. But, in smaller bodies,—one, for instance, composed of five members, sitting around the same table, each under the eye and within reach of the voice of every other member,—a strict observance of all the formalities prescribed by parliamentary usages is not necessary. The question for the court in such cases is whether, in view of the size of the body, the proceedings which were had resulting in the adoption of the motion before the body afforded a guaranty that the sense of that body was fairly taken on that particular motion." State ex rel. Moore v. Archibald, 5 N.D. 359, 66 N.W. 234, 243 (1896).

The conduct of a meeting rests largely within the discretion of the majority. "With but the mayor and six councilmen, all sitting about a single table, within sight and hearing, a strict observance of parliamentary usage, especially adopted for larger bodies, is not essential. The important inquiry always is whether the number required by law have agreed on a particular measure." Mann v. City of LeMars, 109 Iowa 251, 80 N.W. 327, 328 (1899).

"The adoption and observance of one mode, did not preclude them from afterwards pursuing another, which in their judgment is equally or more advantageous. The first resolutions did not perpetually bind them to follow the formalities therein prescribed." Ricau v. Baquie, 20 La. Ann. 67 (1868) (procedures for bids on public works).

[29] Wood v. Town of Milton, 197 Mass. 531, 84 N.E. 332 (1908). See Doggett v. Hooper, 306 Mass. 129, 27 N.E.2d 737 (1940) (further statement of the powers of a moderator).

statutes. No appeal to the meeting was taken from those rules of the moderator. The evidence does not compel the conclusion that a different result would have been reached if these irregularities had not occurred." [30] This decision conforms to the general rule that the moderator of a town meeting has large discretion in providing rules for the government of his meetings, subject only to revision by the town itself.[31]

§ 10.7   Common Parliamentary Rules Applicable

Although it is clear that strict adherence to specific parliamentary rules is not requisite unless imposed on a meeting by its own adoption or by a higher authority, the courts have often applied "commonly recognized rules of parliamentary procedure" [32] in meetings of organizations which did not have previously established rules.

[30] A motion to amend having been adopted, the moderator failed to put the motion as amended to a vote, since he concluded that the motion to amend had been framed in such a way that the sense of the meeting on the subject had really been ascertained and declared. Leonard v. School Dist. 98 N.H. 530, 98 A.2d 635, 636 (1953).

[31] The court held that, where a moderator makes a procedural ruling as to the method of voting which is not contrary to any statute, his ruling stands unless the town itself by vote reverses it. Town of Exeter v. Kenick, 104 N.H. 168, 181 A.2d 638 (1962).

The "duties of the town moderator, and the government of the town meeting" are procedural matters only and not substantive. Blomquist v. Arlington, 338 Mass. 594, 156 N.E.2d 416, 418, 419 (1959) (discussing Robert's Rules of Order).

[32] "The Essex County Democratic Committee either has no constitution or by-laws or their whereabouts are unknown. The statute throws no light on how the proceedings shall be conducted. In the absence of any guide from statute, constitution or by-laws, the commonly recognized rules of parliamentary procedure govern." Egan v. Kelly, 14 N.J. Super. 103, 81 A.2d 413, 414 (1951) (county political committee).

"In the absence of specific regulation to the contrary, the ordinary rules of parliamentary law should be observed in the conduct of the meeting." Randolph v. Mt. Zion Baptist Church, 139 N.J. Eq. 605, 53 A.2d 206, 208 (Ch. 1947) (church meeting).

However, a violation of parliamentary usage will not necessarily annul the action of the body guilty of irregularity. "The course of procedure rests largely with the discretion of the majority, provided the course adopted affords a reasonable guaranty that the sense of the body on the particular measure before it has been fairly taken." State ex rel. Moore v. Archibald, 5 N.D. 359, 66 N.W. 234, 243 (1896).

In the case of an unincorporated voluntary association without a charter, by-laws, or rules of procedure, "[c]ommon parliamentary rules, in use by all deliberative assemblies in this country, may also be resorted to, in the absence of any made by the association itself, in considering the regularity of its proceedings." [33] And in passing on a question of breaking a quorum at a shareholders' meeting, a court held that "ordinary rules of parliamentary procedure" and "ordinary parliamentary usages" will apply.[34] This is an indication that parliamentary principles and procedures, which have become commonly recognized and understood through many years of usage as basic to the maintenance of orderly procedure, will be accepted by the courts as the common law of meetings.[35]

---

[33] Ostrom v. Greene, 161 N.Y. 353, 362, 55 N.E. 919, 922 (1900). The court also said that the association, in the absence of rules, could adjourn its meetings "according to the usual methods of parliamentary bodies."

"In the absence of the adoption of rules of procedure and in the absence of statutory regulation, the generally accepted rules of parliamentary procedure would control." McCormick v. Board of Educ., 58 N.M. 648, 274 P.2d 299 (1954).

Aside from statutory limitations, "the parliamentary body is left free to act according to its custom." Its conduct "is left to general parliamentary procedure or to the particular rules of the legislative body." In construing parliamentary precedents, the court said that "an unbroken legislative practice upon a question partaking so much of the nature of pure parliamentary law would be entitled to weight." Nevins v. City Council, 227 Mass. 538, 116 N.E. 881, 884, 885 (1917).

Where the rules of the board provide that "ordinary parliamentary rules should be observed, and in case any disputed question arose, Cushing's Manual should be taken as authority," the court will require compliance with Cushing in suspending a rule. State ex rel. Krejsa v. Board of Educ., 2 Ohio C.C.R. 510, 515 (Cir Ct. 1887).

[34] Commonwealth ex rel. Sheip v. Vandegrift, 232 Pa. 53, 81 A. 153, 156 (1911).

See Annot., 36 A.L.R. (N.S.) 45.

[35] The meetings of "organizations of human beings for convenience in transacting business, whether the object be to make money or to do charitable or philanthropic work" and whether the organizations are corporations, partnerships, joint stock or voluntary associations, are subject to all applicable laws, depending upon the matter under consideration. The court added this statement: "Common parliamentary rules, in use by all deliberative assemblies in this country, may also be resorted to, in the absence of any made by the association itself, in considering the regularity of its proceedings." Ostrom v. Greene, 161 N.Y. 353, 361, 362, 55 N.E. 919 (1900).

§ 10.8   Parliamentary Manuals as Authority on Procedures

Standard parliamentary manuals may be relied upon as authority to establish the rules and practices of parliamentary law. This doctrine was stated in a recent decision. "While pro tem, we have abandoned Robert's Rules as a mandated guide, resort to that manual for light on relevant parliamentary usages of deliberative assemblies is permissible. . . ." [36] Another case relating to adjournment in the absence of a quorum quotes from Robert's Rules of Order, described as "a recognized authority on parliamentary procedure." [37]

Where a municipal council has adopted Robert's Rules of Order as the rules of parliamentary practice to govern its meetings, when applicable and not inconsistent with standing rules, such Rules will be followed as representative of general parliamentary law as against the usages of the U. S. House of Representatives which are exceptional and contrary to general parliamentary law.[38]

A sensible attitude is found in another case quoting from Trow, *The Parliamentarian*, in construing a question of adjournment of a zoning commission. The court said: "We are not disposed too rigorously to apply technical rules to the action of administrative boards and commissions, but a proper regard for established rules of procedure will cause little trouble and be likely at least to avoid such questions as have arisen in this case." [39]

In a case involving a disorderly meeting of an unincorporated trade union, the court noted that, in the absence of any prescribed rules, "common parliamentary principles in use by all deliberative assemblies may be resorted to in considering the regularity of the proceedings"; that the Constitution specified Robert's Rules of Order; and, therefore, "the trial judge was fully warranted in holding that, as applied to the case at bar, Robert's Rules of Order could be deemed to state common parliamentary principles in general

[36] Posner v. Bronx County Med. Soc'y, 19 App. Div. 2d 89, 241 N.Y.S.2d 540 (1st Dep't), *aff'd*, 13 N.Y.2d 1004, 195 N.E.2d 59, 245 N.Y.S.2d 393 (1963), *citing* Robert's Rules of Order.

[37] *In re Dollinger Corp.*, 51 Misc. 2d 802, 274 N.Y.S.2d 285, 287 (1966).

[38] People *ex rel.* MacMahon v. Davis, 284 Ill. 439, 120 N.E. 326 (1918), *citing* Robert's Rules of Order and Hinds' Precedents.

[39] Strain v. Mims, 123 Conn. 275, 193 A. 754, 757 (1937).

usage without any other affirmative showings to that effect."[40] A trade union case involving the redress of grievances sets forth a legal principle which is also uniquely applicable to meetings of shareholders where rules of order have not been imposed upon or adopted by the meeting. The court said: "Where the method of procedure is not regulated by the law of an association, the procedure should be analogous to ordinary parliamentary proceedings. Gaps in the rules of procedures . . . should be filled by the adoption of fair methods according to accepted principles in similar cases."[41] Another court had held that, in the absence of a constitution, by-laws, or rules for the conduct of meetings, past "usage or custom" as revealed in the testimony cannot be ignored and must be considered by the court.[42]

§ 10.9 Corporate Proceedings

The attitude of the courts toward the application of relevant parliamentary usages and practices in considering the validity of corporate proceedings at meetings of shareholders is entirely consistent with the basic common law of meetings. Robert recommends that every deliberative assembly should adopt some rules of order for the conduct of its business, but notes that the elaborate rules of Congress do not determine common parliamentary law and are not suitable for ordinary assemblies.[43]

Besides complexity and susceptibility to abuse, the strict application of a particular manual of parliamentary rules of order for legislative bodies to corporate shareholder meetings appears impractical for numerous reasons. Ordinarily stockholders' meetings occur only once a year, often in a place different from the location of the previous meeting. The meeting lasts only a few hours, and the business of one meeting is not carried over to a subsequent meeting. In addition, the number and identity of shareholders may differ from meet-

[40] Marvin v. Manash, 175 Ore. 311, 153 P.2d 251, 254 (1944).

[41] Mixed Local of Hotel Employees v. Hotel Employees Int'l Alliance, 212 Minn. 587, 4 N.W.2d 771, 776 (1942).

[42] Ostrom v. Greene, 20 Misc. 177, 183, 45 N.Y.S. 852, 857 (Sup. Ct. 1897), aff'd, 161 N.Y. 353, 55 N.E. 919 (1900).

[43] Robert's Rules of Order, Revised, at 17–20 (1951).

ing to meeting. Shareholders have the right to attend the meeting and participate in its deliberations, but have no duty to do so. There is no reference to or action by committees. Voting is by number of shares held in person or by proxy, and not by individual voice vote. Legislation is not generated from the floor, and proxies solicited by the management usually account for the great majority of shares entitled to vote at the meeting.

§ 10.10   Application of Rule of Fairness

The courts have applied a rule of fairness to prevent or negate the abuse of a parliamentary procedure. Examples include the invalidity of a meeting because the quorum was obtained by trickery [44] and setting aside an election at a special meeting which was jammed through in ten minutes and not conducted in a regular and fair manner.[45] The courts have also set aside an election of directors where the documents relating to the election, the names of the inspectors, and the names of the successful candidates were all decided upon and prepared in advance of the meeting. "The court cannot and will not allow such abortive, undemocratic and illegal election to stand. Justice and fair play require much more." [46]

The rule of fairness also suggests that, where those present at a meeting are not expected to be familiar with the procedures to be followed, an early announcement outlining the basic procedures would be appropriate. Considering this rule, it is the practice in preparation for most larger meetings of stockholders to formulate an agenda and basic rules of order to govern the conduct of the meeting, and to distribute copies of such material to the sharehold-

---

[44] While it is probably true that a meeting would be illegal where the quorum was obtained by "fraud, deceit, duress, or trickery" it is well established that this rule does not apply where the persons who have been tricked attend the meeting and participate in all its proceedings. Dillon v. Berg, 326 F. Supp. 1214 (D. Del.), aff'd, 453 F.2d 876 (3d Cir. 1971).

[45] In re Kirshner, 81 N.Y.S.2d 435 (Sup. Ct. 1948) (setting aside an election of directors at special meeting).

[46] In re Capital Bias Prods., Inc., 28 Misc. 2d 987, 212 N.Y.S.2d 807, 808 (Sup. Ct. 1961).

However, "a harried or contrite conscience" cannot be grounds for nullifying the election of those for whom the stockholders voted. Camp v. Shannon, 162 Tex. 515, 348 S.W.2d 517, 520 (1961).

ers as they enter the meeting hall. The chairman, at the opening of the meeting, will call attention to the rules of order and explain the importance of fair play throughout the meeting.

Also, if it appears likely that there may be disorder which might lead to the imposition of penalties or criminal sanctions, it is suggested that warnings be given by the chairman to the offending member prior to their imposition.[47]

§ 10.11   Application of Parliamentary Law—Evidence

The courts have long recognized that parliamentary law is a branch of the common law consisting of the rules, customs, and usages for the conduct of business by a deliberative assembly. Generally known as common parliamentary law, it can accommodate mandated procedures and also special rules of order designed to meet the needs of assemblies having different purposes.

Throughout this book, reference has been made to parliamentary law in its many manifestations. The hierarchy of parliamentary law as it is applied to almost all deliberative assemblies in this country is headed by the mandated fundamental provisions of the constitution and the organic law, and then gradually steps downward to the usages and customs of the organization, both written and unwritten. Only federal and state legislative bodies and a few other deliberative assemblies in similar circumstances either need or follow individual elaborate parliamentary rules as designed and adopted for themselves only, or as codified in the several standard manuals for general use.

Thus, the general rule of meetings requires the enforcement of only such elementary rules of regularity and fairness as may be needed by the assembly to accomplish the purposes of its creation.

In applying parliamentary law to a particular state of facts, the

---

[47] One court has noted: "Meeting rules are rarely carefully spelled out or well known to the audience. In many cases these rules consist of aged and infrequently used by-laws or tacit understandings and habitual practices, or are otherwise cloaked in obscurity and uncertainty. Even if clear rules can be found, the officials of a meeting commonly suspend or simply ignore such rules to expedite the work of the meeting." The court held that a warning should precede arrest or criminal sanctions. *In re* Kay, 83 Cal. Rptr. 686, 464 P.2d 142, 152, nn. 12 and 13 (1970).

courts have based their findings and conclusions on one or more of the following rules, listed in descending order of rank:

(a) The parliamentary law as prescribed in the federal or state constitution, the organic statutory law, or the charter of the organization,

(b) The parliamentary procedures as set forth in the by-laws or in special rules of procedure adopted by the organization for its own use,

(c) The parliamentary law as codified in a specified parliamentary manual which has been adopted by the organization,

(d) The parliamentary law as explained in one or more parliamentary manuals cited by the court as authority on the subject,

(e) The common parliamentary law as derived from the rules, customs, and usages of the assembly or of deliberative assemblies in general, whether or not recorded in writing, and

(f) The testimony of a qualified parliamentarian who has knowledge of the facts, testifying as an expert witness.

There are ample legal procedures for the pleading of applicable constitutional and statutory parliamentary rules, and for the pleading and proof of parliamentary law as codified in a published manual. However, in the absence of parliamentary rules imposed by some higher authority or adopted by the organization either in its by-laws or by reference to a parliamentary manual, it may be necessary to establish in court the customs, usages, and parliamentary practices of the organization which then constitute the common parliamentary law to be applied to the question at issue.

The customs and usages of various bodies may differ widely or may be quite similar. The testimony of expert witnesses is admissible in evidence to fully expound the customs, practices, and usages of the organization relating to the question at issue.[48]

The testimony of expert parliamentarians who were present during a convention has also been accepted to prove that the proceedings of an organization in convention were regular and in

[48] See, e.g., Walker Memorial Baptist Church v. Saunders, 285 N.Y. 462, 35 N.E.2d 42 (1941), citing Hiscox' Directory (proving the rules, customs, and usages of the ecclesiastical governing body of a religious organization as distinguished from the temporalities and properties of the church).

Ostrom v. Greene, 161 N.Y. 353, 55 N.E. 919 (1900) (proving the rules, usages, and customs relating to quorum, adjournment, notice of meeting, and chairman of a voluntary association).

accordance with the parliamentary rules and usages as understood and adopted by the members in their general bodies. The same court held that extracts from parliamentary authors were inadmissible to show that certain proceedings of the convention were regular and in accordance with parliamentary usage. In excluding the introduction in evidence of parliamentary manuals as such, the court said that "[t]he witnesses who knew the facts and testified to them, and who had qualified as expert parliamentarians, should have been permitted to express their opinions that the proceedings were regular and according to parliamentary usage." [49]

PRESUMPTION OF REGULARITY

§ 10.12 Common Law

The courts have long held that "the law will presume that all things are rightly done, unless the circumstances of the case overturn this presumption." [1] Thus, the regularity and legality of a proceeding taken may be presumed in the absence of evidence to the contrary. [2] This presumption of regularity is applicable to "all tri-

[49] Cranfill v. Hayden, 22 Tex. Civ. 656, 55 S.W. 805, 812, *rev'd on other grounds,* 97 Tex. 544, 80 S.W. 609 (1904) (action for libel and slander against members of Baptist convention for publishing their proceedings in a newspaper devoted to its interests, excluding plaintiff from his rights as a member).

[1] The court also stated: "The same presumptions are, we think, applicable to corporations. Persons acting publicly as officers of the corporation, are to be presumed rightfully in office; acts done by the corporation, which presuppose the existence of other acts to make them legally operative, are presumative proofs of the latter." Bank of the United States v. Dandridge, 25 U.S. (12 Wheat.) 64, 69–70 (1827).

[2] The following cases are illustrative of the presumption of regularity and legality:

"The board is authorized to establish rules and regulations for the transaction of its business. . . . In the absence of any proof to the contrary, it must be presumed that the postponement and the subsequent action were in conformity to its established rules." Masters v. McHolland, 12 Kan. 17, 24 (1873).

A city charter required that ordinances be adopted by a majority vote. The record stated that the ordinance was "adopted by majority vote" without stating the number of aldermen voting in favor. The court stated: "But we think the well settled rule that all things should be presumed to be rightly done applies to such a record as that before us." McCormick v. Bay City, 23 Mich. 457 (1871).

The court remarked that it did not know how the city council meeting was called, but if there was any way the meeting could lawfully be called, it must be presumed that such a way was adopted, and that the meeting was lawfully held. People *ex rel.* Locke v. Common Council, 5 Lans. 11 (N.Y. Sup. Ct. 1871).

A question arose as to whether a town meeting opened on time, with the record showing that the meeting adjourned at 9 A.M., when it was scheduled to open. The court said that "the board was composed of officers acting under the sanction of an oath, and some presumptions may fairly be indulged in favor of the legality of their action." Wisconsin Cent. R.R. v. Ashland County, 81 Wis. 1, 50 N.W. 937, 940 (1891).

It is not necessary that the record show the presence of a quorum. A quorum will be presumed to have been present unless the contrary appears." Coombs v. Harford, 99 Me. 426, 59 A. 529, 530 (1904).

"In the absence of evidence to the contrary, it will be presumed that a stockholders' meeting was held in accordance with the statutes, charter, and by-laws, and the burden is upon one who claims that the meeting is invalid to show facts that render it so." Gentry-Futch Co. v. Gentry, 90 Fla. 595, 106 So. 473, 478 (1925).

It must be presumed that a decision of a constitutional convention was rightly made in accordance with its own rules of procedure. Wells v. Bain, 75 Pa. 39, 55–56 (1874).

In ascertaining whether an "informal" decision has been made by a zoning board, the courts will accord the decision the presumption of regularity. Taub v. Pirnie, 3 N.Y.2d 188, 165 N.Y.S.2d 1 (1957).

Passage of ordinance. "There is no statute requiring the yeas and nays to be called on the adoption of such motion, and as it was declared adopted the presumption must be indulged that the requisite number of votes was cast and the rule legally suspended." State v. Vail, 53 Iowa 550, 5 N.W. 709, 710 (1880).

In the absence of evidence to the contrary, it will be presumed that a shareholders' meeting was held in accordance with the statute, charter, and by-laws. Abbey Properties Co. v. Presidential Ins. Co., 119 So. 2d 74, 77 (Fla. 1960).

When the record shows that a special meeting of a city council was called and held, it is to be presumed that the call was regular, that the service of notice was duly made as required by statute, at least until the contrary is proved. Greeley v. Hamman, 17 Colo. 30, 28 P. 460 (1891).

The record of a city council meeting was corrected and then approved. "The bona fides or truthness of the correction is not questioned, and, in the absence of any showing to the contrary, the verity rather than the falsity of the record will be presumed." Mann v. City of Lemars, 109 Iowa 251, 80 N.W. 327, 328 (1899).

On a motion for a preliminary injunction where there is a sharp issue of fact as to the correctness of corporate minutes relating to the presence of a quorum, the court must presume that the statement in the minutes is correct. Avien, Inc. v. Weiss, 50 Misc. 2d 127, 269 N.Y.S.2d 836 (Sup Ct. 1966).

Where the minutes of meetings of a school board are regular and complete, it will be presumed that all the members received due notice of meetings. Kavanaugh v. Wausaw, 120 Wis. 611, 98 N.W. 550 (1904).

Outside persons are entitled to assume that a proper quorum of directors was summoned and attended. County of Gloucester Bank v. Rudry Merthyr Steam & House Coal Colliery, [1895] 1 Ch. 629.

A loose-leaf minute book in poorly kept condition was held insufficient to overcome the prima facie presumption of regularity which attached to warrants authorized at the meeting. City of Belton v. Brown-Crummer, 17 F.2d 70 (5th Cir. 1927).

"A strong presumption of regularity supports the inference that when administrative officials purport to decide weighty issues within their domain they have consciously considered the issues and adverted to the views of their colleagues." Braniff Airways, Inc. v. CAB, 379 F.2d 453, 460 (D.C. Cir. 1967).

Presumption of validity attaches to public proceedings and the formal recitations of public officials (federal regulatory agency). Willapoint Oysters v. Ewing, 174 F.2d 676, 696 (9th Cir.), cert. denied, 338 U.S. 860 (1949).

A zoning board member is assumed to be adequately informed when voting. State ex rel. Cities Serv. Oil Co. v. Board of Zoning Appeals, 21 Wis. 2d 516, 124 N.W.2d 809, 821, 822 (1963).

Validity of proxies presented at election. Standard Power & Light Corp. v. Investment Associates, Inc., 29 Del. Ch. 593, 51 A.2d 572 (1947).

"A law initiated and adopted by the people, as well as a law enacted by the legislature, is presumed to be constitutional." State v. Meyers, 51 Wash. 2d 454, 319 P.2d 828, 829 (1957).

"There is a presumption in favor of the validity of an ordinance and those questioning this validity have the burden of proof." State ex rel. Balsinger v. Town of Madisonville, 435 S.W.2d 803, 805 (Tenn. 1968).

Presumption of validity concerning municipal procedure does not apply to power to enact ordinance. Simmons v. Holm, 229 Ore. 373, 367 P.2d 368 (1961).

"Every presumption must be in favor of regular action and against irregularity." Presiding officer, but not a member, shall put the question and declare the results of the voting. State ex rel. Southey v. Lashar, 71 Conn. 540, 548, 42 A. 636 (1899), citing Cushing.

It may be presumed that legislative bodies have complied strictly with their own rules. Humphrey v. City of Youngstown, 143 N.E.2d 321 (Ohio 1955).

It will be presumed that a decision of an administrative body was regularly made. Olsen Co. v. State Tax Comm'n, 109 Utah 563 (1946).

Action taken by a municipal body, such as a council, is presumed to be in conformity with its rules. Commonwealth ex rel. Fox v. Chace, 403 Pa. 117, 168 A.2d 569 (1961).

A bill enrolled, authenticated, and approved is presumed to have been passed by the legislature in conformity with the requirements of the constitution unless the contrary affirmatively appears in the journal or other legislative records. State ex rel. Heck's Discount Centers, Inc. v. Winters, 132 S.E.2d 374 (W. Va. 1963).

bunals, judicial, quasi-judicial and administrative." [3] In applying the presumption one court has held that "[r]easonable rules ought to prevail in aid of the accomplishment of the statute's purposes [election of directors], and a certain degree of liberality in favor of a meeting ought to prevail." [4]

Where the record of the proceedings does not show a violation or failure to comply with a legal requirement, it will be presumed that the body complied with all necessary requirements and "the ordinance appearing to be regular, the burden is upon one who denies its validity to show it, and, where the record of the facts, as here, only shows what is required by the statutes and ordinances, the vitiating facts may be shown by evidence other than the record." [5]

The presumption in favor of regularity of all official conduct requires that it be assumed a Congressional committee will not disregard its own rules, or the rules of the House of Representatives.[6] However, this presumption of legality will not overcome a clear affirmative showing of facts to the contrary.[7]

A legislature is presumed to have acted within the limits of its authority. People v. Carmichael, 56 Misc. 2d 931, 288 N.Y.S.2d 931 (Sup. Ct. 1968).

Legislative enactments are presumed to be constitutional, i.e., to be supported by facts known to the legislature. Wiggins v. Town of Somers, 4 N.Y.2d 215, 173 N.Y.S.2d 579 (1958).

There is a "presumption of due passage" to a rule of procedure printed in an authorized city meeting manual. Thorne v. Squier, 264 Mich. 98, 249 N.W. 497 (1933).

[3] United States v. Kamin, 136 F. Supp. 791, 803 (D. Mass. 1956).

[4] Duffy v. Loft, Inc., 17 Del. Ch. 376, 152 A. 849, 853 (1930).

It is a general principle that votes passed at town meetings should be liberally construed. Amey v. Pittsburg School Dist., 95 N.H. 386, 64 A.2d 1 (1949).

[5] Baker v. Combs, 194 Ky. 260, 239 S.W. 56, 59 (1922).

"It is a well recognized rule that the courts must presume that constitutional procedural requirements have been followed by our General Assembly unless the legislative journals themselves show to the contrary." Walther v. McDonald, 243 Ark. 912, 422 S.W.2d 854, 862 (1968).

[6] Randolph v. Willis, 220 F. Supp. 355, 360 (S.D. Cal. 1963).

[7] See, e.g., Brumley v. Town of Greeneville, 33 Tenn. App. 322, 274 S.W.2d 12 (1954) (minutes recorded readings which did not in fact occur); Wright v. Wiles, 173 Tenn. 334, 117 S.W.2d 736 (1938) (passage of bill on three readings).

There is also a presumption that the votes of directors at a meeting are "fairly and honestly cast in good faith for the best interest of the corporation." [8]

[8] Blaustein v. Pan American Petroleum & Transport Co., 174 Misc. 601, 21 N.Y.S.2d 651, 714 (Sup. Ct. 1940), *modified*, 263 App. Div. 97, 31 N.Y.S.2d 934 (1st Dep't 1941).

11

Usage and Custom

§ 11.1 Parliamentary Law Founded on Ancient Usage and Custom

The common law of meetings, generally known as parliamentary law, is founded on ancient usage and custom. Rules of conduct so evolved are in the nature of internal regulations or by-laws "prescribed for a deliberative body for the orderly and convenient conduct of its own proceedings" whether they are "codified in the form of a 'manual,' and formally adopted by the body, or whether consisting of a body of unwritten customs or usages, preserved in memory and by tradition." [1] Usages have become a "kind of common law." [2]

§ 11.2 May Be Written or Unwritten

Custom and practice may be written or unwritten. The Supreme Court has stated that "what Congress may do by express rule it may

[1] The court continued: "It is a principle of the common law of England that the judicial courts have no conusance of what is termed the *lex et consuetudo parliamenti.* . . ." State *ex rel.* Fox v. Alt, 26 Mo. App. 673, 677 (1887) (city house of delegates).

[2] United States v. Macdaniel, 32 U.S. (7 Pet.) 1, 14 (1833).

do also by its custom and practice. There is no requirement, constitutional or otherwise, that its body of parliamentary law must be recorded in order to be authoritative." The court also held it may be presumed that the parliamentary practices of a Congressional committee in the usual course of business conform "to both the written and unwritten rules of the House which created it." [3] Thus, the election of a chairman by the shareholders after the president had unilaterally declared an adjournment against the wishes of a quorum, was approved as being in conformity with "accepted usage and common practice." [4]

In an early English case involving an election of churchwardens, the court, in speaking of the power to adjourn, remarked: "The power must arise from the custom, or common law. Here is no custom found, and I know of no book that shews how it stands at common law." [5] The preceding doctrine is still sound. "In the

[3] Christoffel v. United States, 338 U.S. 84, 91 (1949) (dissenting opinion).

However prudent or advisable, it is not necessary that a corporation should ordain its by-laws by a formal act of legislation, or that they be reduced to writing, unless required by the charter. Taylor v. Griswold, 14 N.J.L. 222, 241 (1834); see Kligerman v. Lynch, 92 N.J. Super. 373, 223 A.2d 511 (1966), cert. denied, 389 U.S. 822 (1967) (distinction between an unwritten rule and a custom of Senatorial courtesy).

[4] In re Dollinger Corp., 51 Misc. 2d 802, 274 N.Y.S.2d 285, 288 (Sup. Ct. 1966).

[5] Stoughton v. Reynolds, 2 Strange 1045, 1047 (K.B. 1736).

Generally, where an ecclesiastical entity does not have the power to prescribe rules by which a pastor may be appointed or discharged, "past and accepted customs" may be relied upon. Spiritual affairs are governed by "ecclesiastical direction, custom, policy, tradition or usage." Evans v. Criss, 39 Misc. 2d 314, 240 N.Y.S.2d 517, 520 (Sup. Ct. 1963).

"There is no central governing body in the Baptist denomination. Since there exists no superior ecclesiastical entity vested with the power to prescribe rules by which a Baptist church may appoint or discharge a pastor, past and accepted customs must be considered in effecting designations and discharges provided they are consistent with statutory law." Hayes v. Board of Trustees of Holy Trinity Baptist Church, 225 N.Y.S.2d 316, 319 (Sup. Ct. 1962), citing Hiscox' Directory.

Parliamentary law applies to church meetings. "The question who may vote depends upon the rules and custom of the particular church." There being no particular custom, the "usual Baptist practice" governs. Randolph v. Mt. Zion Baptist Church, 139 N.J. Eq. 605, 53 A.2d 206, 209 (1947), citing Hiscox' Directory; see Walker Memorial Baptist Church v. Saunders, 285 N.Y. 462, 35 N.E.2d 42 (1941), citing Hiscox' Directory.

absence of express regulations by statute or by-law, the conduct of meetings, including the election of officers, is controlled largely by accepted usage and common practice." [6] Early English law also

---

For a scholarly discussion of custom and usage as derived from English and colonial common law, see People v. Siciliano, 203 Misc. 441, 119 N.Y.S.2d 578 (Sup. Ct. 1952).

[6] The court continued: "The fundamental rule is that all who are entitled to take part shall be treated with fairness and good faith." Matter of Young v. Jebbett, 213 App. Div. 774, 779, 211 N.Y.S. 61 (4th Dep't 1925); *see In re* Election of Dirs. of Bushwick Sav. & Loan Ass'n, 189 Misc. 316, 70 N.Y.S.2d 478, 481 (Sup. Ct. 1947).

When an association has not adopted a constitution or by-laws, the time and manner of conducting elections of officers and their tenure of office are to be determined from the "resolutions" and "usages" of the association. Goller v. Stubenhaus, 77 Misc. 29, 134 N.Y.S. 1043, 1047 (Sup. Ct. 1912).

Aside from limitations imposed by statute, "the parliamentary body is left free to act according to its custom." Nevins v. City Council, 227 Mass. 538, 116 N.E. 881, 884 (1917) (reconsideration of vote).

Usage has established the right of acting by majorities. Damon v. Inhabitants of Granby, 19 Mass. (2 Pick.) 345, 355 (1824) (withdrawal of majority).

In the absence of established regulations, the proceedings are governed by usages and the resolutions adopted from time to time. If none exists, resort may be had to the rules of parliamentary law in common use in all deliberative assemblies. Oestereich v. Schneider, 187 S.W.2d 756 (Mo. 1945).

"Usage and custom (not using these words in any technical sense) must furnish in most cases a sufficiently accurate test of what is reasonable as to the time of proceeding to business. It is not usual to commence business at the exact hour appointed." Kimball v. Marshall, 44 N.H. 465, 467 (1863).

Where an association has no constitution, by-laws, or rules of order, its usages and customs in the conduct of meetings cannot be ignored and are entitled to consideration. Ostrom v. Greene, 20 Misc. 177, 45 N.Y.S. 852 (1897), *aff'd*, 30 App. Div. 621, 52 N.Y.S. 1147 (1898), *aff'd*, 161 N.Y. 353, 55 N.E. 919 (1900) (voluntary association).

The question of quorum at a special meeting to consider reinstatement of a club member "must be determined by precedent and parliamentary usage." Myers v. Union League, 17 Pa. Dist. 301, 304 (C.P. 1908), *citing* Hinds' Precedents and Reed's Rules.

Decisions on the succession of political bodies, as in the case of social or religious divisions, are to be maintained according to the "laws and usages of the body, or, in the absence of these, according to the laws, customs, and usages of similar bodies in like cases, or in analogy to them. This is the uniform rule in such cases." Kerr v. Trego, 47 Pa. 292, 296 (1864) (Philadelphia common council).

A "long acquiescence" in the acts and declarations recognizing a charter

followed custom and past practice in determining what constituted a quorum, by holding that a quorum consists of the number of directors who usually act in conducting the affairs of the company.[7] In fact, it has been held that custom must be recognized even if it may be "bad practice." [8]

It has been noted, for example, that the common-law rule giving but one vote to each shareholder, irrespective of the number of shares he might hold, was abandoned "by long-continued custom and usage" in favor of the general present-day rule of voting by shares.[9] Also, the general rule that a board of directors can act only at a formal meeting does not apply to close or small corporations when the "custom and usages of the directors is to act sepa-

---

supplement might constitute conclusive evidence of assent. Commonwealth *ex rel.* Claghorn v. Cullen, 13 Pa. 133, 141 (1850).

Where there is a mode of voting known to the community, that mode should be followed unless a binding rule to the contrary is shown. *In re* Horbury Bridge, Coal, Iron & Waggon Co., 11 Ch. D. 109 (1879).

Where a public trust is to be executed by a definite number of persons (church corporation), a majority must be present "unless there is a usage or custom to the contrary." Blacket v. Blizzard, 9 Barn. & C. 851, 857 (K.B. 1829).

A Congressional parliamentary practice noted in Robert's Rules of Order, as distinguished from a general parliamentary rule as stated by Robert's Rules, may be followed by a state legislature which had adopted Robert's Rules as to questions not provided for by the House rules. Wright v. Wiles, 173 Tenn. 334, 117 S.W.2d 736, 738 (1938).

In the absence of statute, political parties are governed by their own usages and establish their own rules of procedure. State *ex rel.* Pfeifer v. Stoneking, 74 N.E.2d 759 (Ohio 1946).

The acts of a majority are not binding on the company unless the proceedings are conducted regularly and in accordance with general usage, or in the manner prescribed by the charter and by-laws. *In re* Argus Printing Co., 1 N.D. 434, 48 N.W. 347 (1891); *see* Campbell v. Maund, 5 Adolph. & E. 865 (Ex. Cham. 1836) (right to demand a poll, being a common law incident to election of parish officers, will be recognized wherever it is not excluded by a special custom).

[7] *In re* Tavistock Ironworks Co., L.R. 4 Eq. 233 (1867).

[8] Question of election of vestrymen. "The minute of this meeting is like that of all the others. Their custom has not been to mention the names of the members who attended, or their numbers. It is a bad practice, but there is nothing in the minutes . . . which induces a suspicion that it was not regular." Commonwealth v. Woelper, 3 S. & R. 29 (Pa. 1817).

[9] Proctor Coal Co. v. Finley, 98 Ky. 405, 33 S.W. 188, 190 (1895).

rately or informally and not as a board." [10] And, while the simple majority rule is a basic tenet of our democratic system, "history and practice demonstrate that the rule is not invariable." [11]

§ 11.2.1   Failure To Follow

Failure to follow a long-established practice of re-electing the incumbent directors on unrestricted proxies, after lulling unwitting members into believing that such directors would be re-elected as in the past, has been held to be a ruse which deprived the voters of an opportunity to make a knowledgeable choice of the management they wanted to represent them.[12] And the court has ordered a new election of directors where a minority of protestant members was able to obtain control of an association by taking advantage of a long-continued practice at prior meetings for which there had been general acquiescence and lack of interest, because the membership at large did not have a fair opportunity to express its choice.[13]

[10] Sharon Herald Co. v. Granger, 97 F. Supp. 295 (W.D. Pa. 1951), aff'd, 195 F.2d 890 (3d Cir. 1952).

Although directors act as a board at regularly called meetings, those whom they represent may be estopped from questioning the authority of their officers when acting less formally, if there has been a custom or usage of informality. Superior Portland Cement v. Pacific Coast Cement Co., 33 Wash. 2d 169, 205 P.2d 597 (1949).

[11] Adams v. Fort Madison Community School Dist., 182 N.W.2d 132, 137 (Iowa 1970) (discussion and citations re departure from majority rule).

[12] On appeal the court said: "If the proxy committee, in soliciting such proxies, knew that the long-established practice was not to be followed, and lulled the unwitting members into believing otherwise, then they deprived them of their opportunity to make a knowledgeable choice of the management they wished to represent them." In re Ideal Mutual Ins. Co., 9 App. Div. 2d 60, 190 N.Y.S.2d 895, 897 (1st Dep't 1959).

[13] The court noted that one set of officers had been elected by a "method long used and generally acquiesced in" but then continued: "We are further of the opinion, however, that right and justice require a new election. Because of the long-continued practice at prior annual meetings which had been generally acquiesced in and for which some color of authority may be found in the by-laws, the great mass of members felt no direct interest in the meeting, and took no part therein. A small body of protestant members were thus able, by exercising their strict legal rights, to take control. Under the circumstances, therefore, the membership at large has had no fair opportunity to express its choice." In re Bogart, 215 App. Div. 45, 213 N.Y.S. 137 (4th Dep't 1925).

§ 11.3 Custom Contrary to Law

However, if a custom or practice is contrary to law,[14] or to statutory provisions,[15] or to the charter or by-laws of the organization,[16]

[14] Alleged custom limiting time for rectification of bank mistakes in receipt or payment of money. "If such a custom does exist, it is contrary to law, and ought not to meet with the sanction of a Court of Justice." Gallatin v. Bradford, 4 Ky. 209, 211–12 (1808).

[15] The rules of "tenure of ancient common law offices" based on "ancient usage" have no application to tenure of offices created by the Constitution. "The tenure in those cases depends, in a great measure, upon ancient usage. But with us, there is no ancient usage which can apply to and govern the tenure of offices created by our Constitution and laws. They are of recent origin, and must depend entirely upon a just construction of our Constitution and laws." *Ex parte* Hennen, 38 U.S. (13 Pet.) 230, 260 (1839).

The statutory right of a member to cast a vote in person or by proxy "cannot be vitiated by custom or practice." Flynn v. Kendall, 195 Misc. 221, 88 N.Y.S.2d 299, 301 (Sup. Ct. 1949).

Neither custom and usage, nor parliamentary practices as cited by Cushing's LAW AND PRACTICE OF LEGISLATIVE ASSEMBLIES, can change the general common law of elections as adopted by statute. Cadmus v. Farr, 47 N.J.L. 208 (Sup. Ct. 1885) (majority of quorum may act).

The mere fact that a vote had never been taken in the manner provided by statute (plurality of votes) is not proof that the statute does not apply. Campbell v. Maund, 5 Adolph. & E. 865, 884 (Ex. Cham. 1836).

The fact that the chairman of a previous committee had allowed a member to vote after he moved his residence to another district was not binding as to the future because the member's status was governed by statute. Also, the previous acceptance of a vote by proxy is not a binding precedent. "The action of a particular member, even if he be the chairman of the body, cannot effectuate a new rule of conduct binding on the organization itself." Hart v. Sheridan, 168 Misc. 386, 5 N.Y.S.2d 820, 825 (Sup. Ct. 1938).

[16] Custom and usage cannot affect a written constitution or by-laws. Where the constitution requires a secret ballot, long established custom and usage for an open ballot will not validate a referendum conducted in violation of the constitution. Fritsch v. Rarback, 98 N.Y.S.2d 748 (Sup. Ct. 1950).

An annual meeting, by reason of usage, was held to be a general meeting for the transaction of general business. "A custom or usage so long continued and so invariably pursued has the force of a by-law, and, not being repugnant to any of the provisions of the charter, is valid." Mutual Fire Ins. Co. v. Farquhar, 86 Md. 668, 39 A. 527, 528–29 (1898) (however, there was failure of notice).

Where the charter provided for three directors and custom provided for four, it was held that three directors could decide by majority vote of two to one to

it need not be followed. In a recent case it was argued that a voting rule of the Federal Trade Commission which had been in effect for 40 years, requiring concurrence of only two out of five members of the Commission to reach a decision, should be upheld. The court of appeals did not agree, holding that, with no statutory authority to the contrary, it was necessary that three members concur to enter a binding order of the Commission. The court disposed of the argument in favor of the Commission rule, saying: "[W]e cannot believe, that a long adherence to an improper rule (if indeed it is improper) gives the Commission any vested right to continue such adherence." The Supreme Court reversed in a unanimous opinion, holding that the FTC was not inhibited from following the common-law rule that, in the absence of a contrary statutory provision, a majority of a quorum constituted of a simple majority of a collective body was empowered to act for the body.[17]

It has also been held that custom and practice cannot vitiate constitutional requirements. For example, the possibility that a labor union had in the past submitted multiple constitutional amendments to its membership on a single ballot, and that such procedure over the years may have become a custom and practice, does not make such action free from challenge if in fact it is violative of the union constitution.[18]

§ 11.4 Clear Legislative Intent To Repeal Common Law

Statutory repeal or change in "those doctrines of the common law which are not unsuited to our conditions" require clear legislative intent, and if the intent is not fairly evident, the common law remains in force. Statutory changes so made in the common law do

---

fix the salary of the fourth who abstained. Hax v. Davis Mill Co., 39 Mo. App. 453 (1889).

That a 50 per cent stockholder was content with the status quo in the directorship of the corporation for seven and one-half years did not deprive him of the right to demand cumulative voting when the charter provided for both cumulative voting and for unanimous vote at all meetings of directors or stockholders. Slavin v. A. & G. Manufacturers, Inc., 40 App. Div. 2d 373, 340 N.Y.S.2d 486 (1st Dep't 1973).

[17] Flotill Prod., Inc. v. FTC, 358 F.2d 224, 229 (9th Cir. 1966), rev'd, 389 U.S. 179 (1967).

[18] Young v. Hayes, 195 F. Supp. 911, 916 (D.D.C. 1961).

not extend beyond that which is expressed in its provisions or fairly implied in them.[19]

An attempt to change the common law by the application of usage or custom is void in the absence of clear authority from some legislative enactment. For example, where an ordinance provided that an election be by ballot, "then all the common law rules that apply to that method of acting must be observed, and no rule can be established, by custom or otherwise, that will substantially affect the determination of the majority, otherwise than according to the principles of the common law." [20]

The power of a deliberative assembly to adopt and to change its rules of procedure [21] is in no way limited or impaired by past practices. "Neither custom nor practice of previous councils is of determinative value." [22] The fact that a former practice went unchallenged for many years does not prevent a present determination that such practice need not be followed.[23] On the other hand, it

---

[19] Repeal of common law by statute must be clearly intended, and, if the intent is not clearly evident, the common law remains the rule of decision. Schwartz v. Inspiration Gold Mining Co., 15 F. Supp. 1030, 1034 (D. Mont. 1936).

Rules of common law are not to be changed by doubtful implication, nor overturned except by clear and unambiguous language. Kappers v. Cast Stone Const. Co., 184 Wis. 627, 633, 200 N.W. 376 (1924).

[20] The court previously remarked: "If it be admitted for the sake of argument, that a rule or by-law of a corporation may be established by proof of custom long maintained and acquiesced in by its members" it is clear that "no by-law or rule can be established by custom, which is beyond its authority to adopt by resolution or ordinance." Murdoch v. Strange, 99 Md. 89, 57 A. 628, 629 (1904) (local custom of common council), *quoting* Cushing, Law & Pr. Leg. Assem.

[21] *See* Chapter 9 *supra*.

[22] State *ex rel.* Smith v. Nazor, 135 Ohio St. 364, 21 N.E.2d 124, 126 (1939), *quoting* State *ex rel.* Reed v. De Maioribus, 131 Ohio St. 201, 2 N.E.2d 506 (1936) (city council).

A city council rule that it must complete all business before its term expires was adopted "as a matter of parliamentary custom" and need not be followed as a matter of law. The courts are not required to recognize all "parliamentary rules" that may be adopted by a legislative body. Reuter v. Meacham Contracting Co., 143 Ky. 557, 562, 136 S.W. 1028 (1911).

[23] The board had not adopted any rules of order or procedure, and it had never been the custom to record abstentions as affirmative or negative votes. These proceedings went unchallenged. It was held that they did not prevent

has been held in a case involving a technical parliamentary maneuver that "[a]n unbroken legislative practice upon a question partaking of so much of the nature of pure parliamentary law would be entitled to weight." [24]

A usage or practice of a particular organization, as distinguished from a generally accepted usage or practice which has long been established and preserved by tradition, may be considered for purposes of interpretation, but it will have no common-law standing and need not be followed. In ruling that each shareholder was entitled to one vote regardless of the number of shares held, the court rejected argument founded upon the uniform practice and usage of the company to allow one vote per share, holding that the practice "can have no prescriptive rights founded on immemorial usage; and the validity of any other must depend upon the charter. If this is ambiguous, or doubtful, usage may help us to fix the construction, but cannot alter its terms or change its fundamental constitution." Usage "can never alter or repeal a statute." [25] Similarly, "custom cannot be established by one act only, or a certain course pursued one time only." [26]

---

a determination that abstentions must be counted as negative votes. Cromarty v. Leonard, 13 App. Div. 2d 274, 216 N.Y.S.2d 619, 628 (2d Dep't), aff'd, 10 N.Y.2d 915, 179 N.E.2d 710, 223 N.Y.S.2d 870 (1961).

· The fact that the chairman had been chosen at all previous meetings by consent or by a viva voce vote cannot justify a departure from the by-law provision for a stock vote when the question is first presented Proctor Coal Co. v. Finley, 98 Ky. 405, 33 S.W. 188, 194 (1895).

Fact that town board had consistently adopted ordinances at three separate and distinct meetings does not create a binding practice or custom, because it is within the power of the board to abolish, modify, or waive its own rules. State ex rel. Balsinger v. Town of Madisonville, 435 S.W.2d 803, 805 (Tenn. 1968).

[24] Nevins v. City Council, 227 Mass. 538, 116 N.E. 881 (1917).

[25] Taylor v. Griswold, 14 N.J.L. 222, 241, 251 (1824). See Caffey v. Veale, 193 Okla. 444, 145 P.2d 961, 963 (1944).

In determining whether preferred stock has the right to vote, much weight must be given to continued acquiescence without objection to the matter of not voting. Millspaugh v. Cassedy, 191 App. Div. 221, 181 N.Y.S. 276 (2d Dep't 1920).

[26] Hornady v. Goodman, 146 S.E. 173, 182 (Ga. 1928).

An effort to show that it was contrary to established practice and custom to accept an unsigned ballot at a corporate election will fail where there is no

§ 11.5　Long Custom Likened to By-Law

Long custom within a company may have the force of a by-law. In an early case, company meetings for many years had covered a wide range of subjects and the question arose whether various matters could be considered. The court said: "[U]nder these circumstances, it cannot be doubted that all the members understood and must be regarded as having agreed that at these meetings not only were the directors to be elected, but that any other matters in which the company was concerned could be taken up, considered, and definitely passed upon. A custom or usage so long continued and so invariably pursued has the force of a by-law and, not being repugnant to any of the provisions of the charter, is valid."[27] Conversely, a corporate by-law which has "fallen into disuse" and been disregarded from year to year without dissension or objection is not enforceable in law.[28] And the fact that a certain solicitation of proxies may be a "common manipulative device in modern mass persuasion" is not a defense to a charge that the solicitation is false and misleading.[29]

The practice of corporate directors to solicit proxies in favor of management nominees on the election of directors at an annual meeting of stockholders and to appoint a management proxy committee to vote proxies received, while at the same time also appointing the inspectors of election, was attacked on the ground that such practice "amounts in law and in equity to appointing the present management to be judges in their own case." The court rejected this contention saying: "The practice referred to stands upon the ground of inveterate usage."[30]

---

proof of any practice or custom contrary to the procedure adopted at the election since no similar situation had ever occurred before. State *ex rel.* Dunbar v. Hohmann, 248 S.W.2d 49 (Mo. 1952).

[27] Mutual Fire Ins. Co. v. Farquhar, 86 Md. 668, 39 A. 527, 528–29 (1898).

[28] People v. Albany & S. R.R., 1 Lans. 308, 333 (N.Y. Sup. Ct. 1869), *modified on other grounds,* 5 Lans. 25 (1871), *aff'd,* 57 N.Y. 161 (1874).

[29] Union Pacific R.R. v. Chicago & N.W. Ry., 226 F. Supp. 400, 412 (N.D. Ill. 1964).

[30] Bache v. Central Leather Co., 78 N.J. Eq. 484, 81 A. 571, 572 (1911).

§ 11.6   Legislative History

Legislative history is pertinent in considering the impact of custom and usage. It is a general rule that "[a]n unbroken legislative practice upon a question partaking so much of the nature of pure parliamentary law would be entitled to weight." [31] The right of a legislature to conduct investigations through a committee exists by force of "implication and continued usage" [32] and the customs and practices of a legislative committee are given weight by the courts in construing its rules.[33] General legislative practices are also useful precedents. It has been held that "the practice and usage of other legislative bodies, exercising the same functions, under similar exigencies; and the reasons and grounds existing in the nature of things, upon which their rules and practice have been founded; may serve as an example and as some guide to the adoption of good rules, when the exigencies arise under our constitution." [34] However, the fact that a legislative body has for many years created interim committees by single house resolution with power to act after adjournment, and such usage has never been challenged, does not create a legal right in either house to do so. Usage and custom, no matter how long continued, cannot create a right in the legislature that otherwise it does not possess.[35]

[31] Nevins v. City Council, 227 Mass. 538, 116 N.E. 881, 885 (1917).

It is a rule that "when a statute is susceptible of two interpretations, a long and unvarying construction by administrative officers has a persuasive influence. . . . Where, as here, the language is plain, no custom, however venerable, can nullify the act's clear meaning and purpose." Board of Education v. Montgomery County, 237 Md. 191, 205 A.2d 202, 206 (1964).

[32] Liveright v. Joint Committee, 279 F. Supp. 205, 214 (M.D. Tenn. 1968).

[33] Yellin v. United States, 374 U.S. 109, 116, 117 (1963) (Congressional committee); State ex rel. Todd v. Essling, 268 Minn. 169, 128 N.W.2d 307, 314 (1964) (report of state Senate committee).

However, the court is not bound by a construction arrived at subsequent to the events in controversy. United States v. Smith, 286 U.S. 6 (1932).

[34] Hiss v. Bartlett, 69 Mass. (3 Gray) 468, 475 (1855).

[35] Petition of Special Assembly Interim Committee, 13 Cal. 2d 497, 90 P.2d 304 (Cal. 1939); Fergus v. Russel, 270 Ill. 304, 110 N.E. 130, 28 A.L.R. 1154 (1915).

"The great weight of judicial authority sustains the power of the Legislature to invest its committees with power to function, though the session is over [cases cited]. . . . To the weight of judicial authority is to be added that of

The Supreme Court, in considering the effect of an adjournment of a session of Congress on the right of the President to sign a bill, said that: "Long settled and established practice is a consideration of great weight in a proper interpretation of constitutional provisions of this character."[36] The Court cautions, however, that Congress cannot "unilaterally establish a binding custom" and that it must follow a "uniform policy" to meet the requirement of a "practical construction so positive and consistent as to be determinative."[37]

§ 11.7 Application of Usage and Custom

Usage and custom are of major importance in considering matters relating to the conduct and decorum of meetings;[38] in determining the succession to office in case of a vacancy due to death or removal;[39] in proceedings for the admission of new members to an organization;[40] in deciding whether the time of day for proceeding

---

a practical interpretation ancient and unbroken." Also, "treatises of great weight" give support to the rule that only by statute can a legislative body continue beyond its term. People *ex rel.* Hastings v. Hofstadter, 258 N.Y. 425, 431–32, 180 N.E. 106 (1932), *citing* Cushing, Hinds, Jefferson, and Stubbs.

[36] Okanogan Indians v. United States, 279 U.S. 672, 689 (1928), *citing* State *ex rel.* Corbett v. South Norwalk, 77 Conn. 257, 264, 58 A. 759 (1904) in which the court held that a practice of at least twenty years' duration on the part of the executive department, acquiesced in by the legislative department, while not absolutely binding on the judicial department, is entitled to great regard in determining the true construction of a Constitutional provision, the phraseology of which is in any respect of doubtful meaning.

"Usage cannot alter the law, but it is evidence of the construction given it, and must be considered binding on past transactions." United States v. Macdaniel, 32 U.S. (7 Pet.) 1 (1833).

[37] Eber Bros. Wine & Liquor Corp. v. United States, 337 F.2d 624 (Ct. Cl. 1964), *cert. denied,* 380 U.S. 950 (1965), *quoting* Edwards v. United States, 286 U.S. 482, 487 (1932).

[38] *See* Chapter 13 *infra.*

[39] Upon the death of the president of an organization his duties fall upon the vice president in accordance with general rules of conduct and by "common custom and usage." Application of Davie, 13 Misc. 2d 1019, 178 N.Y.S.2d 740, 742, 744 (Sup. Ct. 1958).

[40] *See* Petition of Serenbetz, 46 N.Y.S.2d 475, 480 (1943), *aff'd,* 46 N.Y.S.2d 127 (Sup. Ct. 1944).

with the business of a meeting was reasonable; [41] in holding that a notice of meeting was not defective for failure to state the place of meeting when the meeting was to be held at the usual and customary place; [42] in approving an established custom of holding board meetings without full notice to all members; and in deciding as a matter of common law whether popular elections are to be decided by a majority or a plurality of votes.[43]

However, custom and practice cannot provide immunity from liability for derelictions of duty. A leading case adjudicating the liability of bank directors states: "No custom or practice can make a directorship a mere position of honor void of responsibility, or cause a name to become a substitute for care and attention." [44]

---

[41] "Usage and custom (not using these words in any technical sense), must furnish in most cases a sufficiently accurate test of what is reasonable as to the time of proceeding to business." Kimball v. Marshall, 44 N.H. 465, 467 (1863).

[42] "It was shown to be the custom for the council to meet in the rear of a bank building in the town of Muenster, and it is undisputed that its meeting place was known to all the members of the council and to the general public. . . ." State ex rel. Oil Operators' Trust v. Hellman, 36 S.W.2d 1002 (Tex. Comm. App. 1931).

[43] "Whether in the absence of any particular provision, the plurality or the majority principle would be recognized as the law, must depend upon the usage in each particular state." State ex rel. Attorney General v. Anderson, 45 Ohio St. 196, 12 N.E. 656, 659 (1887), citing Cushing, Law & Pr. Leg. Assem.

[44] Kavanaugh v. Commonwealth Trust Co., 223 N.Y. 103, 106, 119 N.E. 237, 238 (1918); see People v. Marcus, 261 N.Y. 268, 277, 185 N.E. 97, 98 (1933).

12

Majority and Minority

§ 12.1 Voice of Majority Decides

It has long been the general rule of deliberative assemblies that the will of the majority [1] shall govern. "Our government and our institutions rest on the principle that controlling power is vested in the majority. In the absence of any provision by law to the contrary, the will of any community or association, body politic or corporate, is properly declared only by the voice of the majority." [2]

[1] A meeting consists of the majority and the minority. "A majority cannot separate itself from the minority, and be a quorum. All present are the quorum. *In re* Rapid Transit Ferry Co., 19 Misc. 409, 43 N.Y.S. 538 (Sup. Ct. 1897); *see* Hill v. Town, 172 Mich. 508, 138 N.W. 334, 336–37 (1912), in which the court added: "And a majority of the statutory quorum controls such meeting."

For leading cases on methods of determining the presence of a majority, *see* United States v. Ballin, 144 U.S. 1, 6 (1892); Integration of Bar Case, 244 Wis. 8, 11 N.W.2d 604 (1943).

For distinction between "majority" and "majority vote," *see* § 6.3 *supra.*

[2] State *ex rel.* Duane v. Fagan, 42 Conn. 32, 35 (1875) (school district committee).

Jefferson's Manual states the rule simply: "The voice of the majority decides, for the lex majoris partis is the law of all councils, elections, etc. where not otherwise provided." [3]

Control by the majority is among the "democratic" processes applicable to the election of management.[4] "Where the majority

---

"The fundamental principle of every association for the purposes of self-government is, that no one shall be bound except with his own consent, expressed by himself or his representatives; but actual assent is immaterial—the assent of the majority being the assent of all; and this is not only constructively but actually true; for that the will of the majority shall, in all cases, be taken for the will of the whole, is an implied but essential stipulation in every compact of the sort; so that the individual who becomes a member assents beforehand to all measures that shall be sanctioned by a majority of the voices." Craig v. First Presbyterian Church, 88 Pa. 42, 47 (1879) (church membership meeting), *quoting* St. Mary's Church Case, 7 S. & R. 517 (1822).

"In the absence of express regulation, a proposition is carried in a town meeting, or other legislative assembly, by a majority of the votes cast." Attorney General v. Shepard, 62 N.H. 383, 384 (1882); *see* Laconia Water Co. v. Laconia, 99 N.H. 409, 112 A.2d 58, 59 (1955); *In re* Opinion of the Justices, 98 N.H. 530, 98 A.2d 635, 636 (1953).

Generally, in the absence of statutory or charter restriction, a majority is all that is required for the adoption or passage of any resolution or order properly arising for the action of a collective body exercising administrative functions. Kirkpatrick v. Van Cleave, 44 Ind. App. 629, 89 N.E. 913, 915 (1909).

"It is not to be doubted that, as a general rule, the acts of a majority of a corporation are binding on the whole, when confined to its ordinary transactions, and consistent with the original objects of its formation." Mowrey v. Indianapolis & C.R. Co., 17 Fed. Cas. 930, 931 (No. 9891) (C.C.D. Ind. 1866).

[3] Jefferson's Manual § 501.

"It is a fundamental rule of parliamentary procedure, applicable as well to municipal and electing boards, that a majority of the members of a body consisting of a definite number constitutes a quorum for the transaction of business . . . and it is equally well settled that a majority of the quorum has power to act. . . . This rule derives from the common law and is of universal application unless modified by statute or some controlling regulation or by-law in the particular instance." Hill v. Ponder, 221 N.C. 58, 19 S.E.2d 5, 8 (1942), *quoting* Jefferson's Manual.

[4] A bare majority of votes is sufficient to determine the action of "a board or other parliamentary body in a democratic system." Wesley v. Board of Educ., 403 S.W.2d 28, 29 (Ky. 1966).

"Normally, the majority rule prevails under our democratic processes." Stansberry v. McCarty, 149 N.E.2d 683, 686 (Ind. 1958).

"Outstanding among the democratic processes concerning corporate elections is the general rule that a majority of the votes cast at a stockholders' meeting,

rules, it is true, it may override the wishes and desires of the minority and even become tyrannical and sit in judgment of its own
actions within the organization." [5] "A majority is entitled to control, and the minority, however hard it may be, must submit." [6]
This principle is "in analogy to the established rule at popular
elections" and is applicable to all organizations, whether incorporated or informal, which are not controlled by a higher authority
such as a statute, charter, by-laws, or other regulations.[7]

provided a quorum is present, is sufficient to elect Directors." Standard Power
& Light Corp. v. Investment Associates, Inc., 29 Del. Ch. 593, 51 A.2d 572,
576 (1947).

Procedures adopted by a city council in furtherance of its determination of
whether members are qualified to sit must be consistent with democratic processes and give due recognition to necessary continuance of effective government and the right of the majority to control and rule. Freeman v. Lamb, 33
App. Div. 2d 331, 308 N.Y.S.2d 580 (4th Dep't 1970).

[5] "Courts will not interfere in the majority rule of an organization except to
protect individuals in their contractual relationships, property rights and liberties in connection therewith." Stansberry v. McCarty, 149 N.E.2d 683, 686
(Ind. 1958) (religious society).

[6] Ostrom v. Greene, 161 N.Y. 353, 365, 55 N.E. 919 (1900).

"While the board of directors of a corporation is bound to exercise reasonable business judgment, it is not the prerogative of the minority stockholders
to decide what is reasonable. Minority stockholders cannot exercise the discretion involved in guiding the operations of a corporation." Sanders v. E–Z
Park, Inc., 57 Wash. 2d 474, 358 P.2d 138, 140 (1960).

"The holders of a minority stock interest cannot be permitted to restrain
those holding a majority of the shares from exercising their rights to vote
because their votes would be adverse to the views of the minority." Kentucky
Package Store, Inc. v. Checani, 117 N.E.2d 139, 141–42 (Mass. 1954).

[7] The control is in "the majority of those who attend to their duty and exercise their right; those voluntarily absenting themselves, are held as agreeing to
the vote of the majority of the attending members or voters." Abels v. Mc-
Keen, 18 N.J. Eq. 462, 465 (Ch. 1867) (voluntary association).

It is the general rule that a minority of a select body cannot bind the majority. If all are notified, and the minority refuses or neglects to meet with the
others, a majority of those present may act provided a quorum is present.
Brown v. District of Columbia, 127 U.S. 579 (1888) (board of public works).

It is the fundamental law of corporations that the discretion of those having
the power to act will not be restrained by the court upon the application of a
minority who may entertain a different opinion as to the wisdom of the action
taken. Talbot J. Taylor & Co. v. Southern Pac. Co., 122 F. 147 (W.D. Ky.),
appeal dismissed, 129 F. 1007 (6th Cir. 1903) (action to enjoin corporate
election).

§ 12.2 Majority Rule Not Invariable

There are broad exceptions to the majority rule. "While simple majority rule is a basic tenet in our system, history and practice demonstrate that the rule is not invariable." [8] Typical examples are the election of corporate directors and the common political election where the candidates are elected by a plurality vote instead of a majority vote. An early decision explained: "In this country, where candidates may be numerous, and the votes of the electors divided among a number of different persons, to require a majority to elect would be to prevent a choice in very many cases. Hence it is that a majority is seldom required in a popular election." [9]

"The right of the majority of the members to control the action of the meeting cannot be questioned." American Aberdeen-Angus Breeders' Ass'n v. Fullerton, 325 Ill. 323, 156 N.E. 314, 316 (1927) (election of directors).

"Certainly a minority stockholder disagreeing with the majority had no right to impose his will upon the majority and control the action of the corporation." Lewis v. Matthews, 161 App. Div. 107, 146 N.Y.S. 424, 428 (1st Dep't 1914).

"There is no legal basis whereby a faction of a meeting may ignore the duly elected chairman and the rest of those in attendance, conduct some private maneuvers of their own, and then assert that their actions constitute the official acts of the meeting. . . . It is apparent that courts of equity do not look with favor upon attempts of a minority group to seize control of a corporation by trying to trap the majority without legal advice." Chapman v. Barton, 345 Ill. App. 110, 102 N.E.2d 565, 567–68 (1951).

Holders of a minority of shares, after failure of a stated meeting to elect officers, cannot call a new meeting on their own authority and hold a binding election. Haskell v. Read, 68 Neb. 115, 96 N.W. 1007, *rehearing denied*, 68 Neb. 107, 93 N.W. 997 (1903).

[8] Adams v. Fort Madison School Dist., 182 N.W.2d 132, 137 (Iowa 1970) (school district vote).

[9] State *ex rel.* Attorney General v. Anderson, 45 Ohio St. 196, 12 N.E. 656, 658–59 (1887). The court added: "Whether, in the absence of any particular provision, the plurality or the majority principle would be recognized as the law, must depend upon the usage in any particular state." *Citing* Cushing, Law & Pr. Leg. Assem.

Corporation laws generally provide that directors shall be elected by a plurality of the votes cast at a meeting of stockholders. This conforms with the common law. *See In re* Election of Directors of Rapid-Transit Ferry Co., 15 App. Div. 530, 44 N.Y.S. 539 (2d Dep't 1897).

§ 12.3   Application to Conduct of Meetings

The principle of majority control [10] also applies to the rulings of the chairman while conducting a meeting. When the chairman rules a motion out of order it is his decision that some rule of the body or some practice established by parliamentary usage has been violated. "This question the chairman must decide in the first instance and above him sits the court of final review, the majority who, on an appeal from the ruling of the chair, settle the issue beyond the power of any court to change their decision." [11] Where a presiding officer wrongfully declared the result of a vote and refused to entertain an appeal from his ruling, the majority of members present "were justified in exercising the power of the majority, in the absence of any by-laws or rules of order contrary to such action, by deposing the chairman and proceeding with the business of the meeting. The fact that [people] . . . left the meeting or remained . . . did not affect the power of the majority who remained and constituted a quorum to do business or the legality of their action." [12]

However, where a chairman rightfully refused to accept ballots

---

[10] A committee of non-members appointed by the town to recommend a site for a building is in fact an agency, with powers delegated to the whole number; and "though convenience requires and usage has established the right of acting by majorities, neither will sanction the exercise of the power by minorities." Damon v. Inhabitants of Granby, 19 Mass. (2 Pick.) 345, 355 (1824) (town commissioners or agents).

[11] State *ex rel.* Moore v. Archibald, 5 N.D. 359, 66 N.W. 234, 243 (1896).

The only proper course for those objecting to a ruling of the chairman is to appeal from the ruling and put the matter to a vote of the members. Haskell v. Read, 68 Neb. 115, 96 N.W. 1007.

[12] American Aberdeen-Angus Breeders' Ass'n v. Fullerton, 325 Ill. 323, 156 N.E. 314, 317 (1927).

Where, at a stockholders' meeting for the election of directors, certain persons received the requisite number of votes, the fact that the presiding officer insists on counting certain votes cast otherwise than as they should be counted, announces the result of the election to be otherwise than it really is, issues certificates of election to those not entitled to them, and declares the meeting adjourned, although a majority vote against adjournment, in no way affects the rights as directors of those in fact elected. State *ex rel.* Reed v. Smith, 14 P. 814, 15 P. 386 (Ore. 1887).

from shareholders who had not paid an assessment, and in consequence "was violently interfered with in the discharge of his duties,"
he was justified in refusing to recognize an appeal to the meeting.
"To permit such an appeal to those present and claiming the right
to vote would in effect allow persons to be judges of their own
qualifications and place the election of directors at the mercy of
any body of persons who saw fit to make a claim, however groundless, of the right to participate in the election." [13]

§ 12.4   Exceptions Founded on Higher Authority

Applicable statutes and rules of the body may, of course, provide
that control shall be exercised by other than a majority. For example, it has been held that where the rules of a society do not
allow for majority rule but provide that a moderator should decide
all questions according to the "solid sense" of the meeting, even a
majority of the members cannot proceed without him.[14] Charter
provisions intended to protect the rights of the minority to make
nominations for the election of directors cannot be ignored by the
majority.[15] And there often are statutory requirements that the
votes of more than a majority of the members are required to take
any action which alters the basic structure of the organization.[16]

---

[13] Umatilla Water Users' Ass'n v. Irvin, 56 Ore. 414, 108 P. 1016, 1019
(1910).

[14] Field v. Field, 9 Wend. 395 (N.Y. Sup. Ct. 1832) (Society of Friends).

When a moderator makes a procedural ruling as to the method of voting
which is not contrary to any statute, his ruling stands unless the town itself by
vote reverses it. Town of Exeter v. Kenick, 104 N.H. 168, 181 A.2d 638
(1962).

[15] "A majority of the members cannot by a vote deprive other members of
their rights to nominate candidates as expressly permitted by the Constitution
and Rules of the organization. Any such action by a majority would effectively
impair the rights of the minority members to select and vote for their candidates and thereby unfairly deprive other members of the opportunity assured
them under the Constitution and Rules to nominate candidates for all offices
and to vote for those candidates." Knoss v. Warner, 12 Misc. 2d 1021, 174
N.Y.S.2d 677, 680 (Sup. Ct. 1958).

[16] See, e.g., Hittl v. Buckhout, 13 Misc. 2d 230, 176 N.Y.S.2d 401 (Sup. Ct.
1958), aff'd, 10 App. Div. 2d 719, 199 N.Y.S.2d 444 (2d Dep't 1960) (village
law requiring favorable vote of three-fourths of trustees to amend zoning ordi-

The courts may not always agree. It has been held, for example, that the requirement of unanimous shareholder approval, or 90 per cent approval, of any action in the corporate management area may be "obnoxious to the statutory rule of stock corporation management." The court noted that 90 per cent is substantially the same as unanimous consent and reasoned: "The stockholders may not, by agreement, by-law or even the certificate of incorporation provision as to unanimous action, give the minority interest an absolute permanent all inclusive power to veto." [17]

§ 12.5 Court Recognition of Majority Power

The courts are fully aware of the rights of the majority and of their ultimate success in imposing their control. The principle of majority rule is demonstrated in a court decision approving the action of an international union executive board in declaring void two resolutions adopted at a local union membership meeting by a vote of less than 4 per cent of the members, one of which resolutions sought to overturn an earlier referendum approved by over 45 per cent of the membership, and the other of which would have disenfranchised certain local union members for failure to register at stated times. The board relied on a provision in the by-laws of the local permitting the officers to "correct the situation" when the local is faced with "submitting to unjust, unfair and improper conditions forced upon it by the arbitrary ruling of packed meetings or through the influence of members who control the situation. . . ." The purpose of this provision as viewed by the board was to "prevent a minority from seizing control of a Local by abuse of temporary power and effectuating changes adversely affecting the rights of the majority." The board also held both resolutions invalid in

---

nance); Metzger v. George Washington Memorial Park, Inc., 380 Pa. 350, 110 A.2d 425 (1955) (business corporation law providing vote on amendment of charter).

[17] Eisenstadt Bros. Inc. v. Eisenstadt, 89 N.Y.S.2d 12, 13 (Sup. Ct. 1949).

Corporate by-law requiring unanimous vote of stockholders to elect directors is invalid as contrary to law providing that directors shall be chosen by plurality of votes. Benintendi v. Kenton Hotel, 294 N.Y. 112, 60 N.E.2d 829 (1945); see 48 MICH. L. REV. 875 (1950).

that they violated Robert's Rules of Order (Rule 7) relating to the rights of absentees and permitting the repeal of a referendum only by another referendum. The court upheld the board, holding that the minority was trying to wrest control from the majority in violation of the latter's rights, and making the observation "that the 'right' which plaintiffs [minority] contend has been taken from them is, in effect, the 'right' of a minority group to utilize discriminatory voting procedures to take control of the union contrary to the will of the majority, the very 'right' which the statute was designed to protect against." [18]

When a majority is present and acting at an election of directors, the election should not be prevented by objections of a "purely technical character" interposed by minority stockholders who are disappointed or dissatisfied because of their inability to control the meeting. The court will recognize that a "certain degree of liberality in favor of a meeting ought to prevail. To take any other view would be to encourage the prolongation of internal strife between rival factions and keep the corporation's affairs in such a state of confusion and turmoil that the business which it was organized to conduct will inevitably suffer to the damage of its stockholders." [19] The courts will also recognize the futility of litigation by the minority for the purpose of trying to thwart action which ultimately can lawfully be taken by the majority.[20] One court has suggested that

[18] Guarnaccia v. Kenin, 234 F. Supp. 429, 435–36, 438–39 (S.D.N.Y. 1964).

[19] Duffy v. Loft, Inc., 17 Del. Ch. 376, 152 A. 849, 853 (1930).

[20] MacDougall v. Gardiner, [1875] 1 Ch. D. 13, 25. The court said: "In my opinion, if the thing complained of is a thing which in substance the majority of the company are entitled to do, or if something has been done irregularly which the majority of the company are entitled to do regularly, or if something has been done illegally which the majority of the company are entitled to do legally, there can be no use in having a litigation about it, the ultimate end of which is only that a meeting has to be called, and then ultimately the majority gets its wishes. Is it not better that the rule should be adhered to that if it is a thing which the majority are the masters of, the majority in substance shall be entitled to have their will followed? If it is a matter of that nature, it only comes to this, that the majority are the only persons who can complain that a thing which they are entitled to do has been done irregularly. . . ."

See CURRY (CREW), PUBLIC, COMPANY AND LOCAL GOVERNMENT MEETINGS at 80; SHAW AND SMITH, THE LAW OF MEETINGS at 50.

opposing stockholder factions should be required to fight it out in the corporate arena before going to the courts.[21]

§ 12.6　Protection of the Minority

The power of the majority to control is not absolute. Although the conduct of a meeting rests largely within the discretion and control of the majority, it is subject to the "wholesome restriction" that there is "a reasonable guaranty for fairly taking the sense of the entire body." [22] This power "whether it reside in the majority of the body at large, or of those present at a corporate meeting, or is confined to a select class, is in trust for the benefit of the whole, and must therefore be exercised with discretion." [23]

[21] "If, while the meeting is still in progress, opposing factions may take their disputes to court and require judicial determination of the regularity of the proceedings, eligibility of voters and validity of proxies, the affairs of the corporation may be brought to a standstill by restraining orders, hearings and appeals, courts may be occupied by matters of little or no ultimate consequence, and judicial processes may be employed as tactics for the advantage of one faction or another in their struggle for support of other stockholders. Unless immediate judicial intervention is shown to be essential to protect substantial rights, opposing factions should be required to fight their battles to a conclusion one way or another within the corporate arena before seeking aid of the courts." Salgo v. Matthews, 497 S.W.2d 620, 625 (Tex. 1973).

[22] Mann v. City of LeMars, 109 Iowa 251, 80 N.W. 327, 328 (1899) (meeting of city council).

"The course of procedure rests largely with the discretion of the majority, provided the course adopted affords a reasonable guaranty that the sense of the body on the particular measure before it has been fairly taken." State *ex rel.* Moore v. Archibald, 5 N.D. 359, 380, 66 N.W. 234 (1896).

[23] Granger v. Grubb, 7 Philadelphia 350, 351–52 (C.P. 1870).

"The rule of corporation law and of equity invoked is well settled and has been often applied. The majority has the right to control; but when it does so, it occupies a fiduciary relation toward the minority. . . ." Southern Pacific Co. v. Bogert, 250 U.S. 483, 487–88 (1918).

A shareholder has the legal right to vote even though he has a personal interest. It seems, however, where the action resulting from the votes of the shareholders owning a majority of the stock of a corporation is so detrimental to the corporation itself as to lead to the necessary inference that the interests of the majority lie wholly outside of and in opposition to the interests of the corporation and of the minority of the shareholders, and that such action is a wanton or fraudulent destruction of the rights of the minority, it may be sub-

It can be said, generally: "The holder of the majority of the stock in a corporation owes to the other stockholders and the corporation the duty to exercise good faith, care, and diligence, to conserve the property of the corporation, and to protect the interests of minority stockholders." [24]

Conceding that the principle of majority control is firmly established in considering the conduct of meetings of deliberative assemblies, common parliamentary law has long provided rules designed for the protection of the minority. The majority may not, for example, adjourn an annual meeting of stockholders over the protest of the minority stockholders for the purpose of preventing the minority from exercising their legal right to elect other directors. This would be a "fraud" upon the minority stockholders. "The minority stockholders of a corporation have property rights in the corporation and its assets and management, which the directors, their trustees, may not ignore and set aside. Nor can the majority of the stockholders, broad as their powers are, override the organic law of the corporation for the illegal purpose of preventing the minority from securing the representation in the directory which the shares of stock owned by them enable them to elect." [25] There are also circumstances under which reference by the majority stockholder in its proxy-soliciting material to its "possession of votes that would

---

jected to the scrutiny of a court of equity at the suit of the minority shareholders. Gamble v. Queens County Water Co., 123 N.Y. 91, 98, 25 N.E. 201 (1890).

[24] Steinfeld v. Copper State Mining Co., 37 Ariz. 151, 290 P. 155, 160 (1930).

[25] West Side Hospital v. Steele, 124 Ill. App. 534, 540–42 (1906).

Where a majority of the villagers were opposed to a reorganization and sought to avoid the holding of a town meeting which had been called to implement the statute, it was held that the majority could not adjourn the meeting sine die in an attempt to frustrate the purpose of the meeting. Although the majority has the right to adjourn the meeting, it "must be fairly done, and for no improper purpose." The court commented: "Any other rule would open the door to great abuse of power, and place a loyal minority too much in the power of a disloyal majority." Stone v. Small, 54 Vt. 498, 502 (1882).

The minority, after a lawful adjournment, may not call a new meeting on their own authority and hold a binding election. "To permit this would be to concede to a minority of the shares the power to govern the corporation." Haskell v. Read, 68 Neb. 115, 96 N.W. 1007 (1903).

suffice to end debate" would constitute misleading information in a proxy contest.[26]

Withdrawal of the majority from a duly organized meeting with the intent to destroy its legal existence has received the same unfavorable reception by the court. "A minority must have a right to insist that, after a meeting is organized, the majority shall not withdraw from it, and organize another meeting, at which the minority must appear or lose their rights. Once concede the right, and there is no limit to the number of wrecked meetings which may, at the caprice of a majority, precede the transaction of any business." [27]

§ 12.7   Minority Obligations to Majority

By the same token, the minority has concomitant obligations to the majority.[28] A minority cannot walk out of a meeting for the purpose of breaking a quorum and preventing further business.[29]

[26] "The misleading proxy material deprives the meeting, and the majority stockholder, of the expressions of view and the votes that would have ensued upon truthful disclosure; it is not legally possible to decide what legal consequences flow from the informational defects in the meeting by asserting that the meeting would have been ended in the same resolution no matter what the views or votes of the minority. That is not necessarily the fact and it cannot be the resolving principle of law." Laurenzano v. Einbender, 264 F. Supp. 356, 362 (E.D.N.Y. 1966).

[27] The court continued: "[C]an a majority, constituting less than two-thirds, withdraw from an organized meeting, and thus compel the minority to follow them, or lose their right to defeat the measure? We believe it would be unwise, and unjust as well, to sanction such a rule. It is not essential to the protection of the majority who have the right to vote at the meeting as organized. On the other hand, the contrary rule is necessary for the protection of the minority." In re Argus Printing Co., 1 N.D. 434, 48 N.W. 347, 352–53 (1891).

[28] In a proceeding to oust a municipal official, the court declined to entertain the "right of a minority to resort to parliamentary rules in order to violate a statute." Tillman v. Otter, 93 Ky. 600, 20 S.W. 1036, 1038 (1893) (sinking fund commissioner elected by general council consisting of joint session of councilmen and aldermen).

[29] The court said: "The minority were not justified in leaving the council, and the action of [the president] in declaring the council adjourned was an outrage and cannot be excused. No presiding officer can arbitrarily adjourn a

Nor can a minority prevent an election of directors by declining to participate in an election of inspectors of election.[30] The minority cannot unlawfully adjourn the meeting and then return to the meeting room and elect directors. "It is apparent that courts of equity do not look with favor upon attempts of a minority group to seize control of a corporation by trying to trap the majority without legal advice." [31]

---

meeting in defiance of the majority present. . . . But this does not excuse the illegal action of those who remained. They well knew that they were without a quorum, and the counting of absent members, and recording them as voting on all questions, is also an inexcusable outrage. . . ." Dingwall v. Common Council, 82 Mich. 568, 46 N.W. 938, 939 (1890).

[30] Prigerson v. White Cap Sea Foods, Inc., 100 N.Y.S.2d 881, 885 (Sup. Ct. 1950).

[31] A stockholders' meeting was first adjourned by unanimous vote to enable the president to obtain legal advice as to whether the chairman should be elected by voice vote or by a share vote. At the adjourned meeting another squabble occurred and it was adjourned by a voice vote put by the chairman elected by a voice vote. Western Cottage Piano & Organ Co. v. Burrows, 144 Ill. App. 350 (1908); see Chapman v. Barton, 345 Ill. App. 110, 102 N.E.2d 565 (1951).

Where a corporation failed to give notice of its annual meeting of shareholders as specified in the by-laws, and minority stockholders met without notice at the time and place fixed by the by-laws for the annual meeting and proceeded to elect one of those present to act as chairman and then voted to adjourn to a designated future time and place because there was no quorum present, such "opposition" meeting was invalid for lack of notice and the attending stockholders had no legal authority to adjourn. Gries v. Eversharp, Inc., 69 A.2d 922 (Del. Ch. 1949).

At a meeting of stockholders, some withdrew on the pretext of escaping disorder, for which they were as much to blame at least as the others, but in reality to carry out a preconceived plan to organize the meeting in their own interest. The disorder was begun in an attempt to substitute the chairman who had been properly chosen and who was entitled to continue to preside unless superseded in some orderly and recognized parliamentary manner. The court held that the meeting of the seceders was illegal and that its acts were mere nullities as against the other stockholders. The subsequent invitation to the others to vote at the illegal meeting convened by the seceders was "ineffectual to cure the radical defects of organization." Commonwealth ex rel. Langdon v. Patterson, 158 Pa. 476, 27 A. 998, 999 (1893).

§ 12.8 Parliamentary Concept of Discussion and Persuasion of Opposition

It is a fundamental rule of parliamentary practice that the majority in control of a meeting must respect the rights of the minority to be present throughout all deliberations, to participate in the discussions, and to attempt to win over the majority to its views.[32] Persuasion of the majority is to be expected. "Normally, the majority rule prevails under our democratic processes. It follows that any interested party has a legal right to persuade the majority to accept his views. Meetings are held for the purpose of discussion, argumentation and persuasion, resulting in the enlightenment of all. There can be no legal wrong from such attempts at persuasion." [33]

However, it must be recognized that there are meetings of many groups where it would be physically impossible by reason of num-

---

[32] "It appears to be a fundamental rule of parliamentary practice governing assemblies that the opportunity to deliberate, and if possible, to convince their fellows is the right of the minority, of which they cannot be deprived by the arbitrary will of the majority." The court added that "the matter of a quorum is one separate and apart from the principle that all the members of a deliberative body must have a fair opportunity to participate in its action." The court also held that a written assent of members "will not supply the want of a meeting" as it deprives those interested of the "benefit of mutual discussion, and subjects them to the hazards of fraudulent misrepresentation and undue influence." Terre Haute Gas Corp. v. Johnson, 221 Ind. 499, 45 N.E.2d 484, 489–90 (1942), *modified on other grounds,* 221 Ind. 499, 48 N.E.2d 455 (1943), *quoting* Commonwealth *ex rel.* Claghorn v. Cullen, 13 Pa. 133, 144 (1850).

[33] Stansberry v. McCarty, 149 N.E.2d 683, 686 (Ind. 1958) (religious society).

A shareholder is entitled to have all pertinent and material information, including the views of those who oppose as well as those who favor the matter being considered at the meeting. "Surely stockholders, once informed of the facts, have a right to make their own decisions in matters pertaining to their economic self-interest, whether consistent with or contrary to the advice of others, whether such advice is tendered by management or outsiders or those motivated by self-interest." American Crystal Sugar Co. v. Cuban-American Sugar Co., 276 F. Supp. 45, 50 (S.D.N.Y. 1967).

See Schrank v. Brown, 194 Misc. 138, 86 N.Y.S.2d 209, 211, 212 (Sup. Ct. 1949), *citing* Robert's Rules of Order (fair criticism is the right of members of a union, as it is the right of every citizen).

bers alone, and certainly impractical and wastefully repetitious, to permit every member in attendance to express his views, either briefly or at length, in an attempt to convince others. In considering the validity of a voting trust agreement, the court spoke these words of caution: "An examination of the authorities discloses that there has been a gradual modification of the views of both courts and textwriters upon this subject in modern times. The old theory which seems to dominate the earlier writers, to the effect that every stockholder in a corporation is entitled to have the benefit of the judgment of every other stockholder in the selection of a board of directors, has necessarily been rendered obsolete because of our modern business being conducted by large corporations with thousands of stockholders located in all parts of the country. Manifestly a meeting of the stockholders of such organizations would be not only impracticable but impossible." [34]

It is fundamental law that, in the absence of specific enactment to the contrary, all business requiring the assent of members must be transacted at a duly convened meeting.[35] As to shareholder meetings, it has been held that "the only legal concurrence of stockholders in measures upon which they are called upon to act, is to be expressed at such meeting, after full opportunity to discussion and debate, and full permission to those opposed to any measure favored by the majority, to attempt by persuasion to reverse the prevailing sentiment. As is said by Mr. Brice: 'More than this, they [the minority] can demand a fair hearing, and that their wishes and arguments should be listened to and duly weighed' [citing Green's Brice]. This being the general rule, and one of the most valuable privileges of the members of a corporation, it will never be assumed that the legislation intended to abolish the right except under stress of a clear and imperative enactment to that effect." [36]

The right to be heard entails the corollary right and duty to hear the views of others.[37] In a proxy contest the minority may exercise

[34] Mackin v. Nicollet Hotel, Inc., 25 F.2d 783, 786 (8th Cir. 1928).

[35] See § 1.1 supra.

[36] Reiff v. Western Union Tel. Co., 49 N.Y. Super. 441, 453 (1883).

[37] In a suit to enjoin the sale of church property, the court held that "ordinary rules of parliamentary procedures should be observed in the conduct of the meeting." The by-laws directed that Hiscox' Directory for Baptist Churches should govern the meeting. The court observed that the Directory "recognizes the right of debate," and therefore the two factions "were entitled

the "art of advocacy" and take some liberties with the "whole truth." [38]

The courts recognize that there are circumstances under which the results of a meeting might have been different if all members had been given an opportunity to fully participate in the deliberations. In holding that a meeting was invalid for lack of proper notice, an early English decision held: "The minority might come to resolutions without the majority; or the majority without the minority, who, if they had been present, might have dissuaded or deterred them from such a course." [39]

It is also recognized at law that the views of the minority may have value even where one shareholder owns enough shares to

---

to hear the views of each other" and had "the right to be heard in the hope that their arguments might convince the congregation." The court added that one of the reasons for a notice of meeting was to give members an opportunity for investigation and consideration in preparation for the meeting. Randolph v. Mt. Zion Baptist Church, 139 N.J. Eq. 605, 53 A.2d 206, 208–9 (Ch. 1947).

In an action for libel based on a telegram from one warring faction in a corporate election accusing plaintiff of being "incompetent or worse," it was held that communication was presumptively privileged. Shareholders are entitled to attempt to convert each other as to corporate management. Also, it was held: "That only a minority of the stock of the corporation was voted on at the election of the directors did not make the election illegal; the stockholders attending or represented make a quorum." Ashcroft v. Hammond, 132 App. Div. 3, 116 N.Y.S. 362, 365, rev'd, 197 N.Y. 488, 90 N.E. 1117 (1910).

[38] A letter by a minority shareholder in opposition to management may contain some exaggerations, but is not "a license to lie." SEC v. Okin, 48 F. Supp. 928, 930 (S.D.N.Y.), rev'd, 137 F.2d 862 (2d Cir.), modified, 48 F. Supp. 928 (1943).

"Appellants' fundamental complaint appears to be that stockholder disputes should be viewed in the eyes of the law just as are political contests, with each side free to hurl charges with comparative unrestraint, the assumption being that the opposing side is then at liberty to refute and thus effectively deflate the 'campaign oratory' of its adversary. Such, however, was not the policy of Congress as enacted in the Securities Exchange Act. There Congress has clearly entrusted to the Commission the duty of protecting the investing public against misleading statements made in the course of a struggle for corporate control." SEC v. May, 229 F.2d 123, 124 (2d Cir. 1956).

[39] Dobson v. Fussy, 7 Bing. 305, 311 (C.D. 1831) (meeting of select vestry).

carry any resolution and may be expected to vote in favor of his own resolutions. "It may be that an unfavorable vote from the minority stockholders would have brought about modification or reconsideration of the transactions; in corporate circles, concensus can be a desideratum." [40]

The right of the minority to express its opinion and to attempt to persuade the majority appears to be a matter of internal management of the company, in which the court will hesitate to intervene. Thus, the court will not entertain a petition by an individual shareholder on behalf of himself and the minority to prevent the majority from taking a particular action without first calling a meeting of shareholders for the purpose of discussion and consideration, putting aside all illegality on the part of the majority.[41] Similarly, a majority of the board of directors need not submit to abuse by the minority. The majority directors have the right to take extraordinary actions to protect themselves and the company against harassment by the minority directors, such as the refusal of the minority to follow parliamentary procedures and their taking reprehensible action frequently resulting in the temporary inability of the chairman to proceed with board meetings. And, although an individual director generally has a right to the presence of his own counsel during directors' meetings when he deems it necessary, the majority directors may refuse to allow the minority directors to have their own counsel when the minority has not only failed to follow parliamentary procedures, but has harassed the majority with abusive language in a reprehensible and inexcusable manner.[42]

[40] Laurenzano v. Einbender, 264 F. Supp. 356, 361 (E.D.N.Y. 1966).

[41] "Has a particular individual the right to have it [a meeting] for the purpose of using his power of eloquence to induce the others to listen to him and to take his view? That is an equity which I have never yet heard of in this Court, and I have never known it insisted upon before; that is to say, that this Court is to entertain a bill for the purpose of enabling one particular member of the company to have an opportunity of expressing his opinions *viva voce* at a meeting of the shareholders. If so, I do not know why we should not go further, and say, not only must the meeting be held, but the shareholders must stay there to listen to him and to be convinced by him. The truth is, that is only part of the machinery and means by which the internal management is carried on." MacDougall v. Gardiner, [1875] 1 Ch. D. 13.

[42] Selama-Dindings Plantations, Ltd. v. Durham, 216 F. Supp. 104 (S.D. Ohio 1963), *aff'd sub nom.* Selama-Dindings Plantations, Ltd., v. Cincinnati Union Stock Yard Co., 337 F.2d 949 (6th Cir. 1964).

§ 12.8.1   *Right of Advocacy Cannot Be Abused*

The right of the minority to argue and to persuade the majority must not be abused. Although the majority should "listen to reasonable arguments for a reasonable time" the majority may, after hearing what is to be said, decide that they have "had enough," whereupon the chairman, supported by the majority, may declare the discussion closed.[43]

The court may also put an end to a proxy fight by refusing to intervene to the advantage of either faction. A leading case noted: "The issue was the sharply drawn one of management vs. antimanagement. There are no special circumstances appearing in the case which suggest that this corporation should again be plunged into the midst of a bitter controversy between hostile factions over issues which have been the subject of recent and extensive debate. . . . I can discover no equitable considerations sufficient to warrant the view that the exercise by the majority of its lawful power should be frustrated and the old straw re-threshed." [44] This is consistent with the basic principle that it is not the function of the courts to decide which faction in a proxy fight should prevail. "That judgment is for the stockholders. However, it is the function of the courts to see that that judgment is as well informed as possible, so that when the stockholders are given their annual opportunity to have a voice in the affairs of their corporation, they are fully prepared to evaluate those who would seek to guide the affairs of that corporation." [45]

The right to present one's position and to argue in an attempt to

---

[43] The rule that a majority at a meeting cannot "ride roughshod" over the minority is not applicable to a majority who are "bent on obstructing business and resolved on talking forever." When closure is applied under such circumstances, the court ought not to interfere. "As to the closure, I think if we laid it down that the chairman, supported by a majority, could not put a termination to the speeches of those who were desirous of addressing the meeting, we should allow a small minority, or even a member or two, to tyrannize over the majority," and involve the company in all-night sittings. Wall v. London & N. Assets Corp., [1898] 2 Ch. 469, 481, 483.

See § 16.11 *infra.*

[44] Gow v. Consolidated Coppermines Corp., 19 Del. Ch. 172, 165 A. 136, 147 (1933).

[45] Studebaker Corp. v. Allied Prod. Corp., 256 F. Supp. 173, 190, n.9 (W.D. Mich. 1966).

win over the undecided and convince the opposition is also necessarily limited by such reasonable restraints as may be indicated
or imposed by the character, purpose, and dimensions of the meeting. A rule of reason, and of equal opportunity to participate in
the deliberations within the generally accepted boundaries of the
meeting, is both convenient and necessary to the orderly and expeditious transaction of business. A proper balance between the
rights of the majority and of the minority is the best assurance that
the rights of both will be respected.

13

Decorum at Meetings

§ 13.1   Preservation of Order

The power of an assembly to convene and act implies the right of self-protection and the authority ultimately to discipline those attending the meeting for the purpose of maintaining order. The right of assembly and the right to insure an orderly meeting are essentially related. Common parliamentary law has long recognized that a legislative assembly has all the powers and privileges which are necessary to enable it to exercise in all respects its appropriate functions in a free, intelligent, and impartial manner. "These powers and privileges are derived not from the Constitution; on the contrary, they arise from the very creation of a legislative body, and are founded upon the privilege of self-preservation." Therefore, the powers and privileges which a legislative assembly takes by force and the effect of its creation are to be ascertained by a reference to the common parliamentary law.[1]

[1] *Ex parte* McCarthy, 29 Cal. Rptr. 395, 403 (1866), *citing* Cushing, Law & Pr. Leg. Assem., which lists 13 powers and privileges, including: "3. To estab-

Incidental and appropriate powers of self-protection are implied by the common law.[2] But, "independently of parliamentary custom

---

lish its own rules of proceeding. . . . 6. To preserve its own honor, dignity, purity and efficiency, by the expulsion of an unworthy, or the discharge of an incompetent member. 7. To protect itself and its members from personal violence. 8. To protect itself and its members from libelous and slanderous attacks."

Accord, Bohrer v. Toberman, 227 S.W.2d 719 (Mo. 1950), *citing* Cushing as authority that legislative powers are not derived from the Constitution, but arise from the very creation of a legislative body and are founded on the principle of self-preservation; Moran v. LaGuardia, 270 N.Y. 450, 1 N.E.2d 961 (1936), *citing* Cushing on the effect of a concurrent resolution of the legislature; State *ex rel.* Robinson v. Fluent, 30 Wash. 2d 194, 191 P.2d 241, *cert. denied,* 335 U.S. 844 (1948), *citing* Cushing as authority that a state constitution is not a grant, but a restriction on the powers of the legislature. "The powers and privileges which are necessary to the proper exercise, in all respects, of its appropriate functions, are inherent in the legislature and are to be ascertained primarily by a reference to the common parliamentary law."

[2] In holding that a legislative body has the right to eject a member for "obstruction, interruption, or disturbance" of its proceedings, an Australian court comments: "Even a public meeting would have power to exclude a member disturbing its proceedings. . . ." This power is derived from the common law. "For these purposes, protective and self defensive powers only, and not punitive, are necessary. If the question is to be elucidated by analogy, that analogy is rather to be derived from other assemblies (not legislative), whose incidental powers of self-protection are implied by the common law (although of inferior importance and dignity to bodies constituted for purposes of public legislation), than the British Parliament, which has its own peculiar law and custom, or from Courts of Record, which have also their special authorities and privileges, recognised by law." Barton v. Taylor, 11 App. Cas. 197, 203 (P.C. 1886) (New South Wales).

This common-law power may be formalized in rules of procedure. For example, a church has the right to establish its own practice and rules for the admission and seating of persons and if one refuses to comply with the rules, the church authorities have the right to use reasonable force to evict him. Jones v. State, 219 Ga. 848, 136 S.E.2d 358, *cert. denied,* Jones v. Georgia, 379 U.S. 935 (1964).

"We do hold that a college has the inherent power to promulgate rules and regulations; that it has the inherent power properly to discipline; that it has power appropriately to protect itself and its property; that it may expect that its students adhere to generally accepted standards of conduct; that, as to these, flexibility and elbow room are to be preferred over specificity; that procedural due process must be afforded. . . ." Esteban v. Central Missouri State College, 415 F.2d 1077, 1089 (8th Cir. 1969), *cert. denied,* 398 U.S. 965 (1970).

and usage," a legislative assembly has the power to protect itself and its members; without such authority an assembly would be powerless to accomplish the purposes of its constitution. As the power exists, the assembly must necessarily be "the sole judge of the exigency which may justify and require its exercise." [3]

A body or assembly of persons has the right, without direction or interference by the courts, for its government to adopt a constitution, by-laws, rules, and regulations "which will control as to all questions of discipline, or internal policy and management, and its right to interpret and administer the same is as sacred as the right to make them." [4] Chief Justice Burger has expressed this truth in the following words: "Without civility no private discussion, no

---

A New Zealand case considered a Standing Order of a hospital board which provided that: "The Chairman shall maintain order and any member refusing to obey the orders of the Chair shall be deemed guilty of contempt. The Chairman's decision on any point of order shall be final." The court held that the chairman's decisions were final as regards "the conduct and control of debates." Arcus v. Castle, [1954] N.Z.L.R. 122, 129 (1953).

"To worship God, after the dictates of our consciences, is a privilege that all men claim as a birthright from heaven. . . . The English common law held this privilege so sacred, that it would not justify one in striking even in his own defence, during worship [citation] and it is a principle so clear, that those who unlawfully disturb the devotions of a religious assembly, by any indecency or violence, may be punished by indictment, that authorities are unnecessary to support it." Bell v. Graham, 10 S.C.L. 278, 281 (Constitutional Ct. 1818).

"The principles upon which the disturbance of public worship becomes an offense at common law are these: Every man has a perfect right to worship God in the manner most comfortable to the dictates of his conscience, and to assemble and unite with others in the same act of worship, so that he does not interfere with the equal rights of others. The same law protects this right. . . . The disturbance of public worship . . . is . . . liable to be prosecuted by indictment at the common law." United States v. Brooks, 24 Fed. Cas. 1244, 1245 (No. 14655) (D.C. Cir. 1834).

[3] Hiss v. Bartlett, 69 Mass. (3 Gray) 468, 473, 475 (1855).

[4] State ex rel. Givens v. Superior Court, 233 Ind. 235, 117 N.E.2d 553, 555 (1954) (voluntary trade union association).

But see Duke v. State of Texas, 327 F. Supp. 1218 (E.D. Tex. 1971), rev'd, 477 F.2d 244 (5th Cir., 1973), cert. denied, 415 U.S. 978 (1974) (university's regulations on admission of outside speakers were held to be deficient, and campus security regulations were held unconstitutionally vague; a state court injunction preventing non-students from going onto campus to make speeches was set aside).

public debate, no legislative process, no political campaign, no trial, can serve its purpose or achieve its objective." [5]

The right to preserve order and to discipline includes the right to eject and remove any member whose conduct results in a substantial obstruction of the business of the meeting and, in an appropriate case, includes the right to suspend or expel the obstreperous member from the body. "The ground of justification for the removal of a person who seeks to interrupt or disturb the order and proceedings of others, is that they have the right to the quiet and orderly enjoyment of any lawful business, pleasure and occupation. An intruder has no right to disturb or interrupt, and if he does, it is lawful to remove him and thus restore quiet." [6]

§ 13.2   Duty and Authority of Chairman To Maintain Order

The chairman has the authority and bears the duty and the responsibility to maintain order and to enforce such discipline as may

[5] Opening Remarks, "The Necessity of Civility," 48th Annual Meeting of The American Law Institute, May 18, 1971.

[6] Wall v. Lee, 34 N.Y. 141, 142–43 (1865). The court upheld a charge to the jury "that in every congregation assembled for religious worship, or any other meeting assembled for a lawful purpose, there must necessarily exist the power to preserve order, and to expel and to remove, by necessary force, any person guilty of a *wilful* disturbance of such meeting, who would persist in such disturbances, so that it could not be conducted in an orderly and proper manner," except that the disturbance need not be willful. It concluded: "If the person is guilty of disturbing the meeting, and interrupting its order and decorum, then the application of such force as may be necessary to remove him may be justified. These principles are abundantly sustained by authority."

A statute prohibiting the disturbance of a religious meeting is not a breach of the peace statute as such, "but rather it is a statute which is designed to protect to the citizens of this State the right to worship their God according to the dictates of their conscience without interruption." Ford v. State, 210 Tenn. 105, 355 S.W.2d 102, *cert. denied,* Ford v. Tennessee, 377 U.S. 994.

"Protection of the privilege to assemble peaceably to discuss national issues must encompass security against being assaulted for having exercised it." Robeson v. Fanelli, 94 F. Supp. 62, 69 (S.D.N.Y. 1950) (attempt to disturb and disrupt meeting with intent to deprive plaintiffs of right of free speech and assembly).

The purpose of a statute making disruption of religious services a misdemeanor is to ensure religious freedom. Where defendants acted willfully together to harass and disturb members of a church in their worship service, they effectively denied the members their constitutionally guaranteed right of

reasonably be necessary for that purpose. The means of maintaining order are basically within his discretion.[7] An early English decision [8] puts the matter simply: "Unquestionably, it is the duty of the chairman, and his function, to preserve order and to take care that the proceedings are conducted in a proper manner, and that the sense of the meeting is properly ascertained with regard to any question which is properly before the meeting." This principle of law will always prevail. As noted in a recent decision, "free discussion is impossible if the forum is under the control of superior force, with foreigners patrolling the meeting chamber and exercising the prerogatives of the chair." [9]

A recent New York case stated briefly: "If there was disorder it was incumbent upon the Chairman to quiet the disorder or cease

---

freedom of worship. Central Presbyterian Church v. Black Liberation Front, 303 F. Supp. 894 (E.D. Mo. 1969).

[7] By statute, justices are to preside as moderators at town meetings, and see that they are orderly and regularly conducted, "but the means of maintaining order are left to the discretion of the presiding officers." The court concluded: "Stopping here, there would be little room for question that the justices were well warranted in ordering the plaintiff out of the room, without waiting to put their mandate in writing. The case called for a prompt exercise of their authority, and I can perceive no objection in principle to the manner in which it was exercised." Parsons v. Brainard, 17 Wend. 522, 523 (N.Y. Sup. Ct. 1837).

[8] National Dwelling Soc'y v. Sykes, [1894] 3 Ch. 159, 162.

"It is no doubt the duty of the chairman of a meeting, when a large body of people are gathered together, to do his best to preserve order, and it is equally the duty of those who are acting as stewards or managers to assist him in so doing, but the nature and extent of this duty on both sides cannot be very closely defined a priori, and must necessarily arise out of, and in character and extent depend upon, the events and emergencies which may from time to time arise." Lucas v. Mason, L.R. 10 Ex. 251, 254 (1875).

In speaking of the chairman, the court said: "It is on him that it devolves, both to preserve order in the meeting and to regulate the proceedings so as to give all persons entitled a reasonable opportunity of voting." Regina v. D'Oyly, 12 Adolph. & E. 139, 159 (Q.B. 1840).

[9] The court noted that the right to establish "reasonable rules pertaining to the meeting" under the labor Bill of Rights means the right "to impose reasonable rules to maintain the order and decorum needed to dispose of the business of the meeting," but does not give authority for the takeover by the parent organization. Navarro v. Gannon, 385 F.2d 512, 519–20 (2d Cir. 1967), cert. denied, 390 U.S. 989 (1968) (action to enjoin parent union from assuming control of meeting of local union).

doing business until there was the proper atmosphere for the proper conduct of the meeting. Failure to do this was a grave irregularity." [10] In fact, the right that all members have to attend and participate in the meeting imposes upon the chairman a "duty that is not merely moral or ethical." The members of such meetings have a "positive and substantial right" to demand that the proceedings be conducted with due regard to their respective interests.[11]

§ 13.2.1   Prompt Action

The chairman should act promptly to quell any disturbance. A recent decision notes that "silence of meeting officials in the face of unusual or raucous activity necessarily suggests that the rules of the meeting permit the activity or that the officials do not intend to enforce prohibitory rules to the contrary." [12]

§ 13.2.2   Disturber Cannot Gain Advantage

The disturber must not be permitted to gain any advantage from his unlawful acts. In a recent case, a disturber was removed from a city council chamber and asserted the defense that he had a right to resist removal in order to test the validity of the direction to leave. The court, in holding that the decision of the presiding officer cannot be tested by physical resistance, stated: "Government could not govern if its vital processes could thus be brought to halt. Again, no court would tolerate such interference with its proceedings; the need is the same in the legislative chamber, at the State and at the local level. The chair must have the power to suppress a disturbance or the threat of one, and the power to quell a disturbance would be empty if its exercise could be met by still another disturbance designed to test the officer's judgment." [13]

---

[10] *In re* Ryan v. Grimm, 43 Misc. 2d 836, 840, 252 N.Y.S.2d 521, 525, *aff'd*, 22 App. Div. 2d 171, 254 N.Y.S.2d 462 (4th Dep't 1964), *aff'd*, 15 N.Y.2d 922, 206 N.E.2d 867, 258 N.Y.S.2d 843 (1965) (organizational meeting of political county committee).

[11] SHAW AND SMITH, THE LAW OF MEETINGS at 48.

[12] *In re* Kay, 83 Cal. Rptr. 686, 464 P.2d 142, 152, n.12 (1970) (proceedings for writ of habeas corpus on behalf of persons convicted of disturbing lawful open-air meeting in public park at which congressman spoke).

[13] State v. Smith, 46 N.J. 510, 218 A.2d 147, *cert. denied*, Smith v. New Jersey, 385 U.S. 838 (1966).

§ 13.3   Disturbance of Meetings—Meaning of Terms

What constitutes a disturbance which requires or justifies the imposition of sanctions by the chair? What criteria should the chairman use in deciding whether and to what extent some form of restraint or discipline is necessary or appropriate? Having determined that some action is necessary or desirable, may the chairman act on his own or should he refer the matter to the body? Need he give a warning to the disrupter? If action is to be taken, may the chairman call upon others to assist in enforcing his orders? And what force may be applied in removing the disturber? In resolving these questions it is helpful to look at history.

At common law the deliberate disturbance of a lawful assembly was an indictable offense. "Where people rightfully assemble for worship, or assemble in their township meetings and the like, and probably in all cases where they come together in an orderly way for a lawful object; those who unlawfully interrupt them are indictable at the common law." [14] Many states have embodied this com-

---

A defendant was convicted of being a disorderly person when, at a public hearing of city planning board, he persisted for almost a quarter of an hour in refusing to accept rulings of the chair or to leave the microphone and resume his seat. The defendant quoted Robert's Rules of Order as supporting another speaker who arose for a point of information. The chairman ruled the defendant out of order, stating that the board was not using Robert's Rules. The defendant persisted and the chairman had to rule him out of order three more times. The defendant repeatedly refused to yield the microphone and was finally removed by a police officer. His conviction was upheld. The court stated that "the decision of a chairman may not be tested by resisting his repeated rulings to bring order back into the meeting." State v. Moore, 101 N.J. Super. 419, 244 A.2d 522, 524 (1968).

[14] The court continued: "Here these school directors were lawfully assembled, and in discharge of duties of great importance to the public, and to disturb and interrupt them is an act injurious to the public and a public wrong, and, of course, indictable at common law, although not punished by any Act of Assembly." Campbell v. Commonwealth, 59 Pa. 266, 267 (1868).

The defendant deliberately disturbed a group which had gathered to decorate a Christmas tree. "It will be observed that this indictment is found under common law, and, as such, we are satisfied was maintainable. It is a misdemeanor at common law wantonly to disturb an assemblage of persons met together for any lawful purpose, particularly meetings of a distinctly moral or

mon-law principle into their statutory law.[15] The disturbance of a
meeting may also affect interstate commerce in such a manner as

---

benevolent character." State v. Watkins, 123 Tenn. 502, 504, 130 S.W. 839
(1910).

The disturbing of a congregation assembled for religious worship, by
laughing and talking in a loud voice, and indecent actions, and grimaces during the performance of divine service is a specific misdemeanor in itself, and per
se indictable at common law. State v. Jasper, 15 N.C. 323 (1833).

An early Federal case explains: "The principles upon which the disturbance
of public worship becomes an offence at common law are these: Every man has
a perfect right to worship God in the manner most comfortable to the dictates
of his conscience, and to assemble and unite with others in the same act of
worship, so that he does not interfere with the equal rights of others. The common law protects this right. . . . The disturbance of public worship . . . is
. . . liable to be prosecuted by indictment at the common law." United States
v. Brooks, 24 Fed. Cas. 1244, 1245 (No. 14655) (C.C.D.C. 1834).

Indictment lies at common law for disorderly behavior at town meetings.
The court noted that the disturbance of meetings was a common-law misdemeanor in England. Commonwealth v. Hoxey, 16 Mass. 385 (1820).

Even where a statute does apply, the prosecutor may still proceed under the
common law. People v. Degey, 2 Wheeler Cr. Cas. 135 (N.Y. 1823).

"Common law" offenses are derived from the English common law of breach
of the peace. Heard v. Rizzo, 281 F. Supp. 720 (E.D. Pa. 1968), aff'd, 424
F.2d 279 (3d Cir. 1970).

[15] "The offense of disturbing a public meeting was recognized by the common law as a misdemeanor. Certain like provisions have been enacted into
our statutes. The ordinance in question is a general regulation for all types of
meetings." The court defines "disturbance," with citations. State v. McNair,
178 Neb. 763, 135 N.W.2d 463, 465 (1965) (defendant clergymen and others
found guilty of violating city ordinance proscribing disturbing an assemblage,
for singing and marching within city council chamber and refusing to desist
when the council president called for order and rapped his gavel).

See, e.g., N.Y. PENAL LAW § 240.20(4) providing that a person is guilty of
disorderly conduct when, with intent to cause public inconvenience, annoyance,
or alarm, or recklessly creating a risk thereof: "Without lawful authority, he
disturbs any lawful assembly or meeting of persons."

See also United States v. Woodard, 376 F.2d 136 (7th Cir. 1967) (defendant fell limp on the floor and was carried out of Congressional committee
hearing room by Federal marshals; convicted of disorderly conduct under
Federal Assimilative Crimes Act and Illinois disorderly conduct statute); Central Presbyterian Church v. Black Liberation Front, 303 F. Supp. 894 (E.D. Mo.
1969) (defendants convicted under statute for interruption and disturbance of
religious meeting. Injunction issued. "Their conduct, if condoned, will lead to
a breakdown in this society. It should not be tolerated, and it will be enjoined."); Zwicker v. Boll, 270 F. Supp. 131 (W.D. Wis. 1967), aff'd, 391 U.S.

353 (1968) (defendants convicted of disorderly conduct under Wisconsin penal statute for their actions in protest demonstrations on university campus against employment interviews in campus buildings); State v. Moore, 101 N.J. Super. 419, 244 A.2d 522 (1968) (defendant convicted under New Jersey statute of being a disorderly person at a Newark planning board meeting for refusing to accept rulings of the chair, or to leave the microphone and resume his seat; defendant was arrested and removed by a policeman); People v. Malone, 156 App. Div. 10, 141 N.Y.S. 149 (2d Dep't 1913) (suffragette convicted of disturbing political meeting by persisting to question Woodrow Wilson who had the floor, in disobedience of the chairman and in disregard of his commands; N. Y. Penal Law); In re Kay, 83 Cal. Rptr. 686, 464 P.2d 142 (1970) (defendants convicted by jury for disturbing a lawful meeting, a misdemeanor in violation of state penal code; convictions set aside); State v. Smith, 46 N.J. 510, 218 A.2d 147, cert. denied, Smith v. New Jersey, 385 U.S. 838 (1966) (defendants convicted of violating disorderly persons act at public meeting of city council; with unity of action they arranged themselves on floor outside council chambers and obstructed or interfered with persons lawfully in a public place); State v. Zwicker, 41 Wis. 2d 497, 164 N.W.2d 512, appeal dismissed, 316 U.S. 26 (1969) (defendants convicted of disorderly conduct under Wisconsin statute, arising out of student demonstrations on university campus against employment interviews by chemical manufacturer); United States v. Jones, 365 F.2d 675 (2d Cir. 1966) (defendants chained themselves to iron bars in front of windows on either side of three front entrances to Federal courthouse and caused Federal employees to force their way past the chained persons into the building. Convicted under Federal Assimilative Crimes Act and New York Penal Law); People v. Turner, 48 Misc. 2d 611, 265 N.Y.S.2d 841 (Sup. Ct.), aff'd, 17 N.Y.2d 829, 218 N.E.2d 316, 271 N.Y.S.2d 274 (1966), cert. denied, Turner v. New York, 386 U.S. 773 (1967) (convictions of disorderly conduct under New York statute in connection with a meeting held in a public square to protest involvement in Vietnam war and as to which the police ordered a dispersal).

A disorderly conduct statute is to be interpreted objectively, and not on a basis of the complainant's reaction. The defendant argued, for example, that "political oratory is offensive to many but should not, for that sole reason, be punishable as a crime." The court answered: "We do not think that the statute gauges criminality by the impressions made on an annoyed or disgruntled citizen. Common sense, and [court citations] dictate that language or conduct is to be adjudged to be disorderly, not merely because it offends some supersensitive or hypercritical individual, but because it is, by its nature, of a sort that is a substantial interference with (our old friend) the reasonable man." People v. Harvey, 307 N.Y. 588, 592, 123 N.E.2d 81, 83 (1954).

A person of ordinary intelligence can understand that certain "hard-core" acts may be prohibited. See United States v. Akison, 290 F. Supp. 212 (D. Colo. 1968); Wright v. City of Montgomery, 282 F. Supp. 291 (M.D. Ala. 1968), aff'd, 406 F.2d 867 (5th Cir. 1969), vacated and remanded, 401 U.S. 989 (1971).

A local legislative body has police power to make "all manner of wholesome

to bring such action within the commerce clause of the Constitution.[16] It has been suggested however, that "disputes about meeting or organizational rules or the power or authority of the chairman" should not be resolved by means of a criminal prosecution.[17]

An early case approached the meaningful factors of an unlawful disturbance in the following language: "What shall constitute an interruption and disturbance of a public meeting or assembly, cannot easily be brought within a definition, applicable to all cases; it must depend somewhat on the nature and character of each particular kind of meeting and the purposes for which it is held, and much also on the usage and practice governing such meetings. As the law has not defined what shall be deemed an interruption and disturbance, it must be decided as a question of fact in each particular case; and although it may not be easy to define it beforehand, there is commonly no great difficulty in ascertaining what is a wilful disturbance in a given case. It must be wilful and designed, an act not done through accident or mistake." [18]

---

and reasonable laws, statutes, and ordinances, with penalties or without, not repugnant to the Constitution, as they shall judge to be for the good and welfare of the Commonwealth, and of the subjects of the same. Whatever affects the peace, good order, morals, and health of the community comes within its scope." Brandon Shores, Inc. v. Incorporated Village of Greenwood Lake, 68 Misc. 2d 343, 325 N.Y.S.2d 957, 960 (Sup. Ct. 1971).

As to whether statute or ordinance providing penalty for unlawful disturbance is unconstitutionally vague, see Grayned v. City of Rockford, 408 U.S. 104 (1972) (municipal anti-noise ordinance); Landry v. Daley, 280 F. Supp. 968 (N.D. Ill.), appeal dismissed sub nom. Landry v. Boyle, 393 U.S. 220 (1968) (Chicago ordinance); Turner v. Goolsby, 255 F. Supp. 724, 726 (S.D. Ga. 1966) (state statute).

[16] The disturbance by a union of a meeting held by union members seeking a local charter for the international, and the threatening of the job and personal security of such members, may affect interstate commerce in such a manner as to bring such action within the commerce clause of the Constitution. Johnson v. Local Union No. 58, Internat'l Bro. of Elec. Wkrs., 181 F. Supp. 734 (E.D. Mich. 1960).

[17] The court reasoned that criminal statutes relating to the disturbance of meetings are inapplicable to one who breaches a meeting rule in the good faith belief that the rule is invalid. In re Kay, 83 Cal. Rptr. 686, n. 12, 464 P.2d 142, 152, n. 12 (1970).

[18] Commonwealth v. Porter, 67 Mass. (1 Gray) 476, 478, 480 (1854). The court observed that: "All assemblies, therefore, designed and properly adapted to accomplish these high and generous purposes, whether in the form

In the construction of a statute the words "interrupt" and "disturb" are to be given their plain and ordinary meaning unless the context, or the history of the statute, requires otherwise. Resort to dictionary meaning is permitted. In one case the defendants argued that the statute failed to define "interrupt" or "disturb" and consequently men of common intelligence must necessarily guess at its

---

of deliberative bodies, lectures, or even those characterized as meetings for amusements, if warranted by law, seem thus to be sanctioned and encouraged" by a provision of the Constitutional Declaration of Rights guaranteeing the right to assemble in an orderly and peaceable manner.

"The ordinance in question is a general regulation for all types of meetings. What constitutes a disturbance of a lawful assembly is not susceptible to specific definition, but must depend to some extent upon the nature and the character of the particular assemblage. However, while it may be difficult to specifically define beforehand, there is no problem in determining what constitutes a disturbance in a given case. In the instance of a city council, we hold that any conduct contrary to the normal presentation of business which disturbs or interrupts the orderly progress of the proceedings is a disturbance." State v. McNair, 178 Neb. 763, 135 N.W.2d 463, 465 (1965).

What constitutes a disturbance is not easily defined. "It must depend on the nature and character of each particular kind of meeting and the purposes for which it is held, and much on the usage and practice governing such meetings." The court also cited a dictionary definition that the term "to disturb" means "to throw into disorder; to move from a state of rest or regular order; to interrupt; to throw out of course or order." People v. Malone, 156 App. Div. 10, 141 N.Y.S. 149, 150 (2d Dep't 1913).

Custom may even permit the interruption of a meeting. Defendant parishioner arose during church services and challenged the minister on a point of doctrine. When he asked permission to address the congregation, no audible objection was heard. The court found that the utterance of the minister, when interrupted, was contrary to the doctrines of the church and therefore defendant was within his rights in interrupting to correct the mistake. The court held: "It is manifest from undisputed evidence that defendant interrupted a religious meeting, but it is not every interruption that constitutes a violation of law. Without violating the statute forbidding the interruption of a religious meeting, members of the society may repel a lawless invasion either from without or from within. Under the same principle, a member of a religious society, if permitted by its precepts and usages, may, in a becoming manner, with good motives, interrupt a minister to correct utterances at variance with established tenets or rites. Otherwise, freedom of worship and free speech might be impaired by bigotry and false doctrines. The proper and orderly exercise of these rights, though resulting in a commotion during a religious meeting, is not punishable in a criminal court." Note, however, that this case represents an isolated view. Gaddis v. State, 105 Neb. 303, 180 N.W. 590, 591 (1920).

meaning and thus be left in doubt as to what conduct is prohibited. The court responded: "It is difficult to believe that the defendants are as mystified as to the meaning of these ordinary English words as they profess to be in their brief. Clearly, they have grossly underestimated the powers of comprehension possessed by 'men of common intelligence.' Nevertheless, we treat this contention as having been seriously made." [19]

What constitutes disorderly behavior also depends on the attendant circumstances. " 'Disorderly behavior' are ordinary words in general use. Their meaning, however, is neither rigid or inflexible but depends upon the subject matter to which they relate, the context in which they were employed and the purpose sought to be accomplished by their use." [20] Generally, the offense of disturbing a meeting may be considered as an unlawful interruption or disturbance of an "assemblage of persons met together for any lawful purpose." [21] It has been held that: "Speaking generally, the rule applicable to disturbances of public assemblies is that any conduct which, being contrary to the usages of the particular sort of meeting and class of persons assembled, interferes with its due progress, or is annoying to the assembly in whole or in part, is a disturbance." [22] One may be guilty of disturbing a religious assembly by noise or indecent behavior which merely attracts the notice and attention of persons present, whether the witnesses say they were disturbed or not. "The gravamen of the offense is the indulgence of improper

[19] State v. Wiggins, 272 N.C. 147, 158 S.E.2d 37, 42 (1967), *cert. denied,* 390 U.S. 1028 (1968).

[20] The court also ruled: "The judge was right in instructing the jury that under the statute the plaintiff was disorderly if he failed to observe the ruling of the moderator on a question of order." Doggett v. Hooper, 306 Mass. 129, 27 N.E.2d 737, 740 (1940).

See State v. Davis, 21 Ohio App. 2d 261, 257 N.E.2d 79, 81 (1969) (dictionary definitions of "interrupt" and "disturb," with statement that the definition and meaning of these words "certainly are of common understanding"); State v. Wiggins, 272 N.C. 147, 158 S.E.2d 37, 42 (1967), *cert. denied,* 390 U.S. 1028 (1968) (meaning of "interrupt" and "disturb" when used in conjunction with word "school").

[21] State v. Watkins, 123 Tenn. 502, 130 S.W. 839 (1910).

[22] State v. Mancini, 91 Vt. 507, 101 A. 581, 583 (1917); *see* State v. McNair, 178 Neb. 763, 135 N.W.2d 463, 465 (1965).

conduct, and the attracting of the attention of any part of the assembly thereby; and when these facts occur the offense is complete." [23]

The nature of a meeting necessarily plays a major role in determining whether a given instance of misconduct substantially impairs the effective conduct of a meeting.[24]

A meeting may be unlawfully disturbed by a speaker who is given leave to speak, if his words are intentionally chosen and have a natural tendency to disturb the assemblage. Leave to speak at a religious gathering cannot justify or excuse a violent, passionate, and insulting discourse deliberately made, which by its violence offends the order and decorum essential to religious worship.[25]

§ 13.4   Decision of Jury

Ordinarily, it is for the jury to decide whether conduct at a meeting under all circumstances constitutes a disturbance,[26] and whether the assemblage is a meeting entitled to protection of the law.[27]

[23] Holt v. State, 60 Tenn. 192, 194 (1873).

[24] Generally, to convict for disturbing a meeting, it must be shown that the defendant "substantially impaired the conduct of the meeting by intentionally committing acts in violation of implicit customs or usages or of explicit rules for governance of the meeting, of which he knew, or as a reasonable man should have known." Whether a given instance of misconduct substantially impairs the effective conduct of a meeting depends upon the actual impact of that misconduct on the course of the meeting; the question cannot be resolved merely by asking persons present at the meeting whether any were "disturbed." *In re* Kay, 83 Cal. Rptr. 686, 464 P.2d 142, 150–51 (1970).

[25] The court added: "A member of the assemblage, though he be a member of the particular religious organization having control of the services, is bound to regard its peace and order." Lancaster v. State, 53 Ala. 398, 399 (1875).

[26] Defendant was convicted of disorderly conduct at a dance under a statute prescribing penalty for disturbing any lawful meeting by disorderly or unlawful acts. The court held: "And when persons attending an appointed lawful meeting of any description conduct themselves in a manner lawful in itself, but at variance with the purpose of the gathering and inconsistent with its orderly procedure, it will ordinarily be for the jury to say whether their conduct was such as amounted, in the circumstances, to a disturbance of the peace." State v. Mancini, 91 Vt. 507, 101 A. 581, 583 (1917).

[27] Whether an assemblage alleged to have been disturbed was an assemblage of people met for religious worship within the meaning of the statute was a

§ 13.5 Stockholder Meetings

Responsive answers to many questions of decorum will not easily be found in decided cases directly relating to the conduct of meetings of shareholders and members of a corporation.[28] There are few legal precedents in that area because company meetings, particularly in this country, have in the past been relatively free from the kind of interruptions and disturbances which have resulted in reported litigation, usually in the form of criminal prosecution of the disturber or in civil action by the ejected member or shareholder for illegal ejection or false arrest.[29] Shareholders have been escorted from and carried out of company meetings for persisting in disruptive conduct and refusing to accept the chairman's orders to desist and permit the meeting to continue in reasonably orderly fashion. Generally, the presiding officers have acted responsibly and with restraint, and the persons ejected have not attempted to justify their disruptive conduct by court proceedings.

It is therefore necessary to resort to analogous areas where the courts have been called upon to adjudicate the consequences of interruptions and disturbances at various public and private gatherings. Case law concerning the disturbance of religious assemblies,[30]

---

question properly submitted to the jury. Nix v. State, 27 Ala. App. 388, 173 So. 98 (1937).

Whether a congregation of persons constitutes a religious meeting assembled for religious worship is always a question of fact to be determined by the jury. Cline v. State, 9 Okla. Crim. Ct. App. 40, 130 P. 510 (1913).

[28] It is interesting to note that the Supreme Court in 1891 relied on decisions relating to private corporations and minor legislative bodies in ruling on a question of quorum within the houses of Congress. United States v. Ballin, 144 U.S. 1, 6, 7 (1892).

[29] There are published court decisions on different or related issues in which it has been noted that a shareholder or alleged shareholder was removed from the meeting. See, e.g., Leamy v. Sinaloa Explor. & Dev. Co., 15 Del. Ch. 28, 130 A. 282 (1925) (shareholder objected to legality of meeting with such persistence that he was ejected before any votes were received); Noller v. Wright, 138 Mich. 416, 101 N.W. 553 (1904) (plaintiff claimed to be a shareholder at annual meeting; officers denied this and, on plaintiff's refusal to leave, he was forcibly ejected).

See §§ 14.8 and 15.19 infra.

[30] See Annot., Conduct amounting to offense of disturbing public or religious meeting, 12 A.L.R. 650 (1920).

town meetings,[31] political and social gatherings, and meetings of municipal bodies, unincorporated associations, trade unions, and various other lawful assemblies is useful for this purpose.[32]

§ 13.6　Standard of Decorum Dependent on Setting and Type of Participants

Meetings of different groups have many basic similarities and common objectives. Their stated purposes are to consider and act upon the matters for which the meeting was called. This does not necessarily mean that all meetings must be judged by a single standard of decorum. It is obvious that the conduct of an individual may be proper and decorous in one setting, whereas the same conduct could be highly improper, even unlawfully disturbing, in another setting.[33] Generally, the differences in acceptable conduct

[31] For interesting case references relating to the powers of a town meeting moderator, *see* Doggett v. Hooper, 306 Mass. 129, 27 N.E.2d 737 (1940); Stebbins v. Merritt, 64 Mass. (10 Cush.) 27 (1852).

[32] *See* Note, Character of meeting essential to the offense of disturbing a meeting, 30 L.R.A. (N.S.) 829 (1910).

[33] In upholding convictions for disturbing a Congressional committee meeting, the court held: "It seems unnecessary to add that whether a given act provokes a breach of the peace depends upon the accompanying circumstances, that is, it is essential that the setting be considered in deciding whether the act offends the mores of the community." United States v. Woodard, 376 F.2d 136, 141 (7th Cir. 1967).

In determining whether a union member's freedom of expression had been inhibited by remarks of the presiding officer, it has been held that "this court must consider the setting in which the incident occurred. . . . Not every ungentlemanly remark made by a local union's president to a member" is a violation under the labor Bill of Rights. Broomer v. Schultz, 239 F. Supp. 669, 703 (E.D. Pa. 1965).

In discussing the application of a municipal antinoise ordinance to the disturbance of a school while in session, the court noted: "Different considerations, of course, apply in different circumstances. For example, restrictions appropriate to a single building high school during class hours would be inappropriate in many open areas on a college campus, just as an assembly that is permitted outside a dormitory would be inappropriate in the middle of a mathematics class." Grayned v. City of Rockford, 408 U.S. 104, 120, n. 45 (1972).

In considering whether a mass demonstration meeting of students and faculty in a university building constituted an unlawful disturbance, the court

may be related to the nature and type of meeting, the purpose for which it was convened, its customs and usages of the past, the right of members or shareholders to attend or to be absent, the right of those present to participate in the meeting or to abstain from its proceedings, as well as such statutory powers and limitations as may have been imposed by higher authority.

A case relating to the disturbance of a city council meeting expressed these principles in the following lucid words. "Surely, a man of ordinary intelligence knows the council chamber at the time of a public hearing is a public 'place of assembly.' So, too, such a man knows the 'quiet or good order' of a place depends upon the nature and the purpose and the needs of the meeting. He also knows a legislative chamber from a barroom or a ball park and knows what kind of behavior comports to each." [34]

Even church services may become a public nuisance which the authorities can abate. The court has considered disorderly church services to be of a class of nuisances which are not "nuisances per se" but which may become so by reason of their locality, surroundings, and method of conduct. "It is a question of peace and public order in a thickly populated community. The plaintiffs are entitled to maintain and practice any religious belief or religious principle, or teach any religious doctrine, which does not violate the laws of morality and property, and which does not infringe upon personal rights." But such rights cannot be extended to interfere with the rights of others or to violate peace and good order. [35]

Standards of decorum may also vary according to the type or occupation of the participants. For example, in considering the validity of action taken at a disorderly meeting of union seamen, the court spoke these words: "Having in mind the long smoldering

---

remarked that the university "might reasonably choose to treat this group differently than a dance or county political convention." Cholmakjian v. Board of Trustees, 315 F. Supp. 1335, 1346 (W.D. Mich. 1970).

[34] State v. Smith, 46 N.J. 510, 218 A.2d 147, 152, *cert. denied,* Smith v. New Jersey, 385 U.S. 838 (1966), *see* United States v. Woodard, 376 F.2d 136, 142, n. 6 (7th Cir. 1967).

[35] Services carried on daily in a thickly populated residential area until early hours in the morning wherein worshipers gave forth weird outcries and engaged in loud shouting and incessant noises, and disorderly throngs congregated in the streets, were held to constitute a public nuisance. Morison v. Rawlinson, 193 S.C. 25, 7 S.E.2d 635, 639–40 (1940).

resentment of many of the members toward the incumbent officers and the fact that the membership is composed of seamen, it is not to be expected that the meeting would proceed with the restraint and dignity of a meeting of the 'Ladies' Aid Society'." [36] In a recent case the court upheld an injunction under the labor Bill of Rights restraining a parent international union from assuming control over a meeting of a recalcitrant local union, holding that the members of the local should be "free from inhibiting controls" imposed on the meeting by "hostile outsiders," and that the Act protected them from such "unwanted beneficence." [37]

It has been argued that the statutory words "place of assembly, public or private" should not apply to a basketball game in a high school auditorium but should be restricted to "situations where solemnity or parliamentary order" is required. The court noted that the interpretation of what constitutes "quiet and good order" of any gathering will depend on the "character of the assembly," and that "government may impose a semblance of decorum, suitable to the given circumstances, in order to avert disorder." The court affirmed the conviction of a defendant for disturbing a place of assembly, based on evidence that he gestured obscenely and loudly uttered a lewd chant at the game. "Surely, it cannot be contended, merely because a basketball game is more noisy in nature than a legislative assembly, that spectators at the former may engage in unbridled behavior regardless of its effect on the other persons in attendance." [38] Another recent case, holding that the disturbance of a university commencement address violated a statute relating to the disturbance of a lawful assemblage, noted that: "Standards of acceptable behavior are generally known or can readily be determined, for most gatherings or assemblies, from the general and average conduct and standards of those attending such type of assemblage." The court aptly said: "Standing on a stadium seat at a graduation ceremony and shouting remarks at the Vice President of the United States, with whom you may disagree, is quite a different thing from standing on that same seat at a football game and

[36] Ash v. Holdeman, 13 Misc. 2d 528, 175 N.Y.S.2d 135, 141–42 (Sup. Ct.), *modified,* 5 App. Div. 2d 1017, 174 N.Y.S.2d 215 (3d Dep't 1958).

[37] Navarro v. Gannon, 385 F.2d 512, 519, 520 (2d Cir. 1967), *cert. denied,* 390 U.S. 989 (1968).

[38] State v. Morgulis, 110 N.J. Super. 454, 266 A.2d 136, 139 (1970).

informing the referee that you take exception to his last penalty call." [39]

§ 13.7   Change of Character of Meeting While in Progress

The courts have considered the question whether an assembly of persons initially met for a purpose protected by the law, having subsequently become a meeting or assemblage for some other purpose, loses the protection of the law during the time it met for such other purpose. In a recent case, the President of the United States was presented to and addressed an assembled religious crusade which had been in progress nightly for about a week. Defendant was convicted of the offense of disturbing a religious assembly by participating in an obscene demonstration during the evening the President spoke. In defense, the defendant claimed that the assemblage had "diverted" that evening from a primarily religious function into a political assemblage for political purposes and was, therefore, not entitled to protection of the law during the time that it met for some purpose other than religious worship. The court rejected this argument, holding: "We think the statute protects the assemblage from the time it assembles for worship until it disperses and ceases to be a congregation." [40] The same conclusion was reached in an early decision regarding a church business meeting which was held after the religious services were over.[41]

[39] State v. Davis, 21 Ohio App. 2d 261, 257 N.E.2d 79, 83 (1969).

[40] There was a conflict of testimony as to whether the obscenities took place during the presence of the President or during the choir singing and other religious portions of the meeting. The court observed that "there was a religious assemblage permeated with political overtones by the presence of the President, even though his subject was to a large extent spiritual in its content. On the other hand, we are satisfied that the sizeable majority of those in attendance at the meeting were there for the religious revival that had been under way all week prior to the eventful night." Reynolds v. Tennessee, Tenn. Crim. App. (Sept. 11, 1972), *cert. dismissed and remanded*, Tenn. Sup. Ct. (July 16, 1973), *cert. denied*, 414 U.S. 1163 (1974); *see* dissenting opinion.

[41] A religious congregation assembled to transact church business is entitled to the protection of the law against disturbing public worship. Thus, where the church judicature assembled after the religious services were over, for the trial of an offending member, a disturbance of such assembly is indictable. Protection extends to a religious assembly which might be engaged in public worship or in duties connected with their interests as a church. Hollingsworth v. State, 37 Tenn. 518 (1858).

There may be times within the course of a meeting or assembly at which dissent would be appropriate, whereas that same dissent would be highly objectionable at other times during the same meeting. If such is the case, the burden is on the dissenter to avoid an error in timing. A recent decision states that "one who invites himself to a private place of worship such as a church or synagogue in order to contest the teachings of its pastor, minister, or rabbi, in the presence of a congregation engaged in formal religious worship, should inform himself before doing so whether and when such a disputation would be considered less than offensive." [42] Constitutional rights protecting "unpopular views" do not "imply that persons wishing to exercise the right to express their views may comport themselves in a manner which will constitute disorderly conduct as defined in penal statutes." [43]

§ 13.8 Judicial Proceedings

The rules of decorum and civility in the courts are pertinent to this discussion. In a recent case the Supreme Court pronounced the following doctrine: "It is essential to the proper administration of criminal justice that dignity, order, and decorum be the hallmarks of all court proceedings in our country. The flagrant disregard in the courtroom of elementary standards of proper conduct should not and cannot be tolerated." The court held that a defendant may lose his constitutional right to be present at his own criminal trial if he persists in conduct so disorderly, disruptive, and disrespectful, that

---

[42] The court remarked: "Even a superficial inquiry would make it clear that the Canon of the Mass is a profound solemn experience for those participating in it. Even without any inquiry, it would seem that this is a fact which should be quite evident to any reasonably perceptive observer regardless of his personal religious conviction. The defendant in this case is a well educated man. . . . A stranger who imposes himself upon a congregation in a situation such as this in a way which gives the appearance of intentional obstruction of religious meditation by insulting remarks and bizarre behavior has exceeded the permissible limits of free speech and has infringed upon the rights of others to worship according to the dictates of their conscience." State v. Olson, 178 N.W.2d 230, 232 (Minn. 1970).

[43] People v. Martin, 43 Misc. 2d 355, 251 N.Y.S.2d 66, 67 (Sup. Ct. 1964), aff'd, 15 N.Y.2d 993, 259 N.Y.S.2d 152, cert. denied, 382 U.S. 828 (1965).

his trial cannot be carried on with him in the courtroom.[44] Another recent case holds that the court is not "a public hall for the expression of views, nor is it a political arena or a street. It is a place for trial of defined issues in accordance with law and rules of evidence, with standards of demeanor for court, jurors, parties, witnesses and counsel. All others are absolutely silent nonactors with the right only to use their eyes and ears." [45]

§ 13.9   Political Meetings

A distinction between the meetings of deliberative assemblies and political meetings where the public interest in an "active and critical audience" has long been recognized. In a recent case involving a protest at a holiday celebration in a public park, the court said: "Under most circumstances, of course, ordinary good taste and decorum would dictate that a person addressing a meeting need not be interrupted or otherwise disturbed. The Constitution does not require that any person, however lofty his motives, be permitted to obstruct the convention or continuation of a meeting without regard to the implicit customs and usages or explicit rules governing its conduct. . . . The constitutional guarantees of the free exercise of religious opinion, and of the rights of the people peaceably to assemble and petition for a redress of grievances, would be worth little if outsiders could disrupt and prevent such a meeting in dis-

---

[44] Illinois v. Allen, 397 U.S. 337, *rehearing denied,* 398 U.S. 915 (1970).

Regulation of order and behavior in the courtroom is within the judicial functions of the judge. Skolnick v. Campbell, 398 F.2d 23 (7th Cir. 1968).

"The courts must take such steps by rule and regulation that will protect their processes from prejudicial outside interferences." Sheppard v. Maxwell, 384 U.S. 333, 363 (1966).

The presiding justice may punish the defendant for contumacious behavior committed in the immediate presence of the court. Defendant's return to the courtroom after he had been banned during pendency of his ongoing trial, his subsequent refusal to obey an order to leave, and his provocative language in open court warranted such punishment. Gumbs v. Martinis, 40 App. Div. 2d 194, 338 N.Y.S.2d 817 (1st Dep't 1972).

Business cannot be conducted unless the court can suppress disturbances by immediate punishment. *Ex parte* Terry, 128 U.S. 289 (1888); *see* Cox v. Louisiana, 379 U.S. 536 (1965) (disturbance outside courthouse door).

[45] *In re* Katz v. Murtagh, 28 N.Y.2d 234, 240, 269 N.E.2d 816 (1971).

regard of the customs and rules applicable to it." The court then observed that this inhibition does not mean that a state, in enforcing a statute preventing the disruption of meetings, "can grant to the police a 'roving commission' to enforce Robert's Rules of Order, since other First Amendment interests are likewise at stake." The court found that: "The customs and usages of political conventions may countenance prolonged, raucous, boisterous demonstrations as an accepted element of the meeting process; similar behavior would violate the customs and usage of a church service. Audience participation may be enthusiastically welcomed at a bonfire football rally or an athletic contest, but considered taboo at a solemn ceremony of a fraternal order." Since the nature of the meeting contemplated the acceptance of nonviolent expressions of alternative viewpoints, the court held that a nonviolent protest "did not impair the conduct of the meeting but instead constituted a legitimate element of it." [46]

However, a shareholders' meeting is not a political gathering. In a leading case the court held that it is not the policy of Congress, as enacted in securities legislation, to view disputes between shareholders in a proxy fight as "political contests, with each side free to hurl charges with comparative unrestraint, the assumption being that the opposing side is then at liberty to thus effectively deflate the 'campaign oratory' of its adversary." It follows that the chairman should make every effort to conduct a proxy fight meeting in such manner as to avoid that consequence.[47]

The Supreme Court has said that debate on public issues should be "uninhibited, robust, and wide-open" and may well include "vehement, caustic, and sometimes unpleasantly sharp attacks on government and public officials." [48] However, the same court has well observed that insulting or "fighting" words, and words which by their very utterance inflict injury or tend to incite an immediate breach of the peace, are "no essential part of any exposition of ideas, and are of such slight social value as a step to truth that any benefit

[46] *In re* Kay, 83 Cal. Rptr. 686, 464 P.2d 142, 148, 150, 151 (1970); *see* State v. Morgulis, 110 N.J. Super. 454, 266 A.2d 136 (1970) (disturbance at high school basketball game).

[47] SEC v. May, 229 F.2d 123 (2d Cir. 1956), *aff'g* 134 F. Supp. 247 (S.D.N.Y. 1955).

[48] New York Times Co. v. Sullivan, 376 U.S. 254, 270 (1964).

that may be derived from them is clearly outweighed by the social interest in order and morality." [49]

§ 13.10   Intent To Disturb

Generally, intent to disturb a meeting is not a necessary element in the offense of causing a disturbance, if the offensive acts were done willfully. In reviewing a conviction for disturbing public worship, the appellate court said: "Intent to disturb is not a necessary element of the offense. Any acts which come within the provision of the statute, the natural consequence of which is to disturb, which are done willfully, and which in fact do disturb the people assembled for worship, come under the prohibition of the statute." [50]

[49] Chaplinsky v. New Hampshire, 315 U.S. 568, 572 (1942); *see* State v. Zwicker, 41 Wis. 2d 497, 164 N.W.2d 512, 519 (1969).

[50] Culpepper v. State, 8 Div. 509, 32 Ala. App. 274, 25 So. 2d 56 (1946).

A recent decision interpreting a statute providing that any person who "willfully disturbs or breaks up any assembly or meeting not unlawful in its character" is guilty of a misdemeanor, holds that, generally, if disturbances are occasioned by nonviolent exercise of free expression, the statute will require that defendants be shown to have "engaged in such conduct with knowledge, or under circumstances in which they should have known, that they were violating an applicable custom, usage, or rule of the meeting." The court added: "Not every violation of a general custom or of an explicit meeting rule becomes so grave as to warrant application of criminal sanctions." *In re* Kay, 83 Cal. Rptr. 686, 464 P.2d 142, 151–52 (1970).

When considered criminally, a disturbance must have been willful and "not due to accident or mistake." People v. Malone, 156 App. Div. 10, 14, 141 N.Y.S. 149, 152 (2d Dep't 1913).

Ejection from a meeting, however, is essentially the exercise of a self-protective right, not a punitive sanction, and therefore willfulness or design need not be present. Wall v. Lee, 34 N.Y. 141, 145 (1865).

In an action for false imprisonment against church officers for removing and arresting plaintiff for disturbing a church meeting, allegations in the answer that plaintiff expressed an intention to make the disturbance, and had at previous times made similar disturbances, are not relevant and may be struck out. Beckett v. Lawrence, 7 Abb. Pr. (n.s.) 403 (N.Y. Sup. Ct. 1869).

Defendant was prosecuted for disturbing a religious assembly by singing and hilarity, causing the congregation to erupt in laughter. The court found no intention to unlawfully disturb, but observed: "It would seem that the defendant is a proper subject for the discipline of his church, but not for the discipline of the courts." State v. Linkhaw, 69 N.C. 214, 217 (1873).

Thus, a defendant who appeared at a church in a drunken condition while services were being conducted, and stood on the outside and talked in a loud voice so as to disturb those in attendance, may be guilty of disturbing the church service not because he did not approve of the service but solely because he was under the influence of intoxicating liquor.[51]

In a recent case the defendant was convicted of the offense of disturbing a religious assembly. "He reasons that his only participation was to urge that the demonstration be peaceful, that there was no specific intent on his part to disturb the assembly, and that he did not personally participate in the prohibited acts. We are satisfied that the defendant did not chant obscenities and that his intent was for a peaceful demonstration. Yet, he admits to protesting the appearance of the President, and he admits to participation in the organizing of the protest. The acts of the group under these conditions bring this defendant within the ambit of being an aider and abettor. . . . Thus, we hold that the obscenities from the group and the chanting by the group, which occurred at the assembly during its various religious and non-religious portions, are also his acts by his participation in the group. He cannot escape responsibility for his participation in planning the demonstration by relating he personally himself did not do the unlawful acts, which arose during the event. We find the evidence supports the verdict." On appeal it was held that defendant was guilty as a principal offender, and not merely as an aider and abettor.[52] However, intent is an important factor. "It has long been true that guilt may turn upon the intent with which something itself innocent is possessed or done. A kitchen knife may be a weapon and a chisel a burglar tool, depending on the intent of the holder." These words were written in

---

Act of disturbing a religious ceremony must be willfully done to constitute an offense. Nix v. State, 27 Ala. App. 388, 173 So. 98 (1937).

"The law does not permit us to infer because a person has resorted to violence on some past occasions that he will necessarily do so in the future." Collin v. Chicago Park Dist., 460 F.2d 746, 754 (7th Cir. 1972) (meeting in public park).

[51] Holt v. State, 186 S.E. 147 (Ga. 1936).

[52] Reynolds v. Tennessee, Tenn. Crim. App. (Sep. 11, 1972), *cert. dismissed and remanded,* Tenn. Sup. Ct. (July 16, 1973), *cert. denied,* 414 U.S. 1163 (1974); *see* dissenting opinion.

an opinion holding that the offense of entering a school "with the intent of disturbing classes" was complete upon entry with the forbidden purpose.[53]

An organized scheme designed to create an incident at a religious gathering held in a municipally owned amphitheater has been held unquestionably to be a willful act in violation of a statute prohibiting the disturbance of a religious assemblage.[54] Where defendants acted willfully together to harass and disturb members of a church in their worship service, they effectively denied the members their constitutionally guaranteed right to freedom of worship. "Their conduct, if condoned, will lead to a breakdown in this society. It should not be tolerated, and it will be enjoined." [55]

In a recent case, the court upheld a conviction for disturbing a meeting of a city council. To the defendant's claim that he had the right to appear and protest, the court replied that he had not been denied a chance to be heard. "Rather he was denied a right he seemingly claimed to interfere with the right of others to hear and be heard. He was not ordered removed because he expressed views which displeased the presiding officer. He was ordered out because, in response to the president's call for quiet, he threatened even greater disruption of this public meeting. Whether the forum be the courtroom or the chamber of the legislature itself or of a political subdivision of the State, there must be order. It is frivolous

[53] State v. Young, 57 N.J. 240, 271 A.2d 569, 570, 573, 576 (1970).

[54] Ford v. State, 210 Tenn. 105, 355 S.W.2d 102, *rehearing denied,* 210 Tenn. 114, 356 S.W.2d 726 (1962), *cert. denied,* 377 U.S. 994, *rehearing denied,* Ford v. Tennessee, 379 U.S. 870 (1964).

"We decided that there might be recklessness without willfulness. We are now asked to declare that, if there is recklessness, there cannot be willfulness. We cannot assent to this. An act may be careless, heedless, rash, reckless, and still be willful." Johnson v. State, 92 Ala. 82, 9 So. 539, 540 (1891).

[55] Central Presbyterian Church v. Black Liberation Front, 303 F. Supp. 894, 900–1 (E.D. Mo. 1969).

Demonstrators acting in concert entered a church to disrupt religious services and deprived the members of their rights of freedom of assembly, speech, worship, and enjoyment of their property. They wore semimilitary-type uniforms and carried walkie-talkie equipment and a preprinted list of demands. An injunction was granted. Gannon v. Action, 303 F. Supp. 1240 (E.D. Mo. 1969), *aff'd in part and remanded,* 450 F.2d 1227 (8th Cir. 1971).

to suggest the First Amendment stands in the way of that imperative." [56]

§ 13.11   Time, Place, and Character

An unlawful interruption or disturbance of a meeting or assemblage need not necessarily occur while the members are in session.
Nor is it necessary that the disturbance occur within the confines of
the meeting room.

A meeting can be interrupted and disturbed unlawfully by acts
or events occurring: outside the meeting room; [57] and both within
and without the room; [58] before the meeting actually starts; [59] during

[56] State v. Smith, 46 N.J. 510, 218 A.2d 147, 150, *cert. denied,* Smith v.
New Jersey, 385 U.S. 838 (1966).

[57] The law guards religious meetings so carefully that it makes it an offense
to do certain things within one mile of the place at which meetings are held,
although no actual disturbance be proven to have been occasioned thereby.
The theory of the law is that the doing of these prohibited things within such
close proximity to the place of such meetings is inconsistent with and violative
of the spirit and harmony of such meetings, and the law therefore necessarily
implies a disturbance thereof. Cline v. State, 9 Okla. Crim. Ct. App. 40, 130
P. 510 (1913).

The discharge of a pistol in the near vicinity of a congregation assembled
for divine services is sufficient to justify conviction for disturbing the congregation. Folds v. State, 123 Ga. 167, 51 S.E. 305 (1905).

One defendant was convicted of disturbing a congregation by unhitching
an old shabby horse and buggy and driving up in front of a Sunday school in
session, with the intent of mortifying the prosecuting witness by exhibiting her
"sorry turnout" and causing the people assembled at the Sunday school to laugh
at her discomfiture. Wyatt v. State, 56 Tex. Crim. 50, 119 S.W. 1147 (1909).

[58] Appellant, convicted of disturbing public worship, talked loudly, went
in and out of the building, moved about in the room and "hollered" from outside the window to someone inside, all while church services were in progress.
The conviction was affirmed, the court holding: "It is not a requisite of proof
that the disturbance be within the house or that the religious program or doc-
trinal ceremonies be actually in progress." Culpepper v. State, 8 Div. 509, 32
Ala. App. 274, 25 So. 2d 56 (1946).

A defendant schoolteacher's conduct resulted in the disturbance of and
interference with the quiet and good order of a school assembly when he spoke
several words and made a motioning gesture while walking to the rear and
leaving the auditorium with several students following him out. "This court
is aware that the First Amendment rights of freedom of speech and assembly

an intermission or luncheon period; [60] or after the meeting has ended.[61] Thus, the protection of the law extends not only to the

are available to teachers and students within the schoolhouse as well as without; 'they do not shed such rights at the school house gate' . . . . If defendant's conduct is to be permitted in this instance, then the school authorities must allow any other student or teacher to arise in any other assembly program and speak his mind. This cannot be tolerated." State v. Besson, 110 N.J. Super. 528, 266 A.2d 175, 178, (1970) (note distinction between school building and grounds such as sidewalks and parking lots).

Persons may withdraw from a religious meeting for a temporary purpose without necessarily losing the protection of the meeting. Stovall v. State, 173 Miss. 755, 163 So. 504 (1935) (swearing at deacon of church outside front door while taking collection, not heard by congregation inside).

Noisy demonstrations which disrupt or are incompatible with normal school activities may be prohibited next to a school when classes are in session. In discussing a municipal antinoise ordinance, the court said: "We recognize that the ordinance prohibits some picketing that is neither violent nor physically obstructive. Noisy demonstrations that disrupt or are incompatible with normal school activities are obviously within the ordinance's reach. Such expressive conduct may be constitutionally protected at other places or other times [citations], but next to a school, while classes are in session, it may be prohibited. The anti noise ordinance imposes no such restriction on expressive activities before or after the school session, while the student/faculty 'audience' enters or leaves the school." Grayned v. City of Rockford, 408 U.S. 104, 120 (1972).

[59] A defendant entered a schoolhouse and locked the door from the inside, forbidding entrance to the teacher and pupils. It was held that such action constituted disturbance of a school in violation of statute. The court said: "To interrupt and disturb a school necessarily includes, not only acts which disturb the school while in session, but also those which prevent the school from assembling. A school is as much interrupted or disturbed by preventing the assembly as by breaking it up after it is assembled. The statute is aimed at the protection and peaceable conduct of schools. The fact of calling to order, therefore, is without significance." Douglass v. Barber, 18 R.I. 459, 28 A. 805 (1894).

One who takes possession of the doorstep of a church and by curses and threats prevents a congregation of persons, lawfully assembled for divine service, from entering the church, is guilty of disturbing divine service. Tanner v. State, 126 Ga. 77, 54 S.E. 914 (1906).

Defendants were convicted of disturbing a place of assembly by arranging themselves on the floor outside the city council chambers, thereby obstructing and interfering with passage into the chamber. State v. Smith, 46 N.J. 510, 218 A.2d 147, cert. denied, Smith v. New Jersey, 385 U.S. 838 (1966).

[60] Where a congregation assembled for divine worship had adjourned for dinner on the church grounds after the morning service, with the intention of returning after the meal to the churchhouse for an afternoon service, the con-

gregation had not dispersed while partaking of their dinner but were still assembled for the purpose of divine worship. Folds v. State, 123 Ga. 167, 51 S.E. 305 (1905).

One who disturbed the members of a church while they were eating a basket dinner just outside the church, during a short intermission between the morning and afternoon services, is guilty of disturbing religious worship. "If a congregation is assembled upon the church grounds for religious worship, the statute is applicable, and the assemblage is under its protection, although the disturbance takes place at a time when the religious services are not in progress." Ellis v. State, 10 Ala. 252, 65 So. 412 (1914).

[61] Disturbing conduct may warrant ejection after the meeting has adjourned if the members have not yet left the premises. An early New York court reasoned: "It has been suggested in justification of the plaintiff that at the time of the occurrence the religious services in the church were closed. . . . I do not, however, regard the suggestion, if it were true in fact, of any value. The act of disturbance is within the statute, if the assemblage has met for purposes of religious worship. The religious services need not have been actually in progress." Wall v. Lee, 34 N.Y. 141, 149–50 (1865).

To constitute a disturbance of an assemblage it is not necessary that the disturbance be made during the progress of religious services, if made after the conclusion of the services and the dismissal of the congregation, but while a portion of the people still remain in the house and before a reasonable time has elapsed for their dispersion. Kinney v. State, 38 Ala. 225 (1862).

Defendants attended a school board meeting for a proper purpose but refused to leave within a reasonable time after conclusion of the meeting at 9:30 P.M. upon request of the authorities, and obstructed efforts of school officials to close the school building. People v. Martin, 43 Misc. 2d 355, 251 N.Y.S.2d 66 (1964), aff'd, 15 N.Y.2d 993, 259 N.Y.S.2d 152, cert. denied, 382 U.S. 828 (1965).

Defendants attending a mass demonstration meeting of students and faculty in a university building refused to leave when the building officially closed at 11 P.M. because they "were having a good discussion and wanted to stay." Arrests were made for violation of trespass laws. The court observed that the university "might reasonably choose to treat this group differently than a dance or county political convention." Cholmakjian v. Board of Trustees, 315 F. Supp. 1335, 1346 (W.D. Mich. 1970).

Defendants refused to leave the office of a village urban renewal agency after closing time and after having been requested by police to leave, and were then arrested and physically removed from premises. They were held guilty of disorderly conduct and not entitled to protection of the first and fourteenth amendments. People v. Kern, 56 Misc. 2d 557, 289 N.Y.S.2d 71 (Sup. Ct. 1968).

A defendant who refused to leave after a street protest meeting, and when placed under arrest, ran into a crowd and laid down on the sidewalk and again refused to leave, was held guilty of disorderly conduct. People v. Knight, 35 Misc. 2d 216, 228 N.Y.S.2d 981 (Magistrate's Ct. 1962).

assembly while actually engaged in the conduct of its affairs, but it begins as soon as the members have gathered at the place of meeting and continues until they have dispersed. Persons may withdraw from the meeting temporarily without losing protection of the meeting.[62]

In an early decision involving the disturbance of religious worship, the court held that any act or discourse at or near to the congregation, the natural tendency of which is to disturb the assemblage —to derange its quiet and order—must be regarded as a statutory offense. "Nor is it necessary that the assemblage should have been actually engaged in worship at the moment of the discourse, or of the conduct of which complaint is made. The statute intends its protection shall extend to the assemblage when it is in the act of gathering together at the place appointed for worship; while the exercises are in progress; and until there is a dispersion of the persons who have come together, and they cease to be an assemblage or congregation." [63]

But see State v. Jones, 53 Mo. 486, 489 (1873), holding: "There must be some point of time when the purpose for which the congregation met is ended; and that time has always been understood to be when the head of the congregation dismisses it."

[62] Stovall v. State, 173 Miss. 755, 163 So. 504 (1935).

[63] Lancaster v. State, 53 Ala. 398, 399 (1875).

After church was dismissed and the pastor and part of the congregation were on their way home, the defendant and others engaged in a broil. The defendant by cursing and swearing disturbed those then on the grounds. It was held that the defendant was rightly convicted of disturbing a congregation assembled for religious worship. The court said: "We are of opinion that the object, purpose, spirit and letter of the law are to protect the religious assembly from disturbance before and after services, as well as during the actual service, and so long as any portion of the congregation remains upon the ground; and so believing, we think the defendant was rightly and legally convicted." Dawson v. State, 7 Tex. Ct. App. 59, 60 (1879).

Disturbance of a religious assemblage need not be committed before dismissal of the congregation. "The congregation has the right to convene, worship, and disperse without malicious or willful interruption." State v. Matheny, 122 S.C. 459, 101 S.E. 661 (1919).

Defendants excited and disturbed the congregation after the services were over and the congregation had been dismissed and began to leave, some being still in the church, some in the churchyard, and others having left for home. "It is obvious, from the language of the statute, that the Legislature did not only intend to protect from disturbance a congregation while actually engaged

Where a statute forbade disturbing a religious assembly in whole or in part, any one member is considered a part of the congregation. Thus, a disturbance of one member is sufficient to warrant a conviction under the statute.[64]

---

in worship, but they intended to extend their protection to all 'congregations,' which had 'assembled for the purpose of worshipping,' and this protection continues from the time the congregation assembles until it disperses and ceases to be a congregation." Williams v. State, 35 Tenn. 313, 315 (1855).

See references: Disturbance of Public Meetings, 27 C.J.S. 815–27; Annot., Conduct amounting to offense of disturbing public or religious meeting, 12 A.L.R. 650–59 (1920); Note: Character of meeting essential to the offense of disturbing a meeting, 30 L.R.A. (NS) 829 (1910).

Defendant was convicted of disturbing a religious assembly in violation of a state statute. He contended that the trial court's instructions were defective in that they protected a congregation from being disturbed not only while actually engaged in worship but also while merely assembled for the purpose of worshiping. He reasoned the instructions extended the statute beyond its import so as to protect activities not considered religious. The appellate court held: "We think the statute protects the assemblage from the time it assembles for worship until it disperses and ceases to be a congregation." Reynolds v. Tennessee, Tenn. Crim. App. (Sep. 11, 1972), cert. dismissed and remanded, Tenn. Sup. Ct. (July 16, 1973), cert. denied, 414 U.S. 1163 (1974) (see dissenting opinion).

[64] In a recent case the appellate court approved the following charge to the jury: "It is not necessary that the whole congregation or any part of it, engaged in religious exercises should be interrupted; it is sufficient if one member of the congregation should be interrupted while so engaged." Reynolds v. Tennessee, Tenn. Crim. App. (Sep. 11, 1972), cert. dismissed and remanded, Tenn. Sup. Ct. (July 16, 1973), cert. denied, 414 U.S. 1163 (1974) (dissenting opinion).

The disturbance of any member of a congregation assembled for religious worship is, in law, a disturbance of the congregation. Defendant in a low tone or whisper used insulting and offensive language and called a member of the congregation a liar, while the congregation was engaged in singing. He was unheard and unnoticed by any other members of the congregation. It was held that every individual worshipper in the congregation, as well as the entire congregation, is protected by the statute from rude and profane disturbance during the solemn moments of public worship. "If the whole congregation must be disturbed to make out the charge, not only one person, but a dozen, or any less number of persons than the whole congregation, may be disturbed by a rude, ill-mannered man, without subjecting himself to punishment." State v. Wright, 41 Ark. 410, 414 (1883).

Every individual worshiper in the congregation, as well as the entire congregation, is protected by the statute from rude and profane disturbance dur-

An unlawful disturbance need not be accompanied by noise or excitement, and may occur while the meeting remains "still and silent." [65] Although the disturber may not be noisy, he can disturb and interfere with the conduct of a meeting to the point where the assembly becomes noisy.[66] A disturbance need not be rude, profane, or indecent.[67] In fact, an unlawful disturbance can be caused by inaction or may be "wholly passive," such as by falling limp on the

---

ing the solemn moments of divine worship. McVea v. State, 26 S.W. 834 (Tex. Civ. App. 1894).

Where a statute prohibited the disturbance of a congregation or a "part of a congregation," it was held that any member of the congregation is a part of the congregation. Wyatt v. State, 56 Tex. Crim. 50, 119 S.W. 1147, 1148 (1909).

Swearing at the deacon of a church while he is taking a collection outside the front door, though not heard by the congregation inside, constitutes a disturbance. Stovall v. State, 173 Miss. 755, 163 So. 504 (1935).

"We are of opinion that there is no error in this. Every individual worshiper in the congregation, as well as the entire congregation is protected by the object and policy of our statutes, from rude and profane disturbance during the solemn moments of public worship. And he who thus disturbs one worshiper, cannot, in reason or in law, alledge that he has not disturbed a congregation while engaged in public worship. The protection intended by the law, would amount to little, if the congregation might in detail, through each of the individuals composing it, be disturbed with impunity." Cockreham v. State, 7 Hump. 11, 12, 13 (Tenn. 1846); accord, Nichols v. State, 103 Ga. 61, 29 S.E. 431 (1897).

This line of cases has been described as representing "patently trivial violations of meeting rules and practices." In re Kay, 83 Cal. Rptr. 686, 464 P.2d 142, 151, n.11 (1970); see Annot., 12 A.L.R. 650, 651 (1920) (conduct amounting to offense of disturbing public or religious meeting).

[65] "If the audience had remained still and silent, nevertheless the defendant would have disturbed the meeting when she refused to obey the chairman, and when she prevented the speaker by her attitude and her words from continuing his address after he had closed the incident." People v. Malone, 156 App. Div. 10, 141 N.Y.S. 149, 151 (2d Dep't 1913).

[66] The court said: "[A]lthough he was not noisy, he certainly disturbed and interfered with the conduct of the hearing. His disregard of chairman Booker's repeated rulings and requests that he leave the microphone, his insistence upon his point of order, and the ad hominem remarks he addressed to the chair, disrupted the meeting to the point where the assembly became noisy . . . [and] those in the audience took to the aisles." State v. Moore, 101 N.J. Super. 419, 244 A.2d 522, 524 (1968) (city planning board hearing).

[67] Ford v. State, 210 Tenn. 105, 355 S.W.2d 102 (1962), cert. denied, Ford v. Tennessee, 377 U.S. 994 (1964).

floor and being carried out, as well as by jumping and shouting, causing a general commotion.[68] It is conceivable that those attending an assemblage may speak with others seated nearby and even make certain hand gestures, without causing an unlawful disturbance. And, obviously, "any of those in attendance have the right to remain silent and, by doing so, express their displeasure or dissent

---

[68] Defendant was convicted of disorderly conduct at a Congressional committee hearing. The court said that defendant's action "in falling limp on the floor was an intentional resistance to the authority of those designated to maintain order [U. S. Marshals] on the premises. The jury could find that such disruptive behavior was so unreasonable, given the attending circumstances, as to constitute disorderly conduct within the meaning of the statute." United States v. Woodard, 376 F.2d 136, 140 (7th Cir. 1967).

Defendant was guilty of contempt of court for conduct amounting to obstruction of justice when he refused to rise and approach the bench on direction of the judge but fell limp and lay prostrate on the floor when the court addressed him. Comstock v. United States, 419 F.2d 1128 (9th Cir. 1969).

Several defendants were convicted of disorderly conduct for disturbing a meeting of the city council when, with unity of action, they arranged themselves on the floor outside the council chambers door, thereby obstructing passage into the chambers. One defendant was also found guilty of another charge for resisting efforts to remove him when he locked arms with another person and went limp on the floor. State v. Smith, 46 N.J. 510, 218 A.2d 147, *cert. denied,* Smith v. New Jersey, 385 U.S. 838 (1966).

Defendants chained themselves to heavy ornamental iron bars in front of windows at the sides of the front entrances to the courthouse, causing Federal employees to enter through side entrances. Convictions for disorderly conduct were affirmed. United States v. Jones, 365 F.2d 675 (2d Cir. 1966).

Sitting on the floor in front of a teller's window of a savings and loan association, with the result that customers had to be served elsewhere, constitutes a "disturbance." People v. Weinberg, 6 Mich. App. 345, 149 N.W.2d 248 (1967).

A defendant was convicted of breach of peace for entering a church during a reverential part of the service to "create a dialogue." When told to sit down or leave he went limp, forcing the ushers to haul him outside bodily. The conviction was affirmed. State v. Olson, 178 N.W.2d 230 (Minn. 1970).

A defendant who, after participating in a protest assembly, refused to leave after conclusion of the meeting and laid down on the sidewalk and again refused to move, was held guilty of disorderly conduct. People v. Knight, 35 Misc. 2d 216, 228 N.Y.S.2d 981 (Magistrate's Ct. 1962).

A defendant was arrested while participating in a demonstration in a college campus building, and "went limp" when officers attempted to remove him. His disorderly conduct conviction was sustained. State v. Zwicker, 41 Wis. 2d 497, 164 N.W.2d 512, 515 (1969).

with what is being said." [69] And, when a disturbance occurs, it need not be "complete or enduring" and does not require a "total frustration." [70]

Silence accompanied by objectionable action is a different matter. The disturbance of a congregation engaged in divine service may be by the spoken word or by indecent acting. "One might remain mute, yet by improper conduct interrupt or disturb the service." [71]

Evil thoughts alone do not constitute a disturbance. "Nor would peaceable assembly with evil thoughts do so either. Thus, a quiet meeting in a backroom of two or more persons even if it were to conjure up some future violation of law, is permissible. It is only when such assembly results in the commission of overt acts that it becomes unlawful." [72]

Under some circumstances, the intent to disturb is relevant. In a recent decision involving an interruption and disturbance at a school, the court said, "It is also irrelevant that the defendants marched silently, were not on the school grounds, and neither threatened nor provoked violence. Their actions can admit of no interpretation other than that they were planned and carried out for the sole purpose of attracting and holding the attention of students or teachers" at a time when they should have been engaged in instructional activities.[73]

[69] State v. Davis, 21 Ohio App. 2d 261, 257 N.E.2d 79 (1969) (university commencement exercises conducted at university stadium). A hostile audience is not a basis for restraining otherwise legal First Amendment activity. Collin v. Chicago Park Dist., 460 F.2d 746 (7th Cir. 1972) (meeting in public park).

[70] State v. Smith, 46 N.J. 510, 218 A.2d 147, 152, cert. denied, Smith v. New Jersey, 385 U.S. 838 (1966).

[71] Jones v. State, 219 Ga. 848, 136 S.E.2d 358, 363, cert. denied, Jones v. Georgia, 379 U.S. 935 (1964).

A schoolteacher's conduct was held to result in the disturbance and interference with the quiet and good order of a school assembly, when he spoke several words and made a motioning gesture while walking to the rear and leaving the auditorium with several students following him out. State v. Besson, 110 N.J. Super. 528, 266 A.2d 175 (1970).

A defendant attended a high school basketball game and "gestured obscenely and loudly uttered a lewd chant." He was arrested and quietly led out of the gymnasium. State v. Morgulis, 110 N.J. Super. 454, 266 A.2d 136, 137 (1970).

[72] Hunter v. Allen, 286 F. Supp. 830 (N.D. Ga. 1968), aff'd, 422 F.2d 1158 (5th Cir. 1970), rev'd, 401 U.S. 989 (1971).

[73] State v. Wiggins, 272 N.C. 147, 158 S.E.2d 37 (1967), cert. denied, 390 U.S. 1028 (1968).

A meeting can also be interrupted or disturbed by the wearing of clothing or articles intended to be so distractive as to interfere with the normal progress of the meeting.[74] On the other hand, the character and setting of the meeting must be considered in judging the applicable standards of decorum. For example, the wearing of

[74] Wearing a false mustache at a religious service has been held to be rude or indecent behavior. Williams v. State, 83 Ala. 68, 3 So. 743 (1887).

Wearing an orange lily having a disruptive political implication at a political gathering. Humphries v. Connor, 17 Ir. C.L.R. 1·(1864); see SHAW AND SMITH, THE LAW OF MEETINGS at 17, 25.

Wearing a hat and smoking a cigar at a Salvation Army religious service. Hull v. State, 120 Ind. 153, 22 N.E. 117 (1889).

Use of profane language and smoking a cigarette at a religious meeting conducted by the Salvation Army. State v. Stuth, 11 Wash. 423, 39 P. 665 (1895).

Wearing clothing in disarray at a religious meeting with the intent to cause a disturbance. Green v. State, 56 S.W. 915 (Texas Cr. App. 1900).

The wearing of "freedom buttons" by school children may be prohibited when the wearing, distributing, discussing, and promoting of buttons results in an "unusual degree of commotion, boisterous conduct, a collision with the rights of others, an undermining of authority, and a lack of order, discipline and decorum." Blackwell v. Issaquena County Board of Educ., 363 F.2d 749, 754 (5th Cir. 1966); see Gannon v. Action, 303 F. Supp. 1240 (E.D. Mo. 1969) (demonstrators acting in concert to disrupt church services, including use of semimilitary-type uniforms, walkie-talkie equipment, preprinted list of demands).

But see Tinker v. Des Moines Indep. Community School Dist., 393 U.S. 503 (1969) (holding that the wearing of black armbands in a school as a war protest is "symbolic speech" which is "akin to pure speech" and therefore protected by the first and fourteenth amendments); Stromberg v. California, 283 U.S. 359 (1931) (flag as a symbol of opposition to organized government); Burnside v. Byars, 363 F.2d 744 (5th Cir. 1960) (wearing of "freedom buttons" by school children not prohibited when no disruption of classes); In re Kay, 83 Cal. Rptr. 686, 464 P.2d 142, 150, n. 10 (1970) (examples of rules inconsistent with guarantees of first amendment). See Wright v. Montgomery, 282 F. Supp. 291 (M.D. Ala. 1968), aff'd, 406 F.2d 867 (5th Cir. 1969), vacated, 401 U.S. 989 (1971) ("hard core" conduct, "pure" speech, "symbolic" speech); People v. Street, 20 N.Y.2d 231, 282 N.Y.S.2d 491 (1967) ("nonverbal" expression may be form of free speech).

"We cannot accept the view that an apparently limitless variety of conduct can be labeled 'speech' whenever the person engaged in the conduct intends thereby to express an idea." Discussion of "speech" and "nonspeech." United States v. O'Brien, 391 U.S. 367, 376 (1968).

See Note, Symbolic speech, 43 FORDHAM L. REV. 590 (1975).

a campaign hat or other distinctive clothing and the use of a bull horn at a political gathering, although contributing to the general disorder of the meeting, may not necessarily constitute an illegal disruption.[75] Also, it has been held that the orderly and peaceable carrying of a sign or placard at a political gathering displaying a controversial theme or slogan, but not so controversial as likely to incite a disturbance, is not necessarily an unlawful disruption of a public meeting.[76]

The fact that a person has a proprietary or other financial interest in the company or entity conducting the meeting, and has the right to attend meetings with the privilege of participating in the deliberations, does not give him any greater or any further right or license to disturb the meeting or to interrupt the proceedings. This principle is illustrated by an early New York case in which a parishioner, charged with disturbance and with refusing to be seated or to leave the church when directed, and in consequence taken by the collar of his coat by the priest and another parishioner in an attempt to remove him, argued that he could not be ejected because he was the lessee of the pew which he occupied. The court held that the fact of disturbance, and refusing to depart upon request, were the essential and only elements necessary to justify the attempted re-

[75] *In re* Ryan v. Grimm, 43 Misc. 2d 836, 839–40, 252 N.Y.S.2d 521 (Sup. Ct.), *aff'd*, 22 App. Div. 2d 171, 254 N.Y.S.2d 462 (4th Dep't 1964), *aff'd*, 15 N.Y.2d 922, 206 N.E.2d 867, 258 N.Y.S.2d 843 (1965); *see* State v. Zwicker, 41 Wis. 2d 497, 164 N.W.2d 512, 516 (1969) (bullhorn to lead demonstrators).

[76] Citizen standing at public gathering at which Governor was speaking, with sign on stick publicizing his objection to pollution of a lake. "The claimant was merely exercising his constitutional rights of petition and freedom of speech in a somewhat unusual but perfectly lawful and orderly manner." Pope v. State, 192 Misc. 587, 79 N.Y.S.2d 466, 471 (Sup. Ct.), *aff'd*, 277 App. Div. 1015, 99 N.Y.S.2d 1019 (1st Dep't 1950).

But see University Committee v. Gunn, 289 F. Supp. 469 (W.D. Tex. 1968), *appeal dismissed*, 399 U.S. 383 (1970) (group attempted to disrupt speech of President of United States at a state college, carrying placards and signs which incited disturbance; court held disturbing-the-peace statute unconstitutionally broad).

The passing out of literature criticizing a school and its teachers by a patron thereof lawfully on school premises did not come under the statute when the only disturbance consisted of the reaction of the teachers to their voluntary reading of the literature. Fowler v. State, 93 Ga. App. 883, 93 S.E.2d 183 (1956).

moval of the offender. As to the leasing of the pew, the court said: "That he [parishioner] was the lessee of the pew cannot avail him as a defence, if he violated the decency and order due to the occasion. The grant of a pew in perpetuity does not give the owner an absolute right of property; he has only a qualified interest—the use of the pew for the purpose of sitting therein to hear divine service, and also at meetings of the society held for temporal purposes. . . . He cannot use his pew as a place from which to interrogate the clergyman and fix a quarrel upon him, or in any way interrupt the services. . . . He is as much bound at these times to preserve order and decorum, as a mere stranger or casual hearer." [77]

The courts also look unfavorably on the actions of members and others who attend meetings simply for the purpose of making a disturbance. In sustaining a conviction for disturbing an association meeting, the court remarked: "It is common knowledge that individuals and groups of people frequently attend gatherings simply for the purpose of making a disturbance, in order to attract attention to themselves or some principle that they advocate; such offenders, when convicted should be given severe sentence as a deterrent to others." [78]

§ 13.12   Equitable Relief—Validity of Action Taken

When the proceedings at a meeting become disorderly, the courts have authority to redress any consequent wrong which may have

[77] Wall v. Lee, 34 N.Y. 141, 145, 148–49 (1865).

SHAW AND SMITH, THE LAW OF MEETINGS at 49 suggests that shareholders may have greater rights of attendance and participation where shareholders' rights are concerned. "Where the meeting is one which those present have a specific right to attend, such as a general meeting of the company . . . the question of removal is more delicate."

However, the fact that a person owns shares of a company gives him no right or license to interrupt or otherwise disturb a corporate meeting. All shareholders have an obligation to each other to refrain from any conduct which might impinge upon the right of other shareholders to participate in the meeting in orderly fashion.

[78] People v. Rotunno, 160 Misc. 696, 291 N.Y.S. 364, 365–66 (Sup. Ct. 1936).

See State v. Olson, 178 N.W.2d 230 (Minn. 1970) (entering church during reverential part of service to "create a dialogue"); State v. Young, 57 N.J. 240, 271 A.2d 569 (1970) (lay minister entering school claiming to be a "surrogate father").

been committed.[79] In judging a disorder it has been said that "the race is not to the swift nor the battle to the strong or loud-voiced, but to the orderly." [80] Failure of an aggrieved member to make a motion to establish order in a meeting permeated with noise and disorder may constitute a waiver of such rights as he may have.[81]

Indecorum at a meeting may, but does not necessarily, invalidate the action taken. In a case involving the election of officers by a city council, it was alleged that the proceedings had been "fatally contaminated with indecorum." The court held the election to be valid and said: "If disorderly proceedings should be held to invalidate an election otherwise legal, some legislative bodies could never organize; and, what is more, a minority by rowdyism could forestall action by a worthy majority." [82] However, in another case relating to a union meeting held in confusion and general disorder, the court held that a vote on a motion which was "railroaded" through at a time when there was bedlam in the room was not a lawful or proper vote of the membership.[83]

[79] Where a disturbance is so widespread that ejection of unruly members is not a practical remedy, the chairman may adjourn the meeting. In this case the presiding officer (acting as inspector) withdrew from the meeting due to violent disorder. In setting aside action taken by the members after he withdrew, the court said: "Under the circumstances, he was justified in refusing to further preside or remain in attendance, and we cannot hold that those, whose violent acts caused him to vacate his office as inspector, could take advantage of their own lawless conduct to reorganize the meeting and recount the votes." Umatilla Water Users' Ass'n v. Irvin, 56 Ore. 414, 108 P. 1016, 1021 (1910).

[80] Kerr v. Trego, 47 Pa. 292, 298 (1864) (contest between two factions claiming to be the regularly organized Common Council of Philadelphia).

[81] The chairman of a county political committee waived the right to conduct a meeting and abandoned his candidacy for the office of chairman by abandoning a demand for roll call on a proxy motion and deciding not to further participate in the meeting while a quorum under the rules of the committee remained present. The chairman by his action was not a person "aggrieved" within the election law. McDonough v. Purcell, 44 Misc. 2d 23, 252 N.Y.S.2d 752 (Sup. Ct. 1964).

[82] State ex rel. Reed v. DeMaioribus, 131 Ohio St. 201, 2 N.E.2d 506, 509 (1936).

[83] The union meeting opened with "shouts, protests, confusion and general disorder." The chairman, unable to restore order, declared the meeting in recess and left the room. It was held that the chairman had the right to declare a recess, citing Robert's Rules of Order. Ash v. Holdeman, 13 Misc. 2d 528, 175 N.Y.S.2d 135, 141–42 (Sup. Ct.), modified, 5 App. Div. 2d 1017, 174 N.Y.S.2d 215 (3d Dep't 1958).

Generally, the validity of action taken by vote at a meeting where there is confusion depends not necessarily on the degree of confusion but on whether in fact it may reasonably be concluded that votes were illegally accepted or improperly rejected or that there was an unfair deprivation of the voter's rights to make known his chioce.[84]

§ 13.13   Disorderly Meetings

A meeting or gathering may be used as a vehicle for causing an unlawful disturbance or breach of the peace. The sponsor and the speakers at a meeting may, by their words and their conduct, appeal to fury and incite to disorder and violence both within and outside the meeting hall in violation of statute or ordinance. In a proper case the courts hold that no one will be permitted to use his constitutional privilege of freedom of speech as an instrument for abuse and incitement to violence.[85]

[84] In a decision upholding the validity of a corporate election the court said: "In this case, testimony at the trial and a reading of the minutes of the proceeding reveal that opportunities were given to vote, though some refused to cast their ballots; that an opportunity was given to nominate other candidates for directors, though the sequence in the matter of procedure might be debatable, and that very few persons were in fact disenfranchised, whether intentionally or otherwise. There is no persuasive evidence that the result was affected or that the outcome would have been different if there had been an absence of confusion. This view is buttressed by the fact that there was no opposition slate offered." Dal-Tran Serv. Co. v. Fifth Ave. Coach Lines, Inc., 14 App. Div. 2d 349, 220 N.Y.S.2d 549, 556 (1st Dep't 1961).

[85] See, e.g., Chicago v. Terminiello, 332 Ill. App. 17, 74 N.E.2d 45 (1947), rev'd, 337 U.S. 1 (1949).

14

Ejection from Meetings

§ 14.1 Power To Eject and Punish

Subject only to regulations imposed by a higher authority, an assembly has absolute power to eject from a meeting any person whose conduct results in a substantial obstruction of its business. This right is derived from the fact that the place where an assembly is being held is appropriated to the use of the assembly, and no person is entitled to be present except with its consent. Consequently, if any person refuses to depart when ordered to do so, the assembly may employ sufficient force to remove such person from the meeting.[1]

This power to maintain control over the meeting place is inherent in the body even where those present at the meeting have a specific

---

[1] MODERN RULES OF ORDER at 18 (1964) (originally published as CUSHING'S MANUAL OF PARLIAMENTARY PRACTICE).

396

right to attend, such as the attendance of members at legislative sessions, or at company, lodge, or church meetings.[2]

The powers of a legislative assembly which are necessary and incidental to a free and unobstructed exercise of its appropriate functions, including the power to protect itself and its members, and "[t]o preserve its own honor, dignity, purity and efficiency, by the expulsion of an unworthy, or the discharge of an incompetent member" arise from the very creation of the body and are founded on the principle of self-preservation. These powers are not derived from the Constitution, which is not a grant but is a restriction upon legislative powers. They are recognized under the "common parliamentary law"[3] but exist "independently of parliamentary custom and usage."[4] "The right and power of a state legislature to protect itself against contemptuous and disorderly conduct on the part of non-members cannot be disputed." The legislature has the right to punish for contemptuous behavior and to remove any disorderly person from its meeting place and to enforce such removal. This power is essential to a legislative body and is one which arises from necessity.[5]

§ 14.2 Judicial Review

The inherent right of a legislature to expel, the reason for expulsion, and whether the member had an opportunity to be heard, are matters beyond judicial review. "The power of expulsion is a necessary and incidental power to enable the house to perform its high functions, and is necessary to the safety of the State. It is a power

---

[2] This power and duty also rests with the proprietor of public, social, or amusement premises. For example, in action for assault and battery of a patron of a movie theater who was beaten and ejected by a special police officer for rude and boisterous conduct, the court said: "The jury was also admonished with reference to the right and duty of a theater proprietor to insist that every patron shall conduct himself with proper decorum, so that good order may be preserved, and to that end such proprietor may adopt and enforce reasonable and proper regulations, using if necessary reasonable force to evict a patron who refuses to leave and persists in violating proper and reasonable regulations." McChristian v. Popkin, 75 Cal. App. 2d 249, 255, 260, 171 P.2d 85 (1946).

[3] Ex parte McCarthy, 29 Cal. Rptr. 395, 404, 405 (1866), quoting Cushing, Law & Pr. Leg. Assem.

[4] Hiss v. Bartlett, 69 Mass. (3 Gray) 468, 475 (1855).

[5] Kovach v. Maddux, 238 F. Supp. 835, 840 (M.D. Tenn. 1965).

of protection. A member may be physically, mentally or morally, wholly unfit; he may be afflicted with a contagious disease, or insane, or noisy, violent and disorderly, or in the habit of using profane, obscene and abusive language. It is necessary to put extreme cases to test a principle." The power must exist in every aggregate and deliberative body, in order to exercise its functions, and because without it such body would be powerless to accomplish the purposes of its constitution. "As to the law and custom of parliament, the authorities cited clearly show that the jurisdiction to convict, and also to expel, has long been recognized, not only in parliament, but in the courts of law, for the purposes of protection and punishment." [6] It is a power derived from the common law.[7]

§ 14.3   Power in Presiding Officer

The power to eject or discipline a disrupter for cause may always be exercised by resolution, standing order, or other regulatory action of the assembly. However, this power need not be embodied in a resolution or rule.[8] The right to eject a disruptive person often resides in the presiding officer, whose duty and function is to preserve order and take care that the proceedings are conducted in a

[6] Hiss v. Bartlett, 69 Mass. (3 Gray) 468, 473 (1855), *cited,* Speakership of the House of Representatives, 15 Colo. 520, 25 P. 707, 710 (1891) (*citing* Jefferson, Cushing, Hatsell) (speaker of house may be removed from his office by majority of whole number of members in accordance with common parliamentary law).

[7] The power to expel a member is naturally and even necessarily incident to all legislative bodies which, without such power, could not exist honorably and fulfill the object of their creation. "Such are some of the powers and privileges of a legislative assembly under the law of its creation, or in other words, under the common parliamentary law." *Ex parte* McCarthy, 29 Cal. Rptr. 395, 405 (1866), *quoting* Cushing, Law & Pr. Leg. Assem.

These powers are "protective and self-defensive powers only, and not punitive." They are necessary incidental powers of self-protection "implied by the common law." Barton v. Taylor, 11 App. Cas. 197, 203 (P.C. 1886) (New South Wales).

[8] In an action founded on the expulsion of a disorderly legislator, the court remarked: "It is said they had made no rule on the subject previously. I doubt whether that is necessary. They cannot enlarge their own powers by a rule. Why may they not make a particular rule, when the exigency arises?" Hiss v. Bartlett, 69 Mass. (3 Gray) 468, 472 (1855).

proper manner.[9] This power in the presiding officer may be exercised by him without the authority of an enabling resolution (a) where such power is established by statute,[10] as in the case of a town moderator,[11] (b) where such power is established by custom and practice, as in the case of a priest or clergyman; [12] and (c) where

[9] *See, e.g.*, Lucas v. Mason, (1875) L.R. 10, 251 (holding that it is no doubt the duty of the chairman of a meeting when a large body of people are gathered, to do his best to preserve order, and to cause the removal of any persons who interrupt or disturb the meeting).

[10] The power of the chairman to order the removal of a disturber must not be confused with the common-law or statutory offense of disturbing a meeting. After being removed, the disturber may be subjected to criminal sanctions. *See, e.g.*, People v. Malone, 156 App. Div. 10, 141 N.Y.S. 149 (2d Dep't 1913).

[11] By statute, a "moderator shall preside and regulate the proceedings, decide all questions of order, and make public declaration of all votes." "The powers and duties of a moderator have been fixed by law for more than two centuries." A plaintiff was removed from a town meeting hall for causing noise, laughter, and confusion and failing to observe a ruling of the moderator on a question of order. He was confined in a separate room for an hour, until the meeting had adjourned. The court also held that where the moderator's action was neither malicious nor dishonest, it could not substitute its own judgment for his. Doggett v. Hooper, 306 Mass. 129, 27 N.E.2d 737, 739, 740 (1940); *accord*, Parsons v. Brainard, 17 Wend. 522 (N.Y. 1837) (justice of peace acting as moderator).

"The ample powers possessed by moderators, recognized from earliest times and growing out of the imperative needs of the office, are inconsistent with many incidents of ordinary parliamentary law." Wood v. Town of Milton, 197 Mass. 531, 84 N.E. 332, 333 (1908).

"The moderator, excepting in those matters where he is bound by statute law, rules as he understands that he ought to rule. If his ruling is incorrect, any person who is dissatisfied may appeal to the meeting, and its decision, being not against the statute, is final and conclusive." Hill v. Goodwin, 56 N.H. 441, 454 (1876) (powers of moderator).

[12] "The ground of justification for removal of a person who seeks to interrupt or disturb the order and proceedings of others, is that they have the right to the quiet and orderly enjoyment of any lawful business, pleasure or occupation. An intruder has no right to disturb or interrupt, and if he does, it is lawful to remove him and thus restore quiet." Wall v. Lee, 34 N.Y. 141, 143 (1865).

A plaintiff disturbed a religious meeting by sitting in an area reserved for ladies and was forcibly ejected. The court said: "A religious society has the undoubted right to prescribe such rules as they may think proper, for preserving order, when met for public worship" and concluded that "[t]hey had a right to use the necessary force to remove him." McLain v. Matlock, 7 Ind. 525, 528

such power is established by common law, as in the case of any meeting for a lawful purpose, where the disruptive person persists in disturbing the meeting in disobedience of the chairman and in disregard of his commands to desist.[13] In such case, the mere fact of disturbance and refusal to desist when ordered to do so are sufficient to justify ejection [14] and confinement.[15]

§ 14.4   Concurrence of Body

Where the rules require that concurrence be obtained, the presiding officer does not have the right to eject a disorderly non-member without first obtaining the concurrence of the body. In a recent case it was held that the chairman of a Congressional subcommittee did not have the right, acting alone and without consulting other members of the subcommittee, to remove a witness' attorney from the committee hearing room for failure to conduct himself in an orderly and proper manner, where the rules specified a procedure for obtaining the concurrence of the subcommittee members. The

---

(1856); *accord,* Jones v. State, 219 Ga. 848, 136 S.E.2d 358, 364, *cert. denied,* Jones v. Georgia, 379 U.S. 935 (1964).

A church congregation has the right to admit or exclude members or worshipers according to the expressed will of the group. The court commented that "church brawling" need not be explored either under a statute against disturbing public worship "or under the inherent right of self help where the ejectors use no more force than necessary." Johnson v. State, 7 Div. 720, 173 So. 2d 817, 823, *rev'd,* 7 Div. 650, 173 So. 2d 824 (Ala. 1964).

[13] This class of cases includes the removal of disturbers from meetings of shareholders, union members, political parties and committees, and social clubs, as well as some local public bodies.

[14] In a suit for trespass and assault in attempting to remove a disturber from a church, the court held that nonconformity with the rules and regulations was a justification for the removal of the person refusing compliance and for quelling the disturbance. "The fact of disturbance and refusing to depart upon request, were the essential and only elements necessary to a justification of the trespass and assault." Wall v. Lee, 34 N.Y. 141, 145 (1865).

[15] A person at a town meeting refusing to accept the moderator's ruling on procedures and persisting with a demand that the meeting be conducted under the rules of a certain parliamentary manual is guilty of disorderly conduct within a statute authorizing a moderator to order disorderly persons to withdraw from the meeting and to order the removal and confinement of a person not so withdrawing, until adjournment of the meeting. Doggett v. Hooper, 306 Mass. 129, 27 N.E.2d 737 (1940).

attorney had engaged in a heated exchange with the chairman leading to general turmoil, and he was removed by the marshals, kicking
and screaming, to a waiting police wagon. The court held that such
action by the chairman was not a lawful application of the subcommittee rules which permitted such discipline upon a finding by a
majority of the subcommittee that the attorney for the witness did
not conduct himself in a professional, ethical, and proper manner.
"Although the discipline initiated was within the scope of the rule,
the procedure leading to such discipline clearly was not." [16]

The Constitution of the United States expressly empowers each
House to punish its own members for disorderly behavior, and,
with the concurrence of two-thirds, to expel a member. The Supreme Court has said that "[w]e see no reason to doubt that this
punishment may in a proper case be imprisonment, and that it may
be for refusal to obey some rule on that subject made by the House
for the preservation of order." [17] The power of the House of Representatives to punish a member for contempt was discussed by the
Supreme Court in an early decision which held that the House, by
implication, has the power to punish, since "public functionaries
must be left at liberty to exercise the powers which the people have
intrusted to them. The interests and dignity of those who created
them, require the exertion of the powers indispensable to the attain-
ment of the ends of their creation. Nor is a casual conflict with the
rights of particular individuals any reason to be urged against the
exercise of such powers." [18]

[16] The court opened its opinion with these words: "At the outset, we wish
to make it clear that, although a lawyer has a duty to defend vigorously the
rights of his clients, there is a corollary obligation that he conduct himself with
decorum. And this is equally true whether he be addressing a court or a legislative committee. In neither instance may he so conduct himself that he disrupts
the proceedings and obstructs the orderly administration of the law. At the
same time, the courts and committees before which a lawyer appears are governed by specific rules of order and just as the lawyer must stay within the
boundaries of legitimate legal argument, so too the committee must respect its
own rules." Kinoy v. District of Columbia, 400 F.2d 761, 763 (D.C. Cir. 1968).

[17] Kilbourn v. Thompson, 103 U.S. 168, 189–90 (1881).

See Annot., Power of legislative body to punish for contempt, 79 L. Ed. 809
(1935).

[18] Anderson v. Dunn, 19 U.S. (6 Wheat.) 204, 226 (1821). The court
reasoned as follows: "That a deliberate assembly, clothed with the majesty of
the people, and charged with the care of all that is dear to them; composed of

It may be observed that the power of expulsion has been exercised against a member who used language at a prior meeting "calculated to excite confusion and dissension and who did not "confine himself to the question, but wandered therefrom into indecorous language" and "imputed improper motives" to certain members. Cushing's Manual had been adopted to govern debates. On appeal, it was held that the member could not be expelled under the applicable rule except by prompt action at the meeting when the offensive words were spoken. The member had not been called to order when the offensive words were spoken and he did not refuse to take his seat. Therefore, the expulsion was not valid.[19]

§ 14.4.1   Member or Non-Member

The power of the presiding officer of a legislative body, acting alone and without the authority of a standing order or the concurrence of the body by an enabling resolution, to eject a disturber from the meeting or to punish him for his actions generally depends on whether the disturber is a member of the assembly or a nonmember. As to members it is the general rule that the presiding officer of an elected or appointed legislative assembly, in the absence of such authority or concurrence, does not alone have the power to eject or punish a disorderly legislator except in the case of threatened violence to other members. This parliamentary rule is exemplified in an early case holding that the power of a mayor as presiding officer of a city council extends no further upon the occurrence of

---

the most distinguished citizens, selected and drawn together from every quarter of a great nation; whose deliberations are required by public opinion to be conducted under the eye of the public, and whose decisions must be clothed with all that sanctity which unlimited confidence in their wisdom and purity can inspire; that such an assembly should not possess the power to suppress rudeness, or repel insult, is a supposition too wild to be suggested. And, accordingly, to avoid the pressure of these considerations, it has been argued, that the right of the respective Houses to exclude from their presence, and their absolute control within their own walls, carry with them the right to punish contempts committed in their presence; while the absolute legislative power given to Congress within this district, enables them to provide by law against all other insults against which there is any necessity for providing."

[19] People *ex rel.* Godwin v. American Inst., 44 How. Pr. 468 (N.Y. Sup. Ct. 1873).

indecorum on the part of a member than to bring the facts to the attention of the council, which may, if it sees fit, after the member has been heard, order him to withdraw pending its consideration and action. In one case the unruly member had "conducted himself in an unparliamentary, disorderly, boorish, and insulting manner toward its presiding officer and the council," but it did not appear that he threatened personal injury to any of the other council members. The court held: "When the president [mayor] has called an offending member to order, and stated the matter of the offense to the house, it seems that he has fully discharged his duty and exhausted his powers in the premises. He thereby transmits the further disposition of the matter to the house. The power to punish is not among his prerogatives; that belongs exclusively to the house, and he can never exercise it save as it is expressly ordered by the house." [20]

On the other hand, the chairman with the concurrence of the majority of the body or pursuant to standing orders in effect, may order the ejection of an unruly member. This rule is illustrated in an English case where a member of an urban district council called out "liar" when a vote was being passed. He was behaving in an "abusive and violent manner" and refused to leave the council chamber when requested to do so, and it was necessary to remove him to maintain order in the meeting. The court found that the chairman had acted "in accordance with the rules and standing orders," that he was entitled to order the member removed and that the removal was done "as gently as the circumstances permitted." The court reasoned that the member, upon refusing to withdraw at the lawful order of the chairman, became a "mere trespasser."[21]

---

[20] Thompson v. Whipple, 54 Ark. 203, 15 S.W. 604, 605 (1891), *citing* Cushing's Rules of Pro. & Deb. and Cushing's Law & Pr. Leg. Assem.

[21] Marshall v. Tinnelly, 81 S.J. 903 (1937) (Solicitors' Journal) *cited in* Shackleton at 11.

A member of a colonial legislature was held to have disturbed the assembly when, having already spoken against a motion, he proceeded to debate his objection further after the motion had been amended, such action being contrary to the rules of the body. "It is necessary to distinguish between a power to punish for a contempt, which is a judicial power, and a power to remove any obstruction offered to the deliberations or proper action of a Legislative body during its sitting, which last power is necessary for self-preservation. If a Member of a Colonial House of Assembly is guilty of disorderly conduct in the

There may be some question as to the legality of ejecting a disruptive member if it can be shown that the meeting was not lawfully convened. An early English case held that plaintiff (a parishioner) could not lawfully be thrown out of a meeting of vestrymen because the meeting was not duly noticed. Plaintiff had been asked to leave as an intruder and, on refusal, had been thrashed and forcibly ejected. It was noted that the meeting was held in the parish schoolroom and the plaintiff had as much right to enter the room as the members of the select vestry.[22]

§ 14.5 Enforcement

There are adequate court decisions relating to the enforcement of proper decorum. A leading New York case upheld a misdemeanor conviction of a person who disturbed a lawful assemblage. The defendant, a suffragette, attended a political meeting at which Woodrow Wilson was campaigning for the office of President. During his address she rose from her seat and asked him to state his position on women suffrage. Wilson declined to discuss the question because it was a state issue, and he was present to discuss only national questions. The defendant was requested by the chairman to resume her seat, but she remained standing, repeated her request, and addressed a further question to the speaker relative to the same subject. The meeting was thrown into an uproar and the defendant was ejected, arrested, and convicted. On appeal, the court held that the defendant's offense was her refusal to resume her seat and her persistence in interrogating the speaker "in disobedience of the

---

House whilst sitting he may be removed, or excluded for a time, or even expelled; . . . If the good sense and conduct of the members of Colonial Legislatures prove, as in the present case, insufficient to secure order and decency of debate, the law would sanction the use of that degree of force which may be necessary to remove the person offending from the place of meeting, and to keep him excluded. The same rule would apply, *a fortiori* to obstructions caused by any person not a member." Doyle v. Falconer, L.R. 1 P.C. 328, 340 (1866), *quoted in* Barton v. Taylor, 11 App. Cas. 197 (P.C. 1886).

[22] Dobson v. Fussy, 7 Bing. 305 (D.C. 1831). *See* Leamy v. Sinaloa Explor. & Dev. Co., 15 Del. Ch. 28, 130 A. 282 (1925) (ejection of shareholder who claimed that meeting was illegal); Noller v. Wright, 138 Mich. 416, 101 N.W. 553 (1904) (ejection of shareholder from annual meeting upon refusal of company to recognize his share ownership).

See § 15.19 *infra.*

chairman of the meeting and in disregard of his commands." This constituted a willful disturbance of a public assembly in violation of the New York Penal Law which provided that a person who, without authority of law, disturbed any assembly or meeting not unlawful in character, is guilty of a disdemeanor.[23]

In a Federal case, two persons were removed from the meeting area of a Congressional investigation committee by U. S. marshals and later convicted of disorderly conduct under an Illinois statute. One defendant fell limp on the floor when ordered to leave, and was carried out, while the other defendant jumped to his feet during the hearing and began shouting. The chairman called for order by pounding his gavel and a marshal warned the defendant to be quiet or he would have to leave. When defendant continued his shouting, he was also forcibly removed from the building. In affirming the convictions, the court held that public hearings "must be conducted with decorum" and reasoned that "[i]f each spectator were privileged to shout or even speak at will, pandemonium would likely result." [24]

In another case a newspaper reporter was removed from a meeting of a state legislative committee at the order of the chairman when the committee decided to go into secret or executive session. It was held that although a newspaper publisher has the right to speak out against secret or executive sessions of a legislative committee on routine legislation, its representatives had no right to carry its opposition to the extent of refusing to leave a committee meeting at the request of the chairman. "It [publisher] had no right to offer any physical obstruction whatever to the processes of the Senate or its committees. This much must be conceded." [25] Substantial au-

---

[23] People v. Malone, 156 App. Div. 10, 141 N.Y.S. 149 (2d Dep't 1913).

[24] United States v. Woodard, 376 F.2d 136, 139 (7th Cir. 1967).

[25] Kovach v. Maddux, 238 F. Supp. 835, 840 (M.D. Tenn. 1965).

The presence of a reporter on the floor of a meeting of a board of education is "not a right but a privilege" and he can be removed by order of the president. "That under the rules of the board, reporters were privileged to the floor of the chamber, did not take away the power of the board to revoke the rules. It is argued, that by the rules, the privilege could only be withdrawn by suspension of the rules, or by an amendment, that should have been laid over until the next meeting . . . , but assuming there were such rules, the objection is upon a point of order, which if not taken by a member of the board, could certainly be of no avail to any one else." Corre v. State, 8 Ohio Dec. Reprint 715, 716 (Dist. Ct. 1883).

thority exists for the proposition that coupled with an assembly's power to preserve order is the power to enforce its own disciplinary rulings.

§ 14.5.1   Resistance May Constitute Disorder

A New Jersey case has established the principle that the very act of resistance to a lawful order of removal from a city council meeting, and the noise necessarily generated by the method of removal to which the disrupter put the police officers, did in fact "disturb the quiet and good order within the chamber" and constituted a violation of a disorderly persons statute. The decision of the presiding officer that the defendant intended to disturb the good order of the meeting "cannot be tested by physical resistance." [26]

In a Massachusetts case, a member sought to raise a question of personal privilege at a town meeting and inquired under what rules the meeting was being conducted; the moderator referred to the by-laws, but the member kept on talking and began to read from a parliamentary manual. The moderator ruled him out of order and requested that he be seated, but he kept on talking. The moderator thereupon told him that he would be removed if he said one more word. The member said, "Thank you, sir," whereupon the moderator ordered the member removed from the meeting. The court upheld a jury verdict that the member had disturbed the meeting.[27]

§ 14.6   Priest or Clergyman

The right of a priest or clergyman to take such action as may be requisite to preserve proper decorum at a religious gathering is of long standing at common law. An early case noted that "usage and custom have made it peculiarly the duty of the minister or priest, to conduct the services of religious meetings, to preside over them, to preserve order therein, and act as the organ or spokesman of the congregation." It was held that a parishioner who interrogated the priest and refused to sit down or leave the church when requested

---

[26] State v. Smith, 46 N.J. 510, 218 A.2d 147, *cert. denied*, 385 U. S. 838 (1966).

[27] Doggett v. Hooper, 306 Mass. 129, 27 N.E.2d 737, 739 (1940).

may be removed by the application of force sufficient for that purpose.[28]

If the assembly has adopted rules for the conduct of its meetings which apply to the ejection or expulsion of members, such as a published parliamentary manual, they should be observed.[29]

§ 14.7   Assistance of Stewards and Monitors

It is the duty of the sergeant-at-arms and of those acting as stewards and monitors at a meeting to act for or to assist the chairman in his efforts to preserve order.[30] When stewards have not been

---

[28] Wall v. Lee, 34 N.Y. 141, 146 (1865).

"A religious society has the undoubted right to prescribe such rules as they may think proper, for preserving order, when met for public worship. In this society, the rule was that males and females should sit apart. Persons who do not approve of that mode, have a simple and easy remedy. They can remain away, or retire when informed of the rule. The plaintiff was repeatedly notified of this rule, and requested to conform to it, which he refused to do. They had the right to use the necessary force to remove him. They did so, and that was the arrest complained of." McLain v. Matlock, 7 Ind. 525, 528 (1856).

Evidence showed that defendant had entered a church of which he was not a member and during a reverential part of the service berated the clergyman and refused to sit down or leave when requested by ushers. His conviction for disturbing the peace under municipal ordinance was sustained. State v. Olson, 178 N.W.2d 230 (Minn. 1970).

But see Johnson v. State, 7 Div. 720, 173 So. 2d 817, 822 (Ct. App. Ala. 1965) (questioning the authority of a pastor to invite people out of or into the congregation, in absence of proof of his authority).

[29] Expulsion of a life member for using abusive language at a prior meeting was set aside by the court. The organization had adopted Cushing's Manual, which provided for prompt notice of offensive words and concurrent action calling the member to order. This procedure was not observed. Cushing's Manual did not authorize disciplinary action at a subsequent meeting. People *ex rel.* Godwin v. American Inst., 44 How. Pr. 468, 471 (N.Y. Sup. Ct. 1873).

[30] "It is no doubt the duty of the chairman of a meeting, where a large body of people are gathered together, to do his best to preserve order, and it is equally the duty of those who are acting as stewards or managers to assist him in so doing, but the nature and extent of this duty on both sides cannot be very closely defined a priori, and must necessarily arise out of, and in character and extent depend upon, the events and emergencies which may from time to time arise." Lucas v. Mason, (1875) L.R. 10, 251, 254.

See United States v. Woodard, 376 F.2d 136 (7th Cir. 1967) (U.S. marshals); Hartzog v. United Press Ass'ns, 202 F.2d 81 (4th Cir. 1953), *reversed,*

empowered to assist in maintaining order, the chairman has the power at common law to call upon others to aid him, and the persons so called have an equal right to use force in removing a disturber.[31] The intervention of duly constituted officers to remove a disorderly person from the meeting is not a defense in a prosecution for disorderly conduct.[32] Firm and prompt exercise of authority by the presiding officer is essential to the maintenance of orderly proceedings, including the removal of a disorderly person.[33]

---

233 F.2d 174 (4th Cir. 1956) (alleged ejection by police); McLain v. Matlock, 7 Ind. 525 (1856) (church officer and parishioners); State v. McNair, 178 Neb. 763, 135 N.W.2d 463 (1965) (city clerk as sergeant-at-arms); Beckett v. Lawrence, 7 Abb. Pr. (N.S.) 403 (N.Y. Sup. Ct. 1869) (removal by police officer on order of vestrymen); Corre v. State, 8 Ohio Dec. Reprint 715 (Dist. Ct. 1883) (sergeant-at-arms at board of education); Barton v. Taylor, 11 App. Cas. 197 (P.C. 1886) (New South Wales) (sergeant-at-arms).

[31] Wall v. Lee, 34 N.Y. 141, 145, 146 (1865). The court stated as follows: "It is most appropriate that the minister or priest should preserve order and rebuke all violations of it. As the acknowledged presiding officer of the meeting, it is his duty to check all attempts to interrupt its order, quietness and solemnity, and for this purpose he unquestionably has full power and authority to call upon others to aid him or direct them to remove the offender. In this sense, therefore, he has a greater right to enforce order and use force for that purpose, than any other member of the congregation.

"But usage and custom have made it peculiarly the duty of the minister, or priest, to conduct the services of religious meetings, to preside over them, to preserve order therein, and act as the organ or spokesman of the congregation.

"[There was] error in that part of the charge which instructed the jury that the minister, or priest, had no greater right to use force than any other member of the congregation. In one sense, perhaps, this may be correct, namely that any other member of the congregation had an equal right with the minister, or priest, to use force in removing a disturber of the peace and order of the meeting."

[32] "The conduct of the defendants, not that of the law enforcement agents, occasioned the public disturbances which prompted the prosecution of this case." United States v. Woodard, 376 F.2d 136, 140 (7th Cir. 1967).

See, e.g., State v. Midgett, 8 N.C. App. 230, 174 S.E.2d 124 (1970) (police officers removed disturbers from public school).

[33] Plaintiff was removed from town meeting for objectionable words producing noise, laughter, and confusion. By statute, justices preside at town meetings and see that they are conducted regularly and in an orderly way. They have full authority to enforce obedience to their lawful commands. "Stopping here, there would be little room for question that the justices were well warranted in ordering the plaintiff out of the room, without waiting to

On the other hand, the offense of disturbing a meeting or otherwise interfering with the peace and good order of an assembly, will not be "undone" because the authorities did not have the disturber ejected at once or because the disturber was asked to assist in ending the disorder.[34]

§ 14.8   Company Meetings—Proceed With Caution

The presiding officer at a meeting of stockholders, in approaching the task of ejecting an unruly stockholder, should proceed with caution where the appropriate standard of conduct may be in doubt. Ample warning should always be given by the presiding officer to the disruptive person that he immediately cease his disruptive conduct and that, should he refuse to comply, he will be removed. When it is clearly evident that he will persist in his disruptive behavior and that he will refuse to leave voluntarily, removal should be effected promptly and before the conduct of any other business by the meeting. It is not the custom or practice in this country to secure the support of the meeting before removing a disruptive person. Some writers have suggested, however, that the chairman should first secure the authority of a suspensive resolution, particularly in case of blatant and aggravated obstruction of the orderly conduct of business. It is recommended that, as in all questions of appropriate decorum, the chairman should act responsively considering the attending circumstances.[35]

---

put their mandate in writing. The case called for a prompt exercise of their authority, and I can perceive no objection in principle to the manner in which it was exercised." Parsons v. Brainard, 17 Wend. 522, 523 (N.Y. 1837).

See Robert's Rules of Order at 299; Robert's Rules of Order, Newly Revised (1970) at 542.

[34] State v. Young, 57 N.J. 240, 271 A.2d 569, 576 (1970), cert. denied, 402 U.S. 929 (1971) (offense of entering school for the purpose of disturbing classes).

[35] "In all cases where it is permissible, expulsion should only be used as a last resort. If the conduct of a person is such that the business of the meeting is seriously interfered with, and if, after repeated requests from the chair, the offender still persists in his obstructive methods, it would be desirable for the chairman to warn him of the consequences of his actions. Should the interrupter continue in defiance of these warnings he should be given the opportunity of leaving the meeting voluntarily, and in case of his refusal to leave on

§ 14.9 Warning

Whether the disturber is entitled to a warning that he will be ejected, punished, or subjected to criminal sanctions is not clearly established. It has been held, however, that in instances where the appropriate standard of conduct lies in doubt, a warning and a request that the disturber curtail his conduct should precede arrest or citation. Otherwise individuals would be forced to speculate as to what conduct might entail criminal sanctions. In support of its holding, one court noted that "warnings are commonly given to those who speak out of turn or otherwise disturb or interrupt meetings." [36] If a warning is necessary, it should be given by an authorized person.[37]

---

his own accord, reasonable force should then be used to expel him. It would be desirable to secure the support of the majority of the meeting on this matter, and should there be agreement, the expulsion should be effected expeditiously." SHACKLETON, LAW AND PRACTICE OF MEETINGS at 8–9.

Another writer takes a more conservative view: "Where the meeting is one where those present have a specific right to attend, such as a general meeting of a company or the meeting of a statutory body, the question of removal is more delicate. Any duly constituted assembly has an implied power to act for the protection of the collective interests of those present; and a meeting might properly resolve that a certain member be suspended or excluded if his conduct results in a substantial obstruction of the business of the meeting. Such a resolution could be made effective, if need be, by the exercise of force against the object of it.

"It would appear that in cases of blatant and aggravated obstruction, the chairman could properly direct the expulsion of a member from the meeting without the authority of a suspensive resolution. The expulsion must, however, be in pursuance to the authority which is vested in the chairman in his capacity as chairman. In extreme cases, as where a general uproar had arisen, the chairman may be justified in adjourning the meeting of his own volition." SHAW AND SMITH, THE LAW OF MEETINGS at 47–48.

When the chairman is convinced that an individual is out of order and will persist to be disorderly after a warning, he should request the individual to leave the meeting room. If he refuses to leave, a motion should be initiated by the chairman that the disruptive individual be ejected from the meeting. Cogent reasons are given by the writer in support of this position. See Wetzel, *Conduct of Stockholders' Meeting*, 22 BUS. LAWYER 303 (1967).

See §13.5 *supra.*

[36] *In re* Kay, 1 Cal. 3d 930, 464 P.2d 142, 152, n.13, 83 Cal. Rptr. 686 (1970).

See § 13.2.1 *supra.*

§ 14.10   Disenfranchisement of Ejected Person

Ejection from a meeting when there is unfinished business still to be transacted might well mean temporary or effective disenfranchisement of the ejected member or shareholder. If ejection is justified, however, the courts will not overturn action taken by the meeting after the ejection. In such case, the member must assume the responsibility for the loss of his opportunity to vote.

A different situation is presented when a member is unjustly excluded from voting his shares, as he would be if ejected from a meeting without good cause. Here, disenfranchisement does not stem from his own misconduct and he is entitled to equitable relief from the court on a showing that if permitted to vote, his vote would have changed the result.[38] Thus, to successfully challenge any action taken at a company meeting after his removal, the ejected stockholder must show that his ejection was unjustified, that he was prepared to vote with the minority, and that if he had voted with the minority the final result would have been different.

On the other hand it has been held that action taken at a corporate meeting is not rendered invalid because legal votes were rejected and illegal votes were accepted, if the result would have been the same upon a correction of the errors.[39] There seems to be

---

[37] Johnson v. State, 7 Div. 720, 173 So. 2d 817, *rev'd*, 7 Div. 650, 173 So. 2d 824 (Ala. 1964) (question whether a minister, as pastor of a church, had authority to invite people out of or into the congregation when assembled for worship and to give warning to a disruptive person).

See State v. Besson, 110 N.J. Super. 528, 266 A.2d 175 (1970) (warnings to teacher disturbing a school assembly); State v. Moore, 101 N.J. Super. 419, 244 A.2d 522, 523 (1968) (warning given by police before removal of disorderly person from planning board meeting, and arrest); State v. Smith, 46 N.J. 510, 218 A.2d 147, *cert. denied*, 385 U.S. 838 (1966) (warning by president of city council that citizen speakers be silent or would be asked to leave council chamber); Doggett v. Hooper, 306 Mass. 129, 27 N.E.2d 737, 740 (1940) (warning by moderator of forbidden acts intended by statute).

[38] *See* § 17.13 *infra.*

[39] "As to the receipt of illegal votes and rejection of legal votes little need be said, because, if all the votes which are claimed to have been cast illegally are disregarded, and all the votes which are claimed to have been wrongfully rejected are counted, there still would be voting for the resolution two-thirds of the shareholders present at the meeting." Beutelspacher v. Spokane Sav. Bank, 164 Wash. 227, 2 P.2d 729, 731 (1931).

no difference between the rejection of legal votes and the prevention of a shareholder from voting by lawful removal of the shareholder prior to casting his vote, except that the latter action may also have deprived the shareholder of his opportunity to state his position prior to the tally. Generally, with a majority of voting shares almost invariably being represented by management proxies at meetings of publicly held companies, an ejected minority shareholder must bear a heavy burden if he wishes to overturn a vote taken after he has been lawfully ejected from the meeting room.

§ 14.11   Use of Reasonable Force

The common-law right to direct the removal from the meeting of an obstreperous person whose conduct disturbs the proceedings necessarily includes the power to use all reasonable force to that end.[40] The justification for removing a disruptive person is to restore a proper atmosphere so that the meeting may continue in an orderly fashion. Thus, the right to remove is one of self-protection and is not punitive.[41] The degree of force applied in removing a recalci-

---

[40] See 6 AM. JUR. 2d Assault & Battery § 84 (1963); Annot., 6 A.L.R. 985, 997, 999 (1920).
See § 14.12.1 infra.

[41] "It is necessary to distinguish between a power to punish for a contempt, which is a judicial power, and a power to remove any obstruction offered to the deliberations or proper action of a Legislative body during its sitting, which last power is necessary for self-preservation. If a Member of a Colonial House of Assembly is guilty of disorderly conduct in the House whilst sitting, he may be removed, or excluded for a time, or even expelled; but there is a great difference between such powers and the judicial power of inflicting a penal sentence for the offence. The right to remove for self-security is one thing, the right to inflict punishment is another. . . . If the good sense and conduct of the members of Colonial Legislatures prove, as in the present case, insufficient to secure order and decency of debate, the law would sanction the use of that degree of force which might be necessary to remove the person offending from the place of meeting, and to keep him excluded. The same rule would apply, a fortiori, to obstructions caused by any person not a member. And whenever the violation of order amounts to a breach of the peace, or other legal offence, recourse may be had to the ordinary tribunals." Doyle v. Falconer, L.R. 1 P.C. 328, 340 (1866).
Powers necessary to the existence of a legislative body and the proper exercise of the functions which it is intended to execute are implied by the common law. The power of suspending a member guilty of obstruction or disorderly

trant must be limited to that amount which the occasion reasonably requires. Stern action may be taken when needed to bring about the ejection of the wrongdoer, considering such resistance as need be overcome.[42] In fact, resistance to an order of removal may itself constitute a disturbance of the meeting,[43] and may lead to strong

---

conduct is reasonably necessary for the proper exercise of the functions of a legislative assembly. "Whatever, in a reasonable sense, is necessary for these purposes, is impliedly granted whenever any such legislative body is established by competent authority. For these purposes, protective and self-defensive powers only, and not punitive, are necessary." Barton v. Taylor, 11 App. Cas. 197, 203 (P.C. 1886).

"The power of expulsion is a necessary and incidental power, to enable the house to perform its high functions, and is necessary to the safety of the State. It is a power of protection." The court continued that "as to the law and custom of parliament, the authorities cited clearly show that the jurisdiction to convict, and also to expel, has long been recognized, not only in parliament, but in the courts of law, for the purposes of protection and punishment." Hiss v. Bartlett, 69 Mass. (3 Gray) 468, 473 (1855).

[42] In an analogous case, a railroad passenger was ejected for refusing to show his ticket. It was held that "the conductor may then employ so much force as may be necessary to effect his removal, at the same time using no violence and doing no unnecessary injury. If, however, the passenger refuses to comply, and resists, and injury happens, it is an injury for which the company is not responsible, for it is a result attributable to his own wrongful conduct." Hibbard v. New York & E. R.R., 15 N.Y. 455, 464 (1857).

A plaintiff shareholder was wrongfully forcibly ejected from an annual meeting "using no more force than was necessary to overcome his resistance." The plaintiff recovered in an action for trespass. Noller v. Wright, 138 Mich. 416, 101 N.W. 553 (1904).

A plaintiff, having caused a disturbance and refused to leave a meeting of select vestry on order, was thrashed and thrown out, the thrashing being necessary to get him out. In an action for assault the court held for the plaintiff because the meeting was not legally called. Dobson v. Fussy, 7 Bing. 305 (C.D. 1831).

[43] In a prosecution for violation of a disorderly persons statute, evidence that a person's resistance to efforts to remove him from the meeting was disorderly, and that his conduct, with the noise necessarily generated by the mode of removal to which the disorderly person put police officers, did disturb the quiet and good order within the meeting chamber, was held to be sufficient to sustain his conviction. The decision of the presiding officer to order the removal of a disorderly person cannot be tested by physical resistance. "The chair must have the power to suppress a disturbance on the threat of one, and the power to quell a disturbance would be empty if its exercise could be

measures. "Beating or wounding or the infliction of any form of physical injury is in itself illegal save insofar as such conduct may be rendered necessary by the violent resistance of the traspasser." [44]

In a court decision under the labor Bill of Rights it was held that a union member could not recover damages for injury to his thumb when he resisted being physically ejected from a union meeting and then attempted to regain admittance. He had been suspended from membership for nonpayment of dues and, notwithstanding the illegality of his suspension, the injury was not a direct or a proximate result of a violation of the Act. The trial court held that the suspended member had no right to attend the meeting and that "even though the plaintiff was being illegally disciplined, his remedy was to resort to the orderly process of a union hearing or to the court, not to the use of physical resistance as a means of correcting the error. But for his physical resistance to being excluded, he would not have been injured." [45] The court ruled that "[t]he force and means used for his removal [did] not appear to have exceeded what was reasonable and necessary to accomplish this purpose considering his refusal to voluntarily leave and his resistance to being removed." [46] The appellate court confirmed, holding that the injury to the member "was caused by his improper physical resistance to being excluded from the union meeting at a time when he was suspended. . . ." [47]

---

met by still another disturbance designed to test the officer's judgment." State v. Smith, 46 N.J. 510, 218 A.2d 147, 151, *cert. denied*, 385 U.S. 838 (1966).

The intent of the ejector is an important factor. *See* Noonan v. Luther, 206 N.Y. 105, 108 (1912) (hotel employee was ejected by use of reasonable force).

Convenor of a public meeting in a private hall used no more force than was reasonable to eject a police inspector, and a police officer used no more force than was necessary to protect the inspector and prevent him from being ejected. Thomas v. Sawkins, [1935] 2 K.B. 249.

[44] SHAW AND SMITH, THE LAW OF MEETINGS at 19.

[45] McCraw v. United Ass'n of Journeymen & Apprentices, 216 F. Supp. 655, 659 (E.D. Tenn. 1963), *aff'd*, 341 F.2d 705 (6th Cir. 1965).

[46] *Id.* at 663.

[47] *Id.* at 710.

Defendant went to church for the purpose of getting the church authorities to change the rules and practices as to seating persons. The court charged the jury (a) that a church has the right to establish its own practices and rules for the admission and seating of persons and if one refused to comply with the

§ 14.12   Power To Eject and Keep Excluded

The power to eject a person from the place of meeting includes the power to keep him excluded.[48] Failure to withdraw from the meeting when ordered by the chairman makes the disturber amenable to forcible removal and confinement.[49] The length of time an ejected person may be kept from the meeting depends largely on the attendant circumstances and the time required reasonably to restore the meeting to a deliberative attitude. Recently it was held that a state legislature has the undoubted power to expel any disrupter (non-member) immediately and for a reasonable time to bar him from re-entering.[50] An early English case held that the power

rules the church authorities had the right to use reasonable force to evict him, and (b) that if defendant engaged in loud talking, shouting, and sitting on the floor to induce a change of rules, his desire to change the rules would not constitute a defense. It was held that the evidence authorized these instructions to the jury. Jones v. State, 219 Ga. 848, 136 S.E.2d 358, *cert. denied*, 379 U.S. 935 (1964).

[48] "If the good sense and conduct of the members of Colonial Legislatures prove, as in the present case, insufficient to secure order and decency of debate, the law would sanction the use of that degree of force which might be necessary to remove the person offending from the place of meeting, and to keep him excluded." Doyle v. Falconer, L.R. 1 P.C. 328, 340 (1866), *quoted in* Barton v. Taylor, 11 App. Cas. 197, 203 (P.C. 1886).

[49] A plaintiff was removed from a town meeting hall and confined, by order of the moderator, in a separate room for an hour until the meeting had adjourned, for failure to observe a ruling on a question of order. In a suit for false imprisonment, it was held that arrest of the plaintiff was warranted by law. "The judge was right in instructing the jury that under the statute the plaintiff was disorderly if he failed to observe the ruling of the moderator on a question of order. . . . The defendant was accordingly empowered to have him removed and confined." The moderator will be upheld "when as here, his action was neither malicious nor dishonest" and the court cannot substitute its judgment for his. Doggett v. Hooper, 306 Mass. 129, 27 N.E.2d 737 (1940).

[50] However, the legislature cannot summarily impose a jail sentence for contempt without providing the accused disrupter with some minimal opportunity to appear and to respond to the charge. In contrast, if such conduct took place in a courtroom, the judge might be empowered to impose a jail sentence summarily. Groppi v. Leslie, 311 F. Supp. 772 (W.D. Wis. 1970), *rev'd*, 436 F.2d 331 (7th Cir. 1971), *aff'd*, 404 U.S. 496 (1972). *See connected cases* Groppi v. Froehlich, 311 F. Supp. 765 (W.D. Wis. 1970); State *ex rel.* Groppi v. Leslie, 44 Wis. 2d 282, 171 N.W.2d 192 (1969).

to exclude a member from the meeting hall was limited by "what is required by the assumed necessity," which may extend as far as the whole duration of the meeting or the full sitting of the assembly in the course of which the offense was committed. Power to exclude beyond the current sitting or from future meetings is doubtful. "It seems to be reasonably necessary that some substantial interval should be interposed between the suspensory resolution and the resumption of his place in the assembly by the offender, in order to give opportunity for the subsidence of heat and passion, and for reflection on his own conduct by the person suspended; nor would anything less be sufficient for the vindication of the authority and the dignity of the assembly." The court then commented that "it may very well be, that the same doctrine of reasonable necessity would authorize a suspension until submission or apology by the offending member; which if he were refractory, might cause it to be prolonged (not by the arbitrary discretion of the Assembly, but by his own wilful default) for some further time." As to the habitually disorderly member, the court said: "Powers to suspend toties quoties [as often as occasion shall arise], sitting after sitting, in case of repeated offenses (and, it may be, till submission or apology), and also to expel for aggravated or persistent misconduct, appear to be sufficient to meet even the extreme case of a member whose conduct is habitually obstructive or disorderly." [51]

§ 14.12.1 Improper Ejectment

Should a person be unjustly removed or ejected from a meeting which he was entitled to attend, there are two basic remedies available to him. He may seek a criminal prosecution of the responsible

---

[51] A "sitting" is described as follows: "The sitting of a meeting, as a whole, has a practical unity. It commences with the usual forms of opening, when the Speaker takes the chair; it is terminated by the adjournment of the House." The "service" of members at each sitting is continuous. Barton v. Taylor, 11 App. Cas. 197, 204, 205 (P.C. 1886).

See Doyle v. Falconer, L.R. 1 P.C. 328 (1866) (suggestion that a legislative body has the power to eject a disruptive member "during its sitting"); Corre v. State, 8 Ohio Dec. Reprint 715 (Dist. Ct. 1883) (board resolution excluding news reporter from future meetings for causing disturbance at a former meeting).

officers [52] or commence civil proceedings for vindication of his rights in a court of law or before a regulatory body having jurisdiction [53] He may bring a suit in equity to set aside any action taken at the meeting subsequent to his wrongful ejection, on a showing that he intended to oppose and vote against such action, and that the result of the voting might have been different had he been permitted to state his case and vote with the minority.[54] He may also bring a common-law tort action grounded in assault, battery, and/or false imprisonment, ranging from an action for assault based on a simple laying on of hands with a demand for nominal damages, to an action for assault and battery and perhaps false imprisonment where unreasonable force was used to eject him and keep him in confinement even for a short period.[55] There appears to be no basic differences between criminal and civil proceedings insofar as the use of reasonable force is concerned.

[52] A taxpayer who was attending a public meeting of town trustees, which he had a right to attend, and who was not interfering with the proceedings, was put out of the meeting by the town marshal at the order of the presiding officer largely because he had made himself offensive before the meeting came to order. The marshal took the taxpayer by the coat when he went out but did not use any violence. The presiding officer was found guilty of assault and fined one dollar. The court reasoned that the taxpayer had a right to be at the meeting so long as he did not interfere with the proceedings and that when the marshal took hold of him to put him out the touching was unlawful. "The board of trustees had the undoubted right to maintain order; to remove any one interfering with the transaction of the business; but not arbitrarily to eject, or attempt to eject, one who was not thus offending." O'Hara v. State, 21 Ind. App. 320, 52 N.E. 414, 415 (1898).

[53] See McCraw v. United Ass'n of Journeymen & Apprentices, 216 F. Supp. 655 (E.D. Tenn. 1963), aff'd, 341 F.2d 705 (6th Cir. 1965).

[54] See notes 25 and 26 supra and accompanying text.

[55] RESTATEMENT (SECOND) OF TORTS §§ 13–20, 21–34, 35–45 (1965) (assault, battery, and false imprisonment); PROSSER, TORTS § 9 at 30–34, § 10 at 34–37, § 12 at 48–54 (2d ed. 1955) (battery, false imprisonment).

The ejected person will have several defendants to choose among. They are: the chairman of the meeting; those assisting the chairman voluntarily or under his direction (sergeant-at-arms, vestryman, marshal, usher, etc.); any other person who caused or aided the ejectment; and those who physically laid hands on the ejected person, such as the guard or security officer. See 5 FLETCHER, CYCLOPEDIA OF PRIVATE CORPORATIONS § 2014(1967).

§ 14.12.2   Action for Damages

In a private tort action, there are three acts warranting a claim for damages: (a) where the ejection was unjustified, but where no force, or no more than reasonable force, was used; (b) where the ejection was justified, but more than reasonable force was used; and (c) where the ejection was unjustified, and more than reasonable force was used.[56] The award of damages will follow traditional

---

[56] Plaintiff was ordered to leave the city council chamber when the council resolved itself into a committee of the whole for private deliberations. Plaintiff left the chamber to avoid forcible ejection and brought suit against members of the city council and the marshal to vindicate his right to be present at the meeting, claiming damages for great humiliation, chagrin, and indignity. The jury found for plaintiff and awarded him damages of one cent, which was affirmed on appeal. It was noted that the plaintiff was not forcibly ejected and that he did not predicate his right of recovery upon an assault and battery, nor from physical injury. The action was based on "his right to be present during the session of the city council as a public body while discharging public duties" under an "open door" statute. Acord v. Booth, 33 Utah 279, 93 P. 734 (1908) citing Cushing, Law & Pr. Leg. Assem.; Robert's Rules of Order; and Waples' Handbook Parliament. Pr.

The responsible officers of a corporation who forcibly ejected plaintiff stockholder from an annual meeting of stockholders on the ground that his shares had been cancelled, using no more force than was necessary to overcome his resistance, could not defend an action brought against them for assault on the ground that the plaintiff was a trespasser where it was shown that his shares were valid and he had a right to be present at the meeting. Judgment for plaintiff against corporate officers affirmed on appeal. Noller v. Wright, 138 Mich. 416, 101 N.W. 553 (1904).

Defendants were mayor and chief of police of the city, who served as president and executive officer of the city council. Plaintiff member of the council was conducted out of the council chamber for acting in an "unparliamentary, disorderly, boorish, and insulting manner." In an action for false imprisonment, the mayor and the officer were held liable in damages because they had no inherent authority, according to the usages of deliberative bodies, to order a member to be forcibly ejected from a council merely for disorderly behavior which did not threaten personal injury nor arrest the progress of business. The court concluded that imprisonment of plaintiff was "unnecessary and illegal." There was no question as to the use of reasonable force. Thompson v. Whipple, 15 S.W. 604, 605 (Ark. 1891), citing Cushing's Rules of Pro. & Deb. and Law & Pr. Leg. Assem.

Stockholder attended a meeting called for the election of a director solely in order to protest against the legality of the meeting, consistently taking that

lines. If malice is shown, the jury in its discretion may award exemplary damages.[57]

An action for assault need not involve physical force or injury and may be brought for a mere laying on of hands or for a grievous affront or threat to the ejected person without bodily contact. In determining whether the ejected person has a right of action for assault and battery, evidence of the intent of the ejected person is of vital importance, not on the amount of damages, but on the right

---

position at all times. So persistent was he in objecting to the legality of the meeting that he was ejected before any votes were received. In a proceeding to set aside the election it was held that such stockholder was not present in the sense that his stock could be counted in determining that a quorum was present. A new election was ordered. The use of force was not at issue. Leamy v. Sinaloa Explor. & Dev. Co., 15 Del. Ch. 28, 130 A. 282 (1925).

In an early English case the plaintiff entered a schoolroom when a select vestry was conducting a business meeting and persisted in making a "great noise and disturbance." He refused to depart when requested and when defendants quietly laid their hands upon him he violently resisted and "it then and there became and was necessary to use force and violence for the purpose of removing" plaintiff and he was "forced, pushed, pulled, dragged" out of the room. The court noted that force was "necessarily and unavoidably" given plaintiff "as it was lawful for them to do for the cause aforesaid, doing no unnecessary damage or injury" to plaintiff. It was held that defendants could not justify the assault since they were not duly assembled as a select vestry because one of them did not receive notice of the meeting. Dobson v. Fussy, 7 Bing. 305 (D.C. 1831). *Note:* Presumably the assault would have been justified if there had been a duly assembled meeting.

[57] "Damages, other than nominal, that are recoverable in certain types of tort actions, of which false imprisonment is one, have long been classified as compensatory and punitive in character. Compensatory damages, whether general or special, serve to make good, so far as it is possible to do so in dollars and cents, the harm done by a wrongdoer. Punitive damages, on the other hand, as the name implies, act not by way of compensation but by way of punishment of the wrongdoer and as an example to others. Such damages may be awarded in a proper case only where, and to the extent that, the wrongdoer has acted maliciously, wantonly or with a recklessness that betokens improper motive or vindictiveness. Moreover, even in a case where punitive damages may be warranted by the facts, it is for the jury in its discretion to say whether such damages will be awarded." Sanders v. Rolnick, 188 Misc. 627, 67 N.Y.S.2d 652, 657, *aff'd*, 71 N.Y.S.2d 896 (1st Dep't 1947). *See* McCORMICK, DAMAGES §§ 77, 79, 81, 84, 85 (1935).

of action itself. Evidence that the only purpose of using force was to effect a removal is critical.[58]

The law of agency holds the principal responsible for his agent's torts if the agent acts within the scope of his authority and in furtherance of his principal's interests.[59] Thus, a principal will be liable for the actual injury sustained when these two factors are proven. The principal may be the company.[60] If the agent acts with malice, the principal may be liable for exemplary damages.[61]

§ 14.12.3   Liability of Presiding Officer

The courts have considered the liability of the presiding officer for the ejection of a person from the meeting under various circumstances. It is well established that a chairman is liable in tort if he

---

[58] One court held that an employer had the right to use reasonable force to eject a servant after affording her a reasonable time to leave. "However violent her conduct may have been, he could not inflict violence to her person for punishment or through passion, but simply for the purpose of removing her. Therefore, his intent in using force, which he conceded he used to some extent, was the first thing for him to establish in order to justify what would otherwise have been an assault. True, his testimony on the subject would not have been conclusive, but it was competent." Noonan v. Luther, 206 N.Y. 105, 108 (1912).

[59] RESTATEMENT OF AGENCY § 235 (1934) (if the agent has no intention, at least in part, to perform any service for the principal but only to further a personal end, his act is not within his scope of employment); id. § 236 (so long as there is an intent, even if only subordinate, to serve his principal's purpose, the principal is liable if what is done is within the scope of the agent's authority).

[60] 1 MECHEM, AGENCY § 130 at 91 (2d ed. 1914).

[61] See, e.g., Safeway Stores v. Gibson, 118 A.2d 386 (D.C. Mun. App. 1955), aff'd, 237 F.2d 592 (D.C. Cir. 1956): "[A] principal may be held liable for exemplary damages based upon the wrongful act of his agent only where he participated in the doing of such wrongful act or had previously authorized or subsequently ratified it with full knowledge of the facts. The reasons given for this rule are that since such damages are penal in character, the motive authorizing their infliction will not be imputed by presumption to the principal when the act is committed by an agent or servant, and that since they are awarded not by way of compensation, but as a punishment of the offender and as a warning to him and others, they can only be awarded by one who has participated in the offense. The principal therefore cannot be liable for them merely by reason of wanton, oppressive or malicious intent on the part of the agent." Id. at 388.

ejects from the meeting a member or shareholder, or a person lawfully entitled to be present, without legal justification. The court
has held, for example, that officers of a corporation who caused a
shareholder to be ejected from the meeting on the ground that his
shares had been canceled were liable for a tortious ejectment on a
finding that his shares were valid and that he had a right to be
present.[62]

A more difficult question arises when the ejection is justified, but
excessive force is used. Practically speaking, the chairman may
have little direct control over the manner in which his orders are
carried out. The aggressiveness of the objector and the consequent
turmoil may be such that the chairman has no choice except to
entrust to others the responsibility of removing an unruly person
from the premises, and the decision as to the amount of force required under all the circumstances. A court can decide either that
the agents acted within their scope of authority or that they exceeded their authority when they used force claimed to be excessive
to effect what would otherwise be a proper ejection.

It is submitted that a more limited view of agency should be
adopted. In an early English case the court upheld the authority
of the chairman to quell a disturbance of the meeting. When disorder erupted in the back of the hall at an association meeting,
the chairman ordered: "I shall be obliged to bring those men to the
front who are making the disturbance. Bring those men to the
front." A steward and two policemen acting in good faith and
seemingly on their own initiative in deciding who were the disturb-

---

[62] The plaintiff was forcibly ejected, "using no more force than was necessary to overcome his resistance." The decision does not show whether the
responsible officers directly used force or caused the plaintiff to be removed by
a guard or a sergeant-at-arms. Noller v. Wright, 138 Mich. 416, 101 N.W.
553 (1904).

The mayor of a city, as president of its council, had no authority to order
a member to be forcibly excluded from a council meeting for disorderly or
indecorous behavior which did not threaten personal injury or arrest the progress of business. The mayor and the officer who executed his order were held
responsible in an action for false imprisonment. Thompson v. Whipple, 54
Ark. 203, 15 S.W. 604 (1891).

"Where the trespass complained of is the direct and necessary consequence
of an order given for its committal, the person who gives the order is clearly
liable for the consequences, as much as if the trespass were done by his own
hand. . . ." 2 MECHEM, AGENCY § 1873 at 1457 (2d ed. 1914).

ers, seized the plaintiff, dragged him forward, and caused him to
be bruised and injured. The plaintiff was not in fact one of those
disturbing the meeting. He sued the chairman for assault, and the
court was faced with the question whether the chairman's order
could be interpreted to mean: "Determine who are the disturbers,
and when you have done so, bring forward those whom you so determine to be disturbers." The court, noting that the chairman has
a duty "to do his best to preserve order," held that there was no
evidence of any general or implied authority going beyond the limit
of that created by the express words used by the chairman.[63]

Under principles of agency, the corporation appears liable for an
improper ejection, whether the illegal aspects were due to the unjustified nature of the ejection itself, or to the unreasonable use of
force to accomplish the ejection, or to both. The chairman, when
preserving order, acts as the corporation's agent. Unless he acts

---

[63] Lucas v. Mason, (1875) L.R. 10, 251–54. The court stated: "In the
present case there was no relation of master and servant, or of principal and
general agent, or agent for such cases as might occur in the absence of the
principal, but a particular direction as to a particular matter, and this, in our
judgment, not only prevents the decisions referred to binding us as authorities,
but makes them inapplicable in principle. In the case of master and servant,
the character and duties attaching to the employment are known and defined
beforehand, the servant who is to perform them is selected accordingly. In the
present case no such relationship existed in the first instance, nor did it arise
during the transaction. It is no doubt the duty of the chairman of a meeting,
where a large body of people are gathered together, to do his best to preserve
order, and it is equally the duty of those who are acting as stewards or managers to assist him in so doing, but the nature and extent of this duty on both
sides cannot be very closely defined a priori, and must necessarily arise out of,
and in character and extent depend upon, the events and emergencies which
may from time to time arise. There is no such pre-existing relationship as exists
in the case of master and servant, and there is, we think, no ground for extending
by implication an express authority limited in its terms. The disturbance which
gave rise to the defendant's words took place in the presence of those who
acted upon them. They were nearer to the plaintiff than was the defendant,
and, if in doubt, might have referred to the defendant for further instructions.
It does not, therefore, seem to us that there was any evidence which should
have been submitted to the jury of a general or implied authority going beyond
the limit of that which was created by the express words used, or of any authority to the persons ordered to bring the disturbers forward to exercise a discretion as to who were disturbers."

from malice [64] he acts in furtherance of its interests. Company officials and mercenary guards,[65] when carrying out the chairman's orders, also act for the corporation's benefit and their actions are binding on the principal. In parliamentary law, the person who procures the arrest of another by judicial process, by instituting and conducting the proceedings, is liable to an action for false imprisonment, when he acts without probable cause; but members of the legislative body who did not personally assist in the arrest or imprisonment, nor order the same except by their votes and by participation as members in the official proceedings, cannot be held liable.[66]

§ 14.13 Expulsion of Member

In any discussion of the rights inherent in an organization to maintain order in its deliberations and in the conduct of its affairs,

[64] When a presiding officer acts from malice, he acts against the corporate interests. By maliciously expelling a member, he willfully acts against the purposes for which the meeting was called. See 2 MECHEM, AGENCY §§ 1930–1951 (2d ed. 1914).

[65] RESTATEMENT OF AGENCY § 220(1)–(2) (1934) lists the factors to be considered when determining when an individual is an independent contractor or a servant. Cf. § 227 and comment (servant directed by his master to perform acts for another). See PROSSER, TORTS § 62 at 350–51, n. 5.

See Pinkerton v. Sydnor, 87 Ill. App. 76 (1889); Pinkerton v. Martin, 82 Ill. App. 589 (1898).

The company's position is somewhat analogous to that of a department store which hires a detective agency to police its premises. Almost invariably, the store is liable for the torts of its guards when acting within the scope of their authority. Annot., 35 A.L.R. 677 (1925), 92 A.L.R.2d 61 (1963).

See, e.g., Griswold v. Hollywood Turf Club, 235 P.2d 656 (Cal. Dist. Ct. App. 1951); Alterauge v. Los Angeles Turf Club, 97 Cal. App. 735, 218 P.2d 802 (1950); Safeway Stores v. Gibson, 118 A.2d 386 (D.C. Mun. App. 1955), aff'd, 237 F.2d 592 (D.C. Cir. 1956); Adams v. F. W. Woolworth Co., 144 Misc. 27,·257 N.Y.S. 776 (1932); Szymanski v. Great Atl. & Pac. Tea Co., 79 Ohio App. 407, 85 Ohio Op. 177, 74 N.E.2d 205, 206 (1947); W. T. Grant Co. v. Owens, 149 Va. 906, 924, 141 S.E. 860 (1928).

Police officers may not always honor a chairman's request to intervene. See In re Election of Dirs. of Bushwick Sav. & Loan Ass'n, 189 Misc. 316, 70 N.Y.S.2d 478 (1947) (stockholders' meeting).

Police officer has authority to use his judgment, and failure to obey his directions may constitute disorderly conduct. People v. Galpern, 259 N.Y. 279, 284–85, 181 N.E. 572 (1932).

[66] See Kilbourn v. Thompson, 103 U.S. 168 (1881).

the distinction between expulsion of a member from the organization and ejectment of a member from a meeting must be fully recognized. Expulsion is the more serious and lasting affair. Ejectment may be only temporary.

The power to expel a member is naturally and necessarily incidental to all legislative bodies. An early case noted that "[t]hus by the common parliamentary law the Senate has the power, among other things . . . to preserve its own honor, dignity, purity and efficiency, by the expulsion of an unworthy or the discharge of an incompetent member. . . ." [67]

Generally, the statutory law of membership organizations regulates or provides for the adoption of by-laws governing the censure, suspension, and expulsion of members. Often provision is made for prior notice, the filing of charges, and the granting of an opportunity to be heard before action may be taken to expel a member.

§ 14.13.1   Inherent in Whole Body

The more drastic power to exclude, expel, or disenfranchise a member is inherent in the whole body, and may be exercised by the membership itself or, preferably, by the enforcement of a duly adopted by-law or resolution. [68] An organization may make rules

[67] *Ex parte* McCarthy, 29 Cal. Rptr. 395, 404 (1866), *citing* Cushing. *See* § 9.1, n. 3 *supra*.

[68] "The authorities on the subject unite in saying that corporations such as the one here involved [nonprofit grocers' corporation] have an inherent power to disfranchise their members for any one of three causes, namely, offenses of an infamous character indictable at common law; offenses against the members' duties as a corporator; and offenses compounded of the two. . . . While the power to expel a member is primarily in the whole body of members constituting or representing the corporation, the better view is that such power may be exercised by its directors, trustees, or other officers, by a duly adopted by-law or resolution not contrary to its charter or the law." Gottlieb v. Economy Stores, Inc., 199 Va. 848, 102 S.E.2d 345, 351 (1958).

"In the absence of an express provision in the constitution or by-laws, the power of expulsion belongs to the association, e.g., to the membership at large. By parity of reasoning, therefore, in the absence of any provision as to procedure regulating the filing of charges and subsequent preliminary procedure before trial, they must be filed with the members of the association, as a body, at a meeting of the association, and they, as such body, must prescribe the preliminary procedure." Weinberg v. Carton, 196 Misc. 74, 90 N.Y.S.2d 398, 400 (1949).

See Martire v. Laborers' Local Union 1058, 410 F.2d 32 (3d Cir.), *cert. denied*, 396 U.S. 903 (1969) (expulsion from labor union); Gonzales v. International Ass'n of Machinists, 142 Cal. App. 2d 207, 298 P.2d 92 (1956), *aff'd*, 356 U.S. 617 (1958) (action to obtain reinstatement of former member of union), *citing* Robert's Rules of Order; State *ex rel.* O'Brien v. Petry, 397 S.W.2d 1 (Mo. 1965) (expulsion from guild); Battipaglia v. Executive Comm., 20 Misc. 2d 226, 191 N.Y.S.2d 288 (Sup. Ct. 1959) (petition to review removal "for cause" of chairman of Democratic Co. Comm.); Norman v. Roosevelt Democratic Club, 17 Misc. 2d 219, 184 N.Y.S.2d 980 (Sup. Ct. 1959) (proceeding for order directing political club to restore petitioner as member of board of directors and for order rescinding resolution which expelled petitioner from club); Briggs v. Technocracy, 85 N.Y.S.2d 735 (Sup. Ct. 1948) (expulsion of member from membership corporation without prior notice, statement of charges, or opportunity to be heard is illegal although by-laws make no express provision for a hearing); Yockel v. German–American Bund, 20 N.Y.S.2d 774 (Sup. Ct. 1940) (arbitrary expulsion).

"The right to expel extends to all cases where the offence is such as in the judgment of the Senate is inconsistent with the trust and duty of a member." *In re* Chapman, 166 U.S. 661, 669–70 (1897).

Suspension or expulsion from a membership corporation at a meeting not legally called is invalid. Stein v. Marks, 44 Misc. 140, 89 N.Y.S. 921 (Sup. Ct. 1904).

But see Schrank v. Brown, 194 Misc. 138, 86 N.Y.S.2d 209, 214 (Sup. Ct. 1949) *citing* Robert's Rules of Order, holding that a union convention's jurisdiction to try a local and an individual on charges of slander cannot be implied from the "inherent right" of an association to expel a member for a gross breach of his obligation to support loyally the proper purposes of the association, nor from the "inherent right" of a deliberative assembly to make and enforce its own laws and punish any offending member. *See also* Schrank v. Brown, 192 Misc. 80, 80 N.Y.S.2d 452 (Sup. Ct. 1948) (earlier decision).

An early Massachusetts case relating to the expulsion of a member of the House of Representatives, held: "The power of expulsion is a necessary and incidental power, to enable the house to perform its high functions, and is necessary to the safety of the State. It is a power of protection. A member may be physically, mentally or morally, wholly unfit; he may be afflicted with a contagious disease, or insane, or noisy, violent and disorderly, or in the habit of using profane, obscene and abusive language. . . . As to the law and custom of parliament, the authorities cited clearly show that the jurisdiction to commit, and also to expel, has long been recognized, not only in parliament, but in the courts of law, for the purposes of protection and punishment." Hiss v. Bartlett, 69 Mass. (3 Gray) 468, 473 (1855).

For distinction between exclusion and expulsion, see Powell v. McCormack, 395 U.S. 486 (1969) (exclusion of Congressman); *In re* Milanovics Petition, 162 F. Supp. 890, 892 (S.D.N.Y. 1957), *aff'd*, 253 F.2d 941 (2d Cir. 1958) (exclusion of alien). For distinction between removal of an officer and expulsion of a member, *see* Ostrom v. Greene, 161 N.Y. 353, 362, 55 N.E. 919

by which the admission and expulsion of its members are to be regulated, and the members must conform to these rules.[69] If rules have not been adopted, those of the common law prevail.[70] "But independently of parliamentary custom and usages, our legislative houses have the power to protect themselves, by the punishment and expulsion of a member."[71]

§ 14.14   Non-Members

However, a non-member cannot be punished for disrupting a meeting by the imposition of sanctions unrelated to the meeting itself. For example, a non-member of an Indian tribe cannot be excluded from the Indian reservation for disrupting a committee meeting of the tribal council.[72]

(1900). For distinction between expulsion and voluntary withdrawal, *see* New York Protective Ass'n v. McGrath, 5 N.Y.S. 8, 10 (1889).

[69] The rules of Cushing's Manual, adopted by the corporation to govern its debates, were not observed in the expulsion of a member for using offensive language at a prior meeting. The expulsion was held improper. People *ex rel.* Godwin v. American Inst., 44 How. Pr. 468, 471 (N.Y. Sup. Ct. 1873).

The Speaker of the House of Representatives has ruled that a majority vote of the House would be sufficient to pass a resolution excluding a member and declaring his seat vacant. Powell v. McCormack, 395 U.S. 486, 509 (1969).

For example, the Standing Orders (Ch. XXX) of the Legislative Assembly of New South Wales, Australia, provide that a member may be subject to suspension by the chairman with the concurrence of the assembly if he has (a) persistently and wilfully obstructed the business of the assembly; or (b) been guilty of disorderly conduct; or (c) used objectionable words which he has refused to withdraw; or (d) persistently and willfully refused to conform to the Standing Orders or any of them; or (e) persistently and willfully disregarded the authority of the chairman. NEW SOUTH WALES PARLIAMENTARY HANDBOOK at 141 (7th Ed. 1957)

[70] Any society may make rules by which the admission and expulsion of its members are to be regulated, and the members must conform to those rules. If, however, there are no rules governing the case, those of the common law prevail. Before a member can be expelled, notice must be given him to answer the charges and an opportunity offered to make his defense. Jones v. State, 28 Neb. 495, 44 N.W. 658 (1890).

See 18 AM. JUR. 2d, *Corporations* § 473 (1965) (expulsion of members from corporation); 20 A.L.R.2d 244 (expulsion from social club).

[71] Hiss v. Bartlett, 69 Mass. (3 Gray) 468, 475 (1855).

[72] Dodge v. Makai, 298 F. Supp. 26 (D. Ariz. 1969).

15

Chairman

AUTHORITY TO PRESIDE

§ 15.1 Authority Derived from Assembly

It is essential that a meeting have a presiding officer endowed with authority to conduct its affairs and maintain order. Without a presiding officer acting in his full capacity, the business of a meeting could not be conducted in an orderly fashion and the gathering would be futile. The person duly endowed with authority to control and superintend the meeting is generally styled the chairman.[1]

The chairman derives his authority from the assembly over which he presides. An early decision in the English courts [2] ably stated: "There is not, as far as I know, any case which has ever arisen to guide us in deciding how far the powers of a chairman extend. . . . Public meetings must be regulated somehow; and when a number of persons assemble and put a man in the chair they devolve on him by agreement, the conduct of that body. They attorn to him, as it were, and give him the whole power of regulating themselves individually. This is within reasonable bounds. The chairman collects, as it were, his authority from the meeting."

Another early English case [3] briefly describes the functions and

[1] "The word *chairman* is frequently used to designate the presiding officer, but, not, of any legislative assembly; being more commonly applied to committees, and other assemblies of a temporary character. This term seems to derive its origin from the circumstance that in early times the presiding officer alone was furnished with a chair; because he must necessarily sit by himself, apart from the others, who were provided only with benches. Hence in modern times the presiding officer frequently denominates himself, and is spoken of by others, as the chair." CUSHING, LAW AND PRACTICE OF LEGISLATIVE ASSEMBLIES at 111 (1856).

"The presiding officer, when no special title has been assigned him, is ordinarily called the Chairman, or the President, or, especially in religious assemblies, the Moderator." Robert's Rules of Order at 236.

"The president of a private corporation is, as the term implies, the presiding officer of its board of directors, and of its shareholders when convened in general meeting." Streuber v. St. Mary's Pipe Co., 33 Pa. Co. Ct. 46, 48 (1906).

[2] See CURRY (CREW), PUBLIC, COMPANY AND LOCAL GOVERNMENT MEETINGS at 27 and SHACKLETON, THE LAW AND PRACTICE OF MEETINGS at 53, *both citing* Taylor v. Nesfield (1854) (WILLS ON PARISH VESTRIES at 29 n.).

An American court of the same period said that: "The duty of a moderator is merely to preside and see that the proceedings are conducted in a legal and orderly manner. In doing this, he acts only as the agent of the corporation." Stebbins v. Merritt, 64 Mass. (10 Cush.) 27, 34 (1852).

[3] National Dwellings Soc'y v. Sykes, [1894] 3 Ch. 159, 162, *per* Chitty, J., *quoted in* Shaw and Smith at 46.

"The duty of a chairman of a meeting is to ascertain the sense of the meeting upon any resolution properly coming before the meeting." Second Consol. Trust Ltd. v. Ceylon Amalg. Tea & Rubber Estates, Ltd., 2 All. E.R. 567, 569 [Ch. Div. 1943].

The person who presides at the meeting is the proper individual to decide if and when to adjourn to take a poll. "It is upon him that it devolves, both

powers of the chairman in the following language: "Unquestionably it is the duty of the chairman, and his function, to preserve
order, and to take care that the proceedings are conducted in a
proper manner, and that the sense of the meeting is properly ascertained with regard to any question which is properly before the
meeting."

American common law follows the English concept. "A presiding
officer derives his powers from the assembly over which he presides.
He is only a means for enabling the body to exercise its powers in an
orderly way. His opinion as to what was necessary cannot be taken
as a substitute for the doing of a necessary thing." [4]

---

to preserve order in the meeting, and to regulate the proceedings so as to give
all persons entitled a reasonable opportunity of voting. He is to do the acts
necessary for these purposes on his own responsibility, and subject to being
called upon to answer for his conduct if he has done anything improperly."
Regina v. D'Oyly, 12 Adolph. & E. 139, 159 (Q.B. 1840) (meeting of churchwardens).

"It is, of course, his [Chairman's] duty to take care that the business of the
Board is conducted in a proper manner, but he must be equally careful in his
capacity of Chairman to conduct himself impartially and to see that the opinion
of the meeting is properly ascertained upon any question which is regularly
before the meeting. If he had any misgivings as to whether the meeting was
in order, he might well have obtained the opinion of the Board's solicitor or
even instructed the Board's solicitor to take counsel's opinion." Arcus v. Castle,
[1954] N.Z.L.R. 122, 129 (1953) (hospital board).

"It is no doubt the duty of the chairman of a meeting when a large body of
people are gathered together, to do his best to preserve order, and it is equally
the duty of those who are acting as stewards and managers to assist him in so
doing, but the nature and extent of this duty on both sides cannot be very
closely defined a priori, and must necessarily arise out of, and in character and
extent depend upon, the events and emergencies which may from time to time
arise." Lucas v. Mason, (1875) L.R. 10, 254.

[4] Casler v. Tanzer, 134 Misc. 48, 234 N.Y.S. 571, 579 (1929), *citing* Cushing's Manual.

"The majority attending the meeting was the governing power, not the person who for the time being held the office of president. She was but the agent
of the body to do its lawful will. . . ." Ostrom v. Greene, 20 Misc. 177, 45
N.Y.S. 852, 858 (1897), *aff'd*, 30 App. Div. 621, 52 N.Y.S. 1147 (1898), *aff'd*,
161 N.Y. 353, 55 N.E. 919 (1900).

The chairman's authority "is derived wholly from the assembly itself, and
. . . he is only the means provided for enabling the body to exercise its powers
in an orderly way. His functions are utterly unimportant, save as they are

§ 15.1.1   Must Exercise His Authority

When the presiding officer is designated by statute or charter, he must be permitted to function in that capacity. A leading case holds that when the city charter provided that the mayor shall be an ex officio member of the board and shall preside at all its meetings at which he may be present, his power to preside must be observed. "If, being present at any meeting, he does not preside, then the board is not organized in the manner pointed out by the charter." Thus, when the mayor was present and ready to preside but his authority as presiding officer was openly and persistently disregarded and defied by the members of the board, the proceedings taken were of no avail and were invalid. The court said that "although all the members should be present, if the mayor, being present, does not preside, it would be but an irregular assemblage of persons, unknown to the charter, and whose act, however formally gone through with or however carefully written out, would have no validity to bind the city, or to give title to any appointee." [5]

---

auxiliary to that end." Hicks v. Long Branch Comm'n, 69 N.J.L. 300, 305, 55 A. 250, 251 (1903), *citing* Cushing, Law & Pr. Leg. Assem.

"The right of the majority of the members to control the action of the meeting cannot be questioned. A presiding officer cannot arbitrarily defeat the will of the majority by refusing to entertain or put motions, by wrongfully declaring the result of a vote, or by refusing to permit the expression by the majority of its will. He is the representative of the body over which he presides. His will is not binding on it, but its will, legally expressed by a majority of its members, is binding." American Aberdeen-Angus Breeders' Ass'n v. Fullerton, 325 Ill. 323, 156 N.E. 314, 316 (1927) (nonprofit corporation).

[5] The court noted that "the mayor did not act as presiding officer at all. He did not put the question; he did not declare the result." State *ex rel.* Southey v. Lashar, 71 Conn. 540, 546, 547, 42 A. 636, 638 (1899), *citing* Cushing, Parl. Law *and* Law & Pr. Leg. Assem.

Where the by-laws provide that the president shall preside and the secretary shall keep the minutes, they cannot "function as such" at a special meeting unless it is duly called. In re J. A. Maurer, Inc., 77 N.Y.S.2d 159, 161 (Sup. Ct. 1947).

Where the rector is the only person entitled to call and preside at annual and special meetings, and where he is prevented by another faction from performing his duties, meetings called and presided over by another are illegal. Rector, Churchwardens and Vestrymen v. Manufacturers Trust Co., 18 Misc.

The chairman, unless rules of order to the contrary are adopted for or by the meeting, plays a definite role in determining initially the agenda and the rules of order. An early English court noted, in ruling on the taking of a poll at the election of churchwardens, that those who summon a meeting must necessarily "lay down some order for the proceedings" which are to be followed.[6] In another case the court ruled that the procedure of an election is like everything else at general meetings of shareholders: "[T]he details of the proceedings must be regulated by the persons present, and by the chairman, and if his decision is quarrelled with it must be regulated by the majority of those present. Of course it must be presumed that they do it all honestly and fairly." [7]

The chairman of a state political party has broad powers in designating the time and place for holding required meetings, such as a judicial convention for the nomination of candidates, and his actions will generally be upheld if they are not arbitrary or capricious and the persons entitled to attend the meeting are not prejudiced by his actions.[8] When the chairman of the executive committee of a political party has authority to issue all calls for meetings of the county committee, he may not capriciously or unreasonably refuse to convene the committee and thereby paralyze that body to the detriment of the party.[9]

§ 15.2   Disciplinary Powers—Rules of Order

The chairman has general disciplinary powers over the conduct of the meeting and in case of disorder or great emergency he has the right to declare the meeting adjourned to some other time or place

---

2d 761, 184 N.Y.S.2d 876 (1959), *aff'd,* 9 App. Div. 2d 932, 196 N.Y.S.2d 561, *appeal dismissed,* 10 App. Div. 2d 628, 196 N.Y.S.2d 562 (1960) (church corporation).

[6] Rex. v. Archdeacon of Chester, 1 Adolph. & E. 342, 345 (K.B. 1834).

[7] Wandsworth and Putney Gas-Light & Coke Co. v. Wright, 22 L.T. 404, 405 [1870] (question of procedure used to select scrutiniers), *quoted in* Curry at 110.

[8] Bannigan v. Heffernan, 280 App. Div. 891, 115 N.Y.S.2d 444, *modifying* 203 Misc. 126, 115 N.Y.S.2d 889, *aff'd,* 304 N.Y. 729, 108 N.E.2d 209 (1952) (chairman cancelled meeting because of inadequate seating accommodations).

[9] Thoefel v. Butler, 134 Misc. 259, 236 N.Y.S. 81, 85 (1929).

without a vote of the members.[10] Thus, it appears proper for the chairman to formulate and announce certain simple and reasonable procedures designed to govern the proceedings in an orderly and accustomed fashion, as is often done at deliberative meetings where specific rules of order have not previously been imposed or adopted. If a member or shareholder disagrees with any such rule he can demand an appeal to the meeting when the rules are announced. The majority will then determine the issue, and the rules as adopted will be applicable to the meeting and any adjournments thereof. Unless there is an objection from the floor followed by a successful appeal to the assembled members or stockholders the rules as announced by the chair will govern the proceedings.[11]

Although the chairman has authority to delineate rules of order, and to regulate the discussion, he cannot act arbitrarily. For example, at a shareholders' meeting shareholders present may force an appeal from his ruling, and if he arbitrarily frustrates the majority rule "the assembly has the right to pass him by and proceed to action otherwise," or to remove him from office.[12]

---

[10] Marvin v. Manash, 175 Ore. 311, 153 P.2d 251, 254 (1944), *citing* Robert's Rules of Order § 58.

"If there was disorder it was incumbent upon the chairman to quiet the disorder or cease doing business until there was the proper atmosphere for the proper conduct of business. Failure to do this was a grave irregularity." *In re* Ryan v. Grimm, 43 Misc. 2d 836, 840, 252 N.Y.S.2d 521, *aff'd*, 22 App. Div. 2d 171, 254 N.Y.S.2d 462 (1964), *aff'd*, 15 N.Y.2d 922, 206 N.E.2d 867, 258 N.Y.S.2d 843 (1965).

[11] *See* § 15.8 *infra.*

See State v. Moore, 101 N.J. Super. 419, 244 A.2d 522 (1968) (the Newark Planning Board held a public meeting in the city council chamber to determine whether a certain area was eligible for an urban renewal program. The chairman "outlined the procedure that would govern the hearing" but the defendant insisted that Robert's Rules be followed. The chairman explained that the defendant must follow the procedure set by the Board and that the Board was "not using *Robert's.*" Defendant persisted and he was ruled out of order several times. Defendant continued to interrupt the meeting and was led from the council chamber by a police officer).

[12] A leading case explains that: "The authority of a chairman is derived wholly from the assembly itself, and . . . he is only a means provided for enabling the body to exercise its powers in an orderly way. His functions are utterly unimportant, save as they are auxiliary to that end. When, therefore, his conduct in any particular case has no other aim and effect than to thwart the purpose which his office is designed to assist, there must reside in the as-

Where procedures for a meeting have been established by higher authority, it is incumbent upon the chairman to follow such procedures, especially when the circumstances indicate that the proceedings of the meeting may be challenged if not properly conducted. For example, where the order of business to be followed at the organizational meeting of a county political committee provides that rules are to be adopted to govern the conduct of the meeting, the failure of the presiding officer to observe the order of business and to adopt rules constitutes an "irregularity" under the election laws sufficient to warrant the nullifying of the meeting and the directing of a reconvened meeting.[13] Such dire consequences compel the chairman to be aware of his duties and to carry them out.

The authority and duty of the chairman extends to every facet of the conduct of the meeting. As an officer of the organization,[14] the chairman has broad generally recognized powers. In describing the statutory powers of a New England town moderator, the court said: "The power to serve carries with it the authority to exercise the usual rights possessed by one occupying such a position . . . the duties of which have in the course of years been well and generally known and understood."[15] A moderator "rules as he under-

---

sembly a right to pass him by and proceed to action otherwise. . . . The power is inherent and inseparably attached to the right of the body to convene and act. It is exercisable, when not restrained by some extrinsic law, at the will of the body." Hicks v. Long Branch Comm'n, 69 N.J.L. 300, 55 A. 250, 251 (1903), *citing* Jefferson's Manual, Cushing, Law & Pr. Leg. Assem.

[13] *In re* Ryan v. Grimm, 43 Misc. 2d 836, 252 N.Y.S.2d 521, *aff'd*, 22 App. Div. 2d 171, 254 N.Y.S.2d 462 (1964), *aff'd*, 15 N.Y.2d 922, 206 N.E.2d 867, 258 N.Y.S.2d 843 (1965).

[14] A chairman may be more than a mere presiding officer such as is contemplated under parliamentary law. Van Cleve v. Wallace, 216 Minn. 500, 13 N.W.2d 467 (1944), *citing* Robert's Rules of Order (president of city council is an officer of the city and, in case of vacancy, he becomes the mayor).

See Ketchmark v. Lynch, 107 Ill. App. 2d 36, 246 N.E.2d 133 (1969) (term "corporate authorities" includes mayor or village president; term "alderman" does not include mayor).

[15] Doggett v. Hooper, 306 Mass. 129, 27 N.E.2d 737, 740 (1940).

However, a chairman may be estopped by his own conduct from questioning the legality of a meeting where all the stockholders attended and participated while he occupied the chair. Camp v. Shannon, 162 Tex. 515, 348 S.W.2d 517 (1961) (stockholders' meeting held on wrong day and without sufficient notice).

stands he ought to rule," and if his ruling is incorrect any person who is dissatisfied may appeal to the meeting and its decision will be conclusive.[16]

§ 15.3 Emergent Questions—Motions from Floor

The chairman has "authority to decide all emergent questions which necessarily require decision at the time."[17] For example, where a minority shareholder wishes to place a representative on the board of directors and names a nominee, the other shareholders who are asked to vote on the nominee are entitled to know the background and interests of the nominating shareholder and also of his nominee, and it is reasonable to so provide in the by-laws. The chairman of the meeting has the right and duty to determine whether such by-law requirements have been satisfied and to so declare to the meeting. This authority and duty in the chairman is inherent in his position and cannot be characterized as mere "unbridled discretion." One Federal district court remarked: "Otherwise a shareholder might vote for a nominee not realizing the nominee had been disqualified."[18] The chairman has authority to issue a ruling on the relevancy of a motion within the scope of a notice of a special meeting, and to rule that members of a committee which had recommended a penalty against a member of the body may vote on the member's appeal at a special meeting.[19]

The chairman also, in the absence of higher authority, has the right to determine whether the voting for inspectors of election shall be per capita or per share.[20] However, neither the presiding officer

---

[16] Hill v. Goodwin, 56 N.H. 441, 454 (1876).

[17] *In re* Indian Zoedone Co., 26 Ch. D. 70, 77 (1884), *cited in* Shackleton at 54 and in Shaw and Smith at 46 (resolution at extraordinary general meeting, with chairman's decision on poll entered in minute book. Decision challenged).

[18] McKee & Co. v. First Nat'l Bank, 265 F. Supp. 1, 10 (S.D. Cal. 1967), *aff'd*, 397 F.2d 248 (9th Cir. 1968).

[19] *See* Posner v. Bronx County Medical Soc'y, 19 App. Div. 2d 89, 241 N.Y.S.2d 540, *aff'd*, 13 N.Y.2d 1004, 195 N.E.2d 59, 245 N.Y.S.2d 393 (1963), *reference to* Robert's Rules as adopted by defendant.

[20] Where the statute and by-laws provide that if an inspector neglects to attend an election the "meeting" may appoint an inspector in his place, there is no requirement that stockholders shall vote at all or in any particular manner.

nor the inspectors of election have the power to determine the qualifications of voters at a corporate election or to deny holders of record
the right to vote. When this was done, the court admonished:
"The president usurped powers; the inspectors exceeded their
powers." [21] Acceptance by the chairman of a vote by proxy is not
binding on the organization and does not constitute a basis to sustain
a proxy vote, unless the member had a legal right to vote by proxy.[22]

The chairman should not engage in controversy with members in
attendance at a meeting. However, if he does, his actions are to be
judged according to the circumstances of each case including the
setting in which the incident occurred.[23]

It is the duty of the chairman to rule on motions from the floor
and to make determinations.[24] The chairman cannot prevent the
transaction of business at a meeting by refusing to put motions or by
leaving the meeting. "When she refused to put a motion to the
meeting in respect to a matter concerning which she apparently
differed from the majority, that refusal could not properly stand in

---

"The person or persons presiding at the meeting can determine the right of a
person to vote per capita as well as of his right to vote shares of stock." *In re*
Remington Typewriter Co., 234 N.Y. 296, 299, 137 N.E. 335, 336 (1922).

[21] *In re* Robert Clark, Inc., 186 App. Div. 216, 174 N.Y.S. 314, 316 (2d
Dep't 1919).
The chairman does not have authoritative word on who may vote and when
proxies are valid. *In re* Martin, 34 Minn. 135, 24 N.W. 353 (1885).

[22] Hart v. Sheridan, 168 Misc. 386, 5 N.Y.S.2d 820, 825 (1938).

[23] A chairman at a union meeting was charged with threatening a member
with disciplinary action unless he withdrew his motion for the election of shop
stewards by secret ballot. In determining whether the member's freedom of
expression had been inhibited, the court concluded that it must consider the
setting in which the incident occurred, the statement made by the chairman,
and the effect upon the member. In this case there was no evidence that the
member was intimidated by the statement, that the remark caused him to
yield the floor, or that it inhibited him in speaking at union business meetings.
Broomer v. Schultz, 239 F. Supp. 699, 703 (E.D. Pa. 1965).

[24] The chairman ruled that a motion approving the use of proxies in a political committee election had carried. "It is undisputed that the respondent ruled
that motion had carried. It is undisputed that it was the duty of the respondent
to rule on the motion and make a determination. If the petitioner felt that the
respondent made an error in his determination, then it was his duty to demand
a roll call vote to resolve the question." McDonough v. Purcell, 44 Misc. 2d
23, 252 N.Y.S.2d 752 (Sup. Ct. 1964).

the way of the association going on with its business, nor could her departure from the meeting upon the failure of a motion to adjourn justly operate as a veto upon the further or future deliberations and actions of the association." [25] "A presiding officer cannot arbitrarily defeat the will of the majority by refusing to entertain or put motions, by wrongly declaring the result of a vote, or by refusing to permit the expression by the majority of its will. He is the representative of the body over which he presides." [26]

However, where a shareholders' meeting was split into two opposing factions, each purporting to act upon the election of directors, and the division "prevented the ascertaining and carrying out of the will of those entitled to participate in the election of directors" the court upheld the chairman's refusal to recognize illegal maneuvers and declared: "We think that the law justifies regarding the meet-

---

[25] Ostrom v. Greene, 20 Misc. 177, 45 N.Y.S. 852, 858 (Sup. Ct. 1897), aff'd, 30 App. Div. 621, 52 N.Y.S. 1147 (3d Dep't 1898), aff'd, 161 N.Y. 353, 55 N.E. 919 (1900).

[26] American Aberdeen-Angus Breeders' Ass'n v. Fullerton, 325 Ill. 323, 156 N.E. 314, 316 (1927).

"Certainly the chairman of a meeting cannot paralyze the action of the majority by a refusal to discharge the functions of his office. It would be a monstrous doctrine that one man in a body of several hundred could stop all business until some court . . . had issued a writ of mandamus to compel action on his part, each refusal being followed by the impotence of the majority until some tribunal should come to their aid. When the chairman refused to put the motion . . . all that was left for the majority to do, if they were not to be thwarted in their purpose, was to have some one of their number put the motion, and call for the vote upon it. This was done, and there is no pretense that it worked any injury to the minority, or that it deprived them of any of their rights as members of the board. And it was obvious that the same result would have been reached had the chairman himself put the motion, as it was his duty to do." State ex rel. Moore v. Archibald, 5 N.D. 359, 66 N.W. 234, 343 (1896).

In a New Zealand case, the chairman, having misgivings as to whether the meeting was in order, declared it at an end. The court held the meeting valid and stated: "We hold accordingly that his action in peremptorily declaring the meeting at an end and leaving the room was not justified, and that it was competent for the meeting to go on with the business for which it has been convened and to appoint another Chairman for this purpose." Arcus v. Castle, [1954] N.Z.L.R. 122, 130 (1953), citing National Dwellings Soc'y v. Sykes, [1894] 3 Ch. 159.

ing as having been dissolved without effective action, and that the ends of justice will thereby be best promoted." [27]

§ 15.4 Ministerial Functions

It has been generally held that the duties of the chairman are ministerial only. In an early case it was held that the duties of a moderator "like those of a clerk, are merely ministerial, and can in no way affect the validity of the doings of the corporation or the rights of those claiming under them." [28] Thus, a ruling by the chairman at a company annual meeting that a certain nominee for the office of director would be ineligible to serve under the applicable public utility act was without legal standing. The court concluded that the duties to be performed by the chairman were "ministerial duties, not judicial," and that the chairman, in "presuming to act in a judicial capacity" had "usurped what he must have known was a prerogative of the court where the question would ultimately be decided." [29]

In a dispute between a city council and the mayor as presiding officer, as to whether the council or the mayor was empowered to appoint members to the standing committees, the mayor declared out of order a motion to appoint the committee members and then refused to put to a vote an appeal from his ruling, stating that the mover "had his remedy in the courts." The court issued an order directing the mayor to put the motion to a vote. "The duty of this presiding officer to put such motion did not involve the exercise of

[27] Question of cumulative voting. "The rulings of the president were not upon mere questions of parliamentary practice—of procedure. They went to the matter of legal power. The meeting could not by a mere motion remove a director. Nor could it elect directors otherwise than by the method of cumulative voting." Alliance Co-op Ins. Co. v. Gasche, 93 Kan. 147, 142 P. 882, 883 (1914).

A court will not ordinarily interfere in the conduct of a shareholders' meeting except "when necessary to secure free and full explanation, and an accurate record of the will of the shareholders on the subject in question." Steinberg v. American Bantam Car Co., 76 F. Supp. 426, 436 (W.D. Pa. 1948), *appeal dismissed as moot*, 173 F.2d 179 (3d Cir. 1949).

[28] Stebbins v. Merritt, 64 Mass. (10 Cush.) 27, 34 (1852).

[29] Gilman v. Jack, 148 Me. 171, 91 A.2d 207, 209 (1952).

any discretion; but it was purely ministerial. . . . And in this proceeding he is before this court simply as such presiding officer." [30]

§ 15.5   Judgment and Discretion

Although it is probably sound that a chairman is acting in a ministerial capacity when he is serving as a ministerial officer, such as an inspector of election,[31] there is a large body of case law and other authority which delineates, although not as clearly as may be desirable, specific powers and duties of a chairman in which judgment and discretion are necessary factors. Moreover, ministerial officers have some discretion within the scope of their ministry.[32]

§ 15.6   Putting the Vote

It is a primary duty of the chairman to ascertain the sense or will of the meeting and to record all action taken.[33] While formality is

[30] The court explained: "In effect the proposition of the presiding officer is that he may refuse to put the motion if he thinks that it contemplates action which is ultra vires the body over which he presides. If he can thus prevent action, he practically exercises a veto power, which is not conferred on him by statute, and is not inherent in him as a mere presiding officer. For in effect this would make him by virtue of his right to preside a co-ordinate or a superior branch of the local legislative body." People ex rel. Hayes v. Brush, 110 App. Div. 720, 96 N.Y.S. 500, 502 (1906), citing Cushing, Law & Pr. Leg. Assem.

[31] The chairman ruled that a general proxy was limited in certain respects. "In this instance, the chairman was acting as the judge of the corporate election, which is a purely ministerial function. . . . The chairman cannot limit the use of a proxy which is general in form and appears to be valid on its face. . . . The actions of the chairman violated the fundamental right of a stockholder to be represented by proxy." State ex rel. Hawley v. Coogan, 98 So. 2d 757, 759 (Fla. App.), petition denied, 99 So. 2d 243 (1957), cert. denied, 101 So. 2d 817 (1958).

[32] "While the judges of election are ministerial officers, nevertheless within the scope of their ministry some discretion resides." Young v. Jebbett, 213 App. Div. 774, 211 N.Y.S. 61 (4th Dep't 1925).

The court discussed the question whether an inspector of election acts judicially or ministerially, and concluded that his duties partake of both characters. "Perhaps the truth lies between the two extremes; an inspector being a judicial officer to the extent that his decision is valid until set aside by some competent tribunal." Umatilla Water Users' Ass'n v. Irvin, 56 Ore. 414, 108 P. 1016, 1019, 1020 (1910).

[33] The court also made the following remarks: "In every assembly, small or

not essential, some method of ascertaining the sense of the meeting in an intelligible and authoritative form is necessary.[34] This can only be done by putting the question to a vote according to rules which experience has shown to be adequate. "The proper way to ascertain the wishes of a majority of a deliberative assembly is by a vote of some kind. . . . Silence in such a body under such circumstances does not give consent."[35] Another decision states plainly: "His secret intention to vote for certain persons for directors, with-

---

large, which is governed by parliamentary law, there will be questions of order. These must be, in the first instance, decided by the presiding officer. In every such assembly, when a motion is made, it is the duty of the presiding officer to decide whether or not it is in order. If he deems it to be in order, he entertains it, and proceeds to lay it before the assembly in a proper way. If he deems it to be not in order, he declines to entertain it. . . . Such a decision must be made by the presiding officer, subject to the right of appeal therefrom by any member." State *ex rel.* Southey v. Lashar, 71 Conn. 540, 548, 42 A. 636, 639 (1899), *citing* Cushing, Parl. Law.

In exercising his duty to ascertain the sense of the meeting, the chairman has the power to demand a poll (after a show of hands) which power may be exercised or not according to his decision whether it is necessary. However, the chairman will fail in his duty if he presents a vote by show of hands and fails to demand a poll knowing that the sense of the meeting cannot be truly ascertained in the absence of a poll. Second Consol. Trust, Ltd. v. Ceylon Amalg. Tea & Rubber Estates, Ltd., [1943] 2 All. E.R. 567 (Ch.).

[34] There is no necessity for any particular formality in recording a vote. "A man may give his vote in divers ways, either by writing, or by hand, or by voice, or by conduct: e.g. by nod. The form in which acquiescence is given matters not if acquiescence be actually indicated." Everett v. Griffiths, (1924) 1 K.B. 941, 953, *quoted in* Curry at 60.

[35] A meeting of the church society was held pursuant to regular notice to pass upon the salary of the pastor. "No vote, formal or informal, was called for or taken, and nothing was determined by a majority of voices. . . . Those who spoke, perhaps a dozen in number, were in favor of plaintiff's proposition, but what was the opinion of the hundred who did not speak? What assurance is there that if a vote had been taken the proposition would not have been defeated?" The informal approval of the members was not a valid corporate act. Landers v. Frank Street Methodist Episc. Church, 114 N.Y. 626, 628, 21 N.E. 420 (1889).

When the chairman incorrectly stated the question while putting it to a vote, the original motion as made, seconded, and heard by the members present is the one voted on and carried, not the motion as inaccurately stated by the chairman. Shoults v. Alderson, 55 Cal. App. 527, 203 P. 809 (1921).

out expressing that intention in a legal way, would not elect any one to office." [36]

The method of taking a vote and the handling of ballots may be determined by the meeting in the absence of a statutory or by-law requirement. It is within the competency of the body to prescribe any method of taking the vote which shall be reasonably certain to determine the facts. This may be by roll call, by the passage of members through tellers, by the count of the chairman or the clerk, or by a combination of methods.[37] Thus, the acquiescence of members in the manner of preparing ballots before proceeding to an election must be regarded as controlling.[38] The method of counting votes and ascertaining the results of an election is to be determined by the meeting itself in the absence of a method prescribed by higher authority.[39] For example, a city council has full power to make rules governing the conduct of elections and, in advance of a ballot, has

[36] *In re* Argus Printing Co., 1 N.D. 434, 48 N.W. 347, 352 (1891).

[37] "But how shall the presence of a majority be determined? The Constitution has prescribed no method of making this determination, and it is therefore within the competency of the House to prescribe any method which shall be reasonably certain to ascertain the fact. It may prescribe answer to roll-call as the only method of determination; or require the passage of members between tellers, and their count as the sole test; or the count of the Speaker or the clerk, and an announcement from the desk of the names of those who are present. Any one of these methods, it must be conceded, is reasonably certain of ascertaining the fact, and as there is no constitutional method prescribed, and no constitutional inhibition of any of those, and no violation of fundamental rights in any, it follows that the House may adopt either or all, or it may provide for a combination of any two of the methods." United States v. Ballin, 144 U.S. 1, 6 (1892).

In the absence of statutory requirement, the mode of conducting an election of directors is not material (whether by ballot or viva voce) if done by the proper persons. Fox v. Allensville, C. S. & V. Turnpike Co., 46 Ind. 31 (1874).

[38] "The by-laws provide that the 'mode of taking a vote or ballot on any question shall be in such manner as the meeting shall decide.' And the acquiescence of members in the direction of the president as to the manner in which the ballots were to be prepared before proceeding to an election must be regarded, in the absence of any other action by the meeting, as controlling." People *ex rel.* Thorn v. Pangburn, 3 App. Div. 456, 38 N.Y.S. 217, 219 (1st Dep't 1896).

[39] "No provision is made by statute as to the mode in which, or the persons by whom, the result of an election shall be ascertained. This must necessarily be done by the meeting itself, and, from its character and the numbers who compose it, must primarily be effected by a count of the votes by the moderator or other officers, or by a committee appointed by the meeting, or

the power to determine whether the election should be by a plurality or by a majority.[40] However, when the legislature has expressly dictated the manner in which the vote is to be taken, that manner of voting is not merely directory but is mandatory. If it cannot be shown that the vote was conducted in the manner prescribed, then the action taken is not valid.[41]

Refusal of the chairman to recognize on the floor of the meeting a member who sought recognition for several purposes, including the desire to make a motion for a secret ballot in the election of a chairman, has been held to constitute a "grave irregularity." [42]

---

by its officers with its assent. Such a committee is an instrument of the meeting, and not a distinct counting or canvassing board. No special force can be given to the declaration of the moderator, after such a committee reports the result of the count to him, that an officer is elected. It can amount to no more than a statement by him that the officer appears by such count to be elected. As the meeting is charged with the duty of making an election by a ballot, if a majority of its members desire further examination of the correctness of the result reached by the committee, it must be its right to subject such result to further scrutiny. If the result announced is assented to directly, or perhaps indirectly by proceeding with other business, and an examination of the subject is thus closed, there would be much force in the argument that the election would be fully completed. . . ." Putnam v. Langley, 133 Mass. 204, 205 (1882).

[40] "The council is a deliberative body with prerogatives limited only to positive law. As such it had full power to make reasonable rules governing the election. In advance of a ballot, it could determine whether the election should be by plurality or majority. It could adopt a rule permitting change of votes after a ballot but before announcement of the result by the chair. Neither custom nor practice of previous councils is of determinative value. By common consent and approval it was understood and agreed that the election should be by majority vote, and therefore a majority determined the choice." State ex rel. Reed v. De Maioribus, 131 Ohio St. 201, 2 N.E.2d 506, 509 (1936).

[41] Village of Granville v. Krause, 131 Misc. 752, 228 N.Y.S. 204 (1928).

A general law requiring the election of city officers by viva voce vote controls a charter provision requiring the city council to elect the assessor by ballot. "The statute in the case at bar does not require a secret ballot. On the other hand its manifest purpose is to require public declaration by each member of the joint convention of his vote in order that it may be made a matter of record. Such provision is important. It has the salutary effect of fixing upon each member of the convention who takes part in the proceedings his exact responsibility for the election and provides for an unimpeachable record of his action." Mansfield v. O'Brien, 271 Mass. 515, 171 N.E. 487, 489 (1930).

[42] Ryan v. Grimm, 43 Misc. 2d 836, 252 N.Y.S.2d 521 (Sup. Ct.), aff'd, 22 App. Div. 2d 171, 254 N.Y.S.2d 462 (1964), aff'd, 15 N.Y.2d 922, 258 N.Y.S.2d 843, 206 N.E.2d 867 (1965).

Whether the chairman, having put the vote to those present in person or by proxy, can also cast a vote, depends usually on whether he is a member of the body. The title of chairman or presiding officer does not carry this right to vote; only membership provides that right.[43]

§ 15.6.1   Parliamentary Procedures Followed

The courts have followed generally accepted parliamentary procedures in determining the sense of the meeting. "In every assembly, small or large, which is governed by parliamentary law, there will be questions of order. These must be, in the first instance, decided by the presiding officer. In every such assembly, when a motion is made, it is the duty of the presiding officer to decide whether or not it is in order. If he deems it to be in order, he entertains it, and proceeds to lay it before the assembly in a proper way. If he deems it to be not in order, he declines to entertain it. . . . Such a decision must be made by the presiding officer, subject to the right of appeal therefrom by any member." [44]

---

[43] See Chapter 17 at § 17.1 infra.

[44] State ex rel. Southey v. Lashar, 71 Conn. 540, 42 A. 636, 639 (1899). In this case the motion was ruled out of order; no appeal was taken. The court continued: "To appeal would have been regular and lawful. Not to appeal, but to take another course, was irregular and in violation of parliamentary law. It is the duty of the presiding officer of any assembly 'to put to vote all questions which are regularly moved or necessarily arise in the course of the proceedings, and to announce the result.'" Cushing, Parl. Law is cited.

The presiding officer has the duty to put the question and announce the result of the vote. "The simplest and most expeditious manner of ascertaining the will of any assembly of persons is to call for a viva voce vote upon the question before them. The presiding officer of such assembly, whose duty it is to put the question and announce the result of the vote, when such vote is close, may often be mistaken as to the result of the vote, and may unintentionally make an erroneous announcement. The rule which makes the announcement by the presiding officer of the result of a viva voce vote conclusive, unless a division or a call of the vote is demanded, should only be applied to cases in which the announcement by such officer is honestly made, and should not be invoked in favor of a false and fraudulent announcement, or one that is clearly contrary to the actual result." Gipson v. Morris, 31 Tex. Civ. App. 645, 73 S.W. 85, 88 (1903).

Where the chairman refused to put an amendment to a motion to amend and ruled that the original motion must be voted upon, under a "mistaken idea

§ 15.6.2   Can Member Put Vote?

The question has arisen whether a member has the right to put a motion to vote when the presiding officer fails or refuses to do so. It is a general rule of parliamentary law that the presiding officer is the sole person empowered to put a motion, and that the only proper method of challenging the presiding officer's action is to appeal from his decision refusing to put the motion. In a case involving a point of order, the presiding officer ruled that a certain motion was out of order and illegal and declined to put the motion to vote. A parliamentary skirmish ensued and a member declared that, as a matter of "parliamentary law, or parliamentary usage" if the presiding officer declined to put a motion, any member might put the motion and declare the results. The member called for a rising vote on the adoption of the motion, and it was carried. The presiding officer then instructed the clerk not to record the action as it was illegal, whereupon a member moved that the clerk be directed to record the proceedings and the motion was carried. Connecticut's highest state court held that the proceedings were in violation of parliamentary law, citing Cushing. The court agreed with the argument that, "as an abstract proposition," the presiding officer is the servant of the body over which he presides, not the master, and if he tries to dominate or thwart the will of the assembly, any member can act for him. However, the court rejected the validity of this "high-sounding talk" and held: "If such right exists, it is analogous to the right of revolution—a right to be exercised only when all peaceful and regular methods have been tried and exhausted. Every presumption must be in favor of regular action and against irregularity. Action which violates regular rules of law can never be said strictly to be lawful." [45]

---

as to what the law was," the court disapproved the motion as adopted on the grounds that the conduct of the chairman had "prevented a material question from being brought before the meeting." Henderson v. Bank of Australasia, 45 Ch. D. 330, 346 (C.A. 1890).

[45] The court added: "It is the opinion of this court that all the votes alleged to have been taken at the said meeting of the said board which were not put by the mayor, and the result of which he did not announce, are wholly void. They are void because they violate parliamentary law, and because they violate the commands of the charter of the city." State ex rel. Southey v. Lashar, 71 Conn. 540, 550, 42 A. 636, 638, 639, 44 L.R.A. 197 (1899), citing Cushing, Parl. Law.

The opposing view is expressed in a case involving the regularity of a resolution. A New Jersey court, also citing Cushing, held that "there was no irregularity in the procedure in passing the resolution which should vitiate it. The president of the Board [of commissioners] is only the mouthpiece of the commissioners. It is his duty to put a motion duly made. If he refuses, any member may put it. Any other rule is destructive of legislative functions." A temporary chairman was duly elected to put the question and the motion was carried; the court held that this was a proper procedure on the occasion in question.[46] Another case following this view held that when the presiding officer refuses to put a motion to elect a chairman other than himself, a shareholder may put the motion on his own initiative and the action of a majority will prevail.[47]

§ 15.6.3   All Motions Need Not Be Put

Parliamentary law does not require that every motion made from the floor must be put to a vote by the chairman. He has broad discretion to expedite the meeting in accordance with the apparent will of the majority. It has been held, for example, that the chairman at a union meeting need not put to vote for the third time a motion which had just been defeated for the second time only a month

---

[46] Hicks v. Long Branch Comm'n, 69 N.J.L. 300, 54 A. 568, *rev'd on other grounds,* 55 A. 250 (1903), *accord,* Billings v. Fielder, 44 N.J.L. 381 (1882).

[47] Duffy v. Loft, 17 Del. Ch. 376, 152 A. 849, 852 (1930). The by-laws provided for election of a chairman by the shareholders whenever they deemed it necessary to do so. The court said: "There is good reason for giving to stockholders the power to choose a Chairman, even when the President is present; and especially so if there is a contest for the control of the meeting by two factions and the President is identified with one of them. The Chairman is a very important person in such a situation and the majority should have the power to control the meeting."

During a meeting of the city House of Delegates the speaker put a motion to adjourn and declared it carried. He and others then left the meeting, thereby preventing an appeal. The remaining members, being a quorum, then removed the speaker and elected a new speaker. The city charter was silent as to the term and removal of the speaker. "This office, then, aptly falls within the rule that the incumbent holds merely at the pleasure of the body by which he has been duly elected, and may be at any time removed by them." State *ex rel.* Fox v. Alt, 26 Mo. App. 673, 677 (1887).

before. "The refusal to consider it again so shortly after its second defeat was not an interference with a member's right of free speech, but was a reasonable parliamentary rule."[48] And the chairman need not put to a vote a motion to adjourn which is obviously a "stalling tactic."[49]

Also, if a resolution is offered or a motion made which is clearly beyond the power of the meeting, such as a motion to declare vacant the offices of directors absent from the meeting, the chairman can rule it out of order and also refuse to allow an appeal from his ruling.[50]

§ 15.6.4   Motions Considered Illegal by Chairman

However, when a chairman refuses to put a motion because in his opinion the motion if carried would be illegal, but the motion was not otherwise out of order, the court will not sustain the chairman's refusal to act. "As well might the speaker of a legislative assembly refuse to put the question and call for the vote on the passage of a law because he deemed it unconstitutional." The motion, said the court, presented a "question of law, to be decided by the courts," and not by the chairman. "It was the duty of the chairman to allow the majority of the board to take such action as they might see fit to take. What would be the legal effect of that action was purely a

[48] Broomer v. Schultz, 239 F. Supp. 699, 702 (E.D. Pa. 1965).

[49] Meeting called to vote on a pension plan. Although all essential facts were before the stockholders, a motion was made to adjourn to give plaintiffs an opportunity to present additional facts to an adjourned meeting. "The motion to adjourn was obviously a stalling tactic on the part of those opposed. It might have been more consonant with parliamentary law to have put the motion to adjourn to a vote; failure to do so, however, was not of such serious import as to deprive the dissenting stockholders of any substantial rights." Bresnick v. Home Title Guar. Co., 175 F. Supp. 723, 726 (S.D.N.Y. 1959).

[50] Where, at a corporation meeting, a motion is made to take action which, as a matter of law, is beyond the power of the body, and the president declines to put it on that account, his refusal to entertain an appeal from his ruling is not just ground for removing him and substituting another presiding officer. The court held: "The rulings of the president were not upon mere questions of parliamentary practice—of procedure. They went to the matter of legal power." Alliance Co-op Ins. Co. v. Gasche, 93 Kan. 147, 142 P. 882, 883 (1914).

judicial question, to be decided in another place, and by a different branch of the government." [51]

The mayor as presiding officer of a city council does not have power to refuse to recognize a motion for the adoption of an ordinance, claiming that he has sole power to determine whether or not an ordinance or motion is valid. "Even if the mayor does not believe that a particular motion or ordinance is valid, it can still be considered by the city council. His remedy is not to refuse the right to consider but, rather, to veto the ordinance. . . . Though it may subsequently be proven in court to be invalid, the remedy is in the court house and not in the mayor's office." [52]

Also, when the presiding officer of a common council refused to entertain a motion to appoint committees and then refused to put to a vote an appeal from his ruling, claiming that he, as presiding officer, and not the council over which he presided, was empowered to appoint the committees, the court issued an order directing him to put the motion to a vote on the grounds that the duty of the presiding officer to put motions to a vote did not involve the exercise of any discretion but was purely ministerial.[53] However, where a matter is scheduled to come before a meeting of shareholders as set forth in the proxy-soliciting material, failure to actually present the matter to the assembled shareholders for a vote causes an expiration of the matter so far as that meeting is concerned.[54]

---

[51] With respect to the point of order, the court noted that the chairman merely declared that the motion was illegal, and not that it was out of order. "To declare that a motion violates law, and therefore should not be voted on, is one thing. Such a question neither the chairman nor the majority can pass upon with any legal effect. But to rule that a motion is out of order is to take an entirely different attitude with respect to it. It is a decision that some rule of the body or some practice established by parliamentary usage has been violated. This question the chairman must decide in the first instance, and above him sits the court of final review, the majority who, on an appeal from the ruling of the chair, settle the issue beyond the power of any court to change their decision." State ex rel. Moore v. Archibald, 5 N.D. 359, 66 N.W. 234, 243 (1896) (motion to remove from office the superintendent of a state hospital).

[52] Rudd v. Sarallo, 111 Ill. App. 2d 153, 249 N.E.2d 323, 325 (1969) (Robert's Rules of Order had been adopted to govern procedures).

[53] People ex rel. Hayes v. Brush, 96 N.Y.S. 500, 501 (1906), citing Cushing.

[54] Proxy statement described a stock option plan which was scheduled to come before the meeting. The plan was not presented to the meeting and "ex-

When a chairman wrongfully concludes that a motion to amend a pending election resolution constitutes a substitution rather than an amendment and therefore fails to put the resolution as amended, the court will not sustain the validity of the election. In such a case a city common council adopted a resolution naming three persons to the office of assessor for varying terms. A motion was then made to substitute two of the three names and the motion was passed. The chairman concluded that the original resolution had been replaced by a substitute motion and that its passage made it unnecessary to vote on the original resolution as amended. The court, citing Cushing, held that the motion to replace two of three nominees was an amendment and not a substitution, but that if the motion had provided for a complete substitution of all three nominees the motion would have been a substitution which, when carried, would have accomplished the election of the three nominees named in this amending motion. In refusing to restrain the council from taking further action on the election of assessors the court said: "What the council actually did, and not what the presiding officer thought necessary, is controlling." [55]

§ 15.7   Recognition of Proxies

In ascertaining the sense of the meeting, the chairman is under a duty at law to exercise all the proxies held by him as chairman in accordance with the instructions which they contain.[56]

APPEAL FROM CHAIRMAN'S DECISION

§ 15.8   Motion To Appeal

The decisions and rulings of the chairman, as distinguished from announcements and answers to parliamentary inquiries and other questions, are subject to appeal by any two members, one moving

---

pired" by its own terms. Dillon v. Berg, 326 F. Supp. 1214 (D. Del.), *aff'd*, 453 F.2d 876 (3d Cir. 1971).

[55] Casler v. Tanzer, 134 Misc. 48, 234 N.Y.S. 571, 578 (Sup. Ct. 1929).

[56] Second Consol. Trust Ltd. v. Ceylon Amalg. Tea & Rubber Estates, Ltd., [1943] 2 All. E.R. 567 (Ch.).

the appeal and the other seconding it. The purpose of a motion to appeal is to question and reverse the chairman's decision.[1]

The motion to appeal must be made immediately after the decision to which it refers, and a vote on the appeal must be taken at once. Failure to make a timely appeal is in effect a waiver of the right to appeal. Thus, if any business or debate intervenes, it is too late to appeal.[2] If there is a tie vote on a motion to appeal, the ruling of the chairman prevails.[3] In case of a debatable appeal, the chair-

---

[1] See State ex rel. Southey v. Lashar, 71 Conn. 540, 42 A. 636 (1899) (procedures on appeal from chairman's ruling), quoting Cushing, Law & Pr. Leg. Assem.

[2] Asking for a roll call on a previous nomination is a waiver of the right to appeal from the chairman's ruling that a later nomination was not in order as it was not seconded. The objecting member protested the ruling of the chairman but did not appeal from the ruling. On the contrary, he took the "entirely inconsistent course" of asking for a roll call on the previous nomination. Campbell v. School Comm., 21 A.2d 727, 730 (R.I. 1941).

Where a shareholders' meeting was adjourned by the president in the presence of all the shareholders and no appeal was taken from his ruling, an attempt, after some time spent in consultation, to hold the meeting with less than a majority was not effective. "Right or wrong, the president had adjourned the meeting in the presence of all the stockholders, and no appeal had been taken from his ruling." Haskell v. Read, 68 Neb. 115, 96 N.W. 1007 (1903), quoted and followed, State ex rel. Industrial Fin., Ltd. v. Yanagawa, 484 P.2d 145, 147 (Hawaii 1971).

The making of arrangements to conduct an election of a town officer by balloting at a town meeting did not constitute a commencement of business so as to render it too late to question a vote to adjourn. Before any ballots were given in, the business of balloting was not "commenced." Kimball v. Lamprey, 19 N.H. 215 (1848).

Failure to make timely appeal from a ruling of the chair is a waiver of the right to appeal. In re Doyle, 7 Pa. Dist. 635, 24 Pa. Co. Ct. 27 (1898).

A witness must make his objections to the procedures of a Congressional committee when he appears before the committee. See Shelton v. United States, 404 F.2d 1292 (D.C. Cir. 1968), cert. denied, 393 U.S. 1024 (1969).

But see Henderson v. Bank of Australasia, 45 Ch. D. 330 (C.A. 1890).

However, failure to appeal from the chairman's decision does not estop relief by mandamus. State ex rel. Hawley v. Coogan, 98 So. 2d 757 (Fla.), petition denied, 99 So. 2d 243 (1957), cert. denied, 101 So. 2d 817 (1958).

A basic exception to this general rule is where a by-law, standing rule, or fundamental principle of parliamentary law has been violated, and in such cases a point of order may be raised at any time. See Robert's Rules of Order at 80–81.

[3] See § 17.8 infra.

man is allowed to take part in the debate, which on ordinary occasions he is prohibited from doing.[4] Whether debatable or not, the chairman may state the reasons for his ruling without leaving the chair when stating the question on the appeal.[5] An appeal may be made from a ruling of the chair only at the time the ruling is made, even when another member has the floor.[6]

One court has ruled that, if a member believes that the chairman has made an error in ruling on his motion, then it is his duty to demand a roll-call vote on appeal to resolve the question. Where it appeared from the testimony that the decision of the chairman would have been reversed on an appeal to the assembly, the court noted that the appeal should have been made. "To appeal would have been regular and lawful. Not to appeal, but to take another course, was irregular and in violation of parliamentary law. It is the duty of the presiding officer of any assembly 'to put to vote all questions which are regularly moved, or necessarily arise in the course of the proceedings, and to announce the result.'"[7]

In an early case in North Dakota the court, in considering a ruling that a certain practice established by parliamentary usage was out of order, commented: "But to rule that a motion is out of order . . . is a decision that some rule of the body or some practice established by parliamentary usage has been violated. This question the chairman must decide in the first instance, and above him sits the court

[4] "When a question of order is raised, as it may be by any one member", it is not stated from the chair and decided by the assembly, like other questions, but is decided, in the first instance by the presiding officer, without any previous debate or discussion by the assembly. If the decision of the presiding officer is not satisfactory, any one member may object to it, and have the question decided by the assembly. This is called appealing from the decision of the chair. The question is then stated by the presiding officer on the appeal, namely, shall the decision of the chair stand as the decision of the assembly? And it is thereupon debated and decided by the assembly in the same manner as any other question except that the presiding officer is allowed to take part in the debate, which on ordinary occasions he is prohibited from doing." Cushing's Manual § 154, *quoted in* State *ex rel.* Southey v. Lashar, 71 Conn. 540, 548, 549, 42 A. 636 (1899). *See also* Cushing, Law & Pr. Leg. Assem. § 1464.

[5] *See* Robert's Rules of Order at 82.

[6] *Id.* at 81.

[7] State *ex rel.* Southey v. Lashar, 71 Conn. 540, 549, 42 A. 636, 639 (1899), *citing* Cushing, Parl. Law § 27.

of final review, the majority who, on an appeal from the ruling of
the chair, settle the issue beyond the power of any court to change
their decision." [8]

§ 15.9 Chairman's Ruling Valid Until Reversed

Under English common parliamentary law, the decision of the
chairman is held to be right until the contrary is shown.[9] Where a
statute provides that the decisions of the presiding officer on a point
of order are final, the court will uphold the chairman where he
acted in good faith and a reasonable man would find reason to rule

[8] State *ex rel.* Moore v. Archibald, 5 N.D. 359, 66 N.W. 234, 243 (1896).

Where a constitutional convention violates its own rules of procedure, no
appeal lies to the courts—it is up to the people to accept or reject. The court
will accept the decisions of the convention as final "and leave correction to the
power to which it belongs." Wells v. Bain, 75 Pa. 39, 56 (1874).

The only proper course for those who object to a decision or ruling of the
chair and think they are being "unfairly treated" is to appeal to the assembly
from the "obnoxious ruling" and put the matter to vote. Proctor Coal Co. v.
Finley, 98 Ky. 405, 33 S.W. 188, 192 (1895).

See Henderson v. Bank of Australasia, 45 Ch. D. 330 [62 L.T.R. (n.s.) 869
(1890)], *rev'd on other grounds*, 45 Ch. D. 330 (1890), holding that it is
competent for a member to rise to a point of order and respectfully advise
the chairman of his intention to insist upon his rights to proceed with an
amendment, although his actions may not meet the strict rules of parliamentary
procedure.

In MacDougall v. Gardiner, (1875) 1 Ch. D. 13, a motion to adjourn a
general meeting was moved, and on being put, was declared by the chairman
to be carried. A poll was demanded, but the chairman ruled that there could
not be a poll on the question of adjournment, and left the room. One shareholder sued on behalf of himself and other shareholders praying for a declaration that the conduct of the chairman was illegal. It was held, on demurrer,
that the bill could not be sustained on the ground that internal disputes between shareholders are not the subject of a bill by one shareholder on behalf
of himself and others unless there is something illegal, oppressive, or fraudulent
on the part of the company.

[9] "Whether the objection depends on the form of the document or on the
general point of law, the Court can decide, and is bound to decide, when the
question comes before it, whether the decision of the chairman was right or
wrong; but until the contrary is shewn his decision must be held to be right,
that is to say, the Court must decide the question between the parties, but not
until those who object to his decision satisfy the Court before whom the question comes that his decision was wrong." *In re* Indian Zoedone Co., 26 Ch.
D. 70, 81 (C.A. 1884).

as he did.[10] The courts recognize that it is essential to the prompt and
efficient dispatch of town meeting business that the moderator
exercise his statutory discretionary powers as to the procedure to be
followed at each meeting. "When the moderator makes a procedure
ruling as to the method of voting which, as in the present case, is not
contrary to any statute, his ruling stands unless the town itself by
vote reverses it." And in conclusion the court explained: "Ample
protection against any abuse by a moderator of his powers is afforded
by the fact that the meeting can reverse his decision." Thus, the
right of appeal will expire unless timely exercised.[11] Another court
characterized the power of the body to overrule the chairman as "the
omnipotence of a deliberative assembly." [12]

§ 15.10 Refusal To Recognize an Appeal

Where a political county chairman called a convention to order
and appointed a temporary chairman, contrary to the elective practice of parliamentary law, and then refused to recognize an appeal
from his ruling, the court held that he had "departed from a well
established rule of parliamentary procedure." [13] And, where the

[10] The court held that "a decisive discretion on all matters of procedure in
the council" was committed to the chairman (the mayor) and that his decision
was not the subject of mandamus unless it appeared that he was under a clear
duty to the public to take the opposite course at that time and place. Rex v.
Foley, [1928] Vict. L.R. 1, 5 (1926) (Australian Local Government Act).

[11] Town of Exeter v. Kenick, 104 N.H. 168, 181 A.2d 638, 640, 641
(1962).

[12] Hill v. Goodwin, 56 N.H. 441, 454 (1876) (town meeting). The court
continued: "The moderator, excepting in those matters where he is bound by
statute law, rules as he understands that he ought to rule. If his ruling is
incorrect, any person who is dissatisfied may appeal to the meeting, and its
decision, being not against the statute, is final and conclusive."

See State ex rel. Cole v. Chapman, 44 Conn. 595 (Super. Ct. 1878) (appeal
to convention from decision of mayor was sustained; then mayor ruled corrective resolution out of order and convention again sustained an appeal).

[13] "Absent a provision in the by-laws to the contrary, parliamentary procedure calls for the election of a temporary chairman. When Mr. Kelly [the
defendant–chairman] undertook to exercise his so-called prerogative of appointing a temporary chairman and when he refused to recognize the appeal
from the ruling of the chair, he departed from a well established rule of parliamentary procedure." Egan v. Kelly, 14 N.J. Super. 103, 81 A.2d 413, 414
(1951).

speaker of a city House of Delegates adjourned a meeting on a viva voce vote and then left the room with others, thereby preventing an appeal from his ruling, the remaining members constituting a quorum for the transaction of business had the right to remove him and elect a new speaker.[14]

Thus, refusal of the chairman to permit an appeal to the shareholders from his ruling that certain proper demands from the floor were out of order has been held to deprive the shareholders of a fair opportunity to be heard.[15] In fact, a failure of the chairman to entertain an appropriate appeal from his ruling may justify the majority of members in deposing the chairman and proceeding with the business of the meeting.[16] However, when an appeal is taken from

---

[14] State *ex rel.* Fox v. Alt, 26 Mo. App. 673 (1887).

And where the chair adjourns a meeting at a time when he had a duty to allow it to proceed, and his ruling was sustained by a tie vote on appeal, the losing faction may continue to act as though there had been no adjournment. The winning faction remaining silent cannot question the result. State *ex rel.* Price v. Du Brul, 100 Ohio St. 272, 126 N.E. 87, 90 (1919).

[15] "In the instant case the stockholders were not given the opportunity to pass upon the validity of this by-law changing the manner of nominating directors. When the point was raised the chairman ruled the question out of order. He further refused to submit his ruling to the stockholders for their decision. He then asked if there were any other nominations. This would seem to have been a useless gesture since other nominations were prohibited by the by-law in question, the approval of which the chairman refused to submit to the stockholders. Under such circumstances, it is apparent that those in opposition to management did not have a fair opportunity to be heard." *In re* Scharf, 28 Misc. 2d 869, 216 N.Y.S.2d 775 (Sup. Ct.), *modified,* Scharf v. Irving Air Chute Co., 15 App. Div. 2d 563, 223 N.Y.S.2d 307 (2d Dep't 1961).

[16] The president was mistaken in announcing the result of the election from the report of the tellers. "He was also mistaken in declaring the motion to reject the report of the tellers out of order and refusing to entertain an appeal from his ruling, and the majority of the members present in person and by proxy were justified in exercising the power of the majority, in the absence of any by-laws or rules of order contrary to such action, by deposing the chairman and proceeding with the business of the meeting. The fact that the president, secretary, and treasurer all, or any of them, left the meeting or remained, or that others did either, did not affect the power of the majority who remained and constituted a quorum to do business or the legality of their action. The subsequent proceedings constituted a part of the action of the annual meeting of the association." American Aberdeen-Angus Breeders' Ass'n v. Fullerton, 325 Ill. 323, 156 N.E. 314, 317 (1927).

a ruling of the chair and the ruling is sustained by the assembly, the court will not overrule the assembly even though the ruling of the chair might not have conformed to parliamentary usage.[17]

The chairman need not recognize an appeal from his decisions in all cases. He may deny a demand for an appeal when he believes it would not serve a useful purpose or when he deems it to be merely dilatory. An example would be an appeal from a ruling which, if successful, would not change the result of the voting as declared by the chair.[18] This rule would also apply to an appeal from a decision of the chair ruling a motion to be out of order as frivolous, absurd, or trivial.

Where the president of a corporation, acting as a statutory inspector of elections, ruled that shareholders who had not paid an assessment could not vote (such ruling being correct under statute) and again refused to allow them to vote after the meeting had upheld an appeal from his ruling, the court held that an appeal could be taken only to the courts. "To permit such an appeal to those present and claiming the right to vote would in effect allow persons to be judges of their own qualifications and place the election of directors at the mercy of any body of persons who saw fit to make a claim, however groundless, of the right to participate in the election." [19] Similarly, where the president refuses to allow an appeal from his ruling that the meeting did not have legal power to act in the manner proposed, his refusal will be sustained. "The rulings of the president were not upon mere questions of parliamentary prac-

---

[17] The mayor ruled that a city councilman could not change his vote before the result had been announced. The court remarked that the ruling of the mayor may not have conformed to "parliamentary usage" but that his ruling was sustained by the council. The court added, however, that the ruling of the mayor "has the approval of many deliberative assemblies" and, as applied to municipal elections, seems open to very little objection. Mann v. City of LeMars, 109 Iowa 251, 254, 80 N.W. 327 (1899).

[18] See State ex rel. Hawley v. Coogan, 98 So. 2d 757 (Fla.), petition denied, 99 So. 2d 243 (1957), cert. denied, 101 So. 2d 817 (1958) (appeal, if allowed, would only result in identical vote).

[19] Umatilla Water Users' Ass'n v. Irvin, 56 Ore. 414, 108 P. 1016, 1019 (1910).

See State ex rel. Duane v. Fagan, 42 Conn. 32 (1875) where statute required majority vote to elect school district committee. Meeting upheld ruling of chairman with few dissenting votes that named person had been elected. Court held election not valid, as such person received only 46 out of 97 votes.

tice—of procedure. They went to the matter of legal power. . . . We cannot regard the failure of the president to entertain an appeal on these matters as justifying the selection of another presiding officer." [20]

Another exception has been allowed in the case of an association which did not have a constitution, by-laws, or rules of order. It conducted its affairs in accordance with its own past practices, without the benefit of parliamentary law. The chairman having refused to put a motion and having left the meeting, it was argued that an appeal from the chairman's decision to the body should have been taken. The court answered that the meeting "was acting under no parliamentary regulations requiring that method of procedure." [21]

In a recent case the defendant was found guilty of being a disorderly person when, at a public hearing of a city planning board in the council chamber, he persisted in refusing to accept rulings of the chair and to leave the microphone and resume his seat. The board had adopted its own rules of order and the chairman had outlined the procedures to the meeting, yet the defendant persisted in arguing that Robert's Rules of Order should be followed. The chairman ruled the defendant out of order several times and denied his demands to appeal the rulings to the entire board. A disturbance followed and the defendant was removed and arrested. In affirming his conviction, the court remarked that "the decision of a chairman

---

[20] Alliance Co-op Ins. Co. v. Gasche, 93 Kan. 147, 142 P. 882, 883 (1914).

Where the chairman of a political committee ruled that a member had lost her vote because she moved her residence to a different district, and then refused to permit an appeal from his ruling, the court sustained the chairman, holding that there was no "legal grievance." Hart v. Sheridan, 168 Misc. 386, 5 N.Y.S.2d 820 (1938).

Disallowance by the chairman of a vote by proxy was upheld by the court under articles which provided that every vote not disallowed at the meeting was valid. "Here, all that is done is to take away from a shareholder a right of appeal against a decision disallowing an objection by him against the votes of some other shareholder, and it seems to me quite reasonable that such a question should be allowed to be decided summarily and finally by the chairman, although there should not be the same summary and final effect given to a decision against the right of a shareholder to vote." Wall v. Exchange Inv. Co., [1926] Ch. 143, 148 (1925).

[21] Ostrom v. Greene, 20 Misc. 177, 45 N.Y.S. 852, 858 (Sup. Ct. 1897), aff'd mem., 30 App. Div. 621, 52 N.Y.S. 1147 (3d Dep't 1898), aff'd, 161 N.Y. 353, 55 N.E. 919 (1900).

may not be tested by resisting his repeated rulings to bring back order to the meeting." [22]

CHAIRMAN—CHOOSING, REMOVAL

§ 15.11   Charter and By-Law Provisions

In the absence of provision in the charter or by-laws of the organization naming the chairman or prescribing the method of his selection, the meeting itself should proceed at the time of organization to select the chairman.[1] If a method of selection is imposed by a higher authority it must ordinarily be followed. In an interesting English case, a shareholder was elected to the chair although a director entitled to preside was present in the room. Plaintiff argued that the person elected was not entitled to preside and the proceedings were not regular. The court held the election valid. As to the plaintiff's argument, the court said: "I think probably that is true, but it is not convenient for two persons to talk at the same time. . . . It would have been idle to have gone through the formality of thrusting upon [the director] an honour which he did not desire . . . and the meeting rightly determined who should take the chair." [2] No particular formality is required in the selection process.[3]

However, in an early American case it was held that an election

[22] State v. Moore, 101 N.J. Super. 419, 244 A.2d 522, 524 (1968).

[1] In the absence of rules, a county political committee can appoint anyone as chairman, including those "outside of their ranks." De Camilla v. Connery, 43 Misc. 2d 395, 251 N.Y.S.2d 305, 309 (Sup. Ct), aff'd, 23 App. Div. 2d 704, 256 N.Y.S.2d 986 (3d Dep't 1965).

[2] Catesby v. Burnett, [1916] 2 Ch. 325, 114 L.T.R. (N.S.) 1025.

[3] "A majority of all the stock issued being represented, it was clearly the duty of those present to organize the meeting and proceed with the election." There is good reason to let the shareholders choose the chairman, even when the corporate president is present. The presence of the president ready and willing to preside cannot be said to oust the stockholders of their right to choose a chairman on any such theory that the president's presence makes such a choice unnecessary. "There is good reason for giving to stockholders the power to choose a Chairman, even when the President is present; and especially so if there is a contest for the control of the meeting by two factions, and the President is identified with one of them. The Chairman is a very important person in such a situation and the majority should have the power to control the meeting." Duffy v. Loft, Inc., 17 Del. Ch. 376, 152 A. 849, 851 (1930).

was not legal because: "The president although present, did not preside at the election, nor was there a president pro tempore chosen in his stead; and no person who participated in the proceeding was authorized to receive the ballots, or to declare the result. . . ." [4]

The chairman may be selected by a viva voce vote,[5] but if the by-laws provide for a stock vote the chairman must be elected by such a vote even though the by-law had never previously been invoked in the organization of shareholders' meetings.[6] However, where the by-law provides for a stock vote on a question only when demanded, the chairman may be elected by a viva voce vote in the absence of a demand for a stock vote.[7] Election of a chairman and vice-chairman by secret written ballot may be cured, under a public meeting statute, by a later corrective, open, public vote.[8]

The court continued: "Where no provision is made in the by-laws for a chairman, the meeting itself should proceed to select one. It frequently happens that provision is made for the president to preside at the stockholders' meeting, but, when no such provision is made, a chairman may be selected by the stockholders at the organization of the meeting. The chairman so selected need not necessarily be a stockholder, nor is there any particular formality required in his selection." Commonwealth *ex rel.* Sheip v. Vandegrift, 232 Pa. 53, 81 A. 153, 155, 156 (1911).

[4] State *ex rel.* Guerrero v. Pettineli, 10 Nev. 141, 146 (1875).

[5] "In the absence of a statute or by-law otherwise providing, stockholders may select a chairman to preside at the annual meeting by a viva voce vote. A stock vote is not required to give validity to the meeting. In the present case, even if a stock vote was demandable, the request, coming after the organization had been effected, was too late." Commonwealth *ex rel.* Sheip v. Vandegrift, 232 Pa. 53, 81 A. 153, 156 (1911).

[6] Two factions attempted to organize the shareholders' organization meeting, one by viva voce vote and the other by stock vote, resulting in two separate bodies of shareholders presided over by separate chairmen and each claiming to be the regular meeting. Each faction elected a different board of directors. A by-law provision, not previously invoked, provided for a stock vote. The court upheld this method of voting. The court also noted that a by-law applicable to a "stockholders' meeting" applies as well to a meeting not yet fully organized. "This was certainly a stockholders' meeting as soon as it was called to order, and proceeded to the election of a chairman. It was not an organized meeting, but it was a meeting of the stockholders engaged in the preliminary work of its own organization. . . ." Proctor Coal Co. v. Finley, 98 Ky. 405, 33 S.W. 188 (1895).

[7] Duffy v. Loft, Inc., 17 Del. Ch. 376, 152 A. 849, 851, 852 (1930).

[8] Bassett v. Braddock, 262 So. 2d 425 (Fla. 1972).

§ 15.12   Acquiescence of Meeting

A chairman may take and hold the chair by acquiescence of the meeting without an election or other formal proceeding.[9] It has also been held that the presiding officer of a deliberative body can be elected by the majority of a quorum present even if such number is less than a majority of all the members entitled to vote.[10]

Regardless of the mode of selection, failure to challenge occupancy of the chair immediately after the meeting is organized will be deemed a waiver of all objections.[11] This rule has particular applicability once the objector has acquiesced in the organization of the meeting and has participated in the conduct of its business.[12]

If there is any question as to whether a quorum will be in attendance, the chairman of the meeting should proceed with caution. "In general, the chair is not to be taken till a quorum for business

---

[9] The president assumed to act as chairman of the meeting at the opening morning session, without election to that office. When the meeting reopened in the afternoon, a member moved to reconsider all that had been done, claiming that the meeting had not been properly organized. Commenting on this assertion the court stated: "We think his claim was too late. He had acquiesced in the organization and had participated in the business of the meeting." *In re* Argus Printing Co., 1 N.D. 434, 48 N.W. 347, 352 (1891).

Where no statute or by-law declares the mode in which elections should be conducted and all present agreed to the election of a chairman, the chairman first elected is the rightful chairman. *In re* Pioneer Paper Co., 36 How. Pr. 105 (1864), *appeal dismissed,* 36 How. Pr. 110 (N.Y. Ct. App. 1865).

[10] It was urged in an election of the presiding officer by councilmen that a majority vote was necesary, rather than a plurality of votes, citing CUSHING, LAW AND PRACTICE OF LEGISLATIVE ASSEMBLIES §§ 297, 298. The court did not agree: "But the authority cited does not go to the length here contended for. The author states that the presiding officer of a deliberative body should possess the confidence of the body in the highest practicable degree, and so is required to be chosen by an absolute majority of votes. But it is plain from the context that Mr. Cushing is speaking merely of a usage of electing such officers by a majority vote rather than a plurality of votes. If this usage is anything more than the usual requirements of the law, and if it be an imperative rule, it has no application to the case at hand, for defendant was elected, not by a plurality, but by a majority of the votes cast." Cadmus v. Farr, 47 N.J.L. 208, 217 (1885).

[11] Commonwealth *ex rel.* Sheip v. Vandegrift, 232 Pa. 53, 81 A. 153, 156 (1911).

[12] *In re* Argus Printing Co., 1 N.D. 434, 48 N.W. 347, 352 (1891).

is present; unless, after due waiting, such a quorum is despaired of, when the chair may be taken and the house adjourned." [13]

§ 15.13   Qualifications of Chairman

The chairman of a shareholders' meeting need not be a shareholder unless the prevailing rule requires that he own shares in the corporation.[14] He may be a proxyholder.[15] When the body so consents, an attorney may be the chairman even where the by-laws provide that the president shall preside at all meetings unless otherwise determined by the board of directors.[16] However, the courts recognize the general practice that "from convenience the usage is to elect one of the stockholders to perform the duty." [17] Although

[13] Kimball v. Marshall, 44 N.H. 465, 468 (1863) (election of city clerk), citing Jefferson's Manual and Cushing's Manual.

[14] "The chairman so selected need not necessarily be a stockholder, nor is there any particular formality required in his selection." Commonwealth ex rel. Sheip v. Vandegrift, 232 Pa. 53, 81 A. 153, 156 (1911).

[15] The president may ask a proxyholder (in this case also an attorney) to call the meeting to order and to act for the president. The proxyholder need not be a shareholder. People v. Albany & S. R.R., 1 Lans. 308, 323–24 (Sup. Ct. 1869), modified on other grounds, 5 Lans. 25 (1871), aff'd, 57 N.Y. 161 (1874).

[16] The court noted that on the day of the meeting a large crowd was present and "by mutual consent apparently" an able attorney acted as chairman of the meeting although the by-laws declared the president to be the principal executive officer who should preside at all meetings unless otherwise determined by the board of directors. Warren Rural Elec. Co-op Corp. v. Harrison, 312 Ky. 702, 229 S.W.2d 473, 474 (1950).

[17] To a claim that a corporate meeting was illegally organized by the election as moderator of a person who was not a stockholder, the court said: "The duty of a moderator is merely to preside and see that the proceedings are conducted in a legal and orderly manner. In doing this, he acts only as the agent of the corporation. There is nothing in the nature of the office, which requires him to be a stockholder, although from convenience the usage is to elect one of the stockholders to perform the duty. But his duties, like those of clerk, are merely ministerial, and can in no way affect the validity of the doings of the corporation or the rights of those claiming under them." Stebbins v. Merritt, 64 Mass. (10 Cush.) 27, 34 (1852).

"Where the presiding officer is a member of the body, and, as such member, entitled to vote with the other members, the fact that he was chosen to act as presiding officer would not deprive him of that privilege." Reeder v. Trotter, 142 Tenn. 37, 215 S.W. 400, 401 (1919).

a non-stockholder may serve as chairman of the meeting by appointment of the assembly or of the rightful chairman, it is customary
for the by-laws to provide for succession in case the designated
presiding officer is not persent. The by-law provisions are, of course,
conclusive.

The courts also recognize the general parliamentary principle
that a deliberative body has the power to determine who should
preside over its deliberations, and that any action taken while so
organized is valid whether the occupancy of the chair be de jure
or de facto.[18]

A person not a director of a corporation (although a shareholder) cannot lawfully participate in a directors' meeting as a
director—much less act as chairman or president of the board.[19]

§ 15.14 Temporary Chairman

It is generally accepted in business corporations that the chairman of the board of directors, or the president in the absence of the
chairman, shall preside at meetings of shareholders. This is a
common provision in the corporate by-laws of both public and
private corporations. In other continuous organizations, incorporated or unincorporated, having a management board and elected
officers, it is usual that the charter or by-laws shall designate the
officers who shall preside at meetings of the membership and of
the board. Such organic provisions are controlling in all respects.[20]

In the absence of a provision in the charter or by-laws of an
organization designating the person or officer who shall preside at

[18] The clerk of the city council presided by consent of the members. "The
suggestion has been made that the whole election is invalid because the clerk
was not vested with power to act as presiding officer, and the proceedings
were fatally contaminated with indecorum in conducting the alleged election.
The council had power to determine who should preside over its deliberations,
and whether the clerk held the chair de jure or de facto could not alter the
result." State ex rel. Reed v. De Maioribus, 131 Ohio St. 201, 2 N.E.2d 506,
509 (1936).

[19] Benson v. Keller, 37 Ore. 120, 60 P. 918 (1900).

[20] A temporary presiding officer has the right to vote and to be included
in a statutorily prescribed majority. Brazer v. Borough of Mountainside, 102
N.J. Super. 497, 246 A.2d 170 (1968), aff'd, 104 N.J. Super. 456, 250 A.2d
418 (1969), modified, 55 N.J. 456, 262 A.2d 857 (1970).

meetings, the chairman must be appointed or elected by those present in accordance with commonly recognized rules of parliamentary procedure for deliberative bodies. In an informal meeting the chairman is often a person invited by the conveners to preside. In meetings having more formality, those present generally will appoint a temporary chairman by acclamation or some other convenient method, depending largely on the size and character of the meeting. The selection of a temporary chairman is done by motion, not by nomination. The temporary chairman will preside over the meeting until a permanent chairman has been duly elected and installed.[21]

The chairman of a corporate organization meeting, whether he be styled a temporary chairman or a permanent chairman in the course of being selected, must be given powers appropriate to his position. In a case involving a dispute as to which of two claimants was the lawful chairman of a shareholders' meeting, the court remarked: "In the preliminary organization of every public meeting, this position must be assumed or assigned to some one individual, and, to bring order out of chaos, a certain degree of authority must be conceded to him." [22]

In a leading case involving the organization of a county political meeting the court followed established rules of parliamentary procedure applicable to company meetings, saying that "such is the recognized rule as to corporation meetings and we see no reason why it should not be equally applicable to a political meeting." In that case rival factions attempted to organize a county committee meeting. The County Chairman called the meeting to order and appointed one of the rival candidates as temporary chairman. This brought about disorder and turmoil lasting over an hour, whereupon the County Chairman went into another room and the two factions at separate gatherings conducted their separate elections. The court held: "The Essex County Democratic Committee either has no constitution or by-laws or their whereabouts are unknown. The statute throws no light on how the proceedings shall be conducted. In the absence of any guide from statute, constitution or by-laws, the commonly recognized rules of parliamentary procedure govern." The court then ruled that, absent a provision in the by-

[21] See Sprague v. Bailey, 19 Pick. 436 (Mass. 1837) (moderator *pro tem*).
[22] Proctor Coal Co. v. Finley, 98 Ky. 405, 33 S.W. 188, 191 (1895).

laws to the contrary, "parliamentary procedure calls for the election of a temporary chairman," and when the County Chairman appointed his own temporary chairman and refused to recognize an appeal from his ruling, "he departed from a well established rule of parliamentary procedure." [23]

Another case turned on which of two rival city executive committees was the legal representative of a political party. It appears that rival ward committees had sent delegates to the organization meeting of the city committee. Upon a roll call by the temporary chairman an uncontested delegate asked why seven contested delegates had been seated. The temporary chairman refused to recognize the delegate and ruled that the only item of business then in order was the election of a permanent chairman. No appeal was taken from this ruling, and the dissidents moved to another room and set up a rival committee. The court upheld the ruling of the temporary chairman and also found in favor of his faction because it was supported by a quorum of the uncontested delegates. [24]

In an earlier case a county political committee had appointed a person to open and preside over a convention until the election of a temporary chairman. That person assumed the chair but refused to call the certified roll of delegates on the vote for temporary chairman and instead took a viva voce vote resulting in a volume of voices both for and against the nominee, unsupported by any evidence that those voting had any right to do so. A

[23] Egan v. Kelly, 14 N.J. Super. 103, 81 A.2d 413, 414 (1951).

When the director and minority members of a Board of Selectmen left the room, the remaining selectmen had the right to choose a member to preside over their deliberations. "In such case, *ex necessitate*, the general rule of parliamentary law which governs legislative bodies must apply, so far as to enable the Board to select a presiding officer pro tempore, to conduct its deliberations in due and orderly form. In such case the authority he can exercise will be merely that of a presiding officer. . . ." Billings v. Fielder, 44 N.J.L. 381, 386 (Sup. Ct. 1882).

A provision of the by-laws providing that the president should preside at all meetings, and in his absence a president pro tempore should be chosen, was totally disregarded at a corporate meeting. An election was set aside because the president, although present, did not preside, nor was there a president pro tempore chosen in his stead, and no person who participated in the meeting was authorized to receive the ballots or to declare the result. State *ex rel.* Guerrero v. Pettineli, 10 Nev. 141, 146 (1875).

[24] *In re* Doyle, 7 Pa. Dist. 635, 24 Pa. Co. Ct. 27 (1898).

majority of the delegates refused to accept the temporary chairman so elected and retired to another part of the room where they elected another chairman and proceeded to nominate candidates. The court commented on the danger of taking a viva voce vote under such circumstances and upheld the majority, saying that "the court will ignore the form and consider the substance of things, where the interests of justice seem to require it." With two conventions, so to speak, being held at the same time in one room in an atmosphere of extreme partisanship and confusion, "a liberal allowance must, therefore, be made for lack of formality." [25]

Although a temporary chairman has authority to preside over the meeting until a permanent chairman is elected, he must relinquish his post if the legally constituted chairman arrives at the meeting while he is still presiding as temporary chairman. The ruling case concerns an annual meeting of stockholders called to be held in Wilmington, Delaware, at a stated hour in the morning. The president and other executives left New York by train for the meeting in ample time to arrive before the scheduled meeting time but were delayed by a wreck on the railroad and arrived late. In the meantime certain shareholders present proceeded to elect a temporary chairman and then a board of directors. The court held that no permanent organization of the meeting had been effected and no definite action taken before the arrival of the lawful chairman, and consequently the purported election of a temporary chairman could not divest the legal chairman of his right to preside. Hence, the directors elected at the meeting conducted by the legal chairman after his arrival were duly elected to office.[26] Consequently, the temporary chairman must relinquish the chair when the permanent chairman, designated by vote or by-law, presents himself at the meeting.

§ 15.15   Removal of Chairman—Common Law

In the absence of an express charter or by-law provision governing his tenure, a presiding officer has no definite term of office and may be removed by the body at any time. Certainly, a chairman who is elected by a meeting for the duration and purposes of that

---

[25] French v. Roosevelt, 18 Misc. 307, 41 N.Y.S. 1080, 1082–83 (1896).

[26] Cavender v. Curtiss-Wright Corp., 30 Del. Ch. 314, 60 A.2d 102 (1948).

meeting may be superseded at any time by the will of the meeting. Thus, the body "can elect a president at each meeting, and in so doing would, by implication, remove the preceding president." This is in accordance with "common parliamentary law." [27]

The power to remove a chairman for reasonable cause is incident to a statutory or corporate body at common law. Thus, a chairman who exhibits gross partiality or incompetence or is deliberately obstructive may be removed. [28]

The courts have relied on "common parliamentary law as it existed in this country at the time of the adoption of our constitution" in holding that the duly elected chairman of a statutory, legislative, or deliberative body may be removed with or without cause in the absence of higher authority to the contrary. "From the foundation of representative government in this country the general rule, as announced by standard American authors on parliamentary law, has been that the legislative body of a state, having the power to choose its own speaker from its own members, has also the inherent power to remove such officer at its will or pleasure, unless inhibited from so doing by some constitutional or other controlling provision of law." [29]

[27] Ostrom v. Greene, 161 N.Y. 353, 362, 55 N.E. 919, 922 (1900).

"From the earliest history of legislative bodies the rule of parliamentary law has been that a legislative body having the power to choose its own presiding officer from its own members has also the inherent power to remove such officer at its will or pleasure, unless prohibited by some express constitutional or statutory provision." State ex rel. Childs v. Kiichli, 53 Minn. 147, 54 N.W. 1069, 1070 (1893), quoting Cushing, Law & Pr. Leg. Assem. at § 299.

[28] SHAW AND SMITH, THE LAW OF MEETINGS at 50–51. See JOSKE, THE LAW AND PROCEDURE AT MEETINGS at 28.

[29] Speakership of the House of Representatives, 15 Colo. 520, 25 P. 707, 710, 708 (1891), citing Jefferson's Manual, Cushing, Law & Pr. Leg. Assem. and Hatsell's Precedents (House of Commons).

Where the city charter is silent on the term and removal of the speaker of the city House of Delegates, the speaker may be removed and a new presiding officer elected. "This office, then, aptly falls within the rule that the incumbent holds merely at the pleasure of the body by which he has been elected, and may be at any time removed by them." The court held that this action could be taken even if it violated the rules of the House. "The power that made them can unmake them, or disregard them." State ex rel. Fox v. Alt, 26 Mo. App. 673, 676, 677 (1887).

"The power is inherent and inseparably attached to the right of the body to convene and act. It is exercisable, when not restricted by some extrinsic

The Supreme Court in an early decision confirmed the general principle that offices created by the Constitution and applicable laws are not "ancient common law offices" with tenure protected in great measure by ancient usage. "In the absence of all constitutional provision, or statutory regulation, it would seem to be a sound and necessary rule, to consider the power of removal as incident to the power of appointment." [30]

§ 15.16   Removal of Chairman—Statutory Assembly

The power to remove the chairman of a statutory assembly or incorporated body without reasonable cause must be derived from the organic law or from governing rules or regulations. For example, a chairman selected at the organization of a corporate meeting may not be removed and replaced later in the meeting by a majority who failed to vote at the election of the chairman. The chairman first elected was the rightful chairman.[31] And where, at a corporate meeting, a motion is made which as a matter of law is beyond the power of the meeting, and the chairman refuses to put the motion on that account, his refusal to entertain an appeal from his ruling is not just cause for removing him and substituting another presiding officer.[32]

§ 15.17   Removal for Cause

In a dispute involving an election of directors, the chairman wrongfully declared the result of a vote and refused to entertain an appeal. His removal was sustained. The Illinois court, after citing the chairman's errors, held that the members present in person and

---

law, at the will of the body." Thus, if the chairman fails to exercise his powers in an orderly way, the assembly may pass him by and proceed to take action otherwise. Hicks v. Long Branch Comm'n, 69 N.J.L. 300, 55 A. 250, 251 (1903).

See SHAW AND SMITH, THE LAW OF MEETINGS at 50.

[30] *Ex parte* Hennen, 38 U.S. (13 Pet.) 230, 259 (1839).

[31] *In re* Pioneer Paper Co., 36 How. Pr. 105 (1864), *appeal dismissed*, 36 How. Pr. 110 (N.Y. 1865).

[32] "The rulings of the president were not upon mere questions of parliamentary practice—of procedure. They went to the matter of legal power." Alliance Co-op Ins. Co. v. Gasche, 93 Kan. 147, 142 P. 882 (1914).

by proxy were justified in exercising the power of the majority, in the absence of any by-laws or rules of order contrary to such action, by deposing the chairman and proceeding with the business of the meeting.[33] When a chairman refuses to preside further, the shareholders have the right to proceed with the business of the meeting without him.[34] And when the speaker of a city council put a motion to adjourn and declared it carried by a viva voce vote and then left the room with others, thereby preventing an appeal from his ruling, the remaining members constituting a quorum had the right to remove the speaker and elect a new one.[35]

The chairman may also be removed for his failure to fulfill established rules and regulations. For example, the court has upheld as reasonable a rule of a city political committee that a chairman may be removed without cause or reason when he has absented himself from three consecutive regularly held meetings. The court held that the rules of the committee must be obeyed.[36]

§ 15.18   Death of Chairman

Upon the death of the presiding officer, and in the absence of other provision, his duties fall upon the vice chairman or vice presi-

[33] In speaking of the chairman, the court said: "A presiding officer cannot arbitrarily defeat the will of the majority by refusing to entertain or put motions, by wrongfully declaring the result of a vote, or by refusing to permit the expression by the majority of its will. He is the representative of the body over which he presides. His will is not binding on it, but its will, legally expressed by a majority of its members, is binding. . . . The body has authority to remove its presiding officer and choose another in his place." American Aberdeen-Angus Breeders' Ass'n v. Fullerton, 325 Ill. 323, 156 N.E. 314, 316 (1927).

A political party committee rule that the chairman may be removed by the committee "for cause" does not give the committee unlimited discretion to determine what shall be cause for removal. Battipaglia v. Executive Comm., 20 Misc. 2d 226, 191 N.Y.S.2d 288 (Sup. Ct. 1959).

[34] "We hold that the acts of the president in adjourning or attempting to adjourn said meetings were illegal; that when he refused to preside further at said meetings, the stockholders had the right to proceed with the business of the meeting without him." State ex rel. Ryan v. Cronan, 23 Nev. 437, 49 P. 41, 45 (1897).

[35] State ex rel. Fox v. Alt, 26 Mo. App. 673 (1887).

[36] Kiernan v. Mirante, 53 Misc. 2d 173, 278 N.Y.S.2d 278 (1967).

dent next in line, as the case may be. This is in accordance with the "general rules governing the conduct of associations and corporations, and by common custom and usage." If there is no line of succession, a new chairman would presumably be appointed by the body.[37]

CHAIRMAN—IMMUNITY

§ 15.19 Comments on the Law

The chairman of a voluntary assembly must understand the personal risks he undertakes when he presides at a meeting, especially if the meeting becomes disorderly and it is necessary to eject the person causing the disorder. A chairman as such is not a judge nor a town moderator or a public officer as that term is generally understood.[1] Yet he is often required to make instant rulings on emerging questions of order, many of which would perplex even an experienced judge. The analogy between a judge and the presiding officer at a meeting of a voluntary organization has been recognized by the court in remarking: "Just as a court has the power to decide wrongly as well as rightly, the president on appeal likewise has such power. . . ."[2] It may be argued that a chairman or presiding officer of any meeting being held for a lawful purpose should be entitled to the personal defenses, immunities, and privileges of an arbitrator, a town moderator, or another public or semijudicial parliamentary official.

At common law, judges are immune from liability for damages for acts committed within their judicial discretion. Immunity ap-

[37] *In re* Davie, 13 Misc. 2d 1019, 178 N.Y.S.2d 740, 742, 744 (1958), *citing* Robert's Rules of Order on succession of officers.

See Ostrom v. Greene, 20 Misc. 177, 45 N.Y.S. 852, 858 (1897), *aff'd*, 161 N.Y. 353, 55 N.E. 919 (1900) (on refusal of president to put motion the vice president put motion while president was in chair).

[1] *See,* generally, Prosser, Law of Torts § 126 (3d Ed. 1964).

[2] The court decided that the president's finding that there had been a two-thirds vote in favor of a union member's expulsion from the union could not alone, even if erroneous, justify the member's non-compliance with appeal rules of the union. Gonzales v. International Ass'n of Machinists, 142 Cal. App. 2d 207, 298 P.2d 92, 96 (1956), *aff'd*, 356 U.S. 617 (1958), *citing* Robert's Rules of Order.

See § 13.5 *supra.*

plies even where a judge is accused of acting maliciously and corruptly.[3] In the Federal courts this official immunity is absolute and extends to an officer of minor rank with respect to acts "within the outer perimeter" of that officer's line of duty.[4] However, in many jurisdictions, minor officials are not so immune, or are not immune if malice is established.[5]

The typical town moderator, whose powers and duties have been fixed by law for over two centuries, occupies a unique position in that his power to preside at town meetings and to preserve order is prescribed by statute. Although he is not a judge,[6] his good-faith judgment in deciding questions of order, even if mistaken, is not subject to review by the court.[7] It is clear that a moderator, "excepting in those matters where he is bound by statutory law, rules as he understands that he ought to rule." If his ruling appears incorrect any person who is dissatisfied may appeal to the meeting.

---

[3] This immunity is for the public benefit; judges should be at liberty to exercise their functions with independence and without fear of consequences. Pierson v. Ray, 386 U.S. 547 (1967) (action against police justice for damages based on common law of false arrest).

A trial judge must conduct himself impartially and without preference or hostility toward either side. United States v. Cassiagnol, 420 F.2d 868 (4th Cir.), *cert. denied*, 397 U.S. 1044 (1970).

[4] Skolnick v. Campbell, 398 F.2d 23, 27 (7th Cir. 1968).

See Marshall v. Gordon, 243 U.S. 521 (1917); Skolnick v. Hanrahan, 398 F.2d 27 (7th Cir. 1968).

[5] Skolnick v. Campbell, 398 F.2d 23, 27 (7th Cir. 1968), *citing* Prosser, Law of Torts. At common law, police officers have no absolute and unqualified immunity from liability for false arrest. Pierson v. Ray, 386 U.S. 547 (1967).

[6] "We recognize that in the federal courts the trial judge is not relegated to the position of a mere moderator. He has the duty not only to make rulings of law but also to govern the trial to assure its proper conduct." Here the term "moderator" is used in its common dictionary meaning. *In re* United States, 286 F.2d 556, 561 (1st Cir. 1961), *rev'd*, 369 U.S. 141 (1962).

[7] A plaintiff was removed from a town meeting as a disorderly person for persisting in his demand that a particular parliamentary manual be followed. The trial court instructed the jury that mistakes of judgment made by the moderator not resulting from "willfull, wanton, malicious or dishonest conduct" are not reversible by a court. Doggett v. Hooper, 306 Mass. 129, 27 N.E.2d 737, 739 (1940).

See Parsons v. Brainard, 17 Wend. 522 (N.Y. Sup. Ct. 1837) (authority of justice of peace acting as moderator at town meetings to exercise his authority promptly and without waiting to put his mandate in writing).

Consequently, whether or not the moderator's ruling is "agreeable to parliamentary law" is entirely immaterial.[8]

It would appear from the case law that a town moderator does not have the complete immunity of a judge for his judicial acts, nor the complete immunity of certain high public officers in the performance of their duties. Nevertheless, a moderator is an elected public official with the decisive powers and duties of a presiding officer prescribed by state statute. He is clearly a "public officer" and thus is entitled to the protection of such privileges and immunity as may be consistent with his authority and his responsibilities.

Unless the chairmanship[9] in question qualifies as a "public office,"[10] the chairman may not be deemed a "public officer" and therefore does not have the benefit of immunity from private liability for tortious acts committed in the performance of his duties. There is authority for the proposition that the chairman's interpretation of the constitution of the organization over which he presides is binding on the courts,[11] but it does not follow that a chairman also possesses a judge's immunity.

There are court decisions holding that the chairman and his aids are not liable in damages for assault and battery or for false imprisonment in forcibly removing and confining a disruptive person when the chairman's actions were justified in the performance of his

---

[8] There was no allegation of fraud or lack of good faith. Hill v. Goodwin, 56 N.H. 441, 454 (1876).

[9] The town chairman means the presiding officer and includes the president, priest, rector, sponsor, or other person in charge of the meeting, and all those acting for him or under his direction.

[10] The term "officer" means any person occupying a position identified as an "office" in the charter or by-laws of the organization. NLRB v. Coca-Cola Bottling Co., 350 U.S. 264 (1955).

[11] "The practical and reasonable construction of the constitution and by-laws of a voluntary organization by its governing board is binding on the membership and will be recognized by the courts." However, the court need not accept a "clearly erroneous administrative construction of a definite and unambiguous provision . . ." of the constitution. DeMille v. American Fed'n of Radio Artists, 31 Cal. 2d 139, 147, 187 P.2d 769, 775 (1947), cert. denied, 333 U.S. 876 (1948), quoted and distinguished in Gonzales v. International Ass'n of Machinists, 142 Cal. App. 2d 207, 298 P.2d 92, 98 (1956), aff'd, 356 U.S. 617 (1958).

duties.[12] There is an inference from these cases that the chairman might be liable in tort if his actions were not lawful, and there are some cases to that effect.[13] However, there appear to be no reported cases which clearly define the degree of malfeasance necessary to sustain personal liability or which turn on a finding that tortious intent was or was not present. There are no cases holding a chairman responsible for mistaken rulings which fell short of the

[12] McLain v. Matlock, 7 Ind. 525 (1856) (constable and parishioners removed plaintiff for disturbing religious camp meeting); Doggett v. Hooper, 306 Mass. 129, 27 N.E.2d 737 (1940) (moderator ordered plaintiff removed from town meeting hall for disorderly behavior); Wall v. Lee, 34 N.Y. 141 (1865) (priest and others attempted to remove disruptive member of congregation); Beckett v. Lawrence, 7 Abb. Pr. (N.S.) 403 (N.Y. Sup. Ct. 1869) (vestrymen with duty to preserve order in church removed disorderly person); Parsons v. Brainard, 17 Wend. 522 (N.Y. Sup. Ct. 1837) (justice of peace acting as moderator removed disturber from town meeting); Corre v. State, 8 Ohio Dec. Reprint 715 (Dist. Ct. 1883) (reporter removed from board of education meeting); Campbell v. Maund, 5 Adolph. & E. 865 (Ex. Cham. 1836) (church-warden expelled from vestry room and prevented from being present at meeting); Marshall v. Tinnelly, 81 S.J. 903 (1937) (ejection of member from council meeting by order of chairman pursuant to resolution under authority of standing order). See SHACKLETON, LAW AND PRACTICE OF MEETINGS at 11. See Anderson v. Dunn, 19 U.S. (6 Wheat.) 204 (1821) (suit against sergeant-at-arms of U.S. House of Representatives, for action taken under order of Speaker). (Prosecutions for disorderly conduct and disturbances of meetings are not included in the above list, which is limited to private tort actions.)

[13] Thompson v. Whipple, 15 S.W. 604 (Ark. 1891) (mayor, as presiding officer of city council, and the council executive officer, held liable in damages for false imprisonment due to mayor's having excluded an indecorous council member from the assembly with the assistance of the executive officer, where the power of the mayor extended no further upon the occurrence of indecorum than to bring the facts to the attention of the assembly).

Noller v. Wright, 138 Mich. 416, 101 N.W. 553 (1904) (plaintiff stockholder was forcibly ejected from meeting by controlling group contesting his share ownership. Action for trespass; judgment for plaintiff affirmed).

Dobson v. Fussy, 7 Bing. 305 (C.D. 1831) (plaintiff member of parish thrashed and thrown out of meeting of select vestrymen held in parish schoolroom. Action for assault and battery. Court held for plaintiff because meeting was not valid for lack of due notice to a member, and observed that plaintiff had just as much right to enter the schoolroom as the others, there being no valid meeting).

Acord v. Booth, 33 Utah 279, 93 P. 734 (1908) (plaintiff unlawfully excluded from meeting of city council committee of the whole. Action for damages; judgment for plaintiff affirmed).

exclusion, removal, confinement, or other physical handling of a dissident person.

It may be concluded that a presumption of legality and regularity will prevail with respect to the chairman's conduct, and that all circumstances will be considered including the setting of the meeting, the customs and practices of those in attendance, and the realization that in the course of most meetings resulting in litigation it becomes necessary to reconcile or choose between seriously opposing views.

Giving consideration only to the standing and purpose of a chairman in filling a social and civic need, the conclusion is obvious that the chairman of a meeting, no matter how large or small or for whatever lawful purpose, is entitled to immunity from personal liability for mistakes of law and fact which are made or suffered in good faith, without malice or willful misconduct. Since the start of this century, the dearth of reported litigation in personal damage claims against a presiding officer arising from the removal or confinement of a disturber is a clear indication of the generally accepted thesis that the law favors an orderly conduct of meetings in reasonably acceptable circumstances and with fairness to the purpose of the meeting as well as to its attendants. Furthermore, frequent criminal prosecution of disruptive persons for disorderly conduct after they have been ejected from a meeting by order of the chairman [14] supports the public demand that people have the right to gather together for lawful purposes without disruption from others. The presiding officer of a lawful meeting should be entitled to the benefits and protection of the immunity enjoyed by others having a similar responsibility.

LEGAL ADVICE

§ 15.20   Right To Consult Counsel

The chairman is entitled to consult counsel with respect to parliamentary rules and the legality of meeting proceedings, and may interrupt the meeting to obtain legal advice essential to the orderly and expeditious conduct of business. A New Zealand case suggests

[14] *See, e.g.,* United States v. Woodard, 376 F.2d 136 (7th Cir. 1967); *In re* Kay, 83 Cal. Rptr. 686, 464 P.2d 142 (1970); State v. Smith, 46 N.J. 510, 218 A.2d 147, *cert. denied,* 385 U.S. 838 (1966); People v. Malone, 156 App. Div. 10, 141 N.Y.S. 149 (1913).

that the chairman should take legal advice on emergent questions of law. "It is, of course, his duty to take care that the business of the Board is conducted in a proper manner, but he must be equally careful in his capacity of Chairman to conduct himself impartially and to see that the opinion of the meeting is properly ascertained upon any question which is regularly before the meeting. If he had misgivings as to whether the meeting was in order, he might well have obtained the opinion of the Board's solicitor or even instructed the Board's solicitor to take counsel's opinion." [1]

An English case has ruled that the refusal of a chairman to put a proper amendment which had been duly moved and seconded may invalidate the resolution to which the proposed amendment relates, noting that the effect of the refusal was to withdraw a material and relevant question from the consideration of the meeting. In this case the chairman, after consulting the solicitor of the company, had deliberately ruled that no amendment could be put. The court disagreed and stated in its opinion, "[i]f the advice given to the chairman was that no amendment could be received to the resolution, the advice was erroneous. About that I entertain no doubt whatsoever." [2]

In another case involving a shareholders' meeting for the election of directors, the chairman, confronted with opposing views, refused to proceed with the election without legal advice and announced that the meeting was adjourned until a lawyer could be consulted. The minority proceeded with its voting, and the court ruled the election invalid. "There is no legal basis whereby a fraction of a meeting may ignore the duly elected chairman and the rest of those in attendance, conduct some private maneuvers of their own, and then assert that their actions constitute official acts of the meeting." In conclusion the court declared: "It is apparent that courts of equity do not look with favor upon attempts of a minority group to seize control of a corporation by trying to trap the majority without legal advice." [3]

[1] Arcus v. Castle, [1954] N.Z.L.R. 122, 129 (1953).

See § 7.24 *supra*.

[2] Henderson v. Bank of Australasia, 45 Ch. D. 330, 339 (1890), *rev'd on other grounds* (same citation).

[3] Chapman v. Barton, 345 Ill. App. 110, 102 N.E.2d 565, 567 (1951).

See Western Cottage Piano & Organ Co. v. Burrows, 144 Ill. App. 350 (1908) (stockholder meeting was adjourned to enable the president to take

Where it was impossible to hold a corporate election because two shares were enjoined from being voted and the other shares were evenly divided, the president had authority to adjourn the meeting until the right to vote the shares could be determined and the injunction proceedings could be examined. "We are inclined to think that this was within his powers as presiding officer, in view of the impossibility of doing any business at the meeting." [4]

In a recent case the president refused to put to vote a resolution authorizing the conveyance of property, stating as his reason that he wanted to obtain advice of counsel before he proceeded. The vice president then assumed the chair and called for a vote on the resolution pursuant to a by-law providing that the vice president should perform the duties of the president upon the latter's "refusal to act." The court held on the record that the president did refuse "to act" and that the vice president "properly assumed the chair." [5]

It has been held that the hiring of private counsel to be paid by the corporation whose present management is engaged in a proxy solicitation battle does not afford ground for injunctive relief. [6]

The fact that the chairman may have acted on the advice of counsel does not constitute a defense or justify an illegal act. [7]

---

legal advice as to whether the chairman should be elected by voice vote or by share vote).

[4] Haskell v. Read, 68 Neb. 107, 93 N.W. 997, *rehearing denied*, 68 Neb. 115, 96 N.W. 1007 (1903).

[5] Austin Lake Estates Recreation Club, Inc. v. Gilliam, 493 S.W.2d 343, 348 (Ct. Civ. App. Texas 1973).

[6] *See* Levin v. Metro-Goldwyn-Mayer, Inc., 264 F. Supp. 797 (1967).

[7] *See* People v. Marcus, 261 N.Y. 268, 185 N.E. 97 (1933).

See § 5.7 *supra*.

16

Procedures at Meetings

PROCEEDINGS FROM THE FLOOR

§ 16.1 Methods of Nomination

Parliamentary law recognizes that it is customary in an election of officers and directors to nominate one or more candidates for the positions to be filled.[1] If no method of making nominations is

---

[1] The term "candidate" embraces a decidedly broader class than the term "nominees" literally construed. The word "candidate" is to be understood in its ordinary popular meaning. "Webster defines the word to mean 'one who seeks or aspires to some office or privilege, or who offers himself for the same.' This is the popular meaning of the word 'candidate'. . . . We therefore say, in every-day life, that a man is a candidate for an office when he is seeking some office. It is begging the question to say that he is only a candidate after nomination, for many persons have been elected to office who were never nominated at all." Leonard v. Commonwealth, 112 Pa. 607, 624, 4 A. 220, 224 (1886); *accord*, Commonwealth *ex rel.* Laughlin v. Green, 351 Pa. 170, 40 A.2d 492, 494 (1945).

provided in the by-laws or rules of order, and the meeting has not adopted its own procedure, any member or shareholder may make a motion prescribing the method of nomination. In the absence of such a motion, the chairman may call for nominations from the floor and conduct the meeting and acceptance of nominations in any reasonable fashion.[2]

Where the statute or charter prescribes the method of electing directors, a majority of the members cannot by a vote deprive other members of their right to nominate candidates as expressly permitted.[3] A prescribed method of election is mandatory; even a court of equity may not direct the shareholders to proceed in any other way.[4] In the absence of a prescribed method, the inherent right of a corporation to adopt by-laws for its internal management embraces the power to adopt a by-law or rule regulating the calling and conduct of corporate meetings and the election of directors.[5] An association by-law which provided that nominations may be made only by a nominating committee, or by members in writing at least 10 days prior to the meeting, and that the names of all

---

A nominee was a "good faith" candidate for election as a director although he withdrew his candidacy and then changed his mind and decided to stand for election. Kauder v. United Board & Carton Corp., 199 F. Supp. 420 (S.D.N.Y. 1961).

See A Proposal for the Designation of Shareholder Nominees for Director in the Corporate Proxy Statement, 74 COLUM. L. REV. 1139 (1974).

[2] The organization had adopted Fox's Parliamentary Usage as a parliamentary guide. It provided that a motion to close nominations should be avoided as long as nominations are being made in good faith. The court held that "while an election for office is yet on, a nomination from the floor—that is, at any time—may be made." Hornady v. Goodman, 167 Ga. 555, 146 S.E. 173, 181 (1928).

[3] When the constitution and rules provide that nominations for election of officers and directors shall be made at the regular membership meeting to be held one month prior to the election meeting, action of the board of directors amending the rules and making nominations, followed by adoption of a shareholder motion to close nominations, does not amend the rules and is a nullity. Any attempt to foreclose the right of members to nominate officers and directors to be elected from the membership and to place the power of nomination solely in the board of directors would be unreasonable and invalid. Knoss v. Warner, 12 Misc. 2d 1021, 174 N.Y.S.2d 677 (1958).

[4] People v. Burke, 72 Colo. 486, 212 P. 837 (1923).

[5] McKee & Co. v. First Nat'l Bank, 265 F. Supp. 1 (S.D. Cal. 1967), aff'd, 397 F.2d 248 (9th Cir. 1968).

nominees must appear on the ballots, has been upheld as not depriving the members of their right to participate in the nomination and election of directors.[6]

Nominations should be made according to "a proper and democratic process," such as the nomination at a political convention of two slates of candidates by a complete representation of delegates. Nominations made by conflicting factions not resulting from deliberations of the elected delegates would be irregular.[7]

§ 16.2 Limitations

The courts will approve limitations on the methods and procedures for the nomination and election of officers and directors which are fair and reasonable, but they will set aside any attempt to adopt a rule or an amendment to an existing rule which is calculated to give to one group an unreasonable or unfair advantage over another group of members. The courts consider that reasonable limitations may be adopted to protect the right to vote of all members.[8] In

[6] Booker v. First Federal Sav. & Loan Ass'n, 215 Ga. 277, 110 S.E.2d 360 (1959), *cert. denied,* 361 U.S. 916 (1959).

[7] Bannigan v. Heffernan, 203 Misc. 126, 115 N.Y.S.2d 889, 896, *modified,* 280 App. Div. 891, 115 N.Y.S.2d 444, *aff'd,* 304 N.Y. 729, 108 N.E.2d 209 (1952).

[8] A union constitution and by-law providing that a member cannot nominate anyone for office but himself, and that no member is eligible for nomination or election unless he has been a member for five years and has served a specified number of days at sea, does not violate labor's Bill of Rights which in effect guarantees that members and classes of members shall not be discriminated against in their right to nominate and vote. Calhoon v. Harvey, 379 U.S. 134, *rehearing denied,* 379 U.S. 984 (1964).

The following by-laws provided a "fair system" for the election of trustees: the appointment of a nominating committee of three members of the board of trustees, the posting of nominations made by the nomination committee, an opportunity to be given to other groups to make and post other nominations, full disclosure to the membership of all nominations made long prior to the annual meeting, and a provision that none could be elected unless his nomination was posted. An attempt to violate the stagger system through a by-law amendment abandoning that concept of electing management, which was adopted without sufficient notice at an annual stockholders' meeting, was held void. *In re* Flushing Hosp. & Disp., 27 N.Y.S.2d 207, *aff'd,* 268 App. Div. 749, 28 N.Y.S.2d 155 (2d Dep't 1941), *modified and affirmed,* 288 N.Y. 125, 41 N.E.2d 917, *modified,* 288 N.Y. 735, 43 N.E.2d 356 (1942).

one case, by-laws requiring that independent nominations must be posted and have membership support of at least five per cent of the shares has been upheld as barring the "frivolous nominee" without standing in the way of the "serious candidate." The court in that case stated: "A multitude of candidates might give the appearance of free choice but would destroy the democratic process essential in the government of a corporation." [9]

§ 16.3   Write-ins

Where it is not clearly established that a prior nomination is necessary, nomination for office is not a prerequisite to election.[10]

Failure of a nominating stockholder to fully comply with the detailed requirements of company by-laws regulating the notice of nomination of an opposing slate of directors at a bank's annual meeting of stockholders was held to be in substantial compliance and not so materially deficient as to justify the rejection by management of the opposition slate. The court, in ordering a new election, stated that management's refusal to recognize the opposition nominees was "highly improper and an irregularity that materially affected the outcome of the election." Wolpert v. First Nat'l Bank, 381 F. Supp. 625, 629 (E.D.N.Y. 1974).

A membership corporation's by-laws providing that no candidates for directorships should be voted for except those proposed by nomination of the nominating committee, to be posted not less than two weeks before the annual meeting, or by independent nominations, to be posted not less than five days before such meeting, were held to be not only reasonable but necessary and valid. In re O'Shea, 241 App. Div. 699, 269 N.Y.S. 840 (2d Dep't 1934).

By-laws providing that where the nominating committee has made nominations for directors, no other nominations shall be voted upon at the annual meeting unless made in writing and delivered to the secretary at least 10 days before the meeting are valid. In re City Sav. & Loan Ass'n, 123 N.Y.S.2d 852 (Sup. Ct. 1953).

A proposed by-law amendment requiring that nominations by members be made more than 30 days before an election of directors, but not imposing the same time limit on the nominating committee, has been held to be "arbitrary, unreasonable and unlawful." Bosch v. Meeker Co-Op Light & Power Ass'n, 91 N.W.2d 148, 153 (1958).

A by-law amendment changing the qualifications of directors was held not unreasonable and not unreasonably applied, and therefore valid. McKee & Co. v. First Nat'l Bank, 265 F. Supp. 1 (S.D. Cal. 1967), aff'd, 397 F.2d 248 (9th Cir. 1968).

[9] Stuberfield v. Long Island City Sav. & Loan Ass'n, 37 Misc. 2d 811, 235 N.Y.S.2d 908, 918 (Sup. Ct. 1962).

[10] A by-law providing that nominations for directorships should take place

In the absence of controlling limitations, a person may be elected to office through "write-ins" of his name on the ballot without his name being placed in nomination.[11] The write-in of a name on a ballot may be considered a nomination as well as a vote.[12]

---

at least 10 days before the annual meeting, but which failed to provide that no one could be eligible for election unless so nominated, was held to be directory only and not mandatory. Any attempt to prescribe that no member should be eligible for election who was not nominated 10 days before the meeting would be unreasonable, a "serious impairment of the stockholders' right of free voting," and would therefore be invalid. *In re* Farrell, 205 App. Div. 443, 200 N.Y.S. 95, *aff'd*, 236 N.Y. 603, 142 N.E. 301 (1923).

By-laws requiring that all nominations for the office of director be made by stockholders at the directors' regular meeting in the month next preceding the annual meeting of shareholders does not prohibit shareholders from voting for and electing directors not so nominated. Nomination is not a prerequisite to election unless the by-laws so state; a by-law which relates only to nominations does not limit the manner of electing directors. "We are loath to limit the fundamental right of shareholders to vote for whomsoever they please as directors of their enterprise, unless the limitation of their right is plainer than here appears." Commonwealth *ex rel.* Grabert v. Markey, 325 Pa. 433, 190 A. 892, 893 (1937).

Where the corporate charter provides that in elections each shareholder may cast his votes for "candidates," a by-law which provides that votes can be cast only for "nominees" would be invalid. A candidate is a man who is seeking office whether nominated or not; many persons have been elected to office who were never nominated. "The term 'candidate' embraces a decidedly broader class than the term 'nominees' literally construed." Commonwealth *ex rel.* Laughlin v. Green, 351 Pa. 170, 40 A.2d 492, 494 (1945).

The alleged failure of nomination of candidates for the office of director is not convincing in the light of a certificate of election issued by disinterested inspectors. *In re* Siebenmann, 32 Misc. 2d 92, 222 N.Y.S.2d 707 (1961).

[11] "Ordinarily, of course, a person may be elected to office through 'write-ins' of his name on the ballot; it is not necessary that he should have been placed in nomination." Commonwealth *ex rel.* Laughlin v. Green, 351 Pa. 170, 40 A.2d 492, 494 (1945).

Nomination to office is not a prerequisite to election. Hence, persons not nominated pursuant to by-law provision who received a larger number of votes by write-in ballots were duly elected. *In re* Farrell, 205 App. Div. 443, 200 N.Y.S. 95 (2d Dep't), *aff'd*, 236 N.Y. 603, 142 N.E. 301 (1923).

One need not be nominated to be elected. Ballot is valid when another name is written or pasted on a ballot over the name printed thereon. People *ex rel.* Bradley v. Shaw, 133 N.Y. 493 (1892).

[12] The polls provided that the election of directors should be "by nomination and ballot." The printed ballots used at the election showed nine nominees and

§ 16.4   Information as to Nominees

A corporation has the common-law right to provide in its by-laws, and the management has the authority to require, that information regarding the interests of the nominating shareholder and of his nominee be given to the shareholders who are asked to vote for the nominee. In such case the chairman has the inherent right and duty to decide whether the information requirement has been satisfied and to declare his findings to the meeting. "Otherwise, a shareholder might vote for a nominee not realizing the nominee had been disqualified." [13] This common-law principle has been extended by regulations issued pursuant to statutory authority applicable to the solicitation of proxies for the election of directors or the request for stockholder action.[14] There appears to be no indication that regulations of this kind are intended to be exclusive, and therefore corporations retain their inherent power to adopt other or more restrictive qualifications deemed reasonable.[15] Under SEC

---

provided blank lines for writing in other names, with a notation "The blank lines are for any other name you may care to vote for." The tellers reported that the nine persons having the largest number of votes were five of those whose names were printed on the ballot and four whose names were written in. The court held that the writing in of names on the ballot "might well be called a nomination and ballot because it is itself evidence of both. By simply counting the ballots and names thereon the election, except in the case of a tie vote, is determined." There was a strong dissenting opinion. Wirth v. Fehlberg, 30 R.I. 536, 76 A. 438, 439 (1910).

[13] McKee & Co. v. First Nat'l Bank, 265 F. Supp. 1, 10 (S.D. Cal. 1967), aff'd, 397 F.2d 248 (9th Cir. 1968).

A proxy statement naming eleven directors to be elected is not misleading when the proposed increase in directors (from seven) did not occur because a proposed acquisition did not materialize. Kauder v. United Board & Carton Corp., 199 F. Supp. 420 (S.D.N.Y. 1961).

The naming of four nominees in the notice of meeting, where only two are to be elected directors, is not defective notice since fourteen days' advance notice was requested and some nominees may die, resign, or refuse to run. Catesby v. Burnett, [1916] 2 Ch. 325, 330.

[14] See SEC Regulation 14A, Solicitation of Proxies, and SEC Regulation 14C, Distribution of Information Pursuant to Section 14(c).

[15] National banks are empowered by statute to regulate the manner in which their directors are elected and to prescribe director qualifications. "There is no indication in the statute, cases or legislative history that the statute is or was intended to be exclusive, depriving national banks of their inherent power to

regulations, a proxy statement setting forth certain prescribed information relating to nominees for election must be furnished to security holders from whom proxies are to be solicited. The general practice of listed companies in presenting a management slate of nominees for all offices to be filled by the vote of shareholders was responsible in part for the Federal regulation of proxy solicitation. In an interesting case it was held that the action of the present directors of a corporation in proposing six of their number as candidates for re-election, and in soliciting proxies accordingly, was a matter of business judgment on the part of the present directors and not the subject of judicial review, particularly in the absence of proof that the present directors did not consider the question of whether some outsiders should be designated.[16]

§ 16.5 Nominations from the Floor

Parliamentary law recognizes the validity of nominations made from the floor at an appropriate time or upon request of the chairman [17] notwithstanding the likelihood that the persons so nominated will not be elected. The right to make nominations from the floor is inherent in the membership.[18] Where a provision of the by-

---

adopt other or more restrictive qualifications deemed reasonable." McKee & Co. v. First Nat'l Bank, 265 F. Supp. 1, 5 (S.D. Cal. 1967), aff'd, 397 F.2d 248 (9th Cir. 1968).

[16] Poirier v. Welch, 233 F. Supp. 436 (D.D.C. 1964).

[17] Nominations from the floor should not be made until the presiding officer has called for nominations or has announced that nominations are in order.

[18] It is sometimes provided by statute that whenever a by-law regulating an impending election is adopted or amended by the board of directors, the new by-law must be submitted to the shareholders for action at their next meeting. In one case a by-law amendment in effect prohibited the nomination of directors from the floor, and when shareholders complained that they were not given a chance to pass upon its validity, the chairman ruled the demand out of order and refused to submit his ruling to the shareholders for their approval. The court stated that it would have been a "useless gesture" for the chairman to ask whether there were other nominations under these circumstances, and held that those in opposition to management did not have a fair opportunity to be heard. In re Scharf, 28 Misc. 2d 869, 216 N.Y.S.2d 775, 778, modified on other grounds, Scharf v. Irving Air Chute Co., 15 App. Div. 2d 563, 223 N.Y.S.2d 307 (2d Dep't 1961).

An objection that nominations could not be made at the meeting was denied

laws makes it mandatory that "nominations from the floor shall always be in order," nominations cannot be suspended by a general rule of parliamentary law or practice as set forth in a parliamentary manual which had been adopted as a guide for the organization, or by the adoption of a motion to close the nominations pursuant to such manual.[19]

Failure of the presiding officer to recognize members who wish to make nominations from the floor and to provide adequate facilities for making nominations has been held to be a substantial irregularity which could affect the result of the election and make it impossible to determine who has been elected. When irregularities at a meeting make it impossible to determine who rightfully has been elected, the election may be declared void and a new meeting reconvened for that purpose.[20] When a valid nomination has been made, the meeting cannot reconsider and nominate someone else unless the

---

where there was no restriction upon the method of nominations and no one was prevented from voting for a candidate whose name did not appear on the list. *See In re* Green Bus Lines, Inc., 166 Misc. 800, 2 N.Y.S.2d 556 (Sup. Ct. 1937).

The chairman is required to receive nominations only from members who have the right to vote. State *ex rel*. Devine v. Baxter, 78 Ohio L. Abs. 549, 153 N.E.2d 452 (1958).

[19] The court stated: "The presiding officer at an election of officers is given no discretion as to whether she will or will not entertain such a nomination. . . . We construe this by-law to mean that while an election for office is yet on, a nomination from the floor—that is, at any time—may be made." Hornady v. Goodman, 167 Ga. 555, 146 S.E. 173, 179, 181 (1928), *citing* Fox's Parl. Usage.

[20] It was alleged that the chairman and secretary by prearrangement recognized only certain factions. They denied that they failed to recognize anyone and claimed that the petitioners had bullhorns and were making unnecessary noises and did not stay in their assigned seats. Petitioners proved that they could not get recognition or use either of the two microphones provided in the meeting hall for about 1,500 committeemen present at the meeting. The court noted that the facilities furnished were not adequate. The meeting was in such disorder that the court stated the chairman should have quieted the disorder or ceased doing business until there was a proper atmosphere for the conduct of the meeting. Failure to do this was held to be a grave irregularity. In re Ryan v. Grimm, 43 Misc. 2d 836, 252 N.Y.S.2d 521 (Sup. Ct.), *aff'd*, 22 App. Div. 2d 171, 174, 254 N.Y.S.2d 462 (4th Dep't 1964), *aff'd*, 15 N.Y.2d 922, 206 N.E.2d 867, 258 N.Y.S.2d 843 (1965).

rules of the body so permit.[21] A person may nominate himself. The procedure of seconding a nomination is purely complimentary and is not necessary.

§ 16.6 Closing Nominations

A motion to close nominations, if carried, cuts off further nominations and no person has the right thereafter to make nominations.[22] However, as great freedom should be allowed in the election of officers, an assembly should avoid adopting this motion as long as nominations are being made in good faith.[23] Closing of nominations will not prevent the casting of ballots for persons not nominated.

§ 16.7 Questions from the Floor

It is customary at meetings of shareholders for the chairman to announce that he will entertain comments and questions from the floor regarding the business and affairs of the company at stated intervals during the course of the meeting. Such discussion periods usually follow the introduction of each matter noticed to come before the meeting for its consideration and action, including the election of directors. Each such period is limited to questions and comments germane to the main question.

Another discussion period, which is also open to questions and comments on general matters, is usually held toward the end of the

[21] "Having made one nomination, the party could not, while that remained in force, make another. If it were otherwise, it might keep on until it had as many candidates as voters. No law should countenance such a course. Part of a convention cannot secede from a regular meeting of the nominating body, and make nominations on its own account. Nominations must be the act of the party, not of a clique." People *ex rel*. Simpson v. Board of Police Comm'rs, 10 Misc. 98, 100, 31 N.Y.S. 112, 114 (Super. Ct. 1894).

[22] This rule carries with it the corollary that no person can thereafter address the meeting on the merits of any candidate.

Under parliamentary law, a motion to close nominations requires a two-thirds vote for adoption, and may be amended as to the time when nominations are to be closed.

[23] Hornady v. Goodman, 167 Ga. 555, 146 S.E. 173 (1928), *quoting* Fox's Parl. Usage which had been adopted by the organization as a parliamentary guide.

meeting after the transaction of all business. All questions from the floor are addressed to the chairman.

It is the general practice of the chairman to answer questions put to him from the floor if he knows the answer, or to refer questions to some member of management who is more familiar with the subject posed by the question. It is also customary and proper that the chairman refuse to answer questions in certain areas, and that he limit or generalize his answers to avoid a disclosure of confidential or competitive information.

There are no established standards which can be applied in determining whether and to what extent, or in what detail, a particular question, or a question in a particular area, should be answered. As a strict matter of law, but not necessarily of prudence, the chairman can refuse at the risk of his position to answer any questions put to him and can even refuse to give a reason for not answering. The answering of questions from the floor is therefore largely a matter of courtesy and of common sense, tempered with the recognition that the principal purpose of an annual meeting is to give management an opportunity to account for its stewardship since the last annual meeting and to enable the shareholders to interrogate management on all proper subjects. It is generally irrelevant that the interrogating shareholder owns only a few shares,[24] but a court of equity may deny injunctive relief, which would prevent a scheduled shareholder meeting, to the holder of a single share when such action would seriously upset pending plans of a large corporation and disturb thousands of shareholders.[25] Questions and discussion concern-

[24] In a stockholder's derivative action, it is irrelevant that the plaintiff owns only a few shares. *See, e.g.,* Subin v. Goldsmith, 224 F.2d 753, 761 (2d Cir.), *cert. denied,* 350 U.S. 883 (1955); Breswick & Co. v. United States, 138 F. Supp. 123, 132, n.12 (S.D.N.Y. 1956).

[25] *See* Curtin v. American Tel. & Tel. Co., 124 F. Supp. 197 (S.D.N.Y.), *aff'd per curiam* (2d Cir. Apr. 4, 1954) [unreported—*see* 84 HARV. L. REV. 835, 852 (1971)].

The fact that a shareholder owned only 210 out of 10,000,000 shares should be considered in determining the equities of a shareholder's application to enjoin a meeting. Poirier v. Welch, 233 F. Supp. 436 (D.D.C. 1964).

Where an individual owned no shares, but his wife and brother were substantial shareholders, and he was active as member of a shareholder committee, a studied failure to disclose his activities was a material violation of SEC rules. SEC v. May, 134 F. Supp. 247 (S.D.N.Y. 1955), *aff'd,* 229 F.2d 123 (2d Cir. 1956).

ing the financial statements are of course proper items of business at an annual meeting.[26]

The purpose of a meeting, whether general or special, can be accomplished in a successful fashion in this regard if management accepts and willingly responds to all proper questions, and the individual shareholders willingly accept their share of the responsibility for an orderly and purposeful meeting.

§ 16.8   False and Misleading Questions

Questions from the floor which are based upon false or misleading assumptions or which carry false or misleading implications may be declared out of order and need not be answered by management. It has been held that false and misleading information cast in the form of questions falls within SEC Rule X–14A which forbids the use for proxy solicitation of "any statement" which is false or misleading. Rules applicable to the written word must also be applicable to the spoken word. "To hold that merely by placing a question mark at the end of a sentence the author can circumvent the requirements of fair and complete disclosure would provide an obvious escape from the salutory regulation of the Commission." [27] Furthermore, the addition of the words "in my opinion" does not excuse the making of a false or misleading statement.[28]

Inquiries intended to raise a question in the mind of the average stockholder as to whether the management of the company is in honest and capable hands are proper questions if there is some basis for the inquiries. But if there is no basis for putting such questions, they are misleading and out of order.[29]

[26] *In re* Frankel v. 447 Central Park West Corp., 176 Misc. 701, 28 N.Y.S.2d 505, 506 (Sup. Ct. 1941), *aff'd mem.*, 263 App. Div. 950, 34 N.Y.S.2d 136 (1st Dep't 1942).

[27] SEC v. May, 134 F. Supp. 247, 252 (S.D.N.Y. 1955), *aff'd*, 229 F.2d 123 (2d Cir. 1956). The Court of Appeals held that the Commission has been clearly entrusted with the "duty of protecting the investing public against misleading statements made in the course of a struggle for corporate control."

[28] *See* SEC v. Okin, 137 F.2d 862, 864 (2d Cir. 1943).

[29] "Perhaps it could be argued that each or any one of these questions would not be likely by itself to influence any stockholder to execute the proxy. But taken together one after another as set forth in the 'Time for a Change' letter they certainly would raise a question in the mind of the average stockholder

§ 16.9   Dissenting Stockholder Actions

Over a century ago it was well established at common law that the annual meeting of shareholders was a proper time and place for an aggrieved shareholder to present his complaints against management and to seek action by his fellow shareholders in support of his views. The courts had already established the principle that a shareholder could not bring a derivative action against management without showing with particularity what efforts he had made to get those who control the company to take action, and his reasons for his failure to obtain action or the reasons for not making such effort. This doctrine received careful consideration in an early English case decided in 1843.

In that case two shareholders brought a derivative action against the directors and one shareholder, not a director, charging the defendants with concocting and effecting various fraudulent and illegal actions. The court applied "established rules of law and practice . . . which, though in a sense technical, are founded on the general principles of justice and convenience" in holding that the bill of complaint was fatally defective. The court found that, among other things, the complaining shareholder had not called a meeting of the shareholders or attended at some regular annual meeting and obtained the action of a majority on the matters in issue.[30]

---

as to whether the management of the Company was in honest and capable hands. It is clear that the questions were designed to do just that. If there were some basis for the questions then there could be no objection. But as there is no basis for asking any of them, it seems to me that the questions separately, and as a group, are grossly misleading and constitute a wilful violation of the Regulations." SEC v. May, 134 F. Supp. 247, 254–55 (S.D.N.Y. 1955), aff'd, 229 F.2d 123 (2d Cir. 1956).

[30] Foss v. Harbottle, 2 Harc. 461 (1843), cited in Hawes v. Oakland (Contra Costa Water Co.), 104 U.S. 450, 454 (1882).

"The cases are uniform in holding that there must be a request that the stockholders as a body sue the directors, or that an action be brought for their benefit before an individual stockholder can bring an action in the interest of the corporation, unless the request would be useless and unavailing." Gunn v. Voss, 154 F. Supp. 345, 346 (D.C. Wyo. 1957).

See, e.g., Quirke v. St. Louis–San Francisco Ry. Co., 277 F.2d 705 (8th Cir. 1960) (failure of dissenting shareholder to seek remedy not excused because stockholders were numerous and widely scattered, and because it would be expensive, time-consuming, and impossible to reach them); Heinz v. National

In 1881 the United States Supreme Court, relying on English common law, upheld the rule that a shareholder seeking redress of his grievances or action in conformity to his wishes must make an earnest effort with management to induce remedial action or to show, if he was unsuccessful in obtaining redress from the directors, "that he has made an honest effort to obtain action by the stockholders as a body, in the matter of which he complains." [31]

In a more recent case minority shareholders sued the company and certain officers they accused of misconduct. The bill was filed a few days after the annual meeting of shareholders and alleged, among other irregularities, that the officers had not made a sufficient statement of the current corporate affairs and had refused reasonable information at the meeting. The court dismissed the bill, hold-

---

Bank of Commerce, 237 F.2d 942 (8th Cir. 1916) (dissenting shareholder did not bring matter to attention of shareholders although there had been a meeting since the transaction); Cathedral Estates v. Taft Realty Corp., 228 F.2d 85 (2d Cir. 1955) (demand need not be made on the directors or shareholders where such a demand would be "futile," "useless," or "unavailing"; when the directors and controlling stockholders are antagonistic, adversely interested, or involved in the transaction attacked, a demand on them is presumptively futile and need not be made); Continental Securities Co. v. Belmont, 206 N.Y. 7 (1912) (relief must be sought from directors, but not from shareholders).

See Annot., Pleading and verification requirements in stockholders' derivative suits in federal courts, 15 L. Ed. 2d 1120 (1966).

[31] Hawes v. Oakland (Contra Costa Water Co.), 104 U.S. 450, 461 (1882).

"One of the indispensable prerequisites in Massachusetts is that the stockholder before bringing his suit show that he has resorted to the body of shareholders, except in the one instance where he shows that the majority of the voting stock is under the control of the alleged wrongdoers. It is not enough for him to show that at a particular meeting less than all the stockholders are likely to show up, and that of those who do attend a majority will be corruptly allied with the alleged nefarious directors. Perhaps the reason for the refusal of the Massachusetts court to permit allegations of this type to be treated as sufficient is that they would lead to speculative testimony. Only when a shareholder has actually raised his point at a meeting can one know who will be present, who will vote, and whether those present and voting will be a quorum and will vote independently or under corrupt inducement, favorably or unfavorably. Finally, it *may* be that under Massachusetts law the absentees are counted as if their silence reflects acquiescence and half-hearted approval of whatever is done by a majority of those voting at a meeting attended by a quorum." Carroll v. New York, N.H. & H. R.R., 141 F. Supp. 456, 458 (D. Mass. 1956).

ing that the shareholders had not first exhausted their remedies within the corporation. "The remedy for [the shareholders] lies in the first instance with the directors chosen by the stockholders to manage the corporate affairs. All the matters complained of existed and were known at the stockholders' meeting." The court noted that there was no allegation of any "wrong combination of a majority of the stockholders" but only that they lived at a distance, were ignorant of the situation, and sent their proxies to the president. "The plain remedy for that would be to seek another stockholders' meeting, after informing the other stockholders of the situation and asking them to withdraw their proxies and to attend." [32] These common-law rules and practices are now provided for by Federal statute,[33] and have been extensively litigated.[34] A recent

[32] The court added the following significant words: "A stockholder, in taking stock in the ordinary corporation, submits, within the charter limits, to a guidance of the corporate affairs according to the will of the owners of a majority of the stock and through the directors whom the majority choose." Stone v. Holly Hill Fruit Products, 56 F.2d 553, 554 (5th Cir. 1932).

If the shareholder's complaint is within the control of the shareholders it should be brought to the attention of the shareholders for action. Continental Sec. Co. v. Belmont, 206 N.Y. 7, 99 N.E. 138 (1912); accord, Syracuse Television, Inc. v. Channel 9, 51 Misc. 2d 188, 273 N.Y.S.2d 16 (Sup. Ct. 1966).

In holding that a single member may not absent himself and prevent action by a quorum, the court remarked: "It appears to be a fundamental rule of parliamentary practice governing assemblies that the opportunity to deliberate, and if possible, to convince their fellows is the right of the minority, of which they cannot be deprived by the arbitrary will of the majority." Terre Haute Gas Corp. v. Johnson, 221 Ind. 499, 45 N.E.2d 484, 489 (1942), modified on other grounds, 221 Ind. 499, 48 N.E.2d 455 (1943).

[33] FED. R. CIV. P. § 23 (b).

[34] See, e.g., Quirke v. St. Louis–San Francisco Ry. Co., 277 F.2d 705 (8th Cir. 1960); Gottesman v. General Motors Corp., 268 F.2d 194 (2d Cir. 1959); Cathedral Estates v. Taft Realty Corp., 228 F.2d 85 (2d Cir. 1955). See also Meltzer v. Atlantic Research Corp., 330 F.2d 946 (4th Cir. 1964); Levitt v. Johnson, 334 F.2d 815 (1st Cir. 1964), cert. denied, 379 U.S. 961 (1965); Rogers v. Guaranty Trust Co., 60 F.2d 114 (2d Cir. 1932), aff'g 60 F.2d 106, rev'd on other grounds, 288 U.S. 123 (1933); Heinz v. National Bank of Commerce, 237 F. 942 (8th Cir. 1916).

"It is clear then that the demand is generally designed to weed out unnecessary or illegitimate shareholder derivative suits. This prophylactic device assuredly should not be allowed to frustrate the true derivative suit, the very thing it was designed to protect." Barr v. Wackman, 36 N.Y.2d 371, 368 N.Y.S.2d 497, 505 (1975).

case held that a dissident shareholder who waited eight months after the corporate meeting before going to court to challenge actions taken at the meeting had waived his objections and was guilty of laches.[35]

Although a shareholders' meeting is a proper forum for adversary action, it should not be allowed to become an arena for stockholder disputes in the manner of "political contests, with each side free to hurl charges with comparative unrestraint, the assumption being that the opposing side is then at liberty to refute and thus effectively deflate the 'campaign oratory' of its adversary." [36] This case and others are an indication of the breadth of inquiry which is recognized by the courts to be within the province of the shareholders.

§ 16.10   Proper Subjects for Inquiry

The foregoing are not to be construed, however, to indicate that there are no limitations to shareholder inquiry. The SEC has by

[35] Scheeler v. Buffalo Wire Works Co., 50 Misc. 2d 158, 269 N.Y.S.2d 897 (1966).

Delay in seeking equitable relief until after an annual meeting of stockholders at which an adversary claim could have been asserted may be fatally untimely. Where the dissenting shareholders waited until after a later annual meeting to challenge the validity of an election of directors at an earlier annual meeting, the court held that the proceeding was not timely instituted and the plaintiffs were not entitled to relief. Carter v. Muscat, 21 App. Div. 2d 543, 251 N.Y.S.2d 378 (1st Dep't 1964).

[36] SEC v. May, 229 F.2d 123, 124 (2d Cir. 1956).

Minority shareholder engaged in a proxy contest may practice "the art of advocacy" to gain his objective. A letter to shareholders "must be read with some regard to the fact that it belongs to the class of contentious writings and that the art of advocacy has always taken some liberties with the 'whole truth.' Furthermore, it is a letter by a minority stockholder in opposition to management. That factor does not constitute a license to lie but it does afford the reasonable expectation that under-statement or exaggeration will be answered —a condition not always to be anticipated when the communication reviewed issues from the management." SEC v. Okin, 48 F. Supp. 928, 930 (S.D.N.Y. 1943).

See Levin v. Metro-Goldwyn-Mayer, Inc., 264 F. Supp. 797 (S.D.N.Y. 1967) (denial of motion for preliminary injunction restraining management from soliciting proxies using alleged illegal or unfair methods of communication); see ARANOW AND EINHORN, PROXY CONTESTS FOR CORPORATE CONTROL (2d Ed. 1968).

its rules excluded subjects, within certain defined areas, from the permissible "proper subject" for mandatory inclusion in proxy material.[37] Similarly, the courts have identified certain items of information which it is not "customary" for a business corporation to disclose, if made the subject of inquiry at a meeting of shareholders. In the leading case, Lumbard, C. J., recognizes that the common good is expressed in the legitimate protection by management of confidential information dealing with the accomplishments and hopes of the enterprise.[38]

Generally, questions from the floor and other communications between shareholders and management at a shareholders' meeting are protected by a qualified privilege.[39]

LIMITATION OF DEBATE

§ 16.11   Common Parliamentary Law

Parliamentary law recognizes the right of a deliberative body to limit and to cut off discussion and debate.[1] The purpose of a meeting is to consider and act upon the business for which the meeting was convened. To this end, the discussions and deliberations should be relevant and not repetitive, reasonable in scope and attitude,

[37] SEC Regulation 14A, Solicitation of Proxies, and Regulation 14C, Distribution of Information Pursuant to Section 14(c), under Securities Exchange Act of 1934.

[38] SEC v. May, 134 F. Supp. 247, 253 (S.D.N.Y. 1955), aff'd, 229 F.2d 123 (2d Cir. 1956). It is "not customary" for a publicly owned industrial corporation to disclose: 1. "How much is made" in each major line of products, and how much money is invested in the production facilities for the various items. The court said: "Clearly such disclosure is not customary. In fact such details are generally guarded with care lest competitors be given information which might be harmful to some branch of the company's business." 2. The details of the purchase and sale of particular capital assets. Id.

[39] See § 19.1 infra.

[1] See May's Treatise on the Law, Privileges, Proceedings and Usage of Parliament (16th Ed. 1957), Chapter XX, "Methods of Curtailing Debate," at 475.

Constitution, Jefferson's Manual, and Rules of the House of Representatives (1975), House Doc. No. 416, Rule XVII, § 804 at 525.

Senate Procedure, Rule XXII (1964). Dicey, The Law of the Constitution (10th Ed. 1968) at cixvii. V Hinds' Precedents, Chapter CXX, "The Previous Question," at § 5443.

and subordinate to the purpose of the meeting. When the views of members on a pending question have been heard and the meeting has listened to reasonable arguments for a reasonable time, the meeting may decide that it has heard enough and put an end to further discussion. It is then competent for any member to move the closure ("cloture") of debate—that debate now cease—to avoid prolonged discussion [2] which would only result in the futile thwarting of the expression of the will of the majority. The chairman may accept the motion and, with the sanction of the majority, may declare the discussion closed.

If the closure of debate is not approved by the majority, discussion of the pending question continues. The rights of the minority are protected by the discretionary power in the chairman of refusing to accept a motion for closure.

The power of a presiding officer to accept a closure motion when he concludes that the question has been freely and fully discussed has long been established in English common law. An authoritative English text states simply: "When the views of the minority have been heard, it is competent to the chairman, with the sanction of a vote of the meeting, to declare the discussion closed, and to put the question to the vote." [3]

An Australian text also confirms the power to the chairman, with

---

[2] Closure has been described in the following words: "This is the simplest of the methods of curtailing debate, and first appeared in parliamentary procedure as a means of countering the tactics of an obstructionist minority who persistently protracted discussion to such length as seriously to impede the business of the House of Commons. In its primary form it consists in the motion 'that the question be now put.' After being moved and seconded, it is voted upon without debate. Subject to any regulations affecting the conduct of a meeting, the chairman may refuse to put the motion on the ground that it is an infringement of the rights of the minority; but if, with the general support of the meeting, he *bona fide* allows it to be put, the court will not intervene on the application of the minority [citation]. If the motion is put and carried, the debate which it interrupted is terminated, and the main question is forthwith put." SHAW AND SMITH, THE LAW OF MEETINGS at 69–70, *citing* Wall v. London & No. Assets Corp., [1898] 2 Ch. 469; *see* Shackleton at 80–81; Curry (Crew) at 56, 113; Mays at 475–82. For description of other types of closure, such as "guillotine" closure and "kangaroo" closure, *see* Shackleton at 81; Shaw and Smith at 69–70.

[3] *See* CURRY (CREW), PUBLIC, COMPANY AND LOCAL GOVERNMENT MEETINGS at 113.

the consent of the majority of those present, to cut off debate after reasonable discussion has taken place.[4] Although the chairman, by himself, does not have the right to stop or limit debate, he may put the motion to vote after he has given full opportunity to all who wish to speak and has reason to conclude that no others wish to take the floor. When a vote has been ordered, no further discussion or debate may be permitted.

The principal case [5] dealt with a proposed amalgamation requiring the approval of shareholders. A minority objected to a scheme when presented at an extraordinary general meeting and engaged in various dilatory parliamentary tactics. The chairman, having concluded that the majority had listened to "reasonable arguments for a reasonable time" and had "heard enough," put a motion that the debate should be closed. The motion passed by a majority vote. On appeal, the court refused to overrule, holding the closure of debate to be an internal affair of the company in which the court ought not to interfere. The minority claimed "irregularities," and argued that shareholders desirous of speaking were prevented from so doing. To this the court answered: "It appears that there was a discussion about this matter at a meeting of shareholders of the [company], and, after having heard the views—I do not say of all those who opposed, but of one or two of them—the meeting came to the conclusion that they had heard enough, and did not want to hear any more, and thereupon the chairman declared the discussion closed. That is said to be a matter calling for the interference of this court. I do not think so. I think it would be a very bad precedent that we should interfere in such a case." The court concluded: "After hearing what is to be said, they may say, 'We have heard enough. We are not bound to listen till everybody is tired of talking and has sat down.' There is no reason for supposing that there was any terrorism in this matter, and this appeal must be dismissed

---

[4] The chairman may accept a closure motion although only one person has spoken for and only one has spoken against the proposal. He has a discretion, but should be satisfied that the matter has been reasonably discussed and that the views of the minority have been heard. See JOSKE, THE LAW AND PROCEDURE AT MEETINGS at 31, 48.

[5] Wall v. London & No. Assets Corp., [1898] 2 Ch. 469, 67 L.J. Ch. 596; 76 L.T. 249; 47 W.R. 219, 13 T.L.R. 547 C.A., quoted in Curry (Crew) at 56.

with costs." Chitty, L. J., then stated the following rule: "As to the closure, I think if we laid it down that the chairman, supported by a majority, could not put a termination to the speeches of those who were desirous of addressing the meeting, we should allow a small minority, or even a member or two, to tyrannize over the majority. The case has been put [by the minority] as the terrorism of the majority. If we accepted [this] proposition we should put this weapon into the hands of the minority, which might involve the company in all-night sittings. That seems to me to be an extravagant proposition, and in this particular case there seems to have been nothing arbitrary or vexatious on the part of the chairman or of the majority. I am not, of course, saying that the majority must not listen to reasonable arguments for a reasonable time." This doctrine of common law still prevails, subject only to minor modifications of practice and to rules and regulations adopted by the body fixing the boundaries of debate by time and frequency and the number or percentage of votes necessary for closure.

§ 16.12 Constitutional and Statutory Bodies

Rules providing for limiting or terminating debate are necessary to enable large legislative assemblies with an enormous amount of business to function in an orderly fashion. For example, the U. S. House of Representatives, with hundreds of members having the right to speak even for a limited period of time on every debatable question, would find it impracticable to transact business when the opposing parties are nearly equal, unless the House had effective parliamentary procedure to limit or close the debate.[6]

The power of a legislative body to limit or terminate debate and to invoke closure stems from its inherent right to determine the rules of its own proceedings. This right is unlimited except as controlled by constitutional or dominant statutory provisions, and the courts will not look to the wisdom or folly, the advantages or disadvantages, of the rules so adopted. Generally, public legislative bodies of all ranks have all requisite statutory authority to adopt rules of procedure for the conduct of their meetings and the transaction of business.

[6] *See* ROBERT, PARLIAMENTARY LAW at 68.

§ 16.13   Vote Required

In current American parliamentary practice of legislative assemblies it is a general rule that motions which take away rights or limit freedom of expression of members require more than the usual majority vote. Thus, a motion for "closure" or some other device that will effectively terminate or limit debate in a legislative house, such as a motion for the previous question, generally requires a vote of more than a majority (often two-thirds) of the members present at the meeting. Arguments in favor of requiring more than a mere majority vote have been considered by the courts. One court has asked: "Could it be reasonably argued that any rule for the governing of the proceedings of a legislative house which sought to impose limitations on debate would be invalid if such limitation required more than the majority vote required for the passage of bills? Legislative procedures and rules through the years, of our national Congress as well as of this State and our sister States point emphatically to the contrary. Otherwise, limitation of debate could always be imposed by a simple majority, and a minority could never be heard. Such result is not consonant with full deliberation and hearing essential to legislative tribunals." [7]

A Rule of the U. S. Senate provides that debate on a motion may be cut off (closure) by a vote of three-fifths of the Senators duly chosen and sworn. This Rule may be revoked or changed by the adoption of a motion approved by the vote of only a majority of members present and voting, but such motion is itself subject to unlimited debate unless and until debate on the motion is cut off pursuant to the three-fifths Rule. Thus, an effective filibuster can prevent a change in the Rule unless and until a three-fifths vote is obtained to bring the amending motion to a vote. The due passage of a motion to cut off debate does not preclude subsequent unlimited debate on the adoption of alternative procedures. In the U. S. House of Representatives, however, the "previous question" is the only motion used for closing debate, when ordered by a majority of members voting, a quorum being present. [8]

[7] Opinion of the Justices No. 185, 278 Ala. 525, 179 So. 2d 155, 159 (1965).

[8] U. S. Senate Rule XXII. The vote needed for closure was changed from two-thirds of those present and voting to three-fifths of the members chosen and sworn, March 7, 1975.

U. S. House of Representatives, Rule XVII, § 804.

§ 16.14   Stockholder Meetings

It is established that stock corporations and membership corporations, and in fact most organizations which have annual and special meetings not legislative in character or not in continuous session, have the inherent right to adopt by-laws or regulations permitting the limitation of discussion and debate for the purpose of securing orderly meetings devoted to the consideration, discussion, and resolution of the matters for which the meeting was called.[9]

Some corporations have followed this course by adopting their own rules of procedure for the conduct of stockholder meetings, although it would appear that few have extended their rules to the closing of debate, or to the limitation of debate or discussion according to the duration or frequency of speaking on any one or more subjects.

Most corporations have continued to rely on the common-law doctrine of reasonableness, where discussion and debate are not regulated by the course of events on the floor and may be put to an end by the meeting when it has listened to reasonable arguments for a reasonable time and wishes to proceed with other matters or to adjourn.

Although the American parliamentary practice of legislative assemblies generally requires a vote of more than a simple majority for the closure or limitation of debate, the common law and general corporate usage permit closure or limitation of debate by a shareholders' meeting upon order of the chairman with the concurrence of the shareholders indicated by a simple majority stock vote. The only reason for requiring a two-thirds vote, or any vote exceeding

---

[9] Robert recommends that a two-thirds vote should be required to effect closure of debate at meetings of "ordinary societies" as well as at meetings of legislative assemblies. Robert's Rules of Order at 183 n.

Although the meeting has power to terminate or limit discussion, leaders of factions within the membership or their attorneys do not have the authority to bind their followers to keep quiet. No questions were allowed or discussions permitted at a church meeting to discuss church property. Leaders of the two factions or their attorneys had so agreed. By-laws provided that meetings of the church should be governed by Hiscox' Directory for Baptist Churches. Rules of order in the Directory recognized the right of debate. Randolph v. Mt. Zion Baptist Church, 139 N.J. Eq. 605, 53 A.2d 206 (1947).

a simple majority, to effect closure is that such action may deprive members of their right of discussion or debate to the limit of allotted time. When there is no regulatory limit, the rule of reason prevails. Experience indicates that the rule of reason, as distinguished from an arbitrary allotment of time and frequency, has worked comparatively well especially where the chairman and the assembly have discouraged any tendency to abuse the privileges of the floor.

An inquiry arises whether the question and comment periods of the typical shareholder meeting of a publicly held company may be limited or terminated by order of the chairman without the concurrence of the majority of stockholders present and voting or whether the same rules should be applied to questions and comments as prevail on a closure of debate. The unique procedures of the typical stockholders' meeting accord shareholders the privilege, and perhaps the right, to ask questions and make comments of a general nature as well as to engage in debate on pending motions. This is a deviation from the general parliamentary rule that there should be no speaking from the floor but to a question. There being no question pending during a general discussion period, a motion for the previous question would be irrelevant. However, questions asked and comments made during periods set aside for that purpose immediately following and relevant to a motion before the assembly might well be considered debate inasmuch as questions and comments from stockholders are generally considered a part of the argumentative process.

Although parliamentary practice distinguishes between debate [10] and the asking of questions,[11] the same rules of brevity and expeditious handling should apply to both. Questions asked and comments made by shareholders should be considered for the purposes of elapsed time and relevance to be part of the meeting procedure. Questions and comments, whether on the agenda or of a general nature, are equally time-consuming and often are wholly irrelevant to the business of the meeting. All should be subject to limitation

---

[10] The term "debate," in its strictest sense, is applicable only to what is said on the one side or the other of a question which the assembly is to decide by a vote. In a broader sense, it embraces everything which is said in the assembly by members, whether upon a question pending, or in reference to any other proceeding, matter, or business whatever. See Cushing, LAW AND PRACTICE OF LEGISLATIVE ASSEMBLIES § 1532 at 597.

[11] See Robert's Rules of Order at 186–87.

or closure by appropriate parliamentary proceedings in order to expedite the transaction of business and to assure an orderly meeting.

Custom and usage have not yet placed a specific limit on the speaking time of an individual member or shareholder or on the number of allowable recognitions of the same speaker by the chair, although it is becoming more evident each year that reasonable limitations may sometimes be necessary to protect the right of all members to have an equal opportunity to be heard. The time limit, if any, should vary to suit the circumstances, but should be short on any one question particularly where the proxy-soliciting material and the annual report with its business summaries and financial statements have given the shareholders an opportunity to do their "homework" before coming to the meeting. In case the general question period follows the conclusion of all voting or is resumed at that time, its limitations should be related to the hour, the suitability and further availability of the meeting room, the seriousness of the problem at hand, the urgency of a prompt solution or decision, the extent of which opposing views have been presented, and the evident desire of the remaining shareholders to adjourn and leave the meeting hall.

§ 16.15   Public Hearings

A similar question arises in the conduct of public hearings on pending legislative and executive matters. A New York case has held, for example, that a city council having control over its own proceedings is not required to hear complaints of all aggrieved taxpayers, notwithstanding its power to amend the tax rolls as it may deem proper. In that case the charter allowed but five days to confirm the roll and there was no duty expressly imposed by law to hear the allegations and complaints of all persons interested who might appear. It was acknowledged that five days forbade listening to the allegations and complaints of every dissatisfied taxpayer in the city and that the council in its discretion had the right to refrain from hearing such complaints. The court noted that the council had the right to control its own procedure, which is the "established prerogative of legislative bodies," and that the public could participate in the proceedings only at the pleasure of the council. Otherwise, said the court, "any organized group could disrupt the orderly proceedings of representative government by monopolizing them to the exclusion of the elected representatives of the people."[12] This right of a legislative body to control its proceedings was upheld in a decision holding that the action of a majority of members of a city council in terminating a public hearing on proposed local legislation was not arbitrary or capricious when a reasonable opportunity had been afforded for the presentation to and consideration by council of complete data and arguments for and against the proposal being considered.[13]

§ 16.16   Adjournment To End Discussion

A court decision under the Labor–Management Reporting and Disclosure Act raised the question whether the Act allows limitation upon the freedom of speech and assembly by an arbitrary restriction of the agenda or by a deliberate adjournment of the meeting to prevent a member from speaking.[14] Cases cited included one approving a motion to adjourn a membership meeting while a union member held the floor arguing for a motion to have her rights of arbitration restored,[15] and another relating to the disturbance by an existing local union of a meeting held by members seeking a new local charter from the international union.[16]

---

[12] People ex rel. Powott Corp. v. Woodworth, 172 Misc. 791, 15 N.Y.S.2d 985, 995 (Sup. Ct. 1939), rev'd on other grounds, 260 App. Div. 168, 21 N.Y.S.2d 785 (4th Dep't 1940).

[13] Martin v. Flynn, 19 App. Div. 2d 653, 241 N.Y.S.2d 883 (2d Dep't 1963).

[14] Yanity v. Benware, 376 F.2d 197 (2d Cir.), cert. denied, 389 U.S. 874 (1967). See dissenting opinion of Chief Judge Lumbard at 203, n. 4.

[15] Scovile v. Watson, 338 F.2d 678 (7th Cir. 1964), cert. denied, 380 U.S. 963 (1965).

[16] Johnson v. Local Union No. 58, 181 F. Supp. 734 (E.D. Mich. 1960).

17

Voting at Meetings

VOTING RIGHTS

§ 17.1   Right To Vote

The right to vote is "an affirmative right to express a choice or preference, not merely the right of negation." It is the "right to express the voter's will or preference on a proposed measure, or in the selection of an officer, through ballot, outcry, or other appropriate means by which choice or preference may be made known." [1] The legal effect of voting is a matter of substantive law, not of practice or procedure. [2]

§ 17.2   Voting—Officers

The right to vote in a deliberative assembly is derived from membership, not from office. The mere holding of an office gives no right to vote. Thus, a presiding officer who is not a member, and honorary or emeritus members, have no voting rights. [3] In the corporate area, a chairman of the board of directors and a shareholder while presiding at a shareholders' meeting are entitled to vote as a member and a shareholder respectively. Whether the presiding officer of a constitutional or statutory body can vote at all times, or only under certain circumstances such as a tie, is a matter of organic law. [4]

---

[1] Aldridge v. Franco Wyoming Oil Co., 24 Del. Ch. 349, 14 A.2d 380, 381 (1940), aff'g 24 Del. Ch. 126, 7 A.2d 753 (1939).

The right to vote is a "positive act whereby the person makes known an affirmative or negative position. . . ." Caffey v. Veale, 193 Okla. 444, 145 P.2d 961, 964 (1944).

"A vote is but the expression of the will of a voter; and whether the formula to give expression to such will be ballot or viva voce, the result is the same: either is a vote." People v. Pease, 27 N.Y. 45, 57 (1863), quoted in State ex rel. Shinnich v. Green, 37 Ohio St. 227, 230 (1881).

[2] Blomquist v. Arlington, 338 Mass. 594, 156 N.E.2d 416, 419 (1959), considering Robert's Rules of Order (duties of moderator).

[3] See ROBERT, PARLIAMENTARY LAW at 493, 504, 533.

[4] See § 17.8 infra.

§ 17.3   Shareholders

Every holder of voting shares has the right to vote or to refrain from voting.[5] The right of a shareholder to vote is a basic contractual right [6] inherent in the ownership of shares, and as such is

[5] "Every stockholder has the right to a voice in the affairs of the company by exercising his right to vote. This right belongs to him as a stockholder, but it is not what makes him a stockholder. As a stockholder, he has other rights and he may forego his right to vote without affecting his other rights." Pennroad Corp. v. Ladner, 21 F. Supp. 575, 576 (E.D. Pa. 1937), *rev'd on other grounds,* 97 F.2d 10 (3d Cir. 1938), *cert. denied,* 305 U.S. 618 (1938).

"The ownership of voting stock imposes no legal duty to vote at all." Ringling Bros.–Barnum & Bailey Combined Shows, Inc. v. Ringling, 29 Del. Ch. 610, 53 A.2d 441, 447 (Sup. Ct. 1947). *See* Craig v. Bessie Furnace Co., 19 Ohio N.P. (M.S.) 545, 27 Ohio Dec. N.P. 471 (1917).

A form of proxy which confers discretionary authority with respect to matters as to which a choice is not specified by the shareholder does not deprive the shareholder of his right to abstain from voting. "A stockholder wishing to abstain from having his shares voted on any matter may do so by crossing out the proviso . . . or by other appropriate deletion or assertion." Also, such form of proxy is not against public policy as not affording "sufficient opportunity for 'stockholder democracy,' as being conducive to 'management oligarchy,' and as representing 'SEC czarism.'" Dyer v. SEC, 266 F.2d 33, 39 (8th Cir. 1959).

[6] "The right to vote was a basic contractual right. It was an incident to membership or of the property in the stock, of which the stockholder or member cannot be deprived without his consent." Faunce v. Boost Co., 15 N.J. Super. 534, 83 A.2d 649, 652 (1951).

A New York court has summarized as follows: The stockholders of a corporation have no direct power of management. The shares owned by them represent an investment upon which they are entitled to dividends if earned. Earnings depend on the management. The right to vote for directors, therefore, is the right to protect property from loss and make it effective in earning dividends. Unless the stockholder can protect his investment in this way he cannot protect it at all, and his property might be wasted by feeble administration. He might see the value of all he possessed fading away, yet he would have no power, direct or indirect, to save himself, or the company from financial downfall. The right to vote, it can be argued, enables him to engage in protective measures. Without that right to vote, therefore, he is deprived of an essential attribute of his property. Lord v. Equitable Life Assur. Society, 194 N.Y. 212, 228, 229, 87 N.E. 443 (1909), *citing* Stokes v. Continental Trust Co., 186 N.Y. 285, 78 N.E. 1090 (1906).

a property right.[7] It has been described as "an important and at times a highly valuable incident to the stockholder's shares." [8]

[7] "The right of a stockholder to vote upon his stock at all meetings of shareholders appears to be a right inherent in the ownership of the shares, and as such is a property right." Steinberg v. American Bantam Car Co., 76 F. Supp. 426, 436 (W.D. Pa. 1948), *appeal dismissed as moot,* 173 F.2d 179 (3d Cir. 1949) (action to enjoin election of directors).

"Deprivation of a stockholder's right to vote takes away an essential attribute of his property." DuVall v. Moore, 276 F. Supp. 674, 679 (N.D. Iowa 1967).

Talbot J. Taylor & Co. v. Southern Pac. Co., 122 F. 147, 151 (W.D. Ky. 1903), *appeal dismissed by agreement,* 129 F. 1007 (6th Cir. 1903) (action to enjoin voting of stock at election of directors).

The right to hold annual elections and to vote is inherent in the ownership of stock, and a stockholder of record cannot be deprived of this right upon the allegation that he proposes to vote for purposes which other stockholders may think not to be in the best interests, or even to the detriment of the corporation. Walsh v. State *ex rel.* Cook, 199 Ala. 123, 74 So. 45, 47 (1917).

The right to vote stock having voting powers is ordinarily an incident of its legal ownership. McLain v. Lanova Corp., 28 Del. Ch. 176, 39 A.2d 209, 211 (1944).

The right to vote for directors is one of the most important rights incident to stock ownership, and to deprive a stockholder of the right to vote is to deprive him of an essential attribute of his property. State *ex rel.* Johnson v. Heap, 1 Wash. 2d 316, 95 P.2d 1039, 1042 (1939); *accord,* State *ex rel.* Lidral v. Superior Court, 198 Wash. 610, 89 P.2d 501, 504 (1939).

"It is a basic property right of stockholders to call stockholders' meetings and to select directors." Starr v. Tomlinson, 7 Misc. 2d 916, 166 N.Y.S.2d 629, 631 (1957).

However, the right to vote is not an exclusive property right of common shares, and may be extended to holders of preferred stock by appropriate charter amendment. Metzger v. George Washington Memorial Park, Inc., 380 Pa. 350, 110 A.2d 425, 429 (1955).

[8] Chappel v. Standard Scale & Supply Corp., 15 Del. Ch. 333, 138 A. 74, 77 (1927), *rev'd on other grounds,* 16 Del. Ch. 331, 141 A. 191 (1928) (corporate fight over cumulative voting).

"The right of a qualified shareholder in a corporation to vote, either personally or by proxy, for the directors who are to manage the corporate affairs is a valuable and vested property right. It is one of the most important rights incident to stock ownership and should not be annulled for purely technical reasons." Washington State Labor Council v. Federated American Ins. Co., 474 P.2d 98, 103 (Wash. 1970).

Generally, the right to vote shares at a stockholders' meeting is "an incident to their legal and record ownership." Tracy v. Brentwood Village Corp., 30 Del. Ch. 296, 59 A.2d 708, 709 (1948).

Each shareholder represents himself and his own interest. In no sense does he act as the representative of others.[9] Generally, a shareholder has the legal right to vote as he pleases, or as his self-interest dictates, free of any duty to his fellow shareholders.[10] Mo-

---

Right to vote is an incident of ownership. Reimer v. Smith, 105 Fla. 671, 142 So. 603 (1932).

[9] "A shareholder has a legal right, at a meeting of the shareholders, to vote upon a measure, even though he has a personal interest therein separate from other shareholders. In such a meeting each shareholder represents himself and his own interests solely, and he in no sense acts as a trustee or representative of others." Gamble v. Queens County Water Co., 123 N.Y. 91, 97, 25 N.E. 201 (1890), *quoted and followed in* Windmuller v. Standard Distilling & Distrib. Co., 114 F. 491, 495 (C.C.N.J. 1902) (voting stock on dissolution of company) *and in* Kirwan v. Parkway Distillery, Inc., 285 Ky. 605, 148 S.W.2d 720, 723 (1941) (action by dissenting stockholder for book value of stock on sale of corporate assets).

[10] "The general rule is that a stockholder is not deprived of the right to vote upon a question in which he has an individual interest in the result of the vote apart from his general interest in the corporation. His relation as a stockholder to other individual stockholders and to the body of stockholders is not a fiduciary one. Consequently, when he is called upon to decide at a stockholders' meeting between his own interest as an individual and what may be his interest along with other stockholders in benefiting the corporation, he is free to exercise his own judgment, and to act in accordance with selfish rather than altruistic motives; and further, even though the question for determination by the stockholders be one raised by his acts in his own interest, while an officer or director of the corporation, he is not, as a stockholder, debarred from the full use of the property in his stock, including the right to vote that stock." Also, a stockholder is not disqualified from voting on a question of corporate policy merely because he is related to a person who favors or opposes such policy. DuPont v. DuPont, 251 F. 937, 944 (1918), *modified,* 256 F. 129 (3d Cir. 1919).

"The general rule is that a stockholder has a legal right to vote and dispose of his stock as his self-interest dictates." Borden v. Guthrie, 23 App. Div. 2d 313, 260 N.Y.S.2d 769, 774 (1965), *aff'd,* 17 N.Y.2d 571, 268 N.Y.S.2d 330, 215 N.E.2d 511 (1966).

A stockholder can vote his own stock and dispose of it as he sees fit in his own interest. Berger v. Fogarty, 51 Misc. 2d 628, 273 N.Y.S.2d 620 (1965).

A stockholder can vote his own stock as he pleases for purposes of his own interest. Beutelspacher v. Spokane Sav. Bank, 164 Wash. 227, 2 P.2d 729 (1931).

When voting, each stockholder represents himself and his own interest solely,

tive is generally irrelevant. One court states that the motive of a shareholder which prompts his voting, "however reprehensible or malicious," is not, as a rule, relevant to judicial inquiry.[11] Another court has held that the motive of a shareholder in failing to attend a meeting and to vote is not material.[12]

Accordingly, a shareholder cannot be deprived of the right to vote upon the allegation or surmise that he proposes to vote for purposes which others may think would be detrimental to the interests of the corporation; the court will not presume that shareholders will not exercise their voting rights in a manner which in their judgment will not be conducive to the best interests of the company.[13]

---

and is not a trustee or representative for others. Epstein v. Celotex Corp., 288 A.2d 843 (Del. Ch. 1968).

Stockholders "have the right to exercise wide liberality of judgment in the matter of voting and may admit personal profit or even whims and caprice into the motives which determine their choice, so long as no advantage is obtained at the expense of their fellow stockholders." Heil v. Standard Gas & Elec. Co., 17 Del. Ch. 214, 151 A. 303, 304 (1930).

"It is well settled that it is a stockholder's privilege to vote his shares upon a measure even though he may have a personal interest therein, separate from other shareholders." Wilson v. Rensselaer & Saratoga R.R., 52 N.Y.S.2d 847, 852 (1945).

[11] Kirwan v. Parkway Distillery, Inc., 285 Ky. 605, 148 S.W.2d 720, 723 (1941).

However, where it appears that the actions of the majority may be a "wanton or a fraudulent destruction of the rights" of the minority, such actions may be subject to the scrutiny of a court of equity. Gamble v. Queens County Water Co., 123 N.Y. 91, 25 N.E. 201, 202 (1890).

[12] "Even if petitioner deliberately failed to attend because she did not want to create a quorum, her reason for abstaining, if relevant, is not of a character which should preclude the relief requested." In re Pioneer Drilling Co., 36 Del. Ch. 386, 130 A.2d 559, 561 (1957).

"The motives that may have induced the absence of five of the trustees from the adjourned meeting does not affect the question. . . . However reprehensible their conduct may have been in that respect, the absence of a quorum at the adjourned meeting rendered it impossible for the members present to make any valid appointment." State ex rel. Laughlin v. Porter, 113 Ind. 79, 14 N.E. 883, 884, 885 (1888), citing Cushing, Parl. Law on question of quorum.

[13] Elevator Supplies Co. v. Wylde, 106 N.J. Eq. 163, 150 A. 347 (1930).

A shareholder cannot be deprived of his right to vote upon the allegation that "he proposes to use his legal rights for purposes which other stockholders may think not to the best interests, or even to the detriment, of the corporation." Walsh v. State ex rel. Cook, 199 Ala. 123, 74 So. 45, 47 (1917).

This rule has been tempered where equitable principles are applied, as in cases where there is a fiduciary or other duty among the shareholders. A leading case states the rule as follows: "Generally speaking, a shareholder may exercise wide liberality of judgment in the matter of voting, and it is not objectionable that his motives may be for personal profit, or determined by whims or caprice, so long as he violates no duty owed his fellow shareholders." [14] However, the shareholders' actions resulting from such votes "must not be so detrimental to the interests of the corporation itself, as to lead to the necessary inference that the interests of the majority of the shareholders lie wholly outside of and in opposition to the interests of the corporation and of the minority of the shareholders, and that their action is a wanton or fraudulent destruction of the rights of such minority. In such cases it may be stated that the action of the majority of the shareholders may be subjected to the scrutiny of a court of equity at the suit of the minority shareholders." [15]

The court will not issue a "prophecy" as to whether the vote of

[14] Ringling Bros.–Barnum & Bailey Combined Shows, Inc. v. Ringling, 29 Del. Ch. 610, 53 A.2d 441, 447 (1947), *quoting from* Heil v. Standard Gas & Elec. Co., 17 Del. Ch. 214, 151 A. 303, 304 (Ch. 1930).

"The law is well settled that it is legal for a stockholder to vote his stock for the purchase of property in which he has an interest, unless unfair or improper means are employed which are fraudulent or oppressive toward the other stockholders." Hellier v. Baush Mach. Tool Co., 21 F.2d 705, 708 (1st Cir. 1927); *accord*, Gamble v. Queens County Water Co., 123 N.Y. 91, 98, 25 N.E. 201 (1890).

"The motives which actuated any stockholder in distributing his votes is not a subject of inquiry or control." Chicago Macaroni Mfg. Co. v. Boggiano, 202 Ill. 312, 67 N.E. 17, 18 (1903); *see* Doyle v. Milton, 73 F. Supp. 281, 286 (S.D.N.Y. 1947).

It is not enough to invalidate an election because the conduct of a proxy toward his group "can hardly be squared with the rules of ethics." McLain v. Lanova Corp., 28 Del. Ch. 176, 39 A.2d 209, 212 (1944).

"I am of opinion that although it may be quite true that the shareholders of a company may vote as they please, and for the purpose of their own interests, yet that the majority of shareholders cannot sell the assets of the company and keep the consideration, but must allow the minority to have their share of any consideration which may come to them." Menier v. Hooper's Telegraph Works, (1874) L.R., 9 Ch. App. 350, 354.

[15] Gamble v. Queens County Water Co., 123 N.Y. 91, 98, 25 N.E. 201 (1890).

a shareholder on any matter is an independent vote or a controlled or corrupted vote.[16]

A person acting as a proxy for shareholders may not be a free agent. It has been held in a leading case that it is the duty of a proxy committee "to attend the meeting as well as vote the stock they represent." [17]

One who does not have the right to vote at a corporate election cannot complain of irregularities in the election. It may be otherwise where there has been no right to an election at all.[18]

§ 17.4   Directors

The courts clearly distinguish between the rights of a director–shareholder when voting as a shareholder, and when voting as a director. When voting as a shareholder [19] or as a proxy for other

[16] "The Court will not receive a Gallup-poll type of evidence and issue a prophecy based thereon. Men's votes on such matters as those here in issue cannot be predicated with any accuracy. Only when faced with the responsible task of casting a vote that counts does a shareholder show if he is independent. Plaintiffs, if they wish to succeed, must put the matter to the test of a shareholders' meeting. Then if it appears that the voters were corrupted, coerced, or had conspired with defendants, a court can act in accord with Massachusetts law." Carroll v. New York, N.H. & H. R.R., 141 F. Supp. 456, 458 (D. Mass. 1956).

[17] Duffy v. Loft, Inc., 17 Del. Ch. 376, 152 A. 849, 853 (1930).

Rule 14a–4(c) of the SEC requires that the proxy statement or form of proxy provide, subject to reasonable specified conditions, that the shares represented by the proxy will be voted and that where the person solicited specifies by means of a ballot a choice with respect to any matter to be acted upon, the shares will be voted in accordance with the specifications so made.

[18] See In re Caplan's Petition, 20 App. Div. 2d 301, 246 N.Y.S.2d 913, 916 (1st Dep't 1964) (action to set aside election of director).

"A stockholder cannot be aggrieved by an election in which neither he nor his assignor had a right to participate." In re Scheel, 134 App. Div. 442, 119 N.Y.S. 295, 297 (1909).

[19] There is a "radical difference" when a stockholder is voting strictly as a stockholder and when voting as a director. "When voting as a stockholder he has the legal right to vote with a view of his own benefits and is representing himself only; but, a director represents all the stockholders in the capacity of trustee for them and cannot use his office as director for his personal benefit

shareholders,[20] he has the legal right to vote in his own self-interest and for his own benefit; but as a director he represents all the shareholders and cannot use his office as a director for his personal benefit at the expense of the other shareholders. However, although a shareholder may vote as he pleases, public policy forbids the enforcement of a contract by which a shareholder undertakes to bargain away his right to vote for directors according to his best judgment and in the interest of the corporation.[21]

A shareholder may vote in favor of a certain action at a directors' meeting and then vote against such action at a shareholders' meeting. He has the right to change his mind up to the moment of the final voting of the shareholders.[22] A director has no duty to tell the stockholders how he intends to vote on the election of directors.[23] The motive of a director in voting for a proper resolution is imma-

---

at the expense of the stockholders." Kirwan v. Parkway Distillery, Inc., 285 Ky. 605, 148 S.W.2d 720, 723 (1941).

"A stockholder occupies a position and owes a duty radically different from a director. A stockholder may in a stockholders' meeting vote with the view of his own benefit; he represents himself only. But a director represents all the stockholders; he is a trustee for them; and he cannot use his office for his personal benefit at the expense of any stockholder." Haldeman v. Haldeman, 176 Ky. 635, 197 S.W. 376, 381 (1917).

Directors of a corporation are not precluded from voting as shareholders on the question of directors' salaries merely because they have a personal interest in the question. Green v. Felton, 42 Ind. App. 675, 84 N.E. 166 (1908).

The rule that a director may act where his interest is adverse to that of the corporation does not apply in the case of a stockholder, who may vote as he pleases for purpose of his own interest. Beutelspacher v. Spokane Sav. Bank, 164 Wash. 227, 2 P.2d 729 (1931).

[20] A director properly can vote the stock of other shareholders who, before they signed a proxy, were fairly informed of the issues which were to be considered and voted upon. Smith v. Brown–Borhek Co., 414 Pa. 325, 336, 200 A.2d 398 (1964).

[21] Haldeman v. Haldeman, 176 Ky. 635, 197 S.W. 376, 382 (1917).

[22] Mowrey v. Indianapolis & C. R.R., 17 F. Cas. 930 (No. 9891) (C.C.D. Ind. 1866).

Directors may vote in favor of a contract and still, as stockholders, set up its illegality. Bostwick v. Chapman (Shepaug Voting Trust Cases), 24 A. 32 (Conn. 1890).

[23] Zachary v. Milin, 294 Mich. 622, 293 N.W. 770 (1940) (intention to vote cumulatively).

terial.[24] A "dummy" director may vote against the wishes of the stockholder for whom he acts, with impunity.[25]

A recent case has held that shareholders are entitled to all pertinent and material information whenever called upon to exercise their "right of corporate suffrage" and that, "Surely stockholders, once informed of the facts, have a right to make their own decisions in matters pertaining to their economic self-interest, whether consonant with or contrary to the advice of others, whether such advice is tendered by management or outsiders or those motivated by self-interest." [26]

Since a shareholder is not a fiduciary with respect to his fellow shareholders, unlike a director, he may appoint a proxy to vote for him. The proxy, who need not be a shareholder,[27] becomes a universal agent for this particular purpose.[28]

Votes may not be sold by a director or by a shareholder. A director is a fiduciary. So is a dominant or controlling stockholder or group of stockholders.[29] Although shareholders may agree among

[24] Motive of directors in levying stock assessment for a proper purpose is immaterial. Clark v. Oceano Beach Resort Co., 106 Cal. App. 579, 289 P. 946 (1930).

In voting, corporate directors are presumed to have exercised their judgment in good faith. Epstein v. Celotex Corp., 288 A.2d 843 (Del. Ch. 1968).

[25] "If a 'dummy' director should vote contrary to the wishes of the stockholder who made him a director under a contract that he would by his vote carry out the wishes of the stockholder, there is no law that would invalidate such a vote." Haldeman v. Haldeman, 176 Ky. 635, 197 S.W. 376, 382 (1917).

[26] American Crystal Sugar Co. v. Cuban–American Sugar Co., 276 F. Supp. 45, 50 (S.D.N.Y. 1967) (consideration of proposed merger).

[27] Corporate by-law requiring that all proxies be stockholders is an unwarranted restriction which curtails or destroys voting rights and is not valid. State ex rel. Syphers v. McCune, 143 W. Va. 315, 101 S.E.2d 834, 839 (1958).

[28] Steinberg v. American Bantam Car Co., 76 F. Supp. 426, 436 (W.D. Pa. 1948), appeal dismissed as moot, 173 F.2d 179 (3d Cir. 1949).

Note: This book is primarily interested in the conduct of meetings and therefore does not include a broad study of proxies and their legal aspects.

[29] Pepper v. Litton, 308 U.S. 295 (1939); Seagrave Corp. v. Mount, 212 F.2d 389 (6th Cir. 1954); Chenery Corp. v. SEC, 128 F.2d 303 (D.C. Cir. 1942); Johnson v. American General Ins. Co., 296 F. Supp. 802 (D.C. 1969).

"It is too plain for citation of authority that a director of a corporation cannot barter or sell his official discretion or enter into any contract whatever that will in any way restrict or limit the free exercise of his judgment and discretion

themselves to vote for certain persons, they cannot lawfully accept anything of value for their votes.[30] Some state corporation laws provide that every member of a corporation offering to vote at a shareholders' meeting may on demand be required to take the "customary oath" that he received no promise or money to influence his votes at the meeting.[31]

§ 17.5 Association Members

Members of an association, whether incorporated or unincorporated, have a right to vote that stems from their membership. Unless otherwise provided by organic law or charter, membership in an association is a "privilege and is neither a civil nor property right." [32]

§ 17.6 Political Club Members

The members of a political club may vote in their own interest. "There is no position of trust and confidence which members of a political club so owe to each other that there is an obligation to disclose in advance whatever each intends to do, so long as it is according to law. When rivals for office in a political club are contending for election, they certainly are dealing at arm's length; they are under no obligation to advise their adversaries of how they intend to win. American politics is not a game for people so naive as to do so." [33]

---

in his official capacity, nor can he place himself under any direct and powerful inducement to disregard his duty to the corporation and its stockholders in the management of corporate affairs." Ashman v. Miller, 101 F.2d 85, 91 (6th Cir. 1939).

[30] Drob v. National Memorial Park, Inc., 28 Del. Ch. 254, 41 A.2d 589 (1945); State ex rel. Johnson v. Heap, 1 Wash. 2d 316, 95 P.2d 1039 (1939).

[31] See, e.g., In re Holzer's Petition, 26 Misc. 2d 934, 209 N.Y.S.2d 846 (1960) (stockholder who failed to take oath when challenged was improperly permitted to vote, and therefore the meeting must be annulled).

[32] State ex rel. Givens v. Superior Court, 233 Ind. 235, 117 N.E.2d 553, 555 (1954) (voluntary trade union association).

[33] In re Serenbetz, 46 N.Y.S.2d 475 (1943), aff'd, 46 N.Y.S.2d 127 (1st Dep't 1944).

§ 17.7   Attendance at Meetings

It is well established that the right of a member of a legislative or deliberative society to vote is not dependent upon his attendance at the discussions, debates, or hearings preparatory to the taking of a vote on the matter. However, when members of an administrative body are acting in a quasi-judicial capacity they are clothed with some of the restraints placed on the judicial process.

In considering the propriety of a zoning board acting in executive session with only representatives of the city present, the court held: "Clearly, it is improper for an administrative agency, when acting in a quasi-judicial capacity, to base a decision or finding upon evidence or information obtained without the presence of and notice to the interested parties, and not made known to them prior to the decision. As to a contention that the the absence of a zoning board member from the middle portion of a board hearing disqualified him from voting, the court held that the member's absence in this case was not in itself a jurisdictional defect which disqualified him from voting or which rendered the board's decision void. The court applied the presumption of regularity and assumed in the absence of any showing to the contrary that the member had been adequately informed.[34]

The absence of a member from one or more meetings of a quasi-judicial board or agency raises the question whether the absent member has the right to vote or otherwise participate in the decision. In a recent case, the court concluded that the general rule, in both the Federal and state systems, is that in the absence of specific statutory direction to the contrary, the deciding member or members of an administrative or quasi-judicial agency need not hear the witnesses testify. Here only two members of the five-man board were present. They were joined in the decision by two other members who had read a transcript of the testimony, examined the record, and heard full arguments at the second hearing. The court upheld the decision of the board stating: "The general rule is that it is enough if those who decide have considered and appraised the evidence and the courts feel more satisfied that they have done so

[34] State *ex rel.* Cities Serv. Oil Co. v. Board of Zoning Appeals, 21 Wis. 2d 516, 124 N.W.2d 809, 821, 822 (1963).

if they have heard argument." [35] The prevailing rule is that an absent member may vote if he familiarizes himself with the situation and makes an informed decision.[36]

There are exceptions to the general rule in Federal regulatory boards and commissions where statutory enabling provisions have been construed to permit "notation voting procedures" whereby the body may proceed with its members acting separately and not in meeting, and a member who has considered the issues in a matter may direct an assistant to record his concurrence in a proposed decision. Here, too, the member may rely on subordinates to sift and analyze the facts and prepare summaries and recommendations, and the member may base his decision on these reports without reading the full transcript.[37]

§ 17.8 Tie Vote—Casting Vote

Under common parliamentary law, a resolution or motion receiving an equality of competing votes (a tie vote) would fail of

[35] Younkin v. Boltz, 241 Md. 339, 216 A.2d 714, 715 (1966).

[36] A member of a zoning board who was absent from a first meeting when an appeal was heard need not disqualify himself from voting at a subsequent meeting if he examines the minutes of the first meeting. Albini v. Board of Appeals, 41 Misc. 2d 783, 246 N.Y.S.2d 506 (1964).

A member of a zoning board who was absent during a meeting may vote if he familiarizes himself with the situation and makes an "informed" decision, and in the absence of a "clear" revelation that the body made no independent appraisal and reached no independent conclusion, its decision will not be disturbed. Taub v. Pirnie, 3 N.Y.2d 188, 165 N.Y.S.2d 1, 5 (1957).

It is not objectionable for members of a zoning board who were absent from a public hearing to familiarize themselves with a situation and at a subsequent executive meeting to vote on granting of a permit. Sarber Realty Corp. v. Silver, 205 N.Y.S.2d 30 (Sup. Ct. 1960).

Where a five-man zoning board held a hearing with only three members present and one such member did not participate because he was lawyer for an applicant, the hearing was invalid even though all present agreed to proceed with the hearing and then adjourn for a later discussion by a quorum of the board. Giuliano v. Entress, 158 N.Y.S.2d 961 (Sup. Ct. 1957).

[37] See, e.g., Braniff Airways, Inc. v. CAB, 379 F.2d 453, 461 (D.C. Cir. 1967) and cases cited; T.S.C. Motor Freight Lines, Inc. v. United States, 186 F. Supp. 777 (S.D. Tex. 1960), aff'd per curiam sub nom. Herrin Transp. Co. v. United States, 366 U.S. 419 (1961); Eastland Co. v. FCC, 92 F.2d 467 (D.C. Cir.), cert. denied, 302 U.S. 735 (1937).

adoption,[38] and the presiding officer would have no right or means to break the tie. This result led to difficulties which had to be resolved. Early English law recognized the need for some convenient and workable method of breaking a tie vote to facilitate the enactment of legislation and prevent legislative deadlocks. This problem was solved by the institution of enabling provisions for a second or "casting" vote.[39]

[38] A tie vote is an equality of votes of the affirmative and the negative. ROBERT, PARLIAMENTARY LAW at 576 (1951). In a tie vote the motion is lost. Robert's Rules of Order at 191–92.

Where the board is evenly divided no affirmative action can be taken. Thus, a tie vote on a motion to decline cannot be construed as an approval. *In re* Hackney Pavilion, Ltd., [1924] 1 Ch. 276.

A tie vote does not indicate approval. Anson v. Starr, 198 Misc. 982, 101 N.Y.S.2d 948 (Sup. Ct. 1950).

A petitioner who tied with another candidate for ninth place in an election at a stockholders' annual meeting in which nine directors were to be elected was not elected and not entitled to a writ of mandamus placing him in office as a duly elected director. Grip v. Buffelen Woodworking Co., 73 Wash. 2d 219, 437 P.2d 915 (1968).

A tie vote does not result in a motion being adopted, so it fails to carry. Hager v. State *ex rel.* Te Vault, 446 S.W.2d 43 (Tex. Civ. App. 1969).

[39] "When, as the result of the chairman's giving his vote [as a qualified member], the members on either side become exactly equal, the common law appears to provide no way out of the difficulty. The institution of a second or casting vote, as it is called, is the creature of the statute law introduced for the purpose of avoiding the deadlock which would otherwise ensue." Nell v. Longbottom, [1894] 1 Q.B. 767, 771.

The purpose of a casting vote is to prevent a breakdown of the legislative process. Cromarty v. Leonard, 13 App. Div. 2d 274, 216 N.Y.S.2d 619, 629 (2d Dep't), *aff'd*, 10 N.Y.2d 915, 179 N.E.2d 710, 223 N.Y.S.2d 870 (1961).

A casting vote sometimes signifies the single vote of a person who never votes except in the case of an equality, and sometimes signifies the double vote of a person who first votes with the rest and then, upon an equality, creates a majority by giving a second vote. A "double vote" is not allowed in corporate meetings, except by express statute. People *ex rel.* Remington v. Rector, Churchwardens & Vestrymen, 48 Barb. 603, 606, 607 (Sup. Ct. N.Y. 1866) (meeting of churchwardens), *citing* Curtis on Parliamentary Practice. *See* Arcus v. Castle, [1954] N.Z.L.R. 122 (1953); Second Consol. Trust Ltd. v. Ceylon Amalg. Tea & Rubber Estates, Ltd., [1943] 2 All. E.R. 567.

"A good deal has been said about the right of a presiding officer to cast the deciding vote. The rule as to this is substantially as follows: Where the statute provides that the presiding officer shall cast the deciding vote, in case of a tie, and a member of the organization is chosen as presiding officer, as

Since the advent of the casting vote, numerous variations have been enacted by statute or adopted in constitutional or by-law provisions. The courts have often construed the meaning of various provisions. It has been held that where the presiding officer is a member of the assembly and is entitled to vote with the other members, the fact that he is chosen to act as the presiding officer does not deprive him of that voting privilege.[40] And where a member of a city council is appointed to preside in the absence of the mayor, who could vote only in case of a tie, he does not incur the mayor's disability to vote but may cast his vote as a member.[41]

The right to cast a deciding vote does not of itself make the presiding officer a member of the body.[42] Thus, where a statute or

---

such member, he is entitled to vote, and, in case of an equality, he is entitled to a second vote. If, however, he is not a member of the organization, then he can only cast a vote, even in case of a tie, where he is expressly authorized so to do." Reeder v. Trotter, 142 Tenn. 37, 215 S.W. 400, 402 (1919).

The declaration of a chairman that a certain officer has been elected as a result of a ballot is not equivalent to giving a casting vote. Casler v. Tanzer, 134 Misc. 48, 234 N.Y.S. 571, 579 (Sup. Ct. 1929).

For examples of casting votes, *see* Carroll v. Wall, 35 Kan. 36, 10 Pac. 1 (1886); Small v. Orne, 79 Me. 78, 8 A. 152 (1887); Whitney v. Common Council, 69 Mich. 189, 37 N.W. 184 (1888); Lawrence v. Ingersoll, 88 Tenn. 52, 12 S.W. 422, 424 (1889).

See Annot., Constitutionality and effect of statute relating to deadlock or tie vote in governmental body, 40 A.L.R. 808 (1926).

Where the city council had a tie vote on a question and then called in another councilman to cast his vote to break the tie, the court noted that the "irregularity, if any, was immaterial" and thus legal. Seabolt v. Moses, 247 S.W.2d 24, 26 (Ark. 1952).

[40] Reeder v. Trotter, 142 Tenn. 37, 215 S.W. 400, 401 (1919) (justices of the peace); *accord,* Harris v. People *ex rel.* Squires, 18 Colo. App. 160, 70 Pac. 699, 700 (1902); Whitney v. Common Council, 69 Mich. 189, 37 N.W. 184 (1888); Nell v. Longbottom, [1894] 1 Q.B. 767, 771.

[41] Michael v. State *ex rel.* Welch, 163 Ala. 425, 50 So. 929 (1909).

[42] Hill v. Taylor, 264 Ky. 708, 95 S.W.2d 566, 568 (1936). *See In re* Heafy, 247 App. Div. 277, 285 N.Y.S. 188 (2d Dep't), *aff'd,* Heafy v. McCabe, 270 N.Y. 616, 1 N.E.2d 357 (1936).

The fact that a mayor is designated chairman of the board and may vote when there is a tie does not mean that he is considered a member in establishing a quorum for the transaction of business. City of Somerset v. Smith, 105 Ky. 678, 49 S.W. 456 (1899).

A city charter giving the mayor veto power over ordinances does not alone

charter requires a vote of a majority of all the members to take certain actions, such as the appointment of an official or the granting of a permit, the presiding officer's vote to break a tie is of no effect because he is not a member and cannot be counted in determining whether there was a majority vote.[43]

Statutory or charter provisions enabling the presiding officer to break a tie are not uniform. Conventionally, the presiding officer of a legislative body does not have a vote except in case of a tie.[44] When the presiding officer is a member of the body and has already voted as a member, he does not have the power to cast a second vote to break a tie in the absence of specific statutory or charter authority.[45] The prevailing tendency in this country is to give him

---

give him a casting vote. Markham v. Simpson, 175 N.C. 135, 95 S.E. 106 (1918).

[43] The president of a common council presided at all meetings and could vote in case of a tie, but he was not a member of the council and could not be counted in determining a majority. Merriam v. Chicago, R.I. & P. Ry. Co., 132 Mo. App. 247, 111 S.W. 876 (1908).

A statute requiring vote of a "majority of all the supervisors" means a majority of all members-elect but does not include a "tie-breaker" appointed pursuant to statute. Smiley v. Commonwealth ex rel. Kerr, 116 Va. 979, 83 S.W. 406 (1914).

A statute regulating liquor permits provided that the mayor should not be counted in determining a majority of the council, and therefore his vote could not be counted to break a tie vote in favor of granting a permit. State ex rel. Owen v. McIntosh, 165 Wis. 596, 162 N.W. 670 (1917).

[44] An outstanding example is the Vice President of the United States who, as President of the Senate, can vote only in case of a tie. U.S. Const. Art. I, § 3; see Hill v. Taylor, 264 Ky. 708, 95 S.W.2d 566, 568 (1936); Lake Shore & M.S. Ry. Co. v. City of Dunkirk, 65 Hun 494, 20 N.Y.S. 596 (1892), aff'd, 143 N.Y. 660, 39 N.E. 21 (1894) (a casting vote is limited to a tie vote on a legislative action).

However, a mayor who is disqualified from voting cannot break a tie by casting a vote which would be to his benefit. Township Comm. of Hazlet v. Morales, 119 N.J. Super. 29, 289 A.2d 563 (1972); accord, Grimes v. Miller, 113 N.J.L. 553, 175 A. 152 (1934).

[45] It was argued that the chairman of the state political committee had the right at common law to break a tie. The court said: "We do not read that law as giving any presiding officer the power to break a tie where he is a member of a body and has already voted as such. But such power may be expressly given by statute or a rule." The central committee had the power

that power. One court explains that "while it may not be in accord with strict parliamentary law, it is the prevailing rule in this country that, in case of these municipal boards, a presiding officer, who is also a member, has the legal right, as such member, to vote on questions coming properly before the body for decision and to vote a second time as presiding officer when the law or valid rule of the body itself governing its proceedings confers upon such officer the right to give the casting vote." [46]

Sometimes the presiding officer is required by law to vote when there is a tie.[47] Under a statute providing that a village mayor may vote on all matters coming before the board of trustees and that the mayor shall vote in case of a tie, but that "he shall vote only in his capacity as mayor of the village and his vote shall be considered as one vote," it has been held that the mayor has only one vote, whether he voted voluntarily or to break a tie. "He need not always vote. He is obligated to vote only when there is a tie. In all other instances, he may vote or not as he pleases. But if he does vote, whether voluntarily or by mandate, he has only one vote to cast." [48]

Under some municipal laws the power of the presiding officer to break a tie vote is limited to voting on "resolutions and ordinances submitted to the body." Under such laws the presiding officer's

---

to declare the second vote of the chairman ineffectual to break the tie. O'Neil v. O'Connell, 300 Ky. 707, 189 S.W.2d 965, 968 (1945).

Even where a town charter authorizes the mayor to vote on filling a vacancy, he is not authorized both to vote in the election and then cast an additional tie-breaking vote so as to give him two votes. Aliotta v. Gilreath, 225 Ga. 328, 168 S.E.2d 314 (1969).

[46] Markham v. Simpson, 175 N.C. 135, 95 S.E. 106, 107 (1918), *quoted in* People ex rel. Walsh v. Teller, 169 Misc. 342, 7 N.Y.S.2d 168, 171–72 (1938); *see* People ex rel. Remington v. Rector, Churchwardens & Vestrymen, 48 Barb. 603, 605 (N.Y. Sup. Ct. 1866).

[47] State ex rel. Morris v. McFarland, 149 Ind. 266, 49 N.E. 5, 39 L.R.A. 282 (1898) (county auditor).

The mayor, being unable to break a tie by casting a vote in favor of a resolution of his appointment to another position, sought to avoid the objection by taking no action. The court said: "We fail to see any difference between his casting an affirmative vote or his refraining from voting. The latter, by statute, is the equivalent of the former." Township Comm. of Hazlet v. Morales, 119 N.J. Super. 29, 289 A.2d 563, 567 (1972); *accord,* Grimes v. Miller, 175 A. 152 (N.J. 1934).

[48] Anson v. Starr, 198 Misc. 982, 101 N.Y.S.2d 948, 949–50 (1950).

power to vote is confined to "such as are ordinarily exercised by presiding officers . . . and not as a member of the body." [49]

The right of a presiding officer to give a casting vote in case of a tie vote can only be exercised under precise circumstances. Thus, when a meeting was attended by the mayor and ten out of twelve aldermen, and six voted in favor of the resolution with four voting against, the mayor could not cast a favorable vote and thereby attain the seven affirmative votes needed to adopt the resolution. There being no tie, the mayor had no right to vote.[50] Similarly, where the town charter authorized the mayor to vote on filling a vacancy in the town council consisting of the mayor and six aldermen, the mayor cannot vote in the election to create a tie (3–3 with the mayor voting) and then cast an additional vote to "break the tie." [51]

This overly simple rule has led to unexpected complications. An interesting case involved a city council consisting of the mayor and fourteen aldermen with the mayor having a vote only in case of a tie. One alderman having died, and another being absent, the vote was seven for, five against, and one absent, accounting for the thirteen living aldermen. With a vote of 7 to 5 there was no tie and accordingly the mayor had no right to vote. The court noted that the mayor was deprived of his vote because one of the opposition absented himself, and observed the incongruous situation where a member could have more "legislative strength" while absent than if present and where the mayor becomes a "handicap" because he couldn't vote. The court resolved its dilemma by concluding that the whole council consisted of thirteen members and that the seven votes constituted a majority.[52]

A tie vote can result from the abstention from voting of members

[49] The designation of an official newspaper was not one of the matters upon which he could vote. People ex rel. Argus Co. v. Bresler, 171 N.Y. 302, 308, 63 N.E. 1093 (1902). Similarly, In re Heafy, 247 App. Div. 277, 285 N.Y.S. 188 (2d Dep't), aff'd, Heafy v. McCabe, 270 N.Y. 616, 1 N.E.2d 357 (1936).

[50] In re Dudley, 33 App. Div. 465, 53 N.Y.S. 742 (4th Dep't 1898).

[51] Aliotta v. Gilreath, 225 Ga. 328, 168 S.E.2d 314, 315 (1969).

Where the mayor had the right to vote in an election of officers, and upon questions where there was a tie vote of aldermen, the mayor could vote on the question of dismissal of an officer only when there was a tie vote of aldermen. Aliotta v. Gilreath, 226 Ga. 263, 174 S.E.2d 403 (1970).

[52] Nalle v. City of Austin, 41 Tex. Civ. App. 423, 93 S.W. 141, 144 (1906).

present at the meeting. Early decisions on similar facts often resulted in the same conclusions, based on different legal concepts. In 1885 the court considered the actions of a city council consisting of eight councilmen plus a mayor who could give a casting vote only in case of a tie. At a meeting with all present, four members voted in the affirmative, and four refused to vote either way. The mayor treated those not voting as opposed to those who had voted, and decided the question by a casting vote in the affirmative.[53] In 1889, another court had a case in which a common council of six members met to approve a resolution. Three of the six voted in favor of the resolution, but the other three, although present, declined to vote. The mayor declared that the resolution was adopted, having been approved by a majority (3) of a quorum (4). The court approved, holding that "the mere presence of inactive members does not impair the right of the majority of the quorum to proceed with the business of the body. If members present desire to defeat a measure, they must vote against it, for inaction will not accomplish their purpose. Their silence is acquiescence, rather than opposition. Their refusal to vote is, in effect, a declaration that they consent that the majority of the quorum may act for the body of which they are members."[54] A third case in 1897 came to the same conclusion, following the reasoning in the two previous cases. Here a city council consisted of eight aldermen and a mayor who had the right to vote in case of a tie. With all present at the meeting, four voted in favor while four did not vote, and then the mayor voted in the affirmative to break the tie. The court approved, holding that abstention is a negative vote which can create a tie, and which in turn can be broken by the casting vote of the mayor who was a part of the city council. The court also reasoned that a quorum was present at the meeting and "the proper rule is that those who remain silent shall be deemed to assent to the act of those who do vote."[55] A leading New York case considered a board of supervisors ten in number with a casting vote in the county executive in case of a tie vote. With all being present, the vote was five in favor, four opposed, and one not voting. The chairman ruled that the abstention

---

[53] Launtz v. People *ex rel.* Sullivan, 113 Ill. 137 (1885).

[54] Rushville Gas Co. v. City of Rushville, 121 Ind. 206, 23 N.E. 72, 73 (1889).

[55] State *ex rel.* Young v. Yates, 47 P. 1004, 1006 (Mont. 1897)

should be counted as a negative vote opposed to the adoption of the resolution, thereby creating a tie vote. The county executive voted in the affirmative and the resolution was declared adopted. The trial court held that an abstention may not be counted as a negative vote so as to create a tie. On appeal, the court noted that the "authorities are in conflict" and upheld the ruling of the chairman that the abstention should be treated as a negative vote creating a tie.[56] Similarly it has been held that a tie vote cannot be caused by a blank vote where an odd number of members are present and voting.[57]

When allowed a casting vote, the presiding officer may declare the results of the vote without going through the formality of casting a ballot.[58]

Although there is statutory authority for a casting vote in legislative assemblies and other public bodies, there appears to be no statutory provision for a casting vote at meetings of private organizations or at meetings of shareholders or members of incorporated or unincorporated associations, or in the election of directors or officers of such organizations. Corporation law generally permits the election of a board of directors consisting of an even number of members. The fact that a deadlock may result does not necessarily mean that the law is inadequate and should be remedied, as it could be by the simple expedient of requiring an odd number of directors.[59] At common law, a tie vote at a corporate meeting is a

---

[56] Cromarty v. Leonard, 13 App. Div. 2d 274, 216 N.Y.S.2d 619 (2d Dep't), aff'd, 10 N.Y.2d 915, 179 N.E.2d 710, 223 N.Y.S.2d 870 (1961).

[57] A mayor had the right to give a casting vote in case of a tie. At a meeting 45 aldermen were present; 22 voted for one person, 22 voted for another, and there was one blank ballot. It was held that the mayor could not give a casting vote. Where there is an odd number of members present and participating in the action, there cannot be a tie. State ex rel. Cole v. Chapman, 44 Conn. 595 (Super. Ct. 1878).

[58] Small v. Orne, 79 Me. 78, 8 A. 152 (1887).

The presiding officer may also make an original and a casting vote at the same time, the casting vote being provisional on an equality of votes. Bland v. Buchanan, [1901] 2 K.B. 75, following Nell v. Longbottom, [1894] 1 Q.B. 767.

[59] See Sterling Indus. Inc. v. Ball Bearing Pen Corp., 298 N.Y. 483, 84 N.E.2d 790, 10 A.L.R.2d 694 (1949).

An early case holds that the president of a business corporation does not

deadlock and thus a nullity.[60] Sometimes a tie-vote deadlock can be resolved by continuing the meeting to a subsequent date, which generally can be done without further notice.[61]

One case holds, however, that a tie vote for one of nine director– nominees created a "vacancy" which, when filled by the board of directors without timely objection, was not subject to court review on appeal.[62] There are, of course, statutory provisions in many state corporation laws for equitable relief in case of a deadlock among directors or shareholders.[63]

---

have a casting vote unless provided by statute or by-law. Toronto Brewing and Malting Co. v. Blake, 2 Ontario Rep. 175 (1883).

[60] In re Bruder's Estate, 302 N.Y. 52, 96 N.E.2d 84 (1950) (election of corporate directors); Sterling Indus. Inc. v. Ball Bearing Pen Corp., 298 N.Y. 483, 84 N.E.2d 790, 10 A.L.R.2d 694 (1949) (authorize corporate action); Felice v. Swezey, 278 App. Div. 958, 105 N.Y.S.2d 486, 488–89 (2d Dep't 1951), citing Cushing's Manual § 243 (1947) (nomination for trustee).

See Pacific American Fisheries v. Gronn, 103 F. Supp. 405, 13 Alaska 627 (1952) (incorporation of utility district); Motor Terminals, Inc. v. Nat'l Car Co., 92 F. Supp. 155 (D. Del. 1949), aff'd, 182 F.2d 732 (3d Cir. 1950).

[61] See Shaughnessy v. Metropolitan Dade County, 238 So. 2d 466 (Fla. 1970) (tie vote of zoning board) citing Robert's Rules of Order on quorum.

At a meeting to elect thirteen directors, a majority voted in favor of twelve but there was a tie vote as to the thirteenth director. The meeting was adjourned until counsel could be consulted. The adjournment was held proper as inspectors had not reported before adjournment was taken. In re Newcomb, 42 N.Y. St. Rep. 442, 18 N.Y.S. 16 (Sup. Ct. 1891).

Where a board of directors is prevented from taking action on a demand of a shareholder due to a tie vote, the board being evenly divided between directors representing the only two stockholders, the bringing of a stockholder's derivative action is an appropriate remedy for the disappointed stockholder. Motor Terminals, Inc. v. Nat'l Car Co., 92 F. Supp. 155 (D. Del. 1949); accord, Sterling Indus. Inc. v. Ball Bearing Pen Corp., 298 N.Y. 483, 84 N.E.2d 790 (1949).

[62] Grip v. Buffelen Woodworking Co., 73 Wash. 2d 219, 437 P.2d 915 (1968).

[63] See, e.g., DELAWARE CORP. LAW § 226; NEW YORK BUS. CORP. LAW § 1109.

Where the board of directors and stockholders are so deadlocked that the business of the company can no longer be continued to the advantage of all shareholders, the court will appoint a receiver to liquidate the company. This is a statutory power. Ellis v. Civic Improvement, Inc., 24 N.C. App. 42, 209 S.E.2d 873 (1974).

§ 17.9   Failure To Vote—Abstention

There is a conflict of opinion as to whether the failure to vote of a member present at the meeting, either by his silence or by a declaration that he abstains from voting, is to be wholly disregarded in determining the results of the voting, or whether such silence or abstention is to be treated as a vote, or as an acquiescence in or a disapproval of the results of the votes actually cast. And, if abstention or silence is to be treated as a vote, there is the further question whether it is to be treated as an affirmative or a negative vote, or as a vote on the prevailing side. There is also a question whether the same or a different treatment is to be accorded a silent failure to vote as distinguished from a "pass" vote or a declared abstention from voting.

In considering this problem it is generally acknowledged that all qualified members present at the meeting, whether they vote or remain silent or declare their abstention, are to be counted in determining whether a quorum is present. "Members of a board abstaining from voting are counted for purposes of a quorum, . . . although they may not necessarily be counted in determining whether an issue has been accorded a sufficient vote to constitute the action of a board." [64] This principle alone often resolves the question of abstention. In a case involving an amendment to the by-laws of a political committee, the court, citing Robert's Rules of Order, held that "[t]he failures to vote regardless of the fact that they emanated from committeemen present or absent cannot affect results. A quorum was present and a majority of that quorum adopted the by-laws." [65]

[64] Shaughnessy v. Metropolitan Dade County, 238 So. 2d 466, 468 (Fla. 1970), *citing* Robert's Rules of Order.

Where nine members constituting a quorum were present at the meeting, but only eight votes were cast, the action taken was valid. Members present and not voting are deemed to assent to the action of those who do vote. *In re* Brearton, 44 Misc. 247, 258, 89 N.Y.S. 893 (Sup. Ct. 1904); *accord,* Cromarty v. Leonard, 13 App. Div. 2d 274, 216 N.Y.S.2d 619 at 626 (2d Dep't), *aff'd,* 10 N.Y.2d 915, 179 N.E.2d 710, 223 N.Y.S.2d 870 (1961).

[65] Lamb v. Cohen, 40 Misc. 2d 615, 243 N.Y.S.2d 647, 651 (Sup. Ct. 1963).

"There were seven aldermen. Four were a quorum. Six were present. Three voted for the adoption of the amendment, and the refusal of the other three to vote was inoperative. In the absence of express regulation, a proposi-

It is also the generally accepted practice, particularly in meetings of large groups and of unlimited bodies, not to record the names or the number of votes which could be cast by those present who sit mute and do not declare their votes or declare their abstention. In smaller bodies with a fixed membership, and particularly those bodies which have legislative authority and responsibility, the significance of a member's declaration that he abstains or "passes" may have a serious impact on the legislative productivity of the body, sometimes resulting in the creation of tie votes which must then be broken.

The leading case in New York involved a ten-member county Board of Supervisors, with authority in the County Executive to give a casting vote in case of a tie. Five members voted for a certain appointment, four voted against, and one did not vote. The chairman ruled that the abstention should be counted as a negative vote and directed the clerk so to record it. He further ruled that the County Executive had the power and should cast the deciding vote. The County Executive then voted to approve the appointment and the chairman declared the appointee elected. The abstaining member brought suit to annul the chairman's ruling which "vitalized his abstention into a negative vote." At the court hearing it was established that the board had never adopted any rules of order or procedure; that it was customary for supervisors to abstain from voting; and that it had never been the custom to record an abstention as an affirmative or a negative vote. The lower court held that, while the authorities were in hopeless confusion, an abstention may not be counted as a negative vote so as to create a tie with the right to a casting vote.

The appellate court reversed, holding that, in the absence of a statute or rule providing to the contrary, the abstention should be counted as a negative vote and that the challenged resolutions properly should be regarded as adopted. The dissenting opinion stated firmly, "An abstention is not a vote. Abstention is a common legislative practice. It may be means by which time is gained to gather information and to determine the sentiment of constituents. We

---

tion is carried in a town-meeting, or other legislative assembly, by a majority of the votes cast." Attorney General v. Shepard, 62 N.H. 383, 384 (1882).

cannot inquire into motives of a legislator, nor can we make him vote." [66]

The counting of an abstention as a negative vote was justified in two earlier cases founded on similar facts where the mayor had a right to vote only in a case of a tie. The members of the council were evenly divided with four votes in the affirmative and four not voting, and the major voted in the affirmative. The court reasoned that the council was evenly divided with four voting one way and four not voting, thereby creating a tie, and that the mayor could give a casting vote to break the tie. [67]

[66] Cromarty v. Leonard, 13 App. Div. 2d 274, 216 N.Y.S.2d 619, 623, 628, 629, 631 (2d Dep't), aff'd, 10 N.Y.2d 915, 179 N.E.2d 710, 223 N.Y.S.2d 870 (1961), citing State ex rel. Young v. Yates, 19 Mont. 239, 242–44, 47 P. 1004, 1005, 1006, 37 L.R.A. 205 (1897). To the lower court holding that abstention and absence must be treated alike, the appellate court at 628 quoted from Ray v. Armstrong, 140 Ky. 800, 131 S.W. 1039, 1049 (1910): "If it be held that his not voting had the same effect as if he had been absent, it would belie the facts, for he was not absent." To the argument that in the United Nations an abstention is not counted as a vote, the appellate court at 628 replied: "What is done in that organization of sovereign nations, under the rules of that body, has little relevance to a vote in the Board of Supervisors on matters upon which the Board has a duty to act."

A director who is present and does not vote is counted in the negative for the purpose of determining whether the resolution has been carried by a majority vote. Dillon v. Berg, 326 F. Supp. 1214 (D. Del.), aff'd, 453 F.2d 876 (3d Cir. 1971).

"An abstention is a vote which should be counted in opposition to a resolution. . . ." Downing v. Gaynor, 47 Misc. 2d 535, 262 N.Y.S.2d 837, 840 (1965). But see Smith v. Proctor, 130 N.Y. 319, 322, 29 N.E. 312 (1891) holding that those who do not respond to a roll call should not be counted at all, and certainly not as if they had voted "no."

"The parties are in agreement that the vote was taken in accordance with Robert's Rules of Order. The 1970 edition of Robert's Rules provided that while a member who has an opinion on a question has a duty to vote, he is nevertheless permitted to abstain because he cannot be compelled to vote. The clear implication from that provision is that an abstention is not to be counted as a vote." Rockland Woods, Inc. v. Incorporated Village of Suffern, 40 App. Div. 2d 385, 340 N.Y.S.2d 513, 514 (1973).

[67] State ex rel. Young v. Yates, 19 Mont. 239, 242–44, 47 P. 1004–1006, 37 L.R.A. 205 (1897).

Launtz v. People ex rel. Sullivan, 113 Ill. 137, 144 (1885). The court said: "Why may it not be considered as equivalent to a tie, counting the members who do not vote as voting the contrary way from the mayor? This would be fulfilling the purposes of the law in giving the mayor a casting vote in case of

A conflicting view is represented by a case where the presiding officer (the mayor) declared that "pass" votes were to be counted as affirmative. The vote was one in the affirmative and four "pass" followed by a ruling that the pass votes, not being negative, were affirmative. On appeal the court was faced with the question whether non-action or abstention from voting in the negative amounted to a vote in the affirmative. The court held that the act of voting is a "positive act whereby the person makes known an affirmative or negative position," and that "no presumption should be indulged that a voter who does not vote yea or nay is thereby to be counted among those who vote yea, especially where it is necessary to so count in order to support the adoption of the matter under consideration." [68]

A number of cases not involving a declaration of abstention or the intricacies of creating or breaking a tie vote have been decided on the general premise that "silence means consent." [69] In the case of bodies of indefinite number, it has generally been held that abstention signifies acquiescence. "Those absenting themselves, and those who, being present, abstain from voting, are considered as acquiescing in the result declared by a majority of those actually voting, even though, in point of fact, but a minority of those entitled to vote really do vote." [70] This rule is based on the parlia-

---

a tie." Thus, a majority of votes cast may elect corporate officers, a quorum being present, although a majority of the entire assembly may abstain from voting.

Accord, State ex rel. Morris v. McFarland, 149 Ind. 266, 49 N.E. 5 (1898).

[68] Caffey v. Veale, 193 Okla. 444, 145 P.2d 961, 964 (1944).

[69] Even in the case of an abstention the doctrine of acquiescence has been applied to demonstrate that the abstainer has not been deprived of any substantial right. If the abstainer opposes the resolution, he has the right to vote against and is not aggrieved if his abstention is so recorded. If he tacitly approves the resolution, or is indifferent and does not wish to be recorded as voting one way or the other, he has been deprived of no substantial right since his conduct in refusing to vote amounted practically to acquiescence in the action taken. Also, if he abstains from voting for the purpose of blocking effective legislative action, he should not have the assistance of the court in the avoidance of his legislative duties. Cromarty v. Leonard, 13 App. Div. 2d 274, 216 N.Y.S.2d 619, 630 (2d Dep't 1961), aff'd, 10 N.Y.2d 915, 179 N.E.2d 710, 223 N.Y.S.2d 870 (1961).

[70] Murdoch v. Strange, 99 Md. 89, 57 A. 628, 630 (1904) (blank ballot cast in an election cannot be considered in the total vote, citing Cushing, Law & Pr.

mentary principle that when no response is made in answer to a call by the presiding officer for votes on a question stated, the vote is declared to be affirmative unless objection is made at the time.[71]

The same rule has been applied to bodies of a definite number. In a case construing a statute providing for appointments by the Governor with the approval of the Council, it was held that the exercise of the law-making power is not stopped by the mere silence and inaction of some who are present. Thus, if the councilors who are present should choose to remain silent, or otherwise pass or abstain from voting, their action will not defeat the action of those who do vote, but will be taken as acquiescence or concurrence in an action supported by a majority of votes cast, whether the action be in the affirmative or the negative. [72]

Leg. Assem. for the proposition that all electors have equal rights and one cannot exercise his right so as to hurt another's right and this is the effect of counting a blank ballot in the number of votes cast). *Accord,* Walker v. Oswald, 68 Md. 146, 11 A. 711 (1887).

An early Supreme Court decision relating to a township election on a bond issue held: "All qualified voters who absent themselves from an election duly called are presumed to assent to the expressed will of the majority of those voting, unless the law providing for the election otherwise declares." County of Cass v. Johnston, 95 U.S. 360, 369 (1877).

[71] Under parliamentary practice the question is first put on the affirmative and then on the negative side. The court said: "If silence of the whole assembly is equivalent to a unanimous vote in the affirmative, silence of a part of the members not voting cannot be counted against the express voice of another part voting. . . . Refusing to vote, and neglecting to make known their presence . . . they virtually sanction the acts of those who voted, and waived all objection to their validity. . . . The objection is not one of a miscount of votes, or of a false declaration of record, but of an omission to recognize those who refused to be recognized." Richardson v. Union Congregational Soc'y, 58 N.H. 187, 188, 189 (1877), *citing* Cushing, Parl. Law at 383 (1793).

[72] Opinion of the Justices, 98 N.H. 530, 98 A.2d 635, 636–37 (1953).

Members of city council present and not voting will be deemed to "virtually acquiesce" and assent. *In re* Brearton, 44 Misc. 247, 89 N.Y.S. 893, 899 (1904).

Whoever receives the majority vote, the assembly being sufficient, is elected although a majority of the entire assembly abstains from voting, since their presence suffices to constitute an electing body and their neglect to vote is construed as assent to the majority of those who do vote. State *ex rel.* Roberts v. Gruber, 231 Ore. 494, 373 P.2d 657 (1962).

It has been suggested that those occupying legislative office (board of county supervisors) have some degree of responsibility to exercise their legisla-

The same conclusion is presented in a recent case involving a board of twelve councilmen, with six voting "yea," five "nay," and one "pass" on its first reading. The court reasoned that the six members voting "yea" constituted a majority of the eleven members who voted, and that the "pass" vote must be counted as voting with the six, thereby making seven affirmative votes. [73]

These cases are consistent with the parliamentary concept that an abstention has the effect of a vote on the prevailing side.[74] It must be noted that, under parliamentary law, an abstention is not a true vote and therefore should not serve to break a tie. It could be argued, however, that inasmuch as a resolution fails to pass on a tie vote, an abstention could be considered a vote on the prevailing negative side. In the absence of a controlling statute or rule, all members of a legislative body present and not recorded as voting otherwise, or recorded as passing or as refusing to vote, are presumed to have voted in the affirmative.[75]

---

tive powers in an affirmative way, and to vote on measures presented to them for action. A statutory or "mandatory" duty to elect a chairman and clerk is distinguishable from voting on a resolution. Plantz v. Board of Supervisors, 122 Misc. 576, 580–81, 204 N.Y.S. 27, 30 (1924), *quoted in* Cromarty v. Leonard, 13 App. Div. 2d 274, 216 N.Y.S.2d 619, 627–28 (2d Dep't), *aff'd*, 10 N.Y.2d 915, 179 N.E.2d 710, 223 N.Y.S.2d 870 (1961).

[73] Payne v. Petrie, 419 S.W.2d 761, 763 (Ky. 1967).

But see People ex rel. Floyd v. Conklin, 7 Hun. 188 (N.Y. 1876) where, twelve trustees being present, six voted for relator, four for defendant, one for a third person, and one abstained. It was held not to be a majority as it could not be presumed that the trustee not voting "practically voted" for relator.

An ordinance was passed by a favorable vote of two of five commissioners on a city council with two members abstaining and one member voting against. The court said: "We adopt the rule that a passed vote is to be considered as a vote with the majority, a quorum being present." Northwestern Bell Tel. Co. v. Board of Comm'rs, 211 N.W.2d 399, 404 (N.D. 1973).

[74] *See* Robert's Rules of Order at 193.

[75] Hartford Acc. & Indem. Co. v. City of Sulphur, 123 F.2d 566, 571 (10th Cir. 1941), *cert. denied*, 315 U.S. 805 (1942) (Board of City Commissioners); *accord*, Landes v. State ex rel. Matson, 160 Ind. 479, 67 N.E. 189, 191 (1903) (common council); McCormick v. Board of Educ., 58 N.M. 648, 274 P.2d 299, 308 (1954) (*citing* Robert's Rules of Order); *see* Dyer v. SEC, 266 F.2d 33 (8th Cir. 1959); Caffey v. Veale, 193 Okla. 444, 145 P.2d 961, 962, 964 (1944) (city board).

Failure of the mayor to approve or disapprove a city council resolution on which there is a tie vote is tantamount to an affirmative vote. Grimes v. Miller,

On the other hand, where the controlling statute requires a majority vote of a five-member zoning board to approve the granting of a permit, a vote of two in favor, one against, and one member and the chairman abstaining does not constitute a majority vote and the determination was not valid. A vote of two to one did not constitute a majority; at least three affirmative votes were required to constitute a majority.[76]

Corporation law is more definite. It has been held that shareholders who do not vote at a valid meeting lose their right to be counted in the tally of the voting. "Those who have an opportunity to vote, and refrain, though they have a majority of the stock, must be held to acquiesce in the result of the votes actually cast." [77] A

---

175 A. 152 (N.J. 1934); *accord,* Township Comm. of Hazlet v. Morales, 119 N.J. Super. 29, 289 A.2d 563 (1972).

[76] Gollob v. Bevans, 5 Misc. 2d 958, 161 N.Y.S. 2d 225, 227 (Sup. Ct. 1957) *citing* Robert's Rules of Order.

[77] A shareholder who did not vote because the chairman ruled his proxies were not good was denied relief by the court because he did not exhaust his remedies by asserting his claim of right. *In re* Martin, 34 Minn. 135, 24 N.W. 353, 354 (1885).

A shareholder who deliberately refrains from attending a meeting, and therefore does not vote, virtually consents that election be made by those who choose to exercise their privilege. The petitioner should not be relieved from the consequences of his own deliberate act. *In re* P. F. Keogh, Inc., 192 App. Div. 624, 183 N.Y.S. 408, 413 (1st Dep't 1920).

Those who refuse to vote are deemed to have waived their right. *In re* Pioneer Paper Co., 36 How. Pr. 105 (N.Y. Sup. Ct. 1864), *appeal dismissed,* 36 How. Pr. 110 (N.Y. Ct. App. 1865)

"A common mode of voting in public and corporate assemblies is *viva voce,* or by a show of hands; and when, in answer to a call by the presiding officer for votes for and against a question stated, no response is made, the vote is declared in the affirmative unless objection is made at the time. Cush. Parl. Law. 383, 1793. If silence of the whole assembly is equivalent to a unanimous vote in the affirmative, silence of a part of the members not voting cannot be counted against the express voice of another part voting. If those present having the right and opportunity to vote refused to exercise it, and witnessed, without objection, the passage of a by-law by the usual mode of voting, counting and declaring, the objection of an insufficient or invalid vote, by reason of not counting non-voters present, could not afterwards be made. Refusing to vote, and neglecting to make known their presence and its power to defeat the by-law, they virtually sanctioned the acts of those who voted, and waived all objection to their validity." Richardson v. Union Congregational Soc'y, 58 N.H. 187, 188–89 (1877).

shareholder declining to vote is in that manner "silently giving his consent" to the action of a majority of the votes cast.[78] "This is the settled rule of the common law, as applied to elections in corporate bodies." [79]

However, there is also authority to the contrary holding that it cannot reasonably be implied that failure of a shareholder to vote indicates assent to the action taken by those who voted. It is possible that the abstainer realized that a negative vote or a vocal objection on his part would have little or no effect on the proposed action.[80]

The same rule applies to a municipal body. "If members present desire to defeat a measure, they must vote against it, for inaction will not accomplish their purpose. Their silence is acquiescence, rather than opposition. Their refusal to vote is, in effect, a declaration that they consent that the majority of the quorum may act for the body of which they are members." Rushville Gas Co. v. Rushville, 121 Ind. 206, 23 N.E. 72, 73 (1889).

Members of a voluntary association who do not attend a meeting impliedly give their assent that those who attend should, by majority vote, transact business. Ostrom v. Greene, 20 Misc. 177, 45 N.Y.S. 852, 857 (Sup. Ct. 1897), aff'd mem., 30 App. Div. 621, 52 N.Y.S. 1147 (3d Dep't 1898), aff'd, 161 N.Y. 353, 55 N.E. 919 (1900).

Refusal to vote is virtual consent to having an election by those choosing to exercise their privilege. In re Election of Dirs. of Bushwick Sav. & Loan Ass'n, 189 Misc. 316, 70 N.Y.S.2d 478, 481 (1947).

A stockholder faction which remained silent while others elected directors at a stockholder meeting cannot later question the result. State ex rel. Price v. DuBrul, 100 Ohio St. 272, 126 N.E. 87, 90 (1919).

An assumption that stockholders who failed to vote on a stock option plan at the annual meeting were in opposition to the plan would be unwarranted. Eliasberg v. Standard Oil Co., 23 N.J. Super. 431, 92 A.2d 862 (1952).

[78] In re Union Insurance Co., 22 Wend. 591 (Sup. Ct. N.Y. 1840), quoted in In re Lighthall Mfg. Co., 47 Hun 258 (Sup. Ct. N.Y. 1888).

[79] State ex rel. Shinnich v. Green, 37 Ohio St. 227, 232 (1881).

Members of a voluntary association who absent themselves are held as agreeing to the vote of the majority attending. Thus, a vote of three ayes at a meeting of twenty, where no one dissents, is considered as the affirmative vote of all present. Abels v. McKeen, 18 N.J. Eq. 462, 465 (Ch. 1867).

[80] Braunstein v. Devine, 337 Mass. 408, 149 N.E.2d 628 (1958).

Silence under some circumstances does not necessarily connote consent. In a case involving approval of a pastor's salary, the court commented that some might have opposed the salary and not wished to speak on the subject. Landers v. Frank Street Methodist Episc. Church, 114 N.Y. 626, 21 N.E. 420, 421 (1889).

§ 17.9.1   Dominant Director

A different rule is applicable to the failure of a director to attend meetings, or to vote at meetings he attends, particularly where the abstainer holds a dominant position or has an interest in the transaction to which the voting relates. It is recognized that "a dominating influence may be exerted in other ways than by a vote" and that betrayal may be "by silence as well as by the spoken word." In so stating, the court held that although the refusal of a dominant director to vote on a proposed matter may give the proposal "the form and presumption of propriety," the basic rule of law which holds a trustee to the duty of constant and unqualified fidelity requires him to state his position with candor. Fidelity is not "a thing of forms and phrases." [81]

The fact that a director and president of a corporation, as presiding officer, did not actually vote for the declaration of an unlawful dividend out of capital, did not absolve him from liability.[82]

The failure or refusal to vote has a negative effect where the statute or charter provides that the power to act must be exercised by the affirmative vote of a majority of the "whole number" of the board of legislative body, and the term "whole number" is defined or construed to mean the total number which the body would have were there no vacancies or members disqualified from acting.[83] Where there is a board of nine members, an affirmative vote of at least five would be required to take action. Unless a declared abstention is counted as a vote on the prevailing side, as distinguished from a mere acquiescence in the results, it has the effect of a negative vote.

[81] Globe Woolen Co. v. Utica Gas & Elect. Co., 224 N.Y. 483, 489, 121 N.E. 378 (1918).

An interested director has a duty of full disclosure. Failure to attend the directors' meeting and to vote on the pending resolution in which a director has an interest will not protect the interested director who has failed to divulge pertinent information. This is consistent with the director's duty to fully disclose and withdraw from the board's deliberations. Borden v. Guthrie, 23 App. Div. 2d 313, 260 N.Y.S.2d 769 (1st Dep't).

[82] Union Discount Co. v. Mac Robert, 134 Misc. 107, 234 N.Y.S. 529 (Sup. Ct. 1929).

[83] See, e.g., NEW YORK GEN. CONSTR. LAW § 41 (McKinney 1951), applicable to three or more persons charged with any public duty.

In summation, it seems to be the better rule that those who abstain from voting should not be counted as voting. However, those who neglect to vote should be considered as acquiescing in the result of the voting, the same as if they had voted. Members who remain silent and those who vocally abstain should be deemed to acquiesce in the action taken, but cannot be counted in the tally as voting with the majority.[84]

§ 17.10 Unanimous Vote

Where a "unanimous" vote of a body is required for the approval of a resolution or act, the favorable vote of all present, if constituting a quorum, is generally sufficient to constitute a unanimous vote.[85] One negative vote prevents a unanimous vote.

[84] *See* ROBERT, PARLIAMENTARY LAW at 525.

[85] "Where it is required that a particular action can be taken only by unanimous vote, it is generally held, if there is no further restriction, that it is sufficient if all those at a meeting duly called, constituting a quorum, vote in favor of it." Strain v. Mims, 123 Conn. 275, 193 A. 754, 757 (1937) (zoning commission).

The unanimous vote of the members of a committee consisting of more than a legal quorum, but less than the full committee, is a unanimous decision meeting statutory requirements. Wasserman v. Board of Regents, 13 App. Div. 2d 591, 212 N.Y.S.2d 884, 885 (3d Dep't 1961), *aff'd*, 11 N.Y.2d 173, 182 N.E.2d 264, 227 N.Y.S.2d 649, 653, *cert. denied*, 371 U.S. 861 (1962).

Unanimous consent of a city council means unanimous consent of those present and forming a quorum. Atkins v. Phillips, 26 Fla. 281, 8 So. 429 (1890).

Where a by-law requires unanimous consent it means the unanimous consent only of the members present at the meeting, unless the by-law clearly states that the unanimous consent of all the members of the board is required. Parrish v. Moss, 200 Misc. 375, 106 N.Y.S.2d 577, *aff'd*, 279 App. Div. 608, 107 N.Y.S.2d 580 (1951).

However, an agreement between shareholders that the vote on certain matters must be unanimous, may be void as contrary to a controlling statute. *Cf.* Benintendi v. Kenton Hotel, Inc., 294 N.Y. 112, 60 N.E.2d 829 (1945).

Requirement of "unanimous vote of the board," as distinguished from "unanimous vote of all the directors," can be satisfied by the unanimous vote of all the directors present, being a quorum of the board. Tidewater Southern Ry. v. Jordan, 124 P. 716 (Calif. 1912).

Statute permitting a zoning change by "unanimous vote of the commission" is satisfied if a quorum is present and the action taken is approved by all the members. Gumm v. City of Lexington, 247 Ky. 149, 56 S.W.2d 703 (1933).

By unanimous or silent consent, a deliberative body can expedite its business with little regard for those rules of parliamentary procedure which are intended for the protection of the minority and members absent from the meeting. Thus, it has been held that adoption of a resolution by unanimous vote of a city council dispenses with a requirement that bills be fully and distinctly read on three different days [86] and with a procedure requiring that bills be referred to a committee or that reference to a committee be dispensed with by a three-fifths vote of the council.[87]

§ 17.11 Changing Vote

A member of an assembly has the right to change his vote at any time before the vote has been finally and conclusively announced.[88]

[86] City of El Dorado v. Jacobs, 174 Ark. 98, 249 S.W. 411 (1927).

[87] Baldwin v. City of Martinsburg, 133 W. Va. 513, 56 S.E.2d 886 (1949).

[88] "A stockholder or member may change his vote at any time before the vote is finally announced; and before that time it is proper to permit him to correct his ballot so that it will express his true intention." Zachary v. Milin, 294 Mich. 622, 293 N.W. 770, 772 (1940) (change from straight to cumulative voting).

There may be some question whether a stockholder may change his vote more than once. See State ex rel. Lawrence v. McGann, 64 Mo. App. 225 (1895).

A stockholder may correct a mistake as to his vote before the result of the balloting is finally announced. An announcement of a vote at a stockholders' meeting, made before the meeting was recessed to an adjournment day, was not final when it was especially agreed that the vote was subject to recheck. Wells v. Beekman Terrace, Inc., 23 Misc. 2d 22, 24, 197 N.Y.S.2d 79 (Sup. Ct. 1960).

A city council may make reasonable rules governing an election and can adopt a rule permitting change of votes after a ballot but before announcement of the results by the chair. State ex rel. Smith v. Nazor, 135 Ohio St. 364, 21 N.E.2d 124, 126 (1939).

"In the absence of any controlling bylaw, agreement or other binding provision concerning earlier closing of the polls, a stockholder has the right to change his vote so long as the result has not been finally announced." Salgo v. Matthews, 497 S.W.2d 620, 630–31 (Tex. 1973).

See State ex rel. David v. Dailey, 23 Wash. 2d 25, 158 P.2d 330 (1945) (stockholder changed from straight to cumulative voting thereby being assured of election).

Inspectors of election were ordered by the court to accept and count proxies

Thereafter, a member can change his vote, or cast a vote after first abstaining, only by permission of the assembly, which may be by general consent before any other business is considered. To obtain this permission, a member must make his intention clear to the assembly, which can then taken such further action as a body as it deems proper.[89] Exceptions to the general rule have been made where a change of vote is restricted by the rules of the assembly and where the assembly has sustained a rule by the chairman that a change of vote is out of order.[90] Furthermore, a member cannot change his vote after the meeting has closed or at a later meeting, as such actions would in effect be an attempt to reconsider the matters on which a vote was taken.[91]

An announcement of the vote is not final when it is expressly agreed that the vote is subject to recheck.[92] Generally, announcement of the result of the voting is made by the chairman, but if the statute does not so require, the function of the assembly is "discharged" when the votes are cast and the tally has been made,

---

when presented late but before conclusion of the final count and report. However, the polls cannot be opened after the votes have been counted and the results announced. Young v. Jebbett, 213 App. Div. 774, 211 N.Y.S. 61 (4th Dep't 1925).

[89] Gollob v. Bevans, 5 Misc. 2d 958, 161 N.Y.S.2d 225 (Sup. Ct. 1957), *citing* Robert's Rules of Order.

[90] A member cannot change his vote even before the result of the voting has been announced, unless changed pursuant to a rule or by consent of the assembly. State *ex rel.* Reed v. De Maioribus, 131 Ohio St. 201, 2 N.E.2d 506 (1936).

At a meeting of a city council to elect a street commissioner, two candidates received three votes each, whereupon one councilman desired to change his vote and was ruled out of order by the mayor. An appeal being taken from the decision of the mayor, his ruling was sustained by the council upon a roll being called. The tie was then broken by a vote of the mayor. "The ruling of the mayor, sustained by the council, simply held that a vote could not be changed before the result had been announced. Such a rule has the approval of many deliberative assemblies, and, as applied to the election of municipal officers, seems to be open to very little, if any, objection." Mann v. City of LeMars, 109 Iowa 251, 254, 80 N.W. 327 (1899).

[91] *See* §§ 9.19–9.27 *supra.*

[92] Wells v. Beekman Terrace, Inc., 23 Misc. 2d 22, 197 N.Y.S.2d 79, 82 (Sup. Ct. 1960).

and thereafter members could not change the result by changing their votes.[93]

The rule is different in a popular election whether by ballot or viva voce. The right to change has been denied in both cases. One reason for this difference is that the inspectors cannot be presumed to know how any person voted and, for that reason, the moment the ballot is deposited all control over it is ended.[94]

§ 17.12 Chairman—Rights

It is not within the authority of the chairman to decide who may vote and when proxies are valid.[95] That is the responsibility of the inspectors of election and judges of the voting. Where a member does not have a statutory or charter right to vote by proxy, the chairman cannot create that right by accepting a proxy vote. "The action of a particular member, even if he be the chairman of the body, cannot effectuate a new rule of conduct binding on the organization itself." [96] Nor does the chairman have the right to determine the validity of shares of stock, their ownership, nor their right to vote.[97] The voting rights of a proxyholder who holds a general power cannot be restricted by the chairman to areas specifically designated in the proxy instrument. To do so would violate "the fundamental right of a stockholder to be represented by proxy.[98]

[93] The court noted that the members of the assembly (city council) were "not acting under parliamentary law, but were casting their votes and making their choice as required by specific statute." State *ex rel.* Calderwood v. Miller, 62 Ohio St. 436, 57 N.E. 227, 229 (1900).

[94] State *ex rel.* Lawrence v. McGann, 64 Mo. App. 225 (1895).

[95] A president does not have the "right to determine even the qualifications of stockholders as voters" at the election of directors. *In re* Robert Clark, Inc., 186 App. Div. 216, 174 N.Y.S. 314, 316 (1919).

A chairman does not have authoritative word on who may vote and when proxies are valid. *See In re* Martin, 34 Minn. 135, 24 N.W. 353 (1885).

[96] Hart v. Sheridan, 168 Misc. 386, 5 N.Y.S.2d 820, 825 (Sup. Ct. 1938).

[97] State *ex rel.* Ryan v. Cronan, 23 Nev. 437, 49 P. 41 (1897).

[98] State *ex rel.* Hawley v. Coogan, 98 So. 2d 757, 759 (Fla. 1958), *petition denied,* 99 So. 2d 243 (1957), *cert. denied,* 101 So. 2d 817 (1958) (proxies voted against amendment to amendment of corporate by-laws).

§ 17.13   Acceptance of Illegal Votes—Rejection of Valid Votes

The acceptance of illegal votes and the rejection of valid votes are of no consequence if the result of the voting would not have been changed by a correction of the errors. Thus, an election or other corporate action is not thereby rendered invalid.[99] "It is no

---

[99] "An election or other action at a corporate meeting is not rendered invalid because of the receipt of illegal votes, or the rejection of legal votes, if the result would have been the same had they been rejected or received, as the case may be." Beutelspacher v. Spokane Sav. Bank, 164 Wash. 227, 2 P.2d 729 (1931).

A petition for a declaratory judgment was not sufficient to show illegality of an election of directors even if all the votes cast by the management proxy committee were void, where petition did not show that any other nominations were before the meeting or that the number of votes cast by other members were insufficient to elect. Booker v. First Fed. Sav. & Loan Ass'n, 215 Ga. 277, 110 S.E.2d 360, 363, cert. denied, 361 U.S. 916 (1959).

The acceptance of illegal votes at a previous meeting of a political committee does not constitute a binding precedent at a subsequent meeting. Hart v. Sheridan, 168 Misc. 386, 5 N.Y.S.2d 820 (1938).

An injunction will not be granted against the voting of certain shares by defendants on an allegation that the right to vote such shares had been severed from their ownership, where defendants had uncontested voting rights on sufficient shares to elect directors at the annual meeting. Bache v. Central Leather Co., 78 N.J. Eq. 484, 81 A. 571 (1911).

The court will not direct that a new election be held to correct an alleged grievance which if sustained would not change the results. Burke v. Wiswall, 193 Misc. 14, 85 N.Y.S.2d 187 (Sup. Ct. 1948).

Where a candidate at a corporate election receives a majority of the legal votes cast, the receipt of illegal votes in his favor does not defeat his election. In re Argus Co., 138 N.Y. 557, 34 N.E. 388 (1893).

"It would be a vain and useless act to send the parties back to reach the same result which had already been reached. . . ." Kocke v. Creditors, 25 So. 985 (51 La. Ann. 1899) (creditors' meeting).

The same rule applies to a school district election. Boyes v. Allen, 32 App. Div. 2d 990, 301 N.Y.S.2d 664 (3d Dep't 1969).

"The election is not to be set aside and declared void, merely because two votes were received from persons not entitled to vote, if there was still a majority of legal votes for the ticket declared to be elected." People ex rel. Osborn v. Tuthill, 31 N.Y. 550, 562 (1864).

See SHAW AND SMITH, THE LAW OF MEETINGS at 80, citing Ex parte

objection to an election, that illegal votes were received, unless the illegal votes changed the majority. The mere fact of their existence never voids an election. This is so plain a proposition that it needs no authority to support it. It is the principle adopted and acted upon in all cases of contested elections, whether in the British parliament, the congress of the United States, the legislature of this or any other of the United States. The burden of proof too is always upon the persons contesting the election." [100]

However, where a meeting is conducted under such adverse circumstances that "right, justice and fair play" require a new election, the court may so require. But unless the court may reasonably conclude from the circumstances that shareholders' votes were illegally accepted or improperly rejected resulting in an "unfair deprivation" of shareholders' voting rights, the court generally will not interfere. There must be some "persuasive evidence that the result was affected or that the outcome would have been different" had the adverse circumstances not been present.[101]

The courts are reluctant to interfere with the internal affairs of a corporation after corporate action has been taken, especially where no attempt was made prior to the meeting to correct alleged errors. A recent decision explains: "There is a marked distinction between what a court will do before and after a corporate election. Before an election it will render any necessary assistance to a stockholder to allow him to vote, solicit proxies and the like. But if the election is held without prior application it becomes an unwarranted interference with internal corporate affairs to upset the election absent a

---

Mawby, [1854] 3 E. & B. 718; Colonial Gold Reef, Ltd. v. Free State Road, Ltd., [1914] 1 Ch. 382.

An election of directors will not be set aside because illegal votes were given, unless they were challenged; nor will it be set aside although the votes were challenged, if after deducting all the illegal votes there is still a clear majority in favor of the persons declared to be elected. In re Election of Dirs. of Chenango County Mut. Ins. Co., 19 Wend. 635 (N.Y. 1839).

[100] The court noted, as to the intrusion of illegal votes into the meeting: "The presiding officer should have excluded their votes." Inhabitants of the First Parish in Sudbury v. Stearns, 38 Mass. (21 Pick.) 148, 153, 154 (1838).

[101] Dal-Tran Service Co. v. Fifth Ave. Coach Lines, Inc., 14 App. Div. 2d 349, 220 N.Y.S.2d 549, 556 (1st Dep't 1961).

showing that the relief sought would, if granted, change the result." [102]

The fact that some persons were present at a corporate meeting who were not corporators will not vitiate the proceedings of the meeting, unless it appears that such persons voted, and that their votes were necessary to carry the resolutions which were claimed to be passed.[103] Also, the presence of non-members at a meeting and the casting of votes by the non-members will not void action taken where a majority of the legal votes were cast in favor of the resolution.[104] Although the receipt of illegal votes does not necessarily vitiate the proceedings, the presiding officer should exclude the votes of illegal voters who intrude into the meeting.[105] When a shareholder is unlawfully denied the right to vote his shares, he may be entitled to equitable relief from the courts.[106]

The right of a member of a regulatory board to vote may depend on whether he was a "qualified member" when the deliberative process was completed and the order was signed. Once all members have voted, the order is not nullified because of incapacity of a member occurring before the ministerial act of service.[107]

These general principles of law have also been applied in cases

[102] Goldfield Corp. v. General Host Corp., 29 N.Y.2d 264, 327 N.Y.S.2d 330, 381 (1971).

[103] Madison Ave. Baptist Church v. Baptist Church, 28 N.Y. Super. 649, 650 (1867), aff'd, 31 N.Y. Super. 109 (1869), rev'd on other grounds, 46 N.Y. 131 (1871).

[104] Where a majority of a town board voted for resolution, the presence of a non-member who voted illegally did not void the action where the majority of the legal votes were cast in its favor and a secret ballot was not required by town law. Troy & N.E. Ry. v. K.L.W.M., Inc., 192 N.Y.S. 277 (Sup. Ct.), aff'd mem., 202 App. Div. 768, 194 N.Y.S. 985 (3d Dep't 1922).

[105] "If the unlawful votes changed the majority, then the persons having a majority of lawful votes, by a proper process might be placed in office, instead of those declared to be elected. But the meeting being legal in its inception, the legal voters could maintain their rights in no way but by remaining and exercising their elective franchise." Inhabitants of the First Parish in Sudbury v. Stearns, 38 Mass. (21 Pick.) 148, 154 (1838).

[106] Where the complainant loaned money to a corporation under agreement that he should receive and be entitled to vote shares of stock, he is entitled to equitable relief against other shareholders who refused him permission to vote. Granite Brick Co. v. Titus, 226 F. 557, 565 (4th Cir. 1915).

[107] Braniff Airways, Inc. v. CAB, 379 F.2d 453, 459 (D.C. Cir. 1967).

where the voters have been subjected to unreasonable election rules,[108] misleading proxy material,[109] and misstatements or concealments of fact in a bitterly fought proxy battle.[110]

§ 17.14   Blank Votes

The casting of a blank vote differs from silence and abstention. It has been held that the casting of a blank ballot is an act of "voting" and that the blank ballot must be accepted in counting the number of votes cast.[111] In contrast, it has been held that blank ballots cannot be counted because they do not represent an expression of choice.[112] It has also been held that a majority of the votes

[108] Wirtz v. Local 153, G.B.B.A., 389 U.S. 463 (1968) (union election violating statutory standards which did not affect outcome of election).

[109] Court will not upset merger if satisfied by a "preponderance of probabilities" that the merger would have received a sufficient vote even if the proxy material had not been misleading. "We do not consider that the policy of the '34 Act requires the court to unscramble a corporate transaction merely because a violation occurred." Mills v. Electric Autolite Co., 403 F.2d 429 (7th Cir. 1968), rev'd, 396 U.S. 375 (1970).

See Finkelstein and Robbins, *Mathematical Probability in Election Challenges*, 73 COLUM. L. REV. 241 (1973).

[110] The court reasoned: "A certain amount of innuendo, misstatement, exaggeration and puffing must be allowed as a natural by-product of a bitter campaign." In re R. Hoe & Co., 14 Misc. 2d 500, 137 N.Y.S.2d 142 (1954), aff'd, 285 App. Div. 927, 139 N.Y.S.2d 883 (1st Dep't), aff'd, 309 N.Y. 719 (1955).

A corporate election will not be set aside merely because the election was preceded by a proxy fight. O'Connor v. Fergang, 14 Misc. 2d 1095, 182 N.Y.S.2d 942 (Sup. Ct. 1958).

[111] There were 29 yes votes, 14 no votes, and one blank, or a total of 44 votes cast. The court held that the ayes did not constitute a necessary two-thirds vote of 30. Gonzales v. International Ass'n of Machinists, 142 Cal. App. 2d 207, 298 P.2d 92, 98 (1956), aff'd, 356 U.S. 617 (1958). Cf. Posner v. Bronx County Med. Soc'y, 19 App. Div. 2d 89, 241 N.Y.S.2d 540 (1st Dep't), aff'd, 13 N.Y.2d 1004, 195 N.E.2d 59, 245 N.Y.S.2d 393 (1963).

[112] At a school board election of a superintendent, five voted for A, two voted for B, one for C, and there were three blank ballots. It was held that A was legally elected because he received a majority of the votes cast. Blank ballots cannot be counted. Only by "judicial ingenuity" can a piece of blank paper indicate that the person depositing it in the ballot box was opposed to the election of the person who might have the most votes. Attorney General ex rel. Woodbury v. Bickford, 77 N.H. 433, 92 A. 835, 836 (1914), citing Cushing, Law & Pr. Leg. Assem. § 103.

cast, when all members were present, was sufficient to elect "even though some did not vote or voted a blank ballot." [113]

The law in this area lacks development and certainty. One case holds that a blank ballot is "utterly null and void" but it may, in fact, operate as a vote of assent.[114] Another decision holds that a blank ballot is not technically a vote, but is an act of negation.[115] Yet another case decides that a blank vote cannot create a tie vote when an odd number of members are present and voting.[116]

In any event, one who casts an improperly marked ballot or a "coerced ballot," as distinguished from a blank ballot, should be included in determining those "present and voting" at a meeting.[117]

§ 17.15 Pairing

The practice of "pairing" started in the House of Representatives and was later followed in the Senate. It commenced as an in-

---

[113] State ex rel. Burdick v. Tyrrell, 158 Wis. 425, 149 N.W. 280, 283 (1914) (vote of city council).

Blank votes are ignored in determining the majority of a city council. Van Cleve v. Wallace, 216 Minn. 500, 13 N.W.2d 467, 473 (1944).

[114] "The voter who deposits a blank piece of paper in the ballot box throws away his vote, because the paper he has voted is not expressive of any meaning whatever, and therefore utterly null and void. It is true that a blank ballot may sometimes operate as a vote of assent; not that any presumption as to its meaning may properly be drawn, but because, being ineffective for every purpose, the person casting it has left unopposed the votes of the other electors, and thereby, it may be said assents to the election of the candidate who receives a majority of votes." Murdoch v. Strange, 99 Md. 89, 57 A. 628, 630 (1904), quoting Cushing, Law & Pr. Leg. Assem.

[115] Lawrence v. Ingersoll, 88 Tenn. 52, 12 S.W. 422, 425 (1889) (vote of board of aldermen).

[116] With 45 members of the common council and the mayor present, the vote was 22 for one candidate, 22 for another, and one blank. The tellers did not report the blank to the mayor and he then declared the vote a tie and gave a casting vote viva voce for his choice. It was held that there was no tie because an odd number of members was present. State ex rel. Cole v. Chapman, 44 Conn. 595 (Super. Ct. 1878).

[117] "Certainly, no one could reasonably argue that the voter of an improperly marked ballot, or a coerced ballot, should not be included in determining whether or not a majority of the votes of those 'present and voting' has been obtained." Fritsch v. Rarback, 199 Misc. 358, 98 N.Y.S.2d 748, 752–53 (Sup. Ct. 1950).

dulgence without a rule and was tolerated only by unanimous consent. Pairing has been described as a "clear breach of the rules of the House, a disregard of the Constitution, and a practice open to the grossest abuses." [118] By this practice, two members of opposite political parties voluntarily agree not to vote. Usually both are absent although sometimes one attends but does not vote. This practice has grown to the extent that the pair clerks, unless otherwise instructed, pair all members absent and not voting. On matters requiring a two-thirds vote, the practice is to pair on a basis of two in the affirmative to one in the negative.

As the announcement of pairs in the House Journal does not indicate the attitude of the paired members on the question, many intricate political maneuvers and questions of personal privilege constantly arise. The question of quorum, as affected by pairing, has been submitted to the court in the case of a state legislator who was present at the session but did not vote. The Journal showed that 34 members were present and that one member announced he and an absent member were paired; that he would vote "no" and the absent member, if present, would vote "aye." The proposition was carried by the required vote of "two-thirds of each house" (22 yea and 11 nay). If the member physically present had been considered as "present" for purposes of quorum he would have been a member of the "house" for purpose of voting, and the proposition would have failed for the lack of a two-thirds vote. The court ruled him absent, saying: "The effect of his 'pair' is that for that occasion he is absent." The court noted that each house had the power to adopt "some uniform method within proper limits of determining the question of whether a member present, as shown by the journal, but not voting, should be counted to determine the presence of a quorum." [119] Under recent United States Senate practice, where there are sufficient members present who have announced their pairs and, therefore, withheld their votes, the presiding officer

[118] *See* VIII Cannon's Precedents at § 3076, § 3089, and § 3092; U. S. Constitution; Jefferson's Manual; Rules of the House of Representatives at § 660 and § 765; V Hinds' Precedents at § 5982; Senate Procedure, Precedents and Practices, Senate Doc. No. 44, 88th Cong., at 460.

[119] Opinion of the Justices No. 30, 228 Ala. 140, 152 So. 2d 901, 904 (1964), *citing* May's Treatise on Parliament.

held that a quorum was present for the transaction of business or that the vote was valid.[120]

§ 17.16   Discretionary Vote

The SEC proxy rules require that means shall be provided in the form of proxy whereby the person solicited is afforded an opportunity to specify by ballot a choice between approval or disapproval of each matter or group of related matters to be acted upon (other than the election of directors), and that the proxy may confer discretionary authority with respect to matters as to which the shareholder does not specify a choice.[121]   The court has upheld approval by the SEC of a management proxy form which provided that, unless otherwise indicated by the signing shareholder, such proxy would be voted in accordance with the stated recommendations of management, turning aside the shareholders' arguments that such a blanket form of proxy authority is contrary to public policy as not affording a sufficient opportunity for "stockholder democracy," as being conducive to "management oligarchy," and as representing "SEC czarism."   The unmarked proxy rule was upheld on a finding that the objecting shareholder had not demonstrated that application of the regulation "does not afford a fair opportunity for the operation of corporate suffrage, within the presumable intelligence of ordinary stockholders." [122]

§ 17.17   Dissenting Vote

A dissenting vote [123] has significance only when it protects the dissenter from some liability or when it creates or legalizes a right in favor of the dissenter.   Personal liability of a director for payment

---

[120] Senate Procedure, Precedents and Practices, Senate Doc. No. 93–21, 93d Cong. at 645 (1974).

[121] *See* SEC Rule 14a–4.

[122] Dyer v. SEC, 266 F.2d 33, 39 (8th Cir.), *cert. denied*, 361 U.S. 835 (1959).

[123] A declaration of "not voting" is not a dissent. *See* Zinke v. Hipkins, 193 App. Div. 498, 184 N.Y.S. 802 (1920) (appellate justice).

Refusal to act as director is not a "dissent" under terms of a will. Elger v. Boyle, 69 Misc. 273, 126 N.Y.S. 946 (Sup. Ct. 1910).

of an unlawful dividend is an example of the former; creation of a dissenting shareholder's right to be paid cash exemplifies the latter.

In an election or choice of nominees, votes can be cast for someone but cannot be cast against any person. The negative vote does not exist in an election. The only way to vote against a certain person is to vote for someone else.

A negative vote (as distinguished from a dissenting vote) can, of course, be cast for or against the adoption of a resolution or proposal. In voting on a resolution where personal liability is not involved, a negative vote is merely the recording of the voter's preference.

The statute and case law has been well developed in the imposition of personal liability for the payment of unlawful dividends, such as dividends which impair capital. At common law, directors were not personally liable for payment of unlawful dividends if they acted in good faith.[124] Statutory liability was imposed in many jurisdictions when it became evident that a simple rule of "good faith" did not adequately protect the corporation and its creditors from abuse. Exemption from liability of non-participating and dissenting directors, or limitation of liability to directors "assenting" or "consenting" to the unlawful dividend, is generally provided in the statutory law.[125]

Exercising a shareholder's right of dissent has no parliamentary

---

[124] See Quintal v. Greenstein, 142 Misc. 854, 256 N.Y.S. 462, aff'd, 236 App. Div. 719, 257 N.Y.S. 1034 (1st Dep't 1932).

[125] An Illinois statute imposing liability on "declaring or assenting" directors means that liability exists only if the directors "voluntarily or affirmatively participate or cooperate" in the wrongful payments. Assenting includes the approval and ratification of a dividend after it has been paid. Aiken v. Insull, 122 F.2d 746 (7th Cir. 1941), cert. denied, 315 U.S. 806, rehearing denied, 315 U.S. 829 (1942).

A director need not actively participate in the unlawful payment of a dividend, and is liable even though absent if the dividend was paid with his "sanction." Williams v. Brewster, 117 Wis. 370, 93 N.W. 479, 484 (1903).

North Dakota law holds directors liable for illegal dividends—"except those who have caused their dissent therefrom to be entered at large on the minutes or were not present." Crane–Johnson Co. v. CIR, 105 F.2d 740, 742 (8th Cir. 1939).

The fact that a director is in office only a short period before the meeting at which an unlawful dividend was paid is not a defense if he was present and did not cause his dissent to be entered in the minutes. Quintal v. Greenstein,

significance. It is solely a matter of meeting the applicable statutory requirements.[126]

§ 17.18   Fractional Votes

Where the percentage of the members required for passage of a resolution or bill (*e.g.*, two-thirds) consists of a number of whole votes and a fraction of a vote, the fraction must be raised to the next highest whole number in computing the total votes required. For example, a two-thirds vote of a seventeen-member board of legislators (mathematically $11\frac{1}{3}$) is twelve. In a recent case the county charter required a two-thirds vote of the county board on a number of important items and there was no provision for fractional, weighted, or proportional voting. The board, consisting of eleven members of the majority party and six members of the minority party, voted eleven in favor of a certain appointment and six against. The chairman declared that the appointment had received the necessary two-thirds vote of approval. On appeal from the chairman's ruling, eleven voted to uphold the ruling and six voted

142 Misc. 854, 256 N.Y.S. 462, *aff'd*, 236 App. Div. 719, 257 N.Y.S. 1034 (1st Dep't 1932).

The fact that the president and director, as presiding officer, did not actually vote for the declaration of dividends out of capital did not absolve him from liability. Union Discount Co. v. Mac Robert, 134 Misc. 107, 234 N.Y.S. 529 (Sup. Ct. 1929).

A director who is not present at the meeting which declared an illegal dividend, but is present at a subsequent meeting where the dividend was known but not formally ratified, is nevertheless liable with other directors because he exercised control. City Investing Co. v. Gerken, 121 Misc. 763, 202 N.Y.S. 41 (Sup. Ct. 1924).

Although it did not affirmatively appear that the defendant was present or voted at the meeting declaring an illegal dividend, or did not register his dissent, he is liable because he approved, ratified, and acquiesced in the payment. Walker v. Man, 142 Misc. 277, 253 N.Y.S. 458 (Sup. Ct. 1931).

A director who was not present at the meeting when an illegal dividend was declared and therefore not liable under the statute, does not become liable by approval of minutes at the following meeting at which he was present because approval is only "authentication of the proof of what had happened" at the previous meeting. Hutchinson v. Curtiss, 45 Misc. 484, 92 N.Y.S. 70, 74 (Sup. Ct. 1904).

[126] For definitions of "dissent" in shareholder dissenting proceedings, *see*, *e.g.*, Central–Penn Nat'l Bank v. Portner, 201 F.2d 607 (3d Cir. 1953); Roach v. Stastny, 104 F.2d 559 (7th Cir. 1939).

in the negative. The majority urged the court to conclude that a
two-thirds vote is whatever the chairman as supported by a majority
of the board says it is, so long as the ruling is made in good faith.
The court nevertheless concluded that the chairman's ruling was
"erroneous as a matter of mathematics, legislative usage, parliamentary practice and as a matter of law. Certainly, the common practice is to raise a fractional number to the next highest whole number
in determining minimum voting percentages. . . . As a matter of
mathematics, if a two-thirds vote is necessary for an affirmance,
then that vote should be at least twice as large as the negative vote,
a situation not present on a vote of 11 to 6." [127]   In an earlier case
where the statute required a three-fourths vote of a three-member
town board to authorize emergency action, it was argued that, "since
a town board of three members is incapable of division into three-
fourths," the statute had no application. The court answered: "This
is not correct," and held that a three-fourths vote of a board of
three members is three affirmative votes.[128] This method of calcu-
lation is in conformity with common parliamentary law.[129]

[127] Rippa v. Keane, N.Y. Sup. Ct. Westchester Co. (Sept. 10, 1974).

See, e.g., Savatgy v. City of Kingston, 51 Misc. 2d 251, 273 N.Y.S.2d 1,
aff'd, 26 App. Div. 2d 978, 274 N.Y.S.2d 852 (1966), *aff'd,* 20 N.Y.2d 258,
282 N.Y.S.2d 513 (1967) (a three-fourths vote of a thirteen-member city
council is ten votes); Acquavella v. Lamb, 25 App. Div. 2d 815, *aff'd,* 17
N.Y.2d 839, 271 N.Y.S.2d 280, 218 N.E.2d 321 (1966) (a three-fourths vote
of a nine-member common council is seven votes); Glen Cove Shopping Center v. Suozzi, 8 Misc. 2d 247, 166 N.Y.S.2d 917 (1957) (a three-fourths vote
of a five-member city council is four votes).

Mid-America Cable Corp. v. Metropolitan Government of Nashville, 498
S.W.2d 326 (Tenn. 1972) (twenty-six votes do not constitute a two-thirds vote
of a forty-member council).

[128] "Where, in any instance, a percentage vote of a municipal legislative
body results in so many whole votes and a fraction, it is always necessary to
count the fraction as a whole vote even though this results in a greater percentage of the whole body in such instance than would be the case if the legislative body is equally divisible by said percentage into whole numbers. The
fraction cannot be lopped off or ignored. Therefore, as applied to town boards,
when they are composed of three members and undertake to attach an emergency clause to an ordinance, the practical effect of Sec. 53, supra, is to require
three votes." Bonney v. Smith, 194 Okla. 106, 147 P.2d 771, 773 (1944).

[129] *See* Robert's Rules of Order, Newly Revised, § 43 (1970) at 339;
Robert's Rules of Order, Revised, § 48 at 204 (1951); Demeter's Manual of
Parliamentary Law and Procedure at 36.

§ 17.19   Per Share—Per Capita

At common law each shareholder of a corporation had but one vote at shareholder meetings, no matter how many shares he owned.[130] Voting at corporate meetings was taken by a show of hands, resulting in one vote for each shareholder present. To prevent a distortion of voting control, provision was later made in the charter or by-laws, and by statute, for a vote according to the number of shares held whenever a poll was demanded at a meeting.[131]

There has been a general departure in this country from the common-law rule as applied to ordinary business corporations. It is now well established by state corporation laws that a corporation is competent to provide otherwise in its charter or by-laws within

---

[130] At common law, stockholders are entitled to only one vote each, and not to a vote for every share of stock they respectively own. A by-law declaring each proprietor entitled to as many votes as he has shares, contrary to the charter, is void. A claim of one vote to each share does not rest on the common law and is wholly dependent on the grant of the legislature. Taylor v. Griswold, 14 N.J.L. 222 (1834).

Corporations are creatures of the state and stockholders have only such voting rights as are given them by law, for at common law each stockholder had but one vote no matter how many shares he owned. "When a holder of more than one share claims the right to cast more than one vote he must point to a statute giving him that right." Commonwealth ex rel. Cartwright v. Cartwright, 350 Pa. 638, 40 A.2d 30, 34 (1944).

In re P. B. Mathiason Mfg. Co., 122 Mo. App. 437, 99 S.W. 502, 504 (1907) (common-law rule modified by statute, charter, or by-law).

In re Election of Dirs. and Officers of Rochester Dist. Tel. Co., 40 Hun 172 (N.Y. Sup. Ct. 1886) (motion to adjourn stockholder meeting by majority in number of holders leaving behind minority in number owning a majority of shares).

State ex rel. Fritz v. Gray, 20 Ohio App. 26, 153 N.E. 187, 190 (1925) (majority of shareholders in number cannot withdraw from meeting and prevent owners of majority of shares from electing directors. Statutory modification of common law).

[131] According to common law, "[V]otes at all meetings are taken by a show of hands. Of course it may not always be a satisfactory mode—persons attending in large numbers may be small shareholders, and persons attending in small numbers may be large shareholders, and therefore in companies provision is made for taking a poll, and when a poll is taken the votes are to be counted according to the number of shares. . . . In re Horbury Bridge, Coal, Iron & Waggon Co., 11 Ch.D. 109, 115 (1879).

statutory bounds.[132] In the absence of restrictions to the contrary, it is the prevailing rule that shareholders of a stock corporation are entitled to one vote for each share held. This rule applies irrespective of whether the shares are preferred or common.[133] Nonvoting stock is permitted unless barred by positive law.[134]

Statutory and other organic provisions governing the voting of shares must be read with precision and care. For example, one case holds that a provision in a by-law that "three fifths of all stockholders" shall constitute a quorum means stockholders per capita, and not stockholders in interest.[135] Another case holds that a vote of "three-fourths of all the stockholders" necessary to effect a consolidation means three-fourths of the number of shares and not of the holders.[136]

A statutory requirement that a "majority of stockholders" shall be necessary to take action has been held to mean a majority in

---

[132] "It is true that at common law each shareholder was entitled to but one vote, irrespective of the number of shares he might hold, but it is now established by the best authorities that this rule does not apply at the present day to ordinary business corporations. . . . That there has been a general departure from the common-law rule on this subject is recognized by the ablest text writers." This departure resulted from "long-continued custom and usage." Proctor Coal Co. v. Finley, 98 Ky. 405, 33 S.W. 188, 190 (1895).

Another decision quotes Cook on Corporations: " 'At common law, in public or municipal corporations, each qualified elector has one vote, and only one. This was a natural rule, since each duly qualified citizen voted as a citizen, and not as the holder of stock. But the same rule should not apply to private corporations. Stockholders are interested not equally, but in proportion to the number of shares held by them. Naturally and reasonably each share should be entitled to one vote.' " In re P. B. Mathiason Mfg. Co., 122 Mo. App. 437, 99 S.W. 502, 504 (1907).

[133] State ex rel. Cullitan v. Campbell, 135 Ohio St. 238, 20 N.E.2d 366, 367 (1939) (action to oust respondents from corporate office); State ex rel. Chapman v. Urschel, 104 Ohio St. 172, 135 N.E. 630 (1922) (action to test right to corporate office).

[134] Du Vall v. Moore, 276 F. Supp. 674, 686 (N.D. Iowa 1967).

[135] State ex rel. Schwab v. Price, 121 Ohio 114, 167 N.E. 366 (1929).

[136] Simon Borg & Co. v. New Orleans City R.R. Co., 244 F. 617, 619 (E.D. La. 1917).

"Two-thirds of the stockholders" means two-thirds of the stockholders in interest. Toledo Traction, Light & Power Co. v. Smith, 205 F. 643 (N.D. Ohio 1913).

interest of the stockholders and not a majority in number only.[137]
To be precise, the term "a majority of the stockholders," as ordinarily used, means a majority per capita when the right to vote is
per capita, and a majority of the stock when each share of stock is
entitled to one vote.[138] This view has been stated in other words:
"The ordinary rule in stock corporations is one vote per share of
stock, the ordinary rule in non stock corporations is one vote per
member." [139]

There appears to be no common-law authority for a double-
standard quorum. While a corporation may have power to provide
the number of shares necessary to be present at a stockholders'
meeting to constitute a quorum, it does not have the power, without
statutory authority, to make the additional requirement that the
quorum shall consist also of a certain number of stockholders.[140]

Inspectors of election may be appointed or elected in any manner provided in the charter or by-laws. There is no requirement
at common law that shareholders vote for them at all, or in any
particular manner. Where a statute provides that the "meeting"
may appoint inspectors, courts have held that an election by per-
capita vote of the shareholders present is a valid appointment.
"The person or persons presiding at the meeting can determine the
right of a person to vote per capita as well as his right to vote shares
of stock." [141]

[137] Bank of Los Banos v. Jordan, 167 Cal. 327, 139 P. 691 (1914) (action
to increase or decrease number of directors).

[138] The court stated: "In view of the modern trend in matters of this kind,
it seems to me that the more logical and better interpretation to put upon the
statute is that what constitutes a majority of stockholders and the manner of
voting should be determined in each case by the provisions of the charters of
the merging corporations." Simon Borg & Co. v. New Orleans R.R. Co., 244
F. 617, 619 (1917).

It has been held that a membership corporation does not have power to
issue stock and provide for votes on a per-share basis as if it were a stock corporation. Anderson v. Reid, 19 Misc. 95, 45 N.Y.S. 742 (1897).

[139] Green Gables Home Owners Ass'n v. Sunlite Homes, Inc., 202 P.2d 143,
147 (Cal. 1949). It has also been suggested that the word "stockholders" refers to corporations for profit and the word "members" refers to corporations
not for profit. State ex rel. Fritz v. Gray, 20 Ohio App. 26, 153 N.E. 187,
190 (1925).

[140] State ex rel. Fritz v. Gray, 20 Ohio App. 26, 153 N.E. 187, 189 (1925).

[141] In re Remington Typewriter Co., 234 N.Y. 296, 299, 137 N.E. 335, 336
(1922).

It has been recognized that both per-capita vote and per-share vote have a place in the conduct of modern shareholder meetings which are attended in person by a large number of shareholders, most of whom have delivered proxies in favor of the management. It is generally accepted that all questions coming before the meeting need not necessarily be decided by the shareholders on a per-share vote. It has also been generally accepted that there are certain administrative and procedural matters at a shareholders' meeting which can conveniently and fairly be determined by a per-capita vote. These matters, depending in each case on the circumstances, generally relate to the visual and audio arrangements, and matters of comfort and safety, in which all attending shareholders have equal rights. Included also would be a request by the chairman for concurrence or approval by the meeting of proposed disciplinary action against a disruptive shareholder. It must be recognized, however, that such matters may become subject to a per-share vote upon a proper demand that a poll be taken.[142]

§ 17.20   Disqualification

Disqualification from voting on a pending matter by reason of a personal interest is well established at common parliamentary law. The person so disqualified cannot be counted in making a quorum or in computing a majority of a quorum.[143]

---

[142] "We do not mean to say, of course, that any business transacted at a stockholders' meeting is invalid simply because the vote was not taken and recorded according to the number of shares voting, when there is no division or contest in reference to such matter, or where there was no objection to taking the vote otherwise, and no protest in reference to the result, but we do mean to say, as we have heretofore said, that it is the right of a stockholder to vote upon all matters at such stockholders' meeting in accordance with his interest in the corporation, as represented by the number of shares owned by him, and it is his right to have all questions determined upon that basis." State ex rel. Fritz v. Gray, 20 Ohio App. 26, 153 N.E. 187, 191 (1925).

[143] "The law, however, does not forbid the holding of an office and exercising powers thereunder because of a *possibility* of a future conflict of interest. . . . It has generally been held that the vote of a council or board member who is disqualified because of interest or bias in regard to the subject matter being considered may not be counted in determining the necessary majority for valid action. . . . It is also the rule that where the required majority exists without the vote of the disqualified member, his presence and vote will not invalidate

This rule applies generally to legislators [144] and to corporate directors and others occupying positions of trust. A director who has

---

the result and further that a majority vote need not be invalidated where the interest of a member is general or of a minor character." Anderson v. City of Parsons, 209 Kan. 337, 496 P.2d 1333, 1337 (1972).

See § 6.7.1 *supra* (quorum).

[144] It is "the common parliamentary rule that no member of a legislative assembly shall vote on any question involving his own character or conduct, his right as a member, or his pecuniary interest; but that an interest of the latter description only exists when it is immediate, particular, and distinct from the public interest. . . ." State *ex rel.* Rylands v. Pinkerman, 63 Conn. 176, 28 A. 110, 116 (1893), *citing* Cushing, Law & Pr. Leg. Assem.

"Where the private interests of a Member are concerned in a bill or question he is to withdraw. And where such an interest has appeared, his voice has been disallowed, even after a division. In a case so contrary, not only to the laws of decency, but to the fundamental principle of the social compact, which denies to any man to be a judge in his own cause, it is for the honor of the House that this rule of immemorial observance should be strictly adhered to." Constitution, Jefferson's Manual and Rules of the House of Representatives. H.R. Doc. No. 416 (1975).

"The authorities are generally in accord that a public official is not eligible to participate in a matter which affects his personal pecuniary interest. This is as true of members of municipal councils as it is of judges of courts. Public policy forbids sustaining municipal action based upon a vote of one member of its governing body on a matter which directly and immediately affects him individually." A disqualified vote is an illegal vote and must be subtracted from the otherwise legal votes cast upon the question. Hager v. State *ex rel.* Te-Vault, 446 S.W.2d 43, 49 (Tex. Civ. App. 1969) (recall of councilman).

See Baker v. Marley, 8 N.Y.2d 365, 208 N.Y.S.2d 449, 170 N.E. 2d 900 (1960) (mayor owned small interest in condemned land), *but see* J. J. Carroll, Inc. v. Waldbauer, 219 N.Y.S.2d 436 (Sup. Ct. 1961) (land owned by father of mayor); Benincasa v. Village of Rockville Centre, 215 N.Y.S.2d 575 (Sup. Ct. 1961) (mayor owned contiguous property).

A public officer has the duty of serving the public with undivided loyalty, uninfluenced in his official actions by any private interest or motive whatsoever. He may be disqualified from voting on a matter in which he is personally interested. Whether a particular interest is sufficient to disqualify is a matter of fact, depending upon the circumstances of the particular case. Actual proof of dishonesty need not be shown. The interest which disqualifies is a personal or private one, not such an interest as the public officer has in common with all other citizens. A remote and speculative personal interest will not be held to disqualify. Township Comm. of Hazlet v. Morales, 119 N.J. Super. 29, 289 A.2d 563 (1972) (mayor disqualified from breaking tie with casting vote); *accord*, Grimes v. Miller, 113 N.J.L. 553, 175 A. 152 (1934).

an adverse interest loses his character as a director and his vote is a mere nullity.[145] The rule does not apply to stockholders where there is no trust relation with other stockholders or with the corporation.[146]

There are statutory exceptions to the common parliamentary law, notably in the right of corporate directors to vote upon matters in which they have a personal interest which have been fully disclosed.[147] Also, a "rule of necessity" applies where an administrative body has a duty to act and is the only entity capable of acting in the matter, permitting an interested member to perform his duty to vote.[148]

---

[145] "A director cannot, with propriety, vote in his board of directors, in a matter affecting his private interest; but his fellow directors, who have no personal interest in the matter, may vote. If an interested director does vote, the resolution becomes voidable at the instance of the corporation or the shareholders without regard to its fairness, but this is so providing the vote of the director was essential and necessary to the passage of the resolution." *In re* Franklin Brewing Co., 263 F. 512, 514 (2d Cir. 1920).

See, e.g., Wishon-Watson Co. v. Comm'r, 66 F.2d 52 (9th Cir. 1933) (purchase of corporate assets by directors); Anderson v. Gailey, 33 F.2d 589 (N.D. Ga. 1929) (considering legal proceedings by corporation against director); *In re* Fergus Falls Woolen Mills Co., 41 F. Supp. 355 (D. Minn. 1941), *modified on other grounds*, 127 F.2d 491 (8th Cir. 1942) (dominant director); Colorado Mgmt. Corp. v. American Founders Life Ins. Co., 145 Colo. 413, 359 P.2d 665 (1961) (common directors); Osborne v. Locke Steel Chain Co., 153 Conn. 527, 218 A.2d 526 (1966) (contract between corporation and chairman of the board); Bovay v. Byllesby & Co., 38 A.2d 808 (Del. 1944) (action by trustee in bankruptcy against officers and directors); Bates Street Shirt Co. v. Waite, 130 Me. 352, 156 A. 293 (1931) (voting on salary to member whose presence is necessary to make a quorum); American Discount Corp. v. Kaitz, 348 Mass. 706, 206 N.E.2d 156 (1965) (considering lawsuit against director-trustee); Gieselmann v. Stegeman, 443 S.W.2d 127 (Mo. 1969) (election of officers); Wiberg v. Gulf Coast Land & Dev. Co., 360 S.W.2d 563 (Tex. Civ. App. 1962) (action by corporate director to recover commissions due him under contract with the corporation); Rocket Mining Corp. v. Gill, 25 Utah 2d 434, 483 P.2d 897 (1971) (director was wife of interested party); Sanders v. E-Z Park, Inc., 57 Wash. 2d 474, 358 P.2d 138 (1960) (corporation purchased assets of another, with interested director casting the deciding vote).

But see Bentall v. Koenig Bros., Inc., 140 Mont. 339, 372 P.2d 91 (1962) (no adverse interest shown).

[146] *See* § 17.3 *supra.*

[147] *See* § 6.7.1 *supra.*

[148] "The rule is well settled that where an administrative body has a duty to

VOTING METHODS

§ 17.21   General

A deliberative body, in the absence of higher authority, may prescribe its own method of voting. The body has full power to make reasonable rules and regulations governing the election of directors and officers, and the transaction of business. "In advance of a ballot, it could determine whether the election should be by plurality or by majority. It could adopt a rule permitting change of votes after a ballot but before announcement of the result by the chair. Neither custom nor practice of previous councils is of determinative value. By common consent and approval [in this case] it was understood and agreed that the election should be by a majority vote, and therefore a majority determined the choice." [1]

A deliberative body is often authorized by statute to establish its own voting procedures, including the right to compel a vote by ballot.[2]

Where no method or form of voting is prescribed by statute or by-law, any fair method may be employed. In an early case concerning the election of corporate officers, the ballots were being collected in a hat when it was seized and taken away. The inspectors finished the vote and declared elected those with a majority of votes in the possession of the inspectors. Subsequently the hat was returned and an examination showed the same result. The court held that, where no particular mode of proceeding is required

---

act upon a matter which is before it and is the only entity capable to act in the matter the fact that the members may have a personal interest in the result of the action taken does not disqualify them to perform their duty. It is a rule of necessity which has been followed consistently." Gonsalves v. City of Dairy Valley, 265 Cal. App. 2d 400, 71 Cal. Rptr. 255, 258 (1968).

The rule of necessity was sustained in 1920 when the Supreme Court concluded it could not decline or renounce jurisdiction over a case brought by a United States district court judge concerning an alleged diminution of federal judicial salaries. The court noted that its conclusion was "supported by precedents reaching back many years." Evans v. Gore, 253 U.S. 245, 248 (1920).

[1] State *ex rel.* Reed v. De Maioribus, 131 Ohio St. 201, 2 N.E.2d 506, 509 (1936).

[2] Town of Exeter v. Kenick, 104 N.H. 168, 181 A.2d 638 (1962) (town meeting).

by law and the wishes of the voters have been fairly expressed in an election conducted in good faith, it will not set aside the election on account of the informality in the manner of conducting it.[3]

Where a method or form of an election is not prescribed, a city council may elect by resolution, but when a method is prescribed, such method is mandatory. Where statute provides that appointments shall be determined by vote upon roll call of members, by statement of choice of each member, or by the yeas and nays, an appointment by resolution or ordinance is excluded.[4]

A general statute requiring the election of city officials by viva voce vote is controlling over a charter provision which calls for election by ballot.[5]

A school board, absent some statutory provision, is not required to formally decide school matters by a vote of aye or nay. "Any other method of securing the definite decisions of the respective members is sufficient so long as it enables them to determine whether a majority of the members of the board favor or oppose the proposition."[6]

A statute providing that action shall be taken "by a vote of the city council or, in a town, by vote of the inhabitants thereof" does not require that the vote be by ballot. "According to its terms, the vote might be by voice or by show of hands, as the town meeting may determine. It carries no implication that such vote by the city council be by any other than the common method."[7]

§ 17.22   Viva Voce

The term means "living voice" and signifies voting by speech or outcry as distinguished from voting by ballot.

There are three methods of adopting a resolution by viva voce vote. They are (a) by calling the roll with each member naming his choice; (b) by placing candidates in nomination and then call-

---

[3] Philips v. Wickham, 1 Paige 590 (N.Y. Ch. 1829).

[4] *In re* Heafy, 247 App. Div. 277, 285 N.Y.S. 188, *aff'd,* Heafy v. McCabe, 270 N.Y. 616, 1 N.E.2d 357 (1936).

[5] Mansfield v. O'Brien, 271 Mass. 515, 171 N.E. 487, 488 (1930).

[6] Fleming v. Board of Trustees, 112 Cal. App. 225, 296 P. 925, 926 (1931).

[7] Moloney v. Selectmen of Town of Milford, 353 Mass. 400, 149 N.E. 317, 318 (1925).

ing the roll of members; (c) by naming a candidate by resolution
and the members orally voting for it.[8]

The act of voting, whether done vocally or silently, is included
in the constitutional right of a member of Congress to immunity
from being questioned in any place for any speech or debate in
either house.[9]

A voice vote may be irregular where the question was put with
a loud voice and the same voice put the vote, and it was carried by
those who favored the motion.[10]

The difficulty in ascertaining voice vote is demonstrated in a case
where four witnesses testified—a television cameraman, a radio
newsman, and two newspaper reporters. Three testified that the
nays predominated and the fourth testified that he could not tell
whether the yeas or the nays had predominated. The chairman
had ruled that the motion carried.[11]

"The term 'viva voce,' when applied to elections, is used in opposition or contradistinction to the ballot, and simply means that the
voter shall declare himself by voice, instead of by ballot. In this
country, as a general rule, the people vote by ballot, so that their
action may be secret, free, and untrammeled; their representation
viva voce, so that their action may be public and known to their
constituents. So that when a nomination is made either by written
resolution or oral motion, and each person announces his vote for
or against it by his voice, the vote is viva voce. The manner of
choosing a clerk in this case was left to the discretion of the common
council so long as the vote was viva voce. It could have been done
by calling the roll, and each member naming his choice, or by placing candidates in nomination, and then calling the roll of members,
as was done at the meeting of May 19th, or by naming a candidate
by resolution and calling the roll, and the members orally voting
for or against it, as was done at the meeting of June 2d. Any of
these methods would be voting viva voce. The principle of public,
not secret, voting would be complied with." [12]

---

[8] Walther v. McDonald, 243 Ark. 912, 422 S.W.2d 854, 862 (1968).

[9] Kilbourn v. Thompson, 103 U.S. 168 (1881) (passing between tellers).

[10] See Kerr v. Trego, 47 Pa. 292 (1864).

[11] See McDonough v. Purcell, 44 Misc. 2d 23, 252 N.Y.S.2d 752 (Sup. Ct.
1964).

[12] In re Brearton, 44 Misc. 247, 89 N.Y.S. 893, 899 (1904).

A statute required that ordinances be passed by a majority of members of a city council on a viva voce vote entered in full in the journal. The ordinance received 6 "yea" votes, 5 "nay" votes, and one "pass" vote and was declared to be adopted. It was held that the statute did not affect this case because the term viva voce simply means that the voter declared himself by voice, instead of by ballot. "It appears that less formality is required for a 'viva voce' vote than for a secret or written ballot." [13]

"A common mode of voting in public and corporate assemblies is *viva voce*, or by a show of hands; and when, in answer to a call by the presiding officer for votes for and against a question stated, no response is made, the vote is declared in the affirmative unless objection is made at the time. Cush. Parl. Law 383, 1793. If silence of the whole assembly is equivalent to a unanimous vote in the affirmative, silence of a part of the members not voting cannot be counted against the express voice of another part voting. If those present having the right and opportunity to vote refused to exercise it, and witnessed, without objection, the passage of a by-law by the usual mode of voting, counting, and declaring, the objection of an insufficient or invalid vote, by reason of not counting non-voters present, could not afterwards be made. Refusing to vote, and neglecting to make known their presence and its power to defeat the by-law, they virtually sanctioned the acts of those who voted, and waived all objection to their validity. . . . The objection is not one of a miscount of votes, or of a false declaration and record, but of an omission to recognize those who refused to be recognized." [14]

"The action, then, of Mr. McConaughy in repudiating this roll was a mistake on his part, and the selection of the temporary chairman upon a mere viva voce vote, where there was a volume of voices both for and against the nominee, was apparently unsupported by any evidence of the right of those voting to do so. The danger of taking a vote viva voce under such circumstances is manifest, as no opportunity is presented for an objection to the reception of a vote, and the chairman, even presuming that he had personal knowledge with respect to the authority of any of the delegates, would be utterly unable to determine in the unison of voices whether all of those who participated were entitled to do so. I

[13] Payne v. Petrie, 419 S.W.2d 761, 764 (Ky. 1967).
[14] Richardson v. Union Congregational Soc'y, 58 N.H. 187, 188 (1877).

think, therefore, that when a demand was made for a roll call on the election of the temporary chairman, it should have been recognized by him, and, if such a roll was not at hand, it should have been made up of the certificates of election in the possession of the delegates." [15]

"The simplest and most expeditious manner of ascertaining the will of any assembly of persons is to call for a viva voce vote upon the question before them. The presiding officer of such assembly, whose duty it is to put the question and announce the result of the vote, when such vote is close, may often be mistaken as to the result of the vote, and may unintentionally make an erroneous announcement. The rule which makes the announcement by the presiding officer of the result of a viva voce vote conclusive, unless a division or a call of the vote is demanded, should only be applied to cases in which the announcement by such officer is honestly made, and should not be invoked in favor of a false and fraudulent announcement, or one that is clearly contrary to the actual result." [16]

The court commented as follows: "It may be sufficient to say here that in our changing times ballot voting has been extended to cover many methods beside a written ballot, and that the distinctive line between viva voce and election by ballot is becoming less distinct. The latter is constantly being extended to individual indication by voice which is in turn recorded by a secretary or machine." [17]

§ 17.23   Ayes and Noes

"How is a vote by ayes and noes taken and recorded? By calling the names of those present, and recording such as vote 'aye' as in favor of, and such as vote 'no' as opposed to, the pending resolution. As those who do not vote cannot be recorded as voting, the majority must be determined by comparing the number of those who vote 'aye' with the number of those who vote 'no.' Those who did not vote at all cannot be recorded as voting 'no,' because they did not vote 'no,' and to so record them would falsify the record." [18]

---

[15] French v. Roosevelt, 18 Misc. 307, 41 N.Y.S. 1080 (Sup. Ct. 1896).

[16] Gipson v. Morris, 31 Tex. Civ. App. 645, 73 S.W. 85, 88 (1903).

[17] City of Nevada v. Slemmons, 244 Iowa 1068, 59 N.W.2d 793, 796 (1953).

[18] Smith v. Proctor, 130 N.Y. 319, 322, 29 N.E. 312 (1891).

"It is admitted by plaintiff that there must be a quorum present to do business, or, in this case, to elect the plaintiff to the office he claims. But he claims that it appearing there was a quorum present that morning, and it not appearing there had been an adjournment since, it will be presumed that there continued to be a quorum present. We think this is undoubtedly true,—that the quorum will be presumed until it shall appear there is not one. Cush. Elect. (2d Ed.) 369. This is usually made to appear by what is called a 'division'; and this is usually had after a vote by yeas and nays, when the presiding officer announces the vote and some opposing member doubts the correctness of the announcement and demands a division, —a call of the body. Id. § 1798. And strictly speaking this is what is called a 'division.' Cush. Parl. Law. § 1814. The original purpose of a division was for the purpose of ascertaining who voted 'Aye' and who voted 'No,' and it was effected in this way: the ayes occupied one part of the hall and the noes another, and there remained until the tellers appointed counted them. In this way it came to be called a 'division.' In more modern assemblies it is more usually effected by a call of the house,—a yea or nay vote when each member's name is called. Cush. Elect. § 1615. This mode is used for two purposes,—one to determine on which side the majority voted, and also for the purpose of determining whether there is a quorum present. [Citation] In this case there was no viva voce vote preceding the roll call. With this exception, there seems to have been all done that is usually done before a division, which is now usually had by a call of the roll. Cush. Elect. § 1615. Why this was not done, we do not know. Const. U. S. art. 1, § 5, requries that in all elections under this constitution the vote shall be viva voce. And if this section applies to this election it does not mean a roll call, but a vote by voice, and not by ballot. And if the vote had been taken that way, and announced by the presiding officers in favor of plaintiff, and no division called for, the presumption contended for by plaintiff would have availed him. But when the roll was called, the name of each member voting recorded, and the tellers appointed report the number voting for plaintiff and the number voting against him,—a modern division,—we have the facts, and they must prevail over the presumption which existed in favor of a quorum before that time." [19]

---

[19] State *ex rel*. Stanford v. Ellington, 117 N.C. 158, 23 S.E. 250, 251 (1895).

§ 17.24   Show of Hands

At English common law a show of hands was taken "by counting the persons present who are entitled to vote and who choose to vote by holding up their hands." [20]

"It often happens that, on a shew of hands, the person has a majority, who on a poll, is lost in a minority; and if persons could afterwards recur to a shew of hands, there would be no certainty or regularity in elections." [21]

§ 17.25   Call for Division

The primary purpose of a call for a division of the house is to test the chair's announcement of the vote by some other method such as a vote by show of hands on a motion to postpone indefinitely (24 for and 29 against). The vote was challenged and then a division was called for and taken which resulted in a different vote (60 for and 30 against) showing that the chair's earlier announcement was obviously incorrect.[22]

§ 17.26   Miscellaneous

Other selected aspects of voting at meetings have been the subject of judicial decisions.[23]

[20] Ernest v. Loma Gold Mines, Ltd., [1897] 1 Ch. 1, 6.

[21] Anthony v. Seger, 1 Hagg. Cons. 9, 13 (Consistory Ct. of London 1789), *quoted in part* Shackleton at 41, n. 9.

See Richardson v. Union Congregational Soc'y, 58 N.H. 187, 188–89 (1877); Regina v. Vestrymen and Churchwardens of St. Pancras, [1839] 11 Adolph. & E. 15, 26; 113 E.R. 317.

[22] Pignotti v. Local #3 Sheet Metal Wkrs. Int'l Ass'n, 477 F.2d 825, 831, n.6 (8th Cir. 1973), *citing* Robert's Rules of Order.

See Regina v. Vestrymen and Churchwardens of St. Pancras, [1839] 11 A. & E. 15 (division instead of poll).

[23] A "scattering vote," Keough v. Board of Aldermen, 156 Mass. 403, 31 N.E. 387 (1892).

Proportional voting. Political party had rule that, in each meeting of county committee, each member has voting power in proportion to the last party vote for Governor in his district. However, in the absence of a rule for proportional voting in a city committee or an executive committee, the general rule prevails that each member shall have no vote. Thayer v. Ganter, 174 Misc. 394, 22 N.Y.S.2d 6 (Sup. Ct. 1940).

Voting by delegate rather than in person or by proxy. George v. Holstein-Friesian Ass'n, 238 N.Y. 513, 144 N.E. 776, 206 N.Y.S. 64 (1924).

Split vote. American Hardware Corp. v. Savage Arms Corp., 37 Del. Ch. 59, 136 A.2d 690 (1957).

Division—roll. State *ex rel.* Stanford v. Ellington, 117 N.C. 158, 23 S.E. 250 (1895).

Weighted voting. Seaman v. Fedourich, 47 Misc. 2d 26, 262 N.Y.S.2d 591 (Sup. Ct. 1965); Shilbury v. Board of Supervisors, 46 Misc. 2d 837, 260 N.Y.S.2d 931 (1965), *aff'd,* 25 App. Div. 2d 688, 267 N.Y.S.2d 1022 (1966); McDonough v. Purcell, 44 Misc. 2d 23, 252 N.Y.S.2d 752 (Sup. Ct. 1964).

Vote of union delegates, weighted and counted according to the number in the delegates' local. By-laws named Robert's Revised Manual as parliamentary guide. American Fed'n of Musicians v. Wittstein, 379 U.S. 171 (1964), *rev'g* 326 F.2d 26 (2d Cir. 1963), *aff'g* 223 F. Supp. 27 (S.D.N.Y. 1963).

Unequal numerical groups with equal voting powers. Reed v. Barton, 176 Mass. 473, 57 N.E. 961 (1900) (joint meeting of school committees).

Graduated votes per share, *i.e.,* each share not exceeding five or ten, one vote each, and then diminishing votes as the number of shares increased. Taylor v. Griswold, 14 N.J.L. 222 (Sup. Ct. 1834).

Discussion of "division." State *ex rel.* Stanford v. Ellington, 117 N.C. 158, 23 S.E. 250, 251 (1895), *citing* Cushing, Parl. Law.

Ballot by mail for conducting a labor representation election by secret ballot. NLRB v. Groendyke Transport Inc., 372 F.2d 137, 142 (10th Cir. 1967).

Cumulative voting—did not exist at common law. Hanks v. Borelli, 2 Ariz. App. 589, 411 P.2d 27 (1966).

"Australian" Ballot. *See* Hornady v. Goodman, 167 Ga. 555, 146 S.E. 173, 178 (1928); Town of Exeter v. Kenick, 104 N.H. 168, 181 A.2d 638 (1962).

Roll call described as a "modern division." Moore v. Langton, 92 R.I. 141, 167 A.2d 558, 561 (1961).

"Pass-through voting" and "circular voting" in election of corporate directors. Dal-Tran Service Co. v. Fifth Ave. Coach Lines, Inc., 14 App. Div. 2d 349, 220 N.Y.S.2d 549, 556–57 (1961).

"Pass-through voting." *See* Eisenberg, *Megasubsidiaries: The Effect of Corporate Structure on Corporate Control,* 84 HARV. L. REV. 1577 (1971).

Secret ballot—question whether voting by secret ballot at a notified membership meeting is tantamount to voting in a membership referendum conducted by secret ballot. Local No. 2, Int'l Bro. of Tel. Wkrs. v. International Bro. of Tel. Wkrs., 362 F.2d 891 (1st Cir. 1966).

Where constitution requires a secret ballot, long-established custom and usage for open ballot will not validate a vote conducted in violation of constitution. Fritsch v. Rarback, 98 N.Y.S.2d 748 (Sup. Ct. 1950).

"Notation" voting procedure. Braniff Airways, Inc. v. CAB, 379 F.2d 453, 460 (D.C. Cir. 1967); T.S.C. Motor Freight Lines, Inc., 186 F. Supp. 777, 784–86 (S.D. Tex. 1960), *aff'd per curiam sub nom.* Herrin Transp. Co. v. United States, 366 U.S. 419 (1961); Eastland Co. v. FCC, 92 F.2d 467 (D.C. Cir.), *cert. denied,* 302 U.S. 735 (1937).

"Forced choice" method of voting via a misleading ballot. *See* Young v. Hayes, 195 F. Supp. 911, 916 (D.D.C. 1961).

DUTY TO VOTE

§ 17.27   Common Law

Under common parliamentary law, a member of a deliberative body or assembly does not have a legal obligation to vote. Although it is considered to be the duty of every member in the assembly room who has an opinion on the question to vote accordingly, he may prefer to abstain. No member who was not in the room at that time can vote.[1]

§ 17.28   Directors

It has been established that a corporate director cannot discharge his corporate responsibilities in good faith and with the degree of diligence, care, and skill which an ordinary prudent man would exercise in like circumstances unless he attends and participates in regular and special meetings with reasonable regularity. He can act as a director only by participating in the deliberations of the board and exercising his right to vote. Failure to participate in the decision-making process by refusing or neglecting to vote, resulting in injury to corporate property or a waste of corporate assets, is a sign of dereliction of duty and may constitute tortious action.[2]

A dominant director cannot avoid personal liability for his acts by refusing to vote and allowing the other directors to approve actions in which he has a personal interest. The court has held that

---

[1] See Robert's Rules of Order at 193; CUSHING, MANUAL OF PARLIAMENTARY PRACTICE, New Revised Edition (1925) at 198; DEMETER'S MANUAL OF PARLIAMENTARY LAW AND PROCEDURE, Blue Book Ed. (1969) at 37, 208, 209.

On a call of the roll, it is the practice to record the names of those who answer "present" if they do not wish to vote. The results of the voting are so announced. See Robert's Rules of Order at 197 n.

"The parties are in agreement that the vote was taken in accordance with Robert's Rules of Order. The 1970 edition of Robert's Rules provided that while a member who had an opinion on a question has a duty to vote, he is nevertheless permitted to abstain because he cannot be compelled to vote. The clear implication from that provision is that an abstention is not to be counted as a vote." Rockland Woods, Inc. v. Incorporated Village of Suffern, 40 App. Div. 2d 385, 340 N.Y.S.2d 513, 514 (1973).

[2] See Chapter 5 at § 5.1 supra.

"the refusal to vote does not nullify as of course an influence and predominance exerted without a vote." [3]

§ 17.29 Stockholders

It has been held that a stockholder has no duty to attend or to vote at a meeting of stockholders even though his inaction may frustrate the conduct of corporate business. There being no legal duty to attend or vote, the court will not issue a mandatory injunction to require attendance. [4]

§ 17.30 Public Officials and Legislators

The courts have expressed the opinion that elected legislators have the duty to vote consistent with the legislative intent and that such officials should act and not refrain from acting in the discharge

---

[3] "But the argument is that by refusing to vote, he shifted the responsibility to his associates, and may reap a profit from their errors. One does not divest oneself so readily of one's duties as trustee. The refusal to vote has, indeed, this importance: it gives to the transaction the form and presumption of propriety, and requires one who would invalidate it to probe beneath the surface. . . . A dominating influence can be exerted in other ways than by a vote [citations]." Globe Woolen Co. v. Utica Gas and Elec. Co., 224 N.Y. 483, 489, 121 N.E. 378, 492 (1918); see Subin v. Goldsmith, 224 F.2d 753 (2d Cir. 1955) (defendant–directors dominated and controlled board and had conflicting self-interest).

[4] "The very nature of the corporate form is the creation by statute of an entity separate and apart from the individuals who own, manage and operate it. One who acquires corporate stock obtains an interest in the corporate assets after payment of corporate debts and a right to participate in management which he may or may not exercise. . . . The holder of shares is under no obligation whatever to the corporation other than to make full payment of the consideration for which the shares are issued. . . . As participation by a shareholder in management of corporate affairs is voluntary, it necessarily follows that no shareholder may be compelled to attend or participate in shareholders' meetings. Any different rule would contradict the distinction which separates the corporate existence from the identity of its shareholders and which vests management responsibilities in the directors." Hall v. Hall, 506 S.W.2d 42, 45 (Mo. 1974).

See § 5.8 supra.

of the important duties committed to them.[5] One court has expressed its opinion that "[i]t is an exploded notion that a member of a legislative body such as a city council can be present at a meeting, thus helping to make a quorum of the body, yet defeat the progress of legislation by refusing to vote when the roll is called. . . . Such practice oftentimes might give to one member, and frequently to an attending minority, an opportunity to accomplish by silence what could not be done by speech, and often render presence, though inactive, more powerful than entire absence. The courts, as well as law writers and parliamentarians generally, have adopted the more rational rule that if a member of such a body joins in making a quorum, and sit, his duty is to vote (unless excused for cause). . . ." [6] A recent case holds that a commissioner on a five-member city council has a duty to vote unless excused by law, and that if he does not vote he is to be counted as if he voted with the majority. The court said bluntly: "The duty to vote is present if the member is present." [7] The courts have also

[5] "The courts, as well as law writers and parliamentarians generally, have adopted the more rational rule that if a member of such a body join in making a quorum, and sit, his duty is to vote (unless excused for cause), and he will be counted as present whether or not he refuses to answer the roll call." Cromarty v. Leonard, 13 App. Div. 2d 274, 216 N.Y.S.2d 619, 623, 629, 631, aff'd, 10 N.Y.2d 915, 179 N.E.2d 710, 223 N.Y.S.2d 870 (1961).

It is contemplated that members of a legislative body will ordinarily express an opinion or cast a vote one way or the other on matters coming before them. If they choose to do otherwise, they are in no position to stultify or obstruct the action of others in the performance of their official duty. Opinion of the Justices, 98 N.H. 530, 98 A.2d 635 (1953).

A local draft board can take action only by voting. In re Shapiro, 392 F.2d 397, 400 (3d Cir. 1968).

[6] State ex rel. Young v. Yates, 19 Mont. 239, 47 P. 1004 (1897) (city council), quoted in Cromarty v. Leonard, supra note 5 at 216 N.Y.S.2d 623.

See § 17.8 supra.

Those who are present, and who help to make up the quorum, are "expected to vote on every question." Rushville Gas Co. v. City of Rushville, 121 Ind. 206, 23 N.E. 72, 73 (1889).

[7] "Our conclusion is supported by the better logic of the cases holding that a passed vote is to be counted with the majority, by the argument that a member of a governmental body who is present has a duty to vote and cannot avoid taking a stand (particularly where a statute . . . compels a record of the yeas and nays and does not refer to abstentions), by the importance of pre-

distinguished the "mandatory duty" of a legislative body to elect officers from the mere right of the body to pass a resolution or not pass it, according to the wisdom and judgment of the members.[8]

Although the courts have expressed the opinion that a legislator has the duty to vote under many circumstances, it is generally acknowledged that the courts cannot "make him vote." [9] There is an exception where the legislator may have a statutory obligation to exercise a particular function. For example, when the law provides that the township trustees shall meet biennially on a certain day and appoint a county superintendent, it has been held that mandamus may be invoked to compel the trustees to meet and to so appoint.[10]

Although the court may order an official to meet and act, it will not attempt to control the exercise of discretion in voting. Mandamus generally will not issue to control or regulate a general course of conduct nor will it be granted in anticipation of a supposed omission of duty. It has been held that: "As a general rule mandamus will lie to enforce ministerial acts or duties, and further to require the exercise of discretion, but not to control the discretion."

---

venting impotence of government caused by refusal of members to act, and because such a result avoids the possibility (not hinted at here by the parties) of placement of employees on boards by interested parties for the purpose of obstructive inaction." Northwestern Bell Tel. Co. v. Board of Comm'rs, 211 N.W.2d 399, 404 (N.D. 1973).

See Attorney General v. Shepard, 62 N.H. 383 (1882) (rules of board of aldermen required every member present at meeting to vote when a question was put, unless excused by the board. When called upon by the chairman to vote, three members refused to do so. Their refusal to vote was described by the court as "inoperative").

[8] Plantz v. Board of Supervisors, 122 Misc. 576, 580–81, 204 N.Y.S. 27, 30 (1924) (statutory duty of county supervisors to elect chairman and clerk).

See State ex rel. Young v. Yates, 19 Mont. 239, 47 P. 1004 (1897) (no distinction under law between nomination for office and business proceedings).

[9] Cromarty v. Leonard, 13 App. Div. 2d 274, 216 N.Y.S.2d 619, 631, aff'd, 10 N.Y.2d 915, 179 N.E.2d 710, 223 N.Y.S.2d 870 (1961) (dissenting opinion).

[10] Wampler v. State, 148 Ind. 557, 47 N.E. 1068 (1897), citing Robert's Rules of Order on quorum.

When supervisors neglect to perform any duty required of them at an annual meeting, they may be compelled by mandamus to meet again and to perform. In some cases they may be liable to a penalty for their neglect. People v. Supervisors of Chenango, 8 N.Y. 317 (1853).

Thus, the court will not "regulate the future conduct" of a city council by requiring it to exercise discretion and by "controlling that discretion" by saying "You have to vote, and your vote must be such as is consistent with [the program being considered]. This court cannot substitute its judgment for that of the councilmen." [11]

Sometimes a presiding officer is required by law to vote when there is a tie. Under a statute providing that a village mayor may vote on all matters coming before the board of trustees and that he shall vote in case of a tie, it has been held that the mayor has only one vote whether he votes voluntarily or to break a tie. "He need not always vote. He is obligated to vote only when there is a tie. In all other instances, he may vote or not as he pleases." [12]

The courts have distinguished between compelling attendance at a meeting and coercing the member to vote when he attends. A village council of five members, with two vacancies, needed a quorum of three before it could vote to fill the vacancies. One of the remaining councilmen refused to attend and thus prevented the council from acting. The court said it had not been demonstrated that the dissident councilman "could not be compelled by lawful process to perform his duty of attending a called meeting of the council as distinguished from being coerced to vote" upon attending the meeting. The court remarked: "There is no excuse for the existence of such hiatus. However, a temporary hiatus is preferable to creating a condition whereby two of the remaining councilmen, upon their caprice, whim or fancy, can govern the city." [13]

Statutory requirements that every member present at a meeting shall vote on every question, unless disqualified, are not uncommon.[14] It has also been held that under some statutes, an authorized presiding officer is "expressly required" to discharge the duty of voting in case of a tie.[15]

[11] Mihocka v. Ziegler, 28 Ohio Misc. 105, 274 N.E.2d 583, 584, 585 (1971).

[12] Anson v. Starr, 198 Misc. 982, 101 N.Y.S.2d 948, 949–50 (1950).

[13] Clark v. North Bay Village, 54 So. 2d 240, 242 (Fla. 1951).

[14] See In re Shapiro, 392 F.2d 397 (3d Cir. 1968) (local draft board regulation provided: "Every member present, unless disqualified, shall vote on every question or classification").

[15] County auditor was expressly required to discharge the duty of voting in case of a tie in vote by township trustees. State ex rel. Morris v. McFarland, 149 Ind. 266, 49 N.E. 5 (1898).

The body may, by rule or regulation, require that all members vote aye or nay unless duly excused. The rules of the U. S. House of Representatives, for example, provide that every member shall be present during sittings of the House unless excused or necessarily prevented, and "shall vote on each question put, unless he has a direct personal or pecuniary interest" in the event of such question.[16] However, it has been found impracticable to enforce this provision requiring every member to vote, and the House has not been able to enforce the rule since it was first challenged in 1832.[17] The weight of authority also favors the idea that there is no authority in the House to deprive a member of the right to vote due to a conflict of interest. The member himself should determine that question.[18]

The rules of the United States Senate provide that when the yeas and nays are ordered, each Senator shall without debate declare his assent or dissent to the question, unless excused by the Senate; and that, when a Senator declines to vote on call of his name, he be required to assign his reasons therefor, and the presiding officer shall then submit the question to the Senate for decision, without debate. The Senate is free to accept or reject a request to be excused from voting. When a Senator has declined to vote on call of his name, and, the Senate having refused to excuse him, he again declines to vote, proceedings may be taken against him after the roll call and before the result is announced.[19]

[16] Rule VIII, House of Representatives. In the House of Commons every member must give his vote the one way or the other. *See* reference in Constitution, Jefferson's Manual, and Rules of the House of Representatives (1967), § 505 at 245.

[17] In a case relating to a quorum on a roll call of the house of representatives of North Carolina, the court commented: "And if they were present, whether they could have been compelled to vote is not before us, as there was no such proposition made, so far as we know. But it seems to be conceded that the speaker of the house of representatives of the United States could not compel a member to vote. Nor had he any right to count members present and not voting, to make a quorum, until the houses adopted a rule to that effect." State *ex rel.* Stanford v. Ellington, 117 N.C. 158, 23 S.E. 250, 251 (1895), *citing* Cushing on other points.

[18] Constitution, Jefferson's Manual, and Rules of the House of Representatives (1965), §§ 656–58; V Hinds' Precedents at 497–99; ROBERT, PARLIAMENTARY LAW at 525.

[19] Rule XII, Standing Rules of the Senate, Senate Procedure (1974) at 885–86, 894–95; Senate Manual (1975) at 13, 14.

MOTIVE FOR VOTE

§ 17.31 Legislators

The motive of one who votes or abstains from voting is generally
irrelevant. He may vote in his own self-interest or he may refrain
from voting, unless he is is serving in a representative capacity or
has fiduciary obligations which disqualify him from acting freely.[1]

It is a familiar principle of constitutional law that the courts will
not inquire into the voting motives of elected members of a legislative body, and will not strike down an otherwise constitutional
satute on the basis of an alleged illicit legislative motive. The
Supreme Court has said: "What motivates one legislator to make a
speech about a statute is not necessarily what motivates scores of
others to enact it, and the stakes are sufficiently high for us to
eschew guesswork." [2]

[1] See §§ 17.3 and 17.4 supra.

[2] United States v. O'Brien, 391 U.S. 367, 382, 384 (1968).

It is not "consonant with our scheme of government" for a court to inquire
into the motives of legislators. Tenney v. Brandhove, 341 U.S. 367, 377
(1951).

See Arizona v. California, 283 U.S. 423, 455 (1931) (good collection of
cases on motive for voting).

"We cannot inquire into motives of a legislator, nor can we make him vote."
Cromarty v. Leonard, 13 App. Div. 2d 274, 216 N.Y.S.2d 619, 631 (dissenting
opinion), aff'd, 10 N.Y.2d 915, 179 N.E.2d 710, 223 N.Y.S.2d 870 (1961).

"In a legal sense the object or purpose of legislation is to be determined by
its natural and reasonable effect, whatever may have been the motives upon
which the legislators acted." New York ex rel. Parke, Davis & Co. v. Roberts,
171 U.S. 658, 681 (1898) (dissenting opinion).

"Inquiry into the hidden motives which may move Congress to exercise a
power constitutionally conferred upon it is beyond the competency of courts."
Sonzinsky v. United States, 300 U.S. 506, 513 (1937).

"It should be pointed out that the *application* of the Government in the
Sunshine Law is not dependent upon the good intentions, sincerity of purpose
or noble motives of the public body when it proceeds to act in the shade.
The gravamen is the *doing* of the very act itself rather than the *motivation* for
the doing of the act." IDS Properties, Inc. v. Town of Palm Beach, 279 So.
2d 353, 357 (Fla. App. 1973), aff'd, 296 So. 2d 233 (1974).

Whether a councilman relied on or was influenced by his constituent's
viewpoints is not a matter for judicial inquiry; his motives in voting to adopt
or reject an ordinance may not be inquired into. Breiner v. Los Angeles, 22
Cal. App. 3d 382, 99 Cal. Rptr. 180 (1972).

§ 17.32   Administrative Agencies

The courts will not "probe the mental processes" of members of an administrative tribunal in voting, absent a showing, clearly revealed, that the members did not make an independent appraisal of the pending matter and did not reach an independent judgment.[3] Thus, members of an administrative agency need not indicate the reasons for making their decisions,[4] unless there is a statutory requirement that they indicate the reasons for their action.[5]

The court will not inquire into motives activating members of municipal governing bodies in determining whether action taken is valid, where members are acting within the scope of their powers, unless complaining parties can prove bad faith or fraud. Campbell v. Commissioners, 139 A.2d 493 (Del. 1958).

It is a general rule that the court in passing on the validity of an ordinance will not inquire into the motives of a municipal legislative body. Brumley v. Town of Greeneville, 33 Tenn. App. 322, 274 S.W.2d 12 (1954).

Unanimous rejection of a nomination for whatever reason, including custom of "Senatorial courtesy," is sufficient to meet the "advice and consent" provision of the Constitution. Kligerman v. Lynch, 92 N.J. Super. 373, 223 A.2d 511 (1966), cert. denied, 389 U.S. 822 (1967).

"Council in determining whether its advice and consent should be given to the removal of a public officer may adopt any reasonable methods of forming a proper judgment. . . ." Murphy v. Casey, 300 Mass. 232, 15 N.E.2d 268, 271 (1938).

"The courts cannot inquire into the motive of the defendants in pressing and procuring the enactment of this ordinance, or of the mayor and general council of Atlanta in enacting the same; nor can they set the same aside, if it is not arbitrary and unreasonable, is not ultra vires, or is not unconstitutional." South Georgia Power Co. v. Baumann, 169 Ga. 649, 151 S.E. 513, 515 (1929).

[3] Taub v. Pirnie, 3 N.Y.2d 188, 165 N.Y.S.2d 1, 4 (1957) (zoning board); accord, Kilgus v. Board of Estimate, 308 N.Y. 620, 127 N.E.2d 705 (1955).

[4] A local draft board need not make findings of fact or conclusions of law or indicate reasons for its decision. The court will assume the board relied on whatever factual basis is reflected in the record. If the board states its reasons, and these reasons are found to be legally insufficient to support the board's action, the decision should be found to be without a basis in fact. Owens v. United States, 396 F.2d 540 (10th Cir.), cert. denied, 393 U.S. 934 (1968).

It is "not the function of the court to probe the mental processes" of administrative officers. Morgan v. United States, 304 U.S. 1, 18 (1938), quoted in Braniff Airways, Inc. v. CAB, 379 F.2d 453 (D.C. Cir. 1967).

[5] See, e.g., Board of Educ. v. Montgomery County, 237 Md. 191, 205 A.2d 202 (1964) (reason required for denial of budget item by school board).

In determining whether a majority of a quorum voted in favor of a certain motion or resolution, it is not necessary that the minimum number of affirmative votes were cast for the same reasons. Thus, when two members of a regulatory agency agree and a third concurs in the result, the decision will not be denied enforcement because the third member did not enumerate his grounds or reasons for concurrence.[6] A presumption of regularity prevails,[7] and it may be presumed that when members of a regulatory body make decisions, they have "conscientiously considered the issues and adverted to the view of their colleagues."[8]

§ 17.33   Directors

The same rule applies to the vote of corporate directors in the absence of fraud. If a board of directors has power to adopt a resolution, the motive of its members in doing so is not a "legitimate question for discussion. . . . The courts are concerned with the rights of parties to act, not with the motives that induced them to act. If the legality of the act of a director of a corporation depended upon the motive which actuated him, every act of the directory might be questioned, and its validity would depend, not upon the rights of the parties under the law, but upon the ethical reasons which had induced the directors to exercise their legitimate powers."[9] A board of directors has the power to adopt new reasonable by-laws regulating the conduct of corporate meetings and prescribing qualifications for the office of director including procedures for shareholder nominations of candidates for election as a director in opposition to the management's slate. The purpose, intent, or motive behind the adoption of such by-laws is immaterial and is not a matter of judicial inquiry. The court concluded that "the sole

[6] A commissioner may concur in the result without enumerating the grounds for his concurrence nor the conclusions or findings upon which he based his concurrence. Flothill Products Inc. v. FTC, 358 F.2d 224, 230 (9th Cir. 1966), rev'd on other grounds, 389 U.S. 179 (1967).

[7] Presumption of validity attaches to public proceedings and formal recitations of public officials. Willapoint Oysters v. Ewing, 174 F.2d 676, 696 (9th Cir.), cert. denied, 338 U.S. 860 (1949).

[8] Braniff Airways, Inc. v. CAB, 379 F.2d 453, 460 (D.C. Cir. 1967).

[9] Haldeman v. Haldeman, 176 Ky. 635, 197 S.W. 376, 379 (1917).

question is the reasonableness of the new by-laws and not *why* or *for what reason* they were adopted." [10]

§ 17.34   Stockholders

The court will not inquire into the motives of stockholders in casting their votes at a stockholders' meeting.[11]

POLLING THE VOTE

§ 17.35   Common Law

A vote of some kind is the proper way to ascertain the choice of the members present and entitled to vote at the meeting. The voting may be conducted by various methods such as by a show of hands, by acclamation, by ballot, by division, or by a poll.[1]

A poll, in the strict meaning of the term, is a head count for the purpose of registering the numerical result of the voting. In the parliamentary sense, to poll is to vote, and the poll is the voting or the number of votes cast. The term may also be used to indicate the place where votes are taken.

---

[10] McKee Co. v. First Nat'l Bank, 265 F. Supp. 1, 13 (S.D. Cal. 1967), *aff'd*, 397 F.2d 248 (9th Cir. 1968).

[11] "The question of influence exerted upon other stockholders through the domination and control of the defendants to vote against the resolution and the question of the effect upon stockholders of the letter sent to them . . . would involve an inquiry by the court into the motives which actuated each stockholder in depositing his vote which it is beyond the power or policy of the courts to pursue. Every stockholder was fully informed of the decree of the court by the special master and of the questions involved. He had a right to give his proxy to whomsoever he desired, and his motives for voting, can no more be inquired into now than they could prior to the stockholders' meeting. It must be assumed that every stockholder was reasonably capable of deciding questions of business policy for himself, and if the court could not have determined that for him in advance, it cannot determine it for him now." DuPont v. DuPont, 251 F. 937, 945 (1918), *modified*, 256 F. 129 (3d Cir. 1919).

[1] For discussion of common-law poll, *see* SHACKLETON, LAW AND PRACTICE OF MEETINGS at 40; SHAW AND SMITH, THE LAW OF MEETINGS at 82; JOSKE, THE LAW AND PROCEDURE AT MEETINGS, at 138–39; CURRY (CREW), PUBLIC, COMPANY AND LOCAL GOVERNMENT at 59. *See also* United States v. Ballin, 144 U.S. 1, 6 (1892).

At common law, every member present and voting at the meeting is reckoned as one vote, and the method of determining votes is by a show of hands.[2] At common law, moreover, any voter, however satisfied or dissatisfied with the correctness of the declaration on the show of hands, has the right to demand a poll to obtain an accurate and complete count of the vote and to keep the poll open until all have had the opportunity of attending to record their suffrage.[3] All qualified voters are entitled to vote at the poll, even if they were not present at the meeting.[4]

[2] "We will first of all consider what may be termed the common law of the county as to voting at meetings. It is undoubted, [and counsel admitted] that, according to such common law, votes at all meetings are taken by show of hands." *In re* Horbury Bridge, Coal, Iron & Waggon Co., 11 Ch. D. 109, 115 (1879).

Early English corporation law (Companies Act of 1862) was framed upon the assumption that the mode of voting when a poll was not demanded, then well known, would be "by show of hands—i.e., by counting the persons present who were entitled to vote and who chose to vote by holding up their hands." Accordingly, the chairman must count the vote of each person who holds up his hand as a single vote, not a vote for each proxy held. Ernest v. Loma Gold Mines, Ltd., [1897] 1 Ch. 1.

[3] Regina v. Vestrymen and Churchwardens of St. Pancras, (1839) 11 Adolph. & E. 15.

The court will recognize the right of a majority to demand a poll even where the majority is technically counted as less than three members needed to demand a poll under the articles. Cory v. Reindeer Steamship (Ltd.), (1915) 31 T.L.R. 531.

[4] A resolution was passed at a meeting limiting the right of voting to the persons actually present. The court held: "There is no doubt of the law; that the ratepayers in the vestry are to elect, and that, if a poll be demanded, it should be kept open for all qualified persons. If any single person had been excluded in the present case, it might have been a reason for demanding that the election should be set aside. . . ." Regina v. Rector, Churchwardens & Parishioners of St. Mary, 8 Adolph. & E. 356, 361 (Q.B. 1838).

.There is some question whether persons not present at a show of hands can afterward vote on a poll being granted. In an early English case it was argued that in strictness they could not. "The common law assumption seems to be, that all who have a right to vote are present when the shew of hands is taken. A poll in many cases, as for instance on the question who is to be chairman (if indeed it can be taken at all on such a question), must be confined to parties present at the time when the question arises: and the law must be the same as to other questions." Campbell v. Maund, 5 Adolph. & E. 865, 874 (Ex. Cham. 1836).

Early English corporation law also adopted the means of taking a poll, in corporate voting, to determine the number of votes by shares where a show of hands would not fairly represent the per-share vote.[5] A poll is thus a necessary incident to or an enlargement of the mode of voting by a show of hands.[6] A demand for a poll is a means also of challenging the declaration of the chairman on the results of the voting upon a show of hands.[7] Unless a poll is demanded after a vote by show of hands, the declaration of the presiding officer is generally deemed to be conclusive evidence of the results of the voting and his ruling cannot be impeached.[8]

[5] The court remarked that a show of hands might not always be satisfactory because "persons attending in large numbers may be small shareholders, and persons attending in small numbers may be large shareholders" and therefore provision was made for taking a poll at company meetings, and when a poll is taken the votes are to be counted according to the number of shares. *In re* Horbury Bridge, Coal, Iron & Waggon Co., 11 Ch. D. 109, 115 (1879).

[6] "Under the old system of parliamentary election candidates were chosen upon a show of hands, and a poll was demanded on behalf of him who had the smaller number. A poll is a mere enlargement of the meeting." The court also noted that: "A poll is not a new meeting, but it is a mode of ascertaining the sense of the meeting which is continued for that purpose. . . ." Regina v. Wimbledon Local Bd., 8 Q.B.D. 459, 462, 464 (1882).

"The question, therefore, becomes this: whether the right to demand a poll is by law incidental to the election of a parish officer by shew of hands, where there is no special custom to exclude it?

"And we think such right is, in point of law, a necessary incident, or consequence, to the mode of election by shew of hands, wherever it is not by special custom excluded. Independently of any authority upon the subject, the recourse to a poll, where the population of the parish is large, appears to be the only mode of ascertaining, with precision, the numbers of those who vote on each side, and the right of each elector to vote. Again, it is, under the same circumstances, the only mode by which each individual elector can have the power of expressing his opinion at all; for, in the case of populous parishes, no vestry-room can be large enough to contain the whole body. Still further, where the election is carried on with any warmth of popular feeling, it is the only mode by which a large portion of the community can express their opinion with freedom and security." Campbell v. Maund, 5 Adolph. & E. 865, 879–80 (Ex. Cham. 1836).

[7] *See* State *ex rel.* Stanford v. Ellington, 117 N.C. 158, 23 S.E. 250, 251 (1895).

[8] *In re* Hadleigh Castle Gold Mines Ltd., [1900] 2 Ch. 419, 421–23; *see In re* Gold Co., 11 Ch. D. 701 (1879). This rule does not apply to a false and fraudulent announcement. Gipson v. Morris, 31 Tex. Civ. App. 645, 73 S.W. 85 (1903).

§ 17.36 Chairman

The proper person to grant a poll on the demand of a voter is the chairman,[9] who also has the right to direct a poll without first taking a show of hands and even though a poll was not demanded by a voter. In fact, the duty of the chairman is to ascertain the sense of the meeting upon any resolution properly coming before it, and he possesses the power to demand a poll for that purpose. A chairman who permits a vote by show of hands and fails to demand a poll knowing that the true sense of the meeting cannot be ascertained in the absence of a poll, fails in his duty as chairman and the resolution by show of hands will not properly be carried.[10]

The chairman cannot relieve himself of the duty to conduct a poll by leaving the chair when a doubt has been raised. Where a motion to adjourn a city council was made and carried, but was immediately doubted, the presiding officer had the duty under the council rules at once to resolve the doubt by requiring the members to rise and stand until they were counted. "That would be his duty if there were no such rule." The presiding officer having left the chair and having ceased to preside did not relieve himself of his duty, and the members were obligated to choose someone else to act in his place and to proceed to resolve the doubt. Having resolved the doubt without objection from anybody by deciding that the motion to adjourn was not carried, the meeting may proceed to do business, notwithstanding an irregularity in the procedures resolving the doubt.[11]

[9] "A poll is then demanded: and it is demandable as of right; and the president of the meeting is the person to grant it. In the absence of other business, the poll should be taken immediately: if time does not allow of that, there must be an adjournment for the purpose." The person who presides at the meeting is the proper person to direct the adjournment, not the majority. "It is on him that it devolves, both to preserve order in the meeting, and to regulate the proceedings so as to give all persons entitled a reasonable opportunity of voting." Regina v. D'Oyly, 12 Adolph. & E. 139, 159 (Q.B. 1840).

[10] However, the chairman need not demand a poll unless it might change the result of the voting, as in the case of contesting the right of certain persons to vote or contesting the number of votes cast for and against. Second Consol. Trust, Ltd. v. Ceylon Amalg. Tea & Rubber Estates, Ltd., [1943] 2 All. E. R. 567, 569 (Ch.).

[11] Pevey v. Aylward, 205 Mass. 102, 91 N.E. 315, 316 (1910).

The chairman may also make necessary arrangements for taking a poll if one is demanded. In an early English case involving the election of churchwardens, the notice provided that the meeting would be held in the church but if a poll should be demanded the meeting would be adjourned to the town hall. A poll was demanded and the meeting moved to the town hall. The court held: "This is not properly an adjournment. May not the chairman appoint a convenient place for taking the poll?" [12]

§ 17.37   Demand

The demand for a poll is an abandonment and invalidation of the voting by show of hands, and the voting proper begins with the poll. "Where a poll is demanded, the election commences with it, as being the regular mode of popular elections; the shew of hands being only a rude and imperfect declaration of the sentiments of the electors. It often happens that, on a shew of hands, the person has a majority, who on a poll, is lost in a minority; and if persons could afterwards recur to a shew of hands, there would be no certainty or regularity in elections. I am of the opinion therefor, that when a poll is demanded it is an abandonment of what has

---

The court will not require the chairman to take a poll on the question of adjournment, where the charter gave the chairman power, with the consent of the meeting, to adjourn the meeting and also to take a poll if demanded. This would be an unlawful interference by the court in the internal management of the company. "There was no ground under the articles of the company, or otherwise, for holding that a poll could not be taken upon whether the meeting of the company should be adjourned or not, especially when by the motion for adjournment the question before the meeting was, whether certain important matters should then be discussed and voted, or whether they should be postponed for a long or indefinite time." MacDougall v. Gardiner, (1875) 1 Ch. D. 13, 17.

[12] The court added: "Those who summon a meeting of this kind must necessarily lay down some order for the proceedings; and I think it is competent to them to say that the meeting shall be held in one place, and, in a certain event which may require it, shall be removed to another." Rex v. Archdeacon of Chester, 1 Adolph. & E. 342, 344, 345 (K.B. 1834).

See Rex v. Churchwardens of St. Mary, 1 Adolph. & E. 346 (K.B. 1832) where, on demand for poll, the chairman adjourned the meeting from the schoolhouse to the church, without previous notice of possible adjournment.

been done before; and that everything anterior is not of the substance of the election, nor to be so received." [13]

A demand for a poll should be made immediately upon the conclusion of taking the vote by a show of hands and before the
conduct of any other business, unless otherwise prescribed by regulation.[14] Whether other business has commenced is a question of
fact in each case.[15] The demand for a poll need not be in writing
and does not require a second; and it cannot be withdrawn after a
meeting has come to an end nor privately after it has once been
accepted.[16] However, when a member demands a roll call to resolve the question whether the chair erred in a ruling on a motion
made by the member, and then walks out of the meeting without
pressing his demand, it is obvious that he has waived his right to a
roll call and has abandoned his motion.[17]

The chairman need not conduct a poll unless he believes that it
would serve a useful purpose. The maneuver of demanding a poll
will not serve a useful purpose when the management proxy committee holds sufficient proxies to control the meeting and this fact
is known to the assembled stockholders. Under such circumstances,
it is suggested that the chairman rule the demand out of order as
being a dilatory motion which need not be recognized nor put to a
vote by the chair.

[13] Anthony v. Seger, 1 Hagg. Cons. 9, 13 (Consistory Ct. of London 1789),
quoted in part in Shackleton at 41, n. 9.

[14] *See* Regina v. D'Oyly, 12 Adolph. & E. 139 (Q.B. 1840).

[15] The result of a show of hands on a motion to adjourn was questioned.
Moderator called for a poll, which affirmed a majority vote to adjourn. It was
then moved that the meeting proceed to elect a town representative and the
moderator arranged the ballot box and checklist for that purpose. The vote
was again questioned. It was held that making of arrangements to conduct an
election, including ballot box and checklist, did not constitute commencement
of business if ballots have not yet been received. Kimball v. Lamprey, 19 N.H.
215 (1848).

[16] It was concluded that several persons could demand a poll and that the
demand could not be withdrawn after separation of the meeting. To allow
the demand to be withdrawn privately "might lead to all manner of collusion."
Rex v. Mayor of Dover, [1903] 1 K.B. 668.

[17] The court added: "There is no evidence of any probative value to the
effect that a roll call vote would have been denied if petitioner and his sup-
porters had remained and persisted in their demand." McDonough v. Purcell,
44 Misc. 2d 23, 252 N.Y.S.2d 752, 755 (Sup. Ct. 1964).

BALLOT

§ 17.38 Meaning of Term

A vote may be taken by the use of a ballot. Where a statute or ordinance requires that the method of election shall be by ballot, then all the common-law rules which apply to that method of acting must be observed. No rule can be established by custom or otherwise which would be in derogation of the law, or would substantially affect the determination of the majority, otherwise than according to the principles of the common law.[1]

The terms "vote" and "ballot" are often used interchangeably.[2] More precisely, a ballot is a piece of paper designed to show the voters' choice,[3] while a vote is the choice itself. The word "ballot" primarily signifies "a little ball." As used in statutes providing for

---

[1] Murdoch v. Strange, 99 Md. 89, 57 A. 628 (1904) (holding that a blank ballot cannot be considered in counting the total vote).

A statute may preserve to a town the right to establish procedures for the taking of votes, including the right to compel a vote by ballot. Town of Exeter v. Kenick, 104 N.H. 168, 181 A.2d 638 (1962).

[2] In construing a statute providing a penalty for making a false count of an election, there is no distinction between a miscount of votes and miscount of the ballots themselves, as the words "vote" and "ballot" are to be treated as interchangeable. State v. Doughty, 134 Ark. 435, 204 S.W. 968, 969 (1918).

[3] "The word 'vote' means suffrage, voice, or choice of a person for or against a measure or the election of any person to office. It is not synonymous with 'ballot,' which is merely the means or instrument by which the person votes, or rather expresses his choice or exercises his right of suffrage." Straughan v. Meyers, 268 Mo. 580, 187 S.W. 1159, 1162 (1916).

"A ballot is a form of expression for a candidate to be voted for. If the paper falls short of expressing such a wish, it is defective; certainly, if it expresses nothing, it lacks all of the essential elements of a ballot. If it contains the name of a man who is known to the voter to be ineligible the ballot cannot be counted, because the object of [the] ballot then would be not to elect, but to prevent an election." Murdoch v. Strange, 99 Md. 89, 57 A. 628, 629 (1904) (city council), *quoting* Cushing, Law & Pr. Leg. Assem.

See Johnson v. Clark, 25 F. Supp. 285, 286 (N.D. Tex. 1938) (definition of ballot in public election).

"A ballot may be defined to be a piece of paper, or other suitable material, with the names written or printed upon it of the persons to be voted for." Attorney General *ex rel.* Woodbury v. Bickford, 77 N.H. 433, 92 A. 835, 836 (1914), *citing* Cushing, Law & Pr. Leg. Assem. § 103.

the election of corporate officers when required to be elected by ballot, the word means "a paper so prepared by printing or writing thereon as to show the voter's choice." [4] The word "ballot" is also used as a symbol of secrecy, while "viva voce" is used as a symbol of publicity.[5]

There is no prescribed form of ballot to be used at meetings of deliberative assemblies, although the charter or by-laws of the body may specify a method. In the absence of a prescription, any form of ballet may be used which will show the voter's choice. A form of ballot which may be identified, as by color or symbol, should not be used as its secrecy has been destroyed.[6] In the absence of a charter or by-law requirement, a ballot in a corporate election need not be signed. And, in the absence of proof that an unsigned ballot is contrary to established practice and custom of the corporation, the inspectors may accept an unsigned ballot as being properly cast and valid.[7]

[4] *In re* P. B. Mathiason Mfg. Co., 122 Mo. App. 437, 99 S.W. 502, 504 (1907).

"There are many ways of ascertaining the will of the majority in an election, as, for instance, by a viva voce vote, or by a show of hands, or by dividing the house, or by ballot, and there are various kinds of ballots. The word 'ballot' indicates a little ball, and it is common knowledge that little balls are used in social clubs and other society elections to determine whether a candidate for membership shall be admitted or not, and usually this is determined by the presence of one or more black balls, which are generally sufficient under the rules to defeat the election. In such balloting it is absolutely necessary to name the candidate before the balloting in order that the voters may know for or against whom they are voting. And in balloting with paper ballots marked, respectively, 'Yes,' and 'No,' it would be just as necessary to name the candidate. But, where the name is written or printed on the ballot, it might well be called a nomination and ballot because it is itself evidence of both. By simply counting the ballots and names thereon the election, except in the case of a tie vote, is determined." Wirth v. Fehlberg, 30 R.I. 536, 76 A. 438, 439 (1910).

[5] Payne v. Petrie, 419 S.W.2d 761, 764 (Ky. 1967), *quoting from* Day v. Walker, 124 Neb. 500, 247 N.W. 350, 351 (1933).

[6] The use by one party of ballots with engraved symbols destroys the secrecy of the ballot in that a person offering a ballot without that marking is shown to be anti-party. *See* Commonwealth v. Woelper, 3 S. & R. 29 (Pa. 1817).

Cf. Wood v. Cutter, 138 Mass. 149 (1884) (suggesting that the secrecy of a ballot may be destroyed on a vote to reconsider).

[7] State *ex rel.* Dunbar v. Hohmann, 248 S.W.2d 49 (Mo. 1952).

When a voter marks a ballot in an obviously incorrect manner, such as voting cumulatively under the mistaken impression that votes could be cumulated, the ballot can be examined by the inspectors to determine the voter's intent.[8] The voter of an improperly marked ballot is a person "present and voting" at the meeting.[9]

The writing of a name on a printed ballot raises the presumption that it was the voter's intention to vote for the person whose name was written in, although the voter failed to strike out the name already printed on the ballot. This follows the general rule of law that, where there is any repugnancy between the written and the printed portion of an instrument, the written portion will ordinarily prevail. The intention of the voter may be presumed from or determined by the particular circumstances of each case.[10] When there

---

[8] Cumulative votes were counted as straight votes for the persons designated. Standard Scale & Supply Corp. v. Chappel, 15 Del. Ch. 333, 138 A. 74 (1927), *rev'd on other grounds*, 16 Del. Ch. 331, 141 A. 191 (1928).

[9] "The terms 'members present and voting' must be regarded in their acceptation as including all those members present and who have purported *to vote*. Certainly, no one could reasonably argue that the voter of an improperly marked ballot, or a coerced ballot, should not be included in determining whether or not a majority of the votes of those 'present and voting' has been obtained. Any other result would put a premium upon the deliberate invalidation of the voting in local unions where the prevailing administration did not believe it could succeed and leave only for valid balloting those local unions, where the administration's position was deemed 'safe.'" Fritsch v. Rarback, 98 N.Y.S.2d 748 (Sup. Ct. 1950).

[10] "The intention of the voter is to be inferred, not from evidence given by him of the mental purpose with which he deposited his ballot, or his notions of the legal effect of what it contained or omitted, but by a reasonable construction of his acts. His writing a name upon a ballot in connection with the title of an office, is such a designation of the name for that office as to satisfy the statute, although he omits to strike out a name printed upon it in connection with the same office. The writing is to prevail as the highest evidence of his intention. The judge ought to have charged the jury, as a matter of law, that they were bound to find the fact accordingly from the face of the ballot itself." People v. Saxton, 22 N.Y. 309, 311 (1860), *distinguished in* People *ex rel.* Thorn v. Pangburn, 3 App. Div. 456, 38 N.Y.S. 217 (1st Dep't 1896).

A person may be elected to office through "write-ins" of his name on the ballot; it is not necessary that he should be placed in nomination. Where the constitution provides that shareholders may vote for "candidates," a by-law which provides that votes can be cast only for "nominees" would be invalid. Commonwealth *ex rel.* Laughlin v. Green, 351 Pa. 170, 40 A.2d 492 (1945).

is more than one candidate and the controlling statute permits the shareholder to cast the whole number of his votes for one candidate or distribute them among two or more candidates, the shareholder may write on the ballot the names of the person or persons for whom he desires to vote, and the number of votes he wishes to cast for each individual voted for. When he fails to note the number of votes cast opposite the names of the persons for whom he voted he has "destroyed the efficacy of his ballot." He can complete his ballot by writing in the number of votes cast for each nominee, but if he declines to do so after being offered an opportunity to make the corrective entries, he cannot cause the election to be set aside on the ground that he had been unfairly treated.[11]

Voting at an election conducted by a stock corporation constitutes an open election as opposed to a secret election.[12] A secret ballot is not necessary unless required by law.[13]

Where the by-laws provide that elections of directors shall be by ballot, the fact that it had been the custom in prior years to

---

A by-law providing that nominations for directors should be made at least 10 days before the annual meeting, but not providing that no one could be eligible for election unless so nominated, is directory and not mandatory. Hence, write-in ballots are valid. *In re* Farrell, 205 App. Div. 443, 200 N.Y.S. 95 (2d Dep't), *aff'd,* 236 N.Y. 603, 142 N.E. 301 (1923).

[11] *In re* P. B. Mathiason Mfg. Co., 122 Mo. App. 437, 99 S.W. 502, 504 (1907).

However, a statute providing that if a voter for members of a city council votes for fewer candidates than the number of seats to be filled his vote should not be counted, does not violate the fourteenth amendment. Gordon v. Meeks, 394 F.2d 3 (5th Cir. 1968).

[12] "It must be borne in mind that the vote given at these corporate elections, whether given in writing or *viva voce,* is always essentially an *open* as distinguished from a *secret* vote. In order to enable the inspectors to canvass the vote, they must know how each shareholder voted. . . ." State *ex rel.* Lawrence v. McGann, 64 Mo. App. 225, 233 (1895).

On whether voting by secret ballot at a notified membership meeting is tantamount to voting in a membership referendum conducted by secret ballot, *see* Local No. 2, Internat'l Bro. of Tel. Wkrs. v. International Bro. Tel. Wkrs., 362 F.2d 891 (1st Cir. 1966).

[13] Troy & N.E. Ry. v. K.L.W.M., Inc., 192 N.Y.S. 277, 279 (Sup. Ct.), *aff'd mem.,* 202 App. Div. 768, 194 N.Y.S. 985 (3d Dep't 1922).

Where the constitution requires a secret ballot, an open ballot would be illegal. Fritsch v. Rarback, 98 N.Y.S.2d 748 (Sup. Ct. 1950).

conduct the annual stockholders' meetings in an informal manner
by oral vote or consent will not prevail over the demand of a shareholder that the election be conducted by ballot in accordance with
the by-laws.[14]

§ 17.39 Ballot Box

Possession of the ballot box is sometimes the subject of litigation.
It has been held, for example, that in the absence of a by-law provision to the contrary, it was not improper for the newly elected
president of an incorporated political club thereafter to take charge
of the ballot box containing ballots of the election.[15]

Informality in the handling of the ballot box (in one case a hat)
will not constitute an irregularity sufficient to set aside an election
where the wishes of the voters have been fairly expressed and the
election has been conducted in good faith.[16] On the other hand,
where the ballot box has been tampered with, the court may set
aside the election for fraud and irregularity.[17] Disturbances of
town meetings and repeated attempts to remove ballots from the
ballot box is an offense indictable at common law.[18]

[14] *See* Chapman v. Barton, 345 Ill. App. 110, 102 N.E.2d 565, 567 (1951).

[15] *In re* Serenbetz, 46 N.Y.S.2d 475, 477, *aff'd*, 46 N.Y.S.2d 127 (Sup. Ct.
1944).

Leaving a ballot box in the back seat of a parked car while the driver
(Board agent) was visiting a motel room may violate policy of the NLRB.
Delta Drilling Co. v. NLRB, 406 F.2d 109 (5th Cir. 1969).

[16] Philips v. Wickham, 1 Paige 590 (N.Y. Ch. 1829).

[17] *In re* Societa Mutuo Soccorso San Rocco, 255 App. Div. 815, 7 N.Y.S.2d
337 (2d Dep't 1938).

However, uncorroborated speculation that the ballot box could have been
tampered with is not sufficient to necessitate an evidentiary hearing or to set
aside an election. NLRB v. Capitan Drilling Co., 408 F.2d 676 (5th Cir.
1969).

The right to vote cannot be denied outright, nor destroyed by alteration of
ballots, nor diluted by ballot-box stuffing. *See* Reynolds v. Sims, 377 U.S. 533,
555 (1964).

[18] Defendant attempted repeatedly to take from the ballot box the votes of
electors, and thus behaved himself in a disorderly and indecent manner at the
town meeting. The indictment was held good as at common law, there being
no statute making the act an offence. Commonwealth v. Hoxey, 16 Mass. 385
(1820).

§ 17.40 Ballot—Sufficiency

It is a general principle of parliamentary law that matters submitted to a meeting for consideration and action should be in suitable form for those purposes. In a labor union case it was held that the statutory right of members to vote in referendums of a labor organization "embraces the right to have the referendum submitted in suitable form." Following this principle, a court held that a ballot requiring a single vote on four separate resolutions, all relating to the subject of union dues, was suitable and therefore no injunction would be granted.[19] On the other hand, another court has held that the submission to a union's membership of a ballot in which one proposition embraced 47 different constitutional amendments was improper under the union's constitution. The court upheld the basic rule that "the right to vote extended in the Act is not a mere naked right to cast a ballot." It reasoned that if management of the union can submit amendments for referendum to the membership in any form it may wish, this might very well "open up the way of usurpation of power by union management. . . ." This means, in effect, that "full disclosure be permitted in that the electorate be as fully informed and educated as is possible, and consistent with orderly procedures, as to the pros and cons of the subjects . . . submitted to them for vote." The court acknowledged that, in this case, the prescribed procedure "may be more costly and more time consuming and laborious," and that in the future it may be able to set down more clearly defined standards.[20]

---

[19] Rothstein v. Manuti, 235 F. Supp. 39 (S.D.N.Y. 1963).

Also approved is the use of a separate ballot for voting on 40 questions instead of having them on the official ballot, and the arrangement of voting boxes. Collins v. Town of Derry, 109 N.H. 970, 256 A.2d 654 (1969) (amendment of zoning ordinance).

[20] Young v. Hayes, 195 F. Supp. 911, 917, 918 (D.D.C. 1961).

When the form of a ballot gave a union member no opportunity to vote against a dues increase without also voting against negotiation of a wage increase, the referendum using such a ballot violated the Act. Sertic v. Cuyahoga, Lake, Geauga & Ashtabula Cos., C.D.C., 423 F.2d 515 (6th Cir. 1970).

The fact that two proposals "not wholly unrelated nor incongruous" are on the same ballot title does not render the election void. Moore v. Oklahoma City, 122 Okla. 234, 254 P. 47 (1927).

RESULTS OF VOTING

§ 17.41 Duty of Chairman

At common law it is the duty of the chairman to announce the result of the voting. An early English case stated: "Then, the meeting being held and a shew of hands taken, some one was to declare on whom the nomination had fallen. Who was to do that? Not the body of parishioners who had made the nomination . . . but the person presiding at the vestry, namely, the rector." [1] Under some modern corporation laws the results may be announced by the inspectors of election, the judges of the voting, the clerk, or other authorized person or committee.[2] However, even when the results of the voting are determined by inspectors, it is customary for the chairman to formally declare the results after the inspectors have completed their tabulation and reported the results.

In the case of a city council, the presiding officer should an-

---

See People ex rel. Moore v. Perkins, 56 Colo. 17, 137 P. 55 (1913) (one proposal contingent upon another).

See §§ 17.43 and 17.44 infra.

[1] Regina v. D'Oyly, 12 Adolph. & E. 139, 158, 159 (Q.B. 1840).

"No provision is made by statute as to the mode in which, or the persons by whom, the result of an election shall be ascertained. This must necessarily be done by the meeting itself, and, from its character and the numbers who compose it, must primarily be effected by a count of the votes by the moderator or other officers, or by a committee appointed by the meeting, or by its officers with its assent. Such a committee is an instrument of the meeting, and not a distinct counting or canvassing board. No special force can be given to the declaration of the moderator, after such a committee reports the result of the count to him, that an officer is elected. It can amount to no more than a statement by him that the officer appears by such count to be elected." Putnam v. Langley, 133 Mass. 204 (1882).

[2] For example, the New York Business Corporation Law at § 611 provides that the inspectors of election shall receive, count, and tabulate all votes and "determine the result."

The basic results of the voting at a stockholders' meeting of a registered company must be reported to the SEC on its Form 8K, Item 11. Copies of Form 8K must be filed with the national securities exchanges on which the company's voting securities are listed. See, e.g., N.Y.S.E. Company Manual Sec. A8.

nounce the vote.[3]   However, where pursuant to statute, the function of the council is discharged and completed upon the casting of the votes, an announcement of the results may be made to the council by the council clerk.   In such case a declaration by the presiding officer of the council could neither add to nor detract from that which had already been done.[4]

It is important that the lawfully presiding officer announce the results of the voting, and not someone without authority to do so.[5] In the absence of proper organization and regularity in the conduct of a meeting, including the due authorization of someone to preside and to receive and declare the votes, the meeting may be a nullity and all action taken may be void.[6]

Although it is a function of the chairman to preside and to announce the vote, the election of a presiding officer at the first meeting prior to organization may be conducted by the clerk, according to custom and without objection.[7]   The final results need not be

[3] "The mayor is the presiding officer of the council, and it is his duty to announce the result of a vote of the council according to the fact."   City of Chariton v. Holliday, 60 Iowa 391, 14 N.W. 775, 776 (1883).

When an article has been declared adopted by the requisite vote, it has been "passed" as stated in the notice of meeting (warrant).   Amey v. Pittsburg School Dist., 95 N.H. 386, 64 A.2d 1 (1949).

[4] State ex rel. Calderwood v. Miller, 62 Ohio St. 436, 57 N.E. 227 (1900).

[5] Where a shareholder changed his vote, after an unauthorized person (a stockholder, not the chairman) had announced the results of the first ballot but before the lawfully presiding officer had announced the revised vote of a second ballot, it was held that the change of vote was lawful and should be counted. The court had to determine who was the lawful presiding officer.   Zachary v. Milin, 294 Mich. 622, 293 N.W. 770, 772 (1940).

[6] "But if the meeting had been regularly called the claim of respondents could not be sustained, because there was no organization or regularity in the proceeding . . . the by-laws provides that 'the president, when present, shall preside at all meetings of the company, and at the board of trustees; and in his absence a president pro tempore shall be chosen.'   This provision of the by-laws was totally disregarded.   The president although present, did not preside at the election, nor was there a president pro tempore chosen in his stead; and no person who participated in the proceeding was authorized to receive the ballots, or to declare the result."   State ex rel. Guerrero v. Pettineli, 10 Nev. 141, 146 (1875).

[7] "The suggestion has been made that the whole election is invalid because the clerk was not vested with power to act as presiding officer, and the proceed-

announced immediately after the polls are closed. An established practice of having a preliminary canvass on the day of the election and a more careful recanvass of the ballots by the inspectors on a later day will be accepted by the court as a fair method of determining the results of the voting.[8] However, the refusal of the chair to declare the results of an election when they are available may warrant reconsideration at an adjourned meeting.[9]

The results of a vote taken at a meeting, as announced by the presiding officer after the ballots have been counted, are prima facie the correct results.[10] However, even a declaration by the chairman that a certain person had been elected, followed by a motion that the decision of the chair be sustained which is passed by a viva voce vote with few dissenting votes, will not validate an election which in fact did not meet the statutory requirements of

---

ings were fatally contaminated with indecorum in conducting the alleged election. The council had power to determine who should preside over its deliberations, and whether the clerk held the chair de jure or de facto could not alter the result. If the disorderly proceedings should be held to invalidate an election otherwise legal, some legislative bodies could never organize; and, what is more, a minority by rowdyism could forestall action by a worthy majority." State ex rel. Reed v. De Maioribus, 131 Ohio St. 201, 2 N.E.2d 506, 509 (1936).

[8] Grip v. Buffelen Woodworking Co., 73 Wash. 2d 219, 437 P.2d 915 (1968).

[9] "It follows that the respondent Barton was elected at the first meeting, and should have been declared elected by the chair. The chairman, however, declared that there was no election, and the meeting adjourned. At the adjourned meeting—which was a continuation of the same meeting . . . —it was voted 'to rescind the vote at the previous meeting whereby the convention voted to elect a superintendent of schools,' and this vote is treated by both sides as a rescission of the election, if that was within the power of the meeting.

"We are of opinion that it was within the power of the meeting to rescind its vote." Reed v. Barton, 176 Mass. 473, 57 N.E. 961, 962 (1900).

[10] See Wall v. Exchange Inv. Corp., [1926] Ch. 143 (1925), holding that the decision of the chairman, in bona fide exercise of his powers under the articles to declare the vote, was final and not subject to court review.

At a general meeting duly convened, an extraordinary resolution to wind up voluntarily was declared by the chairman to be carried on a show of hands. No poll was demanded as permitted by the statute. It was held that, apart from fraud, the declaration of the chairman was conclusive and the court would not entertain the question whether the motion was carried by the requisite majority. In re Hadleigh Castle Gold Mines, Ltd., [1900] 2 Ch. 419.

a majority vote.[11] In an election of directors, for example, the burden is upon a dissenter to rebut this prima facie case by facts showing that the requisite number of votes had not been cast for the election of the directors declared to be elected by the chairman.[12]

Every presumption is applied in favor of the regularity of the parliamentary procedures employed. In sustaining a motion to dispense with a rule that an ordinance be read aloud at three successive meetings, the court held: "There is no statute requiring the yeas and nays to be called on the adoption of such motion, and as it was declared adopted the presumption must be indulged that the requisite number of votes was cast and the rule legally suspended." [13] Also, when a stockholders' meeting breaks into two parts, it is reasonable to regard the two as one for the purpose of determining the results of the vote, if that can be done without jeopardizing the accuracy of the vote.[14] But the presumption of regularity in the

[11] State *ex rel.* Duane v. Fagan, 42 Conn. 32, 33–34 (1875).

See State *ex rel.* Reed v. Smith, 14 P. 814, *rehearing*, 15 P. 386 (Oregon 1887) (chairman wrongfully counted votes, announced wrong result, issued wrong certificates of election, and adjourned meeting against majority vote).

[12] "It was alleged that at the meeting and after the ballots had been counted, the president announced that the nominees of management had been elected by a large majority. This declared result of the election is prima facie the correct result. The burden is upon the plaintiffs to rebut this prima facie case by alleging facts showing that the requisite number of members had not voted for the election of the nominated directors." Booker v. First Fed. Sav. & Loan Ass'n, 215 Ga. 277, 110 S.E.2d 360, 363, *cert. denied*, 361 U.S. 916 (1959).

"There can be no doubt that the corporate records in which resolutions of the directors and stockholders are contained are in themselves proof of the regularity of the transactions recorded therein and that the defendants have the burden of meeting that proof. . . . Proxies relied on at the meeting are entitled to the same presumption." Stephens Fuel Co. v. Bay Parkway Nat'l Bank, 109 F.2d 186, 189 (2d Cir. 1940).

See Wall v. Exchange Inv. Co., [1926] Ch. 143 (1925) (articles provided that every vote not disallowed at meeting should be deemed valid).

[13] State v. Vail, 53 Iowa 550, 5 N.W. 709, 710 (1880).

[14] Gow v. Consolidated Coppermines Corp., 19 Del. Ch. 172, 165 A. 136 (1933).

Where stockholders assemble in two bodies and cast their votes at separate polls, the court in ascertaining the result of the election may consider the ballots cast at both polls. *In re* Election of Dirs. of Cedar Grove Cemetery Co., 61 N.J.L. 422, 39 A. 1024 (1898).

passage of a legislative bill (when the record shows it to have been signed by the Speakers of both Houses and approved by the Governor) will not overcome a clear affirmative showing that the bill was in fact defeated by a vote of more than two to one.[15] And where more votes are cast than there are voters present, the results cannot be lawful.[16]

§ 17.42   Erroneous Ruling

An erroneous ruling of the presiding office cannot be corrected by testimony of members present explaining the events as recorded in the minutes. "What the council actually did, and not what the presiding officer thought necessary, is controlling. It is not competent for the members of a legislative body even to give evidence of what they understood was the effect of the action which the record shows they took." The record of the proceedings is controlling on that question. The court then concluded, as to the chairman: "His opinion as to what was necessary cannot be taken as a substitute for the doing of a necessary thing."[17] Comments by the chairman made to the assembled membership relating to action already taken by the members are not relevant. In an early English case, the court expressed its view that "no gloss of the chairman, even if incorrect, and no statement by him as to what was intended . . . could modify or affect" the action taken.[18]

The announcement of an erroneous vote, however, will not be sustained, and will not adversely affect the true result of the vote.[19] "If a vote as to some measure or in an election of officers had been

[15] Wright v. Wiles, 173 Tenn. 334, 117 S.W.2d 736 (1938), *citing* Robert's Rules of Order on motion to table.

[16] There were 39 members present at the opening of the meeting. At the voting, 32 yea votes and 12 nay votes (total 44) were cast. Bushers v. Graceland Cemetery Ass'n, 171 F. Supp. 205 (E.D. Ill. 1958).

[17] Casler v. Tanzer, 134 Misc. 48, 234 N.Y.S. 571, 578, 579 (Sup. Ct. 1929). See § 2.7 *infra*.

[18] Salisbury Gold Mining Co. Ltd. v. Hathorn, [1897] A.C. 268, 276.

[19] The rule that the announcement by the presiding officer of the result of a viva voce vote is conclusive, unless a division or a call of the vote is demanded, cannot be invoked in favor of a false and fraudulent announcement or one that is clearly contrary to the actual result. "No presiding officer should be permitted to arbitrarily or fraudulently defeat the will of the majority of any deliberative assembly by making a knowingly false announcement of the result of a vote, merely because such announcement was not promptly challenged in

illegally announced because of the illegal admission or rejection of certain votes, the court could declare the true result." [20] When a second vote is taken which constitutes a reconsideration of an earlier vote, the results of which were announced by the presiding officer, the second vote will supersede the first vote and the declaration of the presiding officer as to the results of the second vote will be final.[21]

In the case of mistake or fraud in a ballot election, another ballot may be taken and the irregular or fraudulent ballot rejected. However, if an official is in fact elected by a formal ballot, his election cannot be set aside merely because the electors thought that the official was not elected.[22]

---

the manner prescribed by the rules under which the business of such assembly is transacted." Gipson v. Morris, 31 Tex. Civ. App. 645, 73 S.W. 85 (1903).

Where the presiding officer declared that a resolution failed to pass because it did not receive a three-fourths vote, when in fact a majority vote was sufficient and had been obtained; the resolution was held to have been adopted. "The mayor is the presiding officer of the council, and it is his duty to announce the result of a vote of the council according to the fact. . . . The erroneous and arbitrary announcement of the mayor cannot have the effect to nullify the act of a majority of the council." City of Chariton v. Holliday, 60 Iowa 391, 14 N.W. 775, 776 (1883).

But see In re Caratal (New) Mines, Ltd., [1902] 2 Ch. 498, 500, 501, distinguishing earlier decisions which held that "if the chairman by his declaration affirms erroneously or without sufficiently ascertaining the facts but bona fide that a resolution has been carried, the Court cannot go behind that declaration." The court noted: "But those decisions do not apply to a case where the chairman by his declaration finds the figures and erroneously in point of law holds that the resolution has been duly passed."

See also In re Horbury Bridge, Coal, Iron & Waggon Co., 11 Ch. D. 109, 111 (1879), where the articles of the company provided that the chairman's rulings were "sufficient evidence," not "conclusive evidence."

[20] Bridgers v. Staton, 150 N.C. 216, 63 S.E. 892, 894 (1909).

When a town clerk has made a defective or erroneous record of a vote, it is competent for him while in office to amend it according to the truth. Chamberlain v. Dover, 13 Me. 466 (1836).

[21] The court said: "We think that the circumstance that the presiding officer made declaration of the election after the first vote is not decisive. The proceedings covering the two votes constituted a continuous legislative transaction." Mansfield v. O'Brien, 271 Mass. 515, 171 N.E. 487, 489 (1930) (common council).

[22] Where a city official was duly elected to office by the votes of three aldermen, his election will not be set aside by the court on a showing that the aldermen made a mistake of law believing that three votes were not sufficient;

The authority of the presiding officer to determine the results of the voting, and the corollary duty of the members to abide by his decision unless and until reversed or modified by an appeal conducted in accordance with established rules on appeal, in exemplified in a case concerning a union member who was expelled from the union by a trial committee. The verdict of expulsion was first appealed to, and rejected by, the membership and then approved by the membership at a later meeting on a motion to rescind the earlier rejection. The expelled member appealed to the international president claiming that the requisite two-thirds vote of the membership had not been obtained due to the improper counting of a blank ballot as a vote cast. The president upheld the verdict but modified the penalty, whereupon the member took two out of three union appeal steps without success and then started court proceedings. It was held that the member could not appeal to the court without first availing himself of all the review remedies provided by the union constitution. The question before the court was whether the union rules on appeal were violated in any respect or whether further pursuit of internal relief could lawfully be excused. To the claim that union rules had been violated by deciding that the required two-thirds vote had been obtained, the court said: "As to the finding of the president that there was a two-thirds vote in favor of expulsion, such finding, if erroneous, could not alone justify non compliance by petitioner with the appeal rules of the organization. Just as a court has the power to decide wrongly as well as rightly, the president on appeal likewise has such power and a wrong decision is not the violation of the organization's rules on appeal which under [case law] justifies the member in refusing to further follow the union's rules on appeal." The court held, however, that modification of the penalty (including the imposition of an apology) by the president was a violation of the appeal rules and made futile further steps in the appeal procedure. The court then considered the validity of the motion to rescind. The consti-

nor will the election be disturbed by an adverse declaration of the mayor, by failure of the city clerk to certify the election, or by proceedings of the council to defer and reconsider the election. Moreover, after the official had accepted and qualified for the office, the council had no power to reconsider and elect another. State *ex rel.* Burdick v. Tyrrell, 158 Wis. 425, 149 N.W. 280, 282–83 (1914).

tutions of both the international and the local union had adopted Robert's Rules of Order. The court held, first, that in any conflict between Robert's Rules and constitutional provisions, the latter would necessarily prevail, and further, that attempting by a standing vote to rescind an action required to be taken by a secret vote, is a violation of the constitution and of Robert's Rules, which provided that a resolution or other main motion may be rescinded in the same way it had been adopted.[23]

§ 17.43   Proxy Contests

In a proxy contest between opposing factions it is important that management exercise caution and fairness in the ministerial function of processing and preserving all proxies received for use at the meeting, and not take advantage of the information gained from day-to-day tallies as proxies are received and processed. The Rules of the SEC [24] prohibit any solicitation, whether written or oral, which may be "false or misleading" with respect to any material fact, and give as an example: "Claims made prior to a meeting regarding the results of a solicitation." Thus, care should be taken not to release any information on the status or trend of the proxies received prior to the meeting. It should also be remembered that, as a general rule, all proxies except those legally irrevocable, may be revoked at any time before they are exercised.[25]

[23] Gonzales v. International Ass'n of Machinists, 142 Cal. App. 2d 207, 298 P.2d 92, 96 (1956), aff'd, 356 U.S. 617 (1958). The expulsion verdict of the committee was submitted to a meeting of the membership which voted 43–31 against sustaining the verdict. At a later regular meeting a motion to rescind the rejection of the verdict was approved by a standing vote of 38 yes, 4 no. Thereupon a secret ballot vote was taken in a motion to sustain the verdict, resulting in 31 yes, 12 no, and 2 blank ballots. A secret ballot vote was then taken on a motion to expel, resulting in 29 yes, 14 no, and one blank. This last vote failed to meet the requisite two-thirds rule because the blank ballot should have been counted as a vote cast.

See §§ 17.8 and 17.14 supra.

[24] SEC Regulation 14A, Rule 14a–9, note (d).

[25] The SEC proxy solicitation rules require a statement in the proxy statement as to whether the person giving the proxy has the power to revoke it. If the right of revocation before the proxy is exercised is limited or subject to compliance with any formal procedure, such limitation or procedure must be described. SEC Regulation A (Schedule 14A).

See, e.g., NEW YORK BUS. CORP. LAW § 609 (McKinney 1974).

§ 17.44   Challenge

The vote of any person in an election of corporate directors and officers may be challenged, thereby requiring the challenged voter to swear in his vote.[26] If a shareholder at an election is not challenged at the threshold, "the only remaining duty of those conducting the election is to count the ballots and return the number of votes received by the nominees. After that they have no duty to perform."[27]

§ 17.45   Recount

A recount is not an election. It is "a ministerial act only, resorted to for the purpose of establishing accurately the results of the election." Thus, a recount on a day after adjournment of a shareholder's meeting for the election of directors is not a meeting or an adjourned meeting at which directors are elected.[28]

It has long been established that a majority may demand a timely recount of the ballots. "As the meeting is charged with the duty of making an election by a ballot, if a majority of its members desire further examination of the correctness of the result reached by the committee, it must be its right to subject such result to further scrutiny. If the result announced is assented to directly, or perhaps indirectly by proceeding with other business, and an examination of the subject is thus closed, there would be much force in the

[26] See In re Serenbetz, 46 N.Y.S.2d 475, 481, aff'd, 46 N.Y.S.2d 127 (Sup. Ct. 1944) (incorporated political club).

[27] Kauffman v. Meyberg, 59 Cal. App. 2d 730, 140 P.2d 210, 216 (1943).

An election of directors will not be set aside because illegal votes were given unless they were challenged; nor will it be set aside although the votes were challenged, if after deducting all illegal votes there is still a clear majority in favor of the persons declared to be elected. In re Election of Dirs. of Chenango County Mut. Ins. Co., 19 Wend. (N.Y.) 635 (1839).

[28] The court commented: "The practice of having a preliminary canvass on the day of the election and a more careful recanvass of the ballots by the election committee on the following Monday was not an innovation resorted to for this particular election. There was undisputed evidence that this had been the established practice at each annual election since 1955. The ballots were recanvassed so as to be able to make a more careful count, free from the confusion of the annual meeting." Grip v. Buffelen Woodworking Co., 73 Wash. 2d 219, 437 P.2d 915, 917 (1968).

argument that the election would be fully completed." [29] Officers
elected at a town meeting need not suspend their functions pending determination of a petition for a recount. Also, unless there is
authority for a recount and a demand is made, an announcement
of the results of an election will stand as the true results even
though a mistake in the count is afterward discovered.[30]

The chairman may not, in a proper case, declare out of order a
motion to reject the report of the tellers at an election of corporate
directors.[31] However, a recount of ballots cast at an election of
corporate officers should not be had upon suspicion alone. A claim
that the ballots should be examined apparently in the hope that
some irregularity would appear, unsupported by affidavits of tellers
or any showing of irregularity, will not justify a recount of the
ballots.[32]

[29] Putnam v. Langley, 133 Mass. 204, 205 (1882) (town meeting election).

[30] Moloney v. Selectmen of Town of Milford, 353 Mass. 400, 149 N.E. 317
(1925).

[31] The president was mistaken in declaring the results of an election. "He
was also mistaken in declaring the motion to reject the report of the tellers out
of order and refusing to entertain an appeal from his ruling, and the majority of
the members present in person and by proxy were justified in exercising the
power of the majority, in the absence of any by-laws or rules of order contrary
to such action, by deposing the chairman and proceeding with the business of
the meeting." American Aberdeen-Angus Breeders' Ass'n v. Fullerton, 325 Ill.
323, 156 N.E. 314, 317 (1927).

[32] *In re* Serenbetz, 46 N.Y.S.2d 475, 481, *aff'd*, 46 N.Y.S.2d 127 (Sup. Ct.
1944).

Where there is a dispute among the tellers over the vote cast on the first
ballot and a second ballot is thereupon taken, intervention by the court is not
justified unless there is a showing of fraud or bribery. *In re* Nash, 36 Misc.
113, 72 N.Y.S. 1057 (Sup. Ct. 1901).

18

Motions

MOTION PROCEDURES

§ 18.1 Meaning of Term

Generally, action taken at a meeting by the members or shareholders is introduced by a motion. No legislative business should be discussed unless there is a motion before the meeting.

In parliamentary usage, a motion is a proposal that the body take certain action, or that it express itself as holding certain views.[1] The action proposed, if a main motion or part of a main motion, will be in the form of a resolution.[2] Thus, a member moves or

---

[1] See Robert's Rules of Order at 33; Allen v. Wise, 204 Ga. 415, 50 S.E.2d 69, 71 (1948) (definitions of "resolution," "motion," "ordinance").

"The methods by which, under our system of parliamentary law, a Legislature exercises its power and jurisdiction, each in a different way, are, *First.* By motion; *Second.* By resolution; *Third.* By concurrent resolution; *Fourth.* By

proposes that a resolution be adopted or otherwise acted upon. Strictly speaking a motion does not become a resolution until it has been voted upon and adopted. Preambles and resolutions should be complete and precise, but need not specify their end purpose.[3]

Although a resolution is not necessary in all cases [4] an informal discussion will not take the place of a formal resolution.[5]

The courts recognize the difference between a motion and a resolution,[6] but also acknowledge that the use of the terms "motion,"

---

joint resolution; *Fifth.* By bill. Of these methods the motion is the least comprehensive and involves the exercise of parliamentary power in its simplest form. It sets the body in motion and again dissolves it, and is auxiliary merely to the ordinary work of legislation.

"The next in the ascending gradation of parliamentary methods is the *resolution,* which declares some purpose, expresses a will, or prescribes an order, or formulates a command of the legislative body, usually not incidental to the ordinary course of business. A resolution, as well as a motion, is obligatory only upon the house which adopts it, and in this respect is inferior in efficiency to both a concurrent and a joint resolution, each of which is, in its turn, less effective, as the expression of legislative will, than a bill where enacted into a law." Rice v. State *ex rel.* Drapier, 95 Ind. 33, 46 (1883).

[2] In the case of assemblies with paid employees, instructions given to employees are often called "orders" instead of "resolutions"; Robert's Rules of Order at 34.

[3] *In re* Chapman, 166 U.S. 661 (1897) (Congressional investigation).

[4] *See* Butts v. Gaylord State Bank, 156 Misc. 555, 282 N.Y.S. 1 (Sup. Ct. 1935) (assent by all directors at a regular meeting).

[5] Knapp v. Rochester Dog Protective Ass'n, 235 App. Div. 436, 257 N.Y.S. 356 (4th Dep't 1932).

[6] "A motion is a proposition made to the house by a member, which if adopted becomes the resolution, vote, or order, of the house. The form of a motion must consequently be so framed, and its language so expressed, that, if it meets the approbation of the house, it may at once become the resolution, vote, or order which it purports to be. In considering motions in reference to their form, it will be most convenient to treat of the subject affirmatively, by pointing out the several requisites as to form, which a motion ought regularly to possess." CUSHING, LAW AND PRACTICE OF LEGISLATIVE ASSEMBLIES § 1279.

"There is a difference between a motion and a resolution. A motion is a proposal or suggestion looking to action in a deliberative assembly, while a resolution is a statement or verdict, especially a formal expression of the opinion or will of a public assembly, adopted by a vote." De Leuw, Cather & Co. v. Joliet, 327 Ill. App. 453, 64 N.E.2d 779, 784 (1945).

The fact that an action was termed a "motion" instead of a "resolution" is immaterial. There is no difference between a motion and a resolution—"[I]t is

"resolution," "order," and the like, are not as precise as they might be.[7] The election of officers, the appointment of committees, and the adoption of rules by a city council are not "resolutions" and

---

the substance of the corporate act, not the form, that governs." Commonwealth *ex rel.* Fox v. Chace, 403 Pa. 117, 168 A.2d 569, 572 (1961), *citing* Robert's Rules of Order on another parliamentary point.

"A 'resolution,' in the sense used in the charter, is nothing more than the formal expression of the will of the city council, and a 'motion' is a proposal made to evoke action upon the part of the council or other assembly. When the motion had been acted upon, it became the formal expression of the will, or resolution, of the city council." A verbal motion may become a resolution. El Paso Gas, Elec. Light & Power Co. v. City of El Paso, 22 Tex. Civ. App. 309, 54 S.W. 798, 799 (1899), *citing* Cushing, Law & Pr. Leg. Assem. § 1279.

"Legislation by a municipal corporation must be put in the form of an ordinance, and acts that are done in a ministerial capacity and for temporary purposes may be in the form of a resolution. . . . 'The distinction between an ordinance and a resolution is usually considered to be that, while a resolution deals with matters of a special or temporary character, an ordinance prescribes some permanent rule of government.'" Allen v. Wise, 204 Ga. 415, 50 S.E.2d 69, 71 (1948).

[7] *See, e.g.,* Gas & Elec. Securities Co. v. Manhattan & Queens Traction Corp., 266 F. 625, 636 (2d Cir. 1920) (city's legislative power may be exercised by either an ordinance or a resolution, except as otherwise provided by law); California Reduction Co. v. Sanitary Reduction Works, 126 F. 29, 40–41 (9th Cir. 1903) (discussion of words "order," "ordinance," "resolution," "regulation," which are often used to express the same thing).

Where the mayor, having the right to veto ordinances and resolutions of the city council, vetoed a measure which was entitled a motion but was so worded as to clearly indicate a resolution, the veto was legal. The court noted: "By substituting the word 'Resolution' for the word 'Motion,' and inserting the words 'Be it resolved,' immediately preceding the first word of the first line, the document would have the appearance of a formal resolution by the members of council offering it." Allen v. Wise, 204 Ga. 415, 50 S.E.2d 69, 71, 72 (1948).

"In respect of municipal action, a resolution, viewed in the general sense, is merely a proposition offered for adoption by a body; it is the equivalent of a motion; there is no substantial difference between them; a characteristic feature of a resolution is its enacting clause, 'Be it resolved'; it is, generally, not an order, but a mere expression of view upon which an order issues to make it effective." Balacek v. Board of Trustees, 26 N.Y.S.2d 419, 424–25, *rev'd on other grounds*, 263 App. Div. 712, 30 N.Y.S.2d 1007 (4th Dep't 1941), *aff'd*, 288 N.Y. 640, 42 N.E.2d 660 (1942).

thus are not subject to the veto power of the mayor.[8] The difference between a resolution and a legislative bill must be recognized, particularly in the area of statutory interpretation.[9] And, of course, a resolution is not a law.[10]

The courts also recognize the difference between a resolution and a by-law. It has been held that a by-law differs from a resolution, in that "a resolution applies to a single act of the corporation, while a by-law is a permanent and continuing rule which is to be applied on all future occasions."[11] Thus, a resolution which creates a general regulatory rule applicable only to the members of the body may have all the attributes of a by-law.[12]

A resolution is not an ordinance, in that a resolution deals with a matter of special or temporary character whereas an ordinance prescribes some permanent rule of government.[13] Also, it is im-

[8] Morris v. Cashmore, 253 App. Div. 657, 3 N.Y.S.2d 624, 628–29, 633, aff'd, 278 N.Y. 730, 17 N.E.2d 143 (1938) (N.Y. City Council) (following Reed's Rules).

An election by a city council to fill a vacancy (six candidates) does not constitute the adoption of an ordinance or a resolution. If there is only one candidate, it might be considered a motion. State ex rel. Smith v. Nazor, 135 Ohio St. 364, 21 N.E.2d 124 (1939).

Election of a city solicitor is not an "ordinance" or an "order." Pevey v. Aylward, 205 Mass. 102, 91 N.E. 315 (1910).

See Russell Sage College v. Troy, 24 Misc. 2d 344, 198 N.Y.S.2d 391 (Sup. Ct. 1960) (distinction between resolution and ordinance).

[9] A "bill" is a draft of an act of the legislature before it becomes a law and is not a resolution. See Walther v. McDonald, 243 Ark. 912, 422 S.W.2d 854, 862 (1968).

[10] "A resolution is not a law, and in substance there is no difference between a resolution, order, and motion." Allen v. Wise, 204 Ga. 415, 50 S.E.2d 69, 71 (1948).

"An ordinance prescribes some permanent rule of conduct or government, to continue in force until the ordinance is repealed, and is distinctively a legislative act." In re Edgewood Ave., 195 Misc. 314, 90 N.Y.S.2d 131, 139 (Sup. Ct. 1948).

A resolution can be a "plan" under SEC proxy-soliciting rules. Dillon v. Berg, 326 F. Supp. 1214, 1216 (D. Del.), aff'd, 453 F.2d 876 (3d Cir. 1971).

[11] The court continued: "Whether any given rule of action becomes a by-law or a resolution depends upon the solemnity with which it is passed." Hornady v. Goodman, 167 Ga. 555, 146 S.E. 173, 182 (1928).

[12] Mutual Fire Ins. Co. v. Farquhar, 86 Md. 668, 39 A. 527, 529 (1898).

[13] "The distinction between a resolution and an ordinance is that a resolution is an order of the council of a special and temporary character while an ordi-

material that the order of submission to a vote may be in the form
of a resolution, when the resolution contains the essentials of an
ordinance duly passed by the board and signed by the mayor.[14]

§ 18.2 Legislative Language

Generally it is of little significance whether a legislative measure
is couched in language meeting precise formalities when the act
and effect are declaratory of the intent of the enacting body.[15]

---

nance prescribes a permanent rule of government or conduct. . . . It has also
been said that an ordinance is a continuing regulation—a permanent rule of
government—while a resolution is usually declared not to be the equivalent of
an ordinance, but rather an act of a temporary character not prescribing a permanent rule of government, but is merely declaratory of the will of a corporation in a given matter and in the nature of a ministerial act. . . . When the
statute requires that an act of a municipality be done in the form of an ordinance, or if such requirement is implied by necessary or clear inference, the
act can only be done in that form, or perhaps its legal equivalent, and a resolution, especially if not adopted with all the formalities of an ordinance is not
sufficient." Collins v. City of Schenectady, 256 App. Div. 389, 10 N.Y.S.2d
303, 307 (1939).

Although the word "ordinance" usually means a permanent rule of government in the nature of a general village law, it is sometimes used to describe a
"proposed method" of carrying out a municipal project. See O'Flynn v. Village
of East Rochester, 24 N.Y.S.2d 437, aff'd, 262 App. Div. 556, 31 N.Y.S.2d 754
(1941); aff'd sub nom. Village of East Rochester v. Rochester Gas & Elec.
Corp., 289 N.Y. 391, 46 N.E.2d 334 (1943), aff'd, 292 N.Y. 156, 54 N.E.2d
343, cert. denied sub nom. Despatch Shops, Inc. v. Village of East Rochester,
323 U.S. 713 (1944).

[14] Crebs v. Lebanon, 98 F. 549 (W.D. Mo. 1898).

[15] "The law is well settled that a municipal corporation may declare its will
as to matters within the scope of its corporate powers, either by a resolution or
an ordinance, unless its charter requires it to act by ordinance; and generally
it is of little significance whether a legislative measure is couched in the language of an ordinance or of a resolution, where it is enacted with the same
formalities which usually attend the adoption of ordinances. If the action
taken by a municipality amounts to prescribing a permanent rule of conduct,
which is to be thereafter observed by the inhabitants of the municipality, or
by its officers in the transaction of the corporate business, then, no doubt, the
rule prescribed may be more properly expressed in the form of an ordinance,
but it is eminently proper to act by resolution, if the action taken is merely
declaratory of the will of the corporation in a given matter, and is in the nature
of a ministerial act." Alma v. Guaranty Sav. Bank, 60 F. 203, 206 (8th Cir.
1894).

However, where the chairman incorrectly states a motion when putting it to a vote, the original motion as moved, seconded, and heard by the members is the motion voted on and carried.[16] At common law management need not give advance notice of all resolutions it intends to submit to shareholders at a general (annual) meeting.[17]

Where the organic law provides that an act shall be done in a designated manner, such as by ordinance or resolution, this requirement cannot be evaded by giving to the ordinance or resolution the name or form of something else, such as a motion or report. Nor will the mere combining of a motion for the adoption of an act with the act itself, limit the act so as to confine its effect to that of a motion.[18]

"If the mode of the exercise of the power by a municipal corporation is not prescribed by statute the power may be exercised by resolution as well as by ordinance or order. Where, however, the statute prescribes that the method of exercising the power shall be by ordinance, no other method than that so prescribed will suffice to give validity to the action of the municipal governing body. In such case neither a resolution nor a mere verbal motion will suffice." Collins v. City of Schenectady, 256 App. Div. 389, 10 N.Y.S.2d 303, 308 (1939).

Where the mode of exercising a municipal power is not prescribed in the statute conferring the power or in some other statute, the power may be exercised by resolution as well as by ordinance. United States *ex rel.* White v. Walsh, 174 F.2d 49 (7th Cir.), *rev'd,* 338 U.S. 804, *rehearing denied,* 338 U.S. 881 (1949).

A motion need not be made "in the most strict and formal way" or in precise language so long as the chairman and the assembly understand that a definite motion has been made. Henderson v. Bank of Australasia, 45 Ch. D. 330 (C.A. 1890).

[16] Shoults v. Alderson, 55 Cal. App. 527, 203 P. 809 (1921).

[17] Gottlieb v. McKee, 34 Del. Ch. 537, 107 A.2d 240 (1954).

But see § 3.4.2 *supra.*

[18] "In parliamentary procedure a motion may be made which submits a proposed measure for consideration and action. In this case the motion as made proposed the adoption by the council of an administrative measure, temporary in its nature. The fact that the motion as made included the measure to be adopted did not make the enacted measure a 'motion.' There could have been a separate motion to consider, with a vote on this motion, and another and separate vote on the measure proposed. The mere combining of a motion for the adoption of an administrative act, ordinance, or resolution with the act, ordinance, or resolution to be adopted or enacted, does not limit the act, ordinance, or resolution so as to confine its effect to that of a 'motion.' " Allen v. Wise, 204 Ga. 415, 50 S.E.2d 69, 72 (1948).

§ 18.3   Improper Motions

The fact that a motion has been made by a member, in the sense that the member has moved in accepted form that a certain resolution be adopted, does not necessarily mean that a proper motion has been made. Thus, if the motion is to take some action which is beyond the power of the body, the presiding officer may refuse to put it on that account and his further refusal to entertain an appeal from his ruling will be upheld by the courts. In this case the court said that: "The rulings of the president were not upon mere questions of parliamentary practice—of procedure. They went to the matter of legal power." [19]

Also, the fact that a resolution has been made and adopted by the body is not conclusive of its validity. For example, a resolution cannot alter the statutory or common law or violate the dictates of the charter or by-laws of the organization.[20]

§ 18.4   Reading of Resolution or Ordinance

A motion need not necessarily be read in full before being put to a vote, even if a parliamentary manual has been adopted by the body and its rules so provide.[21] It is within the power of

---

Where the statute provides that appointments of officers by a common council should be determined by vote taken by roll call of its members, by statement of choice, or by affirmative or negative vote, an appointment by resolution or ordinance is excluded and invalid. "Putting an administrative act in the clothes or form of a legislative act, i.e., a resolution, does not change its true nature." *In re* Heafy, 247 App. Div. 277, 285 N.Y.S. 188, 192, 195 (3d Dep't), *aff'd*, Heafy v. McCabe, 270 N.Y. 616, 1 N.E.2d 357 (1936).

[19] Alliance Co-op Ins. Co. v. Gasche, 93 Kan. 147, 142 P. 882, 883 (1914).

[20] City charter empowered the council to elect certain officers by a ballot vote. The court held that, when a ballot is required, "then all the common law rules that apply to that method of acting must be observed, and no rule can be established, by custom or otherwise, that will substantially affect the determination of the majority, otherwise than according to the principles of the common law." Murdoch v. Strange, 99 Md. 89, 57 A. 628, 629 (1904), *citing* Cushing, Law & Pr. Leg. Assem.

[21] Parliamentary rules are procedural and their strict observance is not mandatory. "The purpose of a parliamentary procedural rule requiring the reading of a resolution in full before it is voted on is to provide assurance that those whose duty is to vote thereon may have some knowledge of its scope and terms

all deliberative bodies to suspend, abolish, or modify their own rules (as distinguished from statutory or charter provisions), including a rule that every resolution must have two or three readings before its passage.[22] It has also been held that a reading by title

---

before they cast their votes." In this case that purpose was adequately served by informed discussions and a visit to the site in question. City of Pasadena v. Paine, 126 Cal. App. 2d 93, 271 P.2d 577, 579 (1954) (Robert's Rules of Order).

An averment in an action against a city council that a constitutional provision requiring every bill to be read on three separate days, unless dispensed with by two-thirds vote, "is a general rule of parliamentary law" within the rules of the council and a conclusion of the pleader unless accompanied by an averment that the council had adopted it as one of its governing rules. The council itself is the judge of the "general rules of parliamentary law" applicable to its business, and the court cannot declare as a matter of law that it was incumbent upon the council to read an ordinance three times before final passage or that a single reading was sufficient. Landes v. State ex rel. Matson, 160 Ind. 479, 67 N.E. 189, 193 (1903).

Where the rules provide that every "bill" must be read three different times, without suspension of the rules, such reading requirements do not apply to resolutions as they are not bills. Walther v. McDonald, 243 Ark. 912, 422 S.W.2d 854, 862 (1968).

A vote is not a "reading." *See* Brumley v. Town of Greeneville, 33 Tenn. App. 322, 274 S.W.2d 12 (1954).

[22] "It is no objection to the validity of the assessment that the order did not receive, in either branch of the city council, two several readings before its passage, as required by the rules of the city council. It is within the power of all deliberative bodies to abolish, modify or waive their own rules, intended as security against hasty or inconsiderate action." Holt v. City Council, 127 Mass. 408, 411 (1879).

A city council may by its customary practice waive the requirement of oral reading of proposed ordinances. The rule "prescribes merely a rule of parliamentary procedure" and may be waived. Jefferson v. City of Anchorage, 513 P.2d 1099, 1101 (Alas. 1973).

Where a rule requiring that an ordinance be read on three different days was properly suspended by a three-fourths vote of all members of the city council, the ordinance was not invalid because it was not read three times on the same day on which it was passed. Pathe v. Donaldson, 29 Ohio App. 171, 163 N.E. 204 (1928).

An ordinance was read in full at the first meeting and then, at the same meeting under suspension of the rules, was advanced to a second reading and read by title only. The council adjourned to a day certain and the ordinance was again read for the third time and adopted. The procedure was held valid. Property Owners v. City of Anderson, 231 Ind. 78, 107 N.E.2d 3 (1952).

only does not invalidate an ordinance notwithstanding that a rule of the city commission required that an ordinance be read at the meeting at which it was introduced. "It has been decided by the courts of last resort of many states, and also by the United States Supreme Court, that a legislative act will not be declared invalid for non-compliance with rules." [23]

It has been the practice quite uniformly recognized that every bill introduced in a legislative house should be read at least three times, usually on different days, before submission of the question of its passage. The purpose is to inform the legislators of the nature of the proposed enactment and prevent hasty legislation.[24] A stat-

---

"The statute specifically provides that the requirement of a reading on two separate meetings may be suspended by a vote of two-thirds of the members of the board. As shown, the requirement was suspended by a vote of all members of the board. Appellant contends that the Bowling Green council had never adopted any rules and, therefore, could not suspend non-existing rules. We are unable to accept that argument and consider that the statutory suspension was appropriately adopted, and the ordinance was effectively enacted insofar as the reading at two separate meetings is concerned." Payne v. Petrie, 419 S.W.2d 761, 763 (Ky. 1967).

Two readings of a proposed revised ordinance on the same night under suspension of the rules, at a meeting of a city board held at the home of the mayor who was seriously ill, was of no effect because the meeting was not a "public meeting" as contemplated by the statute. Lexington v. Davis, 310 Ky. 751, 221 S.W.2d 659 (1949).

[23] Dayton v. Woodgeard, 110 Ohio App. 326, 187 N.E.2d 921, 925 (1962).

[24] "It is an interesting matter of observation that it was in the middle portion of the preceding century that it became the practice to lay down, in the constitutions of the various states, procedural requirements and restrictions to be observed by legislatures in the process of enacting laws. Previously legislatures had been largely untrammeled in the matter of controlling their own legislative procedure. Many of these comparatively recent constitutional provisions are expressive of regulations which legislatures had anciently prescribed for their guidance. One of these old and commonly adopted rules provided that a bill upon being introduced in a legislative house should be read three times on as many different days before submission of the question of its passage. The writers of our Constitution did not in terms include therein this rule. Yet we think its almost universal adoption and observance by legislative bodies was recognized in the writing of our Constitution, because section 17, above quoted, contemplates a 'last reading' of all bills. The writers of the Constitution evidently contemplated that the legislatures of Iowa would follow this rule, and that they would do so for the accomplishment of its primary purpose, that is, avoidance

ute or charter requiring that all bills be read at certain times is mandatory, and an ordinance or resolution adopted without meeting that requirement is void.[25] However, unanimous adoption of an ordinance by a city council may dispense with a requirement that it be read on three different days.[26]

Passage of an ordinance on its first reading by one council and on its second reading by another and succeeding council is valid.[27] The term "last reading" implies a previous reading or readings and has led to litigation in determining when a "last reading" occurs. It is generally held that the concurrence by one legislative house in amendments to a bill made by the other house constitutes final passage within the meaning of the constitutional requirement that every bill shall be read on three different days and that final passage shall be taken by "ayes" and "nays" on a roll call. The same rule applies to approval by both houses of a conference committee report on amendments to a bill. Thus, the constitutional requirement that bills be read does not apply to amendments so as to compel a further reading of the bills as amended.[28] As one court said: "Amendments

---

of the evils that might follow in the train of enactment of bills immediately upon presentment to the legislative house. The purpose of the rule is to inform legislators, and the people, of legislation proposed by a bill, and to prevent hasty legislation." Scott v. State Bd. of Assessment and Rev., 221 Iowa 1060, 267 N.W. 111, 113 (1936); accord, Carlton v. Grimes, 237 Iowa 912, 922, 23 N.W.2d 883 (1946).

[25] Hatfield v. Meers, 402 S.W.2d 35 (Mo. 1966); Brumley v. Town of Greeneville, 33 Tenn. App. 322, 274 S.W.2d 12 (1954).

[26] Holman v. City of Dierks, 217 Ark. 677, 233 S.W.2d 392 (1950).

[27] Reuter v. Meacham Contracting Co., 143 Ky. 557, 136 S.W. 1028 (1911).

[28] A bill was given three readings in each house before passage and then sent to a conference committee for consideration of amendments. The conference committee report was approved by both houses without further reading. The court approved, holding that the evident constitutional purpose of successive readings had been accomplished before the bill went to conference. Carlton v. Grimes, 237 Iowa 912, 23 N.W.2d 883 (1946).

Adoption of a conference committee report recommending that the house recede from its amendments and that the bill be amended in accordance with a prior report is not compliance with a constitutional requirement that a vote shall be taken immediately after its "last reading" and the yeas and nays be entered on the journal. Smith v. Thompson, 219 Iowa 888, 258 N.W. 190 (1934).

A bill regularly introduced, read once, and advanced to be read a second time on a subsequent day, may be amended while at that stage, either in the

made during the process of enactment do not take from a bill the status obtained by prior readings or make it necessary to begin the reading anew." [29] And it is the rule in amending a bill that it is unnecessary, as each amendment is made, to begin again and read the bill three times as amended.[30] Also, where an amendment does not change the basic character of a bill and, after amendment, the bill still covers the same subject matter as when it was introduced, it is not necessary to proceed with oral reading or publication as if the bill were a new one.[31]

The terms "finally passed" and "final passage" mean the same thing, and that is the vote of either house that completes the passage of the measure. "This meaning accords with the usual practice of parliamentary bodies." [32] Also, the requirements of a statute that every motion, resolution, or ordinance introduced at a meeting should be reduced to writing and read before being voted upon do not apply to the "parliamentary motion" to adopt the resolution. Such motion need not be reduced to writing and read in full.[33]

The presumption of regularity will apply to the reading of motions and resolutions. Although the minutes are silent on the point,

---

mode most frequently pursued, or by substitute offered and adopted in lieu thereof, provided the substitute is not inconsistent with the main purpose and object of the original bill. Hood v. City of Wheeling, 85 W. Va. 578, 102 S.E. 259 (1920).

Where the statute requires that bills and their amendments be printed and that every bill shall be read at large on three different days in each House, the latter requirement that bills be read does not apply to amendments. People ex rel. Sellers v. Brady, 262 Ill. 578, 105 N.E. 1 (1914), citing Jefferson's Manual.

Statutory interpretation is important in deciding questions regarding the reading of bills. For example, where a statute requires two "readings," but the word "passage" relates only to the second reading, an amendment that is permitted between the first and second reading applies only to the second reading and final passage, and not to the first reading. Northwestern Bell Tel. Co. v. Board of Comm'rs, 211 N.W.2d 399, 401 (N.D. 1973).

[29] School Dist. No. 11 v. Chapman, 152 F. 887, 891 (8th Cir.), cert. denied, 205 U.S. 545 (1907).

[30] State ex rel. Davis v. Cox, 105 Neb. 75, 178 N.W. 913, 916 (1920).

[31] Jefferson v. City of Anchorage, 513 P.2d 1099 (Alas. 1973).

[32] Cox v. Stults Eagle Drug Co., 21 P.2d 914, 916 (Ariz. 1933).

[33] Haas v. City of Mobile, 289 Ala. 16, 265 So.2d 564, 569 (1972).

it will be presumed that the resolution was read in full and validly adopted.[34] However, a recital in the minutes that a resolution was passed on three readings can be rebutted on direct testimony of the recorder that the resolution was not in fact read as recited in the minutes.[35]

§ 18.5 Seconding

It is the general practice to require that motions be seconded before they can be stated, thereby preventing time from being taken in considering a matter that only one person favors.[36] However, as a matter of practice, when the chair is certain the motion will be adopted, he may proceed to state and put the question without a second, subject to a point of order insisting that a second be obtained.[37] It has been held that failure to obtain a second does not necessarily amount to a denial or rejection of a motion, particularly where it is unclear whether the body considered there had been a final disposition of the motion.[38] Under early English parliamentary law, a motion put and voted upon has been sustained over an objection that it had not been seconded.[39]

In nominations for office, seconding is purely complimentary and

[34] Baker v. Combs, 194 Ky. 260, 239 S.W. 56 (1922).

[35] Brumley v. Town of Greeneville, 33 Tenn. App. 322, 274 S.W.2d 12 (1954).

[36] A motion may fail for want of a second. *See, e.g.,* Syracuse Television, Inc. v. Channel 9, 51 Misc. 2d 188, 273 N.Y.S.2d 16, 25 (Sup. Ct. 1966). For exceptions to this rule, *see* Robert's Rules of Order at 36–37.

[37] *See* Robert's Rules of Order at 36.

[38] "The failure of a second may have indicated the others desired to more fully consider the question before voting thereon. At least, it is far from clear that this action was considered final by the council or the concerned parties. The trial court concluded the failure to obtain a second did not amount to a denial or rejection of the amendment, and we agree." Smith v. City of Fort Dodge, 160 N.W.2d 492, 498 (Iowa 1968).

[39] A concurring judge remarked: "In my opinion if the chairman put the question without its having been either proposed or seconded by anybody, that would be perfectly good." *In re* Horbury Bridge, Coal, Iron & Waggon Co., 11 Ch. D. 109, 117–18 (1879).

See SHAW AND SMITH, THE LAW OF MEETINGS at 65; SHACKLETON, LAW AND PRACTICE OF MEETINGS at 77.

is not necessary. On the other hand, where the chairman rules that a nomination is out of order because it was not seconded, and the objector "waived" his right to appeal from the chairman's ruling by asking for a roll call on another nominee, the chairman's ruling will stand.[40]

VARIOUS KINDS OF MOTIONS

The courts have at times, but not consistently, had an opportunity to pass upon or interpret various parliamentary motions made during the sessions of deliberative assemblies. Some decisions are founded on common parliamentary law and others on rules which have been established for or by the particular organization. Following is a brief description of various motions which may be expected at the meetings of most deliberative assemblies. For less frequent motions, reference should be made to a standard manual on parliamentary procedure. Relevant court decisions are reported when available.

§ 18.6   To Amend

A motion to amend, in parliamentary usage, is a motion to change or complete the wording of a resolution or proposal by inserting or adding, by striking out, or by striking out and inserting, one or more words or paragraphs. A motion to amend the main motion, being an appendage to another motion, must necessarily take precedence over the motion to which it applies. The motion can be made at any time during the discussion and, when made, further debate on the original motion is out of order.

The proposed amendment must be put to a vote before voting upon the main motion. Regardless of the vote on the amendment, the main motion must be voted upon in any case. If the amendment is carried, the main motion is then referred to as the original main motion as amended.

The chairman should not refuse to put an amendment which is relevant and proper within the scope of the meeting. The refusal of the chairman to put a proper amendment which has been duly

[40] Campbell v. School Comm., 21 A.2d 727 (R.I. 1941).

moved and seconded may invalidate the resolution to which the proposed amendment relates. The effect of such a refusal is to withdraw a material and relevant question from the consideration of the meeting. Accordingly, if the chairman is uncertain whether the amendment is in order he should allow it to be put, as failure to put the amendment may nullify the resolution.[1]

According to parliamentary law, a proposed amendment is "out of order" if it destroys the original question or is irrelevant, absurd, or frivolous; and, when an amendment involves the replacement of one or more paragraphs or the entire resolution, the amendment is a substitute, and so called.[2]

In deciding whether a legislative enactment qualifies as a lawful "amendment," the courts will give full recognition to constitutional and statutory provisions relating to the process of amending a statute or a pending bill. With respect to amending a city charter, it has been said: "This court, as well as the court of appeals, has repeatedly sustained sundry and different kinds of amendments to the former charter, some of which made radical changes in the management of its affairs."[3]

The definitions given the word "amendment" by different courts are substantially the same in effect, but there is no settled rule as to the line of distinction between an amendment and a new act or proposal.[4] The Supreme Court, in considering a city charter, has followed the general rule in holding that a proposed change which does not alter the form of the city government or make extensive changes is an amendment and not a revision requiring intervention

---

[1] Henderson v. Bank of Australasia, 45 Ch. D. 330, *rev'd on other grounds,* 45 Ch. D. 330 (1890).

[2] *See* Robert's Rules of Order at 134–52.

[3] People *ex rel.* Moore v. Perkins, 56 Colo. 17, 137 P. 55, 59 (1913).

[4] "The definitions given the word or term 'amendment' by different courts are substantially the same in effect, but as to determining the exact legal scope, the exact limits of an amendment, or the definite line of distinction between amendments and new acts, and just where an amendment crosses such line and in legal effect becomes a new act there is no settled rule." Moore v. Oklahoma City, 122 Okla. 234, 254 P. 47, 49 (1927).

An ordinance may be repealed by an amendment "striking out" and "inserting." See definitions of "implied repeal," "express repeal," "repeal," "strike out," "amend." St. Louis v. Kellman, 139 S.W. 443 (Mo. 1911).

of a charter convention.[5] In the same sense, a substitute bill which is germane to the original is not a new bill.[6]

A motion to amend should be stated with clarity, preferably in writing, so that its content and import cannot be misunderstood. It has been held, however, that a motion to amend need not be made "in the most strict and formal way" and will be recognized where the chairman understood that it was a motion to amend and asked for a second.[7]

The courts will apply parliamentary law in deciding questions of parliamentary tactics. If the body has adopted a particular code, the courts will give recognition to its provisions. A leading case involving a common council which had adopted Cushing's Manual as a guide quoted from the Manual and held: "From the foregoing provision, it is apparent that an amendment to a motion or resolution takes precedence of the original motion. The original motion cannot be disposed of until the proposed amendment is disposed of, unless the amendment is clearly a substitute for the original motion. A passage of the amendment has no effect other than to amend the original motion, except it is a substitute. Where it simply amends the original motion, and is not a substitute for it, then the original motion must be put." The court concluded that a motion to substitute the names of two out of three nominees designated in a resolution appointing appraisers was an amendment and not a sub-

---

[5] Denver v. New York Trust Co., 229 U.S. 123, 145 (1913).

Minor or formal changes made on the third reading of an ordinance by the city council, which did not result in a material or substantial difference in the ordinance as introduced, will not render the ordinance void. Biltmore Hotel Court v. City of Berry Hill, 216 Tenn. 62, 390 S.W.2d 223 (1965).

A proposed local law adopted by a city common council creating new departments to replace commissions does not create a new charter. Commission of Public Charities v. Wortman, 255 App. Div. 241, 7 N.Y.S.2d 631, aff'd, 279 N.Y. 711, 18 N.E.2d 325 (1938).

Where an ordinance passed on first reading was subsequently amended, but both the original and amended drafts dealing with the same purposes and amendments were not so substantial as to become a new ordinance and the reading of the amended ordinance constituted a second reading as required by the city charter, the ordinance was validly enacted. B & B Vending Co. v. El Paso, 408 S.W.2d 545 (Tex. 1966).

[6] State ex rel. Davis v. Cox, 105 Neb. 75, 178 N.W. 913 (1920).

[7] Henderson v. Bank of Australasia, 45 Ch. D. 330, 343–44, rev'd on other grounds, 45 Ch. D. 330 (1890).

stitution, whereas a motion to substitute all three names would have
been a substitute for the original resolution which, if carried, would
have accomplished the election of the three substitutes.[8]

However, the legislative body has the right to suspend, abolish,
or modify its own parliamentary rules in the course of adopting
an amendment, such as a rule that proposed local laws should be
referred to a special committee of the common council before being
put to a vote.[9]

On the other hand, there is a general rule of statutory construction that, if any section of a pending bill remains, then proposed
new matter and changes are amendatory only. The word "amend"
must be given its usual and ordinary meaning, and thus an amendment may effectually "supplant or destroy" the original motion.[10]
Furthermore, there is a presumption of validity of the amending resolution which "presupposes all necessary procedure was followed." [11]

It is also a "settled principle of parliamentary law" in some jurisdictions that, so long as the enacting words remain in a bill before
a legislative body, the bill can be amended to any extent, even by
striking out all after the enacting words, and by inserting other
words. When a bill passed by one house is thus amended by the
other house, such amendment may be concurred in by the first
house without the three readings required on the original passage.[12]

---

[8] Casler v. Tanzer, 134 Misc. 48, 53, 234 N.Y.S. 571, 577 (Sup. Ct. 1929).

[9] Commission of Public Charities v. Wortman, 255 App. Div. 241, 7 N.Y.
S.2d 631 (3d Dep't), aff'd, 279 N.Y. 711, 18 N.E.2d 325 (1938).

See § 18.4 supra.

[10] The court quoted from Cushing: "A proposition may be amended, in parliamentary phraseology, not only by an alteration which carries out and effects
the purpose of the mover, but also by one which entirely destroys that purpose,
or which even makes the proposition express a sense the very reverse of that
intended by the mover. . . ." State v. Meyers, 51 Wash. 2d 454, 319 P.2d
828, 831 (1957).

[11] Smith v. City of Fort Dodge, 160 N.W.2d 492, 495 (Iowa 1968).

[12] "It is a settled principle of parliamentary law in this state that, so long as
the enacting words remain in a bill, it can be amended to any extent, even by
striking out all after the enacting words, and by inserting other words as a substitute. The constitution does not require every word in an act to have received three readings on three several days. If it did, no important bill ever
became or can become a law. Very few important bills are not amended on
their second reading, and such amendments, when adopted, are not read three
times on three several days. Sometimes, in the house, by unanimous consent,

The courts will not always investigate the character of the original bill or the substitute, or the justice or the policy of the legislation, as that is within the sole control of the Legislature. When the Legislature treats a substitution as an amendment, and so terms it, and no constitutional provision is violated, the court will ordinarily not put a different construction on the legislative action.[13]

It has also been held that a city council's decision as to whether a proposed "amendment" was a true amendment or was in fact a substitute, making it unnecessary to put the original motion, was "a question of parliamentary law" within the judgment of the council and will not be disturbed by the courts.[14]

The term "bill" may mean the bill as it was first introduced, or it may refer to the bill at any time in any of its stages of amendment until finally passed. Thus, a "bill" necessarily includes the amendments. "Under ordinary parliamentary practice, in putting a bill upon its final passage in either house the question is stated, 'Shall this bill pass?' Jefferson's Manual (Barclay's Dig.) 117, 121; Barclay's Digest (Jefferson's Manual) 23. By some authorities it is held to be proper to put the final passage of a question or bill, 'Shall the motion as amended (or bill as amended) pass?' Robert's Rules of Order, § 65. The question, put in either way, 'Shall the bill pass?' or 'Shall the bill as amended pass?' means the same thing. It is

---

and in the senate, upon notice, bills are amended on the third reading. Nothing is more common than to amend by striking out one section and by inserting another, or by striking out several sections and by inserting one or several; and if it be competent to amend by striking out and inserting one, two, three, four sections, clearly it is competent to strike out all the sections, and to insert others, in pari materia. Striking out all after the enacting words, and inserting, is nothing but an amendment, and is governed by the same rules as other amendments." Cantini v. Tillman, 54 F. 969, 975 (D.S.C. 1893); accord, People ex rel. Moore v. Perkins, 56 Colo. 17, 137 P. 55 (1913); Miller v. Ohio, 3 Ohio St. 475 (1854), citing Jefferson's Manual.

[13] Substitution of a new bill of the same character was but an amendment of the original bill, and only required a concurrence of the other house, and did not require the yeas and nays to be taken upon the final passage of a bill as required by the constitution. Brake v. Callison, 122 F. 722 (S.D. Fla. 1903), aff'd, Callison v. Brake, 129 F. 196 (5th Cir.), cert. denied, 194 U.S. 638 (1904), citing Cushing, Law & Pr. Leg. Assem.

[14] Davies v. Saginaw, 87 Mich. 439, 49 N.W. 667, 668 (1891).

always intended to put upon its final passage a motion, resolution, or bill in its final form as amended." [15]

"It is true that under parliamentary law after an amendment is made to a motion, the motion as amended must be put to a vote." However, where an amendment is framed in such a way that its adoption "left no reason to doubt that the sense of the meeting on the subject was really ascertained and declared," failure to put the motion as amended to a vote does not constitute such an irregularity as would justify the granting of an injunction.[16]

Although it is the general rule that all motions should be seconded, an objection that an amendment was not seconded cannot prevail on a showing that it was put and voted upon.[17]

The Association of the Bar of the City of New York has adopted an amendment of its By-Laws limiting the right of the membership to amend any resolution submitted to the meeting which may substantially vary the terms of the resolution as circulated to the membership. The ruling of the chair on this point is not subject to appeal.

The resolution adopting the amended By-Law reads as follows:

RESOLVED, that
Pursuant to Article XXVII of the By-Laws, the following amendment, effective July 1, 1975, will be offered:
Amend Article II of the By-Laws by adding a new Section 5 to read as follows and renumbering the following sections accordingly:
5. *Only the following actions shall be permitted on any resolution submitted to any meeting of the Association:*
    a. *That the resolution be amended, provided that the Chairperson of the meeting rules that the proposed amendment does not substantially vary the terms of the resolution as circulated to the membership. There shall be no appeal from the ruling of the Chairperson;*
    b. *That the resolution be "approved";*

[15] People *ex rel.* Sellers v. Brady, 262 Ill. 578, 105 N.E. 1, 5 (1914).

[16] Leonard v. School Dist., 98 N.H. 530, 98 A.2d 415 (1953), *citing* Robert's Rules of Order.

[17] Simpson v. Berkowitz, 59 Misc. 160, 110 N.Y.S. 485 (1908).

A city charter prohibiting the granting of a franchise until it has been advertised does not prohibit amendments being made after advertisement and before passage. Saginaw Power Co. v. Saginaw, 193 F. 1008 (E.D. Mich. 1911).

    c. That the resolution be "disapproved";
    d. That the resolution be "referred" either to the Executive Committee or to some other Standing or Special Committee of the Association; or
    e. That the Association take "no action or position" on the resolution.

COMMENT: In the opinion of the Special Committee on the Second Century it is "unwise and inappropriate to circularize one resolution, and then to permit the meeting substantially to vary the terms upon which the vote is to be taken." To the extent that the amendments change the position proposed and circulated to the membership, it cannot fairly be said to be a decision on which the membership has had an authentic opportunity to inform itself. Moreover, intelligent drafting cannot be achieved in a large meeting. The remedy is to refer the action back to some competent body, such as the Executive Committee or a Standing or Special Committee, or to take no action or position. It should be noted this is the procedure followed by both Houses of Congress in dealing with the report of a Conference Committee. (The Decision-Making Structure of the Association, 28 Record 98, February 1973).

§ 18.7 To Amend an Amendment

A primary amendment may be amended in the same manner as a main motion. Such an amendment, called a secondary amendment, cannot itself be amended. It takes precedence over the primary amendment and must be disposed of before the primary amendment can be put to a vote.

An amendment to a resolution may be amended at a meeting subsequent to that at which the resolution was passed.[18]

§ 18.8 To Reconsider

The primary purpose of a motion to reconsider a vote taken on a question (whether the motion was carried or lost) is to provide means for correcting errors resulting from hasty action without mature deliberation. A motion to reconsider may be made while another motion is pending, and may interrupt a speaker if necessary. It is debatable only when the motion to which it is applied is debatable.

Some rules provide that a motion to reconsider can be made only

[18] *See In re* Horbury Bridge, Coal, Iron & Waggon Co., 11 Ch. D. 109 (1879).

on the day on which the action was taken or the next day of the
session, and may be made only by a member who voted on the
prevailing side.[19] This rule may be suspended.[20] Generally, a question can be reconsidered only once, and if the motion is lost it
cannot be renewed except by general consent.

Reconsideration cannot be made on a decision which has already
been carried out or is in the process of execution.[21]

Parliamentary procedures for the reconsideration of a question
must be followed with care. For example, where a county board
acting under Robert's Rules adopted a resolution changing a zoning
classification and then, ten days later, adopted another resolution
agreeing to reconsider its earlier action at a future day certain,
failure of the board to receive or act upon a motion to reconsider
on that day did not affect the original resolution. The court remarked that the sole question was one of the controlling "parlia-

[19] "Deliberative assemblies, in order that the will of a majority of its members may be ascertained and registered in an orderly way, must, ex necessitate
rei, be governed by rules of procedure to which each member thereof must
conform. In the absence of special rules of procedure adopted by such an assembly, or for it by an outside power having the right so to do, its procedure
is governed by the general parliamentary law . . . ; Robert's Rules of Order,
Revised, p. 15, one of the rules of which is that, when a motion has been made
and carried or lost, it may be reconsidered on a motion therefor by a member
of the assembly who voted with the prevailing side made 'on the day the vote
to be reconsidered was taken, or the next succeeding day, a legal holiday or
recess not being counted as a day.' Robert's Rules of Order, Revised, p. 156."
Witherspoon v. State ex rel. West, 138 Miss. 310, 103 So. 134, 137 (1925)
(citations omitted).

[20] "It was unquestionably competent for the board to reconsider the vote by
which the ordinance was lost. Parliamentary law requires that the motion to
reconsider be made by one who voted with the majority on the motion proposed
to be reconsidered. But whether this shall be insisted on or dispensed with,
and the motion made by one voting with the majority, rests exclusively in the
discretion of the body whose action it is proposed to reconsider, and no other
tribunal has a right to treat a reconsideration thus moved for as void. A majority could dispense with the rule requiring the reconsideration to be moved
by one who voted with the majority, and if the majority treat the motion as
regularly made, it is to be considered as a tacit suspension of the rule. The
members of the body alone have the right to object to the violation of the parliamentary rule." People ex rel. Locke v. Common Council, 5 Lans. 11, 14–15
(N. Y. Sup. Ct. 1871).

[21] See Casler v. Tanzer, 134 Misc. 48, 234 N.Y.S. 571 (Sup. Ct. 1929);
Robert's Rules of Order at 49–50, 156–65.

mentary rules"—that is, whether the motion was a "simple motion
to reconsider, or a motion recording an agreement to take up the
question of a reconsideration at a later date." [22]

It is a generally accepted parliamentary rule that the vote of a
legislative body to override a veto of the chief executive (whether
successful or not) may not be reconsidered by the body. This practice is, of course, subject to the rules of order of the body. [23]

§ 18.9   To Table

A motion to "lay on the table" is intended to lay aside or suspend
the pending question temporarily until more urgent business has
been considered, retaining the right to resume its consideration
when convenient. [24]   Since this motion has been misused as a method
of cutting off debate and strangling proposals, the assembly should
be alert to avoid these possibilities. This motion has also been
employed as a device to foreclose the reopening of an enacted bill.

In a Tennessee case it appeared that the almost invariable practice of the state legislature was to follow each vote on a bill whether
affirmative or negative, with an entry in the Journal reading: "A

[22] The court said: "According to Robert's Rules . . . the motion of January
10th was a motion entered on the minutes to be considered at a future date.
In discussing the difference between this type of motion and a simple motion
to reconsider, Mr. Robert says that the former motion cannot be voted upon on
the same day on which it is made, but must be taken up and voted upon on
the day in the future fixed by the motion itself, where the regular business
sessions of the assembly are as often as quarterly." First Buckingham Community, Inc. v. Malcolm, 177 Va. 710, 15 S.E.2d 54, 55–56 (1941).

[23] "The motion to reconsider in the case at bar was made and considered in
accordance with a rule of the common council which in its general terms applied to a vote of this kind. A vote on the passing of the measure over the
objections of the mayor, speaking accurately, is not a motion to reconsider the
measure. That vote is upon a new question never before presented to the body,
viz., whether the measure shall be passed notwithstanding the objections of the
mayor. That is a different question from any presented at the earlier stages in
the consideration of the matter. . . . There is considerable diversity amongst
legislative precedents upon this question." Nevins v. City Council, 227 Mass.
538, 116 N.E. 881, 884 (1917) (parliamentary manuals mentioned: Hinds'
Precedents, Cushing, Law & Pr. Leg. Assem., Barclay's Digest, Fish's Manual,
Spofford's Practical Manual, Wilson's Digest Parl. Law).

[24] A motion which has been laid on the table, and not finally acted upon, is
a "subject of deliberation." Coffin v. Coffin, 4 Mass. 1, 21 (1808).

motion to reconsider was tabled." This procedure was used and treated as a "final disposition" of the bill. It was held that a presumption of regularity of the passage of a bill, which had been signed by the Speakers of both Houses and approved by the Governor, supported by the notation that a motion to reconsider had been tabled, would not overcome an affirmative showing that the bill in fact was defeated by a majority of more than two to one.[25]

§ 18.10   To Postpone Indefinitely

A motion to postpone indefinitely is "another method of suppressing a question" or "simply a motion to reject the main question."[26] This motion, made at a town meeting, to postpone indefinitely a resolution that would make a private street a public street, has been described as follows: "Indefinite postponement by a body having only definite present existence is the equivalent of complete disapproval. This conclusion is confirmed by the technical meaning, which the phrase has acquired in parliamentary usage. There is a consensus of opinion among writers upon this subject that it means suppression of the question, and is equivalent to a negative vote."[27]

[25] The rules of the Senate provided that "it shall be a finality when a motion to re-consider is tabled." The rules of the House were silent on this point but named Robert's Rules of Order as a reference on questions not covered by the rules. The court stated that while Robert's "states the general rule to be that a motion to table leaves the measure subject to subsequent further consideration, a foot note states that, 'In Congress it is usual for the member in charge of an important bill as soon as it is passed to move its reconsideration, and at the same time to move that the reconsideration be laid on the table. If the latter motion is adopted the reconsideration is dead and the bill is in the same condition as if the reconsideration had been voted on and lost.'" Wright v. Wiles, 173 Tenn. 334, 117 S.W.2d 736, 738 (1938).

An ordinance of a city council governing rules of procedure provided that a motion to lay on table shall dispose finally of the legislation against which it was made. Humphrey v. Youngstown, 143 N.E.2d 321, 323 (Ohio 1955).

See Goodwin v. State Board of Admin., 210 Ala. 453, 102 So. 718 (1925) (house waived its rule on motion to table).

[26] Robert's Rules of Order at 48, 152.

[27] Wood v. Town of Milton, 197 Mass. 531, 84 N.E. 332, 333 (1908), *citing* Cushing, Crocker, Jefferson, Reed.

Under rules of a city council, the indefinite postponement of a question precluded a further consideration during the entire session of the same subject to

§ 18.11 To Suspend the Rules

The rules of an assembly may be suspended unless they have been imposed by a higher authority.[28] This is often done when the assembly finds it necessary or desirable to take some action that conflicts with the established rules of order. The vote required to suspend the rules depends upon the nature of the rule being suspended and upon the applicable organic law. It appears to be the general rule of parliamentary law that, in the absence of an express

---

which the question referred. Zeiler v. Central Ry., 84 Md. 304, 35 A. 932, 933 (1896).

A vote at an annual town meeting to postpone indefinitely action on articles in the warrant and to appropriate money for the purpose, constitutes rejection of the articles. Commonwealth v. Town of Hudson, 52 N.E.2d 566 (Mass. 1943).

See Ashton v. Rochester, 133 N.Y. 187, 30 N.E. 965 (1892) (*citing* Robert's Rules of Order and Jefferson's Manual) (motion to reconsider and subsequent motion to postpone indefinitely).

[28] "So far as appears, the rules so suspended were not rules prescribed by any superior authority, as by the constitution or laws of the state, but such rules as the council itself had adopted, and which it was authorized to adopt to govern its own proceedings. . . . Such rules might properly be thus suspended by unanimous consent." City of Greeley v. Hamman, 17 Colo. 30, 28 P. 460, 461 (1891), *citing* Cushing, Law & Pr. Leg. Assem.

Rules of order adopted for the government of a city council are "mere rules of procedure adopted by itself for its guidance and convenience. They are no part of its legislative or legal charter, and rest upon no positive prescription of the statutes of the state. Being rules of procedure adopted by the council for its own convenience and government in the enactment of ordinances, it is competent for the council to waive them, and certainly this is so with the consent of all the counsel present . . . such consent, in our opinion, may be implied." Bradford v. Jellico, 1 Tenn. Ch. App. R. 700, 719 (1901).

Another case merely stated: "What rules of procedure the council has adopted are not disclosed by the record. Whatever they are, they may provide for suspension." County Court v. City of Grafton, 77 W. Va. 84, 86 S.E. 924, 925 (1915).

See Property Owners v. City of Anderson, 231 Ind. 78, 107 N.E.2d 3 (1952) (suspension of rules advancing an ordinance to a second reading); Lexington v. Davis, 310 Ky. 751, 221 S.W.2d 659 (1949) (three readings on same subject under suspension of the rules).

However, it has been held that a city council cannot suspend provisions of a city code requiring a waiting period of five days and then adopt an ordinance three days after filing with the clerk. Hukle v. City of Huntington, 134 W. Va. 249, 58 S.E.2d 780 (1950).

authority, the dispensing with or suspension of the rules can only be done by general consent—that is, by unanimous vote in favor or, if proposed informally, by no objection.[29] If done by statute or regulation, suspension of the rules may be by unanimous vote,[30] by two-thirds vote,[31] or even by a majority vote,[32] for limited purposes only,[33] or in any other manner prescribed for that purpose.[34] Also, there may be a tacit suspension of the rules, or their suspension may be implied.[35] An implied suspension may also result from the taking of some parliamentary action in conflict with the rule.[36] A stranger has no standing to question a suspension of the rules.[37]

[29] State *ex rel*. Krejsa v. Board of Educ., 2 Ohio C.C.R. 510 (Cir. Ct. 1887), *citing* Cushing's Manual; *accord*, City of Greeley v. Hamman, 17 Colo. 30, 28 P. 460, 461 (1891), *citing* Cushing's Manual.

[30] Rules provided that they may be suspended by unanimous consent. This was held to mean unanimous consent of members present and forming a quorum. Atkins v. Phillips, 26 Fla. 281, 8 So. 429 (1890) (city council).

[31] A new city council can adopt new rules by a majority vote, although a prior rule had required a two-thirds vote of all members to alter or suspend a rule. Armitage v. Fisher, 74 Hun 167, 26 N.Y.S. 364 (Sup. Ct. 1893).

See Kendall v. Board of Educ., 106 Mich. 681, 64 N.W. 745 (1895) (suspension of rules on two-thirds vote).

[32] An early case disapproved. "If the rules are to be suspended by a bare majority, they have no force as rules." State *ex rel*. Krejsa v. Board of Educ., 2 Ohio C.C.R. 510 (Cir. Ct. 1887).

[33] Suspension of rules by two-thirds of the membership of the city executive committee temporarily only as to time of holding primary elections and conventions. *In re* Doyle, 7 Pa. Dist. 635, 24 Pa. County Ct. 27 (1898).

[34] Parliamentary rules of order "may be amended, suspended, or repealed at the pleasure of the body, or in any manner that it has prescribed for this purpose." Montenegro–Riehm Music Co. v. Board of Educ., 147 Ky. 720, 145 S.W. 740, 743 (1912).

[35] "A majority could dispense with the rule requiring the reconsideration to be moved by one who voted with the majority, and if the majority treat the motion as regularly made, it is to be considered as a tacit suspension of the rule." People *ex rel*. Locke v. Common Council, 5 Lans. 11, 14, 15 (N.Y. Sup. Ct. 1871).

It is competent for a city council to suspend its rules of procedure, certainly with the consent of all the council present. Such consent "may be implied." Bradford v. City of Jellico, 1 Tenn. Ch. App. R. 700, 719 (1901).

[36] Where the rules may be suspended by a two-thirds vote of the members present, the failure to adopt a motion to lay a report on the table, which required a two-thirds vote for passage, resulted in a suspension of the rule. Kendall v. Board of Educ., 106 Mich. 681, 64 N.W. 745 (1895).

[37] A reporter who was ejected from a meeting of a board of education cannot

§ 18.12   Question of Order

A question or point of order arises when a member puts to the chair, whose duty it is to enforce order, the question as to whether there is not then a breach of order.[38] It is also the right and duty of any member who notices a breach of the rules to bring it to the attention of the presiding officer and insist upon its enforcement. The courts will approve parliamentary law in this regard. A recent case citing Robert's Rules of Order held that a question of order takes precedence over the pending question, may be raised when another has the floor, requires no second, may not be amended, and must be decided by the presiding officer without debate, except in doubtful cases when the question is submitted to the assembly.[39]

Just what constitutes a point of order is not easy to define. Where a standing order provides that the chairman's decision on a point of order shall be final, it has been held that: "In our opinion [this standing order] operates to make the Chairman's decision final only in regard to the conduct and control of debates." Thus, it was not a valid point of order within the meaning of the standing order to determine at the outset whether a meeting at which the members have assembled has been validly called or not.[40] In another case, the court distinguished between a declaration by the chairman that a motion was illegal and a ruling that it was out of order: "To declare that a motion violates law, and therefore should not be voted on, is one thing. Such a question neither the chairman nor the majority can pass upon with any legal effect. But to rule that a motion is out of order is to take an entirely different attitude with respect to it. It is a decision that some rule of the body or some practice established by parliamentary usage has been violated."[41]

---

question a suspension of the rules. The objection was upon a point of order "which if not taken by a member of the board, could certainly be of no avail to any one else." Corre v. State, 8 Ohio Dec. Reprint 715, 716 (Dist. Ct. 1883).

[38] *See* Robert's Rules of Order at 79–80.

[39] *In re* Ryan v. Grimm, 22 App. Div. 2d 171, 254 N.Y.S.2d 462 (1964), *appeal denied*, 23 App. Div. 527, 255 N.Y.S.2d 486 (4th Dep't), *motion denied*, 15 N.Y.2d 760, 257 N.Y.S.2d 333, 205 N.E.2d 528, *modified*, 15 N.Y.2d 922, 206 N.E.2d 867, 258 N.Y.S.2d 843 (1965).

[40] Arcus v. Castle, [1954] N.Z.L.R. 122, 129 (1953) (New Zealand).

[41] The court continued: "This question the chairman must decide in the first instance, and above him sits the court of final review, the majority who, on an

In support of the general rule of regularity it has also been held, where a statute provides that the mayor's decision on a point of order is final, that the court will not overrule the mayor where he acted in good faith and a reasonable man would have reason to rule as he did.[42] A point of order questioning the power of the body to suspend its rules cannot be raised by a reporter who was excluded from a meeting of the board of education.[43]

The question or point of order must be raised at the time the breach of order occurs, and not after the motion to which it relates has been discussed.[44]

§ 18.13   Motion—Out of Order

Where a presiding officer refused to put a motion and then refused to entertain an appeal from his ruling on the ground that the motion contemplated the exercise of powers by the body which had been conferred on him, his declaration that the motion was "out of order" was not valid. "I think that this objection in the mind of the presiding officer did not constitute a question of order." [45]

---

appeal from the ruling of the chair, settle the issue beyond the power of any court to change their decision." State *ex rel.* Moore v. Archibald, 5 N.D. 359, 66 N.W. 234, 243 (1896).

See State *ex rel.* Cole v. Chapman, 44 Conn. 595, 601–2 (1878) (city council sustained an appeal from a ruling of the mayor that a resolution was out of order).

[42] The court upheld the mayor in ruling that the city council had no power to deal with a certain matter (readvertise in newspaper) because of lapse of time. Rex v. Foley, [1928] Vict. L.R. 1 (1926).

[43] Corre v. State, 8 Ohio Dec. Reprint 715 (Dist. Ct. 1883).

[44] *See* Robert's Rules of Order at 79, 80. *See also* Henderson v. Bank of Australasia, 45 Ch. D. 330, 340, *rev'd on other grounds*, 45 Ch. D. 330 (C.A. 1890), holding that it was competent for a shareholder, immediately and before voting took place on a resolution, to rise to a point of order and address the chairman.

[45] "In effect the proposition of the presiding officer is that he may refuse to put the motion if he thinks that it contemplates action which is ultra vires the body over which he presides. If he can thus prevent action, he practically exercises a veto power, which is not conferred on him by statute, and is not inherent in him as a mere presiding officer. For in effect this would make him by virtue of his right to preside a co-ordinate or a superior branch of the local legislative body. . . . None will dispute the general power of a presiding officer at the

§ 18.14   To Adjourn

A motion to adjourn is a privileged motion which takes precedence over all other motions except the privileged motion to fix the time to which to adjourn. It is debatable only when adjournment would constitute a dissolution of the meeting and when no time has been fixed for the next meeting. A motion to adjourn cannot be amended nor can any other subsidiary motion be attached to it. A vote on a motion to adjourn cannot be reconsidered, but the motion may be withdrawn.

A motion to adjourn can be repeated if there has been any intervening business. The chair can refuse to entertain a motion to adjourn when it is evidently made for obstructive purposes, as when the assembly has just voted it down and nothing has occurred since to show the possibility of the assembly wishing to adjourn.

§ 18.15   To Take a Recess

A recess is an intermission. A motion to take a recess is a privileged motion. It is not debatable and can have no subsidiary motion applied to it except to amend. The motion can be amended as to the length of the recess. If adopted, it takes effect immediately.

§ 18.16   To Appeal

When a decision by the chairman seems to be in error, any member may appeal from that decision. Appeal must be made immediately after the decision is announced, and not later. The member appealing should rise promptly and without waiting to be recognized, even though another member has the floor. When an appeal is taken, the chairman should state the issue involved, and put the question.

---

objection of a member of the body, or sua sponte, to pass upon the question of the order of a motion under the rules of the body, subject to its review upon appeal from his decision, but in my view of this case this presiding officer could not declare the motion out of order and refuse to put it to a vote, on the ground that it contemplated action ultra vires the body." People *ex rel.* Hayes v. Brush, 96 N.Y.S. 500, 502 (1906), *citing* Cushing, Law & Pr. Leg. Assem.

§ 18.17   To Lay on the Table

This motion is usually made when the assembly has something else before it which is more urgent, and it is desired to suspend consideration of the question and yet retain the right to resume its consideration whenever convenient. The motion is not debatable and cannot be amended.[46]

§ 18.18   Dilatory Motions

The improper use of proper parliamentary procedures clearly made for dilatory purposes should not be permitted. These are motions intended to obstruct, delay, or frustrate the transaction of business in orderly fashion. They are often absurd, frivolous, or mischievous.

The rules of the House of Representatives provide: "No dilatory motion shall be entertained by the Speaker." This rule was adopted in 1890 to make permanent a principle already enunciated in a ruling of the Speaker, who had declared that the "object of a parliamentary body is action, not stoppage of action."[47] The procedures of the United States Senate are in accord.[48]

---

[46] "The object of the motion to lay on the table is stated in Robert's Rules of Order to be to enable the assembly, in order to attend to more urgent business, to lay aside the pending question in such a way that its consideration may be resumed at the will of the assembly as easily as if it were a new question, and in preference to new questions competing with it for consideration. In legislative bodies, and all others that do not have regular sessions as often as quarterly, questions laid on the table remain there for that entire session unless taken up before the session closes. In deliberative bodies with regular sessions as frequent as quarterly the sessions usually are very short, and questions laid on the table remain there until the close of the next regular session, if not taken up earlier. In ordinary deliberative assemblies a question is supposed to be laid on the table only temporarily, with the expectation of its consideration being resumed after the disposal of the interrupting question, or at a more convenient season. When taken up, the question, with everything adhering to it, is before the assembly exactly as when it was laid on the table." People ex rel. MacMahon v. Davis, 284 Ill. 439, 120 N.E. 326 (1918), citing Robert's Rules of Order and Hinds' Precedents.

[47] Constitution, Jefferson's Manual, Rules of the House of Representatives, Rule XVI.10 at § 803, House Doc. 416 (1975).

The report of the committee making the revision of 1890 said: "This clause is merely declaratory of parliamentary law. There are no words which can be framed which will limit Members to the proper use of proper motions. Any

There is little case law on this subject, probably because there
are few attempts to overrule a chairman's decision that a motion is
out of order as dilatory.[49]

---

motion the most conducive to progress in the public business or the most salutary for the comfort and convenience of Members may be used for purposes of
unjust and oppressive delay. The majority may be kept in session for a long
time against reason and good sense, sometimes at the whim of a single Member,
and sometimes for a still longer period, at the will of one-fifth who are misusing
the provision of the Constitution for yeas and nays, by the aid of simple motions proper in themselves, but which are improperly used. In the early days
such prostitution of legitimate motions caused by anger, willfulness, and party
zeal was not so much as named among legislators. To-day the abuse has grown
to such proportions that the parliamentary law which governs American assemblies has found it necessary to keep pace with the evil, and to enable the majority, by the intervention of the Presiding Officer, to meet by extraordinary
means the extraordinary abuse of power on the part sometimes of a very few
Members. Why should an assembly be kept from its work by motions made
only to delay and to weary, even if the original design of the motion was salutary and sensible? Why should one-fifth even be entitled to waste a half hour
of themselves and of four other fifths by a motion to adjourn when the majority
manifestly do not want to adjourn? If the suggestion should be made that
great power is here conferred, the answer is that as the approval of the House
is the very breath in the nostrils of the Speaker, and as no body on earth is so
jealous of its liberties and so impatient of control, we may be quite sure that
no arbitrary interruption will take place, and, indeed, no interruption at all,
until not only such misuses of proper motions is made clearly evident to the
world, but also such action has taken place on the part of the House as will
assure the Speaker of the support of the body whose wishes are his law. So
that in the end it is a power exercised by the House through its properly constituted officer." V Hinds' Precedents, Chapter CXXIV, § 5706 (1907).

See also ROBERT, PARLIAMENTARY LAW at 177; DEMETER, MANUAL OF
PARLIAMENTARY LAW AND PROCEDURE at 58, 123, 130, 161; JOHNSON, TRUST-
MAN AND WADSWORTH, A HANDBOOK OF PARLIAMENTARY LAW at 104–5, 81,
91, 92, 116; FUNK & WAGNALL, BOOK OF PARLIAMENTARY PROCEDURE at 47
(motions commonly abused).

[48] Senate Procedure, Dilatory Motions, at 450, 642, Senate Doc. No. 93–21
(1974).

[49] An appeal from a ruling declaring out of order a motion which is obviously dilatory is not debatable. DEMETER, MANUAL OF PARLIAMENTARY LAW
AND PROCEDURE at 130.

See Schmulbach v. Speidel, 50 W. Va. 553, 40 S.E. 424 (1901); SHACKLE-
TON, THE LAW AND PRACTICE OF MEETINGS at 80.

19

Privilege and Immunity

§ 19.1 Privileged Communications—Stockholders

A shareholder is protected by a qualified privilege in speaking to other shareholders and to management at a meeting. A leading case states the rule: "No doubt a stockholder at such a meeting, speaking to stockholders, may with impunity say things derogatory to an officer or the manager of the company provided that what he says be pertinent to the matter in hand and he speaks in good faith and without malice. His justification rests upon the fact that he is speaking to the stockholders upon a subject in which he and they have an interest."[1] This conforms to the general principle that a communication made bona-fide upon any subject in which the party communicating has an interest, or in reference to which he has a duty, is privileged if made to a person having a corresponding in-

---

[1] Kimball v. Post Publ. Co., 199 Mass. 248, 85 N.E. 103, 104 (1908). The court then said that this privilege does not extend to a newspaper report of the defamatory remarks "made by a stranger, having no interest in the question, to other strangers, called the public, equally without interest." The court also noted that public meetings may be more privileged than private meetings.

For a discussion of English common law on this subject, see the following volumes: SHACKLETON, LAW AND PRACTICE OF MEETINGS at 70–76; SHAW AND SMITH, THE LAW OF MEETINGS at 31–33; CURRY (CREW), PUBLIC, COMPANY AND LOCAL GOVERNMENT MEETINGS at 65–71; JOSKE, THE LAW AND PROCEDURE AT MEETINGS at 10–14.

terest or duty, although it contains matter which without such privilege would be slanderous and actionable.[2]

The privilege is qualified, and may be overcome and defeated by a showing based on evidentiary facts that the defamatory state-

[2] "The principle applicable to cases in which the claim of privilege is set up is well settled. The difficulty lies in its application. No one can be held responsible for a statement or publication tending to disparage the reputation of another, if it is made in the discharge of a social or moral duty, or is required in order to protect one's own interest or that of another. In such cases, all that is necessary to render the words spoken or published privileged is, that they should be communicated, in good faith and without malice, to those who have an interest in the subject matter to which they relate, and a right to know and act on the facts stated." Smith v. Higgins, 82 Mass. (16 Gray) 251, 252 (1860).

This rule applies even though the duty is not a legal one, but only a "moral or social duty of imperfect obligation." Shapiro v. Health Ins. Plan, 7 N.Y.2d 56, 194 N.Y.S.2d 509, 513 (1959); accord, Kemart Corp. v. Printing Arts Res. Lab. Inc., 269 F.2d 375 (9th Cir.), cert. denied, 361 U.S. 893 (1959).

Generally, communications between members of fraternal, social, professional, religious, or labor organizations concerning conduct of other members or officers in their capacity as such are qualifiedly privileged. Willenbucher v. McCormick, 229 F. Supp. 659 (D. Colo. 1964).

The proceedings of a nonofficial public meeting are conditionally privileged for publication. The court said that the meeting was analogous to the New England town meeting with a moderator where all had an opportunity to speak. Borg v. Boas, 231 F.2d 788, 794 (9th Cir. 1956).

Defense of qualified privilege is generally available in libel cases when circumstances correctly or reasonably lead those having common interest in particular subject matters to believe that facts exist which should be called to attention of others sharing that interest. For a case related to a labor union publication's comments on the integrity, etc., of the leadership of a rival union and its president, see DeLury v. WURF, 35 Misc. 2d 593, 230 N.Y.S.2d 848 (Sup. Ct. 1962).

"A communication made between officers within the organizational structure of a church, or a corporation for that matter, made in good faith, on any subject in which the one communicating has an interest or in which there is a duty, is privileged if made to a person having a corresponding interest or duty, even though it contains matter which, without this privilege, would be actionable. Such is the case even though the duty is not a legal one but only a moral or social duty or obligation." Church of Scientology of California v. Green, 354 F. Supp. 800, 804 (S.D.N.Y. 1973).

Statements made by a lawyer for a stockholder to other stockholders or to their attorneys on corporate matters are qualifiedly privileged. Kenny v. Cleary, 363 N.Y.S.2d 606 (Sup. Ct. 1975).

ments were motivated by "actual malice," "actual ill-will," "personal spite," or "culpable recklessness or negligence." [3] Whether
there has been an abuse of privilege is a question for the jury. [4]

§ 19.1.1   Directors and Officers

The courts have applied the doctrine of qualified privilege to
communications by directors, officers, and shareholders made at a

[3] "So long as the statements were motivated not by ill will or personal spite
but by a sincerely held desire to protect the institution, they are not actionable."
Stillman v. Ford, 22 N.Y.2d 48, 290 N.Y.S.2d 893, 897, 238 N.E.2d 304 (1968).

For definitions of "privileged communications" and "conditionally privileged
communications," see Massee v. Williams, 207 F. 222 (6th Cir. 1913); Marsh
v. Commercial and Sav. Bank, 265 F. Supp. 614 (W.D. Va. 1967); Garriga v.
Townsend, 285 App. Div. 199, 136 N.Y.S.2d 295 (3d Dep't 1954).

[4] A union president made a statement at a union meeting directed to the
propriety of the fee charged by the union's attorney. An action was brought
against the president for making the defamatory statement. The court remarked there is no doubt that an officer of a union has a qualified privilege
when he makes a statement informing the union of any supposed dereliction
of duty of its officers. The fact that the plaintiff was the union's attorney,
rather than an officer or member, does not dissipate the immunity the privilege
affords. The court held that it was for the jury to determine whether the president's "motive and the characterization it spawned exceeded the limits the
privilege sets." Manbeck v. Ostrowski, 384 F.2d 970 (D.C. Cir. 1967).

A news association issued a false report that the plaintiff had been forcibly
ejected from a political party executive committee meeting by the police. The
court held on appeal that it was a question for the jury whether the words were
defamatory and actionable. Hartzog v. United Press Ass'ns, 202 F.2d 81 (4th
Cir. 1953), rev'd on other grounds, 233 F.2d 174 (4th Cir. 1956).

Whether a communication between stockholders in relation to the management of a corporation is one of qualified privilege is a question for the jury.
The court should not take a case from the jury unless the facts be undisputed,
and not then unless only one inference can be drawn therefrom. Ashcroft v.
Hammond, 132 App. Div. 3, 116 N.Y.S. 362 (2d Dep't 1909), rev'd on other
grounds, 197 N.Y. 488, 90 N.E. 1117 (1910).

While there are numerous cases in the books in which it is said that as to
privileged communications the good faith of the defendant and the existence of
actual malice are questions of fact for the jury, the expression must not be misunderstood. Those questions are for the jury only where there is evidence in
the case warranting their submission to the jury and the burden of proof is on
the plaintiff. Shapiro v. Health Ins. Plan, 7 N.Y.2d 56, 194 N.Y.S.2d 509
(1959).

shareholders' meeting concerning evidence as to the conduct of certain officers;[5] to a statement of a union president at a union meeting on the propriety of an attorney's fees;[6] to statements made by the chairman of the board discussing company affairs at a meeting of employees;[7] to statements made by a director at a meeting of the

---

[5] Philadelphia, Wilmington & Baltimore R.R. v. Quigley, 62 U.S. (21 How.) 202 (1858).

Statements made before a meeting of stockholders of a railroad company by a member, attributing drunkenness and incapacity to an official, were privileged if made in good faith. The fact that attorneys of the company were present at the meeting, at the request of the president and some of the stockholders, did not take away the privilege. But if such words were spoken to. the attorneys, or to other persons not entitled to hear them, and were not addressed to the stockholders' meeting, they would have been actionable. The question whether the charge was uttered to influence the election of directors was immaterial. Broughton v. McGrew, 39 F. 672 (D. Ind. 1889).

"The president of a business corporation is charged with the duty of safeguarding the legitimate business interests of his company. Of course, it is his duty to make inquiry and to bring to the attention of the stockholders any evidence of dishonesty on the part of any employee, past or present—not excluding stockholders. A call of a stockholders' meeting to present evidence of dishonesty places the president in a position of qualified privilege, both in calling the meeting and in presenting the evidence. His position and the occasion were sufficient to protect him from liability if his charges were made in good faith." Jones v. Hester, 260 N.C. 264, 132 S.E.2d 586, 589 (1963).

[6] Manbeck v. Ostrowski, 384 F.2d 970 (D.C. Cir. 1967).

Statements by an employer representative at a grievance meeting, indicating misappropriation by an employee, were germane to the issue of the employee's reinstatement and were entitled to qualified privilege. Bird v. Meadow Gold Prod. Corp., 60 Misc. 2d 212, 302 N.Y.S.2d 701 (Sup. Ct. 1969).

The remarks of union members and officials at a union meeting are also protected by the Labor–Management Reporting and Disclosure Act. See DeCampli v. Greeley, 293 F. Supp. 746 (D.N.J. 1968).

[7] Where the chairman of the board of an airline corporation called a meeting of pilots and a meeting of employees to discuss affairs and problems of the company, these occasions were privileged in regard to communications by the chairman regarding allegedly improper activity of a former official of the airline. Stephenson v. Marshall, 104 F. Supp. 26, 13 Alas. 657 (D. Alas. 1952).

An office manager had a conditional privilege to discuss at a meeting of insurance agents testimony given by an agent before a Congressional committee. Bander v. Metropolitan Life Ins. Co., 313 Mass. 337, 47 N.E.2d 595 (1943).

board;[8] and to publication by a club in its official magazine that charges had been made against a member at the annual meeting of directors.[9] This privilege is not limited to statements at membership or committee meetings.[10] Communications between shareholders and between company officials may also be conditionally privileged.[11]

However, the privilege of directors and officers of a corporation to communicate with shareholders at the annual meeting on subjects of conduct of certain officers and agents does not extend to

[8] A statement by a director at a meeting of a board of directors of a nonprofit membership corporation that the manager and president were thieves who would "steal pennies from a blind man's cup" was entitled to qualified privilege. McMann v. Wadler, 11 Cal. Reptr. 37, 40, 41, 189 Cal. App. 2d 124 (1961).

[9] Rodger v. American Kennel Club, 138 Misc. 310, 245 N.Y.S. 662 (1930).

See Cranfill v. Hayden, 22 Tex. Civ. App. 656, 55 S.W. 805 (1900), rev'd on other grounds, 97 Tex. 544, 80 S.W. 609 (1904) (action for libel based on publication of proceedings of Baptist convention in newspaper devoted to its interests).

[10] Privilege of church members to discuss qualifications of pastor is not limited to church committee meetings or parish gatherings. Slocinski v. Radwan, 83 N.H. 501, 144 A. 787 (1929).

See Pendelton v. Hawkins, 11 App. Div. 602, 42 N.Y.S. 626 (4th Dep't 1896) (church trustee showed defamatory letter concerning pastor to other trustees and members).

[11] Hamilton v. United States Pipe & Foundry Co., 213 F.2d 861 (5th Cir. 1954) (letter from company official to another official); Stroud v. Harris, 5 F.2d 25 (8th Cir. 1925) (letters between shareholders); Ashcroft v. Hammond, 132 App. Div. 3, 116 N.Y.S. 362, 364 (1909), rev'd on other grounds, 197 N.Y. 488, 90 N.E. 1117 (1910) (telegrams from one shareholder to another objecting to results of election of directors at annual meeting and calling corporation manager "incompetent or worse"; Hemmens v. Nelson, 138 N.Y. 517, 34 N.E. 342 (1893) (report of department director to chairman of board and executive committee).

A minority shareholder's letter to other shareholders, although "contentious," is not "a license to lie," but does "afford the reasonable expectation that understatement or exaggeration" would be answered. SEC v. Okin, 48 F. Supp. 928, 930 (S.D.N.Y.), rev'd, 137 F.2d 862 (2d Cir. 1943).

See World Oil Co. v. Hicks, 46 S.W.2d 394 (Tex. Civ. App. 1932) (letter from director to stockholders composed and sent by order of a majority of directors is entitled to qualified privilege); Stroud v. Harris, 5 F.2d 25 (8th Cir. 1925) (letters from stockholders and bondholders).

the preservation of the evidence in the permanent form of a book for distribution to other corporate personnel or to the community.[12]

English common law denies the privilege to a shareholder who summons a meeting of members and expressly invites news reporters to the meeting; but it recognizes a qualified privilege when reporters are present at a meeting in accordance with custom but not by special invitation. Offensive statements made after the chair has been vacated are not part of the proceedings of the meeting and therefore are not privileged.[13]

§ 19.1.2 News Reporter

A newspaper reporter does not have the personal interest of a shareholder in a corporation's affairs, and thus a shareholder's qualified privilege of communication does not extend to a repetition of the defamatory remarks "made by a stranger [the reporter] having no interest in the question, to other strangers, called the public, equally without interest." [14]

§ 19.1.3 Common Law

The doctrine of qualified privilege is derived from English common law. It is extended to any occasion where the person making

[12] Philadelphia, Wilmington & Baltimore R.R. v. Quigley, 62 U.S. (21 How.) 202 (1858).

[13] Martin v. Strong (1836), 5 Adolph. & E. 535, reported in Shaw and Smith at 33.

A question to shareholders whether the conduct of two directors was "decent" was not a privileged communication because others than the shareholders were invited to attend the meeting and it was stated that the public press would be there. Parsons v. Surgey, (1864) 4 F. & F. 247, reported in Shaw and Smith at 32.

[14] The court noted that the meeting "was simply that of a private corporation invested with no privileges and owing no special duties to the public." Kimball v. Post Publ. Co., 199 Mass. 248, 85 N.E. 103, 105 (1908).

Whether words are defamatory is a question for the jury, and a directed verdict in favor of a news association which had falsely reported that plaintiff had been forcibly ejected from a political party executive committee meeting by police will be set aside on appeal. Hartzog v. United Press Ass'ns, 202 F.2d 81 (4th Cir. 1953), rev'd on other grounds, 233 F.2d 174 (4th Cir. 1956).

the statement has an interest, or a legal, social, or moral duty, to make the statement to the person to whom it is made, provided that the person to whom it is made has a corresponding interest or duty to receive it. This privilege is not limited to statements and discussions made at meetings. The court has held, for example, that the privilege of church members to discuss among themselves the qualifications of their pastor is not limited to committee meetings or parish gatherings. "The idea that the conduct of a minister should be mentioned unfavorably only at church meetings . . . suggests an undesirable departure from the usual course of events."[15]

Generally speaking, a communication made to a private meeting about matters which are of concern to the meeting will be privileged. However, the occasions upon which a public meeting will be privileged are rare, for all the recipients of a statement made at a public meeting can seldom have a common interest or duty with the person making the statement.

Statements made at a meeting convened for the discharge of a public duty, such as a meeting of a borough council, are conditionally privileged; and the mere presence of strangers who have no concern in the duties to be performed will not of itself destroy the privilege.[16]

---

[15] Slocinski v. Radwan, 83 N.H. 501, 144 A. 787, 789 (1929).

[16] Statements made before a New England town meeting in good faith to fellow citizens who had a corresponding interest were privileged. Bradford v. Clark, 90 Me. 298, 38 A. 229 (1897).

Action cannot be maintained without proof of express malice, for words spoken by a selectman in an open town meeting during an election, charging that plaintiff had put two votes in the ballot box. Bradley v. Heath, 30 Mass. (12 Pick.) 163 (1831).

Words spoken at a meeting of a board of guardians which would have been privileged if made in the presence of guardians only, will continue to be privileged if made in the presence of reporters or persons other than guardians. Pittard v. Oliver, [1891] 1 Q.B. 474 (reported in Shackelton at 74; Shaw and Smith at 32).

Statements made by members of a school board while discharging a public duty in a board meeting held to discuss the renewal of a teacher's contract were conditionally privileged. "The subject of that meeting was the alleged misconduct of appellant. . . . The assertions having been made on a conditionally privileged occasion, appellant must then assume the burden of proving the occasion was abused." McClain v. Anderson, 439 S.W.2d 296, 299 (Ark. 1969).

§ 19.2 Immunity from Speech or Debate

Members of Congress and of state legislatures generally have a constitutional immunity from being questioned in any other place for any speech or debate in either House. This privilege is secured, not to protect the members against prosecution for their own benefit, but to support the rights of the people by enabling their representatives to execute the functions of their office without fear of prosecution, civil or criminal.[17] The privilege is not confined to "delivering an opinion, uttering a speech, or haranguing in debate," but extends to "the giving of a vote, to the making of a written report, and to every other act resulting from the nature, and in the execution, of the office . . . without enquiring whether the exercise was regular according to the rules of the house, or irregular and against the rules."[18] Nor does the claim of an unworthy purpose

[17] See, e.g., Gravel v. United States, 408 U.S. 606, rehearing denied, 409 U.S. 902 (1972); Powell v. McCormack, 395 U.S. 486 (1969); United States v. Johnson, 337 F.2d 180 (4th Cir. 1964), aff'd, 383 U.S. 169 (1966); Kilbourn v. Thompson, 103 U.S. 168 (1881); Cochran v. Couzens, 42 F.2d 783 (D.C. Cir.), cert. denied, 282 U.S. 874 (1930); McGovern v. Martz, 182 F. Supp. 343 (D.D.C. 1960); State v. Nix, 295 P.2d 286 (Okla. 1956).

This immunity extends to committee proceedings. Teeney v. Brandhove, 341 U.S. 367 (1951); Stamler v. Willis, 287 F. Supp. 734 (N.D. Ill. 1968); Barsky v. United States, 167 F.2d 241 (D.C. Cir. 1947), cert. denied, 334 U.S. 843 (1948); Coffin v. Coffin, 4 Mass. 1 (1808); Coleman v. Newark Morning Ledger Co., 29 N.J. 357, 149 A.2d 193 (1959); Van Riper v. Tumulty, 56 A.2d 611 (N.J. 1948).

The speech and debate clause of the Constitution was patterned on the English concept of parliamentary privilege. See Scheuer v. Rhodes, 416 U.S. 232 (1974); United States v. Doe, 455 F.2d 753, 759 (1st Cir. 1972).

See Annot., United States Senators' and Representatives' privileges and immunities relating to arrest and to speech or debate, under Art. 1, § 6, cl. 1, of Federal Constitution, 23 L. Ed. 2d 915 (1970); Annot., Privileges and immunities of members of Congress and state legislators—federal cases, 95 L. Ed. 1030 (1951); PROSSER AND WADE, CASES AND MATERIAL ON TORTS (5th Ed. 1971), Ch. 24, at 1117–25; MAY's, THE LAW, PRIVILEGES, PROCEEDINGS AND USAGE OF PARLIAMENT (16th Ed. 1957), Ch. III, at 42.

[18] Coffin v. Coffin, 4 Mass. 1, 27 (1808).

Immunity extends to the act of voting whether done vocally or silently, as passing between tellers. Kilbourn v. Thompson, 103 U.S. 168, 203 (1881).

The voting record of members of Congress and reasons therefor are matters of privilege. Smith v. Crown Publ., Inc., 14 F.R.D. 514 (D.C.N.Y. 1953).

destroy this privilege. "Legislators are immune from deterrents to the uninhibited discharge of their legislative duty, not for their private indulgence but for the common good. One must not expect uncommon courage even in legislators."[19]

While there is respectable authority to the contrary, it is a general rule that the absolute privilege of legislators is limited to the highest legislative bodies, federal and state, and is not applicable to members and officers of subordinate legislative bodies such as municipal councils, public school and state hospital boards, who are protected only by a qualified or conditional privilege.[20]

There has been considerable litigation dealing with the immunity from liability to which judges and various types of governmental officers and public officials are entitled, with respect to acts done within the sphere of their official activities, based on common-law tradition and public policy. The subject of absolute and qualified immunity is still in dispute among constitutional law scholars.[21]

There appears to be no common-law or statutory immunity for officers or directors of business corporations or other non-public organizations. Reported case law does not reveal any decisions in which immunity has been approved for persons who are not acting under some legislative, statutory, or court-appointed capacity.[22]

[19] Tenney v. Brandhove, 341 U.S. 367, 377 (1951).

[20] See McClendon v. Coverdale, 203 A.2d 815 (Sup. Ct. Del. 1964).

[21] At common law, judges could not be held liable in a civil action for acts they performed in the exercise of their judicial function. See, e.g., Bradley v. Fisher, 80 U.S. (13 Wall.) 335 (1871).

Even though some common-law immunities are called "absolute," limitation has always been placed upon them. Common formulations of that limitation have included the requirement that the official's act must have been within the scope of his powers. See Dacey v. New York County Lawyers' Ass'n, 423 F.2d 188 (2d Cir. 1969), cert. denied, 398 U.S. 929 (1970) at 199.

The doctrine of judicial immunity has been extended to other officials while acting in a quasi-judicial capacity. See C. M. Clark Ins. Agency, Inc. v. Maxwell, 479 F.2d 1223, 1228 (D.C. Cir. 1973).

See, e.g., Scheuer v. Rhodes, 416 U.S. 232 (1974) (government officials and national guard); Pierson v. Ray, 386 U.S. 547 (1967) (judges and police officers); Bauers v. Heisel, 361 F.2d 581 (3d Cir. 1966) (list of immunity cases).

[22] See, e.g., Wood v. Strickland, 420 U.S. 308 (1975) (public school officials); Dale v. Hahn, 440 F.2d 633 (2d Cir. 1971) (court-appointed committee for medical patient); Byrne v. Kysar, 347 F.2d 734 (7th Cir. 1965), cert. denied, 383 U.S. 915 (1966) (court-appointed doctors); Estate of Burks v. Ross, 438 F.2d 230 (6th Cir. 1971) (administrator of veteran's hospital).

It has long been a general rule that corporate directors and officers may be personally liable for corporate torts in which they participate. A director who votes at a directors' meeting for, or who directs or otherwise actively participates in, the commission of a tort may be personally liable in damages to the injured or prejudiced party. In a leading case directors of a non-profit corporation who knowingly voted for an invasion of civil rights were personally liable for tortious acts even though they were ignorant of the full consequences of the applicable law. Erroneous decisions of trial courts on the same facts afford the directors no support. Their ignorance of the law "though engendered by lawyers' advice and corroborated by lower federal courts, is no defense." A dissenting opinion remarked: "To hold the directors to a standard of legal acumen greater than that possessed by the federal judiciary would be unconscionable." And, in answer to a contention that the "peculiar nature of the office of a private corporation's director shields him from liability" under the civil rights law, the appellate court held that the law did not "abolish the common law immunities granted some public officials in the performance of their duties." The civil rights act was interpreted as "neither enlarging nor diminishing traditional immunities of public officials" and should be interpreted as "neither enlarging nor diminishing the liability of directors under general corporation law for tortious acts performed nominally by the corporation." [23]

[23] Tillman v. Wheaton-Haven Recreation Ass'n Inc., 517 F.2d 1141, 1143, 1144, 1146, 1151 (4th Cir. 1975). See same case, 410 U.S. 431 (1973), 367 F. Supp. 860 (D. Md. 1973), 451 F.2d 1211 (4th Cir. 1971).

A school board need not "demonstrate greater powers of clairvoyance" than the court. Brewer v. School Board, 456 F.2d 943, 951 (4th Cir.), *cert. denied,* 92 S. Ct. 1778 (1972).

"We agree that a police officer is not charged with predicting the future course of constitutional law." Pierson v. Ray, 386 U.S. 547, 557 (1967) (immunity of judges and police officers).

See Dacey v. New York County Lawyers' Ass'n, 423 F.2d 188 (2d Cir. 1969), *cert. denied,* 398 U.S. 929 (1970) (bar association).

20

Labor Bill of Rights

§ 20.1   Right To Assemble Freely

The common law of meetings has been recognized in a recent federal statute enacting a labor "Bill of Rights." The act includes a provision that members of a labor organization shall have the right to meet and assemble freely, to express any views, arguments, or opinions upon candidates for office or upon any business properly before the meeting, "subject to the organization's established and reasonable rules pertaining to the conduct of meetings."[1]   This

---

[1] LABOR–MANAGEMENT REPORTING AND DISCLOSURE ACT (Landrum–Griffin Act) § 101, 29 U.S.C. § 411 (Supp. I, 1964).

The right to establish "reasonable rules pertaining to the meeting" means the right "to impose reasonable rules to maintain the order and decorum needed to dispose of the business of the meeting." Navarro v. Gannon, 385 F.2d 512 (2d Cir. 1967), *cert. denied,* 390 U.S. 989, *rehearing denied,* 390 U.S. 1046 (1968). *See* Calhoon v. Harvey, 379 U.S. 134 (1964).

During the debate in the Senate on this provision, Senator McClellan read into the record the following statement: "This limitation that the unions might make reasonable rules relating to equal rights and free speech and assembly was implicit in the bill of rights as originally drafted just as it is in the Bill of Rights of the Federal Constitution, *to prevent abuse.*" Guarnaccia v. Kenin, 234 F. Supp. 429, 440 (S.D.N.Y. 1964). *See* Cole v. Hall, 339 F.2d 881 (2d Cir. 1965); Robins v. Rarback, 325 F.2d 929, 931 (2d Cir. 1963) (concurring opinion of Waterman, D. J.); Stark v. Twin City Carpenters Dist. Council, 219 F. Supp. 528 (D. Minn. 1963).

A union member has the statutory right "to express any views, arguments, or opinions" inside or outside of a union meeting, subject to only three general

limiting provision, which has the effect of "tempering the rights so conferred," [2] has been generally accepted to mean the reasonable rules and regulations of "business meetings." [3] Accordingly, it is recognized that "reasonable qualifications" of the Act are permitted in a union's constitution and by-laws. [4]

The statute was not intended or designed to require that labor unions submit to membership vote all matters upon which they are required to act, but only that all members be accorded equal rights to vote in elections and to participate in the deliberations and voting upon the business of membership meetings. [5] "This is not to say that in order to have democratically responsive unions, it is necessary to have each union member make decisions on detail as in a New England town meeting. What is required is the opportunity to influence policy and leadership by free and periodic elections." [6]

Union officials have been held jointly and severally liable for

---

limitations: (1) reasonable union rules relating to the conduct of union meetings; (2) reasonable rules relating to individual responsibility to the union as an institution; and (3) reasonable rules requiring members to refrain from conduct which would interfere with the union's performance of its legal or contractual obligations. Fulton Lodge No. 2 v. Nix, 415 F.2d 212, 218 (5th Cir. 1969).

The 1959 Landrum–Griffin amendments enacted a "code of fairness to assure democratic conduct of union affairs by provisions guaranteeing free speech and assembly, equal rights to vote in elections, to attend meetings, and to participate in the deliberations and voting upon the business conducted at the meetings." NLRB v. Allis–Chalmers, 388 U.S. 175, 181 (separate opinion), *rehearing denied*, 389 U.S. 892 (1967).

See *Pre-Election Remedies Under the Landrum–Griffin Act: "The Twilight Zone" Between Election Rights Under Title IV and the Guarantees of Titles I and V*, 74 COLUM. L. REV. 1105 (1974).

[2] Guarnaccia v. Kenin, 234 F. Supp. 429, 440 (S.D.N.Y. 1964). See Hickey, *The Bill of Rights of Union Members*, 48 Geo L.J. 226, 236 (1959).

[3] Note, *Bill of Rights of Members of Labor Organizations, 1959–1964*, 40 NOTRE DAME LAWYER 86, 94–95 (1964).

[4] See, e.g., Calhoon v. Harvey, 379 U.S. 134 (1964); Williams v. International Typographical Union, 423 F.2d 1295 (10th Cir. 1970); Rosen v. District Council, 198 F. Supp. 46, 49 (S.D.N.Y. 1961), *aff'd*, 326 F.2d 400 (2d Cir. 1964).

[5] Cleveland Orchestra Comm. v. Cleveland Fed'n of Musicians, 193 F. Supp. 647, 650 (N.D. Ohio 1961), *aff'd*, 303 F.2d 229 (6th Cir. 1962).

[6] Aikens v. Abel, 373 F. Supp. 425, 437, n. 11 (W.D. Pa. 1974). Nor was the statute intended to create a right to call meetings of the union

damages resulting from their abuse of union meeting and voting parliamentary procedures to gain their unlawful objectives.[7]

"Although freedom of speech is a union member's right that is protected by section 101(a)(2) of the act, the exercise of the right at union meetings must accommodate itself to the union's correlative right to conduct its meetings in an orderly fashion in accordance with its previously established rules. The statute itself places these conditions upon the right of a member."[8] In fact, it is clearly established that membership in a union constitutes acceptance of the jurisdiction of the act. "In accepting membership, the members subject themselves to the provisions of the constitution and by-laws; and recognition of this subjection is expressly disclosed" in the act.[9]

§ 20.2　Representative Court Decisions

The courts in considering the extent and application of the act have decided a number of cases related to the holding and conduct of meetings. They have, for example:

---

membership; it is more appropriately applicable in this regard to "rump sessions" than to a general right to hold meetings. Yanity v. Benware, 376 F.2d 197, 199 (2d Cir.), *cert. denied,* 389 U.S. 874 (1967).

[7] Three union officials who decided to force members of a local union to join a national union pension plan whether the majority wanted the plan or not, and finally succeeded in getting an affirmative membership vote after three earlier defeats in as many months, were held by the court to have violated the union members' statutory rights to an equal right to vote and to have that vote be meaningful. Abusive parliamentary tactics had been employed by the officials, including delay in calling a meeting mandated by the membership, denial of equal rights to participate in meetings, blatant refusal to implement a union vote, and denial of the right to vote as if the officials had stuffed the ballot box itself. The officials were held liable for damages in an amount equal to the amount of money that had been deducted from the wages of members and paid into the pension fund. Pignotti v. Local #3 Sheet Metal Wkrs. Int'l Ass'n, 343 F. Supp. 236 (D. Neb. 1972), *aff'd,* 477 F.2d 825 (8th Cir. 1973).

[8] Scovile v. Watson, 338 F.2d 678, 680–81 (7th Cir. 1964), *cert. denied,* 380 U.S. 963 (1965). *See* Stark v. Twin City Carpenters Dist. Council, 219 F. Supp. 528 (D. Minn. 1963).

The scope of freedom of speech guaranteed to union members under the labor Bill of Rights is broader than that guaranteed by the Constitution. Reyes v. Laborers' Int'l Union, 327 F. Supp. 978 (D.N.M. 1971).

[9] Cleveland Orchestra Comm. v. Cleveland Fed'n of Musicians, 303 F.2d 229, 230 (6th Cir. 1962).

Held that freedom of expression of a union member on union matters is an individual right subject only to individual enforcement; [10]

Approved a motion to adjourn a membership meeting while a union member held the floor arguing in favor of a motion to have her rights of arbitration restored; [11]

Approved a voting system by delegates weighted and counted according to the number of members in the local which the delegate represented; [12]

Let stand a by-law depriving a union member of the right to nominate anyone for office but himself and prescribing certain service requirements for nominees; [13]

Held that there is nothing in the act guaranteeing equal rights which purports to guarantee that all proposed amendments to a union constitution would be accorded the same procedural treatment, and that the act was not violated even if the membership, as alleged, was not given all of the information it needed for voting intelligently, and even if the resolution in question was rushed through the convention in disregard of custom and the union constitution; [14]

Held that a union can establish rules for the orderly adjudication of grievances and appeals, and that a union member claiming a denial of his right to express his views and arguments on union business at union meetings must first exhaust his internal remedies before the jurisdiction of the court can be invoked; [15]

Refused to take jurisdiction, until all administrative procedures had been pursued, over a demand by an international union that candidates for president of the local submit to a complete physical examination before being allowed to continue as a candidate, although there was no such provision in the constitution or by-laws of the local union, and such demand was not uniformly applied; [16]

[10] Broomer v. Schultz, 239 F. Supp. 699, 702, 703 (E.D. Pa. 1965).

[11] Scovile v. Watson, 338 F.2d 678 (7th Cir. 1964), cert. denied, 380 U.S. 963 (1965).

[12] American Fed'n of Musicians v. Wittstein, 379 U.S. 171 (1964), rev'g 326 F.2d 26 (2d Cir. 1963), aff'g 223 F. Supp. 27 (S.D.N.Y. 1963); accord, Zentner v. American Fed'n of Musicians, 237 F. Supp. 457 (S.D.N.Y.), aff'd, 343 F.2d 758 (2d Cir. 1965).

[13] Calhoon v. Harvey, 379 U.S. 134 (1964).

[14] Coleman v. Brotherhood of Ry. & Steamship Clerks, 340 F.2d 206 (2d Cir. 1965).

[15] Harris v. International Longshoremen's Ass'n, 210 F. Supp. 4 (E.D. Pa. 1962), aff'd, 321 F.2d 801 (3d Cir. 1963).

[16] Jackson v. International Longshoremen's Ass'n, 212 F. Supp. 79 (E.D. La. 1962).

Refused to interfere with a by-law amendment submitted by referendum which would give inactive members of a union the same voting opportunity as active members, and call for a single vote on four separate resolutions relating to the subject of union dues; [17]

Held broadly that the courts do not have general supervision over the conduct of union elections and do not have jurisdiction over a suit to enjoin a union from committing certain "electoral abuses" where no denial of the right to vote is involved; [18]

Held that the courts will take cognizance of an attempted denial of the right to vote as distinguished from a "mere infirmity or irregularity" in the conduct of the election; [19]

Held that, while a union may set up procedural and even substantive conditions or restrictions on a member's right to vote, it may not do so indefinitely or arbitrarily so as to establish a permanent class of membership not entitled to vote; [20]

Held that an action of a union executive board in voiding a local's resolutions requiring voting in person, or registration during business hours in order to vote by mail, did not violate the act by denying working members an equal right to vote; [21]

Held that a union member could not recover damages for personal injury when he resisted being put out of a union meeting after he had been suspended from membership for nonpayment of dues, notwithstanding the illegality of his suspension, as such injury was not a direct or proximate result of a violation of the act; [22]

---

[17] Rothstein v. Manuti, 235 F. Supp. 39 (S.D.N.Y. 1963). *See* Young v. Hayes, 195 F. Supp. 911 (D.D.C. 1961).

[18] Robins v. Rarback, 325 F.2d 929 (2d Cir. 1963). *But see* concurring opinion of Waterman, C. J., commenting that he regarded the act "as being broad enough to protect union members from election practices which, if unchecked, would serve to render balloting at union elections a vain act." *Id.* at 932. *See* Barunica v. United Hatters, 321 F.2d 764 (8th Cir. 1963).

[19] Unanswered allegations that union officers printed 750 ballots for a union election involving 250 voters without accounting for the surplus, and that the election judge concealed the election box long enough to allow tampering and substitution, was considered sufficient to warrant injunctive relief. Beckman v. Local No. 46 Int'l Ass'n of Bridge, S. & O. I. Workers, 314 F.2d 848 (7th Cir. 1963).

[20] Acevedo v. Bookbinders & Machine Operators, 196 F. Supp. 308, 311 (S.D.N.Y. 1961).

[21] Gurton v. Arons, 339 F.2d 371 (2d Cir. 1964).

[22] McCraw v. United Ass'n of Journeymen & Apprentices, 216 F. Supp. 655 (E.D. Tenn. 1963), *aff'd*, 341 F.2d 705 (6th Cir. 1965).

Refused to enjoin use of a ballot requiring a single vote on four separate resolutions; [23]

Held improper a single ballot embracing 47 different constitutional amendments in violation of a provision in the union constitution providing that the membership shall vote on each subject separately; [24]

Held that the method of selecting union officials is not a matter for the courts, that the failure of the union executive committee to submit a constitution and by-laws to the members for adoption as required by the act was not within the jurisdiction of the court for the application of injunctive proceedings in the absence of a showing of imminent and irreparable harm; [25]

Held that a union member, pursuant to his right of free speech, has the right to speak, publish, and disseminate his views on various matters even to the extent of defaming the officers of the union; [26]

Held that a union member could not be suspended and denied the right to attend and participate in union meetings by reason of his conduct in picketing the union offices with signs criticizing the local's officials.[27]

§ 20.3   Application of Reasonable Rules

It is evident from the decided cases that the courts and the legislatures have a profound respect for the established rules and regulations of social and business organizations and other deliberative bodies and assemblies which have been adopted for the purpose of establishing and hopefully assuring the orderly conduct of business. The courts favor the establishment by local organizations of reasonable rules pertaining to the conduct of their affairs, and they encourage the settlement of all issues at the local level wherever possible.

Following this policy, it has been held that the labor Bill of Rights does not grant broad supervisory powers to the courts. The

[23] Rothstein v. Manuti, 235 F. Supp. 39 (S.D.N.Y. 1963).

[24] Young v. Hayes, 195 F. Supp. 911 (D.D.C. 1961).

[25] Broomer v. Schultz, 239 F. Supp. 699 (E.D. Pa. 1965).

[26] Speech protected by Bill of Rights is different from that protected by the Constitution, in that constitutionally protected speech does not include libelous utterances. Salzhandler v. Caputo, 316 F.2d 445 (2d Cir.), *cert. denied,* 375 U.S. 946 (1963). *See* Leonard v. M.I.T. Employees' Union, 225 F. Supp. 937 (D. Mass. 1964).

[27] Gartner v. Soloner, 220 F. Supp. 115 (E.D. Pa. 1963).

right to equal suffrage has been established. "But the guaranty of the equal right to vote is surely not a general commission for the federal courts to review the constitution and by-laws of the union. As long as no claim is made that provisions of the constitution and by-laws are being applied in such a way as to deny equality in voting, there is nothing in Section 101 which authorizes consideration of these documents. Section 101 grants no power to the courts to examine into whether by-laws were lawfully adopted or repealed." [28]

Consistent with this judgment, it has also been held that the federal courts are not empowered to control and direct the entire conduct of union elections "on the theory that the right to vote is a right to cast an 'effective' vote, and that a vote cannot be effective unless the election is properly conducted in all its aspects." [29] However, it is recognized that the right to vote extended in the labor Bill of Rights is the "right of a meaningful vote" [30] and not a "mere naked right to cast a ballot." [31]

A recent case, dealing with a local union's parliamentary moves to gain approval of its international union's objectives, holds that the power of a union official cannot be used to adopt rules the effect of which is to deny the members the right to an equal vote. It was held that the action of the general president of the international union in calling for a vote on a union-sponsored pension plan following three defeats by the local union of the same plan at previous meetings within three months, and adoption of a motion to postpone indefinitely, was violative of the statutory rights of union members to an equal right to vote and to having the vote be meaningful. In the same decision the court held that delay by the

[28] Gurton v. Arons, 339 F.2d 371, 374 (2d Cir. 1964).

[29] Robins v. Rarback, 325 F.2d 929, 930 (2d Cir. 1963), *cited in* Guarnaccia v. Kenin, 234 F. Supp. 429, 441 (S.D.N.Y. 1964).

[30] Union members have the right to participate freely in the government of their union, including the right to vote "yes" or "no" on increases of dues or assessments. Sertic v. Cuyahoga, Lake, Geauga & Ashtabula Cos., C.D.C., 423 F.2d 515 (6th Cir. 1970).

[31] The court held that the union management may not submit amendments in any form they wish as that may well open up the way to usurpation of power and the imparting to the membership "via the ballot an almost 'forced choice' method of voting." Young v. Hayes, 195 F. Supp. 911, 916 (D.D.C. 1961).

president of the local union in calling a special meeting of members mandated by a petition submitted by members in accordance with the constitution, denied the plaintiff equal rights and privileges to participate in meetings of the local union.[32]

§ 20.4 Parliamentary Questions

The labor Bill of Rights has raised some interesting parliamentary questions. In a recent decision the majority ruled that legislative history indicated that the right of assembly conferred by the statute was intended to enable union members to meet outside their regular union meetings for the purpose of discussing pending union affairs without fear of reprisal, and that the statute was not intended to create a right to call meetings of the union membership. In a dissenting opinion Lumbard, C.J., noted that "whether a meeting was required by the union constitution or by-laws would generally be a much easier issue to determine than whether a member was improperly denied a chance to speak." He then entered a footnote, questioning: "Under that holding, does a presiding officer at a union meeting violate Section 101(a)(2) by deliberately limiting the agenda so as to prevent discussion of a particular issue? or by deliberately adjourning the meeting to prevent a member from speaking? . . . And how broadly are the union meetings which the majority holds are not protected by Section 101(a)(2) defined? For example, under the majority's holding, could a local union lawfully seek to prevent dissident members from meeting to appeal to higher union bodies or to seek a charter for a new local?" In answer, it may be assumed that the statute has not repealed common parliamentary law. The presiding officer at a union meeting could not deliberately limit the agenda so as to prevent discussion nor could he deliberately adjourn a meeting without concurrence of the body to prevent a member from speaking.[33]

Parliamentary law has been followed in considering the regularity of proceedings at a union meeting under the labor Bill of Rights. In a legal proceeding founded on a union member's motion

[32] Pignotti v. Local No. 3, Sheet Metal Wkrs. Int'l Ass'n, 343 F. Supp. 236 (D. Neb. 1972), aff'd, 477 F.2d 825 (8th Cir. 1973).

[33] Yanity v. Benware, 376 F.2d 197, 203, n. 4 (2d Cir.), cert. denied, 389 U.S. 874 (1967).

that stewards be elected at membership meetings rather than appointed by the president, the court refused to grant a preliminary injunction as there was no showing of imminent and irreparable harm. The court observed that the same motion had been defeated for the second time only a month before and, in upholding the president for refusing to again submit to the meeting another identical motion, held: "The refusal to consider it again so shortly after its second defeat was not an interference with a member's right of free speech, but was a reasonable parliamentary rule." [34]

A most meaningful court decision applicable to the conduct and decorum of union meetings upheld a preliminary injunction restraining a parent union from assuming control of a local union meeting. The appellate court in an opinion by Lumbard, C.J., held that rights of speech and assembly secured by the labor Bill of Rights encompass the right to assembly, consult, and decide matters of concern to the local union under the supervision of their own chosen officers and "without the inhibiting presence and control by international officials." The court said that the best guaranty of "full freedom to criticize, to dissent, and to oppose," is to let the local meeting be run by its own officials and to prevent "hostile outsiders" from attempting to "manage the meeting, determine who may attend, and who is to be recognized." The court concluded by repeating in lucid language a fundamental principle of parliamentary law that "free discussion is impossible if the forum is under the control of superior force, with foreigners patrolling the meeting chamber and exercising the prerogatives of the chair." [35]

[34] Broomer v. Schultz, 239 F. Supp. 699, 702 (E.D. Pa. 1965).

A union member was ruled out of order by the chairman for again arguing the legality of certain seniority provisions of the union's constitution and by-laws at a regular membership meeting, and after several years of debate on the same subject at previous membership meetings and a membership vote not to continue the practice. The court held that the member was "properly ruled out of order pursuant to the union's rules for conducting its meetings in an orderly fashion." Patterson v. Tulsa Local No. 513, 446 F.2d 205, 210 (10th Cir. 1971), cert. denied, 405 U.S. 976, rehearing denied, 406 U.S. 951 (1972).

[35] The court said that the rights of union members are also "protected against incursion, or subversion by the individual's own representatives, the officers of his union." Navarro v. Gannon, 385 F.2d 512, 518–19, 520 (2d Cir. 1967), cert. denied, 390 U.S. 989, rehearing denied, 390 U.S. 1046 (1968).

21

Corporate Structure

CHARTER DOCUMENTS

§ 21.1   Charter

It is firmly established at law that the charter and by-laws of an organization together constitute a contract between the organization and its members and among the members themselves.[1] Its

[1] "The certificate of incorporation, constitution and by-laws of the corporation, constitute a contract between the corporation and its stockholders inter sese." Faunce v. Boost Co., 15 N.J. Super. 534, 83 A.2d 649, 651 (1951).

The constitution, by-laws, and the contents of the certificate of membership, taken together, form the contract between the association and its members. Farmers' Loan & Trust Co. v. Aberle, 18 Misc. 257, 41 N.Y.S. 638 (1896).

"A corporate charter is a contract between the corporation and the State. It also regulates and defines the rights of its stockholders, and is, therefore, in

provisions are binding with equal force on each party.[2] An incorporated organization has certain additional contractual rights and
obligations derived from the enabling laws of its state of incorporation.[3]

The charter and by-laws are, however, different structural members of the organizational body [4] and have distinctly different purposes and functions.[5] The charter, subject only to its organic law,[6]

---

some respects a contract between them individually." Aldridge v. Franco
Wyo. Oil Co., 24 Del. Ch. 349, 14 A.2d 380 (1940), aff'g, 24 Del. Ch. 126,
7 A.2d 753, 758 (1939).

Palmer v. Chamberlin, 191 F.2d 532, *rehearing denied*, 191 F.2d 859 (5th
Cir. 1951); Du Vall v. Moore, 276 F. Supp. 674, 680 (N.D. Iowa 1967).

The constitution of a union is a contract with the members. Adams v. In-
ternational Bro. of Boilermakers, 262 F.2d 835 (10th Cir. 1959); Gonzales v.
International Ass'n of Machinists, 142 Cal. App. 2d 207, 298 P.2d 92, 99
(1956), aff'd, 356 U.S. 617 (1958); DeMille v. American Fed'n of Radio
Artists, 31 Cal. 2d 139, 187 P.2d 769 (1947); Harris v. National Union of
Marine Cooks & Stewards, 98 Cal. App. 2d 733, 221 P.2d 136 (1950).

However, charter and by-law provisions are not binding when they are
violative of law or are unworkable or unenforceable. Weisblum v. LiFalco
Mfg. Co., 193 Misc. 473, 84 N.Y.S.2d 162, 166 (1947).

See Annot., Charter and by-laws as contracts, 14 A.L.R. 1446 (1921), 20
A.L.R. 2d 344, 352–80 (1951).

[2] "When this appellant became a member of the brotherhood, he was bound
in duty and in honor to give allegiance to its constitution and by-laws, and he
had a reciprocal right to insist that the organization should fairly apply to him
the provisions of the same laws by which he was bound. The constitution and
by-laws establish the contract between the organization and the members and
their provisions are binding with equal force on each party." Engle v. Potts-
ville D. B. of L. E., 66 Pa. Super. 356, 362 (1916).

[3] "Where a corporation is created under state law, every pertinent provision
of the constitution and the law is impliedly written in and composes a part of
its charter." Aldridge v. Franco Wyo. Oil Co., 24 Del. Ch. 349, 14 A.2d 380,
381 (1940), aff'g, 24 Del. Ch. 126, 7 A.2d 753, 758–59 (1939).

[4] "Charter provisions are structural, and the courts have a right to inquire
whether they have been complied with. Parliamentary rules are merely procedural, and with their observance the courts have no concern. They may be
waived or disregarded by the legislative body." South Georgia Power Co. v.
Baumann, 169 Ga. 649, 151 S.E. 513, 515 (1929).

[5] A leading case holds that "the charter is an instrument in which the broad
and general aspects of the corporate entity's existence and nature are defined,
so the by-laws are generally regarded as the proper place for the self-imposed
rules and regulations deemed expedient for its convenient functioning to be

is the fundamental constitution of the organization. Its requirements are mandatory [7] and cannot be ignored or overridden by an act of a majority of shareholders, broad as their powers may be,[8] or by the adoption of a contrary by-law.[9]

An early case held that the charter of a corporation "is the measure of its powers and privileges, and, where the mode of exercising any of its functions is therein prescribed, it must be strictly pursued." [10] However, where it is contrary to fundamental rights, a charter provision may be illegal.[11]

---

laid down." Gow v. Consolidated Coppermines Corp., 19 Del. Ch. 172, 165 A. 136, 140 (1933).

[6] The provisions of all corporate charters are subject to the limitations imposed by the constitution and statutory law. "The relation between a corporation and its shareholders is contractual. [citations] In determining the agreement, the statutes governing corporations, their organization, and all of the provisions of the charter are a part of the contract." Du Vall v. Moore, 276 F. Supp. 674, 680 (N.D. Iowa 1967).

The provisions of all corporation charters are subject to the limitations imposed by the constitution of the state of incorporation. State ex rel. Syphers v. McCune, 101 S.E.2d 834 (W. Va. 1958).

A municipal corporation established for political purposes possesses no powers except such as have been expressly or by implication given by the law creating it. Murdoch v. Strange, 99 Md. 89, 57 A. 628 (1904).

[7] "It is settled that charter requirements, prescribing the method to be pursued by a municipal body, are mandatory, and unless complied with, any attempted exercise of power is void." Rutherford v. Nashville, 168 Tenn. 499, 505, 79 S.W.2d 581, 584 (1935).

[8] "The minority stockholders of a corporation have property rights in the corporation and its assets and management, which the directors, their trustees, may not ignore and set aside. Nor can the majority of the stockholders, broad as their powers are, override the organic law of the corporation for the illegal purpose of preventing the minority from securing the representation in the directory which the shares of stock owned by them enable them to elect." West Side Hosp. v. Steele, 124 Ill. App. 534, 540 (1906).

[9] See Gentry-Futch Co. v. Gentry, 90 Fla. 595, 106 So. 473 (1925) (by-law providing that no business should be transacted at any meeting without there being 75 per cent of the stock represented at the meeting is void where the statute provides that a majority of the stock constitutes a quorum).

[10] Mutual Fire Ins. Co. v. Farquhar, 86 Md. 668, 39 A. 527, 529 (1898).

[11] "Fair criticism is the right of members of a union, as it is the right of every citizen. A provision of a union constitution, which would suppress protests of members against actions of their officers which such members regard as improper or opposed to their best interests, would be illegal and unenforceable." Schrank v. Brown, 192 Misc. 80, 80 N.Y.S.2d 452, 455 (1948).

The charter will normally provide and define the voting rights of members and of the various classes of shareholders.[12] Some classes may be excluded by the charter from voting except in respect to such matters as to which the right to vote cannot be denied.[13]

Those who become members of the organization are bound by the rules and regulations then in effect. It has been held that: "By becoming a member of a union the worker, in effect, makes a contract to be governed by the constituion and by-laws and rules of the organization."[14] It has also been held that a construction of the constitution and by-laws by the governing board is binding on the membership and will be recognized by the courts.[15]

Whenever it is proposed to depart from well established corporate practices, including the "democratic processes concerning corporate elections," the charter provisions on which deviation is

[12] *See, e.g., In re* Hausner's Petition, 198 N.Y.S.2d 982 (1960) (voting rights of shareholders are fixed by corporate charter and by-laws and are immune from change except by amendment).

Preferred shareholders are entitled to vote, the same as common, unless the right is expressly withheld. Millspaugh v. Cassedy, 191 App. Div. 221, 181 N.Y.S. 276 (1920).

Charter and by-law provisions limiting voting procedure to certain classes of stock constitute a contract binding on shareholders. St. Regis Candies v. Hovas, 8 S.W.2d 574 (Tex. 1928).

[13] State v. Guaranty Sav. Bldg. & Loan Ass'n, 225 Ala. 481, 144 So. 104, 108 (1932).

[14] Smith v. General Truck Drivers, 181 F. Supp. 14, 17 (S.D. Cal. 1960).

When plaintiffs became members of the union "they became so upon the conditions set forth in its constitution and by-laws, and if dissatisfied with the administration, and enforcement of such conditions they cannot invoke the power of a court of equity for such enforcement, unless their civil or property rights are invaded." State *ex rel.* Givens v. Superior Court, 233 Ind. 235, 117 N.E.2d 553, 555 (1954).

Where a local union is affiliated with an international union, members of the local are bound by the constitution of the international. Navarro v. Gannon, 385 F.2d 512 (2d Cir. 1967), *cert. denied,* 390 U.S. 989, *rehearing denied,* 390 U.S. 1046 (1968).

[15] DeMille v. American Fed'n of Radio Artists, 31 Cal. 2d 139, 187 P.2d 769, 775 (1947), *quoted and distinguished in* Gonzales v. International Ass'n of Machinists, 142 Cal. App. 2d 207, 298 P.2d 92, 98 (1956), *aff'd,* 356 U.S. 617 (1958).

founded must be unambiguous, clear, and understandable.[16] A charter may, of course, be amended in a proper proceeding.[17]

§ 21.2   By-Laws—Power To Enact

By-laws do not ordinarily have the organic and structural qualities of a charter or a certificate of incorporation, and are subordinate to both.[18] They are more in the nature of rules and regulations

[16] "Words and phrases employed by incorporators in drafting a certificate should be given their common accepted meaning, unless the context clearly requires otherwise or unless legal phrases having a special meaning are used. But where the language is not expressed with that clarity of expression which permits of but one reasonable interpretation, the language must be said to be ambiguous, and resort must be had for assistance through certain well-established legal rules of construction. . . . Outstanding among the democratic processes concerning corporate elections is the general rule that a majority of the votes cast at a stockholders' meeting, provided a quorum is present, is sufficient to elect Directors. . . . If this rule is not to be observed, then the charter provision must not be couched in ambiguous language, rather the language employed must be positive, explicit, clear and readily understandable and susceptible to but one reasonable interpretation, which would indicate beyond doubt that the rule was intended to be abrogated." Standard Power & Light Corp. v. Investment Associates, Inc., 29 Del. Ch. 593, 51 A.2d 572, 576 (1947).

[17] See, e.g., Metzger v. George Washington Memorial Park, Inc., 380 Pa. 350, 110 A.2d 425 (1955).

[18] As between the charter and the by-laws, the charter must control. Christal v. Petry, 275 App. Div. 550, 90 N.Y.S.2d 620 (1949), aff'd, 301 N.Y. 562, 93 N.E.2d 450 (1950).

A by-law requiring three-fourths of the issued stock for a quorum is void in the face of a statute stating that one-half of the issued stock constitutes a quorum. Gentry-Futch Co. v. Gentry, 90 Fla. 595, 106 So. 473 (1925).

A by-law which deprives a shareholder of his statutory voting rights is null and void. In re Crown Heights Hosp., 183 Misc. 563, 49 N.Y.S.2d 658, 660 (Sup. Ct. 1944).

See Darrin v. Hoff, 99 Md. 491, 58 A. 196 (1904) (state statute prohibited by-laws "inconsistent with law").

An early decision held that a by-law of a municipal corporation is void which might "so hamper and cripple its powers as to disable it from performing those duties enjoined or authorized by the laws of the state," and that a subsequent resolution or act of the corporation which was done within the scope of the organic law has the effect of repealing the objectionable by-law. Ex parte Mayor etc. of Albany, 23 Wend. 277, 280 (N.Y. 1840).

which have been adopted to govern and regulate the conduct of intraorganization affairs,[19] and also constitute a contract between the corporation and its members.[20] A court decision describes the by-laws in the following words: "Provisions in corporate by-laws may, generally speaking, be divided into two classes (a) those that are mere regulations governing the conduct of the internal affairs of the corporation. These may be repealed, altered and amended at

---

"When a by-law is adopted, it is as much the law of the corporation as if its provisions had been a part of the charter." *In re* Siebenmann, 32 Misc. 2d 92, 222 N.Y.S.2d 707, 709 (Sup. Ct. 1961).

[19] "All regulations of a company affecting its business, which do not operate upon third persons, nor in any way affect their rights, are properly by-laws of the company. Rules and regulations which operate upon and affect the rights of others are not within the operation of the principle of by-laws." Brumfield v. Consolidated Coach Corp., 240 Ky. 1, 40 S.W.2d 356, 361 (1931).

Parliamentary rules are "merely in the nature of by-laws, prescribed for a deliberative body for the orderly and convenient conduct of its own proceedings." State *ex rel.* Fox v. Alt, 26 Mo. App. 673, 677 (1887).

A leading case notes that the matter of fixing and altering the number of directors "has been generally regarded as a particularly appropriate one to be committed to by-laws for regulation." Gow v. Consolidated Coppermines Corp., 19 Del. Ch. 172, 165 A. 136, 139, 140 (1933).

[20] "A by-law is in the nature of a contract among shareholders and becomes a law of the corporation unless its provisions violate some provision of law or is unworkable or unenforceable." Weisblum v. LiFalco Mfg. Co., 193 Misc. 473, 84 N.Y.S.2d 162, 166 (Sup. Ct. 1947).

The by-laws of a corporation constitute a contract between the different members of the corporation. Bushway Ice Cream Co. v. Fred H. Bean Co., 284 Mass. 239, 187 N.E. 537, 540 (1930).

The by-laws of a labor union are a contract between members on which they can rely. Estes v. Tomkins, 371 P.2d 86 (Okla. 1962).

A by-law operates as a contract between the corporation and its members. State *ex rel.* Brewster v. Ostrander, 212 Ore. 177, 318 P.2d 284 (1957).

A by-law will prevail over a foreign law "for the reason that it amounts to an agreement between the stockholders." Brown v. Republican Mountain Silver Mines, Ltd., 55 F. 7, 10 (C.C.D. Colo. 1893), *rev'd*, 58 F. 644 (8th Cir. 1893).

By-laws of an association are a contract among the members. In the absence of express provision, the by-laws cannot be altered or amended without the consent of all members. Gordon v. Tomei, 144 Pa. Super. 449, 19 A.2d 588 (1941).

the will of the majority unless a greater vote is required by the by-laws themselves or by statute. (b) Provisions in the nature of a contract which are evidently designed to vest property rights *inter se* among all stockholders. These cannot be repealed or changed without the consent of the other parties whose rights are affected." [21] An organization has broad latitude in adopting by-laws. "It is a general rule that a corporation may enact any by-law for its internal management so long as such by-laws are not contrary to its charter, a controlling statute, its articles of incorporation, or violative of any general law or public policy. Subject to the above qualifications, a corporation may adopt by-laws regulating the calling and conduct of corporate meetings and election of its officers." [22] In a decision holding that the power of the SEC to enact rules requiring management to give notice in its proxy statement of a security holder's proposal could not be frustrated by a corporate by-law requiring that notice of such proposal be given in the notice of meeting, the court remarked: "The power conferred on the Commission by Congress cannot be frustrated by a corporate by-law." [23]

By-laws are presumptively valid.[24] They are part of the "fundamental law" of the company [25] and have been likened to a legislative act. A by-law differs from a resolution, in that a resolution applies

---

[21] Bechtold v. Coleman Realty Co., 367 Pa. 208, 79 A.2d 661, 663 (1951); *accord,* Metzger v. George Washington Memorial Park, 380 Pa. 350, 110 A.2d 425 (1955).

Where there are conflicting by-laws, the more specific will control. Am. Center for Educ. v. Cavnar, 26 Cal. App. 3d 26, 102 Cal. Rptr. 575 (1972).

[22] Booker v. First Fed'l Sav. and Loan Ass'n, 215 Ga. 277, 110 S.E.2d 360, 362, *cert. denied,* 361 U.S. 916 (1959).

"By-laws adopted under authority of this section must, of course, not be inconsistent with the charter of the corporation and the purposes for which the corporation was created, must not infringe the common or statute law of the state, must be reasonable, must not defeat or impair any vested right of its stockholders or members, and must not be contrary to public policy." Hornady v. Goodman, 167 Ga. 555, 146 S.E. 173, 181 (1928).

[23] SEC v. Transamerica Corp., 163 F.2d 511, 518 (3d Cir. 1947), *cert. denied,* 332 U.S. 847 (1948).

[24] *See* McKee & Co. v. First Nat'l Bank, 265 F. Supp. 1, 4 (S.D. Cal. 1967), *aff'd,* 397 F.2d 248 (9th Cir. 1968).

[25] *See* Commonwealth *ex rel.* Sheip v. Vandegrift, 232 Pa. 53, 81 A. 153, 154 (1911).

to a single act of the corporation, while a by-law is a permanent and continuing rule which is to be applied on all future occasions.[26]

By-laws need not be in writing. "However prudent and advisable, it is not necessary, that a corporation should ordain its by-laws by a formal act of legislation, nor that they should reduce them to writing, unless required to do so by the charter."[27] And it should be noted again that, although in writing, a by-law which has fallen into disuse and been disregarded year after year without objection, may not be enforceable.[28]

Generally, by-laws adopted for the conduct of the internal affairs of an organization cannot affect the interests of third parties and defeat their just claims against the organization.[29] Strangers may or may not be bound by the by-laws, depending in each case on the circumstances.[30] For example, the published by-laws and rules of a public body, such as the rules of a school board relating to public bids, have been held to be binding on those who dealt with the

[26] Hornady v. Goodman, 167 Ga. 555, 146 S.E. 173, 181, 182 (1928), *citing* Fox's Parl. Usage.

[27] Taylor v. Griswold, 14 N.J.L. 222, 241 (1834). The court held that, although immemorial usage may help in the construction of fundamental provisions, it cannot alter or repeal.

[28] "The by-laws, which required the inspectors to be stockholders of the company, had fallen into disuse, and had been disregarded by the continued election from year to year, by the stockholders of persons not stockholders for inspectors. The same persons had been chosen for the three previous successive years as such inspectors, without dissent or objection, and I much doubt whether said by-law was ever of any force or validity, and whether the directors could thus restrict the choice of inspectors." People v. Albany & S. R.R., 1 Lans. 308, 333 (N.Y. Sup. Ct. 1869), *modified on other grounds*, 5 Lans. 25 (1871), *aff'd*, 57 N.Y. 161 (1874).

On the other hand, it has been held that "no by-law or rule can be established by custom, which is beyond its authority to adopt by resolution or ordinance." Murdoch v. Strange, 99 Md. 89, 57 A. 628 (1904).

[29] The power to adopt by-laws is necessarily incident to a corporation, but it is not intended that the interest of third persons can be affected and their just claims defeated by the operation of a by-law. Mechanics' & Farmers' Bank v. Smith, 19 Johns. 115, 124 (N.Y. 1821).

[30] *See* Pfister v. Gerwig, 122 Ind. 567, 23 N.E. 1041 (1890) (member of mutual insurance company must abide by by-laws in force when he becomes member).

board.[31] It has also been held that the by-laws of a church can be collaterally attacked in an action by the church against the pastor.[32]

The power to adopt rules and by-laws for the conduct of its internal affairs is inherent in every entity and in all assemblies organized for a lawful purpose. An early Supreme Court decision stated the basic rule. "To corporations, however erected, there are said to be certain incidents attached, without any express words or authority for this purpose; such as the power to plead and be impleaded, to purchase and alien [sic], to make a common seal, and to pass by-laws." [33] The power to adopt by-laws is ordinarily in the shareholders or members of a company, but such power may be delegated to the directors.[34] "A corporation derives its existence from the state, but its by-laws come into existence through the action of its members. [citation] They are laws made by the corporation itself." [35] The power of a corporation to adopt by-laws is usually expressed in the general corporation laws of the several states.[36]

Members of an organization are presumed to have knowledge of

[31] *See* Montenegro–Riehm Music Co. v. Board of Educ., 147 Ky. 720, 145 S.W. 740 (1912).

[32] In an action by a church to restrain the defendant from acting as pastor, the court held that "the rule against collateral attack does not apply to corporate by-laws. A corporation derives its existence from the state, but its by-laws come into existence through the action of its members. . . . They are laws made by the corporation itself and consequently can be directly challenged, as the by-laws upon which the plaintiff relies were challenged." Hopewell Baptist Church v. Craig, 143 Conn. 593, 124 A.2d 220 (1956).

[33] Bank of the United States v. Dandridge, 25 U.S. (12 Wheat.) 64, 67 (1827).

Every corporation has an inherent right to adopt by-laws for its internal government and to regulate the conduct and prescribe the rights and duties of its members toward itself and among themselves in reference to the management of corporate affairs. McKee & Co. v. First Nat'l Bank, 265 F. Supp. 1 (S.D. Cal. 1967), aff'd, 397 F.2d 248 (9th Cir. 1968); Olincy v. Merle Norman Cosmetics, Inc., 200 Cal. App. 2d 260, 19 Cal. Rptr. 387 (1962).

But see Taylor v. Griswold, 14 N.J.L. 222 (1834) (question whether a by-law allowing voting by proxy was an incidental corporate power).

[34] Bennett v. Hibernia Bank, 47 Cal. 2d 540, 305 P.2d 20, 27 (1957).

[35] Hopewell Baptist Church v. Craig, 143 Conn. 593, 124 A.2d 220, 223 (1956).

[36] *See, e.g.,* Benintendi v. Kenton Hotel, Inc., 294 N.Y. 112, 60 N.E.2d 829, 832 (1945); Hornady v. Goodman, 167 Ga. 555, 146 S.E. 173, 181 (1928).

its by-laws.[37] Thus, a person who becomes a member of an organization is legally bound by the constitution, by-laws,[38] and rules [39] in force when he acquires membership, even if he has no actual notice of their existence or terms. He is also entitled to the benefit and protection of the by-laws then in effect.[40] Where, for example, the by-laws provide that Cushing's Manual shall govern all debates, the rules and procedures so adopted should be observed.[41]

§ 21.3   By-Laws—Power To Amend

The power to amend and to repeal the by-laws rests in the members or shareholders, and may be exercised directly by them or by the board of directors or other subordinate body having delegated power to so act.[42] Where the by-laws provide that they can be

[37] *See, e.g., In re* Unexcelled, Inc., 28 App. Div. 2d 44, 281 N.Y.S.2d 173 (1st Dep't 1967).

[38] Cleveland Orchestra Comm. v. Cleveland Fed'n of Musicians, 303 F.2d 229 (6th Cir. 1962) (labor union); Pfister v. Gerwig, 122 Ind. 567, 23 N.E. 1041 (1890) (mutual insurance company); Green v. Felton, 42 Ind. App. 675, 84 N.E. 166 (1908) (private corporation); Morrill v. Little Falls Mfg. Co., 53 Minn. 371, 55 N.W. 547, 549 (1893) (business corporation); Merchants' Ladies Garment Ass'n v. Coat House of William M. Schwartz, Inc., 152 Misc. 130, 273 N.Y.S. 317 (N.Y.C. Mun. Ct. 1934) (membership corporation).

[39] Rosen v. District Council No. 9, 198 F. Supp. 46 (S.D.N.Y. 1961) (prescribed procedural methods for taking disciplinary action against members).

[40] "Those who become members of the corporation are entitled to assume that faith will be kept with them in observance of the by-laws and to resist infractions of them, and to enforce their rights accordingly." Bushway Ice Cream Co. v. Fred H. Bean Co., 187 N.E. 537, 540 (Mass. 1933).

[41] Cushing's Manual provided that, if offensive words are not noticed at the time and any other business intervenes before notice is taken of the words which gave offense, the words are not to be written down nor the member using them censured. This rule was not observed. People *ex rel.* Godwin v. American Institute, 44 How. Pr. 468 (N.Y. Sup. Ct. 1873).

[42] Those parts of the by-laws of a corporation which are "mere regulations governing the conduct of the internal affairs" may be repealed, altered, and amended at the will of the majority unless a greater vote is required by the by-laws themselves or by statute. But by-law provisions "in the nature of a contract" designed to vest property rights among shareholders cannot be repealed or changed without the consent of those whose rights are affected. Metzger v. George Washington Memorial Park, Inc., 380 Pa. 350, 110 A.2d 425, 429 (1955), *quoting* Bechtold v. Coleman Realty Co., 367 Pa. 208, 79 A.2d 661 (1951).

amended by the directors only at a regular meeting, an amendment adopted at any other meeting will be invalid.[43]

This is an inherent power, as the power to adopt includes and implies the power to amend and to repeal. "It is the general rule that, in the absence of specific provision to the contrary, the body which has the power to adopt a by-law also has the power to amend one adopted." [44] However, a by-law requiring a two-thirds vote of shareholders to amend a by-law fixing the number of directors may be ineffective where the statute permits a simple majority vote to amend unless the charter provides otherwise.[45]

The power to amend includes the power to waive. "But even if the council had acted out of harmony or in contradiction of the rules of the manual, it did no more than it legally might do, since such body is not bound to act in accordance with its rules or by-laws. Such bodies may, and perhaps do, oftener than otherwise, waive them." [46]

Early common law recognized that the power to enact by-laws is a "continuous" right residing in the membership and thus a body cannot limit future actions of the same or any subsequent body by the enactment of "irrepealable" rules or procedures.[47] Directors

---

Where the statute permits a change in the number of directors by amendment of the by-laws, or by a resolution of the shareholders if there is a by-law in effect providing for change by resolution, a simple resolution of the shareholders not acting under a by-law will not effect the change. Model, Roland & Co. v. Industrial Acoustics Co., Inc., 16 N.Y.2d 703, 261 N.Y.S.2d 896, 209 N.E.2d 553 (1965).

See Lamb v. Cohen, 40 Misc. 2d 615, 243 N.Y.S.2d 647 (Sup. Ct. 1963) (by-laws amended by a majority vote of political committee at a meeting with a quorum present).

[43] Moon v. Moon Motor Car Co., 17 Del. Ch. 176, 151 A. 298 (1930).

[44] See State ex rel. Brewster v. Ostrander, 212 Ore. 177, 318 P.2d 284, 290 (1957).

Rules of procedure "in the nature of by-laws" prescribed for a deliberative body may be amended at will. "The power that made them can unmake them, or disregard them." State ex rel. Fox v. Alt, 26 Mo. App. 673, 677 (1887).

[45] Model, Roland & Co. v. Industrial Acoustics Co., Inc., 16 N.Y.2d 703, 261 N.Y.S.2d 896 (1965); accord, Gentry-Futch Co. v. Gentry, 90 Fla. 595, 106 So. 473 (1925).

[46] City of Sedalia v. Scott, 104 Mo. App. 595, 78 S.W. 276, 280 (1904), citing Cushing's Manual.

[47] "The power of the society, derived from its charter and the laws under which it was organized, to enact by-laws, is continuous, residing in all regular

have the "right and power to adopt new bylaws and change their thinking in the matter." [48] Although they may be amended, they are considered to be "permanent and continuing in nature" and must be observed until legally changed.[49]

Although the body has power to amend the by-laws, a court of equity will not approve a change calculated to give to one group an unreasonable or unfair advantage over another group. "The method used in the adoption or amendment of a by-law may be legal, but the courts are not constrained to sanction an unlawful result though achieved by legal means." [50]

§ 21.4 By-Laws—Reasonableness

Generally, the by-laws of an organization must be fair and reasonable [51] and must be reasonably applied.[52] By-laws cannot be "nuga-

---

meetings of the society so long as it exists. Any meeting could, by a majority vote, modify or repeal the law of a previous meeting, and no meeting could bind a subsequent one by irrepealable acts or rules of procedure. The power to enact is a power to repeal; and a by-law, requiring a two thirds vote of members present to alter or amend the laws of the society, may itself be altered, amended, or repealed by the same power which enacted it." Richardson v. Union Congregational Soc'y, 58 N.H. 187, 189 (1877); *cited with approval*, Hornady v. Goodman, 167 Ga. 555, 146 S.E. 173, 182 (1928).

Although a corporation has the right by organic statute to adopt by-laws, it need not provide a method for amending. Thus a by-law requiring unanimous vote to amend is not forbidden by statute. Benintendi v. Kenton Hotel, Inc., 294 N.Y. 112, 60 N.E.2d 829 (1945).

Every corporation may by statute make by-laws, but it need not provide for amending. The State is interested to see that by-laws are not inconsistent with public policy, but "once proper by-laws have been adopted, the matter of amending them is, we think, no concern of the State." Prigerson v. White Cap Sea Foods, Inc., 100 N.Y.S.2d 881, 884 (Sup. Ct. 1950).

[48] McKee & Co. v. First Nat'l Bank, 265 F. Supp. 1, 12 (S.D. Cal. 1967), *aff'd*, 397 F.2d 248 (9th Cir. 1968).

[49] Bosch v. Meeker Co-Op Light & Power Ass'n, 253 Minn. 77, 91 N.W.2d 148, 152 (1958). The court set aside a proposed amendment of the by-laws relating to the nomination of directors as "arbitrary, unreasonable and unlawful."

[50] *In re* Flushing Hosp. and Disp., 288 N.Y. 125, 41 N.E.2d 917, *modified*, 288 N.Y. 735, 43 N.E.2d 356 (1942).

[51] Bosch v. Meeker Co-Op Light & Power Ass'n, 91 N.W.2d 148, 152 (Minn. 1958) (nominations for director); Gottlieb v. Economy Stores, Inc., 199 Va. 848, 102 S.E.2d 345, 353 (1958) (expulsion of member). *See* Selama–Dind-

tory and vexatious, unequal, oppressive, or manifestly detrimental to the interests of the corporation"; if so, they are void.[53] They must not be "unworkable or unenforceable." [54] They must not be "repugnant to the laws of the state" [55] nor conflict with common law,[56] and must not be inconsistent with the charter of the organiza-

---

ings Plantations, Ltd. v. Durham, 216 F. Supp. 104 (S.D. Ohio 1963), aff'd sub nom. Selama–Dindings Plantations, Ltd. v. Cincinnati Union Stock Yard Co., 337 F.2d 949 (6th Cir. 1964) (recording proceedings of directors' meetings). See also Ruggles v. Illinois, 108 U.S. 526 (1882), followed in Illinois Central R.R. v. Illinois, 108 U.S. 541 (1882); Conlee Construction Co. v. Cay Construction Co., 221 So. 2d 792 (Fla. 1969) (majority vote of controlled board); Commonwealth v. Woelper, 3 S. & R. 29 (Pa. 1817) (appointment of inspectors); Granger v. Grubb, 7 Phila. 350, 351–52 (C.P. 1870).

[52] The by-laws of a corporation are presumptively valid. The validity of a by-law is purely a question of law and not of fact. Thus, the question whether a by-law is void because is it unreasonable is a question of law for the court and not a question for the jury. By-laws must be applied reasonably and without discrimination. And, if by-laws are reasonable, the purpose, intent, or motive behind their adoption is not a matter of judicial inquiry. McKee & Co. v. First Nat'l Bank, 265 F. Supp. 1 (S.D. Cal. 1967), aff'd, 397 F.2d 248 (9th Cir. 1968).

[53] Granger v. Grubb, 7 Phila. 350, 351 (C.P. 1870).

[54] Weisblum v. LiFalco Mfg. Co., 193 Misc. 473, 84 N.Y.S.2d 162, 166 (Sup. Ct. 1947).

[55] State ex rel. Moore v. Archibald, 5 N.D. 359, 66 N.W. 234, 242 (1896).

A corporation may adopt reasonable by-laws not "in conflict with the laws of this state or the United States" to enable it to carry out its purposes. Gottlieb v. Economy Stores, Inc., 199 Va. 848, 102 S.E.2d 345, 352 (1958); accord, In re Lighthall Mfg. Co., 47 Hun 258 (N.Y. Sup. Ct. 1888).

Voting rights of stockholders may be determined by by-laws which are not in conflict with the law of the state. Commonwealth ex rel. Cartwright v. Cartwright, 350 Pa. 638, 40 A.2d 30 (1944).

[56] When the Constitution gave each House the right to determine its own rules of proceeding, "it was never held for a moment that such a right included the power to change any existing statute or common law." The Constitution being silent as to a quorum, the question arises whether a majority may fix a greater number. "For the body itself to attempt to fix a greater number is for the body to attempt to change a rule of the common law. . . . But it is well established in this state that even a statute law (much less a rule of procedure) that seeks to alter a principle of the common law must do so in plain and direct terms." Heiskell v. City of Baltimore, 65 Md. 125, 4 A. 116, 119 (1886). See Murdock v. Strange, 99 Md. 89, 57 A. 628 (1904).

In the absence of other appropriate indication of legislative will, the common law forms part of the laws of the State to which the by-laws of a corporation.[57] These qualities have been combined in a court decision holding that the by-laws of a corporation "must, of course, not be inconsistent with the charter of the corporation and the purposes for which the corporation was created, must not infringe the common or statute law of the state, must be reasonable, must not defeat or impair any vested right of its stockholders or members, and must not be contrary to public policy."[58] It has been held that a corporate by-law which disturbs a vested right is ipso facto not reasonable.[59]

The validity of a corporate by-law is a question of law, not of fact. In an early case it was held that evidence is not admissible in a jury trial to determine whether a by-law is reasonable or not.[60]

---

tion must conform. Ruggles v. Illinois, 108 U.S. 526 (1882), *followed in* Illinois Central R.R. v. Illinois, 108 U.S. 541 (1882).

[57] "It cannot be denied, that a by-law contrary to the charter, is void from the beginning; and that as to usage, it can never alter or repeal a statute. . . ." Taylor v. Griswold, 14 N.J.L. 222, 251 (1834).

Where a charter required that by-laws be adopted by the incorporators when two-thirds of their members were present, the adoption of by-laws by the directors was not valid. Thayer v. Herrick, 23 Fed. Cas. 899 (No. 13868) (C.C.D. Minn. 1876).

A by-law requiring a quorum of two-thirds of the shares at a special meeting was not authorized by the certificate of incorporation and was in direct opposition to stock corporation law. *In re* William Faehndrich, Inc., 2 N.Y.2d 468, 141 N.E.2d 597, 161 N.Y.S.2d 99 (1957).

"It is uniformly held that the by-laws of a corporation may not conflict with the articles of incorporation." State *ex rel.* Brewster v. Ostrander, 212 Ore. 177, 318 P.2d 284, 289 (1957).

[58] Hornady v. Goodman, 167 Ga. 555, 146 S.E. 173, 181 (1928).

Where by-laws of a corporation are invalid by reason of their inconsistent and conflicting provisions, a question of quorum will be governed by the corporation law and not according to the common-law rule which would apply to a voluntary association without rules. New York Elec. Wkrs. Union v. Sullivan, 122 App. Div. 764, 107 N.Y.S. 886 (1st Dep't 1907).

[59] Vernon Manor Co-op Apartments v. Salatino, 15 Misc. 2d 491, 178 N.Y.S.2d 895 (West. County Ct. 1958).

[60] It is the "acknowledged canon that rules and by-laws must be reasonable. And all which are nugatory and vexatious, unequal, oppressive, or manifestly detrimental to the interests of the corporation, are void. . . . This is a question for the Court solely, and upon a trial before a jury, it is not admissible to allow them to determine upon the evidence whether a by-law is reasonable or not." Granger v. Grubb, 7 Phila. 350, 351–52 (C.P. 1870); *accord,* Commonwealth v. Worcester, 20 Mass. (3 Pick.) 461, 473 (1826).

On the other hand, where the reasonableness of a by-law is a mere matter of judgment, and one on which reasonable minds must necessarily differ, it has been held that a court would not be warranted is substituting its judgment for the judgment of those who have exercised their authority to make by-laws.[61]

§ 21.5 By-Laws—Labor Unions

When one becomes a member of a union "he agrees to be governed by the union constitution, by-laws and rules, not inconsistent with rights and procedures established by the Act [Federal statute]; and the constitution and by-laws of the union express the terms of the contract which define the privileges secured and the duties assumed by those who become members."[62] The membership may, at the very least, compel a member to give obedience to the by-laws and regulations until they are successfully challenged either intramurally or before a court or administrative agency.[63] Recognition of this principle is expressly provided by the Federal statutes and, since the rights of members are subject to the constitution and by-

---

The validity and reasonableness of a by-law is a question of law for the court and not a question of fact for the jury. McKee & Co. v. First Nat'l Bank, 265 F. Supp. 1, 4 (S.D. Cal. 1967), aff'd, 397 F.2d 248 (8th Cir. 1968).

"The reasonableness of such regulations is a question of law for the court and not for the jury." Brumfield v. Consolidated Coach Corp., 240 Ky. 1, 40 S.W.2d 356, 362 (1931).

However, it has been held that "the courts have no visitorial power to determine whether the by-laws of a voluntary association are reasonable or unreasonable." Green v. Felton, 42 Ind. App. 675, 84 N.E. 166, 170 (1908).

[61] See McKee & Co. v. First Nat'l Bank, 265 F. Supp. 1, 4 (S.D. Cal. 1967), aff'd, 397 F.2d 248 (9th Cir. 1968).

[62] Cleveland Orchestra Comm. v. Cleveland Fed'n of Musicians, 303 F.2d 229 (6th Cir. 1962).

The constitution and by-laws of an unincorporated association express the terms of a contract which define the privileges secured and the duties assumed by those who have become members. Fritsch v. Rarback, 98 N.Y.S.2d 748 (Sup. Ct. 1950); accord, Polin v. Kaplan, 257 N.Y. 277, 177 N.E. 833 (1931).

[63] "Generally it seems the least that membership can compel is obedience to the By-laws and regulations until successfully challenged either intramurally or before a court or administrative agency. By becoming a member of a union, the worker, in effect, agrees to be governed by the Constitution and By-laws of the organization." Carroll v. Associated Musicians, 235 F. Supp. 161, 172 (S.D.N.Y. 1963).

laws, the remedies provided by such documents must be exhausted before the Federal courts may properly be called upon for relief under the Act.[64]

OFFICE OF SECRETARY

§ 21.6 Secretary

The secretary occupies an important position in the regulatory functions of a deliberative body. He need not be, but often is, a member of the board of directors.[1]

The powers and duties of the secretary are usually specified in the by-laws or code of regulations of the organization, but in the absence of such specification they may be determined from time to time by the body without a formal resolution.[2] The principal duties of the secretary are to record all action taken at meetings as declared by the presiding officer, issue notices and certificates, and maintain custody over the records of the body.[3] These have been held to be ministerial functions involving no judicial discre-

---

[64] See Rizzo v. Ammond, 182 F. Supp. 456 (D.N.J. 1960).

[1] See Streuber v. St. Mary's Pipe Co., 33 Pa. County Ct. 46, 48 (1906).

The powers and duties of the officers of a corporation are often prescribed in the general corporation law of the state of incorporation and in the by-laws. Reference should be made to these authorities.

[2] Cole v. City of Kanopolis, 159 Kan. 304, 153 P.2d 920, 922 (1944) (clerk of city council).

The duties of the president and the secretary "as officers of the corporation are confined to the power that created them, and their duty primarily is to the same power—the board of directors—which is the governing body of the corpo-ration." Streuber v. St. Mary's Pipe Co., 33 Pa. County Ct. 46, 48 (1906).

[3] "The presence of the clerk is not necessary to the validity of a meeting, nor does it follow that he cannot record any proceedings unless he were present. If it did, it would follow that if he were called out for any time whatever, the proceedings must stop until he returned and the same would be true of all other clerks, whose duty it is to keep minutes and make entries of any proceed-ings. The village clerk was the keeper of the records, and it was his duty to see that nothing was entered on them, but what he was fully satisfied was proper, and that no person, without his authority, should presume to enter any thing as records or minutes of the proceedings of the meeting. He is made not only the keeper of the records, but also the certifying officer as to copies." Hutchinson v. Pratt, 11 Vt. 402, 419 (1839).

tion.[4] However, when the secretary is directed to send notices of meetings, it is "his duty and responsibility to see to it that they [are] proper." [5]

The chairman may serve as secretary and record the minutes of the meeting; in doing this he does not invalidate the action taken at the meeting.[6]

[4] Distinction between a judicial and a ministerial act is whether the act involves discretion. Texas State Board of Dental Examiners v. Fieldsmith, 242 S.W.2d 213 (Tex. 1951).

The town clerk refused to record the proceedings of a meeting. Mandamus was issued. "A subordinate officer, whose duties are simply ministerial, cannot judge for himself whether the rulings of the moderator are correct. . . . The duty of the defendant, as town-clerk, to record the doings of the annual meeting *as declared* by the moderator, is purely a ministerial duty, involving the exercise of no judicial discretion whatever." Hill v. Goodwin, 56 N.H. 441, 448, 452 (1876).

Generally, the secretary of a corporation is merely a ministerial officer, as distinguished from the president and vice-president, who are executive officers. Emmerglick v. Philip Wolf, Inc., 138 F.2d 661 (2d Cir. 1943).

The secretary's call of a meeting, pursuant to directive, is ministerial and not discretionary. Cullum v. Board of Educ., 15 N.J. 285, 104 A.2d 641 (1954).

The secretary has no right to call a special meeting on his own motion, no power to pass on a written request for a meeting, no power to hire a hall, or to fix a date, or to take any steps which pertain to the office of the chairman. He is merely a ministerial officer. *In re* Davie, 13 Misc. 2d 1019, 1021, 178 N.Y.S.2d 740, 743 (1958) (Robert's Rules of Order had been adopted by county political committee).

The duties of a moderator, "like those of clerk, are merely ministerial, and can in no way affect the validity of the doings of a corporation or the rights of those claiming under them." Stebbins v. Merritt, 64 Mass. (10 Cush.) 27, 34 (1852).

The duty of city clerk to issue and file a certificate of appointment was "ministerial" and no part of the appointing power. State *ex rel.* Burdick v. Tyrrell, 158 Wis. 425, 149 N.W. 280, 283 (1914).

Calling a meeting of directors or of stockholders is a "plain ministerial duty" whether the call is to be issued by the secretary or the president. State *ex rel.* Dendinger v. Kerr Gravel Co., 158 La. 324, 104 So. 60, 61 (1925).

[5] *In re* 74 & 76 West Tremont Ave. Corp., 10 Misc. 2d 662, 173 N.Y.S.2d 154, 156 (Sup. Ct. 1958).

[6] "Simply because the chairman of the meeting of the board of trustees acted also as its scribe would, in our opinion, operate to invalidate neither the action of the meeting nor the minutes of that action as taken down and recorded by him." Budd v. Walla Walla Print. & Publ. Co., 2 Wash. Terr. 347, 7 P. 896, 897 (1885).

The absence of the secretary or clerk cannot "effectively frustrate the wishes of the majority," and the board members have the clear right to perform his ministerial acts,[7] or the chairman may appoint someone to act in his place. "It must, from necessity, be in the power of any corporation, whether public or private, to appoint a person as cleark, *pro tem,* for the purpose of making the entries of what was done by them."[8] Absence of objection to the temporary appointment of a secretary of a meeting is conclusive as to the validity of his appointment.[9]

In the absence of authority to the contrary, the secretary or clerk holds his office at the will of the appointive power and he may be removed by that power without cause.[10] He may, of course, be removed for cause.[11]

§ 21.7   Minutes

Minutes are the records or reconstruction of the proceedings of a meeting. "The very purpose of minutes is to transcribe into per-

[7] Requirement of the secretary's signature on a notice of meeting is directory and not mandatory. Cullum v. Board of Educ., 15 N.J. 285, 104 A.2d 641 (1954).

[8] Hutchinson v. Pratt, 11 Vt. 402, 420 (1839); *accord,* State *ex rel.* Patty v. McKee, 20 Ore. 120, 126, 25 P. 292, 294 (1890) (requirements of a statute in relation to who shall be secretary are "directory merely, and not mandatory").

Temporary clerk duly sworn may continue in office as clerk until successor is sworn. School Dist. in Stoughton v. Atherton, 12 Met. 105 (Mass. 1846).

Absence of the town clerk does not invalidate the business transacted at a town board meeting. To hold otherwise "would be merely glorifying form and ignoring substance." Roth v. Loomis, 54 Misc. 2d 39, 281 N.Y.S.2d 158, 160 (Sup. Ct. 1967).

[9] "When the chairman announced the appointment in the presence of the meeting, and the secretary served, without a single objection from any one, the act of the chairman became the act of the meeting." State *ex rel.* Patty v. McKee, 20 Ore. 120, 25 P. 292, 294 (1890).

See Chapman v. Barton, 345 Ill. App. 110, 102 N.E.2d 565 (1951) (employee served as recording secretary of stockholders' meeting without objection).

[10] *See Ex parte* Hennen, 38 U.S. (13 Pet.) 230, 260 (1839). The court reasoned that, in the absence of statutory regulation, the power of removal is incident to the power of appointment (court clerk appointed by judge).

[11] "The failure of an officer to do his duty may be a cause for his removal, but it does not of or by itself remove him or create a vacancy in his office." State *ex rel.* Clifford v. McMullen, 46 Ind. 307, 310 (1874) (township trustee).

manent and official form the actions at a meeting of the organization." [12] The current minute book, or the minutes of the last annual meeting, and the minutes of any intervening special meeting, should be produced or be readily available at each meeting of stockholders.[13] Minutes are the property of the organization, not of the clerk or any other person.[14]

There is judicial authority that "a corporation can only speak through its minutes." [15] Clearly, the minutes of a meeting are prima

[12] Chapin v. Crullis, 299 Mich. 101, 299 N.W. 824, 826 (1941).

The office of a legislative journal is to record the proceedings of the house, and authenticate and preserve the same. Moore v. Langton, 167 A.2d 558, 562 (R.I. 1961).

The minutes of meetings and by-laws of public bodies are usually open to the inspection of any interested person. Lehrman v. Board of Examiners, 22 Misc. 2d 348, 350, 195 N.Y.S.2d 478, 479 (1959).

Open meeting statutes often provide that any session of a municipal body which takes action required by law or rule to be recorded in the minutes or journal, is a meeting which must be open to the public. See Beacon Journal Publ. Co. v. Akron, 3 Ohio St. 2d 191, 209 N.E.2d 399 (1965).

See Minneapolis Star and Tribune Co. v. State, 282 Minn. 86, 163 N.W.2d 46 (1968) (right of newspaper to examine minutes of State Board of Medical Examiners).

[13] The president refused to call the annual meeting of stockholders. "The president also refused to produce the minute book of the corporation before any such meeting. Which is again an untenable position. The stockholders and directors of the corporation are entitled to have the minute book, and all other books, brought before their meeting." State ex rel. Dendinger v. Kerr Gravel Co., 158 La. 324, 104 So. 60, 61 (1925).

[14] "The property of the records is in the parish. The clerk is the officer designated by law to hold and keep them; and if a stranger gets possession of them, the parish may take them from him by proper action, or recover damages for their destruction or retention." Inhabitants of the First Parish in Sudbury v. Stearns, 21 Pick. 148, 151 (Mass. 1838).

[15] South Georgia Power Co. v. Baumann, 169 Ga. 649, 655, 151 S.E. 513, 516 (1929).

It is the rule "that the governing body of a municipal corporation such as a board of education can speak only through its records and can confer authority to make or terminate contracts only by proper proceedings at a meeting regularly called and held when its acts are duly recorded and authenticated." Lewis v. Board of Educ., 348 S.W.2d 921, 923 (Ky. 1961).

A city council can speak only by its records, and where the record is produced parol evidence is inadmissible to supply omissions or to contradict its provisions. Erlanger v. Berkemeyer, 207 F.2d 832, 835 (6th Cir.), cert. denied, 346 U.S. 915 (1953); accord, People ex rel. Reilly v. City of Kankakee,

facie evidence of what took place at the meeting, the resolutions adopted, the proceedings followed, and the business transacted.[16]

---

288 Ill. App. 192, 6 N.E.2d 260 (1937); Kelly v. Galloway, 156 Ore. 321, 68 P.2d 474 (1937).

The records of the proceedings of a school board cannot be contradicted by parol evidence. Lingle v. Slifer, 8 Ill. App. 2d 489, 131 N.E.2d 822 (1956).

"The actions of the legislative or governing body of a municipal corporation are expressed in the minutes of the body, recorded as they take place by its clerk. . . . The minutes, and records of the proceeding constitute sufficient compliance with the statute of frauds." Bochino v. Palmer, 203 N.Y.S.2d 301, 304, 305 (Sup. Ct. 1960).

"Where there is a record, it cannot be added to or varied by parol, but the record will be deemed to be evidence of all that was done and that nothing more was done." Hutchinson v. Pratt, 11 Vt. 402, 421 (1839).

A town clerk, having only ministerial duties, "must record the doings of the annual meeting as declared by the moderator." Hill v. Goodwin, 56 N.H. 441, 452 (1876), *citing* Cushing's Manual.

It must be proved by the journal itself that the resolution was adopted by the requisite vote; such fact cannot be proved by extrinsic evidence. The only legal evidence is the record of the proceedings kept in accordance with law. *In re* South Market St., 76 Hun 85, 27 N.Y.S. 843 (1894).

[16] Hartford Acc. & Indem. Co. v. City of Sulphur, 123 F.2d 566, 571 (10th Cir. 1941), *cert. denied*, 315 U.S. 805 (1942).

"Ordinarily, the minutes of corporate meetings are prima facie evidence, and usually held to be the best evidence of what they purport to show as to the corporate business transacted at such meetings. . . . Of course, such minutes are subject to contradiction, and it is permissible to show by parol what were the actual proceedings, if the minutes do not correctly record them." Gentry-Futch Co. v. Gentry, 90 Fla. 595, 106 So. 473, 478 (1925).

"A corporation commonly speaks through its records. [citation] The minutes of the meeting of a corporation's board of directors are a part of such corporate records, [citation] and are prima facie evidence of the facts stated. [citation]" Stipe v. First Nat'l Bank, 208 Ore. 251, 301 P.2d 175 (1956).

The minute books of a corporation or an unincorporated association are "competent evidence" of action taken at the meeting. Francis v. Perry, 82 Misc. 271, 144 N.Y.S. 167, 168 (Oneida County Ct. 1913).

It is clearly competent to show from the journals of either branch of the legislature that a particular act was passed or not passed. Moore v. Langton, 167 A.2d 558, 562 (R.I. 1961).

Where minutes of a meeting at which a resolution was adopted had been read and approved at a subsequent meeting, and the company had itself pleaded the resolution, it could not thereafter successfully urge its invalidity. Kilsby v. Aero-Test Equip. Co., 301 S.W.2d 703 (Tex. 1957).

Shareholders are bound by corporate resolutions in the minutes. Wright v. Phillips Fertilizer Co., 193 N.C. 305, 136 S.E. 716 (1927).

This is often a statutory presumption.[17] One court states simply: "The parliamentary history of an act or bill in the legislative journals is the only evidence that is recognized by the courts in this state, and the journals cannot be aided or contradicted by other documents or evidence of any kind."[18]

In proving that a meeting was held and that certain action was taken at the meeting, the best evidence is the original minutes as contained in the minute book. A copy of the minutes as certified by the secretary is not competent.[19]

§ 21.7.1   Presumed Correct

The minutes of a meeting as written are presumed to be correct in the absence of a contrary showing.[20] As stated in an early

---

However, in a shareholder's action against the directors, recitals in the minutes of a directors' meeting are not binding on the stockholder. Gallagher v. Perot, 122 Misc. 845, 848, 202 N.Y.S. 441, 446 (Sup. Ct. 1923).

Corporate records in which resolutions of the directors and stockholders are contained are in themselves proof of the regularity of the transactions recorded therein. Stephens Fuel Co. v. Bay Parkway Nat'l Bank, 109 F.2d 186, 189 (2d Cir. 1940).

The minutes of a meeting are the best evidence of the proceedings and actions taken at the meeting, and the statements thereof appearing in the minutes are not subject to collateral attack or to be contradicted by the officials. City of Coral Gables v. Sackett, 253 So. 2d 890 (Fla. App. 1971).

[17] See, e.g., Shamel v. Lite Prods. Sales, Inc., 131 Cal. App. 2d 33, 279 P.2d 1020, 1022 (1955) (statute provided that minutes of meeting are "prima facie evidence of the . . . due holding of such meetings, and of the facts or actions stated therein").

However, where the statute or charter provided that the votes of members shall be recorded in the minutes, and the minutes failed to so record the vote, the facts could not be proved by extrinsic evidence. In re South Market St., 75 Hun 85, 27 N.Y.S. 843, 846 (1894).

The articles of a company provided that the declaration by the chairman that a resolution was carried, recorded in the minute book, was "sufficient evidence" unless a poll was demanded. In re Horbury Bridge, Coal, Iron & Waggon Co., 11 Ch. D. 109 (1879).

[18] People ex rel. Sellers v. Brady, 262 Ill. 578, 105 N.E. 1, 6 (1914), citing Jefferson's Manual and Robert's Rules of Order on other points.

[19] In re Mandelbaum, 80 Misc. 475, 141 N.Y.S. 319 (Sup. Ct.), aff'd, 159 App. Div. 909, 144 N.Y.S. 1128 (1st Dep't 1913).

[20] This presumption of regularity extends to all necessary implications. For example, if the minutes show that a special meeting had been called it will be

opinion, "The verity rather than the falsity of the record will be presumed." [21] Parol evidence is not admissible to alter or contradict the record of a legislative body as actually made in its journal,[22] and cannot be introduced to supplement the minutes of a city council meeting for the purpose of showing what the presiding

presumed that the call of the meeting was duly and regularly made. Greeley v. Hamman, 17 Colo. 30, 28 P. 460 (1891), *citing* Cushing, Law & Pr. Leg. Assem. on suspension of rules.

"The presumption that public officials properly perform their duties will not serve to establish that certain procedure for validity of action taken by the city commission, required by the charter, took place at a meeting, where there is a duty that the proceedings be recorded, if the minutes of the meeting show the required procedure was not taken, or fail to show that such required procedure was observed. Nor have we overlooked the established rules that the minutes of a meeting of such a city commission are the best evidence of the proceedings and actions taken at the meeting, and that statements thereof appearing in the minutes are not subject to collateral attack or to be contradicted by the officials. Those rules apply to statements which are made in the minutes that certain procedures, proceedings or actions were or were not taken or performed. But such rules do not have application to matters required to have been done to import validity to commission action where, notwithstanding the duty to report them, the minutes are silent thereon or so imperfectly drawn as not to reveal whether the required action was performed, or are so drawn as to leave the matter in doubt and in issue." City of Coral Gables v. Sackett, 253 So. 2d 890, 896 (Fla. App. 1971).

"It is an uncontroverted fact that the minutes, at the time of the hearing, had been signed and bore the signatures of the mayor and clerk. Therefore a presumption of regularity and validity arose." City of Biloxi v. Cawley, 278 So. 2d 389, 390 (Miss. 1973).

Recital in the records of a special meeting that it was "called by the chairman for the purposes of ordering an election" as to issuing bonds, is, in the absence of proof to the contrary, sufficient evidence that the time and purpose of the meeting was given to each member of the board. Stockton v. Powell, 10 So. 688 (Fla. 1892).

[21] Mann v. City of LeMars, 109 Iowa 251, 255, 80 N.W. 327 (1899).

It is clearly for those who object to the minutes to impeach their contents. *In re* Indian Zoedone Co., 26 Ch. D. 70, 80 (1884).

[22] Portland Gold Mining Co. v. Duke, 191 F. 692 (8th Cir. 1911).

Minutes and records of a private corporation are admissible to prove its acts, but they can be rebutted by parol evidence. Rueb v. Rehder, 24 N.M. 534, 174 P. 992 (1918).

Articles providing that minutes signed by a chairman are "conclusive evidence without any further proof of the facts therein stated" are binding. Kerr v. Mottram, Ltd., [1940] 1 Ch. 657.

officer intended by his rulings. "What the council actually did, and not what the presiding officer thought necessary, is controlling. It is not competent for the members of a legislative body even to give evidence of what they understood was the effect of the action which the record shows they took. The record of the proceedings is controlling on the question." [23] Also, the corporate secretary's construction of a resolution cannot prevail over the plain terms thereof.[24]

§ 21.7.2   Parol Evidence

In the absence of recorded minutes, parol evidence is competent to show what transpired at a meeting.[25] Competent testimony is

[23] Casler v. Tanzer, 134 Misc. 48, 234 N.Y.S. 571, 578 (1929).

The official check at a town meeting showed 706 registered voters present. Only 348 votes were cast, which was less than the by-law quorum of 400. To an argument that a quorum was not present, the court said: "Parol evidence could not be received to contradict the record." Del Prete v. Board of Selectmen, 351 Mass. 345, 220 N.E.2d 912, 913 (1966), citing Robert's Rules of Order.

Parol evidence "in direct contradiction to the record" is not admissible. "It differs entirely from the case of the admission of parol evidence to show the existence of certain facts omitted to be stated upon the record. . . ." School Dist. in Stoughton v. Atherton, 12 Met. 105, 113 (Mass. 1846).

It is not competent for individual legislators to "give evidence of what they understood was the effect of the action which the record shows they took. This must be gathered from the whole record of their proceedings. . . ." Whitney v. Common Council of Village of Hudson, 69 Mich. 189, 201–2, 37 N.W. 184, 189 (1888).

[24] Kilsby v. Aero-Test Equip. Co., 301 S.W.2d 703 (Tex. 1957).

[25] Resolution was not formally entered upon the minute books, and nothing but a pencil memorandum was made of the proceedings at the meeting. The court held that no objection could be made to the validity of the resolution. "The testimony shows clearly what took place at this meeting. . . . The failure to enter this resolution at the time it was adopted did not affect its validity, as most corporate acts can be proved as well by parol as by written entries." Handley v. Stutz, 139 U.S. 417, 422 (1891).

"Proceedings of a corporate meeting of stockholders or directors are facts and they may be proved by parol testimony when they are not recorded." Tuttle v. Junior Bldg. Corp., 228 N.C. 507, 46 S.E.2d 313, 317 (1948).

"If no minutes are kept, or if the record is incomplete, action at a meeting of the directors may be proved by parol evidence." Redstone v. Redstone Lumber & Supply Co., 101 Fla. 226, 133 So. 882, 884 (1931).

also admissible in supplementing the minutes where a matter has been omitted [26] and to "explain ambiguities, to correct errors or to

---

"What is resolved upon at a meeting of a board of directors of a private corporation may be proven by the record of the proceedings of the board, if one is kept and the proceedings entered, but if a record is not kept, or the proceedings are not recorded, parol evidence is admissible to show what was resolved upon, and by what vote it was carried." Ten Eyck v. Pontiac O. & P.A. R.R., 74 Mich. 226, 41 N.W. 905, 906 (1889).

Corporate resolutions can be proved by parol testimony when they are not recorded. Wright v. Phillips Fertilizer Co., 193 N.C. 305, 136 S.E. 716 (1927).

"The acts of corporations may be proved in the same way as the acts of individuals. If there be no record evidence, they may be proved by the testimony of witnesses; and even where no direct evidence of such acts can be given, facts and circumstances may be proved from which the acts may be inferred." Moss v. Averell, 10 N.Y. 449, 454 (1853).

The testimony of those present at the meeting can also be used to rebut the minutes. Keough v. St. Paul Milk Co., 205 Minn. 96, 285 N.W. 809 (1939).

Where a city council may act without formal resolution, the absence of a formal resolution in the minutes is insufficient to establish that a certain act was unauthorized. Cole v. City of Kanopolis, 159 Kan. 304, 153 P.2d 920, 922 (1944).

The minutes of a meeting are not exclusive evidence of what took place at the meeting. An unrecorded resolution may be proved. In re Fireproof Doors, Ltd., [1910] 2 Ch. 142, 149.

"The minute book of an unincorporated association is competent evidence of action taken by the association at a meeting." Francis v. Perry, 82 Misc. 271, 144 N.Y.S. 167 (Oneida County Ct. 1913).

Corporate books including the stock certificate book, stock ledger, and minute book showing proceedings at meetings of trustees are admissible in evidence. Blake v. Griswold, 103 N.Y. 429, 434 (1886).

In the absence of a record it might be competent to show by parol the proceedings of a meeting. Where there is a record, it cannot be added to or varied by parol, but the record will be deemed to be evidence of all that was done and that nothing more was done. Hutchinson v. Pratt, 11 Vt. 402, 421 (1839).

[26] "We think that corporate minutes are prima facie evidence of the proceedings which transpired at the meeting, but that competent testimony is admissible in supplementing such minutes where a matter has been omitted." Phoenix Fin. Corp. v. Iowa–Wisconsin Bridge Co., 2 Terry (41 Del.) 130, 16 A.2d 789, 794 (1940).

Where corporate minutes, authorizing sale of property by corporation to director, did not show all transactions that took place at a corporate meeting or were not complete, the omission could be supplied by parol evidence. Green River Mfg. Co. v. Bell, 193 N.C. 367, 137 S.E. 132 (1927).

Parol evidence may be put in evidence to show the existence of certain facts

supply omissions." [27] Where the oral testimony is in conflict—for example, about which of two persons was first elected—the court may accept the sequence of events as shown in the minutes of the meeting.[28]

The court will take judicial notice of the journals of a state legislature to ascertain whether a bill has been constitutionally enacted.[29] An enrolled Act of Congress, signed by the Speaker of the House and by the President of the Senate and approved by the President becomes an authenticated Act and is complete and unimpeachable. It is not competent for an objector to show, from the journals of the House, from the reports of committees, or from other documents printed by the authority of Congress that the enrolled bill contained a section that does not appear in the enrolled Act.[30]

---

omitted from the recorded minutes. School Dist. in Stoughton v. Atherton, 12 Met. 105 (Mass. 1846).

Contentions that the minutes of a meeting of a school committee were deliberately recorded in such a way as to deprive the petitioner of the right of appeal based on the record itself, and that certain happenings were intentionally omitted from minutes, were held without merit in view of evidence. Campbell v. School Committee, 67 R.I. 276, 21 A.2d 727 (1941).

[27] Wear v. Harrisburg Steel Corp., 7 Dauph. Co. 82, 97 (1956).

The minutes of a stockholders' or directors' meeting are not conclusive and errors therein may be explained by extraneous evidence. Petrishen v. Westmoreland Fin. Corp., 394 Pa. 552, 147 A.2d 392 (1959).

Minutes may be sufficiently ambiguous to require evidence to rebut direct testimony of the recorder that an ordinance was not in fact read. Brumley v. Greenville, 33 Tenn. App. 322, 274 S.W.2d 12 (1954).

Extrinsic evidence may be considered to prove that a legislature failed to comply with constitutional requirements in case of ambiguity, omission, or conflict in legislative journal. State ex rel. Heck's Discount Centers, Inc. v. Winters, 132 S.E.2d 374 (W. Va. 1963).

[28] The court also noted that the minutes of directors' meetings are prima facie correct. Young v. Janas, 103 A.2d 299, 303 (Del. Ch. 1954).

[29] Callison v. Brake, 129 F. 196, 200 (5th Cir.), *cert. denied,* 194 U.S. 638 (1904). *See* Ottowa v. Perkins, 94 U.S. 260 (1876) (judicial notice of legislative journals).

The court will take judicial notice of a legislative charter. Simmons v. Holm, 229 Ore. 373, 367 P.2d 368 (1961).

The journal may be looked to in determining the regularity of passage of a bill. Wright v. Wiles, 173 Tenn. 334, 117 S.W.2d 736 (1938), *citing* Robert's Rules of Order.

[30] Field v. Clark, 143 U.S. 649 (1891).

This conforms to the common-law rule that an enrolled bill, nothing to the contrary appearing on its face, is an absolute verity, is conclusive of its textual content and of its lawful enactment, and cannot be impeached by the legislative journals or evidence extrinsic of the journals.[31] However, newspaper accounts are not official records or legislative history; they represent individual sentiments that are privately evaluated and edited before release and thus are an unreliable source for charter or legislative interpretations.[32]

The meeting itself must be authentic. The introduction into evidence of so-called minutes of a shareholders' meeting is insufficient to establish that a meeting was held where the evidence clearly shows that no meeting was actually held. "Minutes cannot make a meeting if none was in fact held." [33]

Where a legislative act is defectively certified for failure to show that the requisite number of members were present on passage of the act, resort may be had to the legislative journals to prove the facts. *In re* Week's Estate, 109 App. Div. 859, 96 N.Y.S. 876 (2d Dep't 1905), *aff'd*, 185 N.Y. 107, 77 N.E. 993 (1906).

[31] The court also discussed the "journal-entry rule" that the enrolled bill is not a verity but is prima facie evidence that the legislature met all constitutional requirements. The journals are admissible to rebut the prima facie presumption. Carlton v. Grimes, 237 Iowa 912, 927, 23 N.W.2d 883 (1946).

See Young v. Galloway, 177 Ore. 617, 164 P.2d 427 (1945) (discussion of "journal-entry rule" and "enrolled bill rule").

But see Integration of Bar Case, 244 Wis. 8, 11 N.W.2d 604 (1943) (legislative journals may be resorted to for purpose of showing that enrolled bill is either erroneous or valid).

Silence of the journal on matters not required to be entered of record does not conflict wtih the presumption of regularity of the passage of a bill afforded by the enrolled bill. State *ex rel.* Davis v. Cox, 105 Neb. 75, 178 N.W. 913 (1920).

[32] Dayton Newspapers, Inc. v. City of Dayton, 23 Ohio Misc. 49, 259 N.E.2d 522 (1970).

See Cox v. Stults Eagle Drug Co., 21 P.2d 914 (Ariz. 1933); Smith v. Thompson, 219 Iowa 888, 258 N.W. 190 (1934).

See School Dist. No. 11 v. Chapman, 152 F. 887 (8th Cir.), *cert. denied*, 205 U.S. 545 (1907).

[33] "The mere submission of so-called minutes of a shareholders' meeting is insufficient to establish the fact of such a meeting where the evidence clearly shows, as it does here, that no meeting within the intendment of the Louisiana corporation law was held or contemplated in the purely informal discussions held" at place and date. *In re* Louisiana Inv. and Loan Corp., 224 F. Supp. 274, 276 (E.D. La. 1963), *aff'd*, 342 F.2d 999 (5th Cir. 1965).

Written minutes of a directors' meeting are required by some general corporation laws [34] but not by all.[35]   In fact, a school board, absent some statutory restraint, can act without the formality of recording its proceedings in written minutes.[36]   This conforms to the basic principle that it is "irrelevant to the validity of a corporate act, duly authorized, that no record of it is made in the corporate books." [37]   Also, in the absence of a statutory or charter re-

---

Minutes showing that regular meetings had been held authorizing borrowings from bank were fictitious, having been written in the lawyer's office as though the company had acted in due and formal manner. The court commented: "No such thing. There was no meeting. No one was present." People v. Marcus, 261 N.Y. 268, 286, 185 N.E. 97 (1933).

Pretended corporate minutes which intentionally and falsely recited that a meeting had been held at a certain time, which were signed and conceived in fraud, were null and void. Gieselmann v. Stegeman, 443 S.W.2d 127 (Mo. 1969).

[34] See, e.g., NEW YORK BUS. CORP. LAW § 624 which provides: "Each corporation shall keep correct and complete books and records of account and shall keep minutes of the proceedings of its shareholders, board and executive committee, if any. . . . Any of the foregoing books, minutes or records may be in written form or in any other form capable of being converted into written form within a reasonable time."

[35] See, e.g., NLRB v. Crosby Chemicals, Inc., 274 F.2d 72 (5th Cir. 1960) (Mississippi corporation law).

"I am aware of no law or statute requiring the keeping of minutes by a private corporation, or that, if such minutes are kept, they shall be signed or attested by any officer." Woodhaven Bank v. Brooklyn Hills Imp. Co., 69 App. Div. 489, 74 N.Y.S. 1023, 1025 (2d Dep't 1902).

[36] At a timely meeting attended by all the members of a school board, at least a majority orally declared their decision not to re-elect plaintiff as a teacher and the clerk formally notified plaintiff in writing of the board's decision. No minutes of the meeting were kept. "This formal action, however, has never been held to require strict adherence to the technical procedure approved by 'Robert's Rules of Order.' Nowhere has it been held that a business proposition must necessarily be decided by a school board by means of the formal vote of the members indicated by the signs aye or nay. Any other method of securing the definite decisions of the respective members is sufficient so long as it enables them to determine whether a majority of the members of the board favor or oppose the proposition. Nowhere has it been held the proceedings of a school board are invalid unless they are formally recorded. In the absence of a statute requiring this to be done, it is unnecessary." Fleming v. Board of Trustees, 112 Cal. App. 225, 296 P. 925, 926 (1931).

[37] Sugden v. Shaffer, 100 F.2d 457 (2d Cir. 1938).

quirement regulating the keeping of minutes or journals, the entries may be "of a most cursory nature." [38] Certainly, the deliberations of those present need not be recorded.[39] In recording minutes of a directors' meeting, the secretary, though under an obligation to keep the minutes "faithfully," need not include in the minutes everything that is said so long as there is an accurate description of what took place.[40]

There are no statutory or regulatory guidelines covering the form and content of the minutes of corporate meetings. Suggested forms may be found in several publications.

The pattern of stockholder meetings is relatively uniform, with the designation of nominees in the proxy statement, their nomination at the meeting and their election by written ballot. All other action taken at the meeting by vote of the shareholders is recorded according to the affirmative and negative votes cast. Discussion periods are noted, but the minutes generally do not record the comments, questions or answers.

There is no standard or preferred pattern of minutes of a directors' meeting, except that all formal action taken by resolution of the board, and all financial statements and committee reports received and approved, are recorded in the minutes. A record is made of the directors present, of those absent, and of those abstaining and dissenting from any formal action taken. However, there is a wide

[38] A constitutional provision directing each house to keep journals of its own proceedings does not require entries to be made of every action taken on proposed amendments to pending bills. The best evidence of the text and content of any bill enacted is the enrolled bill authenticated by the signatures of the presiding officers, signed and approved by the governor, and deposited in the office of the secretary of state. Carlton v. Grimes, 237 Iowa 912, 921, 23 N.W.2d 883 (1946).

A formal resolution is not required to validate action taken at a directors' meeting when all directors have knowledge of the facts and the corporation received the benefits. Rubenstein v. Nourse, 70 F.2d 482 (8th Cir. 1934).

[39] "Agencies are no more bound to enter for the record the time, place, and content of their deliberations than are courts." Braniff Airways, Inc. v. CAB, 379 F.2d 453, 460 (D.C. Cir. 1967).

[40] Field v. Oberwortmann, 16 Ill. App. 2d 376, 148 N.E.2d 600, *cert. denied,* 358 U.S. 833 (1958).

Minutes of a board meeting may be "highly informative." Escott v. Bar-Chris Constr. Corp., 283 F. Supp. 643, 694–95 (no written minutes, missing minutes, incomplete minutes).

divergence in the treatment of discussions among the directors present at a meeting, in the recording of informal reports from management and the expressed opinions of individual directors. Some boards prefer minutes which record only the essentials; other boards also prefer a summary or cursory mention of items and topics considered or reported. It is apparent that the form and content of the minutes of a meeting of the board of directors reflects the style of the chairman, the preference of the secretary and the advice of general counsel.

Formal resolutions are not the only evidence of action taken. "Everything that was said and done, the entire setting of the occasion, may help in determining the authorization intended to be conferred and the purpose to be carried out and effected." [41]

Although formality and completeness have useful probative value, the courts will recognize that substance is more effective than form. This is particularly true in closed or small corporations which act informally. Proof of their activities need not be confined to the formal minutes of a meeting but may be established by other means.[42]

However, where there is a contest between the members who were present at the meeting as to what actually took place, the testimony of witnesses sworn and examined and cross-examined in court will be accorded greater weight by the court than notes prepared at and after the meeting by persons present to serve as official minutes, but which had not been officially approved and made the recorded minutes.[43] Although the minutes of a particular organization are customarily not as complete as might be desired, and thus might be considered "bad practice," they are evidence in

[41] *In re* Norton's Will, 129 Misc. 875, 224 N.Y.S. 77, 87 (Sup. Ct. 1927) (dividend distributions).

[42] Sharon Herald Co. v. Granger, 97 F. Supp. 295, 301 (W.D. Pa. 1951) *aff'd,* 195 F.2d 890 (3d Cir. 1952).

[43] Such writings were merely self-serving statements. Chapman v. Barton, 345 Ill. App. 110, 113, 102 N.E.2d 565, 566 (1951).

Minutes may not be convincing evidence when they are proven to be incorrect in several particulars. Where minutes showed the presence of a trustee who testified that he was not present, they are unreliable. United States v. Smith, 523 F.2d 771 (5th Cir. 1975).

disputes between members and are sufficient to prove that a meeting was duly held.[44] Where there are two sets of minutes it may be necessary to decide which set is to be recognized. In one case, the court recognized the original minutes and rejected the other set which had been rewritten with indications of tampering.[45] Yet, where a company kept duplicate minutes for the convenience of shareholders living in a different city and there was a dispute as to which were the correct minutes, both were admissible in evidence, even though one set was not signed or attested by any officer.[46]

Approval of the minutes of the previous meeting does not constitute a "legislative act." It is a mere acknowledgment that the secretary had correctly recorded that which occurred at the meeting.[47] Approval of prior minutes is not a legalization of invalid acts recorded in the minutes.[48]

---

[44] "The minute of this meeting is like that of all the others. Their custom has not been to mention the names of the members who attended, or their numbers. It is a bad practice, but there is nothing on the minutes of the meeting at which this bye-law was passed, which induces a suspicion that it was not regular." Commonwealth v. Woelper, 3 S. & R. 29 (Pa. 1817) (church corporation).

Minutes need not be written with complete reporting of the facts, but they should recite or reasonably imply the conclusive facts. *See* Blum v. Latter, 163 So. 2d 189, *writ refused,* 167 So. 2d 301 (La. 1964).

[45] Rice & Hutchins v. Triplex Shoe Co., 16 Del. Ch. 298, 147 A. 317 (1929), *aff'd,* 17 Del. Ch. 356, 152 A. 342 (1930).

[46] "I think that the mere omission of the keeper of the minutes to sign them did not render them incompetent upon the question as to whether the corporation had done a certain act at this meeting; for it was but the absence of attestation, and not of a certificate requisite to validity." Woodhaven Bank v. Brooklyn Hills Imp. Co., 69 App. Div. 489, 74 N.Y.S. 1023, 1026 (2d Dep't 1902).

[47] Hornady v. Goodman, 167 Ga. 555, 146 S.E. 173, 182 (1928).

Approval of minutes of previous meeting is only the "authentication of the proof" of what happened at the meeting. Hutchinson v. Curtiss, 45 Misc. 484, 92 N.Y.S. 70 (Sup. Ct. 1904).

[48] Approval of minutes of a preceding directors' meeting is nothing more than an acknowledgment that the secretary had properly recorded the acts of the board and is not a legalization of invalid acts recorded therein. Colorado Management Corp. v. American Founders Life Ins. Co., 145 Colo. 413, 359 P.2d 665 (1961).

§ 21.7.3   Corrections

The minutes of a meeting are usually prepared and signed after the event.[49] They may be corrected "as might be necessary to truthfully exemplify what had been done."[50] The secretary, being a servant or agent of the body, may be directed by the body to correct any mis-entries which have been made.[51] Also, the court will, in a proper case, compel the correction of erroneous minutes.[52] One court has held that, if the minutes as certified by the clerk are

---

[49] Teperman v. Atcos Baths, Inc., 6 Misc. 2d 162, 163 N.Y.S.2d 221, 224 (1957), aff'd, 7 App. Div. 2d 854, 182 N.Y.S.2d 765 (2d Dep't 1959).

See Stanley v. Board of Appeals, 168 Misc. 797, 5 N.Y.S.2d 956 (Sup. Ct. 1938) (document signed by members was dated one month before the meeting).

[50] Minutes are prima facie evidence, subject to correction. Gentry-Futch Co. v. Gentry, 90 Fla. 595, 106 So. 473 (1925).

Minutes of a city council meeting may be corrected by resolution at the following meeting. Mann v. City of LeMars, 109 Iowa 251, 80 N.W. 327, 328 (1899).

A defect in certifying copies of a legislative journal may be cured by a subsequent legislative act. In re Stickney, 185 N.Y. 107, 77 N.E. 993 (1906).

The board of directors is within their rights in correcting the minutes to show their official action. Bown v. Ramsdell, 139 N.Y. Misc. 360, 249 N.Y.S. 387, 392 (Sup. Ct. 1931).

Where minutes are incorrectly dated, the date can be corrected as the wrong date was "simply a clerical error, which affected nothing." Hatcher-Powers Shoe Co. v. Bickford, 212 Ky. 163, 278 S.W. 615, 619 (1925).

It is competent for a town clerk to rectify any error in the record to state the proceedings truly. This power is confined to the person whose duty it was originally to make the record, and only while he is in office. Boston Turnpike Co. v. Pomfret, 20 Conn. 589 (1850).

[51] Hutchinson v. Pratt, 11 Vt. 402, 419 (1839).

[52] Correction of minutes of zoning board. "The board by erroneous entry in its minutes cannot render lawful what is in fact unlawful. The error merely serves to confuse public officers and others who may rely upon the minutes and to hamper proof of legal rights and enforcement of the law." Smidt v. McKee, 262 N.Y. 373, 379, 186 N.E. 869 (1933); accord, Steers Sand & Gravel Corp. v. Village Board, 129 N.Y.S.2d 403, 404 (1954).

Mandamus is a proper remedy to compel the rewriting of minutes to correctly state what happened. State ex rel. Lovell v. Tinsley, 236 S.W.2d 24 (Mo. 1951); Smidt v. McKee, 262 N.Y. 373, 186 N.E. 869 (1933).

incorrect, the members of the body have a duty to have the minutes corrected upon their reading at the next meeting.[53]

The time of making a correction in the minute book is not material if the entry faithfully shows what was done.[54] The Supreme Court has validated a corporate resolution formally entered upon the minute book two years after its adoption, when the omission was first discovered.[55] However, the legal effect of a resolution adopted by the board of directors, expressing and embodying an agreement with retiring officers, cannot be changed or affected by a memorandum entered on the records after adjournment of the meeting without the knowledge or consent of the other parties.[56]

The minutes of a corporate meeting are ordinarily authenticated by the signature of its secretary, but it is not necessary that they be signed or otherwise attested. "The mere fact that these particular minutes were not signed did not warrant their rejection." [57]

---

[53] State v. Rulon, 169 N.E.2d 640 (Ohio 1960).

"There is no question that a County Council has a right to correct the minutes of its council meetings and make *nunc pro tunc* entries where errors have occurred by the secretary in properly recording the same. Modifications and amendments may be made where no intervening vested rights are involved. No private vested rights are here involved, and the County Council is at liberty and even has the duty to correct its own records or clarify them." State *ex rel.* Wineholt v. LaPorte Superior Court, 249 Ind. 152, 230 N.E.2d 92, 95 (1967).

A statute requiring that the clerk "make an accurate record of all the proceedings" of the city council contemplated that the council had control of its own record and that until the record had been approved at the next succeeding regular meeting of the council, it was open to such modifications as might be necessary to truthfully exemplify what had been done. Mann v. City of LeMars, 109 Iowa 251, 255, 80 N.W. 327 (1899).

[54] Caldwell v. Dean, 10 F.2d 299 (5th Cir. 1926).

Minutes may be amended at any time to make them conform to the facts, although the personnel of the board has changed and a long time has elapsed. Lingle v. Slifer, 8 Ill. App. 2d 489, 131 N.E.2d 822 (1956).

[55] Nothing but a pencil memorandum was made at the time of the meeting; testimony clearly proved what took place. "The failure to enter this resolution at the time it was adopted did not affect its validity, as most corporate acts can be proved as well by parol as by written entries." Handley v. Stutz, 139 U.S. 417, 422 (1891).

[56] Schlens v. Poe, 128 Md. 352, 97 A. 649 (1916).

[57] Woodhaven Bank v. Brooklyn Hills Imp. Co., 69 App. Div. 489, 74 N.Y.S. 1023, 1025 (2d Dep't 1902).

The signing of minutes by the directors does not give them "the characteristics of a contract." [58] And the fact that the chairman of the meeting acted also as its scribe does not invalidate either the action taken or the minutes as recorded by him.[59] Authentication merely facilitates proof of the correctness of the minutes. Failure of the proper officer to sign the minutes, due to mere inadvertence, does not invalidate the action taken at the meeting.[60] Minutes appearing regular on the face of the record ordinarily cannot be challenged by the officers who had certified them.[61] A director not present at a meeting who signed the minutes as a member of the board is bound by the minutes, and the time when he signed is immaterial.[62]

The corporate minutes are part of the corporate records notwithstanding the fact that the secretary did not pen the minutes with his own hand but adopted and signed minutes as dictated at the time of the meeting by a director–attorney. And the fact that the minutes were not read by the directors prior to the secretary's signature did not invalidate them.[63]

---

[58] Mastin Realty & Mining Co. v. Commissioner, 130 F.2d 1003, 1006 (8th Cir. 1942).

[59] Budd v. Walla Walla Print. & Publ. Co., 2 Wash. Terr. 347, 7 P. 896 (1885).

[60] Teperman v. Atcos Baths, Inc., 7 App. Div. 2d 854, 182 N.Y.S.2d 765 (2d Dep't 1959).

[61] Charles R. Hedden Co. v. Dozier, 99 N.J. Eq. 543, 133 A. 857 (1926), aff'd, 100 N.J. Eq. 560, 135 A. 915 (1927).

[62] Vance v. Mutual Gold Corp., 6 Wash. 2d 466, 108 P.2d 799 (1940).

[63] Teiser v. Swirsky, 137 Ore. 595, 2 P.2d 920, rehearing denied, 4 P.2d 322 (1931).

"The objection to the regularity of the entry in the minute book, that it was made by a stranger, and never read to and approved by the board, is obviated by the fact that the entry was made under the direction of the secretary, from a minute made by him at the time on a loose sheet of paper, and after entry was compared with this sheet by him. It is not necessary that the minutes of a corporation should be written up by the secretary in his own handwriting, or that they should be approved by the board. And in fact, if it was shown that the resolution had been passed by the board when lawfully assembled, it would be valid, although never entered upon the minutes." Wells v. Rahway White Rubber Co., 19 N.J. Eq. 402, 404 (Ch. 1869).

§ 21.7.4   Statutory Requirements

It is important that the minutes of meetings comply in all respects with statutory and charter prescriptions, especially where the rights of third parties are involved. For example, a constitutional provision that no bill shall become a law unless on its final passage the vote be taken by "ayes and noes" and the names of those voting shall be entered on the journal, is mandatory, and a failure to comply with it is fatal.[64] However, it is not necessary that a single book called a journal be kept. "Both the letter and spirit of the law are observed if a permanent public record is maintained in some reasonable form." [65]

In a similar situation, it was held that a mere recording in the minutes of the vote as "all voting aye" [66] or as "carried by full yea vote" [67] does not comply with the village charter and the resolutions were not carried. On the other hand, it has been held that a constitutional provision requiring that the ayes and nays on final passage of a bill must be entered in the journal is only directory to the legislation and not imperative.[68] And, where the constitution does not require more than a declaration of the result in a legislative journal, a mere showing that the resolution was adopted is sufficient and the yeas and nays need not be recorded in the journal.[69] But

[64] Portland Gold Mining Co. v. Duke, 164 F. 180 (8th Cir. 1908).

Where the Constitution requires that a bill be presented to the governor for executive action it must be physically delivered. City of Rye v. Ronan, 67 Misc. 2d 972, 325 N.Y.S.2d 548 (Sup. Ct. 1971), aff'd, 338 N.Y.S.2d 384 (1st Dep't 1972).

[65] Bigham v. City of Rock Island, 120 Ill. App. 2d 381, 256 N.E.2d 897, 899 (1970).

[66] In re South Market St., 75 Hun 85, 27 N.Y.S. 843 (Sup. Ct. 1894).

An ordinance to quiet adverse title to real estate failed to legally pass where there was a failure to comply with a city charter requirement that voting by yeas and nays be recorded. O'Neil v. Tyler, 3 N.D. 47, 53 N.W. 434 (1892).

[67] State v. Rulon, 169 N.E.2d 640, 645 (Ohio 1960).

[68] People v. Supervisors of Chenango, 8 N.Y. 317 (1853).

[69] "The direction that the vote be entered on the journals does not require more than a declaration of the result and is complied with by the showing in the Senate Journal that the resolution was adopted. Had the framers of our constitution intended, as appellee contends, that the yeas and nays be recorded in the journal, they would have said so in those words. . . ." Walther v. McDonald, 243 Ark. 912, 422 S.W.2d 854, 862, 863 (1968).

where a statute requires that the minutes show the vote of each member upon every question, it may be concluded that each member must openly announce his vote at the time he gives it.[70]

The rights of third parties have been protected. A typical case holds that a city cannot escape liability on a contract because the vote of each member of the city council was not recorded.[71]

A statutory requirement that a full and accurate journal of the proceedings of a deliberative body be kept would seem to be merely directory and not a condition precedent to the validity of a contract regularly entered into. "The mere failure of the clerk to properly record the resolution authorizing the contract would certainly not authorize the municipality to repudiate it."[72] In fact the recording of minutes is a "ministerial act," and thus the failure to comply with a statutory requirement that minutes be recorded and that such records be open to public inspection will not per se invalidate any action taken by the body which is otherwise valid.[73] Also, in the

---

Where the minutes of a council meeting showed that all seven members were present, an entry in the minutes stating "Voted yes all" sufficiently shows how many voted for and against. Giesel v. City of Broadview Heights, 14 Ohio Misc. 70, 236 N.E.2d 222 (1968).

[70] Board of Educ. v. State Bd. of Educ., 79 N.M. 332, 443 P.2d 502 (1968).

[71] Statute provided that all votes in city council on ordinances and resolutions for payment of money "shall be by ayes and nays and the vote of each member shall be permanently recorded in the proceedings of the council." This was not done. The court remarked: "We therefore conclude that the city cannot at this time escape liability because of its own failure to keep proper records of its business transactions." Carr v. City of Anchorage, 243 F.2d 482, 483 (9th Cir. 1957).

"Failure of the board of directors of a corporation to record their action will not affect the validity of the acts done by them." Redstone v. Redstone Lumber & Supply Co., 101 Fla. 226, 133 So. 882, 883 (1931).

A corporation may be bound by an agreement not expressly authorized by the by-laws or minutes. Authority to bind the corporation is a jury question. Cary v. U. S. Hoffman Mach. Corp., 148 F. Supp. 748, 751 (D.D.C. 1957).

See Handley v. Stutz, 139 U.S. 417, 422 (1891); Crebs v. City of Lebanon, 98 F. 549 (W.D. Mo. 1898).

[72] Town of Graham v. Karpark Corp., 194 F.2d 616, 622 (4th Cir. 1952).

[73] "It is clear that the board of township trustees is required by statute to keep a record of its proceedings. If the trustees refused to keep such a record, a court could order them to do so upon the request of any interested party. However, we hold that the omission of making a record of the proceedings of

absence of any law or statutory imposition requiring the keeping of minutes and the signature or attestation of minutes by an officer, the failure of a corporation to have minutes of meetings of shareholders and directors does not affect the "corporate existence." [74]

A typographical error in the record need not prejudice the validity of a resolution. It has been held that the power of a committee to act is not lost because a resolution of the parent body purporting to extend such power misstates the number of the original resolution conferring the authority, where the context and circumstances show plainly the authority intended to be conferred. [75] Action taken at a meeting of shareholders is effective even if the minutes have not yet been signed. "From their very nature, minutes of meetings record the events which took place at the meeting and are usually prepared and signed after the event. The time which elapses between the holding of the meeting and the preparation of the minutes may vary." [76]

A statute which requires public "meetings" and also requires that a board keep minutes of its "proceedings" and "examinations," and also of its "other official actions," gives the impression that the board is also to function outside of a public meeting or hearing. "All of these things, the minutes, the records of the examinations

---

the township trustees does not, *per se,* invalidate the action of the township trustees, which is otherwise valid." Thomas v. Board of Trustees, 5 Ohio App. 2d 265, 215 N.E.2d 434, 436 (1966).

[74] Gale–Hasslacher Corp. v. Carmen Contracting Corp., 219 N.Y.S.2d 212, 216 (Sup. Ct. 1961).

[75] Sinclair v. United States, 279 U.S. 263, 296 (1929).

An obvious error in the title does not render an act invalid under a constitutional mandate that the subject of a bill be clearly expressed in the title. School Dist. No. 11 v. Chapman, 152 F. 887 (8th Cir.), *cert. denied,* 205 U.S. 545 (1907); *accord,* Sinclair v. United States, 279 U.S. 263 (1929).

Clerical errors in a legislative journal may be disregarded. *See* Crawford v. Gilchrist, 64 Fla. 41, 59 So. 963 (1912), *citing* Jefferson's Manual on parliamentary questions.

[76] Teperman v. Atcos Baths, Inc., 6 Misc. 2d 162, 163 N.Y.S.2d 221, 224 (1957), *aff'd,* 7 App. Div. 2d 854, 182 N.Y.S.2d 765 (2d Dep't 1959).

The fact that the minutes of a meeting of the board of directors at which a corporate mortgage was authorized were not written up and attested by the officers cannot be invoked to defeat the mortgage. Sorge v. Sierra Auto Supply Co., 47 Nev. 217, 218 P. 735 (1923), *rehearing denied,* 221 P. 521 (1924).

and the records of other official actions are stated to be public
records." [77]

PROXIES *

§ 21.8   Common Law

There is no common-law right of a stockholder or member of a
corporation to vote by proxy,[1] although it has been generally recognized that an interested party may always be represented by his
attorney.[2] The right to vote by proxy is not a general right, but is
a special right derived from some specific statutory provision or
from the charter, by-laws, or other agreement among members.[3]

[77] Sullivan v. Northwest Garage & Storage Co., 223 Md. 544, 165 A.2d 881
(1960).

* This writing does not include a study of proxy solicitation as regulated by
the SEC, the New York Stock Exchange, and the American Stock Exchange,
except in limited pertinent areas. Reference should be made to Regulations
14A, 14B, and 14C and certain releases of the SEC under the Securities Exchange Act of 1934; special sections of the Public Utility Holding Company
Act of 1935 and the Investment Company Act of 1940; the New York Stock
Exchange Company Manual, Sec. A8; and the American Stock Exchange Company Guide, Part 7.

See also, e.g., Annot., Proxies—Securities Exchange Act. Proxies provision
of § 14 of Federal Securities Exchange Act (15 U.S.C. § 78n)—federal cases.
12 L. Ed. 2d 1235 (1965).

[1] Harben v. Phillips, 23 Ch. D. 14, 32, 35 (C.A. 1882); *accord,* Robbins v.
Beatty, 240 Iowa 80, 67 N.W.2d 12, 17 (1954); Taylor v. Griswold, 14 N.J.L.
222, 226 (1834); Dal-Tran Service Co. v. Fifth Ave. Coach Lines, Inc., 14
App. Div. 2d 349, 220 N.Y.S.2d 549, 554 (1st Dep't 1961); Hart v. Sheridan,
168 Misc. 386, 5 N.Y.S.2d 820 (Sup. Ct. 1938) (political committee).

Robert's Rules of Order (at 200) states that voting by proxy is "allowed
only when authorized by the by-laws or charter." *See* SHACKLETON, LAW AND
PRACTICE OF MEETINGS at 148; Williston, *History of the Law of Business Corporations Before 1800,* 2 HARV. L. REV. 105, 149, 158 (1888).

[2] "Although the attorneys voiced the motions and nominations it is clear they
were acting for their respective clients, who were present and acquiesced in all
the proceedings." *In re* Shulman's Petition, 151 N.Y.S.2d 819, 823 (Sup. Ct.
1956).

[3] *See, e.g.,* Robbins v. Beatty, 240 Iowa 80, 67 N.W.2d 12, 17 (1954) (articles authorized voting by written proxy); Klein v. United Theaters Co., 80
Ohio App. 173, 75 N.E.2d 67, 70, *aff'd,* 148 Ohio St. 306, 74 N.E.2d 319
(1947) (right granted by statute).

Corporate directors have not been empowered by statute to act by proxy, and do not have the common-law right to do so.[4]

The right of a member to cast a vote in person or by proxy, specifically provided by statute, "cannot be vitiated by custom or practice." Nor does the failure to use a proxy vote at prior meetings, or a failure to include in the notice of meeting a statement that proxy votes would be accepted, establish a binding precedent.[5]

The person who claims the right to vote by proxy must show his authority for that purpose.[6] It may be presumed that a proxy appearing to be authentic should normally be accepted.[7] However, it has been held unlawful and a "gross violation of the public policy" to permit or contract for the separation of the voting power of corporate stock from its ownership.[8]

Where a statute permits voting by proxy, proxies should be recognized even if the by-laws do not specifically provide for voting by proxy. Vliet v. Smith, 2 Misc. 2d 713, 153 N.Y.S.2d 1014 (Sup. Ct. 1956).

A lawyer's honest legal opinion that certain proxies are invalid is not a tortious interference with the right to vote by proxy; something more in the nature of bad faith or fraudulent actions must be shown before liability can be established. McDonough v. Kellogg, 295 F. Supp. 594 (W.D. Va. 1969).

[4] In re Acadia Dairies, Inc., 15 Del. Ch. 248, 135 A. 846 (1927).

[5] Flynn v. Kendall, 195 Misc. 221, 88 N.Y.S.2d 299, 301 (Sup. Ct. 1949).

"The right of a stockholder to vote his stock is clear; so, too is his right to be represented by a legitimate proxy. Where, as here, the stockholder's physical presence at the meeting is for the purpose, among others, of confirming rather than revoking the proxy, there is no basis for refusing recognition of the stockholder's representatives." In re Manacher, 205 Misc. 513, 133 N.Y.S.2d 265, 266, aff'd, 283 App. Div. 1048, 131 N.Y.S.2d 914 (1954).

[6] Dal-Tran Serv. Co. v. Fifth Ave. Coach Lines, Inc., 14 App. Div. 2d 349, 220 N.Y.S.2d 549, 555 (1961); Philips v. Wickham, 1 Paige 590, 598 (N.Y. Ch. 1829); Craig v. First Presbyterian Church, 88 Pa. 42, 47 (1879).

Proxies relied on at a meeting are entitled to the presumption of regularity. Stephens Fuel Co. v. Bay Parkway Nat'l Bank, 109 F.2d 186 (2d Cir. 1940).

[7] Levin v. Metro-Goldwyn-Mayer, Inc., 221 A.2d 499 (Del. Ch. 1966).

[8] A proxy committee should not vote shares borrowed from another stockholder for the sole purpose of voting and thereafter immediately return such shares to the true owner. "If a stockholder executes a proxy, the person to whom it runs is the stockholder's agent, and he must vote in accordance with the instructions given either openly or tacitly to him by the real owner of the shares. The agency is of such a character that it may be abrogated by the appearance of the shareholder in person at the meeting, or by the execution of a subsequent proxy which would cancel the former one; the whole situation being

Statutes authorizing the voting by proxy usually require that the proxy be in writing.[9]

§ 21.9 Revocation

Generally, every proxy may be revoked in whole or in part at any time before it is exercised. There is some authority that a proxy need not be revoked in the formal manner provided in the proxy but may be revoked orally or by conduct.[10] A proxy may be revoked by the execution of a later proxy, by another writing, or by an appearance of the record holder at the meeting for the purposes of representing himself. A proxy is not revoked by the mere physical presence at the meeting of the shareholder who issued the proxy—for instance, when the shareholder is present to confirm rather than to revoke the proxy.[11] Nor does the granting of a proxy

---

entirely under the control of the stockholder himself. The situation as to the stock complained of in this case is very different. Here the stockholder has divested himself of the right to vote at stockholders' meetings and has sold the right or given it away to persons who may vote it wholly in opposition to his wishes, and thus the power to appoint a proxy degenerates from a scheme for the best method of conducting the business of the company into a mere device for maintaining the control." Bache v. Central Leather Co., 78 N.J. Eq. 484, 81 A. 571, 572 (1911).

[9] Klein v. United Theaters Co., 148 Ohio St. 306, 74 N.E.2d 319 (1947).

No special form of proxy is required by New York law, but there is a statutory requirement that a proxy be in writing. *See* Prince v. Albin, 23 Misc. 2d 194, 200 N.Y.S.2d 843 (Sup. Ct. 1960).

Reference should be made to the applicable state corporation statute which usually requires that proxies be in writing.

[10] Flagg-Utica Corp. v. Baselice, 14 Misc. 2d 476, 178 N.Y.S.2d 860 (Sup. Ct. 1958).

A proxy once given can be revoked by a stockholder personally appearing at a meeting and casting a contrary vote or by giving a later proxy indicating a different vote. Elgin Nat'l Industries v. Chemetron Corp., 299 F. Supp. 367 (D. Del. 1969).

[11] *In re* Manacher, 205 Misc. 513, 133 N.Y.S.2d 265, *aff'd*, 283 App. Div. 1048, 131 N.Y.S.2d 914 (1954).

See Flagg-Utica Corp. v. Baselice, 14 Misc. 2d 476, 178 N.Y.S.2d 860 (Sup. Ct. 1958); Leamy v. Sinaloa Explor. & Dev. Co., 15 Del. Ch. 28, 130 A. 282 (1925) (shareholder attended meeting solely in protest against legality of meeting, and was ejected before votes were received).

to another denude the stockholder of his status of a principal or his rights as a stockholder.[12]

The word "proxy" has a double meaning. Robert explains: "A proxy is a power of attorney given by one person to another to vote in his stead. It is also used to designate the person who holds the power of attorney."[13] A proxyholder has been described under the law of agency as a "universal agent for a particular purpose."[14] Since the relationship created by a proxy is one of principal and agent, it is subject to the duties and liabilities of agency in general.[15] Thus, the person designated in a proxy has a fiduciary obligation to

[12] Ohlstein v. Hillcrest Paper Co., 24 Misc. 2d 212, 195 N.Y.S.2d 920 (Sup. Ct. 1959).

[13] Robert's Rules of Order at 200.

See Bache v. Central Leather Co., 78 N.J. Eq. 484, 81 A. 571 (1911) (discussion of nature and characteristics of proxy).

"A proxy is neither a prospectus nor a registration statement." Robbins v. Banner Industries, Inc., 285 F. Supp. 758, 762 (S.D.N.Y. 1966).

[14] "A universal agent is one appointed to do all that a principal may personally do and may lawfully delegate the power of so doing." Steinberg v. American Bantam Car Co., 76 F. Supp. 426, 439 (W.D. Pa. 1948), *appeal dismissed as moot,* 173 F.2d 179 (3d Cir. 1949).

A proxy is an agent representing and acting for his principal, as distinguished from a trustee. Cliffs Corp. v. United States, 103 F.2d 77, 80 (6th Cir.), *cert. denied,* 308 U.S. 575 (1939).

A proxy to "vote and act" for the undersigned stockholder at all meetings of stockholders for five years has been held to be insufficient to constitute a waiver of the statutory requirement of a notice of meeting. Société Anonyme D'Innov. C. v. American Alcolac Corp., 8 Misc. 2d 166, 171 N.Y.S.2d 149 (Sup. Ct. 1957).

"A proxy is an authority by one, having a right to do a certain thing, to another to do it." Manson v. Curtis, 223 N.Y. 313, 119 N.E. 559 (1918).

[15] "A proxy is the grant of authority by a shareholder to someone else to vote the former's shares. . . . Any stockholder of record having the right and entitled to vote may be represented and vote by a proxy appointed by an instrument in writing. . . . The relationship created by a proxy is one of principal and agent and is subject to the duties and liabilities of agency in general. . . . Consequently, a proxy may not vote in favor of resolutions which benefit himself at the expense of or against the principal's interest. . . . Thus if the proxies were improperly voted, or if they exceeded their authority, the parties to complain are the stockholders who gave the proxies. The stockholders may repudiate the acts of a proxyholder which were in excess of their authority, if timely made, and likewise, the stockholders may elect to ratify such acts. A vote cast at a meeting of the stockholders under such circumstances will be deemed ratified by any subsequent conduct of the stockholder

carry out the wishes of the granting stockholders to the best of his ability.[16]

Although a proxyholder may be and often is himself a member or shareholder, he need not be;[17] and a by-law attempting to so limit persons authorized to act as proxies is invalid.[18] Members of a society who cannot transfer their membership to another should not be allowed to appoint any proxy who is not a member of the organization.[19]

§ 21.10 Authority

The extent of authority granted to a proxyholder depends upon the enabling provisions of the proxy instrument.[20] A proxy that is

---

inconsistent with an intention to repudiate it. . . . It has also been stated that a proxyholder's vote in support of unlisted extraordinary action would be sustained where it was beneficial to the corporation's immediate financial needs." Abbey Properties Co. Inc. v. Presidential Ins. Co., 119 So. 2d 74, 77, 78 (Fla. D. Ct. App. 1960) (also holding that Robert's Rules of Order do not apply to stockholder meetings unless specified).

[16] "The person designated in a proxy has a fiduciary obligation to carry out the wishes of the stockholders to the best of his ability. However, it will be presumed that what the attorney does in the proper exercise of the power conferred expresses the will of the stockholders. . . . It must be assumed that the stockholders expected that their proxies would be voted in accordance with the wishes of the majority of the board of directors, since they represent the management." Hauth v. Giant Portland Cement Co., 33 Del. Ch. 496, 96 A.2d 233, 235–36 (Ch. 1953).

[17] In the absence of a statute or by-law, a proxyholder need not be a stockholder. Gentry-Futch Co. v. Gentry, 90 Fla. 595, 106 So. 473 (1925); accord, People v. Albany & S. R.R., 1 Lans. 308, 323–24 (N.Y. Sup. Ct. 1869), modified on other grounds, 5 Lans. 25 (1871), aff'd, 57 N.Y. 161 (1874).

[18] Under a statute providing for an election by shareholders "either in person or by proxy," the shareholder is at liberty to select any person to act in whom he might be willing to confide the exercise of this privilege. In re Lighthall Mfg. Co., 47 Hun 258, 263 (N.Y. Sup. Ct. 1888).

However, there is considerable authority in support of charter and by-law provisions requiring that a proxyholder be a member. Curry (England) at 148; Joske (Australia) at 144; Shaw and Smith (England) at 84, 158; see Second Consol. Trust Ltd. v. Ceylon Amalg. Tea & Rubber Estates, Ltd., [1943] 2 All. E.R. 567 (Ch.); Companies Act of 1948 § 136(i).

[19] See Robert's Rules of Order at 200.

[20] Where a meeting is adjourned and the notice of adjourned meeting is not broad enough to cover all the items of business contained in the notice of the

general in form need not identify a specific meeting and may be used at any general or special meeting during the term of its validity.[21] Also, a general proxy which gives the proxyholder all the powers the grantor would have possessed had he been present personally at the meeting authorizes the proxyholder to vote on a motion to materially change a proposed amendment to the corporate by-laws. It has been deemed error for a chairman, acting as the judge of the voting (a ministerial function), to rule that a proxyholder could not vote on such a motion unless his proxy instrument specifically authorized him to vote.[22]

However, where the proxy instrument limits the authority of the proxyholder to vote "at any election," he does not have the right to do anything except to vote and to perform incidental voting functions. He cannot, for example, call a special meeting of share-

---

original meeting, the authority of a proxy who was appointed to attend the adjourned meeting does not authorize him to vote upon any matter other than the particular matter mentioned in the notice of adjourned meeting. "The notice of the adjournment was not necessary, but, being sent with notice of the particular business to be then done, it has the effect of limiting that which might be lawfully done to the business thus noticed." Synnott v. Cumberland Bldg. Loan Ass'n, 117 F. 379, 385 (6th Cir. 1902).

[21] Molloy v. Bemis Bros. Bag Co., 174 F. Supp. 785, 794 (D.N.H. 1959), aff'd in part, vacated in part, 283 F.2d 32 (1st Cir. 1960).

"The proxies were general. They authorized the attorneys therein mentioned . . . 'to attend and vote' at the meeting 'with all the powers the undersigned would possess if personally present.' . . . When the stockholders gave general proxies to the Higgins representatives and placed no limitations upon the extent of the power conferred thereby, it must be assumed that the proxies were authorized to vote upon all matters that might come before the meeting in the ordinary and usual course." Stockholders who give a general proxy to a proxy committee "must be presumed to have approved of the announced goal" of the committee. Gow v. Consolidated Coppermines Corp., 19 Del. Ch. 172, 165 A. 136, 142, 147 (1933).

Unless restricted by its terms or some statutory provision, a proxy confers on the grantee a discretion unlimited either in character or in duration, until revoked. Venner v. Chicago City Ry. Co., 258 Ill. 523, 101 N.E. 949 (1913).

[22] The court held: "The chairman cannot limit the use of a proxy which is general in form and appears to be valid on its face. . . . The actions of the chairman violated the fundamental right of a stockholder to be represented by proxy." State ex rel. Hawley v. Coogan, 98 So. 2d 757, 759 (Fla. App.), petition denied, 99 So. 2d 243 (1957), cert. denied, 101 So. 2d 817 (1958).

holders as the power to call a meeting "cannot be implied from the general authority given to vote their stock." [23]

Since the right to vote by proxy exists only by statutory authority and may be limited by the proxy instrument, the scope of permissible conduct of a proxyholder must depend on the clear meaning of the applicable statute and the proxy instrument. The primary purpose of a proxy is to delegate to another person the right to vote, and it is arguable that the proxyholder should be able to speak and perhaps to move on any proposition or subject on which he can cast a vote. But in the absence of a statutory or contractual extension of authority beyond the mere right to vote, the authority of the proxyholder to act ends at that point. However, it has been held that a proxyholder has the right, if requested by the presiding officer, to take the chair and call the meeting to order. [24]

§ 21.11   Presumption of Regularity

In the absence of evidence to the contrary, it will be presumed that proxies presented and voted at a meeting were regularly executed by the persons entitled to vote and are valid. [25] All acts performed by a proxyholder within the boundaries of his appointment are binding upon the shareholder he represents. The shareholder is estopped from thereafter questioning the regularity of the proceedings, [26] and is bound by and chargeable with the acts of the proxy-

[23] Josephson v. Cosmocolor Corp., 31 Del. Ch. 46, 66 A.2d 35, 36 (Ch. 1949).

[24] People v. Albany & S. R.R., 1 Lans. 308 (N.Y. Sup. Ct. 1869), *modified on other grounds*, 5 Lans. 25 (1871), *aff'd*, 57 N.Y. 161 (1874).

[25] Stephens Fuel Co. v. Bay Parkway Nat'l Bank, 109 F.2d 186 (2d Cir. 1940); Standard Power & Light Corp. v. Investment Associates, Inc., 29 Del. Ch. 593, 51 A.2d 572, 580 (1947) (forged proxy); Gentry-Futch Co. v. Gentry, 90 Fla. 595, 106 So. 473, 478 (1925).

[26] A vote by proxy is as binding on the shareholder as his own vote, unless it be shown that such vote was cast in furtherance of fraud or collusion. McClean v. Bradley, 299 F. 379 (6th Cir.), *cert. denied*, 266 U.S. 619 (1924).

"Any irregularity in the proceedings, or calls of the meeting, if there were any, which could have been waived by [the shareholder] if personally present could be waived by his proxy, and such waiver was binding upon him." Columbia Nat'l Bank v. Mathews, 85 F. 934, 942 (9th Cir. 1898).

Any irregularity in the proceedings or call of a meeting which could have been waived by the stockholder if personally present can be waived by his

holder.[27] However, a shareholder may sue to set aside a corporate transaction disclosed in the proxy statement even if his proxy voted in favor of ratifying such action, when the shareholder did not know that the ratifying resolution would be presented and the management proxy statement said that it did not know of any other matters to come before the meeting.[28]

§ 21.12　Dates and Inspection

Generally, later proxies revoke earlier proxies from the same record holders.[29] The court will confirm the findings of an election proxy committee in counting proxies where the committee acted honestly and in good faith.[30] However, where a proxy contest is won by a slight margin due to the shifting of votes by the acceptance of later dated proxies, a court of equity might consider the circumstances sufficient to order a new election.[31]

---

proxy, and such waiver is binding on him. If the shareholder wishes to repudiate action taken by his proxy, he must act with reasonable diligence. Synnott v. Cumberland Bldg. Loan Ass'n, 117 F. 379 (6th Cir. 1902).

"The stockholders may repudiate the acts of a proxyholder which were in excess of their authority, if timely made, and likewise, the stockholders may elect to ratify such acts." Abbey Properties Co., Inc. v. Presidential Ins. Co., 119 So. 2d 74, 78 (Fla. 1960).

[27] A stockholder is bound by the act of her proxy "even though she had no personal knowledge of it, because he was her agent and she is chargeable with his knowledge." Gray v. Aspironal Labs., 24 F.2d 97 (5th Cir. 1928).

[28] Gottlieb v. McKee, 34 Del. Ch. 537, 107 A.2d 240 (1954).

Where directors voting as stockholders could properly vote their own stock in favor of ratification and exoneration, they similarly could properly vote the stock of other stockholders who before they signed a proxy were fairly informed of the issues which were to be considered and voted upon. Smith v. Brown-Borhek Co., 414 Pa. 325, 200 A.2d 398 (1964).

[29] Execution and postmark dates were held sufficient evidence of subsequent execution. Standard Power & Light Corp. v. Investment Associates, Inc., 29 Del. Ch. 593, 51 A.2d 572 (1947).

Normally, envelopes are guides when two conflicting proxies bear the same date, or where proxies are undated. Levin v. Metro-Goldwyn-Mayer, Inc., 221 A.2d 499 (Del. Ch. 1966).

[30] Burke v. Wiswall, 193 Misc. 14, 85 N.Y.S.2d 187 (Sup. Ct. 1948).

[31] See In re Scharf, 28 Misc. 2d 869, 216 N.Y.S.2d 775, modified on other grounds sub nom. Scharf v. Irving Air Chute Co., 15 App. Div. 2d 563, 223 N.Y.S.2d 307 (2d Dep't 1961).

It is clear that any qualified person at the meeting may call for the inspection of proxies and may challenge any proxies he concludes are not valid.[32] And, of course, proxies claimed to have been wrongfully obtained may be challenged by the persons who gave the proxies.[33] Failure to challenge a proxy constitutes a waiver of all objections.[34]

TELLERS AND INSPECTORS OF ELECTION

§ 21.13 Appointment

Parliamentary law recognizes the practice of appointing tellers from each side of the question to count the votes of members in the affirmative and negative and to report the results to the presiding officer.[1]

It is the general practice in corporation law to appoint inspectors of election and judges of the voting at stockholder meetings and at the meetings of incorporated associations. However, the use of inspectors is not mandatory in the absence of a statutory, charter, or by-law requirement. Many states have enacted statutory provisions relating to the appointment, as well as the powers and duties of inspectors, thereby replacing or reflecting case law. The requirements of the particular state of incorporation should be studied and observed.[2]

---

[32] Molloy v. Bemis Bros. Bag Co., 174 F. Supp. 785, 794 (D.N.H. 1959), *aff'd in part, vacated in part*, 283 F.2d 32 (1st Cir. 1960).

[33] Dal-Tran Serv. Co. v. Fifth Ave. Coach Lines, Inc., 14 App. Div. 2d 349, 220 N.Y.S.2d 549, 555 (1961).

[34] Molloy v. Bemis Bros. Bag Co., 174 F. Supp. 785, 794 (D.N.H. 1959), *aff'd in part, vacated in part*, 283 F.2d 32 (1st Cir. 1960).

[1] The rules of the House of Representatives provide that the Speaker shall, if he doubts a voice vote, or a count is required by at least one-fifth of a quorum, to "name one or more from each side of the question to tell the Members in the affirmative and negative; which being reported, he shall rise and state the decision." Constitution, Jefferson's Manual and Rules of the House of Representatives, 93d Congress, 2d Session, § 630, House Doc. 416 (1975).

See Cushing, Law & Pr. Leg. Assem. §§ 1801–3.

[2] *See, e.g.*, NEW YORK BUS. CORP. LAW §§ 610, 611.

When the statute requires the appointment of "inspectors," the use of the plural has been construed to require that two or more inspectors be appointed

If there is no higher authority providing for the appointment or election of inspectors, the shareholders present or represented by proxy may do so at their discretion. This is a common-law right.[3] Where the powers and duties of inspectors are not stated or fixed at the meeting, and are not regulated by law, their standing is controlled "largely by accepted usage and common practice."[4] Unless otherwise provided by law, there is no requirement that a majority of all qualified inspectors must act.[5]

When the by-laws provide for the appointment of inspectors and judges by the chairman of the meeting, all appointments depend for their validity on the right of the chairman legally to preside.[6] If the office of inspector becomes vacant, or if an inspector is absent or fails to appear for duty, the shareholders present or their proxies

---

and that an election of directors be void when only one legally appointed inspector presided. *In re* Remington Typewriter Co., 203 App. Div. 65, 196 N.Y.S. 309, 310 (1st Dep't), *rev'd on other grounds*, 234 N.Y. 296, 137 N.E. 335 (1922); *see* Bache v. Central Leather Co., 78 N.J. Eq. 484, 81 A. 571 (1911) (powers and duties of inspectors).

[3] When there are no regulations governing the election of directors, the right of choosing the inspectors or judges of election is vested in the stockholders, and not in the directors. Directors in assuming that function against the will of the stockholders present, "mistook their duty and exercised a function not warranted by law." State v. Merchant, 37 Ohio 251, 254 (1881).

Where inspectors are appointed by the board of directors, a majority is required; two of nine directors are not sufficient. *Ex parte* Willcocks, 7 Cow. 402 (N.Y. 1827).

Where the corporate procedure fails to accomplish the purposes contemplated so that the office of inspector becomes vacant, it is competent for the stockholders themselves to exercise the power of election and provide for the appointment of inspectors for that purpose. These are "common law rights incident to any corporation." *In re* Wheeler, 2 Abb. Pr. N.S. 361, 364 (N.Y. 1866).

[4] Burke v. Wiswall, 193 Misc. 14, 85 N.Y.S.2d 187, 190 (Sup. Ct. 1948), *quoting* Young v. Jebbett, 213 App. Div. 774, 779, 211 N.Y.S. 61, 66 (1925).

[5] Plaintiff alleged irregularities in an election—18 inspectors were named, 14 actually watched the polls, 8 met to count the votes and declare the results. The same 8 heard an appeal, and 7 signed the return. The court upheld the procedure, holding that it was not the intention of the law that a majority of qualified inspectors must act. State v. Huggins, 16 S.C.L. 139 (1824).

[6] *See* Cavender v. Curtiss–Wright Corp., 30 Del. Ch. 314, 60 A.2d 102 (1948) (appointment of inspectors by person claiming to be temporary chairman later rescinded by lawful chairman).

may appoint temporary inspectors by a per-capita vote.[7] And where the inspectors refuse to serve or fail to perform their duties, they may be replaced in the manner of appointment provided in the by-laws.[8]

§ 21.14   Who May Act

Unless otherwise specified by higher authority, an inspector need not be a shareholder,[9] and a person is not disqualified as an inspector because he is an officer of the organization.[10] It is questionable whether a candidate for office may be an inspector at his own election.[11] Although the practice has been approved, a strong dissent

[7] New York law provided, for example, that if an inspector neglected to attend an election, the "meeting" could appoint an inspector in his place. There was no requirement that stockholders vote for inspectors at all or in any particular manner and therefore the presiding officer had the right to determine whether votes should be per capita or per share. "In case an inspector of election fail to appear at the election, the 'meeting' may appoint an inspector in his place. The non-appearance of an inspector may be very unexpected. The Legislature evidently intended to provide or permit the place of an absent inspector to be filled by an immediate appointment through a per capita vote of those present at the meeting, and entitled to participate therein. It is just as easy to determine who the stockholders are for a per capita vote as for a stock vote." *In re* Remington Typewriter Co., 234 N.Y. 296, 298, 137 N.E. 335, 336 (1922); *accord,* Prigerson v. White Cap Sea Foods, Inc., 100 N.Y.S.2d 881, 885 (Sup. Ct. 1950).

[8] Gow v. Consolidated Coppermines Corp., 19 Del. Ch. 172, 165 A. 136 (1933).

[9] It is recommended that professional inspectors be engaged whenever there is a serious proxy contest.

[10] Where the charter of a corporation prohibits directors from acting as inspectors of election, other officers of the company are not excluded. *In re* Election of Dirs. Chenango County Mut. Ins. Co., 19 Wend. 635 (N.Y. 1839).

The judging of a corporate election is a "purely ministerial function." State *ex rel.* Hawley v. Coogan, 98 So. 2d 757, 759, *petition denied,* 99 So. 2d 243 (1957), *cert. denied,* 101 So. 2d 817 (1958); *see* Umatilla Water Users' Ass'n v. Irvin, 56 Ore. 414, 108 P. 1016 (1910) (statute provided that president of corporation shall act as inspector of elections and certify who are elected directors).

[11] *See* Haslam v. Carlson, 46 R.I. 53, 124 A. 734 (1924) (appointment of a substitute teller to take the place of a teller who had been nominated for director is valid when done prior to the casting of ballots).

has been expressed.[12] The fact that inspectors were first designated as tellers is of no consequence if it was the intent that they were to act as inspectors and their duties were identical.[13]

Although the law may provide that inspectors shall be sworn before entering upon their duties, this requirement is directory only, and an election will not be void if the inspectors are not sworn.[14]

It is generally agreed that inspectors of election and judges of the voting are ministerial officers, generally without discretionary power.[15] Inspectors are "without power to determine any disputed

---

[12] "The judge of an election, who is at the same time a candidate, has a direct interest in the event, and cannot be viewed in any other light than as judging in his own cause. It is no answer that his decision may be examined by superior authority; so may those of any inferior tribunal." The majority approved the practice on the grounds that the duties of an inspector are not judicial in character but rather ministerial. Commonwealth v. Woelper, 3 S. & R. 29, 43 (Pa. 1817) (dissenting opinion).

An early common-law case held that the mayor could be a candidate for town councillor if he refrained from acting as a returning officer and appointed another in his place. Queen v. White, L.R. 2 Q.B. 557 (1867).

[13] Data-Guide, Inc. v. Marcus, 16 Misc. 2d 541, 181 N.Y.S.2d 945 (Sup. Ct. 1958).

[14] An election of directors will not be set aside merely because the inspectors are not sworn. In re Election of Dirs. Chenango County Mut. Ins. Co., 19 Wend. 635 (N.Y. 1839).

An election of directors will not be invalidated because the oath of inspectors was not in writing. In re Zenitherm Co. 95 N.J.L. 297, 113 A. 327 (1921).

A statute requiring the oath of inspectors to be filed with the county clerk is directory only, and the failure to so file does not invalidate the election. Union Nat'l Bank v. Scott, 53 App. Div. 65, 66 N.Y.S. 145 (1900).

An election of directors will not be set aside on a summary application to the court on the ground that the inspectors were not sworn. They are inspectors de facto. In re Election of Dirs. Mohawk & Hudson R.R., 19 Wend. 135 (N.Y. 1838).

Similarly, an election of directors is not invalid and may not be set aside as irregular because the oath actually administered to them was not subscribed by them. In re Wheeler, 2 Abb. Pr. N.S. 361 (N.Y. 1866).

An election may be set aside for irregularities in appointing inspectors and in taking the vote. Regina v. Vestrymen and Churchwardens of St. Pancras, (1839) 11 Adolph. & E. 15.

[15] Standard Power & Light Corp. v. Investment Associates, Inc., 29 Del. Ch. 593, 51 A.2d 572 (1947); aff'g, 29 Del. Ch. 225, 48 A.2d 501 (1946); Gow v. Consolidated Coppermines Corp., 19 Del. Ch. 172, 165 A. 136 (1933); Data-Guide, Inc. v. Marcus, 16 Misc. 2d 541, 181 N.Y.S.2d 945 (1958); Prigerson

question." [16] This has been described as an untenable position because the refusal to act may in fact be determinative.[17]

§ 21.15   Authority

Although inspectors of election and judges of the voting are
ministerial officers, they have some latitude and may exercise discretion within the scope of their ministry in the performance of their
duties. A leading case states simply: "The duties of the inspectors
are an admixture of *ministerial* and *judicial*." [18] Recognition of such

---

v. White Cap Sea Foods, Inc., 100 N.Y.S.2d 881, 885 (Sup. Ct. 1950); *In re*
Lake Placid Co., 274 App. Div. 205, 81 N.Y.S.2d 36, 39 (1948), *appeal
denied,* 298 N.Y. 932 (1949); *In re* Cecil, 36 How. Pr. (N.Y.) 477 (1869).

It has been suggested that a statutory inspector is a public officer and an
appeal from his rulings can only be taken to the courts. Umatilla Water Users'
Ass'n v. Irvin, 56 Ore. 414, 108 P. 1016, 1019 (1910).

It has been held that a town clerk, having only ministerial duties involving
the exercise of no judicial discretion, must record the minutes of the annual
meeting "as declared by the moderator." Hill v. Goodwin, 56 N.H. 441, 445,
452 (1876).

[16] Prigerson v. White Cap Sea Foods, Inc., 100 N.Y.S.2d 881, 885 (Sup. Ct.
1950).

[17] Where the inspector of election refused to count certain challenged votes
and to certify the election, the court held that the inspector "had no right to
take the position that he would refuse to count the votes challenged on the
ground that he had no power or authority to determine the question of the
challenge and dispute. In so doing he was in fact deciding the matter against
the majority stockholder. An inspector of elections is a ministerial officer; he
has no power to determine any disputed question. . . . When a vote is challenged the inspectors shall require the production of corporate books as evidence of the right to vote. If it appears therefore that he has the right, the
vote must be counted and the election certified." Data-Guide, Inc. v. Marcus,
16 Misc. 2d 541, 181 N.Y.S.2d 945, 946 (1958).

[18] *In re* Election of Dirs. Mohawk & Hudson R.R., 19 Wend. 135, 145 (N.Y.
1838).

Inspectors may correct mistakes when it can be done without prejudicing
the right of others. "While the judges of election are ministerial officers, nevertheless within the scope of their ministry some discretion resides." Young v.
Jebbett, 213 App. Div. 774, 779, 211 N.Y.S. 61 1925).

"The inspectors do no more than receive and count the votes. But it is said
that the inspectors are judges, and may decide the election as they please by
the admission or rejection of votes. Their office is ministerial rather than judi-

discretionary authority on the part of the inspector best serves the
interest of stockholders in the prompt resolution of proxy contests.
The functions of the inspectors in determining the result of an election ought not to be interrupted while opposing factions litigate. If
he errs, the losing party may resort to the courts.[19] Should an ap-

---

cial. The charter declares who may vote, and the inspectors are bound by it.
To be sure they must in some cases exercise their judgment, when a question
arises on the construction of the charter. But so must every ministerial officer,
when a question arises on the extent of his powers. If an inspector refuses a
vote, the injured person is not without remedy. The decision of the inspector
may be examined before some competent tribunal." Commonwealth v. Woelper, 3 S. & R. 29, 33 (Pa. 1817).

"Perhaps the truth lies between the two extremes; an inspector being a
judicial officer to the extent that his decision is valid until set aside by some
competent tribunal." Umatilla Water Users' Ass'n v. Irvin, 56 Ore. 414, 108
P. 1016, 1020 (1910).

Practical necessity requires that inspectors be authorized to employ reasonable means to ascertain the identity and number of shareholders present. "In
the case of most corporations having numerous shareholders, it is unlikely that
inspectors could be found who would be able to recognize at sight all, or even
a large part, of the shareholders. Practical necessity requires that inspectors be
authorized to employ reasonable means to ascertain the identity and number of
stockholders present. The obtaining of such information in writing from persons known to the inspectors and believed by them to be worthy of credence is
manifestly a reasonable means for this purpose and is not cause to disregard
the presumptive correctness of their finding." Atterbury v. Consolidated Coppermines Corp., 26 Del. Ch. 1, 20 A.2d 743, 749 (1941).

"The action of the inspectors went beyond the scope of their lawful authority. The master properly held that the office of inspector is a ministerial and
not a judicial one." Gow v. Consolidated Coppermines Corp., 19 Del. Ch. 172,
165 A. 136, 147 (1933).

[19] "Plaintiffs' contention that the function of an election inspector is purely
ministerial rather than judicial has support in opinions from several jurisdictions, but most of the statements to this effect must be taken in context to
mean that the decision of the inspector is not binding on the court in subsequent
litigation to review the election. Other courts have recognized that election
inspectors have a measure of discretion and have refused to disturb their findings even after the election if made fairly, honestly and in good faith. . . . .
The function of the inspector is to determine the result of the election accurately and declare the result promptly so that the affairs of the corporation may
go forward, and in performing that function he must make some sort of decision on whatever problems may arise, including validity of proxies tendered to
him." Salgo v. Matthews, 497 S.W.2d 620, 627–28 (Tex. 1973).

In an earlier election the inspectors issued their report tabulating and de-

peal from the inspectors' report be made, it falls within the jurisdiction of the courts.[20] "Contested elections and particularly contested incidents relating to the voting at elections must, for the most part, be litigated summarily. In such proceedings courts are interested in the merits rather than in the technique."[21]

---

claring the vote after accepting a ballot received 29 minutes later than the hour for closing as specified in the notice of meeting. The chairman of the meeting ruled that the late ballot could not be counted and directed the inspectors to issue a "correct" report. On mandamus, the court held that, when results are properly certified by the inspectors to the chairman, the latter has no right to reject or alter the returns. State ex rel. Dunbar v. Hohmann, 248 S.W.2d 49, 50 (Mo. 1952).

The discretion of inspectors of elections extends to granting all shareholders a reasonable opportunity to vote, and to this end they may keep the polls open and continue to take votes after the stated closing hour. "The trustees acted properly in taking the requisite time, notwithstanding they were called on to close the poll at one o'clock. I much doubt whether the time could in virtue of a by law be tied up to a certain hour of the day; but in this case it was not attempted. I have no doubt, that in case of actual necessity, the business might have been extended even to the next day. Every principle of construction is in favor of full time, otherwise business may be badly done by being hurried, or embarrassed or defeated by the raising of dilatory objections and protracted examination and discussion. In re Election of Dirs. Mohawk & Hudson R.R., 19 Wend. 135, 147 (N.Y. 1838).

[20] In a Delaware case, the court overruled a chairman who had decided that no nominees in a corporate election had received a majority of the votes, and reinstated the inspector's decision that certain opposition nominees had been elected. Standard Power & Light Corp. v. Investment Associates, Inc., 29 Del. Ch. 593, 51 A.2d 572 (1949).

A statutory inspector (the president) is in effect a "public officer" and an appeal from his ruling could only be taken to the courts. Umatilla Water Users' Ass'n v. Irvin, 56 Ore. 414, 108 P. 1016 (1910).

However, an early Massachusetts case suggests that the presiding officer has some control over the inspectors. In the election of a tax collector by the city council, the tellers ruled that an illegal ballot had prevented any candidate from receiving the necessary majority, and the mayor ordered a new election on a finding that no one had received a majority. The court held that the decision of the mayor was a reasonable one and that "it was for the tellers in the first instance, and then for the mayor, to make the decision." Keough v. Board of Aldermen, 156 Mass. 403, 31 N.E. 387, 388 (1892); see American Aberdeen-Angus Breeders' Ass'n v. Fullerton, 325 Ill. 323, 156 N.E. 314 (1927) (chairman rejected report of tellers and refused to entertain appeal from his ruling).

[21] Young v. Jebbett, 213 App. Div. 774, 778, 211 N.Y.S. 61 (3d Dep't 1925).

Where, pursuant to a state statute, the president is acting as an inspector of election for directors at a shareholders' meeting and a violent interference with the discharge of his duties then ensues, the reasonable expectation that further violence will occur justifies his decision not to further preside or remain in attendance, and to vacate his office as inspector. In such event, the dissidents could not "take advantage of their own lawless conduct to reorganize the meeting and recount the votes." [22]

§ 21.16   Duties

The principal duties of inspectors in an election of directors is to distribute the ballots, collect them, count the vote, and report the results of the vote.[23] They do not determine whether a quorum is present.[24] They must exclude from their consideration all extraneous matters, such as the intent of the voter.[25]

Inspectors can amend their original report to correct a mistake, as by including shareholders who had not but should have been counted, but they cannot reopen a meeting to permit more people to attend and to vote. Inspectors may also keep the polls open after

[22] Umatilla Water Users' Ass'n v. Irvin, 56 Ore. 414, 108 P. 1016, 1021 (1910).

[23] Tellers who fail to report to a stockholders' meeting that they had rejected certain ballots and give the grounds for rejection "failed in their duty" under the by-laws which provided they should receive and count the ballots cast and report the results. However, if this irregularity does not affect the results of the election, it will not be declared void. Haslam v. Carlson, 46 R.I. 53, 124 A. 734 (1924).

[24] "Inspectors have nothing to do with counting for a quorum, or dealing with anything in their official capacity, other than the ballots deposited in the box, which it is their duty to count and tally, and therefrom to certify their returns." In re Gulla, 13 Del. Ch. 23, 115 A. 317, 319 (1921).

An election is incomplete if the meeting is adjourned before the inspectors make their formal report. In re Newcomb, 42 N.Y. St. Rep. 442, 18 N.Y.S. 16 (Sup. Ct. 1891).

[25] "The defendant cannot be deprived of her right to vote the number of shares of stock which she claims a right to vote upon the allegation or surmise that she proposes to exercise her legal right for purposes which others may think would be detrimental to the interests of the corporation. The defendant's right to vote the number of shares of stock which she claims she is entitled to vote is for determination of the inspectors of election at the stockholders' meeting." Elevator Supplies Co. v. Wylde, 106 N.J. Eq. 163, 165, 150 A. 347 (1930).

the time for closing if the extra time is needed to give those ready to vote an opportunity to do so.[26] Inspectors may accept and count proxies when presented late but before the final count has been concluded and reported.[27] They cannot pass upon the genuineness

[26] "Authorities are cited for the proposition that where the inspectors have closed the polls, counted the votes and announced the result of a vote it is then too late to open the polls and receive the votes of any who have not voted. However this may be, the inspectors' report of the existence or non-existence of a quorum is not a matter of voting or balloting. The inspectors in amending their report did not reopen or purport to reopen a meeting to permit more people to attend, but merely attempted to remedy what they deemed to be mistakes which they had made in counting the persons who already had been there. No valid reason appears why they should not be permitted to do this. Moreover, the essential question is whether there was a quorum at the meeting, and in a review proceeding of this character, this court may inquire into the actual facts." Atterbury v. Consolidated Coppermines Corp., 26 Del. Ch. 1, 20 A.2d 743, 745 (1941).

"In the absence of express regulations by statute or by-law, the conduct of meetings, including the election of officers, is controlled largely by accepted usage and common practice. The fundamental rule is that all who are entitled to take part shall be treated with fairness and good faith. That rule, we think, permits the correction of a mere mistake, when it can be made without prejudice to the rights of others, and before the final vote is announced. While the judges of election are ministerial officers, nevertheless within the scope of their ministry some discretion resides. So in [citation] it was held not improper for inspectors to keep the election open as long, within a reasonable discretion, as was necessary to receive the vote of those present." Young v. Jebbett, 213 App. Div. 774, 211 N.Y.S. 61, 66 (1925).

[27] "Had the disputed proxies in question been offered for filing while the polls were open, it would have been the duty of the judges of election to receive them, and to count the vote cast under their authority. The fact that the revenue stamps were not canceled did not invalidate them. [citation] It is a fair inference from the facts before us that a majority of the judges of election omitted to receive and file the proxies when presented because they thought they had no right to do so under the law, and, since there was therefore no basis for the vote cast on those shares, that they omitted to recognize that vote. If it was the duty of the judges to file the disputed proxies when they were presented, and to treat them as they would have done had they been filed when the polls were still open, then we think the petitioner was not premature in seeking to enforce the performance of that duty. The disputed proxies here were formally offered 24 hours after the polls were closed. The evidence before us shows that the delay was due solely to an oversight. The proxies were actually at the meeting, and in the custody of one of the judges of election. They had continued in that custody until they were offered. Although the polls had closed, the meeting was still in existence, awaiting the report of the

or validity of proxies except as to irregularities appearing on the face,[28] and they are controlled exclusively by the record of the stock ledgers in determining who may vote.[29] The neglect to keep a stock book permits common-law evidence of who are stockholders.[30]

---

judges. On the record before us, there is no indication that the proxies were upon their face irregular; there is no suggestion of fraud. We think the judges of election should have received and filed the proxies and counted the vote cast thereunder." Young v. Jebbett, 213 App. Div. 774, 779, 211 N.Y.S. 61, 65, 66 (1925).

[28] Gow v. Consolidated Coppermines Corp., 19 Del. Ch. 172, 165 A. 136 (1933).

"The inspectors entirely mistook their powers and duties. They are purely ministerial officers.

"When a proxy apparently executed by the stockholder, regular in form was presented to them, they had no right to refuse to receive the vote, or assume to themselves the power of a judicial tribunal to try its genuineness. If it were apparently the act of the stockholder, and regular upon its face, that ended the matter so far as the inspectors were concerned. If for any reason, not apparent upon its face, it was invalid, redress must be sought from the courts after the election, if its being used worked any detriment." In re Cecil, 36 How. Pr. (N.Y.) 477, 478 (1869); see In re Commonwealth v. Woelper, 3 S. & R. 29 (Pa. 1817) (inspectors were allowed to reject a ballot if it was attached to another ballot or if anything other than a name was written on it).

[29] "So far as the corporation is concerned, the books control." Raible v. Puerto Rico Indus. Dev. Co., 392 F.2d 424 (1st Cir. 1968) (vote on a corporate merger).

"The general and better rule is that the person in whose name stock stands on the books is entitled to vote it; that the books of the company are conclusive upon the inspectors as to who are entitled to vote; and that neither inspectors nor stockholders can successfully dispute the right of any one to vote who appears by the company's books to be the holder of stock legally issued. Upon any other rule it would never be known who were entitled to vote until the courts had settled the dispute." Morrill v. Little Falls Mfg. Co., 53 Minn. 371, 55 N.W. 547, 550 (1893).

Holders of shares of stock in a corporation, who appear to be such on the stockbooks at the date of a meeting of stockholders, are prima facie entitled to vote the stock. Bernheim v. Louisville Property Co., 221 Fed. 273 (W.D. Ky. 1914) (record date not fixed).

Stock record books are conclusive upon the inspectors of election as to the right to vote. But that record is not binding upon the court in a legal proceeding relating to the qualification of directors. In re Ringler & Co., 204 N.Y. 30, 97 N.E. 593 (1912).

[30] Union Nat'l Bank v. Scott, 53 App. Div. 65, 60 N.Y.S. 145 (3d Dep't 1900).

Holders of record cannot be disfranchised by the presiding officer or by the inspectors, as they do not have the power to pass upon the qualifications of voters. When holders of record were denied the right to vote, the court said: "The action of the inspectors was beyond their power. Indeed, the president had no right to determine even the qualifications of stockholders as voters at the election." The court concluded: "The president usurped powers; the inspectors exceeded their powers." [31]

Shares registered in the name of a broker or in a "street name" may be voted by the record holder. The fact that the broker is subject to voting limitations by the New York Stock Exchange or other regulatory body is not binding on the inspectors of election unless the proxy is so restricted.[32]

It has been held that, if the right of a shareholder to vote is not challenged at the threshold, "the only remaining duty of those conducting the election is to count the ballots and return the number of votes received by the nominees. After that they have no duty to perform." They cannot decide that some of the ballots cast for the successful candidate were illegal, and thus favor the minority.[33]

[31] *In re* Robert Clark, Inc., 186 App. Div. 216, 174 N.Y.S. 314, 316 (2d Dep't 1919).

[32] *See* New York Stock Exchange Company Manual at A-143 stating when a member organization (stock broker) may, and may not, vote proxies without first receiving its customer's instructions.

"An equitable owner of shares who permits them to stand in his broker's name impliedly authorizes the broker to vote them; any other rule would lead to hopeless confusion. . . . The fact that brokers may be obliged, under the rules of the New York Stock Exchange or under any other requirement of law or regulation, to obtain the consent of their customers before voting the stock does not alter the rule in this respect; the presumption being that in the absence of proof to the contrary, of which there was none in this case, consent had been obtained." *In re* Pressed Steel Can Co., 16 F. Supp. 329, 336 (W.D. Pa. 1936).

"Hence, the real owners must be taken to know that one of the consequences of permitting their stock to be held in the name of a nominee is that the latter will normally have the power to vote the shares without obtaining the consent of the owners, and that the corporation will recognize the registered owner as the true owner, at least under circumstances such as here. Although the partners did not attempt to vote the shares, they were present and in a position to demand that their right to do so be recognized. It follows that the shares registered in the names of the partnerships should be counted." Atterbury v. Consolidated Coppermines Corp., 26 Del. Ch. 1, 20 A.2d 743, 749 (1941).

[33] Kauffman v. Meyberg, 59 Cal. App. 2d 730, 140 P.2d 210, 216 (1943).

The findings and determinations of inspectors are entitled to credence and have a "presumptive correctness." [34] In the exercise of their powers and duties inspectors and judges are controlled "largely by accepted usage and common practice," and "when judged and not found wanting in the light of those essential and controlling elements of fairness, honesty and good faith, no sound reason presents itself for disturbing their results." [35]

The right of contesting parties at a corporate election to demand the appointment of proxy examiners and tellers selected by them, for the purpose of participating in and observing the counting of proxies, is enforceable through the equity jurisdiction of the court. [36]

[34] Atterbury v. Consolidated Coppermines Corp., 26 Del. Ch. 1, 20 A.2d 743, 748 (1941).

[35] Burke v. Wiswall, 193 Misc. 14, 85 N.Y.S.2d 187, 190–91 (Sup. Ct. 1948), *quoting* Young v. Jebbett, 213 App. Div. 774, 211 N.Y.S. 61, 66 (4th Dep't 1925).

[36] *See* Ellsworth v. Carr-Consolidated Biscuit Co., 90 F. Supp. 586 (M.D. Pa. 1950) (court refused to take jurisdiction of foreign corporation).

Appendix

Company Meetings—
Selected Procedures

NEED FOR ORDERLY PROCEDURES

A shareholders' meeting is a form of deliberative assembly. The broader aspects of the law of shareholders' meetings are now being developed through the evolutionary processes by which custom and practice become established and acquire legal significance. During the past thirty years, and especially within the last decade, there has been a rapid and steady increase in shareholder participation in the meetings of many publicly held companies. This movement has already become a significant influence on the development of the law and it will continue to have a bearing on future developments as they unfold on the floor and on the dais of the meeting hall.

Custom, in the sense of established usage having the force of law, is in the process of development. Decorum, in the sense of usage required by the essentials of civility and common courtesy, without which shareholders' meetings cannot properly serve their intended purpose, is now being defined. A workable arrangement of procedures and customs must be developed so that all lawful meetings will be able adequately to serve their intended and proper purposes. The ultimate purpose of a deliberative meeting remains the same— to ascertain the sense of the members on each matter properly brought before the meeting for consideration and action through the process of orderly deliberation.

The modern concepts of "corporate democracy" and "corporate suffrage" seek the establishment and acceptance of orderly proce- dures and usages at shareholders' meetings which will give all share- holders, both large and small, whether silent or vocal, timid or aggressive, a reasonable opportunity to participate actively or to be passive, as they individually may prefer, in the deliberations of the meeting. For each privilege of one shareholder to take the floor and speak, there is the concomitant duty to allow all others an opportunity to do likewise within reasonable limits and without in- terruption. And, for every privilege of a shareholder to occupy the floor in debate, there is a predominant right of all shareholders peacefully to sit and listen without discord or disruption.

RULES OF ORDER FOR SHAREHOLDERS' MEETINGS

Every corporation has an inherent and continuous power to adopt Rules of Order governing the conduct of shareholders' meetings. Every assembly for which Rules of Order have not been imposed by the corporation has the power to formulate and adopt its own Rules of Order governing the conduct of its meetings.

Rules of Order are necessary effectively to enable the chairman to conduct the meeting in an orderly and convenient fashion and to ascertain the sense and will of the meeting upon all matters prop- erly coming before it for consideration and action.

So long as the Rules do not violate any constitutional provisions or fundamental rights, and there is a reasonable relation between the methods of proceeding established by the Rules and the orderly results sought to be attained, the Rules will be absolute and beyond the challenge of all concerned, even if it might be said that some other rule would be better, more accurate, or even more just.

In the absence of Rules of Order imposed upon or established by an assembly for the conduct of its business, meetings of the assem- bly may be conducted in accordance with the precedents of previous meetings or, in the absence of precedents, according to established usages and customs. In the absence of established usages and customs, in whole or in any particularity, the meeting should be conducted in accordance with the common law applicable to the proceedings of similar deliberative bodies, generally known as parliamentary law.

Following are some of the generally accepted rules of order and standards of decorum which are applicable to shareholders' meetings and other deliberative assemblies convened for business purposes, as distinguished from the meetings of deliberative assemblies which have legislative, religious, fraternal, or social objectives.

1. Speakers must rise to gain recognition from the chairman. When recognized, the speaker should give his name and state whether he is a shareholder in person, a proxy, a fiduciary, or a voter in some other capacity.
2. Speakers must not address the chairman until recognized, except to obtain the floor.
3. Speakers must not rise until after the floor has been yielded by the previous speaker. It is out of order to be standing when another has the floor.
4. All speakers must address their remarks to the chairman. Speakers may not address other shareholders or members of management for any reason whatsoever. However, with the consent of the chairman, speakers may address questions or comments on accounting and auditing matters directly to a representative of the corporation's certified public accountants if a representative is present at the meeting.
5. Where two or more speakers rise at about the same time to claim the floor, all other things being equal, the speaker who is first observed by the chairman after the floor has been yielded will be recognized and will become entitled to the floor.
6. Where it is evident that several speakers wish to be heard and the chairman decides that the interests of the assembly require the floor to be assigned to a claimant who was not the first to rise and be observed, the chairman may recognize speakers according to any method or pattern which in his opinion will permit all opposing views to be adequately expressed.
7. The chairman need not recognize any speaker more than once while the same question or motion is before the meeting or during any discussion period, particularly so long as any member who has not spoken desires the floor. When all who desire to speak have spoken, a member may speak a second time by leave of the chairman.

8. By leave of the chairman a member who has already spoken on a motion may speak again thereon in order to clear up any misunderstanding as to some material part of his former remarks, but he is not entitled to interrupt another speaker for that purpose or to introduce new matter or arguments.

9. The mover of a debatable motion has the right of reply, but he may not introduce new matter.

10. After a speaker has become entitled to the floor he cannot be interrupted by another member even to receive an explanation. The speaker does not lose his right to the floor by interruptions, and the interrupting member does not obtain the floor thereby.

11. No person may address the meeting upon any question after it has been finally put to a vote.

12. All resolutions presented from the floor for consideration and action should be in writing, signed by the mover, and delivered to the chairman or the secretary before the opening of the meeting.

13. Every resolution must be read to the meeting before it is put to a vote.

14. All persons present who are entitled to vote shall have a reasonable opportunity of voting. All voting shall be on a share basis unless the organic law of the corporation provides otherwise.

15. Where a resolution has been presented and the chairman is of the opinion that such resolution does not present a single question or a series of related questions on which the assembly may clearly vote, he may suggest to the mover that the resolution be divided, recast, or withdrawn.

16. When a motion has been duly made and seconded and the chairman is uncertain whether the assembly understands the intent and substance of the motion, the chairman may request the moving member to explain his motion for the enlightenment of the assembly, or the chairman may, if he chooses, undertake such explanation or, in the alternative, request that the motion be withdrawn.

17. Before any subject is open for discussion or debate, it is necessary: first, that a motion be made; second, that the motion be seconded (with certain exceptions); and third, that the question be stated by the chairman.

18. When a motion has been duly made and seconded it is the duty of the chairman, unless he rules the motion out of order, immediately to state the question. After the question has been stated by the chairman, the motion is before the assembly for consideration and action.

19. There should be a discussion period immediately after every debatable motion and prior to the taking of a vote on such motion. All speakers must limit their remarks to the merits of the motion.

20. There should be a discussion period immediately after the nomination of directors and prior to the taking of a vote. All speakers must limit their remarks to the qualifications of the persons nominated.

21. Except during periods of general discussion, each speaker must limit his remarks to the merits of the immediately pending question. Remarks should be brief and concise. The chairman should see that the discussion does not drift from the merits of the matter before the meeting.

22. All duly constituted company meetings have the implied power to act for the protection of the collective interests of those present.

23. The chairman derives his authority from the consensus of those present at the meeting over which he presides. The chairman has the power and duty inherent in his position to issue such rulings during the meeting as may reasonably be intended to facilitate the conduct of its business in an orderly fashion and enable the chairman to ascertain the sense of the meeting on all matters coming before it for consideration and action. He must decide all emergent questions which require a decision at the time.

24. Where it is evident that discussion must be curtailed to enable a meeting to achieve its purposes within a reasonable time, the chairman has the power to apportion time for discussion so that as many speakers may be heard as the circumstances permit. The chairman may also declare discussion closed when it is evident that all opposing views on the issue have been adequately expressed and any further discussion would be repetitious, redundant, or dilatory. The chairman's decision to close or limit debate or discussion (but not to apportion time) may be subject to the concurrence of a simple majority stock vote of the stockholders present and voting, upon a proper demand.

25. A person wishing to speak on a point of order must do so immediately, and so state in his opening words. The person then addressing the chair must resume his seat, as also must the person making the point of order as soon as he has concluded his appeal to the chair.

26. It is essential that a meeting be conducted in an orderly manner. The maintenance of order is one of the primary duties of the chairman. He should at once suppress all offensive acts or remarks. He is entitled to call a person to order. If a person persists

in being obstreperous or disorderly or in disturbing or interfering with the orderly conduct of the meeting, the chairman may
call upon him to take his seat or to withdraw from the meeting.
The chairman may also direct the removal of any person who refuses to take his seat or to withdraw when so directed by the
chairman, and for this purpose the chairman may direct the use
of such force as may be necessary to eject such person and to
keep him excluded. The chairman has the authority to detail
members to remove the disturber, or to call upon officials designated for that purpose. The person using force to eject a person
who has disturbed a meeting may not use harsher measures than
are necessary to remove such person, taking into consideration
the nature and degree of resistance by the disturber which must
be overcome.

Note: In company meetings the most prevalent acts of disturbance appear to be: interruption of the chairman when presiding;
refusal to sit down and be quiet when so ordered by the chairman;
refusal to surrender the microphone when ordered to do so; interruption of the person rightfully having the floor; quarreling with
another person on the floor of the meeting; use of a distractive instrument such as a bullhorn; attempting to talk too long or too often;
and refusal in various ways to recognize the equal rights of others
to participate in the discussions and deliberations of the meeting.

SIMPLE FORM OF MINUTES FOR
ANNUAL SHAREHOLDERS' MEETING

CHAIRMAN: Will the meeting please come to order. My name is [name];
I am cahirman of [name of company]. In the name of the board of
directors, I welcome all of you to this our [number] annual meeting
of stockholders.

CHAIRMAN: May we please have the secretary's report.

SECRETARY: The notice of the meeting was duly and properly mailed and
here is the affidavit to that effect. According to the tabulation made
before the meeting, there is a total of at least [number] shares represented at this meeting by proxy, equivalent to about [number] per cent
of the shares entitled to be voted at the meeting. This is more than
needed for a quorum, so we can proceed with the meeting. The report
to stockholders will show the final number of shares represented at
this meeting in person and by proxy.

CHAIRMAN: I declare a quorum present and that this is a duly constituted meeting. I wish to thank the stockholders for this splendid representation.

I will first introduce the representatives of our transfer agent and our independent public accountants:

[Names of individuals and the companies they represent]

I will now introduce the persons on the dais with me and ask them to stand when I introduce them:

[Introductions]

The agenda of the meeting is fairly simple. We have established that the meeting has been duly called and that a quorum is present for the conduct of business. As stated in the Notice of Meeting and further described in the Proxy Statement, there are three items of business on the agenda. I will present those items now and they will be discussed and voted upon later one at a time. The items are:

First, the election of [number] directors.

Second, ratification of the selection of independent public accountants.

Third, the stockholder proposal on [subject] if presented.

There will be four discussion periods during the course of the meeting, one for each of the three items I have mentioned, and the fourth will serve for a general discussion of further matters appropriate to Company affairs.

Ballots will be distributed to stockholders who wish to vote in person on any item. Signed ballots will be gathered for delivery to the inspectors.

Now, let me explain the arrangements. There are four microphones in this room for the convenience of stockholders who wish to take the floor. Two are located in the center aisle and two are in the lateral aisles. There is an usher at each microphone who will assist you with its use under the coordination of the chairman, and generally assist stockholders in gaining recognition. In the interest of conducting an orderly meeting and giving all stockholders present an opportunity to ask questions and to make comments if they wish to do so, I ask that a few simple Rules of Order be observed during this meeting as they have been at past annual meetings.

If you wish to address the meeting, please go to the microphone nearest you and give the usher your name and tell him the city from which you come. The usher will, at the earliest appropriate time, signal the chairman to gain recognition for you. When recognition is extended, you will then be introduced to the meeting and the microphone will be made available for your use. Please confine your questions and your comments to the single subject of the agenda then being considered.

Questions and comments on other subjects and on general matters should wait their time in the order of business which has been outlined. Every stockholder will have a full opportunity at some time during the meeting to ask such questions and make such comments as he may wish. In fairness to the stockholders who may wish to address the meeting, it is requested that no stockholder take the floor more than once on the same subject until all other stockholders who wish to speak on that subject have had an opportunity to do so.

I urge that all stockholders try to make their comments as brief as possible.

Each speaker who observes these few basic rules should be permitted to conclude his remarks in his own fashion, without interruption. Those who may differ from the speaker will themselves be given an opportunity to speak in their turn and, I hope, without interruption.

The Secretary will keep the record. A summary report of the proceedings at this meeting will be mailed to all stockholders as usual.

SECRETARY: The inspectors have the certified list of common stockholders of record at the close of business on [record date], showing the names of the stockholders in alphabetical order, and the post office address and the number of shares of common stock held by each. This list is open for inspection and will be filed with the records of the Company at the conclusion of the meeting.

CHAIRMAN: The inspectors have signed the required oath and have presented it to the secretary.

We will now proceed with the election of [number] directors. Mr. Secretary, will you please read the names of the nominees set forth in the Proxy Statement.

SECRETARY: The persons nominated are:

[Names of nominees]

CHAIRMAN: Before asking for a second of the nominations, the meeting is open for discussion on matters relating to the election of directors. Please limit your questions to this area. Questions on other subjects will be answered during the general discussion period.

[Discussion period]

That completes the discussion. Is there a second?

STOCKHOLDER: I second the nominations and move that they be closed.

CHAIRMAN: All those in favor of the motion that the nominations be closed will please say "aye," opposed "no." The motion is carried. Mr. Secretary, will you please furnish a ballot to those who wish to vote in person and collect them after they have been filled out. Stockholders who have already sent in their proxies need not vote again in person.

SECRETARY: Will those desiring to vote please raise their hands. Please distribute the ballots. After you have marked your ballot, please hold it up so it can be collected.

CHAIRMAN: It is important that we pause a moment to check whether all stockholders desiring to vote have turned in their ballots.

[Management Proxy Committee signs its ballot]

We now seem to have all the ballots so we will proceed with the meeting.

CHAIRMAN: We are now ready to discuss and vote on ratifying the selection of [name of firm] as independent public accountants. Mr. Secretary, will you please read the resolution to be voted upon.

SECRETARY: The resolution reads as follows:

[Reads resolution from ballot]

CHAIRMAN: Before asking for a second of the proposal, are there any questions or discussion of this proposal? If so, please limit your comments or questions to the proposal.

[Discussion of proposal]

That completes the discussion. Is there a second?

STOCKHOLDER: I second the motion.

CHAIRMAN: Mr. Secretary, will you please distribute the ballots so that those present can vote on the proposal.

SECRETARY: Will those desiring to vote in person please raise their hands. Please distribute the ballots. After you have marked your ballot, please hold it up so that it can be collected.

[Management Proxy Committee signs its ballot]

CHAIRMAN: We are now ready to discuss and vote on a proposal relating to [subject] made by [name], a stockholder. Would the stockholder care to introduce his [or her] resolution?

[Stockholder reads resolution from ballot or Proxy Statement]

Before asking for a second, are there any questions or discussion of the resolution? If so, please limit your comments or questions to the resolution.

[Discussion of resolution]

That completes the discussion. Is there a second?

STOCKHOLDER: I second the motion.

CHAIRMAN: Mr. Secretary, will you please distribute the ballots so that those present can vote on the proposal.

SECRETARY: Will those desiring to vote please raise their hands. Please distribute the ballots. After you have marked your ballot, please hold it up so that it can be collected.

[Management Proxy Committee signs ballot; pause to
check whether all ballots have been received]

CHAIRMAN: While the votes are being tallied, the meeting will proceed to the discussion of other matters. The reading of the minutes of the previous annual meeting held on [date] is now in order.

STOCKHOLDER: I move that the reading of the minutes be waived.

CHAIRMAN: Do I hear a second to that motion?

STOCKHOLDER: I second the motion.

CHAIRMAN: Before asking for a vote on that motion, let me state that the minutes are here on the table and can be read by any interested stockholder. Now on the motion. Will those in favor say "aye," opposed "no." The motion is carried.

SECRETARY: I would like to submit a copy of the Annual Report for [year].

CHAIRMAN: At this point, I wish to talk for a few minutes about our Company and add some comments on an important piece of legislation before Congress. My comments may answer as well as promote questions in the general discussion period which will follow.

[Chairman gives his report]

The meeting is now open for general discussion.

[General discussion]

The inspectors have completed the count of the vote and are ready to report the results for the election of directors, the selection of auditors, and the resolution concerning [subject].

INSPECTOR: A total of [number] votes were cast, and the following persons were elected directors of the Company:

[Name those elected]

CHAIRMAN: The foregoing persons are declared the duly elected directors of the Company, to hold office until the next annual meeting of stockholders and until their respective successors shall be elected and shall qualify.

INSPECTOR: The tabulation of the ballots on the ratification of the selection of [name of firm] as independent public accountants for the Company and subsidiaries for [year] shows that [number] shares were voted in favor of the proposal and [number] shares were voted against the proposal.

CHAIRMAN: The votes in favor of the proposal represent more than a majority of the common shares voted and it is therefore adopted.

INSPECTOR: The tabulation of the ballots concerning [subject] shows that [number] shares were voted for the resolution and [number] shares were voted against the resolution.

CHAIRMAN: The votes in favor of the resolution represent less [more] than a majority of the common shares voted and the resolution has therefore failed [been adopted].

SECRETARY: I have here the regular report from the inspectors covering the election of directors and the two proposals. This report will be filed with the records of this meeting.

CHAIRMAN: If there is no further business, a motion to adjourn is in order.

STOCKHOLDER: I move the meeting adjourn.

CHAIRMAN: All in favor please say "aye," opposed "no."

The meeting is adjourned.

EMERGENCY STATEMENT BY CHAIRMAN EXPEDITING SHAREHOLDERS' MEETING DURING DISORDER OR DISRUPTION

CHAIRMAN: This disturbance interferes with the orderly procedures of our annual meeting, and makes it necessary to expedite the conduct of the business for which this meeting was called.

I remind you that a quorum is present and that this meeting has been duly called and is lawfully convened. The Management Proxy Committee has received proxies representing more than a majority [number or per cent] of the common stock entitled to vote, with instructions to vote most of these shares for the election of the nominees for directors named in the Proxy Statement, and to vote in accordance with Management's recommendations on the other items of business listed in the Notice of Meeting and more fully described in the Proxy Statement.

The secretary, who is a stockholder and a member of the Management Proxy Committee, will now vote all Management proxies in accordance with Management's recommendations except only as instructed to the contrary on the proxy cards received by the Committee.*

This means that, despite the disruption, we still have a lawful meeting with full authority to act; and this meeting has acted.

The requisite vote having been taken, the Chair declares that the Management's nominees have been duly elected as directors, that the selection of auditors has been ratified, and that the stockholder proposal on [resolution] has failed.

Shareholders and valid proxyholders present at this meeting who also wish to record their votes may do so by obtaining ballots from an usher, marking and signing them, and returning them to the secretary or any usher, within the next half-hour.

In view of the continuing disruption, I declare the meeting adjourned.

* Secretary signs all requisite ballots.

Note: If it appears that order might be restored within a reasonable time, the chairman may wish to order a recess for a stated period (such as a half-hour) and then open the meeting for general discussion and questions, but not for voting on any matter. This procedure is not recommended except when it is to the benefit of the shareholders.

MOTIONS FROM THE FLOOR

If a stockholder rightfully having the floor makes a proper motion, the chairman should entertain the motion and put it to a vote. The chairman need not initiate or ask for comments or questions from the floor regarding the proposed resolution, but if the motion is debatable the chairman should permit any stockholder to advocate or oppose the motion upon gaining the floor and being recognized for that purpose. In a proper case, a stockholder not satisfied with a voice vote may demand a poll.

The following format is suggested for relatively small orderly meetings.

STOCKHOLDER: Mr. Chairman, I move that the stockholders recommend to management that the following action be taken [proposed action].
CHAIRMAN: You have heard the motion. Is there a second?

STOCKHOLDER: I second the motion.

CHAIRMAN: A motion has been made and seconded relating to [proposed action]. You have heard the motion as presented by the proposing stockholder. We will now take a vote. All in favor of this motion please so indicate by rising and stating your names and the number of shares voted in favor of the motion. [A record is taken of the affirmative votes.]

All opposed, please rise and state your names and the number of shares voted against the motion. [A record is made of the negative votes.]

A vote having been taken, the Chair announces that the motion has been carried [has failed].

The following format is suggested for larger meetings when management holds sufficient proxies to control the meeting.

STOCKHOLDER: Mr. Chairman, I move that the stockholders recommend to management that the following action be taken: [proposed action].

CHAIRMAN: You have heard the motion. Is there a second?

STOCKHOLDER: I second the motion.

CHAIRMAN: A motion has been made and seconded relating to [proposed action]. You have heard the motion as presented by the proposing stockholder. We will now take a vote on this motion.

All in favor of this motion please so indicate by saying "aye." [The chairman and secretary observe the voice vote and appraise its strength without recording the names and number of shares voted.]

All in opposition to this meeting please so indicate by saying "no."

CHAIRMAN: I observe that the Management Proxy Committee has voted its proxies [for] against the motion, and therefore I declare that the motion has [been adopted] failed of adoption.

APPEAL FROM CHAIRMAN'S RULING

STOCKHOLDER: I don't agree with the chairman's ruling and I appeal the ruling to the assembled stockholders.

CHAIRMAN: A stockholder has moved to appeal the ruling of the chairman that his motion to [brief description of ruling] is out of order. The motion to appeal is not debatable, and I will put the motion to an immediate vote.

All stockholders in favor of the motion to overrule the chairman please so indicate by saying "aye."

All stockholders opposing the motion, please so indicate by saying "no."

I observe that the Management Proxy Committee has voted its proxies against the motion. As the Committee holds proxies for more than a majority of the shares entitled to vote, the Chair declares that the motion has failed.

We will now proceed with the meeting.

REMOVAL OF DISRUPTIVE SHAREHOLDER— DIRECTIVES OF CHAIRMAN

[Two or more stockholders are seeking recognition or claiming the microphone]

CHAIRMAN: Mr. X [recognized stockholder], you have been recognized by the Chair and you are entitled to the microphone. Mr. Y, you have *not* been recognized by the Chair and you do not have the floor. You are *not* entitled to use the microphone. Please step aside and await your turn to be recognized.

[Y persists]

Mr. Y, you are out of order. I again ask that you step aside and await your turn. I direct you to stop disrupting the speaker who rightfully has the floor.

[Y still persists]

Mr. Y, I have told you that you are out of order and have asked you to step aside. You still persist in disrupting the meeting. I now ask that you leave the vicinity of the microphone and return to your seat.

[Y still persists]

Mr. Y, I am telling you for the third time that you are out of order. Your refusal to take your seat constitutes disorderly conduct. Unless you return to your seat promptly, I shall order you to leave the room. If you do not leave voluntarily I will order that you be removed.

[Y fails to leave the room]

Mr. Y, you have persisted in your disorderly conduct in spite of the rulings of the Chair. It is now necessary and proper that you be removed from the meeting room so that the meeting may proceed in orderly fashion. I direct the guard [marshal, sergeant-at-arms, officer] to remove Mr. Y from the meeting room.

Although the Chairman has the right and duty to eject a disorderly person from the meeting room, there may be at times circumstances which suggest the desirability of obtaining the concurrence of the assembly. If that is done, the following format is suggested.

CHAIRMAN: The Chair will entertain a motion that Mr. Y be ejected from the meeting because he persists in his disorderly conduct. A vote will be taken on this motion.

STOCKHOLDER: I move that the stockholders approve and direct the removal of Mr. Y from this meeting room because he has persisted in disrupting the proceedings of this meeting.

CHAIRMAN: Is there a second?

STOCKHOLDER: I second the motion.

CHAIRMAN: All in favor of this motion say "aye." All opposed so signify by saying "nay." * The motion is carried, and Mr. Y will be removed from the meeting room.

    I direct the guard to remove Mr. Y from the meeting room.

   * A stock vote is appropriate, but a voice or standing vote will suffice in the absence of a demand for a stock vote or for a poll.

Note: The offender should be escorted from the room with the use of only such amount of force as reasonably may be necessary, taking into account the resistance encountered. If the offending person is a woman, due regard must be had for her as the manner of removing a woman from the meeting might be objectionable where it would not be in the case of a man.

It is suggested that the officer removing the offending stockholder be in uniform or be identified as an officer by a badge or other insignia. Also, in the case of a woman being removed, it is preferable that the officer be a policewoman or a uniformed matron. If it is not feasible to obtain the services of a qualified matron, a male officer may be employed provided he acts under the immediate command and in the presence of a policewoman, matron, nurse, or other qualified woman.

INSTRUCTIONS FOR GUARDS

(It is recommended that the instructions for guards be printed or typed and delivered to the security force.)

1. Remain on call in the [defined] Area throughout the meeting.
2. Act only pursuant to instructions of the security representative. The security representative must be alert at all times to directions of the presiding officer and the secretary and will be responsible for assuring that guards act promptly and effectively in carrying out those directions.
3. In the event security measures are necessary, the security representative will request that guards don their armbands and act with the dignity and composure needed. Guards should not run or act with undue haste.
4. Ordinarily, if it should be necessary to remove a female stockholder from the meeting, a policewoman should undertake the task. Male guards are not to touch any female person for any reason whatsoever, unless so directed by the security representative to assist in a particular situation under the direct supervision and in the presence of a policewoman, matron, nurse, or other qualified woman.
5. Ordinarily, if it should become necessary to remove a male stockholder from the meeting, the male guards will undertake the task. A policewoman should not be involved in the removal of a male person from the meeting.
6. After three warnings by the presiding officer, he or the secretary, on signal, will direct the security representative to effect removal. Should physical removal become necessary, the guard or matron, with armbands visible, will first identify himself or herself (to the individual to be removed) as private security and request the individual to accompany him or her quietly and peacefully.
7. If the individual refuses to leave, he or she may be first taken gently by the arm and repeatedly asked to accompany the guard or matron. Under no circumstances may the offending person be pushed with enough force to cause him or her to lose balance or fall, or be struck any blow.
8. If the offending person becomes violent or abusive, the guard or matron shall not retaliate in kind, but shall continue impassively to induce the person to leave. The guard may block the aisle with his person to prevent the offender from approaching the Chair.
9. If the offending person refuses to move or falls limp on the floor, he or she may be carried out of the meeting room as gently as circumstances will permit.
10. It must be remembered that the only legally permissible force which can be used is "reasonable" force—which is only that

amount necessary to effect removal taking into account the degree of resistance.

11. The distance a person will be taken from the meeting room and the length of time such person will be excluded will be determined by the presiding officer or the secretary, and communicated to the security representative.

12. The guards may be called upon to prevent nonqualified persons from entering the meeting room.

13. If the meeting is adjourned by the presiding officer due to disorder, the guards and matrons will assist in keeping order and clearing the meeting room.

DEMAND FOR POLL

Any stockholder has the right to question the results of a voice vote as announced by the chairman, and may demand a poll. This maneuver will not serve any useful purpose when the Management Proxy Committee holds sufficient proxies to control the voting at the meeting. It is suggested, under these circumstances, that the chairman rule the demand out of order as being a dilatory motion.

Glossary

Amend To modify or change a resolution by inserting, by striking out, or by inserting and striking out, one or more words, paragraphs, or sections. When the amendment effectively replaces the resolution with another, it is called a substitute. See also *Rescind*.

Assembly A group of persons having a common interest, present together in a meeting for the transaction of business.

Carried Voting outcome in which a motion is adopted.

Casting vote A vote by the presiding officer, created by statute or regulation (not recognized by parliamentary law), for the purpose of breaking a deadlock in a legislative assembly due to a tie vote. Corporation law makes no provision for a casting vote.

Charman; Chair The presiding officer or chairman of an assembly, convention, legislative or deliberative body, board of directors, or committee. The presiding officer is designated the chairman or the chair regardless of his title and whether he is standing or sitting.

Commit To refer to a committee.

Committee One or more members of a legislative or deliberative body officially appointed and charged with examining into defined matters referred to them by the body and reporting the results of their investigations and recommendations.

Committee of the whole All the members of an assembly sitting as a committee to obtain the advantage of less formal rules of order and debate.

Decorum Good order; the proprieties.

Dilatory Intended or tending to accomplish improper delay; misuse of parliamentary procedures or debate for the improper purpose of gaining time or delaying a decision.

Division The separation of members of a deliberative body to take a vote, as by passing between tellers, by roll-call vote, or by rising to be counted.

Division of the question The separation of a motion or resolution containing more parts than one into two or more parts in order to debate and vote on the parts as separate questions. A division must separate the motion or resolution into self-sustaining parts. Often the only mode of separating a complicated question is by moving amendments.

Executive Committee A committee of the board of directors having all or much of the power and authority of the board of directors between meetings of the board. This committee is usually established by the by-laws, and is often authorized by state corporation laws.

Executive Session Deliberation of a legislative body or committee in private, without the presence of non-members. The term was derived from the practice of the United States Senate to meet in private when considering presidential matters.

Ex Officio By virtue of the office; from the office. Holding an office by reason of holding another office, such as the president being a member ex officio of specified committees.

Floor A member "has the floor" by recognition of the presiding officer and thereby has the exclusive right to speak or make a motion for such length of time and such purpose as the rules permit.

Germane An amendment is germane to the resolution it proposes to amend, and thus is in order, when it is in close relationship with the resolution.

Immunity Immunity from speech and debate (absolute or qualified) is generally granted to legislators, judges, and various types of governmental officers and public officials, but not to officers or directors of business corporations. See *Privilege*.

Majority More than half of any number. A majority vote is more than half of the votes cast for a particular motion or candidate. A majority of stockholders is a majority in stock interest and not a majority in number alone.

Meeting An assemblage of members of an organization from the time they are called to order until they adjourn, with the only separations being recesses for a few minutes. A recess or separation for an afternoon or evening meeting or for a longer period is a termination of the meeting, so a convention scheduled for several days may have two or three meetings a day. A meeting of stockholders, whether regular or special, together with its adjourned meetings is usually a session. See *Session*.

Minutes The official record of the proceedings and the business transacted at the meeting. A corporation "speaks" through its minutes.

Motion   The method by which a member submits a proposed resolution for the consideration and action of the meeting. For convenience and rank, motions are divided into classes to which reference should be made where parliamentary tactics are routine.

Pass   A bill or resolution is said to "pass" when it is enacted by the legislative body, or when its adoption has been approved by the requisite vote; also, when the bill proceeds from one legislative step to another.

Pass vote   A voice expression of abstention from casting an affirmative or negative vote.

Plurality   When more than two choices are available in a vote, the one receiving the most votes has a plurality. When there are only two choices, the one receiving the greater number has a majority. A plurality may well be less than a majority.

Point of order   Verbal opposition directed against present actions to be taken by the meeting and deemed to be contrary to the rules, practices, and precedents of the assembly. A member is "in order" when the rules are observed, and "out of order" when the rules are violated. A point of order is made when a member objects to an action or proceeding as being out of order. See *Question of order.*

Poll   The casting or recording of votes of a body of persons; the result of the counting of votes; the number of votes cast; the place where the votes are cast. In corporation law it is the general practice at stockholder meetings to vote by ballot on all items of business listed in the notice of meeting and described in the proxy statement. Other matters, such as the approval of prior minutes or the appointment of tellers and judges of the voting may be by voice vote of stockholders present in person or by proxy.

Preamble   An introductory clause at the beginning of a statute or resolution stating some of the reasons for its enactment and the objects sought to be accomplished.

Previous question   The object of moving the "previous question" is to cut off debate and secure immediately a vote on the pending question. The previous question is the only motion used for closing debate in the United States House of Representatives. It is suitable for closing debate at a stockholders' meeting.

Privilege (qualified)   The protection of a person from liability for communicating in good faith on any subject in which he has an interest, or in reference to which he has a duty, to a person having a corresponding interest or duty, although it contains matter which without such privilege would be slanderous and actionable. A director or shareholder is protected by a qualified privilege in speaking to other directors and shareholders and to management on company matters. See *Immunity*.

Proxy A statement or power of attorney signed by a stockholder of record authorizing another (who need not be a stockholder) to act at a meeting for the signor, as in casting a vote. Proxies were not recognized at common law; they were authorized by statute for use by stockholders, but not by corporate officers or directors.

Public meeting A meeting of a local governing body (city council, school board, public authority) which by statute must be open to the public when any resolution, regulation, or other formal action is to be adopted or voted upon. Such statutes are sometimes known as "open door" or "in the sunshine" laws.

Putting the question The act of the presiding officer submitting the pending question to the meeting for a vote. "Stating the question" means informing the meeting of the pending question.

Question Any proposal submitted to a meeting for decision such as a "motion," "resolution," or "proposition."

Question of order Request by a member who rises and asks the chair to rule without debate whether a certain present proceeding or action is out of order. Normally the chair decides on a question of order, but the chair may put the question in the form of a motion and call for a vote, in which case the motion may be debatable. Decisions of the chair may be appealed to the assembly. See *Point of order*.

Quorum Such a number of the members of an assembled body, or such a number of shares represented at a stockholders' meeting, as must be present at a meeting to transact business.

Ratify A motion to make valid (approve or confirm) an action previously taken by an official or committee, or action taken by an insufficient number of the main body. An action which was initially void cannot be retroactively cured.

Recess An intermission in an assembly meeting. At a stockholders' meeting a recess normally would be only for a few minutes, as while collecting or counting ballots. After a recess, business is resumed at the point of its interruption.

Recognize; Recognition Permission given by the presiding officer before a member can take the floor or use the microphone to make a motion or speak in debate. Recognition may be by announcing the member's name, by a nod of the head, or by hand signal.

Rescind To cancel an earlier action, resolution, or decision; to amend by striking out an entire resolution that has been previously adopted.

Rising vote   Voters rise and stand until counted. Same as "standing vote."

Roll-call vote   A vote by calling the alphabetical roll of members. This method is time-consuming and not suitable for stockholders' meetings.

Rules of order   Written rules of parliamentary procedure formally adopted by an assembly or organization relating to the orderly transaction of business at meetings. Basically, rules of order closely correspond to the common parliamentary law modified to meet the needs of the organization. Rules of order may also be pronounced by the presiding officer prior to the opening of the meeting.

Second; Seconder   Parliamentary law generally requires that motions be seconded before they can be stated and put to a vote. Many motions do not require a second and any corporation or private organization may dispense with the requirement of a second.

Session   The time during which a legislative body or other assembly sits for the transaction of business, as a session of Congress which commences on a day certain and ends when the Congress finally adjourns. A session may consist of several meetings or of just one meeting. A stockholders' meeting together with its adjourned meetings constitutes one session. See also *Meeting*.

Sine die   Without day; without assigning a day for a further meeting. When a meeting is adjourned sine die it is dissolved and the session of the assembly is ended.

Special meeting   A meeting not regularly held (monthly, quarterly, annually) but called for a special purpose which must be clearly set forth in the call.

Standing committee   A committee having a continuing existence or one established for a stated period of time.

Standing rules   Rules adopted by an organization concerning operating procedures which are of lesser importance or permanence than the constitution or by-laws, such as the time, day, or date on which meetings are held, the place of meetings, the opening procedures, and order of business. Standing orders should include only those procedures which do not affect the rights of members.

Sunshine laws   See *Public meeting*.

Table; Tabling   A motion to table the pending motion holds the tabled motion in the hands of the secretary until it is brought up again by a motion to "take from the table." This permits the meeting to consider more urgent business until it is convenient to renew consideration of the tabled motion with priority over new business.

Tellers Members (one or two from each side of the question) appointed by the chair or otherwise designated by the rules, to count the votes and report the results to the presiding officer. Many state corporation laws provide that the election of directors be conducted by inspectors or judges of election appointed by the chairman or the assembly. Generally, inspectors are not stockholders or members of management. They are often representatives of the corporate transfer agent. Inspectors customarily take an oath of office and file a signed certificate with the secretary of the meeting. Tellers are not required to report the results of voting under oath.

Tie vote An equality of affirmative and negative votes cast on any motion. The motion fails on a tie vote.

Two-thirds vote Where two-thirds of the total number of votes cast are necessary for a decision, as distinguished from a vote of two-thirds of those present, or a two-thirds vote of all the members. Where a two-thirds vote is required it should be taken by a division or by ballot, and not by a voice vote.

Voice vote; Via voce (living voice) Voting by speech or outcry as distinguished from voting by division or by ballot; a vote taken by calling for "ayes" and "noes" and judged by whichever side is the more numerous based on volume of voice response.

Bibliography

BARCLAY, HUGH. *Digest of the Laws of Scotland, with special reference to the office and duties of a justice of the peace.* 3d ed. rev. and enlarged. Edinburgh: T. & T. Clark, 1865.

CAIN, T. E. *Charlesworth's Company Law.* 9th ed. London: Stevens & Sons, 1968.

CANNON, CLARENCE. *Cannon's Precedents of the House of Representatives of the United States.* Washington: Government Printing Office, 1935.

CROCKER, GEORGE GLOVER. *Principles of Procedure in Deliberative Bodies.* 2d ed. G. P. Putnam's Sons, 1894.

CURRY, T. P. E. (CREW, A.). *Public, Company and Local Government Meetings.* 19th ed. London: Jordan & Sons, Ltd., 1956.

CUSHING, LUTHER STEARNS. *Elements of the Law and Practice of Legislative Assemblies in the United States of America.* First ed. Boston: Little, Brown & Co., 1856.

———. *Lex Parliamentaria Americana.* 9th ed. Boston: Little, Brown & Co., 1907.

———. *Manual of Parliamentary Practice.* Boston: William J. Reynolds & Co., 1855.

———. *Cushing's Manual of Parliamentary Practice.* Ed. by Albert S. Bolles. Philadelphia: The John C. Winston Co., 1928.

DICEY, A. V. *The Law of the Constitution.* 10th ed. London: Macmillan & Co., Ltd., 1968.

FISH, GEORGE T. *American Manual of Parliamentary Law.* New York: Harper & Bros., 1907.

FOX, EMMA A. *Parliamentary Usage for Women's Clubs.* 4th ed. Detroit, Mich.: Maurice W. Fox, 1939.

GREGG, FRED M. *Handbook of Parliamentary Law.* 3d ed. Boston: Ginn & Co., 1940.

HINDS, ASHER C. *Rules of the United States House of Representatives.* Washington: Government Printing Office, 1907.

JOHNSON, R. B., TRUSTMAN, B. A., and WADSWORTH, C. Y. *Town Meeting Time; A Handbook of Parliamentary Law.* Boston: Little, Brown & Co., 1962.

ROBERT, HENRY MARTYN. *Parliamentary Law.* New York: Appleton-Century-Crofts, 1951.

———. *Parliamentary Practice.* New York: Appleton-Century-Crofts, 1949.

———. *Robert's Rules of Order, Revised.* Seventy-Fifth Anniversary Edition. New York: Scott, Foresman and Co., 1954.

———. *Robert's Rules of Order, Newly Revised.* New York: Scott, Foresman & Co., 1970.

SHACKLETON, F. *The Law and Practice of Meetings.* 3d ed. London: Macdonald & Evans, Ltd., 1956.

SHAW, S., and SMITH, E. D. *The Law of Meetings.* 3d ed. London: Macdonald & Evans, Ltd., 1956.

STURGIS, ALICE FLEENOR. *Standard Code of Parliamentary Procedure.* New York: McGraw-Hill, Inc., 1950.

WHITNEY, BYRL ALBERT. *Parliamentary Procedure.* Washington: R. B. Luce, 1962.

WILSON, OLIVER MORRIS. *Digest of Parliamentary Law.* 2d ed. Philadelphia: Kay & Bros., 1869.

INDEXES

Index of Cases

Index of Subjects